International Human Rights and Canadian Law – Legal Commitment, Implementation and the *Charter*

by

William A. Schabas, OC, LLD
National University of Ireland, Galway

&

Stéphane Beaulac, PhD (Cantab)
University of Montreal

THOMSON
™
CARSWELL

Library and Archives Canada Cataloguing in Publication

Schabas, William A., 1950-
    International human rights and Canadian law : legal commitment, implementation and the Charter / William A. Schabas, Stéphane Beaulac.—3rd ed.

Previous eds. published under title: International human rights law and the Canadian Charter.

Includes bibliographical references and index.
ISBN-10: 0-459-24418-3
ISBN-13: 978-0-459-24418-7

    1. Human rights. 2. Human rights—Canada. 3. Canada. Canadian Charter of Rights and Freedoms. I. Beaulac, Stéphane II. Title.

KE4381.5.S28 2006   342.7108'5   C2006-906241-2
KF4483.C519S28 2006

Composition: Computer Composition of Canadian Inc.

THOMSON

CARSWELL

One Corporate Plaza
2075 Kennedy Road
Toronto, Ontario
M1T 3V4

Customer Relations:
Toronto 416-609-3800
Elsewhere in Canada/U.S. 1-800-387-5164
Fax 1-416-298-5082
World Wide Web: http://www.carswell.com
E-mail: carswell.orders@thomson.com

Foreword

It is with great pleasure that I write these few words of introduction to what promises to be an important and influential contribution to Canadian legal literature. The original edition of this book, published by William Schabas in 1991, examined a phenomenon that was still very much in its infancy. Now, fifteen years later, the role of international (and comparative) law has become a standard element in judicial methodology. I witnessed the process first hand, as a member of the Supreme Court of Canada from 1987 to 2002.

We now live in an increasingly globalized legal world. Judges around the world deal more and more with similar issues and often look at the precedents of other courts, particularly in those countries where constitutions are of recent vintage and where little caselaw exists to guide them. While comparative law is not binding, it can be a source of ideas and inspiration. When faced with the interpretation of constitutional issues, international law provides much of the framework and may bring a perspective which might help bring about a consensus or strengthen a dissenting opinion. But the engine that drives this dynamic process seems to lie as much with national courts, especially those with responsibility for interpreting and applying constitutional norms, as it does with the international bodies.

Stéphane Beaulac worked with me in 1995-1996 as a law clerk at the Supreme Court of Canada. Together with William Schabas, a law professor whom I have known and admired for many years, he has examined the relevant material in the Canadian cases and the international authorities. The writers state their views in a forthright and clear manner, reflecting the views of the courts but also contributing their own insights and arguing for innovative interpretations.

This material is of great intrinsic interest to lawyers, judges and policy makers. But it is also important because it helps to move the goalposts on the great issues of our time, including equality and human rights, in particular the rights of women and children. These were matters that drove much of my own judicial philosophy and vision of the law, as a member of the bench, and continue to motivate my work. Canada has in many ways set examples for other countries to follow, and we can all be proud of our contribution to this process. Much, however, still remains to be done.

Claire L'Heureux-Dubé

Preface

This is the third edition of a book that first appeared in 1991, some fifteen years ago. Human rights law was still if not in its infancy barely into its early adolescence. The various international adjudicative bodies, such as the European Court of Human Rights and the Human Rights Committee, were in the course of developing a modest body of caselaw. There were a handful of advisory opinions and only a couple of contentious judgments of the Interamerican Court of Human Rights. International human rights treaties were slowly gathering ratifications. As for the International Criminal Court, and the *ad hoc* tribunals for the former Yugoslavia, Rwanda and Sierra Leone, they were barely a twinkle in the eye of a few determined law professors. The momentum was modest, and the corpus of international human rights law still relatively meager, at least by today's standards. A relatively obscure aspect of this developing body of law was its application by national courts.

Among the very first domestic jurisdictions to make reference to international human rights law sources were the Canadian courts. For reasons that are still mysterious, some clairvoyant Canadian judges began to consult these innovative new international sources and even, occasionally, to cite them in their rulings. A great impetus came with the enactment of the *Canadian Charter of Rights and Freedoms*, in 1982, although there is evidence of the phenomenon many years before that defining moment in Canadian law. Really, the *Canadian Charter* was simply part of the whole process, because it too was influenced by developments in international human rights law.

It is now clear that Canadian courts were pioneers in a movement of judicial globalization that has captured the imagination of jurists around the world. The intermingling of national and international law, in the enforcement by the courts of human rights norms, has become relatively common. In some sense it is a confirmation of the universality of human rights that was first proclaimed in the Universal Declaration of Human Rights, in 1948, and reaffirmed in the 1993 Vienna Declaration.

The first edition of this book saw itself as a contribution to this process. Didactic in tone, perhaps overly so, it had the ambition of familiarizing Canadian judges and lawyers with a body of law that, because of its relative novelty, few of them had ever studied. The book examined the handful of Canadian cases that had referred to international human rights sources, searching for patterns in the analysis and explanations of the rationale behind such references. At the time, there were a few hundred Canadian judicial decisions with references to human rights law, although most of the citations were quite perfunctory in nature and, in some cases, somewhat erroneous or entirely inaccurate.

Today, few Canadian lawyers and judges need to be introduced to international human rights law. Most have now studied it as part of their training, or learned of it in special courses, or at conferences. References to international human rights law in the judgments of the Supreme Court of Canada are virtually expected when issues of fundamental rights and freedoms are being considered. In 1991, the Supreme Court might look to international sources as part of its inquiry, viewing them as useful and interesting, if sometimes curious and of doubtful authority. As the international tribunals have matured, so the attitude of judges in Canada – and elsewhere too – has changed to one of greater deference. Increasingly, they see the task as one of harmonizing Canadian law with international law.

This change of perspective is perhaps most sharply demonstrated in the evolving caselaw on capital punishment which, in Canada, was debated in a series of extradition cases. In 1991, in *Kindler* and *Ng*, when the matter was first studied, the Supreme Court found international law to be of interest but, ultimately, its final ruling was out of synch with evolving international jurisprudence. A decade later, in *Burns and Rafay*, the Court was endeavoring to ensure the concordance of Canadian law with the international position.

All of this means that the objective and the philosophy of the third edition of this book can no longer be the same as it was fifteen years ago, when the first edition appeared, or ten years ago, when the second was published. Today, the body of law that it considers is well-established, not fragile and uncertain. Nor is it a question of helping the uninformed to discover unfamiliar sources. Nevertheless, the original structure seems to have stood the test of time, and remains much the same.

The first chapter takes an historical perspective, describing the evolution of international human rights law from a Canadian standpoint. Even here, there is much that is new, particularly research resulting from materials released in the National Archives of Canada only recently. The second chapter discusses the theoretical basis of reference to international human rights law. In this area, practice has largely confirmed the rationale of judges for reference to international law. It has also effectively disposed of some of the theories that circulated in the early years. The third chapter considers the sources of international human rights law. They are infinitely richer than they were a decade or so ago, both because of the dramatic growth of the institutions that then existed, and because of the establishment of new bodies and mechanisms. The final chapter reviews the Canadian caselaw. Many of the newer cases reflect the increasing maturity of the analysis. They also tackle issues that have moved from the avant-garde to the mainstream. The first two editions were supplemented with an extensive collection of documents, as well as tables that analysed the reported caselaw. The Internet has made these materials so easily accessible that there can now be no need to reproduce treaties and other relevant instruments. As for the caselaw, on-line data bases have greatly diminished the significance of reported caselaw in the traditional sense of a limited list of decisions carefully selected by expert editors. Moreover, analysis of its contents is facilitated by powerful search engines. The value added to the first two editions of this book that resulted from fastidious research in poorly indexed cases is no longer valuable at all. So most of these parts of the book have been dropped, victims of technological progress.

When the first editions were published, William Schabas was a professor in the Département des sciences juridiques of the Université du Québec à Montréal, as well as a practicing member of the Québec bar and a member of the Quebec Human Rights Tribunal. In 2000, he left Canada to participate in the establishment of the Irish Centre for Human Rights, located in Galway at the National University of Ireland. Out of concern that he was a bit too remote to tackle a third edition on his own, he and Stéphane Beaulac have joined forces in an academic partnership. The latter has a Ph.D. in international law from the University of Cambridge, England, and is a former law clerk to Madame Justice Claire L'Heureux-Dubé at the Supreme Court of Canada. A specialist in Canadian constitutional law as well as international law, Professor Beaulac is on the Faculty of Law at the University of Montreal.

William Schabas would like to express his appreciation to the Université du Québec à Montréal, where he remains a *professeur associé*, as well as to his new institution, the National University of Ireland, Galway, and to his colleagues at the Irish Centre for Human Rights. As he did in the earlier editions, he would also like to thank his wife Penelope, for her assistance and support.

Stéphane Beaulac, for his part, is grateful to the University of Montreal for its constant institutional support and, in particular, to the George Stellari Fund for the financial aid provided. Two fantastic research assistants participated in this project, Brendan Naef and Stéphanie Garon, to whom credit is due. Finally, a word of thanks to his wife Olga and his three sons (Sasha, Jacob, Stéphane Jr.) for their inspiration.

William A. Schabas and Stéphane Beaulac
Montreal and Galway, June 2006

Table of Contents

Table of Cases

European Court of Human Rights

European Court of Justice

Human Rights Committee

International Court of Justice

International Criminal Court

International Criminal Tribunal for Rwanda

International Criminal Tribunal for the former Yugoslavia

International Military Tribunal

Permanent Court of International Justice

Special Court for Sierra Leone

National Courts

Australia

Canada

Germany

India

Ireland

New Zealand

South Africa

Zimbabawe

1

Historical Context: *Magna Carta* to the *Canadian Charter*

The protection of the human rights and fundamental freedoms of Canadians from government action and legislation was substantially enhanced by the proclamation of the *Canadian Charter of Rights and Freedoms* on 17 April 1982.[1] In a departure from the English parliamentary tradition, legislation in violation of rights and freedoms could be declared inoperative by the courts,[2] subject to an unlikely override by Parliament pursuant to the *Charter*'s "notwithstanding clause".[3] Canadian courts may also be petitioned for an appropriate remedy when these rights and freedoms are violated by government action, even where no formal statutory recourse exists.[4] It has often been said that proclamation of the *Charter* provides Canada with a judicial system "like that of the United States". But the recent preoccupation of Canadian politicians and jurists with the constitutional protection of human rights and fundamental freedoms certainly owes as much to the rapid

---

1 RSC 1985, Appendix II, No. 44 (hereinafter *Canadian Charter* or *Charter*).

2 *Constitution Act, 1982*, being Schedule B of the *Canada Act 1982* (UK) 1982, c. 11, [RSC 1985, Appendix II, No. 44, s. 52]; exceptionally, such legislation had been declared inoperative even prior to the *Canadian Charter*: *R*. v. *Drybones*, [1970] SCR 282, 71 WWR 161, 10 CRNS 334, 9 DLR (3d) 473; *Reference Re Alberta Statutes*, [1938] SCR 100, [1938] 2 DLR 81.

3 *Ibid.*, s. 33. The "notwithstanding clause" was occasionally invoked during the 1980s, most notoriously by Quebec's National Assembly following the judgment of the Supreme Court of Canada in a case concerning legislation aimed at protecting the French language: *Ford* v. *Attorney-General of Quebec*, [1988] 2 SCR 712, 54 DLR (4th) 577, 19 QAC 69, 36 CRR 1, 90 NR 84, 10 CHRR D/5559, 13 ACWS (3d) 7, 6 WCB (2d) 186. Since then, however, the federal and provincial parliaments have been deferential without exception to the judgment of the courts.

4 *Canadian Charter, supra* note 1, s. 24(1); *R*. v. *Mills*, [1986] 1 SCR 863, 58 OR (2d) 544*n*, 16 OAC 81, 29 DLR (4th) 161, 26 CCC (3d) 481, 52 CR (3d) 1, 67 NR 241, *per* Lamer J.

1

and dramatic evolution of international law since the Second World War as to any judicial osmosis from the south.

1.1   The Genesis of Human Rights Protection

Long before the proclamation of the *Charter*, Canadians proudly declared that the "unwritten constitution" they had inherited from English law, and whose genealogy could be traced to a confrontation between King John and some dissident barons in 1215, provided protections that were unequalled elsewhere in the world.[5] "The evolution of our democratic tradition can be traced back to the Magna Carta (1215) and before, through the long struggle for Parliamentary supremacy which culminated in the English Bill of Rights in 1688-89", wrote the Supreme Court of Canada in the *Secession Reference*.[6] The Americans were the first to understand that common law protections were insufficient. They were frustrated by the fact that the fabled rights and freedoms sanctified by English judges did not seem to extend to the colonies, and made sure that the citizens of their new republic were protected by a constitution. Of course, there is no doubt that *Magna Carta*,[7] the *Petition of Right*[8] and the *Bill of Rights of 1689*[9] inspired those who drafted the United States Bill of Rights and who, in their turn, furnished a model for the French revolutionaries.[10] As more and more countries followed the model of constitutional entrenchment of fundamental rights and freedoms, Canada was very much a holdout until, finally, the *Canadian Charter* was adopted. Since then, even the Westminster Parliament has taken steps towards a rather modest form of entrenchment of human rights

---

5   *Reference re Alberta Legislation, supra* note 2.

6   *Reference re Secession of Quebec*, [1998] 2 SCR 217, 161 DLR (4th) 385, 55 CRR (2d) 1, para. 63.

7   *Magna Carta*, (1215) 17 Joh.

8   *Petition of Right*, (1627) 3 Car. I, c. 1.

9   1 Wm. & Mary, 2d Sess. (1689) v. 2; See: Irving Brant, *The Bill of Rights, Its Origin and Meaning*, Indianapolis: Bobbs-Merrill, 1965.

10   *The New Cambridge Modern History*, Vol. VIII, Cambridge: Cambridge University Press, 1968, at 676; the United States Library of Congress possesses two original drafts of the *Déclaration des Droits de l'homme et du citoyen* which were submitted by the Marquis de Lafayette to Thomas Jefferson, who was the United States's ambassador in Paris during the summer of 1789, for his comments. One of the copies bears remarks penned by Jefferson: see Allessandro Passerin D'Entrèves, *Natural Law*, 2nd ed., London: Hutchison, 1970, at 53-55. For the various versions, including those in which Jefferson was involved, see Stéphane Rials, *La déclaration des droits de l'Homme et du citoyen*, Paris: Hachette, 1988.

within the British Isles.[11] In practice, even the British have done indirectly what they balked at doing directly: by their participation in the system of the European Court of Human Rights, they provide their citizens with what is very close to a form of constitutionalized protection of human rights.[12] In one case, the Supreme Court of Canada spoke of *Magna Carta* being reinforced by the *European Convention on Human Rights*.[13]

The primary subject of this book is not, however, Canadian constitutional law. This study is concerned with international human rights law, a branch of the broader discipline of public international law. The term "international law" apparently owes its origin to Bentham, and has prevailed since then over the more ancient expression "law of nations" or *jus gentium*. The adjective "public" was added in an 1802 translation of Bentham, helpfully distinguishing the field from that of "private international law", which we more properly refer to as "conflict of laws".[14] As a general rule, the latter regulates the application and interrelationship of domestic legislation rather than generating an autonomous normative system.[15] However, so-called "private international law" matters may be regulated by treaty, as in the case of child abduction. There the line between public and private international law is thin indeed.

Modern-day international human rights law can trace its origins to a variety of sources. The authorities have explained that natural law provides for certain norms of human conduct, and in this sense international law can be said to provide a degree of protection of rights and freedoms since the time of Bodin, Grotius, Vattel, and even before.[16] There were early references to issues that we would today see as falling within the ambit of the international protections of human rights. For example, the *Peace of West-*

---

11 The *Human Rights Act, 1998* (UK), 1998, c. 42, which incorporated the *European Convention on Human Rights* into the domestic law of the United Kingdom, received Royal Assent on 9 November 1998 and came into force on 2 October 2000. The relationship between the *Convention* and the *Human Rights Act* was noted in *R.* v. *Clay*, [2003] 3 SCR 735, at para. 32.

12 See: A.W. Brian Simpson, *Human Rights and the End of Empire, Britain and the Genesis of the European Convention*, Oxford: Oxford University Press, 2001.

13 *Blencoe* v. *British Columbia (Human Rights Commission)*, [2000] 2 SCR 307, 190 DLR (4th) 513, [2000] 10 WWR 567, 23 Admin LR (3d) 175, 38 CHRR 153, 3 CCEL (3d) 165, 77 CRR (2d) 189, 81 BCLR (3d) 1, at para. 151.

14 Alain Pellet & Patrick Daillier, *Droit international public*, 6th ed., Paris: LGDJ, 1999, p. 37.

15 *Serb Loans*, PCIJ, Series A, Nos. 20-21, pp. 41-42.

16 Allessandro Passerin D'Entrèves, *Natural Law, supra* note 10, at 53-55. On the role of natural law for Jean Bodin and Emer de Vattel, respectively, see Stéphane Beaulac, "The Social Power of Bodin's 'Sovereignty' and International Law", (2003) 4 *Melbourne Journal of International Law* 1, and Stéphane Beaulac, "Emer de Vattel and the Externalization of Sovereignty", (2003) 5 *Journal of the History of International Law* 237.

phalia of 1648, often used as the reference for the beginning of modern public international law, provided certain guarantees for religious minorities.[17] Other contemporary treaties contemplated the protection of Christian minorities within the Ottoman empire.[18] One of them, the 1713 *Treaty of Utrecht*, applied to Canada, and ensured certain rights of francophone Roman Catholics within British North America.[19] Article 14 states that:

> It has been expressly agreed that in all the territory and colonies which by virtue of this treaty must be ceded or returned by [the King of France], the subjects of the said King will have the liberty of leaving within a year with all their movable properties. Those who, nevertheless, would choose to stay and remain under the domination of Great Britain, must be able to enjoy the exercise of the Roman Catholic religion, in so far as the laws of England permit it.

Along the same lines, pursuant to article 4 of the *Treaty of Paris* of 1763, the King of Great Britain declared that he ". . .agrees to grant to the inhabitants of Canada the freedom of the Catholic religion: consequently [he] will give the most precise and most effectual order, that his new Roman Catholic subjects may profess the worship of religion according to the rites of the Romish church, as far as the laws of Great Britain permit".

In the nineteenth century bilateral and multilateral agreements were reached outlawing slavery.[20] The *General Act of the Berlin Conference on Central Africa* affirmed that the slave trade was forbidden "in conformity with the principles of international law".[21] Two highly specialized interna-

---

17 *Treaty of Peace between Sweden and the Empire*, signed at Osnabruck, 14(24) October 1648; Dumont VI, Part 1, p. 469, arts. 28-30; *Treaty of Peace between France and the Empires*, signed at Münster, 14(24) October 1648, Dumont VI, Part 1, p. 450, art. 28. On the *Peace of Westphalia* and its socially constructed significance upon the consciousness of international law, see Stéphane Beaulac, "The Westphalian Model in Defining International Law: Challenging the Myth", (2004) 8 *Australian Journal of Legal History* 181; and Stéphane Beaulac, "The Westphalian Legal Orthodoxy – Myth or Reality?", (2000) 2 *Journal of the History of International Law* 148.

18 For example: *Treaty of Peace between Russia and Turkey*, signed at Adrianople, 14 September 1829, BFSP XVI, p.647, arts. V, VII.

19 *Treaty of Peace and Friendship between France and Great Britain*, signed at Utrecht, 11 April 1713, Dumont VIII, Part 1, p. 339, art. 14; *Definitive Treaty of Peace between France, Great Britain and Spain*, signed at Paris, 10 February 1763, BFSP I, pp. 422, 645, art. IV.

20 See, *e.g.*, *Treaty Between Her Majesty and the United States of America, to Settle and Define the Boundaries Between the Possessions of Her Britannic Majesty in North America, and the Territories of the United States; for the Final Suppression of the African Slave Trade; and for the Giving up of Criminals, Fugitive from Justice, in Certain Cases*, 9 August 1842, [1952] CTS 12, cited in *United States* v. *Allard*, [1991] 1 SCR 861, reconsideration refused, (July 11, 1991), Doc 20626 (SCC) .

21 Paul Sieghart, *The International Law of Human Rights*, Oxford: Clarendon Press, 1983, at 13.

tional agreements on labour and working conditions were adopted in 1906.[22] The international law of armed conflict dealt with the rules of war and the protection of the wounded, prisoners and, to a more limited extent, civilian noncombatants, and was codified in the Hague Conventions of 1899[23] and 1907.[24] It addressed certain issues concerning vulnerable civilians, who were caught "in the crossfire", so to speak. Thus, the law of armed conflict also provides early recognition of issues that would subsequently become quite central to the international protection of human rights. Eventually, it would begin to be called "international humanitarian law", reflecting this evolution in its vocation.

The armistice of 1918 brought with it renewed international attention to rights and freedoms.[25] The new Soviet leaders had aroused not only their own citizens but much of what we now call the "third world", and the Allies felt compelled to answer Lenin's stirring appeal by declaring that the post-war world would provide international protection of national rights and working conditions. Part I of the *Treaty of Versailles* incorporated the *Covenant of the League of Nations*, which guaranteed freedom of conscience and religion in League mandate countries (*i.e.*, former German colonies), and more generally ensured that "fair and humane conditions of labour"

22 *Convention on Night Work for Women in Industrial Employment*, reached at Berne, Switzerland, 26 September 1906, 2 Martens (III) 861; *Convention on Use of White (Yellow) Phosphorus for Matches,* reached at Berne, Switzerland, 26 September 1906, 2 Martens (III) 872. By 1914, the Canadian Parliament had begun taking steps to give effect to these international agreements: SC 1914, c. 12. As an indication of how attitudes have changed, it is interesting to note that a restriction on night work for women, originally serving a humanitarian aim, would no doubt now be considered discriminatory. Much later in the century, in 1966, Canada ratified *ILO Convention No. 45 Concerning the Employment of Women in Underground Work in Mines of Any Kinds*, Cmd. 5033, 154 BSP 351, only to denounce the treaty twelve years later as violating the equality of women, in the following terms: "The Government of Canada is aware that at the time of its adoption, Convention 45 was intended to prevent exploitation of women workers and was thus considered a step toward social progress. However, it is now considered within the various jurisdictions of Canada that the Convention limits the employment opportunities of women and that it is, therefore, in contradiction to the principle of equality of treatment and opportunity between men and women, to which the Government of Canada attaches great importance." Cited in "Consideration of Reports Submitted by States Parties under Article 18 of the Convention – Initial Reports of States Parties/Canada", UN Doc. CEDAW/C/5/Add.16 (1983) p. ix.

23 *International Convention with Respect to the Laws and Customs of War by Land*, [1942] CTS 6.

24 *International Convention Concerning the Laws and Customs of War by Land*, signed at The Hague, 18 October 1907, ratification of United Kingdom deposited 27 November 1909, TS 9(1910) Cmd. 5030, P. (1910) CXII 59, 100 BSP 338, 25 HCT 596, 3 Martens (V) 461.

25 See, generally, Paul Gorden Lauren, *The Evolution of International Human Rights, Visions Seen*, 2nd ed., Philadelphia: University of Pennsylvania Press, 2003, pp. 90-102.

and the rights of indigenous populations would be defended by League members.[26] Wilson had apparently wished to go even further in the international protection of human rights and freedoms with the *Treaty of Versailles*, but backed off gingerly when the Japanese delegates to the Peace Conference insisted upon guarantees against racial discrimination.[27] Wilson's cowardice provoked riots in American cities where the frustrations of African-Americans were already manifesting themselves.[28]

Treaties adopted after the war concerning eastern Europe provided for protection of minority rights, the right to life, freedom of religion, equality before the law, and the prohibition of anti-Semitism.[29] The *Treaty of Versailles* also contemplated an idea that did not then prove particularly effective, but that would eventually take on dramatic proportions: the individual criminal responsibility of perpetrators of human rights abuses.

After the First World War, ongoing attention to the rights of labour was ensured by the establishment of the International Labour Organization (ILO), an arm of the League of Nations, created by Part XIII of the *Treaty of Versailles*. The International Labour Organization was responsible for scores of conventions dealing with the rights of labour and working conditions; the first, giving effect to one of Wilson's wartime promises, guaranteed an eight-hour working day.[30] Several of the labour conventions motivated Canadian lawmakers.[31] During the 1930s, the Canadian Parliament sought to legislate on such matters as unemployment insurance as part of the "Bennett new deal". There was a flurry of ratification of several of the ILO conventions early in 1935, followed by federal legislation that the Prime Minister defended as a measure to comply with Canada's interna-

26 *Treaty of Peace between the Allied and Associated Powers and Germany (Treaty of Versailles)* made at Versailles, 28 June 1919, TS 4 (1919) Cmd. 153, P. (1919) LIII 127, 112 BSP 1, 29 HCT. 603. The *Treaty of Versailles* and other post-war conventions were incorporated in Canadian law by the *Treaties of Peace Act, 1919* , SC 1919 (2nd sess.) v. 30.
27 John Humphrey, *Human Rights and the United Nations: A Great Adventure,* Dobbs Ferry, New York: Transnational, 1984, at 11.
28 Paul Gorden Lauren, *supra* note 25, p. 100.
29 *e.g.*, *Treaty of Peace between the United States of America, the British Empire, France, Italy and Japan, and Poland,* [1919] TS 8; *Treaty between the Principal Allied and Associated Powers and Roumania,* (1921) 5 LNTS 336; *Treaty between the Principal Allied and Associated Powers and Czechoslovakia,* [1919] TS 20; *Treaty between the Principal Allied and Associated Powers and the Serb-Croat-Slovene State,* [1919] TS 17.
30 *ILO Convention No. 1 Limiting the Hours of Work in Industrial Undertakings to 8 per Day and 48 per Week,* (1949) 38 UNTS 18.
31 Early efforts by the Canadian provinces to give effect to the labour conventions are discussed in Bryce M. Stewart, *Canadian Labour Laws and the Treaty,* New York: Columbia University Press, 1926, at 36 and ff.

tional obligations under those conventions.[32] The statutes were declared to cover matters whose pith and substance were under provincial jurisdiction and consequently declared *ultra vires* by the Judicial Committee of the Privy Council.[33] During the Second World War, the ILO briefly transferred its headquarters from Geneva to Montreal, and was located on the McGill University campus for the duration of the conflict.

The 1930s also witnessed the country's first halting steps at the legislative protection of human rights.[34] There were some initial moves at anti-discrimination legislation in Ontario during the early 1940s,[35] although Saskatchewan took the real pioneering step with the enactment of a human rights code in 1947.[36] Yet Canada at the time was in many ways a quite repressive society, and its human rights record compared unfavourably in several respects with that of the United States and the United Kingdom. For example, legislation enacted pursuant to the *War Measures Act*[37] went well beyond that of Canada's closest allies in prohibiting political activity and in ordering the internment of "enemy aliens".[38] In February 1942, the Cabinet ordered the removal of all Japanese Canadians from an area within 100 miles of the Pacific coast, despite the fact that senior military and Royal Canadian Mounted Police officials opposed such a measure on the grounds that the Japanese minority was no threat to security. More than 20,000 persons, many of them born in Canada, were persecuted during the war on this basis, forced to leave their homes and live in internment camps.[39] Cabinet decrees also denied the right to vote to Canadians of Japanese descent. The racist treatment of Canadians of Japanese origin did not end with the surrender in the Pacific theatre, and it was only in 1949 that

---

32 John Mainwairing, *The International Labour Organization, A Canadian View*, Ottawa: Supply and Services Canada, 1986.

33 *AG Canada* v. *AG Ontario (Labour Conventions Case)*, [1937] AC 326, [1937] 1 DLR 673, [1937] 1 WWR 299 (Canada P.C.).

34 *Insurance Act*, SO 1932, c. 24, s. 4: "Any licensed insurer which discriminates unfairly between risks within Ontario because of the race or religion of the insured shall be guilty of an offence." Such laws as *An Act to prevent the further introduction of Slaves and to limit the term of contracts for servitude within this Province*, 1793, SUC (2d sess.) v. 7, can be considered as the ancestors of our modern human rights legislation.

35 *Racial Discrimination Act, 1944*, SO 1944, c. 51.

36 *Saskatchewan Bill of Rights Act, 1947*, SS 1947, c. 35.

37 RSC 1927, c. 206.

38 Harold Laski, "Civil Liberties in Great Britain and Canada during War", (1942) 55 *Harvard Law Review* 1006.

39 Ken Adachi, *The Enemy that Never Was: A History of Japanese Canadians*, Toronto: McClelland & Stewart, 1991; Barry Broadfoot, *Years of Sorrow Years of Shame: The Story of Japanese Canadians in World War II*, Toronto: Doubleday, 1977; Ann Gomer Sunahara, *The Politics of Racism: The Uprooting of Japanese Canadians During the Second World War*, Toronto: Lorimer, 1981. See also: *Co-operative Committee on Japanese Canadians* v. *Canada (Attorney General)*, [1947] AC 87 (Canada PC).

discriminatory measures were finally repealed, and those interned allowed to return without restriction to British Columbia, and their right to vote restored.[40] Within Quebec, the *Padlock Law*[41] operated to prohibit the activities of communists and Jehovah's Witnesses.[42] In late 1945, following the revelations of Soviet embassy employee Igor Gouzenko, several suspects were arrested secretly and held *incommunicado*, without access to counsel or to family and friends. Under the *Continuation of Transitional Powers Act, 1945,*[43] which replaced the *War Measures Act*[44] at the close of the war, *habeas corpus* was suspended. Those detained were subsequently questioned, without the assistance of legal counsel, before a secret royal commission composed of two sitting Supreme Court judges.[45]

The Second World War marked a turning point in both international and Canadian law dealing with human rights and fundamental freedoms. Unlike the First World War, whose origins and whose *raison d'être* still remain clouded in machiavellian wrangling, confusion and misunderstanding, the Second World War was an international struggle against barbarism, genocide, totalitarianism and national oppression. Tens of millions were roused to enormous sacrifice by the promise of a new world order. The Second World War was pervaded with a moral authority its predecessor had lacked. The *Atlantic Charter*, signed by the United Kingdom and the United States only a few months before the latter's entry into the war, contained human rights proclamations of a general nature.[46] It acknowl-

---

40   SOR/48-92, Canada Gazette II, pp. 733-734, s. 3.

41   *Act respecting Communist Propaganda*, LQ 1937, c. 11.

42   William Kaplan, *State and Salvation, The Jehovah's Witnesses and Their Fight for Civil Rights*, Toronto: University of Toronto Press, 1989; M. James Penton, *Jehovah's Witnesses in Canada, Champions of Freedom of Speech and Worship*, Toronto: Macmillan, 1976. See also: *Saumur* v. *City of Quebec*, (1953) [1953] 2 SCR 299, [1954] 4 DLR 641; *Roncarelli* v. *Duplessis*, [1959] SCR 121, 16 DLR (2d) 689.

43   LC 1945 (2nd sess.) v. 25. Also: *Continuation of Transitional Measures Act, 1947*, LC 1947, c. 16.

44   *Supra* note 37.

45   M.H. Fyfe, "Some Legal Aspects of the Report of the Royal Commission on Espionage", (1946) 24 *Canadian Bar Review* 777; Amy Knight, *How the Cold War Began, The Gouzenko Affair and the Hunt for Soviet Spies*, Toronto: McClelland & Stewart, 2005. On the anti-Communist climate in general, see: Reg Whitaker & Gary Marcuse, *Cold War Canada: The Making of a National Insecurity State, 1945-1957*, Toronto/Buffalo/London: University of Toronto Press, 1994.

46   *Atlantic Charter*, [1942] CTS 1; signed on 14 August 1941 by Franklin D. Roosevelt and Winston Churchill (both signatures in the original are in Roosevelt's handwriting). No official version exists: *New Cambridge Modern History*, Vol. XII, Cambridge: Cambridge University Press, 1968, pp. 811-812. The *Atlantic Charter* has been referred to on several occasions by the Canadian courts: *Re Drummond Wren*, [1945] 4 DLR 674, [1945] OR 778 (HC); *Re Noble and Wolf*, [1948] 4 DLR 123, [1948] OR 579 (HC), affirmed, [1949] 4 DLR 375, [1949] OR 503 (CA), reversed, (1950) 1950 CarswellOnt 127 (SCC);

edged the right of all peoples to choose the form of government under which they wished to live, called for "improved labour standards, economic advancement, and social security", and declared that all states should abandon the use of force.[47] The *Atlantic Charter* was agreed to by Roosevelt and Churchill aboard the British battleship *Prince of Wales* in Placentia Bay, just off the coast of Newfoundland. Earlier that year, in his state of the union address, Roosevelt had proclaimed that the post-war system would be built upon "four essential human freedoms":

> The first is freedom of speech and expression – everywhere in the world.
> The second is freedom of every person to worship God in his own way – everywhere in the world.
> The third is freedom from want – which, translated into world terms, means economic understandings which will secure to every nation everywhere a healthy peacetime life for its inhabitants everywhere in the world.
> The fourth is freedom from fear – which, translated into international terms, means a world-wide reduction of armaments to such a point and in such a thorough fashion that no nation will be in a position to commit an act of physical aggression against any neighbour – anywhere in the world.

Franklin D. Roosevelt's stirring and immortal words were reprised in the preamble of the *Universal Declaration of Human Rights*: "Whereas disregard and contempt for human rights have resulted in barbarous acts which have outraged the conscience of mankind, and the advent of a world in which human beings shall enjoy freedom of speech and belief and freedom from fear and want has been proclaimed as the highest aspiration of the common people."[48]

In the middle of the following year, as the war drew to a close, diplomats meeting in San Francisco adopted the *Charter of the United Nations*,[49] which placed unprecedented emphasis on human rights. The *Charter* provided several references to human rights, and declared that "promoting and en-

---

Bhadauria v. *Board of Governors of Seneca College*, (1980) 105 DLR (3d) 707, 27 OR (2d) 142, 11 CCLT 121, 9 BLR 117, 81 CLLC 14,003 (CA), reversed, [1981] 2 SCR 181, 124 DLR (3d) 193, 2 CHRR D/468, 17 CCLT 106, 81 CLLC 14,117, 22 CPC 130, 14 BLR 157, 37 NR 455; *Board of Governors of Seneca College* v. *Bhadauria*, [1981] 2 SCR 181, 124 DLR (3d) 193, 2 CHRR D/486, 17 CCLT 106, 81 CLLC 14,117, 22 CPC 130, 14 BLR 157, 37 NR 455; *R.* v. *Finta*, (1989) 50 CCC (3d) 236, 64 CR (3d) 223, 44 CRR 23 (Ont HC), additional reasons at, (1987) 50 CCC 236 (Ont HC); *Canada Trust Co.* v. *Ontario Human Rights Commission*, (sub nom. *Leonard Foundation Trust, Re*) (1990) 37 OAC 191, 69 DLR (4th) 321 (CA).

47 On the role of the *Atlantic Charter* in the development of international human rights, see Elizabeth Borgwardt, *A New Deal for the World, America's Vision for Human Rights*, Cambridge and London: Harvard University Press, 2005, pp. 14-45.

48 *Universal Declaration of Human Rights*, GA Res. 217 A (III) UN Doc. A/810.

49 *Charter of the United Nations*, [1945] CTS 7, TS 67 (1946) Cmd. 7015, P. (1946-7) XXV 1, 145 BSP 805.

couraging respect for human rights and for fundamental freedoms for all without distinction as to race, sex, language, or religion" was among the purposes of the United Nations. To the dismay of many, the great powers reneged on earlier commitments to include a declaration of human rights within the *Charter* itself. Well before the San Francisco Conference in June 1945, at which the *United Nations Charter* was adopted, foreign ministries, academics and non-governmental organizations were at work preparing draft declarations of human rights designed to form part of the post-war legal regime and, ideally, to be contained within the constitutive document of the new organization.[50] One such initiative came from diplomat Escott Reid, who was part of Canada's delegation to the Dumbarton Oaks Conference, in August 1944. The first chapter of his "draft charter" was entitled "The rights of every man". Reid prepared the text following Dumbarton Oaks, in the hope that the Department of External Affairs might circulate it in preparation for the San Francisco Conference. The proposal was not taken up, and senior bureaucrat Hume Wrong apparently considered it a "wasted effort" although the Department did allow Reid to publish his proposal anonymously.[51] It was in fact circulated to the delegates at San Francisco in a pamphlet issued by the Free World Research Bureau entitled "The Constitution of the United Nations".[52] In February 1947, Reid also managed to slip references to his human rights proposals into a speech he drafted for Louis St. Laurent, who was then Secretary of State for External Affairs. St. Laurent's address was delivered to the Montreal branch of the United Nations Association, at a meeting attended by Eleanor Roosevelt, who had just been designated chair of the "nuclear" Commission on Human Rights of the United Nations.[53]

The compromise at San Francisco was to make ample reference to human rights in the *Charter* but to postpone adoption of anything substantive. Three years later, the United Nations General Assembly adopted the *Universal Declaration on Human Rights*,[54] in effect completing the work it had left unfinished at San Francisco. The *Universal Declaration of Human Rights* forms the centrepiece of the international law of human rights and

---

50 Louis B. Sohn, "How American International Lawyers Prepared for the San Francisco Bill of Rights", (1995) 89 *American Journal of International Law* 540; Johannes Morsink, "World War Two and the Universal Declaration", (1993) 15 *Human Rights Quarterly* 357; Hersh Lauterpacht, *An International Bill of the Rights of Man*, New York: Columbia University Press, 1945.

51 Escott Reid, *Radical Mandarin: The Memoirs of Escott Reid*, Toronto/Buffalo/London: University of Toronto Press, 1989, at 192.

52 National Archives of Canada MG 31, E 46, Vol. 3.

53 Escott Reid, *On Duty, A Canadian at the Making of the United Nations, 1945-1946*, Toronto: McClelland and Stewart, 1983, pp. 18-23.

54 *Universal Declaration of Human Rights*, *supra* note 48.

fundamental freedoms.[55] Eleanor Roosevelt and the Commission over which she presided had been assigned principal responsibility for the preparation of two human rights documents, a declaration and a covenant or treaty.[56] Canada was not then a member of the Commission, and did not in fact seek election to that body until 1963.[57] But the work of the Commission was driven by a remarkable Canadian, John Peters Humphrey, who had left his position as dean of the McGill University Faculty of Law in order to pilot human rights work within the United Nations. Humphrey was assigned the task of preparing an initial draft declaration of human rights. He submitted a forty-eight-article text, which was essentially a synthesis of all existing human rights provisions in national constitutions throughout the world as well as the various proposals received by the United Nations. The original of the Humphrey draft can be found in the archives of McGill University, together with most of Humphrey's papers from the period.

The preparation of the text of the *Declaration* was subsequently assigned to a small drafting committee, in which French jurist René Cassin

55 See: Gudmundur Alfredsson & Asbjorn Eide, eds., *The Universal Declaration of Human Rights – A Common Standard of Achievement*, The Hague: Kluwer Academic, 1999; Peter Baehr, Cees Flinterman & Mignon Senders, eds., *Innovation and Inspiration: Fifty Years of the Universal Declaration of Human Rights*, Amsterdam: Royal Netherlands Academy of Arts and Sciences, 1999; Gudmunder Alfredsson & Asbjorn Eide, eds., *The Universal Declaration of Human Rights: A Commentary*, Oslo: Oxford University Press/ Scandinavian University Press, 1992; René Cassin, "La Déclaration universelle et la mise en œuvre des droits de l'homme", (1951) 79 *Receuil de cours de l'Academie de droit international* 237; John Humphrey, "The Universal Declaration of Human Rights: Its History, Impact and Judicial Character", in Bertrand G. Ramcharan, ed., *Human Rights: Thirty Years After the Universal Declaration,* The Hague: Martinus Nijhoff, 1984.

56 UN Doc. E/CN.4/SR.1*. For a history of the work of the Commission on Human Rights in the drafting of the *Universal Declaration*, see Jean-Bernard Marie, *La Commission des droits de l'homme de l'O.N.U.*, Paris: Pedone, 1975. Other works dealing with the history of the *Declaration* include: Alfred Verdoodt, *Naissance et signification de la déclaration universelle des droits de l'homme*, Louvain/Paris: Nauwelaerts, 1963; Glen Johnson, "La rédaction de la Déclaration universelle (1946-1948)", in *La Déclaration universelle des droits de l'homme*, Paris: UNESCO/L'Harmattan, 1991, at 21-78; Johannes Morsink, *The Universal Declaration of Human Rights: Origins, Drafting, and Intent*, Philadelphia: University of Pennsylvania Press, 1999; Mary Ann Glendon, *A World Made New, Eleanor Roosevelt and the Universal Declaration of Human Rights*, New York: Random House, 2001; Paul Gorden Lauren, *The Evolution of International Human Rights, Visions Seen*, 2nd ed., Philadelphia: University of Pennsylvania Press, 2003, pp. 199-232; William Korcy, *NGOs and the Universal Declaration of Human Rights*, New York: St. Martin's Press, 1998.

57 Canada served on the Commission from 1963-1965, but its contribution during those years was unremarkable. It was elected again in 1975, and has been a member of the Commission since then, with a couple of two-year breaks.

played a pivotal role.[58] By June 1948, after three intense sessions, the Commission managed to adopt its final text, which then passed to the Economic and Social Council for what was only perfunctory consideration. The Council sent the draft to the General Assembly, whose autumn 1948 session was held in Paris at the Palais de Chaillot. During sessions of the General Assembly, the *Declaration* underwent comprehensive scrutiny and debate, most of this in the meetings of its Third Committee. Over the course of October and November 1948, the Third Committee voted no fewer than 1,400 times on various proposals and amendments, before finalizing the text on 7 December 1948. Although no Member States voted against the *Declaration*, there were seven abstentions, six from the Soviet Union and its allies, and Canada.[59] Three days later, the General Assembly adopted the text of the *Declaration*, with forty-eight Member States, including Canada, voting in favour. There were no contrary votes, although eight delegations, those of the Soviet Union, Bielorussia, Ukraine, Bulgaria, Romania, Albania, South Africa and Saudi Arabia, abstained.[60] A separate vote by show of hands was held on article 26, concerning the right to education, and on article 27, which protects the right to cultural life. Canada abstained on both provisions, as it had done in the Third Committee.[61]

1.2   Canada and the Adoption of the *Universal Declaration of Human Rights*

As the *Universal Declaration of Human Rights* was being drafted, the House of Commons proposed the creation of a Special Joint Committee of the Senate and the House of Commons on Human Rights and Fundamental Freedoms, with a mandate "to consider the question of human rights and fundamental freedoms, and the manner in which those obligations accepted by all members of the United Nations may best be implemented".[62] The resolution added:

> And, in particular, in the light of the provisions contained in the Charter of the United Nations, and the establishment by the Economic and Social Council thereof of a Commission on Human Rights, what is the legal and constitutional situation in Canada with respect to such rights, and what steps, if any, it would be advisable to take or to recommend for the purpose of

---

58 René Cassin, *supra* note 55. See: Eric Pateyron, *La contribution française à la rédaction de la Déclaration universelle des droits de l'homme, René Cassin et la Commission consultative des droits de l'homme*, Paris: La documentation française. 1998.

59 UN Doc. A/C.3/SR.178, p. 880.

60 Two Member States, Honduras and Yemen, were not present at the time of the vote.

61 National Archives of Canada RG 25, Vol. 3701, File 5475-DR-40, No. 611, 13 December 1948.

62 *Hansard*, 26 May 1947.

preserving in Canada respect for and observance of human rights and fundamental freedoms.

The Committee held seven sessions during June and July 1947, considering a range of documents including the 48-article initial draft of the *Universal Declaration* whose authorship is attributed to John Humphrey.[63] Lester B. Pearson, who was then Under-Secretary of State for External Affairs, wrote the Secretary-General of the United Nations, Trygvie Lie, informing him of the Special Joint Committee and asking authorization for Humphrey to appear as a witness.[64] In Humphrey's testimony before the Committee, he modestly described the 48-article draft as being produced by the "secretariat".[65]

The Legal Adviser to the Department of External Affairs, E.R. Hopkins, explained that the *Declaration* "would eventually be submitted to the General Assembly of the United Nations and approved by a Resolution of that body, in which case it would have only a quasi-juridical force, a moral force having the character of a strong recommendation. It would however be of a highly persuasive nature."[66] He distinguished the *Declaration* with a full-blown human rights treaty, which was also being considered and which would, in contrast with the *Declaration*, bind States parties that had ratified or acceded to it. In turn, Humphrey also sought to appease the anxious parliamentarians by insisting upon the non-binding nature of the *Declaration*, stating that "a resolution of the General Assembly has no binding effect on international law", although he added prudently: "I think it would be an element in the building up of international jurisprudence. You cannot take

---

63 "Draft Outline of the International Bill of Rights (Prepared by the Division on Human Rights)", Appendix D, pp. 57-62, UN Doc. E/CN.4/AC.1/3. See also: "Memorandum from Lester B. Pearson to Louis St. Laurent", 18 June 1947, National Archives of Canada RG 25, Vol. 3700, File 5475-W-40.

64 "Letter from Lester B. Pearson, USSEA to Trygvie Lie, June 16, 1947", National Archives of Canada RG 25, Vol. 6281, 5475-W-40, [Pt. 1.1]. Also: "Letter from Trygvie Lie to Lester B. Pearson, June 26, 1947", National Archives of Canada RG 25, Vol. 6281, 5475-W-40, [Pt. 1.1].

65 Canada, Special Joint Committee of the Senate and the House of Commons on Human Rights and Fundamental Freedoms, *Minutes of Proceedings and Evidence*, Ottawa: King's Printer, 1947, p. 90. He also conceded that "the final project, [was] elaborated by Professor Cassin for the drafting committee", (p. 96) adding that "Professor Cassin used the secretariat documents as the basis of this draft, in that some of the sections are textually the same", (p. 97). Humphrey told the Commission: "Professor Cassin, who is president of the Commission, and who was familiar with the French position and the French member of the Commission on Human Rights was asked to take the secretariat draft and rewrite it with the idea of presenting something that could be put forward in the form of a declaration." (p. 105).

66 *Ibid.*, p. 13.

it for granted that it would have no legal significance at all."[67] The Committee requested that provincial attorneys general and heads of Canadian law schools be solicited for their views on the power of the federal Parliament to enact a comprehensive Bill of Rights applicable to all of Canada, and recommended that a joint committee be appointed to resume its work at the next session.[68]

The Special Joint Committee of the Senate and the House of Commons on Human Rights and Fundamental Freedoms spent several sessions examining the draft *Declaration*, article by article. The proceedings are a revealing guide to prevailing attitudes on human rights matters, and on the nervousness with which much of Canada's political elite approached the question. Among the few real proposals to emerge was the suggestion that "the name of God should be embodied" in the *Declaration*. One honourable member urged that where draft article 1 referred to "dignity and rights", the words "and rights" should be replaced with "being vested by their Creator with unalienable rights."[69] An apparent consensus emerged recommending that Cassin's text of article 1 be replaced with the following: "All men are born free and equal in dignity being vested by the Creator with unalienable rights. They are endowed by Him with reason and conscience, and should act towards one another like brothers."[70]

When attention turned to the non-discrimination provision of the draft *Declaration*, that eventually became article 2, some parliamentarians expressed concern about how this might apply to Canadians of Japanese descent, and to Amerindians.[71] At one point, the chair noted: "Somewhere in these articles there is the right of movement of citizens within their own country, and if you wish to have a law preventing a movement of the Japanese from one part of the country to the other which we have at the present time it could well be argued it is contrary to this *Declaration*."[72] A Member of Parliament from British Columbia quickly interjected that there was no human rights violation in the treatment of the Japanese, who had been interned not because of "race" but because of "loyalty or subversive

---

67 *Ibid.*, p. 93. Many years later, Humphrey was one of the more outspoken advocates of the view that the *Universal Declaration* constitutes a codification of customary norms and is thus binding on all States: John P. Humphrey, "La nature juridique de la Déclaration universelle des droits de l'Homme", (1981) 12 *Revue générale de droit* 397; John P. Humphrey, "The Universal Declaration of Human Rights: Its History, Impact and Judicial Character", *supra* note 55; John Humphrey, "The International Bill of Rights: Scope and Implementation", (1976) 17 *William & Mary Law Review* 527.
68 *Ibid.*, p. v.
69 *Ibid.*, p. 52.
70 *Ibid.*, p. 59.
71 *Ibid.*, p. 72.
72 *Ibid.*, p. 75.

attitudes".[73] As for aboriginal peoples, it was questioned whether the *Declaration*'s democratic rights provision (eventually, article 21) might entitle them to vote (status Indians were not allowed to vote in Canada until 1960).[74] Senator Gouin explained that "they have the right to choose to be wards of the state and not vote, or to vote and have freedom".[75]

Concern was expressed about the right to life provision (article 3 in the final draft). Cassin had intentionally omitted reference to the death penalty, with the view that the *Declaration* would evolve into an abolitionist instrument.[76] Unaware of Cassin's intentions, the Committee chair noted: "Certainly there is an exception in countries which have capital punishment. I suppose that is covered by a subsequent section and so therefore all the *Declaration* amounts to is that everyone has the right to life, except those whose lives are taken away by process of law."[77] But a member of the Committee, Marquis, was skeptical: "It seems to me that we are going as far as advocating the removal of capital punishment."[78] Marquis was also intrigued by the possibility that the prohibition of torture or other cruel, inhuman and degrading treatment or punishment (article 5 of the final draft) might outlaw hanging, but the chair reassured him.[79] Members of the Committee also concluded that flogging would not be prohibited by the provision.[80]

The economic and social clauses of the *Declaration*, which are found in articles 22-26 of the final version, were treated with considerable levity by the Committee. Member of Parliament John Hackett described the right to an adequate standard of living as being "a statement of political economy, not human rights".[81] When it came to the right to rest and leisure (article 24 in the final version), Senators and MPs joked about whether vacations should be compulsory. The chair said "they should be frequent and they should be long".[82]

The Special Joint Committee of the Senate and the House of Commons on Human Rights and Fundamental Freedoms reconvened in April 1948,

---

73 *Ibid.* In fact, no Japanese-Canadian was ever charged with subversive activities.

74 *Canada Elections Act*, SC 1960, c. 39, s. 14.

75 Canada, Special joint committee of the Senate and the House of Commons on Human Rights and Fundamental Freedoms, *Minutes of Proceedings and Evidence*, Ottawa: King's Printer, 1947, p. 72.

76 UN Doc. E/CN.4/AC.1/SR.2, p. 10. This is discussed in William A. Schabas, *The Abolition of the Death Penalty in International Law*, 3rd ed., Cambridge: Cambridge University Press, 2003.

77 *Supra* note 65, p. 76.

78 *Ibid.*, p. 77.

79 *Ibid.*

80 *Ibid.*, p. 96.

81 *Ibid.*, p. 155.

82 *Ibid.*, p. 157.

and learned that the Canadian government had received a report from the United Nations Commission on Human Rights on its December 1947 session,[83] with a request for comments on the evolving drafts.[84] Secretary of State for External Affairs St. Laurent had replied to the Secretary-General of the United Nations, on 1 April 1948, explaining that Canada sought the advice of Parliament before expressing its views. St. Laurent indicated a hint of reticence within the Government, launching the suggestion that the United Nations might consider postponing the adoption of the *Declaration* for at least another year.[85] In its report to Parliament, the Committee concluded: "Although not legally binding upon States, such a document, being a statement of principles, will tend to influence the course of legislation in States which consider themselves morally bound by its provisions, and will, therefore, promote human rights and fundamental freedoms."[86] The Committee noted that it had not attempted to redraft the entire *Declaration*, but simply to examine critically the principles set out in the working draft generated by the Commission at its December 1947 session. The report states:

> Your Committee considers that the *Declaration* would be more effective if stated in a shorter, more concise form. As there is no assurance that any specific draft prepared by your Committee would be accepted by the United Nations, your Committee does not suggest any particular revision of the draft submitted but recommends that the Government, in presenting its views to the United Nations, have in mind the views of members of your Committee as reported in the record of proceedings evidence.[87]

Canada was rather proud of the fact that its elected officials had reviewed the draft *Declaration*, something that few, if any, of the other members of the United Nations had apparently taken the trouble to do. At the August 1948 meeting of the United Nations Economic and Social Council, a Canadian delegate, L.A.D. Stephens, referred to the work of the Joint Parliamentary Committee, and told the gathering that the Committee "had been able to report on [the draft *Declaration*] in highly favourable terms". Conveying one of the suggestions to emerge from the Committee's deliberations, he said that Canada "fully agreed" with an amendment to article 1 that would indicate the "Creator" as the source of rights, and pledged that "the Canadian delegation to the General Assembly would be anxious to

---

83 UN Doc. E/600.
84 *Hansard*, 13 February 1948.
85 Canada, Special Joint Committee of the Senate and the House of Commons on Human Rights and Fundamental Freedoms, *Minutes of Proceedings and Evidence*, Ottawa: King's Printer, 1948, pp. 22, 51.
86 *Ibid.*, p. 207.
87 *Ibid.*

support such an amendment".[88] Stephens also singled out article 23 (article 26 in the final version) dealing with the right to education. He said that the provision might have been more appropriate in a UNESCO resolution. A reference to incitement to discrimination (article 7 in the final version) was described as being vague, and Stephens said it should either be clarified or deleted.[89] As for the economic and social rights clauses (articles 22-26 in the final version), the Canadian representative said that they went beyond the purpose of the *Declaration*, and became, in effect, a proclamation of governmental responsibilities. "A simple general statement of the right to social security would have been preferable." But Stephens cautioned that these were only minor criticisms, "and did not detract from the admiration which the Canadian delegation felt for the *Declaration* in general". According to Stephens, Canada "would support the *Declaration*, with the necessary modifications, in the conviction that its adoption would add to the sum total of human dignity, happiness and decency".[90]

The draft *Universal Declaration* was also studied by an interdepartmental committee on human rights. The Committee urged that "Canada must take a firm stand for the adoption of a Declaration of Human Rights by U.N. To oppose the document is tantamount to denying its principles."[91] Perhaps even more than the Parliamentary Committee, the interdepartmental committee was painfully aware of the shortcomings of Canadian legislation. Under draft article 3, which concerned the right to equality, the committee noted that much Canadian legislation dealing with elections appeared to be discriminatory. For example, it observed that the British Columbia *Provincial Elections Act* disqualified Japanese, Indians, Doukhobors, Hutterites and Menonites from voting, the Alberta *Elections Act* denied the right to vote to Indians, and the Dominion *Elections Act* prevented Eskimos and Indians resident on reservations from voting. The Committee also noted that Hutterites in Alberta could not purchase land, and that "[t]he Common Law of Quebec discriminates in certain respects against women".[92] The Committee's recommendation was that "[i]f this article is

---

88 UN Doc. E/SR.216, p. 655.
89 In its final version, article 7 of the *Declaration* states: "All are entitled to equal protection against any discrimination in violation of this Declaration and against any incitement to such discrimination."
90 UN Doc. E/SR.216, p. 655.
91 "Inter-Departmental Committee on Human Rights, Draft International Declaration on Human Rights", National Archives of Canada RG 25, Vol. 6281, 5475-W-40, [Pt. 1.1].
92 Quebec now has some of the most progressive family law provisions in the developed world. But under the *Civil Code* then in force, which was essentially unchanged from the version adopted in 1861, and that was based on the French *Civil Code*, married women were deprived of their civic identity, and could not even enter into contracts without the consent of their husbands.

adopted, it may be necessary in Canada to consider statutes which will prohibit discrimination". With respect to the right to life (article 4 of the draft, article 3 of the final version), the interdepartmental committee said that "[a]s a general principle it is satisfactory but it should be borne in mind that a revision of the laws of capital punishment may become necessary if it is adopted". On the presumption of innocence, the committee noted problems with reverse onus provisions in Canadian criminal law, and re-called that persons had been interned during wartime without any hearing. Other comments referred to the Quebec *Padlock Law*, and various discrim-inatory measures against religious minorities, such as Jehovah's Witnesses, Hutterites and Mennonites. On the right to work, the committee observed: "It is accordingly doubtful if Canada can subscribe to the Article in its present form without a change of Government policy."[93]

There were public signs of opposition within Canada, notably in a resolution of the influential Canadian Bar Association, adopted 3 September 1948, stating that "the said draft *Declaration* ought to be examined with the utmost care in all its juridical aspects before further action is taken, so that there may be no misunderstanding as to the meaning and effect thereof".[94] The 1948 Convention of the Association, which had opened with a disgrace-ful defense of Quebec's "padlock law" by keynote speaker Premier Maurice Duplessis, exuded an obsessive antagonism to the whole question of judicial protection of human rights.[95] The Duplessis speech was followed by the presidential address of John T. Hackett, a Montreal lawyer and federal member of Parliament for the Conservative Party, consisting principally of a cynical diatribe on the draft declaration. For Hackett,

> These human rights and fundamental freedoms exist in Christian civilization. They do not exist elsewhere. They have never existed elsewhere.[96]

His message was that protection of human rights would be achieved not by declarations under the aegis of the United Nations but by the promotion of Christianity.

During the sessions of the General Assembly, and of its Third Com-mittee, at which the final draft of the *Declaration* was debated, Canada did not participate very actively. Despite initial promises to present a range of

---

93 *Supra* note 91.
94 *The 1948 Yearbook of the Canadian Bar Association and the Minutes of Proceedings of the Thirtieth Annual Meeting*, Ottawa: National Printers Limited, 1949, p. 142.
95 *Ibid.*, p. 19. Walter S. Tarnopolsky interpreted the proceedings in the Canadian Bar Association somewhat more charitably, downplaying the organization's hostility to hu-man rights: Walter S. Tarnopolsky, *The Canadian Bill of Rights*, 2nd ed., Toronto: McClelland and Stewart, 1975, pp. 6-7.
96 *Ibid.*, pp. 100, 142.

amendments, Canada never did take any such initiatives.[97] A telegram dated 28 September 1948 from E.A. Côté, a member of the Canadian delegation already present in Paris, to George Ignatieff, in the United Nations Division of External Affairs, states that "[w]e do not feel [the *Declaration*] can be supported".[98] On 7 October 1948, the delegation received a discouraging telegram, and a day later a personal message arrived from Louis St. Laurent indicating the Acting Prime Minister's serious misgivings about the *Declaration*. "We were advised not to take a prominent part in the discussion on individual articles, until our position on the *Declaration* as a whole had been further clarified", recapitulated a subsequent report from Paris.[99] The Canadian delegation read the signals from Ottawa without difficulty and, on 11 October 1948, wrote back: "In accordance with your instructions the Canadian delegation will not sponsor nor support the early passage of the Declaration on Human Rights in its present form."[100] When the Third Committee came to the provisions dealing with economic and social rights (articles 22-26 in the final version), Canada made an important statement indicating its unhappiness with the provisions, and invoking the spectre of provincial jurisdiction:

> After careful consideration, the Canadian delegation has come to the opinion that it should abstain from voting on these four articles, but we wish immediately to stress the fact that no one should interpret our abstention as an opposition to the principles set forth in Article 20 [article 22 in the final version] and in those three immediately succeeding articles. We wish to make it clear, however, that, in regard to any obligations that may arise under the Declaration of Human Rights, the Federal Government in Canada will not invade the field of provincial jurisdiction, particularly in regard to education. It is for this reason that I shall abstain on these articles.[101]

---

97 "Report on Draft Declaration of Human Rights up to the 23 November – (Articles 1 to 22, inclusive) November 25, 1948", National Archives of Canada RG 25, Vol. 3700, File 5475-DM-1-40 No. 31, p. 5, para. 8.

98 "Telegram from Coté to Ignatieff, September 28, 1948", National Archives of Canada RG 25, Vol. 3699, File 5475-DG-2-40, No. 63.

99 *Ibid.*

100 National Archives of Canada RG 25, Vol. 3701, File 5475-DR-40, No. 165, 11 October 1948.

101 For the original text, see: "Report on Draft Declaration of Human Rights. . .", *supra* note 97. For the précis in the summary records: UN Doc. A/C.3/SR.138, pp. 500-501. Also: National Archives of Canada RG 25, Vol. 3700, File 5475-DN-40, No. 402, 16 November 1948; National Archives of Canada RG 25, Vol. 3699, File 5475-DG-2-40, No. 458, 22 November 1948.

As pledged, Canada subsequently abstained in the vote on all of the economic and social rights.[102] The Canadian delegation report described article 23, which recognizes the right to work, as the "most contentious single article of the *Declaration*".[103] This was an evident exaggeration because the provision as a whole was carried handsomely, by thirty-nine votes, with only Canada and China abstaining, and the United States opposing.[104]

The *Universal Declaration* contains no provision dealing with the rights of ethnic minorities, although one had been drafted by the Sub-Commission on the Prevention of Discrimination and Protection of Minorities,[105] and it was defended by Yugoslavia, the Soviet Union and Denmark in the Third Committee.[106] Many States were uneasy with the issue because of the failure of the League of Nations minorities protection system and the suspicion that it had been exploited by Nazi warmongers.[107] Canada's representative in the Third Committee made an important statement in opposition to the inclusion of a minority rights clause in the *Declaration*, based on the questionable premise that Canada had no problems in this area:

> Some attempt has been in the Committee, to define the word "minority", and thus give its proper context in these resolutions. It has been stated that the problem of minorities may arise as the result of the arrival in a country of new settlers from a foreign country, or it may arise from the unfavourable circumstances in which certain indigenous national groups may find themselves.
>
> I can say quite confidently that for Canada the problem of minorities, regarded in *either* of these two ways, does not exist; that is to say it is not pre-set in the sense that there is discontent. In the first place, Canada is a country made up of English speaking and French speaking Canadians, and I trust by the very use of these words I am making clear that neither of these groups falls in the category of a "minority" referred to in these draft resolutions. These two peoples, who comprise the greatest number of Canadian citizens, carry on their

---

102 "Report on Draft Declaration of Human Rights. . .", *ibid.*, p. 15; "Final Report, Item 58, Universal Declaration of Human Rights, Supplementary to and continuing Interim Report submitted under cover of despatch No. 31 of 25th November from Chairman of the Canadian Delegation, by J.H. Thurrott, Second Secretary at the Canadian Embassy in Brussels, sent to George Ignatieff, December 21, 1948", National Archives of Canada RG 25, Vol. 3700, File 5475-DM-1-40, pp. 2, 7.

103 "Final Report, Item 58, Universal Declaration of Human Rights. . .", *ibid.*, p. 5.

104 *Ibid.*, p. 689.

105 UN Doc. E/CN.4/52, pp. 9-10.

106 Albert Verdoodt, "Influence des structures ethniques et linguistiques des pays membres des Nations Unites sur la rédaction de la Déclaration universelle des droits de l'homme", in *Liber Amicorum Discipulorumque René Cassin*, Paris: Pedone, 1969, pp. 403-416.

107 Pablo de Azcarate, *League of Nations and National Minorities*, Washington: Carnegie Endowment for International Peace, 1945; Patrick Thornberry, *International Law and the Rights of Minorities*, Oxford: Clarendon Press, 1991; Thomas D. Musgrave, *Self Determination and National Minorities*, Oxford: Clarendon Press, 1997.

lives and activities with complete amity one towards the other, and each has its own language and makes use of its own educational facilities and contributes its own cultural tradition to our country.[108]

Canada's representative did not return to the subject of indigenous peoples, although he did discuss the status of immigrants:

> There were many European and non-European immigrants in Canada. They were free to worship as they pleased and to speak their own language. The Government's policy was one of voluntary assimilation, looking forward to the day when the immigrant would regard himself as a Canadian citizen. While Canadians were free to use whatever language they wanted, the question of education remained within the jurisdiction of each province and the federal Government neither wished nor was able to interfere in that connection.[109]

In the end, the General Assembly decided to leave the question for another day[110] and, of course, an important minority rights provision was finally included in the *International Covenant on Civil and Political Rights.*[111] Canada also voted against another unsuccessful Yugoslav proposal, seeking to add a national rights provision to the *Declaration,* on the grounds that it was superfluous.[112]

Some popular mythology persists about Canada's heroic record in these early days of human rights. For example, the Standing Senate Committee on Human Rights, in its 2001 report, said that "Canada was at the table and played a key role in the drafting of the *Universal Declaration of Human Rights. . .*"[113] John Humphrey was more reserved. Many years after the Paris session of the General Assembly, he wrote: "I knew that the international promotion of human rights had no priority in Canadian foreign policy."[114]

---

108 "Final Report, Item 58, Universal Declaration of Human Rights. . .", *supra* note 102, Appendix H.

109 UN Doc. A/C.3/SR.162, p. 729.

110 GA Res. 217 C (III). See: William A. Schabas, "Les droits des minorités: Une déclaration inachevée", in *Déclaration universelle des droits de l'homme 1948-98, Avenir d'un idéal commun,* Paris: La Documentation française, 1999, pp. 223-242; Johannes Morsink, "Cultural Genocide, the Universal Declaration, and Minority Rights", (1999) 21 *Human Rights Quarterly* 1009.

111 *International Covenant on Civil and Political Rights,* (1976) 999 UNTS 171, [1976] CTS 47, art. 27. In one of its first rulings, the Human Rights Committee concluded that Canada was in breach of article 27 of the *Covenant.* The case dealt with discrimination against aboriginal women: *Lovelace* v. *Canada,* [1983] Can. Hum. Rts. Y.B. 305, 68 ILR 17.

112 "Final Report, Item 58, Universal Declaration of Human Rights. . .", *supra* note 102, p. 10.

113 The Senate: *Promises to Keep: Implementing Canada's Human Rights Obligations,* Ottawa, December 2001, p. 14.

114 John P. Humphrey, *Human Rights and the United Nations: A Great Adventure,* Dobbs Ferry, New York: Transnational, 1984.

Certainly, the public profile, in terms of Canadian participation in the General Assembly debates, suggested real indifference. But behind the scenes, there was much trepidation in Canada about the *Declaration*, which was discussed by the Cabinet on two occasions prior to the vote in the General Assembly.

Lester B. Pearson, who was serving as Minister of External Affairs, prepared a telegram of instructions for the delegation in Paris. He wrote that "it would be difficult for us to oppose actively the adoption of a *Declaration* strongly supported by the United States and the United Kingdom" but added that "we would not, repeat not, wish to be responsible in any way for its adoption in its present form at this session of the General Assembly". Pearson urged the delegation to secure a complete revision of the draft that would exclude Soviet amendments, adding that "[a]ll attempts by Soviet States to amend it would have to be voted down. Such a declaration might be a useful weapon in the cold war." If that failed, Pearson advised the delegation to attempt to have the draft referred to a body of international jurists, preferably the International Law Commission, which had just been set up, noting that "[y]ou will no doubt be aware of the resolution passed recently by the Canadian Bar Association". As a last resort,

> . . . it is our view that in the absence of instructions to the contrary, you should abstain from voting for the adoption of the draft in its present form, explaining that the present declaration is so ambiguous in some of its articles as to raise genuine doubts regarding the meaning and effect of its provisions. You might also indicate that under the constitutional arrangements in Canada, as a federal state, the field of human rights is one in which the provinces of Canada are directly concerned, and that accordingly the Canadian delegation feels particularly anxious that, even though the *Declaration* will not have an absolutely juridical force, its terms should not be such as to invite disputes in their interpretation.[115]

Pearson had left instructions that the draft cable be discussed with the Acting Prime Minister, Louis St. Laurent, and that it be sent only if the latter agreed. Notes in the archives indicate that St. Laurent "suggested certain minor alterations which were incorporated". When the powerful J.W. Pickersgill of the Privy Council Office returned St. Laurent's comments on the telegram to George Ignatieff of the Department of External Affairs, he suggested that a supplementary telegram be sent to the delegation setting out "Mr. St. Laurent's misgivings regarding the *Declaration*".[116] St.

115   National Archives of Canada RG 25, Vol. 3701, File 5475-DR-40, No. 110, 8 October 1948.

116   "Memo to Secretary of State for External Affairs, October 14, 1948", National Archives of Canada RG 25, Vol. 3701, File 5475-DR-40.

Laurent reviewed a second draft cable prepared by Ignatieff, pencilling an additional sentence that went to the heart of his worries:

> I am particularly concerned about the uses which could be made of text of articles 17, 18, 19 and 22 [freedom of speech, freedom of association, freedom of assembly, and the right to employment in the public service] as an undertaking not to discriminate against communists because of their political views and of article 27 as obliging a state to provide higher education to everyone at the cost of the state if he cannot pay for it.[117]

St. Laurent decided to bring the matter to Cabinet. On November 8, Ottawa asked for Pearson's recommendations on the course to follow, in preparation for the November 17 Cabinet meeting.[118] Pearson replied that referring the draft declaration to the International Law Commission, a delaying tactic that had initially appealed to Ottawa, "would be overwhelmingly defeated"[119] because "[n]early all the other delegations – including the United Kingdom and the United States – are anxious to get the *Declaration* approved by this Assembly".[120] Pearson noted that the version to be adopted would most certainly contain "features found objectionable in the original text by the Parliamentary Committee and by the Canadian Bar Association". He also referred to the economic and social clauses of the draft *Declaration* "which raise questions of provincial jurisdiction in Canada". Pearson proposed that Canada make a general statement in the Third Committee on the economic and social clauses, "emphasizing our constitutional position and our consequent inability to vote in favour of these articles". The Cabinet decided that Canada was to abstain in the vote on the economic and social clauses, on the ground that their subject matter was not within the jurisdiction of the government of Canada; to abstain on the same ground at the plenary session from voting on the resolution for adoption of the draft declaration as a whole; and to explain clearly the Canadian constitutional difficulties, possibly making reference to the view that the

---

117 "Hand-written memo to file by Acting Prime Minister of Canada", National Archives of Canada RG 25, Vol. 3701, File 5475-DR-40.

118 National Archives of Canada RG 25, Vol. 3701, File 5475-DR-40, No. 217, 8 November 1948.

119 Another member of the delegation, R.G. Riddell, wrote to Reid in Ottawa: "such a proposal will be defeated. Even so, the Canadian delegation would then probably be in a better position to explain our abstention on the Declaration as finally approved by Committee III." See: "Progress Report on Committee III, November 1, 1948", National Archives of Canada RG 25, Vol. 3699, File 5475-DG-2-40.

120 See UN Doc. A/C.3/SR.108, p. 201, where a member of the Canadian delegation, Macdonnell, said: "In view of the limited time at the Committee's disposal, he thought the Committee might consider the possibility of postponing the discussion on the declaration of human rights to another session of the Assembly, or of referring it for study to another organ of the United Nations."

whole declaration might well be referred for further study to the International Law Commission.[121] It was an improvised, amateurish strategy that showed just how out of touch Canada's political leaders were at the time with respect to the evolving values of the international community.

Pearson was unhappy with the Cabinet decision. He warned Ottawa of the dangers of abstention, acknowledging that he was the source of the original idea, but that there was now a concern Canada would be associated with a group of unsavoury states.[122] Cabinet reconsidered the matter the following week, and decided that Pearson was to

> stat[e] clearly in the Assembly that, while the government were generally favourable to the objectives set out in the *Declaration*, the subject matter thereof was largely outside the jurisdiction of the government of Canada; furthermore, in supporting the resolution, the government relied upon the provisions of article 28 [the limitations clause, which became article 29(2) in the final version] as a safeguard against any unacceptable interpretation of certain other articles of the declaration.[123]

A telegram to Pearson reporting on the Cabinet position explained that many ministers felt that "the language and scope of the declaration are thoroughly objectionable for numerous reasons and that the adoption of the declaration in anything like the present form may do more harm to the cause of the United Nations and of freedom than if no (repeat no) Declaration were adopted at all". Moreover,

> [q]uite apart from the question of provincial jurisdiction, the Cabinet holds strongly to the view that the language is sometimes so lacking in precision as to make some articles incapable of application. Article No. 19 [subsequently 21], conferring the right to public employment irrespective of political creed, must be read as requiring the employment of Communists in the government service, while Article 16 [subsequently 18] would permit the unrestricted activities of sects like Jehovah's Witnesses.[124]

Pearson changed his mind yet again, deciding it would be better to abstain in the vote in the Third Committee, but then cast a positive vote in the General Assembly. His strategy was authorized by Ottawa and, to the

---

121 "Cabinet Conclusions, November 17, 1948", National Archives of Canada RG 2, A5a, Vol. 2642; also: "Memorandum of Cabinet Decision, November 17, 1948", National Archives of Canada RG 25, Vol. 3701, File 5475-DR-40.

122 National Archives of Canada RG 25, Vol. 3701, File 5475-DR-40, No. 461, 23 November 1948. Also: "Memorandum of Escott Reid to Assistant Under-Secretary of State for External Affairs, November 23, 1948", RG 25, Vol. 3701, File 5475-DR-40.

123 "Cabinet Conclusions, November 24, 1948", National Archives of Canada RG 2, A5a, Vol. 2642; also: "Memorandum of Cabinet Decision, November 24, 1948", National Archives of Canada RG 25, Vol. 3701, File 5475-DR-40.

124 National Archives of Canada RG 25, Vol. 3701, File 5475-DR-40, No. 294, 25 November 1948.

shock and dismay of many observers, including John Humphrey, Pearson duly abstained when the final text of the *Universal Declaration* was proposed in the Third Committee, on 7 December 1948. Pearson promptly explained in a cable to Ottawa:

> There was considerable surprise at the association of Canada with the Slavs. It certainly is regrettable that it had to occur but in view of the messages from Ottawa, we felt that we had no alternative. I hope that no misunderstanding arises in Canada over the situation. We will, however, make an explanatory statement at the plenary session and as agreed, change our vote in favour of the resolution.[125]

A little later in the day, he sent another telegram:

> All members present voted for the Declaration, none against, and the seven abstentions consisted of Canada and the Soviet Six. Chang (China), Malik (Lebanon) and Humphrey of Secretariat are at a loss as to why we should have taken this stand. I shall probably make a statement in the plenary to put this matter into proper perspective, though it will probably appear that the Canadian representative on Committee III is the sacrificial goat.[126]

The next day, Pearson informed Ottawa that the delegation had been urgently approached by the United Kingdom and the United States who had stressed "the propaganda importance of getting on record some statement of the rights which were being denied to people daily within the Soviet bloc as so great that they were prepared to accept the declaration in its present form. They regarded our abstention as a serious weakening of the propaganda position which they were hoping to achieve." Pearson also informed them that Canada would change its vote in the plenary General Assembly, something which soon must have become an open secret in Paris.[127] According to historian Robert Spencer, Canada's abstention was an "embarrassing association with the Soviet group" that "caused a mild sensation".[128] John Humphrey wrote:

---

125 National Archives of Canada RG 25, Vol. 3701, File 5475-DR-40, No. 560, 7 December 1948.

126 "Daily reports of delegation meetings, December 7, 1948", National Archives of Canada RG 25, Vol. 3700, File 5475-DN-40, No. 562. Earlier in the day, a laconic telegram to Ottawa from the Canadian delegation had announced: "Convention (sic) adopted December 6th (sic) with no contrary votes, 7 abstentions (including Canada)". National Archives of Canada RG 25, Vol. 3699, File 5475-DG-2-40, No. 566, 7 December 1948.

127 According to National Archives of Canada RG 25, Vol. 3700, File 5475-DN-40, No. 579, 9 December 1948, the Canadian delegation had already "told certain press representatives here privately that we will vote for the resolution in the plenary session".

128 Robert A. Spencer, *Canada in World Affairs, 1946-1949*, Toronto: Oxford University Press, 1959, pp. 162-163. The phrase "mild sensation" was used in the Canadian Press wire story: *The Globe and Mail*, 8 December 1948, p. 1.

It was the Canadian abstention which shocked everyone, including me. The Canadians had given me no warning, and I was quite unprepared for what happened. Although I knew that the international promotion of human rights had no priority in Canadian foreign policy, it had never occurred to me that the government would carry its indifference to the point of abstaining in such an important vote. I could hardly have prevented the scandal even if the delegation had taken me into their confidence, but I could at least have warned them of the company in which they would probably find themselves.[129]

There is a suggestion in the documents in the National Archives of Canada of some consternation in Ottawa because Pearson had abstained in the Third Committee without making any explanatory comment.[130] Whether or not this was an intelligent approach, Pearson had clearly informed Ottawa that he would follow such a course.[131] Cabinet was immediately notified of the developments, and of Pearson's intention to vote in favour of the draft declaration in the plenary General Assembly, making a statement at that time. Cabinet again endorsed Pearson's actions.[132] Pearson and Brooke Claxton exchanged cables over the next few days, fine tuning the speech that was to be delivered in the General Assembly.[133]

Prior to the vote on the *Universal Declaration* as a whole, Pearson addressed the General Assembly – over which only a few years later he would preside – explaining the Canadian concerns and reservations.[134] He said that Canada regarded the document as one inspired by the highest ideals, and that the great goal of the United Nations must be to move towards full and universal application of the principles set out in the draft instrument. He continued:

> The Draft Declaration, because it is a statement of general principles, is unfortunately, though no doubt unavoidably, often worded in vague and imprecise language. We do not believe in Canada that legislation should be placed on our statute books unless that legislation can indicate in precise terms the obligations which are demanded of our citizens, and unless those obligations can be interpreted clearly and definitively in the courts. Obviously many of the clauses of

---

129   John P. Humphrey, *supra* note 114.
130   "Memo from Escott Reid to Brooke Claxton, December 8, 1948", National Archives of Canada RG 25, Vol. 3701, File 5475-DR-40.
131   National Archives of Canada RG 25, Vol. 3701, File 5475-DR-40, No. 534, 3 December 1948.
132   "Cabinet Conclusions, December 8, 1948", National Archives of Canada RG 2, A5a, Vol. 2642.
133   "Brooke Claxton to Lester B. Pearson", National Archives of Canada RG 25, Vol. 3701, File 5475-DR-40, No. 366, 9 December 1948; "Lester B. Pearson to Brooke Claxton", RG 25, Vol. 3701, File 5475-DR-40, No. 596, 9 December 1948.
134   UN Doc. A/PV.182, 81-91. The speech can also be found at: *External Affairs*, I, January 1949, pp. 23-24; Robert Alexander Mackay, *Canadian Foreign Policy, 1945-1954*, Toronto: McClelland & Stewart, 1971, pp. 163-165.

this Draft Declaration lack the precision required in the definition of positive obligations and the establishment of enforceable rights. For example, Article 22 [article 21 in the final version] which gives the right to public employment to people irrespective of political creed might, unless it is taken in conjunction with Article 31 [article 29 in the final version], be interpreted as implying an obligation to employ persons in public service even if it was their stated and open desire and intention to destroy all the free institutions which this Declaration of Rights is intended to preserve and extend.

Pearson said that "some of the difficulties and ambiguities" in the *Declaration* might have been avoided had it been reviewed by a body of international jurists, such as the International Law Commission, adding "we regret that the general desire to expedite this important matter has made such a reference impossible". Then, no doubt because the Soviets were proposing just such a delay, Pearson distanced himself from them with a bit of cold war rhetoric. He explained that human rights were protected in Canada by a combination of statute law and judicial decisions, and that "[w]hile we now subscribe to a general statement of principles such as that contained in this Declaration, in doing so we should not wish to suggest that we intend to depart from the procedures by which we have built up our own code under our own federal constitution for the protection of human rights".

Pearson attempted to clarify the issue of provincial jurisdiction, noting that Canada had abstained on certain articles adopted in committee because these were not within federal government powers. Ottawa was not seeking to invade areas of provincial authority, he said. He concluded:

> Because of these various reservations on details in the Draft Declaration, the Canadian Delegation abstained when the Declaration as a whole was put to the vote in committee. The Canadian Delegation, however, approves and supports the general principles contained in the Declaration and would not wish to do anything which might appear to discourage the effort, which it embodies, to define the rights of men and women. Canadians believe in these rights and practice them in their communities. In order that there may be no misinterpretation of our position on this subject therefore, the Canadian delegation, having made its position clear in the committee, will, in accordance with the understanding I have expressed, now vote in favour of the resolution, in the hope that it will mark a milestone in humanity's upward march.

In his diaries, John Humphrey described this statement as "[o]ne of the worst contributions", and "a niggardly acceptance of the Declaration because, it appeared from Mr. Pearson's speech, the Canadian government did not relish the thought of remaining in the company of those who, by abstaining in the vote, rejected it".[135] But Pearson's speech met with ap-

---

135 Alan John Hobbins, ed., *On the Edge of Greatness, The Diaries of John Humphrey,*

proval in the Canadian press. The *Montreal Star* noted, erroneously, that "the whole issue has been examined in this country and found to lie in the provincial, rather than the federal, field", and it congratulated Pearson for the reservations he formulated in the General Assembly.[136] *Le Devoir* also reflected the ambivalence of the Canadian government position, and complained that the text was incomplete in that it provided insufficient protection to confessional schools.[137] Others were more positive. Within a few weeks of the adoption of the *Declaration*, Northrop Frye editorialized prophetically in the *Canadian Forum* that "it is a magnificent Declaration of faith, which may in the long run do much to force statesmen to examine their conscience (and public opinion) before they undertake to suppress the basic freedoms and rights of their peoples".[138]

1.3   Complaints of Human Rights Violations Filed Against Canada at the United Nations

Some of the latent hostility to the *Universal Declaration of Human Rights* within Canada's foreign policy establishment can be seen almost immediately following its adoption. On 13 December 1948, Thomas A. Sutton, Chairman of the Eldorado Shareholders' Committees, sent a copy of the *Universal Declaration* to the Department of External Affairs in the context of complaints about the expropriation of the company's capital stock, which was effected by an Order in Council in January 1944. An External Affairs memorandum to the Legal Adviser that followed a few days later noted cynically: "The attached correspondence from the Chairman of the Eldorado Shareholders' Committees represents the first fruits of them that slept and brought forth the Declaration on Human Rights."[139]

Although the *Charter of the United Nations* did not specify any content for the human rights and fundamental freedoms that it pledged to promote and respect, it took little time for persons who felt their freedoms had been infringed upon by their own governments to petition the organization. There was no formal mechanism for such complaints, and initially the Commission on Human Rights took the position that these were simply inadmissible. Article 2(7) of the *Charter* said the United Nations was to steer clear of matters that were "essentially within the domestic jurisdiction of any state". The conservative view considered such petitions to be simply inadmissible,

---

First Director of the United Nations Division of Human Rights, Volume I, 1948-1949, Montreal: McGill University Libraries, 1994, at 90-91.

136   *Montreal Star*, 13 December 1948, p. 14.

137   *Le Devoir*, 11 December 1948, p. 1.

138   *Canadian Forum*, Vol. XXVIII, No. 336, January 1949, p. 219.

139   Memo of 17 December 1948, signed H. Hay, National Archives of Canada RG 25, Vol. 3690, 5475-W-4-40, Part 1.

and it prevailed in the early work of the Commission. The United Nations did, however, inform the government concerned that a petition had been filed, although it did not require that any action be taken. In the late 1940s, the Economic and Social Council decided upon a rather informal and non-threatening procedure by which such complaints would be "brought to the attention" of the Commission on Human Rights on a confidential basis.[140] And so it was that, like others around the world in the Member States of the United Nations, Canadians began to complain to the United Nations.

The first recorded petition found in the National Archives of Canada is from an unnamed individual who immigrated from Germany before the War, and who said she and her son had suffered bodily injury at the hands of the local police, resulting in disablement.[141] Another complained that a weekly newspaper started by trade union leaders in 1946, "with the aim of furthering the workers' movement and striving to promote a policy of peace and international friendship in support of the United Nations," was suppressed by the police and could not be printed or distributed within Quebec. The Attorney-General's repression of the publication took place without due process of law and no proper hearing, it was alleged.[142]

A petitioner from Georgetown, in what was then British Guiana, complained he was being denied entry to Canada because his wife was "Asian".[143] At the time, Canadian immigration regulations imposed strict quotas on the admission of "Asians" to the country. When the Department of External Affairs transmitted to petition to the Department of Immigration, it received a stern lecture in reply from C.E.S. Smith, who was director of the Immigration Branch: "I wish to first mention that it is not a fundamental human right of an alien to enter Canada. It is a privilege and Canada is perfectly within her rights in selecting immigrants whose admission will contribute to the economic and/or cultural well-being of the Canadian people."[144] In another case, a complaint arrived from Belgrade submitted by a

---

140 ECOSOC Res. 75(V), para. (b).

141 "Communication from *individual*", "Letter, dated 30 October 1947, addressed to the Commission on Human Rights", National Archives of Canada RG 25, Vol. 3690, 5475-W-4-40, Part 1

142 "Communication from *individual*", "Letter, dated 18 March 1948, addressed to the Secretary-General", National Archives of Canada RG 25, Vol. 3690, 5475-W-4-40, Part 1

143 "UNSG Letter SOA 317/02 to PermRep, Oct 4, 1954", National Archives of Canada RG 25, Vol. 6282, 5475-W-6-40, [Pt. 1.2].

144 "Letter 1-54-7082 from C.E.S. Smith, Director, Immigration Branch to USSEA, November 17, 1954", National Archives of Canada RG 25, Vol. 6282, 5475-W-6-40, [Pt. 1.2].

petitioner who claimed he had obtained political asylum in Canada but could not re-enter because he had left Canada of his own free will.[145]

Another complaint, from the various international labour organizations including the World Federation of Trade Unions, challenged the sending of United States seamen to break a strike in Canada, claiming these were "terrorist measures against members of the Canadian Seamen's Union".[146] Allegations about the treatment of the striking Canadian seamen came from trade union bodies in Albania, Czechoslovakia, Italy and Yugoslavia.[147] Some complaints were filed by Doukhobors within Canada.[148] A petitioner in the United States alleged that in a reply from a hotel in Quebec, he had been informed that the clientele was restricted to Christians only.[149] The Congress of Canadian Women charged that material issued by the United Nations Commission on the Status of Women suggested that full political rights were enjoyed by women in Canada. The Congress asked the Commission to make corrections, considering that Indian women had no political rights at all, and that women in Quebec were not allowed to vote in municipal elections.[150] There was a complaint that the African-American singer Paul Robeson had been prevented from leaving the United States and coming to Canada, noting that this violated articles 13(2) and 19 of the *Universal Declaration of Human Rights*. A note in the file says: "I don't think we should reply. Perhaps RCMP would like a copy of her letter."[151]

Another petition found in the National Archives of Canada concerns a complaint about elections on an Indian reservation at the Village Huron in

145 "UNSG Letter SOA 317/02 to PermRep, June 25, 1954", National Archives of Canada RG 25, Vol. 6282, 5475-W-6-40, [Pt. 1.2]; "Letter from M. Krycun to Government of Canada, July 22, 1954", RG 25, Vol. 6282, 5475-W-6-40, [Pt. 1.2]
146 "Communication from *Non-Government Organizations, International Organizations*", "Cable, dated 9 April 1949, from World Federation of Trade Unions, addressed to the Secretary-General", National Archives of Canada RG 25, Vol. 3690, 5475-W-4-40, Part 1.
147 National Archives of Canada RG 25, Vol. 3690, 5475-W-4-40.
148 "Letter from Gilles Sicotte, Legal Division, to Political Co-ordination Section, June 29, 1955", National Archives of Canada RG 25, Vol. 6282, 5475-W-6-40, [Pt. 1.2]; "Letter from M. Cadieux, UN Division, to Legal Division, July 5, 1955", National Archives of Canada RG 25, Vol. 6282, 5475-W-6-40, [Pt. 1.2].
149 "Communication from *Individuals*", "From *United States of America*. Letter dated 8 June 1949 addressed to the Director of the Division on Human Rights", National Archives of Canada RG 25, Vol. 3690, 5475-W-4-40
150 "Letter SOA 149/3/02 from UNSG to PermRep, June 1, 1950", National Archives of Canada RG 25, Vol. 3690, 5475-W-4-40.
151 "Letter from Jean Carlson, Lake Cowichan Peace Council, Feb 6, 1952 to External Affairs Department", National Archives of Canada RG 25, Vol. 3690, 5475-W-4-40.

Lorette, Quebec.[152] Jules Sioui had been filing applications with the United Nations about issues concerning the rights of aboriginal peoples since 1948.[153] Sioui was a real thorn in the side of the Department of External Affairs. For decades, representatives of Canada's aboriginal peoples had used international fora to advance their rights. In the 1920s, they had petitioned the League of Nations, provoking a reply from the Canadian government that was published in the Official Journal. Sioui was apparently a regular presence at the United Nations headquarters in New York, where the Canadian mission kept a close eye on him.[154] He led a delegation that met with United Nations senior legal counsel Oscar Schacter, submitting a petition and invoking the ECOSOC resolution.[155] Ottawa informed its permanent mission in New York that criminal charges had been laid against Sioui, adding: "He is 90 per cent white, speaks French, but little English. Around 50 years of age, suave, good manners and dress, but has a criminal record, including a homosexual charge and one under defence of Canada regulations."[156] The mission must have leaked some of this material to inquiring journalists because it wrote back to Ottawa that when one interested reporter "found out the nature of the charges pending against Mr. Sioui, he dropped the entire matter forthwith".[157]

Officials in the Department sometimes seemed genuinely moved by the complaints, and frustrated that they were being treated in what was essentially a perfunctory manner. On 8 July 1952, a petition was received from L. Pronk, who had immigrated to Canada with his family from the Netherlands, only to be deported upon arrival.[158] The Immigration Branch was consulted, but it brushed off the matter as an unfortunate consequence of official policy.[159] M.W. MacLellan of the United Nations Division noted

---

152 "Letter to UNSG from Eugène Sioui, Village Huron, Lorette Québec, received January 20, 1954", National Archives of Canada RG 25, Vol. 6282, 5475-W-6-40, [Pt. 1.2]; "Letter No. 775 from PermDel to USSEA, Aug 29, 1955", National Archives of Canada RG 25, Vol. 6282, 5475-W-6-40, [Pt. 1.2].

153 "Letter V-146 from Bruce Keith, Acting USSEA to Permanent Delegation, Frebruary 23, 1954", National Archives of Canada RG 25, Vol. 6282, 5475-W-6-40, [Pt. 1.2].

154 "Telegramme from Info Office, Cdn Con Gen, NY, to Info Div, EXTOTT, Oct. 1, 1948", National Archives of Canada RG 25, Vol. 6281, 5475-W-6-40, [Pt. 1.1].

155 "Telegramme from Info Office, Cdn Con Gen, NY, to Info Div, EXTOTT, Oct. 4, 1948", National Archives of Canada RG 25, Vol. 6281, 5475-W-6-40, [Pt. 1.1].

156 "Telegramme from Info Div, EXTOTT, to Info Office, Cdn Con Gen, NY, to Oct. 1, 1948", National Archives of Canada RG 25, Vol. 6281, 5475-W-6-40, [Pt. 1.1].

157 "Letter from Acting USSEA to R.L. MacInnes, Secretary, Indian Affairs Branch, October 23, 1948", National Archives of Canada RG 25, Vol. 6281, 5475-W-6-40, [Pt. 1.1].

158 "Letter SOA 317/02 from UNSG to PermRep, August 22, 1952", National Archives of Canada RG 25, Vol. 6281, 5475-W-6-40, [Pt. 1.1].

159 "Letter D.79497 from C.E.S. Smith, Director, Immigration Branch to USSEA, September 22, 1952", National Archives of Canada RG 25, Vol. 6281, 5475-W-6-40, [Pt. 1.1].

that Canadian policy was to send a reply to the Secretary-General "in cases of a valid nature", but

> [i]n my opinion, the reply sent to us by Citizenship and Immigration would give the impression to non-sympathetic individuals of being a good example of discrimination based on undisclosed information and expressed in typical officialese. By contrast the translation of Mr. Plonk's letter is a very lucid, human and moving appeal, containing statements which taken by themselves, make Citizenship and Immigration's action difficult to understand. Certainly Citizenship and Immigration's letter does little to clarify the matter.[160]

MacLellan advised that "in view of the propaganda possibilities of these two letters", it might be advisable not to reply to the Secretary-General or, alternatively, that Citizenship and Immigration might "consider disclosing more information".[161] Eventually, a letter was sent to the Secretary-General noting that "this matter has been referred to the appropriate government department for investigation and such action as is necessary".[162]

The petition that appeared to make Canadian officials most uncomfortable was filed in October 1948. A non-governmental organization representing Canadians of Japanese descent petitioned the United Nations arguing that the continuation of measures adopted during the war indicated that they were taken for other than military reasons, and that they constituted racial discrimination.[163] For example, one Order in Council deprived Canadians of Japanese descent of the right to vote. Why it remained in force more than three years after the unconditional surrender of Japan was indeed difficult to explain. Yet the Federal Cabinet had renewed the Order as recently as March 1948.

It was unclear whether Canada was expected to reply to the Commission on Human Rights. The Economic and Social Council, to which the Commission on Human Rights was responsible within the United Nations hierarchy, was being forwarded a list of communications concerning human rights compiled by the Secretary-General. These were studied by an Ad Hoc Committee on Communications, which at the time consisted of representatives of Chile, France, Lebanon, the Soviet Union and the United States,

---

160 "Memorandum from M.W. MacLellan (UN Division) to Mr. Summers, October 8, 1952", National Archives of Canada RG 25, Vol. 6281, 5475-W-6-40, [Pt. 1.1].

161 *Ibid.* Also: "Memorandum from G.B. Summers to Consular Division, October 16, 1952", National Archives of Canada RG 25, Vol. 6281, 5475-W-6-40, [Pt. 1.1].

162 "Letter No. 59 from SSEA to UNSG, November 3, 1952", National Archives of Canada RG 25, Vol. 6281, 5475-W-6-40, [Pt. 1.1].

163 "Memorandum for American and Far Eastern Division, concerning 'Complaints forwarded to Human Rights Commission by Residents of Canada'", File 5475-W-4-40, 3 November 1948, National Archives of Canada RG 25, Vol. 3690, 5475-W-4-40, Part 1.

and a report presented to the Commission.[164] The entire procedure was shrouded in confidentiality, however, reflecting the tremendous discomfort of various states with this unprecedented development in international relations.

The adoption of the ECOSOC policy coupled with the receipt of a growing number of petitions confronted External Affairs with a policy decision. The United Nations Division asked for advice from the Legal Division, questioning whether the petitions should be circulated to the relevant departments.[165] R.C. Ormerod of the Commonwealth Relations Office wrote:

> There are or course different opinions about the present powers of the Human Rights Commission with regard to petitions and the position will remain obscure at least until a Covenant is drawn up and approved, together with accompanying measures for "Implementation". For the time being, in our view, there can be no question of enforcing the observance of human rights, and we think that the Human Rights Commission can do no more now than take note of petitions. An implied contradiction between the documents on this point seems to exist as Resolution 75(V), to which you draw attention, does not authorise the Commission to act as arbitrator, let along judge. . . We consider, therefore, that the Canadian Government are not in any way *bound* to reply to any communication passed to them. . .[166]

Officials in External Affairs still thought it might be wise to consult with the British and the Americans, and find out how they were handling similar matters. Initially, the Canadians felt that a reply might "be regarded in certain quarters as undignified and possibly an infringement of national sovereignty".[167] Officials in the Department of External Affairs found the British view to be "rather obscure", and thought "something more helpful" might be obtained from the Department of State, in Washington.[168] They were aware that the Order would be allowed to lapse early in 1949, and they decided simply to wait out the matter. Department of State officials, in answer to Canadian inquiries, "stressed the lack of power of the Commission

---

164 UN Doc. E/800, para. 20.
165 "Memorandum for Legal Division from Untied Nations Division, October 28, 1948", National Archives of Canada RG 25, Vol. 3690, 5475-W-4-40, Part 1. Also: "Letter No. 3387 from George Ignatieff for the Acting SSEA to High Commisioner for Canada, London, December 6, 1948", National Archives of Canada RG 25, Vol. 3690, 5475-W-4-40, Part 1.
166 "Letter U.2410/93 from R.C. Ormerod , Commonwealth Relations Office to Halstead, [Canadian HC], January 12, 1949", National Archives of Canada RG 25, Vol. 3690, 5475-W-4-40, Part 1.
167 "Memo of November 27, 1948, David M. Johnson", National Archives of Canada RG 25, Vol. 3690, 5475-W-4-40, Part 1.
168 "Letter of Frederic Judd, High Commissioner, to SSEA, 17 Jan, 1949", National Archives of Canada RG 25, Vol. 3690, 5475-W-4-40, Part 1.

on Human Rights to take any action in regard to complaints concerning
Human Rights", and said Canada was not compelled to reply but could do
so, although the United States had no intention of replying to similar petitions.[169]

A.R. Menzies wrote to Mike Burwash of the United Nations Division
of External Affairs with a pencilled note saying: "We shall await your advice
as to whether a reply should be sent to Secr-Gen. *If* we do I recommend that
we wait until J. orders-in-council lapse on April 1, 1949."[170] J.W. Holmes
replied to Menzies: "I would certainly agree with your recommendation that
any reply sent to the United Nations should be withheld until after April 1,
when the Canadian leopard will have partially changed his spots so far as
the Japanese are concerned." He added that a recommendation from the
Legal Adviser should be followed to the effect that "some sort of reply"
should be sent "after the magic date of April".[171] The Department of External
Affairs decided it would be prudent not to reply to the Japanese organizations until after the Orders-in-Council had been allowed to lapse.[172] Menzies
made a pencilled notation to the file: "No action taken." [173] There is no
record of any reply being provided.

Debate within the Department continued about how to address the
complaints. One concern was not how to respond to the substance of the
petition but rather what spin, if any, to put on a reply to the United Nations
Secretary-General. Canadian officials took note of the views of Hersh Lauterpacht, who wrote: "The examination of complaints and petitions is essential to the proper fulfilment of the task of the Commission and must be
considered as inherent in the task of the United Nations to encourage and
promote the observance of human rights and freedoms."[174] Eventually, it
was decided to send a polite and rather terse reply to the Secretary-General:
"The Secretary of State for External Affairs thanks the Secretary-General
for notice of these communications. The Canadian Government, as in all

---

169 "Letter of G.L. Magann, February 19, 1949", National Archives of Canada RG 25, Vol.
     3690, 5475-W-4-40, Part 1.
170 "AR Menzies to Mike Burwash, February 2, 1949", National Archives of Canada RG
     25, Vol. 3690, 5475-W-4-40, Part 1.
171 "J.W. Holmes to AR Menzies, March 1, 1949", National Archives of Canada RG 25,
     Vol. 3690, 5475-W-4-40, Part 1.
172 "Memorandum from UN Division, J.W. Holmes, to Legal Division, July 16, 1949",
     National Archives of Canada RG 25, Vol. 3690, 5475-W-4-40, Part 1.
173 "J.W. Holmes to AR Menzies, March 1, 1949", National Archives of Canada RG 25,
     Vol. 3690, 5475-W-4-40, Part 1.
174 "Memorandum for UN Division to Legal Division, December 11, 1950", National
     Archives of Canada RG 25, Vol. 6281, 5475-W-6-40, [Pt. 1.1].

similar cases, is giving its attention to these matters."[175] Some years later, Saul F. Rae of the United Nations Division of the Department of Foreign Affairs confirmed that Canadian policy was basically to ignore such communications:

> Our policy with regard to these communications has, in fact, been to ignore the Secretary-General's notes enclosing human rights allegations, or, latterly, to send a non-commital, form reply. . . [T]his policy has been the subject of discussions in the past and the suggestion has been made that each case might be considered on its merits. The matter was once put up to the Under-Secretary, but I can find on the file no indication of any decision being taken. [. . .] The de facto policy, therefore, is clearly one of no reply, and the line of precedents is unbroken. In addition, the Department's general policy is one of scepticism about the desirability of the whole concept of communications concerning violations of human rights. At the eighth session of the General Assembly, for example, our Delegation voted against an Egyptian resolution in the Third Committee which requested the Commission on Human Rights to transmit to governments for their comments communications alleging violations of human rights serious enough to justify such references and to transmit to the Economic and Social Council such communications and replies to the by governments as the Commission considers should be brought to the attention of the Council. Our lack of enthusiasm for communications may also be reflected in our comments on the draft Covenants on Human Rights which are now being prepared and will eventually be published by the United Nations.[176]

1.4   The *Universal Declaration* Prompts Changes in Law and Policy

The influence of the *Universal Declaration of Human Rights* was soon being felt in national law. The constitution of newly independent India included constitutional guarantees patterned on the *Universal Declaration of Human Rights*. When other British possessions attained sovereignty, these members of the "new Commonwealth" adopted similar laws.[177] As a

---

175 "Memorandum from UN Division, J.W. Holmes, to Legal Division, July 25, 1949", National Archives of Canada RG 25, Vol. 3690, 5475-W-4-40, Part 1; "Memorandum from Legal Division to UN Division, July 26, 1949", National Archives of Canada RG 25, Vol. 3690, 5475-W-4-40.

176 "Memorandum from S.F. Rae, United Nations Division, to Consular Division, January 13, 1954", National Archives of Canada RG 25, Vol. 6282, 5475-W-6-40, [Pt. 1.2].

177 This phenomenon is mentioned in several Canadian cases: *R.* v. *Therens*, [1983] 4 WWR 385, 148 DLR (3d) 672, 5 CCC (3d) 409, 33 CR (3d) 204, 20 MVR 8, 23 Sask R 81, 5 CRR 157 (CA), affirmed, [1985] 1 SCR 613 at 686 (DLR); *British Columbia (AG)* v. *Craig*, (1984) (sub nom. *R.* v. *Carter*) 4 DLR (4th) 746, 9 CCC (3d) 173, 36 CR (3d) 346 (BC SC), affirmed, (1984) 1984 CarswellBC 532 (CA), affirmed, (1986) 1986 CarswellBC 706 (SCC) at 753 (DLR); *Black* v. *Law Society of Alberta*, [1986] 3 WWR

State Party to the *European Convention on Human Rights*, the United Kingdom had extended the protection of that instrument to its colonies. It would have been an anomaly for the latter, as decolonization progressed, to withdraw the guarantees in the *Convention* from their citizens. For example, in 1961 the European Commission of Human Rights noted with satisfaction that the Republic of Cyprus, in attaining independence from London, had adopted a Constitution that "very closely follows" the *European Convention*.[178]

In 1948, Justice O'Halloran of the British Columbia Court of Appeal argued for a constitutional charter modelled on the *Universal Declaration of Human Rights*.[179] However, Canadian politicians made little headway towards such a document, and during the 1950s the initiative in civil liberties fell to constitutional lawyers who succeeded in obtaining a series of landmark decisions from the Supreme Court of Canada.[180] Canadian interest in legislative protection of rights and freedoms revived in the late 1950s and, in September 1958, Bill C-60 for the *Recognition and Protection of Human Rights and Fundamental Freedoms* was presented to Parliament by the new Conservative government.[181] At the time, Prime Minister John Diefenbaker told the Commons: "The measure that I introduce is the first step on the part of Canada to carry out the acceptance either of the international declaration of human rights or of the principles that activated those who produced that noble document."[182] Diefenbaker spoke of the *Universal Declaration of Human Rights*, citing *in extenso* the preamble of that instrument which he said "sets forth clearly and unmistakably, as does the preamble of the United Nations charter, the greatness of human rights and the determinant that the preservation of human rights is on the peace of the world".[183]

591, 27 DLR (4th) 527, Alta LR (2d) 1, 68 AR 259, 20 Admin LR 140, 20 CRR 177 (CA), affirmed, [1989] 1 SCR 591, at 541 (DLR).

178 (1961) 4 European Convention on Human Rights Yearbook 654. Part II of the Cyprus constitution which deals with fundamental freedoms was reproduced in (1960) 3 European Convention on Human Rights Yearbook 678.

179 W.O. O'Halloran, "Inherent Rights", (1947-48) *Obiter Dicta*; see also W.G. How, "Case for a Canadian Bill of Rights", (1948) 26 *Canadian Bar Review* 497.

180 *Saumur* v. *City of Quebec*, (1953) [1953] 2 SCR 299, [1954] 4 DLR 641; *Birks* v. *City of Montreal*, [1955] SCR 799, 113 CCC 135, [1955] 5 DLR 321; *Switzman* v. *Elbling*, [1957] SCR 285, 7 DLR (2d) 337, 117 CCC 129; *Chaput* v. *Romain*, [1955] SCR 834, 114 CCC 170, 1 DLR (2d) 241; *Roncarelli* v. *Duplessis*, [1959] SCR 121, 16 DLR (2d) 689.

181 Maxwell Cohen, "Bill C-60 and International Law – The United Nations Charter – Declaration of Human Rights", (1959) 37 *Canadian Bar Review* 228.

182 *Debates*, HC 1960, at 5645. Cited by Justice Belzil in *R.* v. *Big M Drug Mart Ltd.*, [1984] 1 WWR 625, 5 DLR (4th) 121, 9 CCC (3d) 310, 28 Alta LR (2d) 289, 49 AR 194, 7 CRR 92 (CA), affirmed, [1985] 1 SCR 295, p. 149 (DLR).

183 *Debates*, HC 1960, at 5644.

The draft legislation relied heavily on the *Universal Declaration of Human Rights* as well as on the text of the *European Convention on Human Rights*.[184] But the influence of the American tradition came to prevail in the version Parliament eventually adopted in 1960, including the name of the statute itself, the *Canadian Bill of Rights*.[185] Moreover, American jurisprudence enjoyed considerable popularity in the judicial interpretation of the *Canadian Bill of Rights*. The influence of United States law was no doubt enhanced by the fact that its Supreme Court, presided over by the Chief Justice Earl Warren, was in a period of great dynamism. At the time, the law in the United States provided, in many respects, a far more exciting model for progressive measures favouring the promotion of human rights than did the fledgling international institutions.

In 1966, the work that the United Nations General Assembly had begun with the *Universal Declaration* was complemented with two draft multilateral treaties. It had initially been planned to adopt a single treaty, known as the "covenant", in order to give binding legal effect to the norms set out in the *Universal Declaration*. In fact, in 1947 and 1948 the Commission on Human Rights laboured in parallel on drafts of both a declaration and a covenant. It soon reached agreement on a text of the *Universal Declaration* but finalizing a treaty proved more elusive. The Commission studied the draft in annual sessions until 1954, when it reported to the General Assembly. In turn, the General Assembly's Third Committee spent several years reviewing the materials, and only finished its work in 1966. Meanwhile, what had began as one treaty ended up in three distinct pieces. In the early 1950s, the United States and the United Kingdom argued that some of the rights in the *Universal Declaration*, specifically the economic and social rights listed in articles 22 to 27, had no place in a binding treaty. These were aspirational objectives or policy goals, they argued, rather than legally enforceable norms. But there was much opposition to this within the United Nations, both from the then socialist bloc and from the emerging countries of the Third World. A compromise was reached, by which the single covenant was split in two. The result was the *International Covenant on Civil*

---

184   *Re Trumbley and Fleming*, (1986) (sub nom. *Trumbley* v. *Fleming*) 29 DLR (4th) 557, 55 OR (2d) 570, 15 OAC 279, 24 CRR 333, 21 Admin LR 232 (CA), affirmed, (1987) 1987 CarswellOnt 948 (SCC), affirmed, (1987) 1987 CarswellOnt 947 (SCC), affirmed, (1987) 1987 CarswellOnt 949 (SCC) at 585 (OR) *per* Morden JA.

185   RSC 1985, Appendix III. For example, the drafters apparently set aside the formulation of the "cruel and unusual treatment or punishment" provision found in the new international instruments in favour of the more laconic wording of the Eighth Amendment to the United States *Constitution* and its predecessor, the English *Bill of Rights* of 1689: *Miller and Cockriell* v. *R.*, [1977] 2 SCR 680, 31 CCC (2d) 177, 38 CRNS 139, 70 DLR (3d) 324, [1976] 5 WWR 711, 11 NR 386, *per* Laskin CJ.

and Political Rights[186] and the *International Covenant on Economic, Social and Cultural Rights,*[187] both of which were adopted by the General Assembly in 1966. Yet a third instrument was also prepared, the *Optional Protocol to the International Covenant on Civil and Political Rights,* which provided for a right of petition by individuals to an international adjudicative body, the Human Rights Committee. Together, the *Universal Declaration,* the two *Covenants* and the *Optional Protocol* became known as the "International Bill of Rights". Decades later, yet a fifth instrument was added to the "Bill", the *Second Optional Protocol to the International Covenant on Civil and Political Rights Aiming at Abolition of the Death Penalty.*[188]

In order to prepare for ratification of the *Covenants* and the *Optional Protocol,* the Canadian government undertook a process of consultation with the provincial governments.[189] So began a mechanism which continues to the present day. Most human rights treaties concern issues of both federal and provincial jurisdiction, and Canada cannot therefore implement obligations that are undertaken on the international level without the cooperation of the provinces. The actual act of ratification remains a prerogative of the federal government, however. After some discussion, all of the provinces concurred. Canada acceded to the two *Covenants* and to the *Optional Protocol*[190] on 19 May 1976.[191] In international law, this bound Canada to ensure

---

186   *International Covenant on Civil and Political Rights,* (1976) 999 UNTS 171, [1976] CTS 47. On the *Covenant* generally, see: Manfred Nowak, *Covenant on Civil and Political Rights: CCPR Commentary,* 2nd ed., Kehl: Engel, 2005; Dominic McGoldrick, *The Human Rights Committee, Its Role in the Development of the International Covenant on Civil and Political Rights,* 2nd ed., Oxford: Clarendon Press, 2000; Sarah Joseph, Jenny Schultz and Melissa Castan, *The International Covenant on Civil and Political Rights – Cases, Materials, and Commentary,* 2nd ed., Oxford: Oxford University Press, 2005.

187   *International Covenant on Economic, Social and Cultural Rights,* (1976) 993 UNTS 3, [1976] CTS 46.

188   *Second Optional Protocol to the International Covenant on Civil and Political Rights Aimed at Abolition of the Death Penalty,* UN Doc. A/RES/44/128, annex. Cited in: *Kindler* v. *Canada,* [1991] 2 SCR 779, 67 CCC (3d) 1, 84 DLR (4th) 438, 6 CRR (2d) 193; *United States* v. *Burns and Rafay,* [2001] 1 SCR 283, 195 DLR (4th) 1, [2001] 3 WWR 193, 151 CCC (3d) 97, 39 CR (5th) 205, 81 CRR (2d) 1, 85 BCLR (3d) 1.

189   In 2004, a private member's bill (Bill C-260) was proposed aimed at prohibiting the federal government from negotiating or concluding a treaty "without consulting the government of each province", to the extent that the international agreement dealt with matters of provincial jurisdiction. It was defeated in Parliament in September 2005. See: *Crossing Borders; Law in a Globalized World,* Ottawa: Law Commission of Canada, 2006, p. 19.

190   *Optional Protocol to the International Covenant on Civil and Political Rights,* (1976) 999 UNTS 171, [1976] CTS 47; acceded to by Canada pursuant to Privy Council decision No. 1976-1156, 18 May 1976.

191   It would also have been open to Canada to sign the *Covenants* and the *Protocol,* as a preliminary step, and then complete this with ratification. In the case of some interna-

the respect of the two *Covenants* from the date they formally entered in force, three months later, on 19 August 1976.

The new obligations were more than mere professions of noble sentiments. Canada was required, pursuant to article 2(2) of the *International Covenant on Civil and Political Rights*,

> Where not already provided for by existing legislative measures, each State Party to the present Covenant undertakes to take the necessary steps, in accordance with its constitutional processes and with the provisions of the present Covenant, to adopt such legislative or other measures as may be necessary to give effect to the rights recognized in the present Covenant.

And to ensure, pursuant to article 2(3), that all Canadians had a remedy against the violation of *Covenant* rights:

> Each State Party to the present Covenant undertakes:
>
> (a) To ensure that any person whose rights or freedoms as herein recognized are violated shall have an effective remedy, notwithstanding that the violation has been committed by persons acting in an official capacity;
> (b) To ensure that any person claiming such a remedy shall have his right thereto determined by competent judicial, administrative or legislative authorities, or by any other competent authority provided for by the legal system of the State, and to develop the possibilities of judicial remedy;
> (c) To ensure that the competent authorities shall enforce such remedies when granted.

In the case of the *International Covenant on Economic, Social and Cultural Rights*, the corresponding provisions required, somewhat more cautiously:

> Each State Party to the present Covenant undertakes to take steps, individually and through international assistance and co-operation, especially economic and technical, to the maximum of its available resources, with a view to achieving progressively the full realization of the rights recognized in the present Covenant by all appropriate means, including particularly the adoption of legislative measures.

Furthermore, the covenants established an obligation to make regular reports to United Nations bodies on the protection of human rights and on progress in implementing the new treaties. On 29 October 1979 Canada made a declaration pursuant to article 41 of the *International Covenant on Civil and Political Rights* accepting the Human Rights Committee's jurisdiction over interstate complaints. Canadian legislation for the first time expressly

---

tional treaties, for example the *Rome Statute of the International Criminal Court*, this was the approach favoured by the Canadian government.

referred to the *International Covenant on Civil and Political Rights* in 1988.[192]

In 1968 a White Paper entitled *A Canadian Charter of Human Rights* was tabled in Parliament by the then Justice Minister Pierre Elliott Trudeau.[193] Trudeau noted that 1968 had been declared International Human Rights Year by the United Nations. This offered Canada the opportunity to take a lead in the promotion of human rights, he said:

> The preamble of the United Nations Charter declares that the peoples of the United Nations are determined "to reaffirm faith in fundamental human rights, in the dignity and worth of the human person, in the equal rights of men and women". As a reflection of this determination, the United Nations in 1948 adopted the Universal Declaration of Human Rights. Since that date some fifteen separate conventions or treaties have been sponsored by the U.N. dealing with particular rights of a more specialized character. Only last year, however, were those rights which are generally regarded as "fundamental" formulated into two Covenants, (The International Covenant on Economic, Social and

---

192 *Emergencies Act*, SC 1988, c. 29: the preamble states: "AND WHEREAS the Governor in Council, in taking such special temporary measures, would be subject to the Canadian Charter of Rights and Freedoms and the Canadian Bill of Rights and must have regard to the International Covenant on Civil and Political Rights, particularly with respect to those fundamental rights that are not to be limited or abridged even in a national emergency. . ." The preamble to the *Canadian Multiculturalism Act*, SC 1988, c. 31, states: "AND WHEREAS Canada is a party to the International Convention on the Elimination of All Forms of Racial Discrimination, which Convention recognizes that all human beings are equal before the law and are entitled to equal protection of the law against any discrimination and against any incitement to discrimination, and to the International Covenant on Civil and Political Rights, which Covenant provides that persons belonging to ethnic, religious or linguistic minorities shall not be denied the right to enjoy their own culture, to profess and practise their own religion or to use their own language. . ."

193 H. Carl Goldenberg was appointed Special Counsel to the Minister of Justice for the project; five part-time advisors were named: Gerald LeDain, Mark MacGuigan, Barry Strayer, Gérard La Forest and Jean Beetz (*Globe and Mail*, 23 June 1967); all five were eventually named to the Bench, and each subsequently rendered judgments on the *Canadian Charter* that drew upon international law sources. With regard to former Justice Gérard La Forest in particular, see G.V. La Forest, "The Expanding Role of the Supreme Court of Canada in International Law Issues", (1996) 34 *Canadian Yearbook of International Law* 89; and Michel Bastarache, "The Honourable G.V. La Forest's Use of Foreign Materials in the Supreme Court of Canada and His Influence on Foreign Courts", in Rebecca Johnson & John P. McEvoy, eds., *Gérard V. La Forest at the Supreme Court of Canada, 1985-1997*, Winnipeg: Canadian Legal History Project, 2000, pp. 433-447.

Cultural Rights; The International Covenant on Civil and Political Rights) open for signature and ratification by all states.[194]

The proposal seemed more influenced by the *European Convention on Human Rights* than by the treaties adopted within the United Nations system, which barely figure in the accompanying commentary. The *European Convention* seems to have attracted attention because of its influence upon post-independence constitutions within the Commonwealth. But even the *European Convention* did not seem to inspire much enthusiasm. With respect to freedom of expression, for example, Justice Minister Trudeau referred to article 10 of the *European Convention on Human Rights* as an example of an enumeration of specific exceptions, but he said the weakness of such an approach was "its lack of flexibility and the difficulty of adopting the language to changed circumstances. For this reason the simple form of description is recommended."[195]

Drafters of the successive versions of the *Charter*, as negotiations progressed, drew upon the international authorities, specifically the *Universal Declaration of Human Rights*, the *European Convention on Human Rights*, and the *International Covenant on Civil and Political Rights*. For example, the *Statement of Conclusions of the Third Constitutional Conference* of 1971 included a clause that has no counterpart in the United States *Bill of Rights* and that was clearly patterned on provisions of the *Universal Declaration of Human Rights* and the international treaties adopted in its wake:

It was agreed to entrench in the Constitution the following basic political rights;

(a) universal suffrage and free, democratic elections at least every five years;
(b) freedom of thought, conscience and religion;
(c) freedom of opinion and expression;
(d) freedom of peaceful assembly and association.

The exercise of these freedoms may be subject only to such limitations as are prescribed by law and as are reasonably justifiable in a democratic society in the interests of national security, public safety, health or morals or the fundamental rights and freedoms of others.[196]

---

194 Pierre Elliott Trudeau, *A Canadian Charter of Human Rights*, Ottawa: Queen's Printer, 1968, p. 12. See also: Lester B. Pearson, "Federalism for the Future: A Statement of Policy by the Government of Canada", in Anne F. Bayefsky, *Canada's Constitution Act 1982 & Amendments, A Documentary History*, Vol. I, Toronto: McGraw-Hill Ryerson, 1989, pp. 61-74, at 66.

195 Pierre Elliott Trudeau, *ibid.*, at 17.

196 *Hansard*, 1971, Appendix "A", p. 3268-9; Walter S. Tarnopolsky, *The Canadian Bill of Rights*, 2nd ed., Toronto: McClelland and Stewart, 1975, at 18; clearly the forerunner of section 1 of the *Canadian Charter*.

A similar provision appeared later that year in the text known as the "Victoria Charter", adopted by the Federal-Provincial First Minsiters' Conference.[197] The attentive reader will no doubt discern the embryo of section 1 of the *Canadian Charter of Rights and Freedoms*.

In his report to the 1978 Federal-Provincial First Ministers' Conference, Federal Justice Minister Otto Lang argued that the right to property had been recognized in section 1 of the *Canadian Bill of Rights* in too absolute a manner, and defended the reformulation in the *Constitutional Amendment Bill* (C-60) of 1978 whereby it was reduced to the "use and enjoyment of property without deprivation except in accordance with law".[198] He said this was more consistent with the *Universal Declaration of Human Rights*, which protects individuals against arbitrary deprivation of property.[199] Lang also referred to the *Universal Declaration of Human Rights*, as well as to the *International Covenant on Civil and Political Rights*, to justify recognition of the right of the individual to equality before the law and to equal protection of the law in the draft charter.[200] He noted as well that the panoply of legal rights being proposed "find their counterparts in the several international instruments".[201] He said that the protection against arbitrary detention, imprisonment or exile had not been included in earlier proposals for the Charter, but that it was found in the *Universal Declaration of Human Rights* and that "it would thus seem appropriate to retain it in the Charter".[202]

The draft resolution on constitutional amendment, submitted to the two houses of Parliament on 6 October 1980, contained several references to international human rights law. The explanatory notes stated that several of the legal rights listed in sections 7-14 of the draft Charter had not previously been recognized in Canadian law, although "some now find expression in the *International Covenant on Civil and Political Rights* (the U.N. Covenant) to which Canada became a party in 1976".[203] The notes to section 11, which is broadly similar to the final text, indicated that paragraphs (a), (b),

---

197 "Canadian Constitutional Charter, 1971", in Anne F. Bayefsky, *supra* note 194, at pp. 214-219, at 214. The Special Joint Committee on the Constitution said that it had "reservations with respect to the general qualification on the fundamental freedoms in Article 3 of the Victoria Charter": *ibid.*, p. 242.

198 Inclusion of a right to property had been proposed by the Special Joint Committee on the Constitution: "Final Report, 16 March 1972", in Anne F. Bayefsky, *ibid.*, at 238.

199 "The Canadian Charter of Rights and Freedoms, Division III of the Constitutional Amendment Bill", in Anne F. Bayefsky, *ibid.* pp. 499-529, at 504-505.

200 *Ibid.*, p. 505.

201 *Ibid.*

202 *Ibid.*, p. 506.

203 "Proposed Resolution for Joint Address to Her Majesty the Queen Respecting the Constitution of Canada, Tabled in the House of Commons and the Senate, October 6, 1980", in Anne F. Bayefsky, *supra* note 194, pp. 743-761, at 747.

(c), (f) and (g) "assure new rights of an accused in such proceedings and are drawn from similar provisions now found in the U.N. Covenant".[204]

The influence of international sources in the final version of the *Canadian Charter* is uncontested[205] and has, since April 1982, been commented upon on numerous occasions by the courts.[206] The significance of international authorities in *Charter* interpretation was explained by Chief Justice Brian Dickson in his dissenting opinion in *Re Public Service Employee Relations Act*:[207]

> A body of treaties (or conventions) and customary norms now constitutes an international law of human rights under which the nations of the world have undertaken to the standards and principles necessary for ensuring freedom, dignity and social justice for their citizens. The *Charter* conforms to the spirit of this contemporary international human rights movement, and it incorporates many of the policies and prescriptions of the various international documents pertaining to human rights. The various sources of international human rights law – declarations, covenants, conventions, judicial and quasi-judicial decisions of international tribunals, customary norms – must, in my opinion, be relevant and persuasive sources for interpretation of the Charter's provisions.

Pre-*Charter* references to international human rights law had been rare and perfunctory.[208] The first celebrated case, *Re Drummond Wren*,[209] remained an isolated decision, disdained by other judges[210] and spurned by the Supreme Court of Canada[211] until Justice Bertha Wilson, then of the Ontario Court of Appeal, and Chief Justice Bora Laskin, of the Supreme Court of

---

204 *Ibid.*, p. 748.
205 Robin Elliott, "Interpreting the Charter – Use of the Earlier Versions as an Aid", (1982) 16 *Charter Edition University of British Columbia Law Review* 11.
206 "Thus it can be seen that the *Canadian Charter* was not conceived and born in isolation. It is part of the universal human rights movement": *R.* v. *Big M Drug Mart, supra* note 182, per Belzil J.
207 *Re Public Service Employee Relations Act (Alberta)*, [1987] 1 RCS 313, 51 Alta LR (2d) 97, [1987] 3 WWR 577, (sub nom. *A.U.P.E.* v. *Alberta (Attorney General)*) 28 CRR 305, 38 DLR (4th) 161, (sub nom. *Reference re Compulsory Arbitration*) 74 NR 99, 78 AR 1, [1987] DLQ 225, 87 CLLC 14,021, at 348 (RCS).
208 There are only two references by the Supreme Court of Canada: *Miller and Cockriell* v. *R.*, *supra* note 185, where Chief Justice Laskin referred in passing to the *Universal Declaration of Human Rights*, and found it of no relevance in interpreting the "cruel and unusual" provisions of the *Canadian Bill of Rights*; *Ernewein* v. *Minister of Employment and Immigration*, [1980] 1 SCR 639, 103 DLR (3d) 1, 14 CPC 264, 30 NR 316, *per* Pigeon J., dissenting, who found that the *Immigration Act, 1976* had incorporated the *Convention on the Status of Refugees* into Canadian law.
209 [1945] 4 DLR 674.
210 *Noble* v. *Wolf and Alley*, [1951] SCR 64, [1951] 1 DLR 321; *Re Noble and Wolf*, [1948] 4 DLR 123, [1948] OR 579 (HC), affirmed, [1949] 4 DLR 375, [1949] OR 503 (CA), reversed, (1950) 1950 CarswellOnt 127 (SCC).
211 *Noble* v. *Wolf and Alley, ibid.*

Canada, explained its importance in the history of human rights jurisprudence.[212]

When the *Canadian Charter* was proclaimed in 1982, many believed it would considerably enhance the importance of international human rights law in Canadian jurisprudence,[213] and experience has shown they were not wrong.[214] Maxwell Cohen and Anne F. Bayefsky, in a seminal article published in the *Canadian Bar Review*, described the *Charter* as a "bridge between municipal law and international law to a degree, and with an intensity, not heretofore known in any of the multitude of links between Canadian and international legal orders".[215]

Over the nearly twenty-five years since the proclamation of the *Charter* on 17 April 1982, Canadian courts have cited international human rights instruments and jurisprudence in hundreds of reported cases.[216] The process began in the lower courts in the years following enactment of the *Charter*.

---

212 *Bhadauria* v. *Board of Governors of Seneca College*, (1980) 105 DLR (3d) 707, 27 OR (2d) 142, 11 CCLT 121, 9 BLR 117, 81 CLLC 14,003 (CA), reversed, [1981] 2 SCR 181, 124 DLR (3d) 193, 2 CHRR D/468, 17 CCLT 106, 81 CLLC 14,117, 22 CPC 130, 14 BLR 157, 37 NR 455; *Board of Governors of Seneca College* v. *Bhadauria*, [1981] 2 SCR 181, 124 DLR (3d) 193, 2 CHRR D/486, 17 CCLT 106, 81 CLLC 14,117, 22 CPC 130, 14 BLR 157, 37 NR 455; see also *Canada Trust Co.* v. *Ontario Human Rights Commission*, (sub nom. *Leonard Foundation Trust, Re*) (1990) 37 OAC 191, 69 DLR (4th) 321 (CA).

213 Maxwell Cohen & Anne F. Bayefsky, "The Canadian Charter of Rights and Freedoms and International Law", (1983) 61 *Canadian Bar Review* 265. Cohen and Bayefsky predicted a generation of lawyers who would "roam the law schools and the government departments to find those once exotic footnotes of international law", at 268. See also: Errol P. Mendes, "Interpreting the Canadian Charter of Rights and Freedoms: Applying International and European Jurisprudence on the Law and Practice of Fundamental Rights", (1982) 20 *Alberta Law Review* 383; John E. Claydon, "The Application of International Human Rights Law by the Canadian Courts", (1981) 30 *Buffalo Law Review* 727; John E. Claydon, "International Human Rights Law and the Interpretation of the Canadian Charter of Rights and Freedoms", (1982) 4 *Supreme Court Law Review* 287; and Guy Tremblay, "La Charte canadienne des droits et libertés et quelques leçons de la Convention européenne des droits de l'homme", (1982), 23 *Cahiers de Droit* 795.

214 According to Justice G.V. La Forest of the Supreme Court of Canada, in a speech to the Canadian Council on International Law, 22 October 1988: "The experience of our Court since 1982 shows this prediction, [*i.e.*, of Cohen and Bayefsky] to have been largely correct." G.V. La Forest, "The Use of International and Foreign Material in the Supreme Court of Canada", *Proceedings, XVIIth Annual Conference, Canadian Council on International Law*, 1988, pp. 230-241.

215 Maxwell Cohen & Anne F. Bayefsky, *supra* note 213, at 268.

216 A table of some 400 decisions was provided in the second edition of this book, which was published in 1996. The references are now too numerous to bear listing in any concise yet comprehensive fashion. In any event, preparation of such a list in the early 1990s seemed helpful, given the difficulty in finding such materials in the various series of reported caselaw. Today, electronic data base technology makes this material readily accessible.

The language of the new *Charter* was innovative and unfamiliar. Academics provided training that directed Canadian judges to the international sources, and some of them responded with enthusiasm. No doubt it was also exciting for trial judges to begin to interpret a new instrument in the absence of hardened caselaw from the appellate courts. Soon, however, the first *Charter* cases had worked their way up to the Courts of Appeal and eventually the Supreme Court of Canada. Since then, the Supreme Court of Canada has kept the initiative in terms of reference to international human rights law sources. In the five-year period following the *Singh* decision in 1985, the Supreme Court of Canada referred to international sources in some fifty-nine judgments dealing with *Charter* interpretation. Not infrequently, international authorities were cited by more than one judge within the same judgment. Occasionally, members of the court even differed about how to interpret international treaties and jurisprudence.[217]

If the reference to international authority is new, the use of comparative law in interpreting Canadian statutes is most certainly not. Indeed, because of the English and French origins of Canadian law, reference to foreign legislation and jurisprudence is logical and well-accepted. Despite the fact that appeals to the Judicial Committee of the Privy Council came to an end in the late 1940s,[218] recent decisions of the House of Lords are still influential in Canadian criminal law. In civil law, editions of the *Civil Code of Quebec* generally provide cross-references to the corresponding articles in the Napoleonic Code, and French doctrine and jurisprudence are cited by the courts as authority, although now rather exceptionally.[219] Prior to proclamation of the *Charter* in April 1982, Canadian jurists were also familiar and not at all uncomfortable with citations from both Commonwealth and United States sources on civil liberties matters, especially following enactment of the

---

217 *RWDSU* v. *Saskatchewan*, [1987] 1 SCR 460, 38 DLR (4th) 277, [1987] 3 WWR 673, 87 CLLC 14,023, 74 NR 321, [1987] DLQ 233 (headnote), 56 Sask R 277; *United States of America* v. *Cotroni*; *United Statess of America* v. *El Zein* (sub nom. *El Zein c. Centre de Prévention de Montréal*) [1989] 1 SCR 1469, (sub nom. *United States v. Cotroni*) 48 CCC (3d) 193, (sub nom. *United States v. El Zein*) 96 NR 321, (sub nom. *El Zein c. Centre de Prévention de Montréal*) 42 CRR 101, (sub nom. *El Zein c. Centre de Prévention de Montréal*) 23 QAC 182.

218 *AG Ontario* v. *AG Canada (Privy Council Appeals)*, [1947] AC 127, [1947] 1 All ER 137 (Canada P.C.).

219 See for example the decision of Justice Beetz in *C (G)* v. *V-F (T)*., 78 NR 241, 9 QAC 241 (sub nom. *C. (G.)* v. *V.-F.(T.)*) [1987] 2 SCR 244, (sub nom. *V.-F.(T.)* v. *C. (G.)*) 9 RFL (3d) 263, at 263 (SCR).

Canadian Bill of Rights.[220] Their ongoing affinity for United States *Bill of Rights* jurisprudence has been well demonstrated under the *Charter.*[221] The openness of Canadian courts to the use of international sources has most certainly been conditioned by this longstanding comparative law tradition.

A bit like a fable, the modesty of Canadian judges in their willingness to accept guidance from other jurisidictions ultimately proved to be to their great credit internationally. The bold and innovative decisions of post-*Charter* Canadian courts, which was inspired by international and comparative law sources in the protection of human rights and fundamental freedoms, have themselves become influential in the courtrooms of the world. There are now many examples of judges in a wide range of jurisdictions referring to Canadian jurisprudence. Let one suffice.

When the Supreme Court of Canada effectively reversed its position on the question of extradition to a country where the death penalty might be imposed, it drew upon many important developments in international law, including a ruling of the Constitutional Court of South Africa.[222] The Supreme Court cited *S.* v. *Makwanyane* et al., the 1995 ruling of the newly-minted South African Constitutional Court that declared capital punishment to be contrary to the right to life and the cruel punishment provisions of the country's interim constitution.[223] The South African Constitutional Court was deeply influenced by its Canadian counterpart. *Makwanyane* was only its second judgment, and it referred to twelve Canadian cases, essentially the leading *Charter* decisions at the time. Two Canadian decisions were not exactly helpful, because in 1991 the Supreme Court had refused to follow the approach taken by the European Court and to deny extradition in the absence of an assurance that capital punishment would not be carried out.[224] The South African judges tried to extract the best from *Kindler*, citing it as authority for the proposition that capital punishment constitutes a serious

---

220 J.M. MacIntyre, "The Use of American Cases in Canadian Courts", (1966) 2 *University of British Columbia Law Review* 478; Paul Bender, "The Canadian Charter of Rights and Freedoms and the United States Bill of Rights: a Comparison", (1982) 28 *McGill Law Journal* 811; Jamie Cameron, "The Motor Vehicle Reference and the Relevance of American Doctrine in Charter Adjudication," in Robert J. Sharpe, ed., *Charter Litigation*, Toronto & Vancouver: Butterworths, 1987, p. 69; and Peter W. Hogg, "The Charter of Rights and American Theories of Interpretation", (1987) *Osgoode Hall Law Journal* 87.

221 *Law Society of Upper Canada* v. *Skapinker*, [1984] 1 SCR 357, 9 DLR (4th) 161, 11 CCC (3d) 481, 53 NR 169, 3 OAC 321, 20 Admin LR 1, 8 CRR 193.

222 *United States* v. *Burns and Rafay*, [2001] 1 SCR 283, 195 DLR (4th) 1, [2001] 3 WWR 193, 151 CCC (3d) 97, 39 CR (5th) 205, 81 CRR (2d) 1, 85 BCLR (3d) 1, at para. 67.

223 *S.* v. *Makwanyane*, 1995 (3) SA 391, (1995) 16 *Human Rights Law Journal* 154.

224 *Kindler* v. *Canada*, [1991] 2 SCR 779, 67 CCC (3d) 1, 84 DLR (4th) 438, 6 CRR (2d) 193; *Reference re: Ng Extradition (Can.)*, [1991] 2 SCR 858, 67 CCC (3d) 61, 84 DLR (4th) 498.

impairment of human dignity.[225] But not only was it fitting that when the Supreme Court of Canada reversed its position, a decade later, it acknowledged its debt to the South Africans. And barely months after *Burns and Rafay*, the South African Constitutional Court returned the favour:

> Recently, in *Minister of Justice* v. *Burns*, the Supreme Court of Canada had occasion to reconsider its attitude to the extradition of fugitives to a country where they would fact the death penalty. It had previously held by a majority of that Court in *Kindler* v. *Canada (Minister of Justice)* and *Reference re Ng Extradition (Canada)* that there was no obligation on Canada before extraditing a suspect to a country that has the death penalty to seek an assurance from the receiving state that the death penalty will not be imposed. In a unanimous judgment the Court held in *Burns* that in the light of developments since the decisions in *Kindler* and *Ng*, there is now an obligation on the Canadian government. . .[226]

And what were those developments. *Makwanyane* was one of them!

---

225 *S.* v. *Makwanyane, supra* note 223, para. 60.

226 *Mohamed* et al. v. *President of the Republic of South Africa* et al., CCT 17/01, 28 May 2001, para. 46 (references omitted).

2

Theoretical Underpinnings of the Use of International Human Rights Law Before Canadian Courts

The judicial basis of reference by Canadian courts to international human rights law has given rise to considerable debate. Several theories or conceptual approaches have been advanced in order to justify resort to international law by Canadian courts.[1] Where international legal instruments have been expressly referred to in Canadian law, the proposition that the norms they comprise are directly incorporated is not particularly controversial. Reference within a statute may in effect add certain rules of international law to the Canadian legislation,[2] but there are few examples of such references in Canadian laws or regulations that could support a theory of direct incorporation. The *Canadian Charter* itself makes only one express reference to international law, in section 11(g), referring to the prohibition of retroactive criminal prosecution. Customary international human rights law is also readily recognized to be a part of Canadian law, but once again there is little concrete authority to support this theoretically unchallengeable proposition.

---

1 As a preliminary issue, the Supreme Court of Canada has made it quite clear that Canadian courts are competent to pronounce on questions of international law. See: *Reference re Secession of Quebec*, [1998] 2 SCR 217, 161 DLR (4th) 385, 55 CRR (2d) 1, paras. 22-23.

2 This is indeed the case for the provisions of the *Criminal Code*, RSC 1985, c. C-46, sections 7(3.76) and 7(3.77), on the international criminal law offence of "crime against humanity". See *Mugesera* v. *Canada (Minister of Citizenship and Immigration)*, [2005] 2 SCR 100.

The suggestion that international human rights norms have been introduced into Canadian law by implication presents the greatest interest for litigants. Such a thesis was enthusiastically advanced by scholars in the early years of *Charter* interpretation,[3] although it has met with a more lukewarm acceptance by the courts. They have generally rejected the notion of implicit implementation, adopting the more cautious view whereby international human rights law is a valid contextual aid to the interpretation of the *Charter* and other relevant legislation, including human rights codes and statutes dealing with immigration, labour and criminal law.

In fact, no theory is particularly helpful in explaining the frequent reference to international human rights law by Canadian judges in the application of the *Canadian Charter* and of other legislation relevant to the protection of human rights and fundamental freedoms. Rarely, if ever, do the courts actually provide any justification for their use of international law.[4] Such references have never seemed particularly controversial, and perhaps for this reason no explanation was thought to be useful. It would appear that Canadian judges do not consider international human rights law

---

3 John E. Claydon, "The Application of International Human Rights Law by the Canadian Courts", (1981) 30 *Buffalo Law Review* 727; John E. Claydon, "International Human Rights Law and the Interpretation of the Canadian Charter of Rights and Freedoms", (1982) 4 *Supreme Court Law Review* 287; Errol P. Mendes, "Interpreting the Canadian Charter of Rights and Freedoms: Applying International and European Jurisprudence on the Law and Practice of Fundamental Rights", (1982) 20 *Alberta Law Review* 383; Daniel Turp, "Le recours au droit international aux fins de l'interprétation de la Charte canadienne des droits et libertés: un bilan jurisprudentiel", (1984) 18 *Revue juridique Thémis* 353; Ann M. Hayward, "International Law and the Interpretation of the Canadian Charter of Rights and Freedoms: Uses and Justifications", (1985) 23 *University of Western Ontario Law Review* 9.

4 One notable exception was the decision of the Supreme Court of Canada in *Baker* v. *Canada (Minister of Citizenship and Immigration)*, [1999] 2 SCR 817, 174 DLR (4th) 193, 14 Admin LR (3d) 173, 1 Imm LR (3d) 1, 243 NR 22, at paras. 69-71 and 79-81, where L'Heureux-Dubé J. for the majority and Iacobucci J. for the minority actually explained their respective positions with regard to use of unimplemented treaty norms. See Stephen J. Toope, "The Uses of Metaphor: International Law and the Supreme Court of Canada", (2001), 80 *Canadian Bar Review* 534; Stephen J. Toope, "Inside and Out: The Stories of International Law and Domestic Law", (2001) 50 *University of New Brunswick Law Journal* 11; Hugh Kindred, "Canadians as Citizens of the International Community: Asserting Unimplemented Treaty Rights in the Courts", in Stephen G. Coughlan & Dawn Russell, eds., *Citizenship and Citizen Participation in the Administration of Justice*, Montreal: Thémis, 2002, pp. 263-287; René Provost, "Le juge mondialisé: légitimité judiciaire et droit international au Canada", in Marie-Claude Belleau & François Lacasse, eds., *Claire L'Heureux-Dubé à la Cour suprême du Canada, 1987-2002*, Montreal: Wilson & Lafleur, 2004, pp. 569-603; and Stéphane Beaulac, "Recent Developments on the Role of International Law in Canadian Statutory Interpretation", (2004) 25 *Statute Law Review* 19.

to be incorporated in any sense that might be "binding" upon them.[5] Rather, to use an expression coined by Chief Justice Dickson in an early effort at rationalizing the resort to international law, they find such sources to be "relevant and persuasive".[6] To attempt an analogy, it would be as *comparative law* that judges refer to the international sources, albeit a body of comparative law with particular importance and credibility.[7]

The failure to go further has dismayed some specialists in the field of international law, who had hoped for a more theoretically robust approach that would in some sense join together international and domestic legislation.[8] The danger with this concept is that it actually tends to restrict the usefulness of international law sources. It requires judges to provide a relatively rigorous analysis not only of the content of the norms, be they treaty norms or customary norms, and then establish the direct legal effect of such norms within Canada. The more relaxed comparative law type of approach that has been followed by the courts allows them great flexibility.[9] They may consult sources in regional systems with which Canada is unconnected, as well as the wealth of "soft law" documents where new international law standards may be emerging.

Much of international human rights law, especially in its pure form of international treaty or convention, constitutes a low common denominator of the world community. This is not always appropriate for Canadian so-

---

5   On how little is gained by placing the discourse within a "binding vs. non-binding" dichotomy, see Stéphane Beaulac, "Arrêtons de dire que les tribunaux au Canada sont "liés" par le droit international", (2004) 5 *Revue juridique Thémis* 359.

6   *Reference Re Public Service Employee Relations Act (Alberta)*, [1987] 1 RCS 313, 51 Alta LR (2d) 97, [1987] 3 WWR 577, (sub nom. *A.U.P.E.* v. *Alberta (Attorney General))* 28 CRR 305, 38 DLR (4th) 161, (sub nom. *Reference re Compulsory Arbitration*) 74 NR 99, 78 AR 1, [1987] DLQ 225, 87 CLLC 14,021, at 349-350, *per* Dickson CJ, dissenting.

7   A similar argument has been put forward by Karen Knop, "Here and There: International Law in Domestic Courts", (2000) 32 *New York University Journal of International Law & Policy* 501.

8   See: Elisabeth Eid & Hoori Hamboyan, "Implementation by Canada of its International Human Rights Treaty Obligations: Making Sense out of the Nonsensical", in *Legitimacy and Accountability in International Law – Proceedings of the 33rd Annual Conference of the Canadian Council on International Law*, Ottawa: Canadian Council of International Law, 2005, 175-191; Irit Weiser, "Undressing the Window: Treating International Human Rights Law Meaningfully in the Canadian Commonwealth System", (2004) 37 *University of British Columbia Law Review* 113; and Jutta Brunée & Stephen J. Toope, "A Hesitant Embrace: The Application of International Law by Canadian Courts", (2002) 40 *Canadian Yearbook of International Law* 3. See also the invitation by Justice Louis LeBel (writing extra-judicially with Gloria Chao) to articulate a theoretical approach to international law: Louis LeBel & Gloria Chao, "The Rise of International Law in Canadian Constitutional Litigation: Fugue or Fusion? Recent Developments and Challenges in Internalizing International Law", (2002) 16 *Supreme Court Law Review (2nd)* 23.

9   See: Stéphane Beaulac, "National Application of International Law: The Statutory Interpretation Perspective", (2003) 41 *Canadian Yearbook of International Law* 225.

ciety, where many aspects of human rights law and practice are more advanced and are, in several areas, often on the cutting edge.[10] In other words, the failure of Canadian courts to adopt a theoretical concept by which some international human rights law is actually binding upon them may actually have enhanced the dynamism of the law and, in turn, strengthened the protection of human rights and fundamental freedoms within the country.

2.1   Direct Application of International Human Rights Norms Before Domestic Courts

The classic formulation of the sources of international law is article 38(1) of the *Statute of the International Court of Justice*. It sets out the three principal sources:

(a)   international conventions, whether general or particular, establishing rules expressly recognized by the contesting States;
(b)   international custom, as evidence of a general practice accepted as law;
(c)   the general principles of law recognized by civilized nations.

The *Statute of the International Court of Justice* indicates that legal scholarship and judicial decisions are "subsidiary means for the determination of rules of law."

The list is not exhaustive. For example, a source of international law that is of growing importance is decisions of the United Nations Security Council, adopted pursuant to article 25 of the *Charter of the United Nations* and binding upon all Member States. Unilateral acts, such as a declaration of support for legal principles comprised in a resolution of the General Assembly or reservations to international treaties, may also create legal rights and obligations.

Although the enumeration in article 38 of the *Statute of the International Court of Justice* is often presented as a statement of the sources of international law it is actually a guide to the applicable law that the International Court of Justice is authorized to apply. In this regard, it is not the only such attempt to define the law applicable before international tribunals. Of more recent vintage, the *Rome Statute of the International Criminal Court* also contains a statement of applicable law that is somewhat different than that of the *Statute of the International Court of Justice*.[11] Article 21(1) of the *Rome Statute* refers specifically to one treaty, the *Statute* itself, but it also authorises the Court to apply "where appropriate, applicable treaties and

---

10   See: Anne W. La Forest, "Domestic Application of International Law in *Charter* Cases: Are We There Yet?", (2004) 37 *University of British Columbia Law Review* 157, at 208.
11   *Rome Statute of the International Criminal Court*, UN Doc. A/CONF.183/9.

the principles and rules of international law, including the established principles of the international law of armed conflict" and,

> Failing that, general principles of law derived by the Court from national laws of legal systems of the world including, as appropriate, the national laws of States that would normally exercise jurisdiction over the crime, provided that those principles are not inconsistent with this Statute and with international law and internationally recognized norms and standards.

There is no explicit reference to "customary international law" although such an apparent gap is addressed with the expression "principles and rules of international law". Indeed, it might be taken as an implicit reference to article 38(1) of the *Statute of the International Court of Justice*. Nor does the *Rome Statute* even mention the writings of publicists, although this would seem to be no obstacle to the use of academic literature. The very first significant judicial decision of the International Criminal Court, issued in early 2006, made abundant reference to scholarly writings.[12]

2.1.1   Conventional Human Rights Norms

International conventions, which are the first source of public international law listed in the *Statute of the International Court of Justice*, go by a variety of titles: treaty, protocol, covenant, act, charter and pact are commonly used. A treaty is "an international agreement concluded between States in written form and governed by international law, whether embodied in a single instrument or in two or more related instruments and whatever its particular designation."[13] Canada is a party to a large number of conventional human rights instruments.

Although the *Charter of the United* Nations, which is the treaty at the centre of the modern system of public international law, contains several references to the protection of human rights, it provides little information about the normative content of human rights. The first international treaty of the United Nations system devoted exclusively to human rights was the *Convention on the Prevention and Punishment of the Crime of Genocide.*[14] Its text was adopted by the General Assembly of the United Nations on 9 December 1948, only hours before the *Universal Declaration of Human Rights.* The *Genocide Convention* entered into force in 1951, following the deposit of the twentieth ratification. Canada was not among the initial States

---

12 *Situation in the Democratic Republic of Congo* (Case ICC-01/04), Décision sur les demandes de participation à la procédure de VPRS 1, VPRS 2, VPRS 3, VPRS 4, VPRS 5 et VPRS 6, 17 January 2006, para. 50, fn. 49.

13 *Vienna Convention on the Law of Treaties*, (1969) 1155 UNTS 331, [1980] CTS 37, 8 ILM 679, art. 2(1)(a).

14 *Convention for the Prevention and Punishment of the Crime of Genocide*, (1951) 78 UNTS 277, [1949] CTS 27.

party to the *Convention*. It signed the *Convention* on 28 November 1949, but only ratified the instrument on 3 September 1952.[15] The *Genocide Convention* was followed by the *Convention Relating to the Status of Refugees*,[16] which was adopted on 28 July 1951 and entered into force three years later. Canada acceded to the *Refugee Convention* on 4 June 1969 (accession is an act by which a State binds itself when it has not taken the preliminary step of signature). The process launched by the drafting of the *Universal Declaration of Human Rights* led to the two *International Covenants* and five other specialized treaties, dealing with racial discrimination, discrimination against women, the prevention of torture, the rights of the child and the rights of migrant workers and their families. Several of the treaties have additional protocols that complete their provisions with supplementary procedural or substantive obligations.

In addition to the treaties of the United Nations system, there are also a range of conventional instruments within other universal systems involving the protection of human rights, of which the most important are the *Geneva Conventions* and the *Rome Statute of the International Criminal Court*. There are also regional systems for the protection of human rights, that of the Organization of American States being the most important as far as Canada is concerned.

The human rights treaty systems are discussed in detail in Chapter 3. This chapter is concerned with the legal status of such treaties within Canada.

2.1.1.1   The Transformation of Treaty Norms by Implementing Legislation

In many legal systems, ratification of or accession to an international treaty makes the legal norms that it contains directly enforceable before the courts of the country in question. Such states are described with the adjective "monist", because domestic law and international law make up a coherent and holistic body of norms. This is not, however, the case in Canada, which follows the so-called "dualist" English Parliamentary tradition. Foreign relations are the prerogative of the executive, which has the power to bind the State as a matter of international law. International obligations are not enforceable before the courts of the land unless they have been implemented

---

15   Ratification was approved by motion in Parliament. See: HC Debates, 1952, pp. 2430-2443; Senate Debates, 1952, pp. 311-315.

16   *Convention Relating to the Status of Refugees*, (1954) 189 UNTS 137, [1969] CTS 29.

by Parliament.[17] In an April 2002 opinion, the Legal Bureau of the Department of Foreign Affairs wrote:

> It is the legislative implementation of treaties that affords Parliament its main role in the treaty process: if new legislation must be passed, or existing legislation amended, it is Parliament that must pass or amend the legislation according to usual parliamentary practices. A practice has developed for the federal government to table annually in Parliament international treaties that have come into force for Canada in the previous year. This practice fell into disuse for a number of years, but has resumed since 1999 in accordance with a Standing Order of the Parliament. This practice is voluntary: it is not required by any statute or constitutional provision.
>
> There is no legal requirement for Parliamentary approval prior to international ratification of a treaty. On occasion, international agreements were brought to the attention of Parliament before ratification, and their approval sought by joint resolution. The decision on whether to seek Parliamentary approval was made, in each instance, by the Government of the day. This practice has now fallen into disuse: the last Parliamentary resolution approving an international treaty was passed in 1966.[18]

Canadian courts have repeatedly referred to the dualist principles, by which governmental ratification or accession to treaty obligations do not in any way alter the law applicable within the country and before its courts.[19] As the Judicial Committee of the Privy Council stated in the *Labour Conventions* case:

> It will be essential to keep in mind the distinction between (1.) the formation, and (2.) the performance, of the obligations constituted by a treaty, using that words as comprising any agreement between two or more sovereign States. Within the British Empire, there is a well-established rule that the making of a treaty is an executive act, while the performance of its obligations, *if they entail alteration of the existing domestic law*, requires legislative action. Unlike some other countries, the stipulations of a treaty duly ratified do not within the Empire, by virtue of the treaty lone, have the force of law. If the national executive, the government of the day, decide to incur the obligations of a treaty

---

17 *The Parlement Belge*, (1878-79) 4 PD 129; *Malone* v. *Commissioner of Police of the Metropolis*, [1979] 2 All ER 620, [1979] Ch. 344, 69 Cr App R 168. See the comments of Justice Tarnopolsky in *R.* v. *Videoflicks Ltd.*, (1984) 14 DLR (4th) 10, 15 CCC (3d) 353, 34 RPR 97, 9 CRR 193, 48 OR (2d) 395, (sub nom. *Edwards Books & Art Ltd.* v. *R.*) 5 OAC 1 (CA), reversed, (1986) 1986 CarswellOnt 1012 (SCC).

18 Colleen Swords, ed., "Canadian Ratification Practice", (2002) 40 *Canadian Yearbook of International Law* 491.

19 *Re Arrow River and Tributaries Slide & Boom Co. Limited*, [1932] SCR 495, 39 CRC 161, (sub nom. *Arrow River & Tributaries Slide & Boom Co., Re*) [1932] 2 DLR 250, at 260-261 (DLR); *Francis* v. *R*, [1956] SCR 618; *Capital Cities Communications Inc.* v. *Canadian Radio-Television Commission*, [1978] 2 SCR 141, 81 DLR (3d) 609, 36 CPR (2d) 1, 18 NR 181; and, again recently, *Baker* v. *Canada*, *supra* note 4.

which involve alteration of law they have to run the risk of obtaining the assent of Parliament to the necessary statute or statutes. . .[20]

In Canada, federalism has given this principle a further twist. Although the treaty-making power is formally an attribute of the Sovereign, it is actually wielded by the federal government. In theory at least, the federal Parliament could encroach upon provincial jurisdiction by making treaties dealing with matters under section 92 of the *Constitution Act, 1867* and, more specifically, issues affecting property and civil rights. When the federal government sought to introduce unemployment insurance as part of the Bennett "new deal" in 1935, it argued that the matter was one of federal jurisdiction because Canada was a party to certain International Labour Organization conventions requiring such legislation. Actually, the treaties had been ratified only weeks before introduction of the draft legislation. Ratification provided the federal government with a pretext to attempt to invade an area hitherto of provincial jurisdiction. In the *Labour Conventions* case, the Judicial Committee of the Privy Council refused to allow the proposed legislation. Parliament's treaty-making power was confined to the subject matter of section 91 of the *British North America Act*, and the federal government could not, by ratifying or acceding to an international convention dealing with the rights of labour or other human rights, pierce the watertight compartment of provincial jurisdiction.[21] Despite jurisprudential hints that the Supreme Court is prepared to reconsider the matter,[22] and no shortage of sometimes incredulous learned criticism by legal scholars,[23] Lord Atkin's *dictum* in the *Labour Conventions* case remains a valid statement of Canadian law.[24]

Canada's treaty obligations under human rights instruments can therefore bind the courts if they meet two tests. They must be reflected in legislation, either expressly or by necessary implication, and such legislation must be an enactment of the legislature having jurisdiction over the subject matter of the treaty. One of the principal human rights instruments to which Canada is bound on the level of international law is the *International Cov-*

---

20 *AG Canada* v. *AG Ontario (Labour Conventions Case)*, [1937] AC 326, [1937] 1 DLR 673, [1937] 1 WWR 299 (Canada P.C.), at 347-348 (AC) (emphasis added).
21 *Ibid.*
22 *MacDonald* v. *Vapor Canada Ltd.*, [1977] 2 SCR 134, 66 DLR (3d) 1, 22 CPR (2d) 1, 7 NR 477; *Schneider* v. *R*, [1982] 2 SCR 112, 139 DLR (3d) 417, 43 NR 91.
23 Maxwell Cohen & Anne F. Bayefsky, "The Canadian Charter of Rights and Freedoms and International Law", (1983) 61 *Canadian Bar Review* 265, at 292-293.
24 For a confirmation of the principle dealing with international human rights law, see: *Immeubles Claude Dupont Inc.* v. *Québec (PG)*, [1994] RJQ 1968 (SC). In the context of international environmental law, see: Stéphane Beaulac, "The Canadian Federal Constitutional Framework and the Implementation of the Kyoto Protocol", (2005) 5 *Revue juridique polynésienne (hors série)* 125.

enant on Civil and Political Rights.[25] Two federal enactments refer specifically to the *Covenant*, both of them in their preambles.[26] It may reasonably be argued that the effect of such reference is to incorporate the provisions of the *Covenant* into Canadian statute law, at least those parts of it that are relevant to the legislation in question. For example, the *Emergencies Act*, by its preambular reference to the *Covenant*, may be deemed to incorporate article 4 of that instrument, which prohibits the suspension of certain rights that are deemed non-derogable. Consequently, any exercise of authority pursuant to the *Emergencies Act* by, for example, the federal Cabinet, would be obliged to respect the limits imposed by article 4 of the *Covenant*. Nevertheless, a preamble is intended to assist in interpretation rather than create binding norms. It is also not unreasonable to view such references as a reminder of the persuasive force of Canada's international obligations rather than as a somewhat oblique effort to formally incorporate treaty obligations into domestic statutes.

Besides the *Covenant*, international human rights instruments are directly referred to in other Canadian statutes. For example, the *Crimes Against Humanity and War Crimes Act*[27] cites the *Rome Statute of the International Criminal Court*.[28] The *Immigration and Refugee Protection Act*[29] makes reference to the *Convention Relating to the Status of Refugees* in the definition of "Convention refugee", at section 96, and somewhat less explicitly in the enumeration of refugee objectives in section 3(2)(b):

> (2) The objectives of this Act with respect to refugees are
>
> [. . .]
>
> (b) to fulfil Canada's international legal obligations with respect to refugees and affirm Canada's commitment to international efforts to provide assistance to those in need of resettlement [. . .]

---

25 *International Covenant on Civil and Political Rights*, (1976) 999 UNTS 171, [1976] CTS 47.

26 *Emergencies Act*, SC 1988, c. 29; *Canadian Multiculturalism Act*, SC 1988, c. 31. In *Re Boyd and Earl & Jennie Lohn Ltd.*, (1984) 11 DLR (4th) 265, 47 OR (2d) 111 (HC), the Attorney General of Ontario apparently produced a letter from the provincial government indicating that it did not consider the *International Covenant on Civil and Political Rights* to be legally binding on provincial legislation, a position it may be possible to justify in a highly technical way (because strictly speaking Ontario is not a party to the *Covenant*) but which makes no real sense, given Ontario's endorsement of the *Covenant* and its regular participation in the preparation of periodic reports on the *Covenant's* application to the Human Rights Committee of the United Nations.

27 *Crimes Against Humanity and War Crimes Act*, SC 2000, c. 24.

28 UN Doc. A/CONF.183/9.

29 *Immigration and Refugee Protection Act*, SC 2001, c. 27.

Section 3(3)(f) says the *Act* "is to be construed and applied in a manner that [. . .] (f) complies with international human rights instruments to which Canada is signatory". In *Ernewein* v. *Minister of Employment and Immigration*, Justice Pigeon of the Supreme Court of Canada found that "the Provisions of the Convention were adopted and became part of the law of Canada by being thus referred to in an Act of Parliament".[30] Justice Wilson of the Supreme Court of Canada, in her reasons in the *Singh* decision, which rallied two other members of the bench, expressly approved of these comments.[31]

International human rights law has assumed an important role in the refugee determination process, pursuant to the *Immigration Act*,[32] which since 28 July 2002 has been replaced by the *Immigration and Refugee Protection Act*. The definition of a refugee focuses on the notion of "persecution", which a learned commentator on refugee matters, Professor James Hathaway, has described as "sustained or systemic violation of basic human rights demonstrative of a failure of state protection".[33] Justice Rouleau of the Federal Court considered that "in extreme circumstances" a breach of the *International Covenant on Economic, Social and Cultural Rights*[34] could constitute persecution, and hence justify a refugee claim.[35] The courts have also found international law to be relevant in determining whether a refugee claimant belongs to a "particular social group", such as parents wishing to assert their fundamental right to determine the number, spacing and timing of their children.[36] International instruments are also

---

30 *Ernewein* v. *Canada (Minister of Employment and Immigration)*, [1980] 1 SCR 639, 103 DLR (3d) 1, 14 CPC 264, 30 NR 316, at 658 (SCR).

31 *Singh* v. *Canada (Minister of Employment and Immigration)*, [1985] 1 SCR 177, 17 DLR (4th) 422, 58 NR 1, 14 CRR 13, 12 Admin LR 137, at 193 (SCR).

32 *Immigration Act*, RSC 1985, c. I-2, s. 2(1). In *Canada (AG)* v. *Ward*, (1990) 67 DLR (4th) 1, 10 Imm LR (2d) 199 (FCA), reversed, [1993] 2 SCR 689, at 15 (DLR), Justice Urie of the Federal Court of Appeal, echoing the words of Chief Justice Dickson in *Reference Re Public Service Employee Relations Act (Alberta)*, [1987] 1 RCS 313, 51 Alta LR (2d) 97, [1987] 3 WWR 577, (sub nom. *A.U.P.E.* v. *Alberta (Attorney General)*) 28 CRR 305, 38 DLR (4th) 161, (sub nom. *Reference re Compulsory Arbitration*) 74 NR 99, 78 AR 1, [1987] DLQ 225, 87 CLLC 14,021, said that the *Refugee Convention* was "persuasive" although not "binding" in "forming a logical construction of the Convention refugee definition".

33 James Hathaway, *The Law of Refugee Practice*, Toronto: Butterworths, 1991, at 104-105.

34 *International Covenant on Economic, Social and Cultural Rights*, (1976) 993 UNTS 3, [1976] CTS 46.

35 *Ramirez* v. *Canada (Solicitor General)*, (1988) 88 FTR 208 (TD).

36 *Chan* v. *Canada (Minister of Employment and Immigration)*, [1995] 3 SCR 593, at 646 (SCR).

regularly used to assist in applying the "exclusion clauses" that accompany the *Convention* refugee definition.[37]

The *An Act to amend the Canada Labour Code* refers, in the preamble to Part V,[38] to *I.L.O. Convention No. 87*,[39] which protects freedom of association. The preamble was inserted at the suggestion of the Woods Task Force on labour relations.[40] It even makes reference to the adjudication procedure before the International Labour Organization Freedom of Association Committee. This might be deemed to imply that the caselaw of the body is also incorporated into Canadian law, although that has not been the position taken by the majority of the Supreme Court of Canada.[41] In a decision of the Canada Labour Relations Board, the majority considered that the reference in the preamble to the *Convention* "enlightened" the interpretation of the *Code*. But a dissenting member cautioned: "I am mindful of the significance of Canada's endorsement of this and other international labour conventions. It is still necessary, however, to determine the extent to which Parliament has actually implemented the convention by examining the language of the Code itself."[42] There is no serious suggestion in Canadian caselaw that the preambular reference alone actually incorporates some or all of the provisions into Canadian law.

2.1.1.2   *Implementation by Implication is Not Domestic Transformation*

An argument has been made that the *Covenant* and the other human rights instruments to which Canada is a party are incorporated into Canadian law by *implication*, the implementing legislation being the *Charter* itself or some other specific enactment.[43] This comes close to Chief Justice Dickson's statement in *Reference re Public Service Employee Relations Act* to the effect that the *Charter* provides a protection that is generally comparable

---

37 Pursuant to a proposal in the *Handbook on Procedures and Criteria for Determining Refugee Status*, Geneva: Office of the United Nations High Commissioner for Refugees, 1988, para. 60. See, for example: *Maslova* v. *Canada (Minister of Citizenship and Immigration)*, (1994) 86 FTR 34 (TD).

38 *An Act to amend the Canada Labour Code*, SC 1972, c. 18: "And Whereas the Government of Canada has ratified Convention No. 87 of the International Labour Organization concerning Freedom of Association and Protection of the Right to Organize and has assumed international reporting responsibilities in this regard."

39 *ILO Convention (No. 87) Concerning Freedom of Association and Protection of the Right to Organize*, (1950) 68 UNTS 17, [1973] CTS 14.

40 *Télévision Saint-François Inc.*, (1981) 43 di 175 (Can LRB).

41 *Reference Re Public Service Employee Relations Act*, *supra* note 32.

42 *Canadian Broadcasting Corp.*, (1990) 83 di 102, 91 CLLC 16,007 (Can LRB), reconsideration refused, (1991) 1991 CarswellNat 1022 (Can LRB), affirmed, (1992) 1992 CarswellNat 105 (Fed CA), affirmed, (1995) 1995 CarswellNat 265 (SCC).

43 Maxwell Cohen & Anne F. Bayefsky, *supra* note 23.

to that in human rights treaties which bind Canada. However, it is clear that the Chief Justice did not fully accept the implementation by implication thesis.

In an article published shortly after the coming into force of the *Charter*, Maxwell Cohen and Anne F. Bayefsky argued that Canadian courts ought not to look for legislation that expressly implements the *International Covenant on Civil and Political Rights* and other treaties to which Canada is a party but rather they should:

> [c]onsider the words of the domestic provision and of the convention together with extrinsic evidence in order to determine whether the purpose of the enactment was to implement the convention or give it legal effect in domestic law. The appropriate question for our courts to ask therefore, is whether a provision of the Charter was included in order to give effect to Canada's international obligations.[44]

This idea of treaty transformation on the basis of pre-existing domestic legal norms is now often referred to as "passive incorporation" or "incorporation by complacence".[45] Such an alternative is irreconcilable with the long-standing position in Canada, based on the "dualist" model, which requires implementing legislation to give legal effect domestically to treaty norms.[46]

A study of the preparatory work of the *Charter* reveals the influence on its drafters of the international models.[47] Justice Belzil of the Alberta Court of Appeal has said the *Charter* was meant to "dovetail" with the

---

44 *Ibid*, at 303 [footnotes omitted].
45 See: Irit Weiser, "Effect in Domestic Law of International Human Rights Treaties Ratified without Implementing Legislation", in *The Impact of International Law on the Practice of Law in Canada – Proceedings of the 27th Annual Conference of the Canadian Council on International Law*, The Hague: Kluwer Law International, 1999, p. 132, at 137-139; Elizabeth Brandon, "Does International Law Mean Anything in Canadian Courts", (2002) 11 *Journal of Environmental Law & Practice* 399, at 418; G. van Ert, "What is Treaty Implementation?", in *Legitimacy and Accountability in International Law – Proceedings of the 33rd Annual Conference of the Canadian Council on International Law*, Ottawa: Canadian Council of International Law, 2005, pp. 165-174.
46 The traditional proposition that domestic transformation of international treaty norms needs to be done through legislation comes from the *AG Canada* v. *AG Ontario (Labour Conventions Case)*, [1937] AC 326, [1937] 1 DLR 673, [1937] 1 WWR 299 (Canada P.C.), at 347. See also: Ruth Sullivan, *Sullivan and Driedger on the Construction of Statutes*, 4th ed., Markham, Ontario & Vancouver: Butterworths, 2002, at 430.
47 Referred to by Lamer CJ in *B. (R.)* v. *Children's Aid Society of Metropolitan Toronto*, [1995] 1 SCR 315, 122 DLR (4th) 1, 176 NR 161, at 34-350 (SCR). See particularly the document prepared by Minister of Justice Otto E. Lang, dated August 1978, entitled *Constitutional Reform: Canadian Charter of Rights and Freedoms*, which is reproduced in Anne F. Bayefsky, *Canada's Constitution Act 1982 & Amendments, A Documentary History*, Toronto: McGraw-Hill Ryerson, 1989, at 499.

International Covenant on Civil and Political Rights.[48] Justice Watt of the Ontario Court of Appeal stated that "a textual comparison and a review of the evidence before the Special Joint Committee of the Senate and House of Commons on the Constitution, 1981-82, confirm that the *International Covenant on Civil and Political Rights* was an important source of the terms chosen" by the *Charter*'s framers.[49] Recently, Justice Cumming of the Ontario Superior Court of Justice wrote: "Undoubtedly, the Charter gives effect to many of Canada's obligations under international law."[50]

The drafting of the *Charter* was somewhat influenced by the comments of members of the United Nations Human Rights Committee who, during presentation of Canada's initial report pursuant to article 40 of the *Covenant* in March 1980, remarked upon what they considered to be glaring shortcomings in Canadian legislation.[51] Four years later, when the complementary report was presented, Canadian officials referred to articles 1, 8, 10 11(b), 15 and 24 of the *Charter* as examples of provisions that had been inspired not only by the *Covenant* itself but by the comments of the members of the Committee. At the same time, Canadian representative Martin Low told the Human Rights Committee that the *Covenant*, although not formally incorporated in Canadian law, could be used as an aid to interpreting ambiguous provisions of domestic law and even the *Charter*.[52]

If the role and influence of the *Covenant* in the drafting of the *Charter* is inescapable, there are also significant and substantial differences that militate against the implication approach (or passive incorporation in general[53]). Some rights found in the *International Covenant on Civil and Political Rights* do not appear expressly in the *Charter*, such as the right to privacy,[54] and the right of persons belonging to ethnic, religious or linguistic minorities to enjoy their own culture, to profess and practise their own religion, or to use their own language.[55] Those of the *International Covenant on Economic, Social and Cultural Rights* are totally excluded. In some

---

48 *Reference Re Public Service Employee Relations Act (Alberta)*, (1984) [1985] 2 WWR 289, 35 Alta LR (2d) 124, (sub nom. *Reference re Compulsory Arbitration*) 57 AR 268, 85 CLLC 14,027, 16 DLR (4th) 359 (CA), at 389 (DLR).

49 *Re Corporation of the Canadian Civil Liberties Association and Minister of Education*, (1988) 64 OR (2d) 577 (Div Ct), reversed, (1990) 1990 CarswellOnt 1078 (CA).

50 *Mack* v. *Canada (Attorney General)*, (2001) 55 OR (3d) 113 (SC), affirmed, (2002) 60 OR (3d) 737, 217 DLR (4th) 583, 96 CRR (2d) 254, 165 OAC 17 (CA), leave to appeal refused, (2003) 319 NR 196n (SCC), at para. 35.

51 UN Doc. CCPR/C/SR.558, para. 12.

52 UN Doc. CCPR/C/SR.559, para. 23.

53 On why "passive incorporation" is misguided, see: Stéphane Beaulac, "National Application of International Law: The Statutory Interpretation Perspective", (2003) 41 *Canadian Yearbook of International Law* 225, at 245-248.

54 *International Covenant on Civil and Political Rights*, *supra* note 25, art. 17.

55 *Ibid.*, art. 27.

cases, the wording of texts is inspired by common law provisions rather than the international model. For example, the guarantee against "cruel and unusual punishment" that is found in section 12 of the *Charter* is borrowed from the English *Bill of Rights* of 1689 and the Eighth Amendment to the United States Constitution; the *Universal Declaration of Human Rights*,[56] in article 5, and the *International Covenant on Civil and Political Rights*, in article 7, refer to "cruel, inhuman and degrading treatment or punishment".[57]

Several examples of implementation of international human rights norms by implication seem to exist in the *Criminal Code*,[58] but they are not real cases of domestic incorporation of treaty obligations. The prohibition of hate propaganda, set out in section 319 of the *Code*, is clearly inspired by the *International Convention on the Elimination of All Forms of Racial Discrimination*,[59] even though the provision may not adequately give effect to the obligations set out in article 5 of that instrument. In *R. v. Andrews*,[60] Justice Peter D. Cory, then of the Ontario Court of Appeal, wrote that the hate propaganda provisions of the *Criminal Code* (s. 319) were enacted so as to respect (though he did not say "incorporate") Canada's undertakings pursuant to the *Convention*. Likewise, section 318, which criminalizes public incitement to genocide,[61] gives partial effect to international obligations imposed by the *Convention for the Prevention and Punishment of the Crime of Genocide*.[62] But the Canadian legislation speaks of "advocating genocide", whereas the *Convention* uses the terms "direct and public incitement to commit genocide". Some of the other underlying acts that form part of the crime of genocide, such as killing and causing serious bodily or mental harm, were already part of Canadian criminal law at the time the *Convention* was ratified in 1951. But the *Genocide Convention* also requires states to punish as genocide two other acts, preventing measures of birth within a

---

56 *Universal Declaration of Human Rights*, GA Res. 217 A (III) UN Doc. A/810.

57 *R. v. Shand*, (1977) 13 OR (2d) 65 (CA), leave to appeal refused, (1976) 13 OR (2d) 65n (SCC); *R. v. Buckler*, [1970] 2 OR 614 (PC, Cr Div).

58 RSC 1985, c. C-46.

59 *International Convention on the Elimination of All Forms of Racial Discrimination*, (1969) 660 UNTS 195, [1970] CTS 28. The *Convention* inspired amendments to the *Criminal Code* creating the new infraction of hate propaganda: *Act to Amend the Criminal Code*, SC 1969-70, c. 39. The *Convention* is referred to specifically in the preamble to the *Multiculturalism Act*, SC 1988, c. 31.

60 (1989) 43 CCC (3d) 193, 65 OR (2d) 161, 28 OAC 161, 65 CR (3d) 320, 39 CRR 36 (CA), affirmed, (1990) 75 OR (2d) 481n (SCC).

61 The offense was added to the *Criminal Code*: *Act to Amend the Criminal Code*, SC 1969-70, c. 39.

62 *Convention on the Prevention and Punishment of the Crime of Genocide*, (1951) 78 UNTS 277, [1949] CTS 27. Cited in *Mugesera* v. *Canada (Minister of Citizenship and Immigration)*, [2005] 2 SCR 100.

group and forcibly transferring children from one group to another, and these have never been the subject of legislation. Arguably, such acts might engage other criminal offences under Canadian law.

Certainly, there are isolated instances in Canadian law where there is little doubt that treaty obligations were legislatively transformed. For example, following ratification of the *Convention Against Torture and Other Cruel, Inhuman or Degrading Treatment or Punishment* in 1987,[63] the *Criminal Code* was amended to add section 269.1, which deals specifically with torture.[64] At first glance, the provision would appear to be superfluous, because acts of torture are clearly contemplated by other provisions of the *Code*, such as assault. However, the amendment was coupled with another provision giving Canadian courts universal jurisdiction over torture, as required by the *Convention*, and entitling them to judge individuals accused of acts of torture even where these take place outside Canada. Several international instruments, as well as customary international law, require that states cooperate in the prosecution of those responsible for gross violations of human rights, crimes against humanity and war crimes.[65] In order to give effect to this obligation, sections 7(3.71)-(3.76) of the *Criminal Code* were enacted in 1987.[66] The *Immigration and Refugee Protection Act* says that its objectives include the offer of safe haven to "those at risk of torture or cruel and unusual reatment or punishment"[67], and provides the definition of torture contained in article 1 of the *Convention Against Torture and Other Cruel, Inhuman and Degrading Treatment or Punishment.*[68]

Similarly, provincial legislation may constitute domestic transformation of international human rights norms. The *Ontario Human Rights Code*[69] and the Yukon Territory *Human Rights Act*[70] refer explicitly to the *Universal Declaration of Human Rights*. The Saskatchewan Court of Appeal has held that the province's human rights legislation gives effect, in a general sense, to Canada's and Saskatchewan's international obligations.[71] A provision of

---

63 *Convention Against Torture and Other Cruel, Inhuman or Degrading Treatment or Punishment*, UN Doc. A/39/51, p. 197, REIQ (1984-89) no (1987) (16) p. 870.

64 *Criminal Law Amendment Act (Torture)* SC 1987, c. 13.

65 See: M. Cherif Bassiouni & Edward M. Wise, *Aut dedere aut judicare, the Duty to Extradite or Prosecute in International Law*, Dordrecht/Boston/London: Martinus Nijhoff, 1995.

66 See: *R.* v. *Finta*, [1994] 1 SCR 701, 88 CCC (3d) 417, 112 DLR (4th) 513, 150 NR 370, at 729 (SCR), *per* La Forest J.

67 *Immigration and Refugee Protection Act*, SC 2001, c. 27, s. 3(2)(d).

68 *Ibid.*, Schedule.

69 RSO 1990, c.H.19, preamble.

70 SY 1987, c. 3, s. 1.

71 *Canadian Odeon Theatres Ltd.* v. *Saskatchewan Human Rights Commission and Huck*, 18 DLR (4th) 93, (Sask CA), leave to appeal refused [1985] 1 SCR vi (note) at 736 (WWR).

Quebec's *Labour Code* dealing with appropriate indemnities in case of dismissal or lay-off, and three provisions of its *Labour Standards Act* dealing with wrongful dismissal, were deemed to be "inspired" by Recommendation No. 119 of the International Labour Organization.[72]

Sometimes, legislation has been enacted in order to give effect to a finding by the Human Rights Committee that Canada is in breach of its obligations under the *International Covenant on Civil and Political Rights*. It would seem reasonable to conclude that such legislation is intended to give effect to the *International Covenant on Civil and Political Rights*, even if no direct reference is made to the instrument. In 1985, the *Indian Act*[73] was amended by the repeal of section 12(1)(b),[74] which denied Indian status to aboriginal women who had married non-aboriginal men, although the same was not the case for aboriginal men who married non-aboriginal women. The Human Rights Committee had previously found such legislation to be incompatible with article 27 of the *International Covenant on Civil and Political Rights*, which enshrines certain rights of ethnic, religious and linguistic minorities.[75] The government reported back to the Human Rights Committee that appropriate adjustments were being made. The Canadian government declared: that "as a result of the decision of the Human Rights Committee in regard to communication No. 24/1977 brought by Sandra Lovelace, Canada is anxious to amend the Indian Act so as to render itself in fuller compliance with its international obligations pursuant to article 27 of the *International Covenant on Civil and Political Rights*".[76] While there is no doubt that the amending legislation was a response to the views of the Committee, the courts have had difficulty identifying the provision of the *Covenant* that the 1985 amendment was meant to implement.[77]

---

72 *Cappco Tubular* v. *Montpetit*, [1990] CT/TT 286 (Labour Court) at 291. ILO Recommendations are non-binding texts that accompany the Conventions and often expand upon the obligations contained therein.

73 RSC 1970, c. I-6.

74 *An Act to amend the Indian Act*, SC 1985, c. 27, s. 4. The debate about various provisions of the *Indian Act* literally preoccupied judicial interpretation of the *Canadian Bill of Rights*, RSC 1985, Appendix III, and at least indirectly influenced the drafters of the *Canadian Charter*. In *Law Society of British Columbia* v. *Andrews*, [1989] 1 SCR 143, 56 DLR (4th) 1, [1989] 2 WWR 289, 36 CRR 193, 25 CCEL 255, 10 CHRR D/5719, 34 BCLR (2d) 273, 91 NR 255, at 171 (SCR) Justice McIntyre described the *Indian Act* as part of the "linguistic, philosophic and historical context" of section 15 of the *Charter*.

75 *Lovelace* v. *Canada*, [1983] Can. Hum. Rts. Y.B. 305, 68 ILR 17. See: Anne F. Bayefsky, "The Human Rights Committee and the Case of Sandra Lovelace", [1982] *Canadian Yearbook of International Law* 244.

76 UN Doc. CCPR/C/OP/2, p. 224, [1984-85] *Canadian Human Rights Yearbook* 373.

77 *Batchewana Indian Band* v. *Batchewana Indian Band* [1994] 1 FC 394 (TD) at 414 [FC], varied, [1997] 1 FC 689 (CA), leave to appeal allowed, (1997) 215 NR 239n, [1999] 2 SCR 203, reconsideration refused, (2000) 2000 CarswellNat 2393 (SCC), note 18.

In 1993, the Quebec government amended provisions of the *Charter of the French Language*[78] following a finding by the Human Rights Committee that there had been a violation of article 19 of the *Covenant* (freedom of expression).[79] In this case, there was little doubt about legislative intent. The Quebec National Assembly had defied an earlier ruling to the same effect from the Supreme Court of Canada.[80] It seemed more impressed by the international body than by the country's highest tribunal!

Canadian courts are increasingly aware of the consequences of violations of the *International Covenant on Civil and Political Rights* and other treaties where there exists an individual petition mechanism. But the possibility that Canada will be embarrassed before an international tribunal in no way changes the state of domestic law. According to Justice Strayer of the Federal Court, in *Henry* v. *Canada*:

> With respect to the plaintiff's argument concerning the *International Covenant on Civil and Political Rights*, important as such an international instrument is, and even though its breach can expose this country to complaints made directly to the United Nations by individuals under the *Optional Protocol*, it does not have the force of law within Canada and is not enforceable by Canadian courts. At times it may be helpful in interpreting domestic law, but I am unable to see how it is of assistance in this case.[81]

Courts in the United Kingdom have taken the same view of decisions by the European Court of Human Rights. In *Tease* v. *O'Callaghan*, the High Court of the Isle of Man held that despite a successful petition to the European Court, the domestic law remained in force unchanged.[82]

Canadian courts have often insisted that international instruments such as the *International Covenant on Civil and Political Rights* and the *Universal Declaration of Human Rights* have no direct effect on Canadian law

---

78 *Loi modifiant la Charte de la langue française*, LQ 1993, c. 40.

79 *Ballantyne and Davidson, and McIntyre* v. *Canada* (Nos. 359/1989 and 385/1989), UN Doc. CCPR/C/47/D/385/1989, UN Doc. A/48/40, Vol. II, p. 91, 14 *Human Rights Law Journal* 171, 11 *Netherlands Quarterly of Human Rights* 469.

80 *Ford* v. *Québec (PG)*, [1988] 2 SCR 712, 54 DLR (4th) 577, 19 QAC 69, 36 CRR 1, 90 NR 84, 10 CHRR D/5559.

81 *Henry* v. *Canada*, [1987] 3 FC 429, 10 FTR 176, 29 CRR 149 (TD), per Strayer J.

82 *Tease* v. *O'Callaghan*, [1982] 4 EHRR 232 (Isle of Man High Court). The European Court had held that whipping, which was provided for in the domestic law, was in violation of article 3 of the *European Convention on Human Rights*, (1955) 213 UNTS 221, ETS 5, in *Tyrer* v. *United Kingdom*, 25 April 1978, Series A, No. 26, 2 EHRR 1, 59 ILR 339. Interestingly, the Isle of Man High Court relied on the Privy Council decision in the Canadian *AG Canada* v. *AG Ontario (Labour Conventions Case)*, [1937] AC 326, [1937] 1 DLR 673, [1937] 1 WWR 299 (Canada P.C.).

because they have not been legislatively incorporated into Canada's law.[83] The latest forceful statement confirming that implementation by implication (or passive incorporation) of treaty norms is not domestic transformation comes from a 2002 Ontario Court of Appeal decision in *Ahani v. Canada (Attorney General)*.[84] At the centre of the dispute was whether or not the *Optional Protocol to the International Covenant on Civil and Political Rights*[85] was part of the law of the land, applicable to the deportation case

---

83 See: *Gagnon and Vallières* v. *R.*, [1971] Que CA 454, 14 CRNS 321; *Re Minister of Employment and Hudnik*, (1979) [1980] 1 FC 180, 103 DLR (3d) 308 (CA); *Re Dixon and Manitoba Labour Board*, (1981) 127 DLR (3d) 752, 12 Man R (2d) 431 (QB); *Dolack* v. *Canada (Minister of Manpower and Immigration)*, [1982] 1 FC 396 (TD), reversed [1983] 1 FC 194, 140 DLR (3d) 767, 45 NR 146 (CA); *Collin* v. *Kaplan*, [1983] 1 FC 496, 143 DLR (3d) 121, 1 CCC (3d) 309, 2 CRR 352 (TD); *Vincent* v. *Canada (Minister of Employment and Immigration)*, [1983] 1 FC 1057, 148 DLR (3d) 385, 48 NR 214 (CA), leave to appeal allowed, (1983) 53 NR 315 (SCC), affirmed, [1985] 2 SCR xiii (SCC); *Re R. and Warren* (1983) 35 CR (3d) 173, 6 CRR 82 (Ont. HC); *Re Mitchell and R.* (1983) 150 DLR (3d) 449, 6 CCC (3d) 193, 35 CR (3d) 225,42 OR (2d) 481 (HC); *Evans* v. *Kingston Penitentiary*, (1987) 30 CCC (3d) 1, 55 CR (3d) 276 (Ont HC); *(AG) Canada* v. *Ward*, (1990) 67 DLR (4th) 1, 10 Imm LR (2d) 199 (FCA), reversed, [1993] 2 SCR 689; *Charran* v. *Canada (Minister of Citizenship and Immigration)*, (1995) 28 Imm LR (2d) 282 (TD); *R.* v. *Demers*, (1999) 176 DLR (4th) 741, 137 CCC (3d) 297 (BC SC), affirmed, (2003) 102 CRR (2d) 367 (BC CA), leave to appeal refused, (2003) 321 NR 399n (SCC); *Mack* v. *Canada (Attorney General)*, (2001) 55 OR (3d) 113 (SC), affirmed, (2002) 60 OR (3d) 737, 217 DLR (4th) 583, 96 CRR (2d) 254, 165 OAC 17 (CA), leave to appeal refused, (2003) 319 NR 196n (SCC); *De Guzman* v. *Canada (Minister of Citizenship and Immigration)*, (2004) 257 FTR 290, 245 DLR (4th) 341, 40 Imm LR (3d) 256 (TD), affirmed, (2005) 51 Imm LR (3d) 17 (CA), leave to appeal refused, (2006) 2006 CarswellNat 1694 (SCC), at para. 53. *Contra*, see *Bouzari* v. *Islamic Republic of Iran*, (2004) 71 OR (3d) 675 (CA), leave to appeal refused, (2005) 2005 CarswellOnt 292 (SCC).

84 *Ahani* v. *Canada (Attorney General)*, (2002) 58 OR (3d) 107, 91 CRR (2d) 145, 19 Imm LR (3d) 231 (CA), leave to appeal refused, (2002) 2002 CarswellOnt 1651 (SCC). The *Ahani* case was considered with the *Suresh* case at the Supreme Court of Canada: *Suresh* v. *Canada (Minister of Citizenship and Immigration)*, [2002] 1 SCR 3, 208 DLR (4th) 1, 37 Admin LR (3d) 159, 90 CRR (2d) 1; *Ahani* v. *Canada (Minister of Citizenship and Immigration)*, [2002] 1 SCR 72, 208 DLR (4th) 57, 90 CRR (2d) 47. Unlike *Suresh*, the petitioner Ahani was not given a new deportation hearing and, having exhausted all domestic remedies, he petitioned the United Nations Human Rights Committee under the *Optional Protocol* to the *International Covenant of Civil and Political Rights*. In an interim order, the Human Rights Committee requested Canada to stay the deportation until the full consideration of Ahani's case, but this was refused by the federal government. See: *Ahani* v. *Canada* (No. 1051/2002), UN Doc. CCPR/C/80/D/1051/2002. The second Canadian judicial proceeding, which reached the Ontario Court of Appeal (the Supreme Court of Canada refused leave to appeal), sought an injunction to suspend his deportation order, invoking in support the interim order from the Human Rights Committee. The application was denied.

85 *Optional Protocol to the International Covenant on Civil and Political Rights* , (1976) 999 UNTS 171, [1976] CTS 47.

at hand. Both the majority and the dissent reached the inescapable conclusion that the international legal norms contained therein had no domestic
legal effect in Canada. Justice Laskin, for the majority, wrote quite bluntly
"Canada has never incorporated either the Covenant or the Protocol into
Canadian law by implementing legislation. Absent implementing legislation, neither has any legal effect in Canada."[86] It would lead to an "untenable
result", he further wrote, to "convert a non-binding request, in a Protocol
which has never been part of Canadian law, into a binding obligation
enforceable in Canada by a Canadian Court."[87]

2.1.2   Customary International Human Rights Law

The *Statute of the International Court of Justice* refers to "international
custom, as evidence of a general practice accepted as law", but the expression commonly used in judgments of the Court is "customary international
law"[88] or simply "customary law".[89] Sometimes, the Court will also describe
a norm as being "of a customary character"[90] or "of a customary nature".[91]
The formulation of "evidence of a general practice accepted by law" is
usually stated in another manner, as a requirement that customary international law be established with reference to "state practice" and *"opinio
juris"*. In the *North Sea Continental Shelf cases*, the International Court of
Justice held that for a customary norm to be determined, "there must exist
extensive and uniform state practice underpinned by *opinio juris sive ne-
cessitatis"*.[92]

In an early case, the International Court of Justice said that a party who
invokes customary international law

> . . .must prove that this custom is established in such a manner that it has
> become binding on the other party [. . .] that the rule invoked [. . .] is in
> accordance with a constant and uniform usage practiced by the States in ques-
> tion, and that this usage is the expression of a right appertaining to the State
> granting asylum and a duty incumbent on the territorial State. This follows

---

86 *Ahani* v. *Canada (Attorney General)*, *supra* note 84, para. 31.
87 *Ibid.*, para. 33.
88 For recent examples, see: *Case Concerning Armed Activities on the Territory of the
    Congo (Democratic Republic of the Congo* v. *Uganda)*, 19 December 2005, paras. 162,
    172, 219, 244, 267, 300.
89 *Ibid.*, para. 217. Also: *Legal Consequences of the Construction of a Wall in the Occupied
    Palestinian Territory, Advisory Opinion*, [2004] ICJ Reports 172, para. 89.
90 *Ibid.*, para. 213.
91 *Ibid.*, para. 214.
92 *Prosecutor* v. *Erdemović* (Case No. IT-96-22-A), Joint Separate Opinion of Judge
    McDonald and Judge Vohrah, 7 October 1997, para. 49, referring to: *North Sea Conti-
    nental Shelf Cases (Federal Republic of Germany* v. *Denmark* and v. *Netherlands)*, [1969]
    ICJ Reports 4, para. 73-81.

from Article 38 of the Statute of the Court, which refers to international custom "as evidence of a general practice accepted as law".[93]

Some authorities suggest four components of this analysis: a concordant practice by a number of states with reference to a type of situation falling within the domain of international relations; a continuation or repetition of the practice over a considerable period of time; a conception that the practice is required by or consistent with prevailing international law; and general acquiescence in the practice by other states.[94] State practice will be identified with reference to official governmental conduct, including legislation, international and national judicial decisions, recitals in treaties and other international instruments, a pattern of treaties in the same form, the practice of international and regional governmental organizations such as the United Nations and the Organization of American States and their organs, domestic policy statements, press releases and official manuals on legal questions.[95] Some authorities note that State practice generally comprises any acts or statements by a state from which views about customary laws may be inferred.[96] This makes the reasoning somewhat tautological, with the distinction between "practice" and expressions of opinion difficult to untangle. Often, international courts turn to the treaties themselves as evidence of customary international law.[97]

The Ontario Court of Appeal has endorsed the position taken by the Attorney General of Canada that customary law consists of a "practice among States of sufficient duration, uniformity and generality [. . .] that States consider themselves legally bound by the practice".[98]

2.1.2.1   Identifying Norms of Customary International Law

Customary law binds States in the same way as convention law or treaties. It is based on their consent, but with the distinction that proof of such consent does not rely on the existence of a formal written instrument.

---

93 *Asylum Case (Colombia v Peru)*, [1950] ICJ Reports 266, at 276-277.

94 Yearbook of the International Law Commission, 1950, Vol. II, p. 26, para. 11. See similarly Ian Brownlie, *Principles of Public International Law*, 5th ed., Oxford: Clarendon Press, 1998, at 5.

95 James L. Brierly, *The Law of Nations: An Introduction to the International Law of Peace*, 6th ed., Oxford: Clarendon Press, 1963 , at 61-62.

96 Malcolm N. Shaw, *International Law*, 4th ed., Cambridge: Cambridge University Press, 1997, at 66.

97 For example: *Case Concerning Armed Activities on the Territory of the Congo, supra* note 88, para. 172, 219; *Legal Consequences of the Construction of a Wall, supra* note 89, para. 89; *Domingues* v. *United States of America*, Report No. 62/02, Merits, Case 12.285, 22 October 2002, paras. 55-68.

98 *Mack v. Canada (Attorney General)*, (2002), 217 DLR (4th) 583, 96 CRR (2d) 254, 165 OAC 17 (CA), leave to appeal refused, (2003) 319 NR 196n (SCC), para. 22.

The great difficulty with customary norms, especially when human rights are concerned, is the definition of their scope. It is easier to demonstrate the existence of customary norms when these concern matters directly relevant to issues that normally arise between sovereign states, such as the delimitation of maritime borders or the treatment of diplomats. There is a reciprocal element in their behaviour that is not necessarily present when the issue is their treatment of individuals and their respect for human rights norms.

The International Court of Justice has held that common article 3 to the *Geneva Conventions*, which prohibits murder of all kinds, mutilation, cruel treatment and torture, taking of hostages, humiliating and degrading treatment and ensures due process, expresses norms of customary international law.[99] Echoing a conclusion of the International Military Tribunal at Nuremberg, in 1946,[100] the Court has said that the provisions of the Regulations annexed to the 1907 *Hague Convention* are part of customary international law.[101] It has also declared that freedom from slavery and racial discrimination "have entered into the body of general international law".[102] In a recent case concerning acts that could amount to aggression, committed in the territory of a neighbouring state, the International Court referred to the 1970 United Nations Declaration on Principles of International Law Concerning Friendly Relations and Co-operation Among States in accordance with the Charter of the United Nations: "Every State has the duty to refrain from organizing, instigating, assisting or participating in acts of civil strife or terrorist acts in another State or acquiescing in organized activities within its territory directed towards the commission of such acts, when the acts referred to in the present paragraph involve a threat or use of force."[103] Moreover, "no State shall organize, assist, foment, finance, incite or tolerate subversive, terrorist or armed activities directed towards the violent overthrow of the regime of another State, or interfere in civil strife in another State". The Court said that "[t]hese provisions are declaratory of customary international law", noting that this was acknowledged by all parties to the proceedings.[104] In a case concerning immunities, the International Court of

---

99 *Military and Paramilitary Activities in and Against Nicaragua (Nicaragua* v. *United States)*, [1986] ICJ Reports 14, paras. 218, 255, 292(9).

100 *France* et al. v. *Göring* et al., (1946) 22 IMT 203, 13 ILR 203, 41 *American Journal of International Law* 172, p. 219 *(AJIL)*.

101 *Legal Consequences of the Construction of a Wall in the Occupied Palestinian Territory*, *supra* note 89, para. 89; *Case Concerning Armed Activities on the Territory of the Congo*, *supra* note 88, paras. 217, 219.

102 *Barcelona Traction, Light & Power Co. (Belgium* v. *Spain)*, [1970] ICJ Reports 3, paras. 33-34.

103 GA Res. 2625 (XXV).

104 *Case Concerning Armed Activities on the Territory of the Congo*, *supra* note 88, paras. 162, 300.

Justice said it had examined State practice, including national legislation and those few decisions of national higher courts, such as the House of Lords or the French Court of Cassation but that it was "unable to deduce from this practice that there exists under customary international law any form of exception to the rule according immunity from criminal jurisdiction and inviolability to incumbent Ministers for Foreign Affairs, where they are suspected of having committed war crimes or crimes against humanity".[105]

The Inter-American Commission on Human Rights, in a 1987 case involving execution of individuals for crimes committed while under the age of eighteen, attempted to interpret article I of the *American Declaration of the Rights and Duties of Man*[106] in light of customary international law. Counsel for two American prisoners argued that although article I of the *Declaration* was textually silent on the subject of the death penalty, the *travaux préparatoires* of several international instruments prohibiting such executions indicated they were in fact norms of customary international law.[107] The Commission said that it was convinced by the United States government's argument that there is no norm of customary international law establishing eighteen to be the minimum age for imposition of the death penalty. In light of the widespread ratification of the *American Convention on Human Rights*[108] and the *International Covenant on Civil and Political Rights*,[109] as well as the practice of many states, including various jurisdictions within the United States, the Commission concluded that such a norm was "emerging".[110] But it added that even if a customary norm did exist, it would not bind a state which had protested the norm.[111] Because the United States government had proposed ratification of the *American Convention on Human Rights* with a reservation to article 4(5) stating that the United States "reserves the right in appropriate cases to subject minors to procedures and penalties applicable to adults", the Commission considered that it had protested the formation of a customary norm, to the extent one could be found.[112] But in 2002, the Inter-American Commission on Human Rights

---

105 *Case Concerning the Arrest Warrant of 11 April 2000 (Democratic Republic of the Congo v. Belgium)*, 14 February 2002, para. 58.

106 *American Declaration of the Rights and Duties of Man*, OAS Doc. OEA/Ser. L./V/II.23, doc. 21, rev. 6.

107 *Roach and Pinkerton* v. *United States* (Case No. 9647) Resolution No. 3/87, reported in: OAS Doc. OEA/Ser.L/V/II.71 doc. 9 rev. 1, p. 147, *Inter-American Yearbook on Human Rights, 1987*, Dordrecht/Boston/London: Martinus Nijhoff, 1990, p. 328, 8 *Human Rights Law Journal* 345, para. 37.

108 *American Convention on Human Rights*, (1979) 1144 UNTS 123, OASTS 36.

109 *International Covenant on Civil and Political Rights*, (1976) 999 UNTS 171, [1976] CTS 47.

110 *Roach and Pinkerton* v. *United States*, *supra* note 107, para. 60.

111 *Ibid.*, para. 52.

112 *Ibid.*, para. 53.

returned to the issue of juvenile executions, revising the view of customary international law that it had expressed in its 1987 ruling:

> The overwhelming evidence of global state practice as set out above displays a consistency and generality amongst world states indicating that the world community considers the execution of offenders aged below 18 years at the time of their offence to be inconsistent with prevailing standards of decency. The Commission is therefore of the view that a norm of international customary law has emerged prohibiting the execution of offenders under the age of 18 years at the time of their crime.[113]

In its General Comment on reservations, the Human Rights Committee proposed a list of customary international human rights norms: the prohibition of slavery, of torture and cruel, inhuman or degrading treatment or punishment, the right to life, protection against arbitrary arrest and detention, freedom of thought, conscience and religion, the presumption of innocence, the right to a fair trial, prohibition of execution of pregnant women or children, prohibition of advocacy of national, racial or religious hatred, the right of persons of marriageable age to marry, the right of minorities to enjoy their own culture, profess their own religion or use their own language.[114] The United States courts have also declared certain human rights norms to be customary law.[115] In an objection filed protesting a reservation by Yemen to the *International Convention on the Elimination of All Forms of Racial Discrimination*, Canada stated that it "believes that the principle of non-discrimination is generally accepted and recognized in international law and therefore is binding on all states".[116]

Customary international law has received significant attention in the recent caselaw of the international criminal tribunals for the former Yugoslavia, Rwanda and Sierra Leone.[117] The three tribunals have relied upon determinations of customary international law in the determination of the content of punishable crimes so as not to infringe the principle of non-retroactivity of criminal offences. For example, a Trial Chamber of the International Criminal Tribunal for the former Yugoslavia looked at a va-

---

113 *Domingues* v. *United States of America*, *supra* note 97, para. 84.

114 "General Comment No. 24 (52), Issues relating to reservations made upon ratification or accession to the Covenant or the Optional Protocols thereto, or in relation to declarations under article 41 of the Covenant", UN Doc. CCPR/C/21/Rev.1/Add.6, para. 8.

115 *DeSanchez* v. *Banco Central de Nicaragua*, 770 F.2d 1385 (5th Cir.1985); *Filartega* v. *Pena-Irala*, 630 F.2d 876 (2d Cir.1980); *Rodriguez-Fernandez* v. *Wilkinson*, 654 F.2d 1382 (10th Cir.1981).

116 Multilateral Treaties deposited with the Secretary-General, UN Doc. ST/LEG/SER.E/ 13 (1995).

117 Generally, on the three international tribunals, see: William A. Schabas, *The UN International Criminal Tribunals: the former Yugoslavia, Rwanda and Sierra Leone*, Cambridge: Cambridge University Press, 2006.

riety of international humanitarian law codes, conventions and other instruments as evidence that a customary legal prohibition on torture had "crystallised".[118] But another Trial Chamber said torture intended to "humiliate" the victim was not within the Tribunal's subject matter jurisdiction because it is not mentioned in any of the principal international instruments prohibiting torture.[119] The Appeals Chamber has ruled that the requirement in article 5 of the *Statute of the International Criminal Tribunal for the former Yugoslavia* that crimes against humanity be "committed in armed conflict" and the requirement in article 4 of the *Statute of the International Criminal Tribunal for Rwanda* that crimes against humanity be perpetrated "on national, political, ethnic, racial or religious grounds" are both inconsistent with contemporary interpretations.[120] In *Mugesera*, the Supreme Court of Canada said that "[t]hough the decisions of the [International Criminal Tribunal for the former Yugoslavia] and the [International Criminal Tribunal for Rwanda] are not binding upon this Court, the expertise of these tribunals and the authority in respect of customary international law with which they are vested suggest that their findings should not be disregarded lightly by Canadian courts applying domestic legislative provisions".[121] The Court referred to judgments of the Tribunals as a justification for reconsidering its own caselaw with respect to the content of customary international law.

Recently, the Ontario Court of Appeal considered the customary law status of the prohibition of racial discrimination, in a suit filed against the Government of Canada by descendants of Chinese immigrants concerning the so-called "head tax", which was only abolished in 1947. The Court began by acknowledging the lamentable history of discrimination:

> In the Quebec Secession Reference, the Supreme Court of Canada observed that although the protection of minority rights has played an essential part in the design of Canada's constitutional structure, our record for upholding such rights has by no means been spotless. In this regard, Canada's treatment of people of Chinese origin who sought to immigrate to this country between 1885 and 1947 represents one of the more notable stains on our minority rights tapestry. For the first 38 of those years, until 1923, Parliament passed a series of laws that required persons of Chinese origin to pay a duty or "head tax" upon entering Canada. The tax, which grew progressively from $50 in 1885 to

---

118 *Prosecutor* v. *Furundžija* (Case No. IT-95-17/1-T), Judgment, 10 December 1998, para. 137.

119 *Prosecutor* v. *Krnojelac* (Case No. IT-97-25-T), Judgment, 15 March 2002, para. 108.

120 *Prosecutor* v. *Tadić* (Case No. IT-94-1-AR72), Decision on the Defence Motion for Interlocutory Appeal on Jurisdiction, 2 October 1995, para. 141; *Prosecutor* v. *Tadić* (Case No. IT-94-1-A), Judgment, 15 July 1999, para. 305.

121 *Mugesera* v. *Canada (Minister of Citizenship and Immigration)*, [2005] 2 SCR 100, at paras. 126, 133.

$500 in 1903, was meant to be prohibitive and it placed Canada beyond the reach of many. But not enough, apparently, for the government of the day, which explains why the tax was abolished in 1923 and replaced by legislation that for the next 24 years, until its repeal in 1947, effectively barred all but a select few Chinese people from immigrating to Canada.[122]

The lawsuit relied on the claim that the prohibition of racial discrimination had been a norm of customary international law prior to 1947, when the offensive legislation was repealed. The Court of Appeal accepted the position taken by the Attorney General of Canada that no such customary norm existed prior to 1947, and that evidence of the abhorrence of racial discrimination only indicated "pockets of enlightenment in an era when the protection of human rights did not figure prominently on the international scene".[123] The Court referred to an article by John Humphrey describing the "revolutionary" transformation in human rights law that took place with the adoption of the *Charter of the United Nations*, in 1945, and the *Universal Declaration of Human Rights* three years later. For the Court, this helped to establish that a customary international legal norm prohibiting racial discrimination did not exist earlier.[124]

Customary law has the great advantage over treaty law in that it is binding on all states. Thus the law governing the international responsibility of states for the treatment of aliens is binding on all states by virtue of their membership in the international community. This law, as already indicated, has recently undergone significant changes. For the traditional minimum objective international standard (which was sometimes higher than national standards) has been replaced by a new standard under which foreigners and nationals are entitled to the same treatment. This new standard is set forth in the *Universal Declaration of Human Rights* which, whatever its drafters may have intended in 1948, is now part of the customary law of nations – not because it was adopted as a resolution of the General Assembly but because of juridical consensus resulting from its invocation as law on countless occasions since 1948 both within and outside the United Nations. The *Universal Declaration of Human Rights* has now become the authentic interpretation of the human rights provisions of the *Charter* which neither catalogues nor defines the human rights to which it refers.

As some of these examples demonstrate, often the search for customary norms leads almost inexorably back to written instruments. Many non-binding or "soft-law" declarations adopted by international bodies such as the United Nations General Assembly and the Commission on Human Rights are viewed as written codifications of customary law. There is some-

---

122   *Mack v. Canada (Attorney General)*, *supra* note 98, para. 1.
123   *Ibid.*, para. 25.
124   *Ibid.*, para. 28.

times a tendency among human rights lawyers to exaggerate the scope of customary norms; given the absence of convincing evidence of state practice or of *opinio juris*, they are simply wished into existence. Critical of over-optimistic assessments of the scope of customary rules, Theodor Meron has drawn attention to a "tendency to ignore, for the most part, the availability of evidence of state practice (scant as it may have been) and to assume that noble humanitarian principles that deserve recognition as the positive law of the international community have in fact been recognized as such by states. The 'ought' merges with the 'is', the *lex ferenda* with the *lex lata*."[125]

2.1.2.2   Jus Cogens *and* Erga Omnes

Discussion of customary international law is often accompanied by two Latin expressions, *jus cogens* and *erga omnes*. They are often confused, and are seeming used interchangeably by many, although they have quite distinct meanings and consequences. Each term describes a category of customary international legal norms. *Jus cogens* indicates those norms that are so important as to be hierarchically superior even to conflicting treaty norms. *Erga omnes* expresses the legal interest that States may have in the enforcement of important rules of customary international law.

The term *jus cogens* is used in the *Vienna Convention on the Law of Treaties* to designate a "peremptory norm of general international law".[126] This is defined as "a norm accepted and recognized by the international community of States as a whole as a norm from which no derogation is permitted and which can be modified only by a subsequent norm of general international law having the same character". Thus, *jus cogens* norms constitute a category of customary international law that is hierarchically superior and that, in effect, trump inconsistent provisions of treaty law. According to the *Vienna Convention*, "[a] treaty is void if, at the time of its conclusion, it conflicts with a peremptory norm of general international law."[127] Fundamental human rights norms have frequently been described as *jus cogens*. For example, judgments of the international criminal tribunals have occasionally referred to specific norms as being *jus cogens*, such as

---

125   Theodor Meron, "The Geneva Conventions as Customary Law", (1987) 81 *American Journal of International Law* 348, at 361.

126   *Vienna Convention on the Law of Treaties*, (1969) 1155 UNTS 331, [1980] CTS 37, 8 ILM 679, art. 53. See: Lauri Hannikainen, *Peremptory Norms (Jus Cogens) in International Law: Historical Development, Criteria, Present Status*, Helsinki: Lakimiedliiten Kustannus, 1988.

127   *Ibid.*

the prohibitions of genocide[128] or torture.[129] The Appeals Chamber of the International Criminal Tribunal for the former Yugoslavia "note[d] that in human rights law the violation of rights which have reached the level of *jus cogens*, such as torture, may constitute international crimes".[130] In one judgment, a Trial Chamber of the International Criminal Tribunal for the former Yugoslavia, presided by Judge Antonio Cassese, said "most norms of international humanitarian law, in particular those prohibiting war crimes, crimes against humanity and genocide, are also peremptory norms of international law or *jus cogens*, i.e. of a non-derogable and overriding character".[131] The Inter-American Commission on Human Rights has held that the prohibition of juvenile executions is a norm of *jus cogens*. It used this to overcome the argument by which the United States had persistently objected to the formation of a customary norm.[132]

The role of *jus cogens* norms in international law is not a simple matter to determine and, as Ian Brownlie has noted, "many problems of application remain".[133] The International Court of Justice resisted even acknowledging the concept until a perfunctory reference appeared in a February 2006 ruling.[134] In his individual opinion, *ad hoc* Judge John Dugard explained:

> Norms of *jus cogens* are a blend of principle and policy. On the one hand, they affirm the high principles of international law, which recognize the most important rights of the international order – such as the right to be free from aggression, genocide, torture and slavery and the right to self-determination;

---

128 *Prosecutor* v. *Kayishema* et al. (Case No. ICTR-95-1-T), Judgment and Sentence, 21 May 1999, para. 88; *Prosecutor* v. *Jelisić* (IT-95-10-T), Judgment, 14 December 1999, para. 60 (which claims – erroneously – that the International Court of Justice, in its 1951 advisory opinion on the *Genocide Convention*, "placed the crime on the level of *jus cogens* because of its extreme gravity"); *Prosecutor* v. *Krstić* (Case No. IT-98-33-T), Judgment, 2 August 2001, para. 541; *Prosecutor* v. *Stakić* et al. (Case No. IT-97-24-T), Decision on Rule 98*bis* Motion for Judgment of Acquittal, 31 October 2002, para. 20; *Prosecutor* v. *Brođanin* (Case No. IT-99-36-T), Judgment, 1 September 2004, para. 680.

129 *Prosecutor* v. *Delalić* et al. (Case No. IT-96-21-T), Judgment, 16 November 1998, para. 225; *Prosecutor* v. *Furundžija* (Case No. IT-95-17/1-T), Judgment, 10 December 1998, paras. 155-157l; *Prosecutor* v. *Kunarac* et al. (Case No. IT-96-23-T and IT-96-23/1-T), Judgment, 22 February 2001, para. 466.

130 *Prosecutor* v. *Delalić* et al. (Case No. IT-96-21-A), Judgment, 20 February 2001, para. 172, fn. 225.

131 *Prosecutor* v. *Kupreškić* (IT-95-16-T), Judgment, 14 January 2000, para. 530.

132 *Domingues* v. *United States of America*, Report No. 62/02, Merits, Case 12.285, 22 October 2002, para. 85.

133 Ian Brownlie, *Principles of Public International Law*, 6th ed., Oxford: Clarendon Press, 2003, p. 490.

134 *Case Concerning Armed Activities on the Territory of the Congo (New Application: 2002) (Democratic Republic of the Congo* v. *Rwanda)*, Jurisdiction of the Court and Admissibility of the Application, 3 February 2006, para. 64.

while, on the other hand, they give legal form to the most fundamental policies or goals of the international community – the prohibitions on aggression, genocide, torture and slavery and the advancement of self-determination. This explains why they enjoy a hierarchical superiority to other norms in the international legal order. The fact that norms of *jus cogens* advance both principle and policy means that they must inevitably play a dominant role in the process of judicial choice.[135]

Judge Dugard put aside the concept of *jus cogens* as it is presented in the *Vienna Convention* and instead outlined its usefulness within the context of judicial lawmaking. Rather than use *jus cogens* to trump existing treaty provisions, which is in any event a concept that is difficult to apply to international human rights law, he argued that international courts should use *jus cogens* as a guide to the exercise of their discretion "within the interstices of the law in a molecular rather than a molar fashion".[136] Examples might be a rejection of immunity in the case of serious crimes, or the primacy of the concept of self-determination.

The Supreme Court of Canada considered whether the prohibition of torture was a *jus cogens* norm in *Suresh*. With some caution, it concluded:

> Although this Court is not being asked to pronounce on the status of the prohibition on torture in international law, the fact that such a principle is included in numerous multilateral instruments, that it does not form part of any known domestic administrative practice, and that it is considered by many academics to be an emerging, if not established peremptory norm, suggests that it cannot be easily derogated from.[137]

The expression *erga omnes* addresses the question of legal interest. It is of particular relevance to international human rights law because it establishes the interest of States in the protection and enforcement of human rights within other States. In the *Barcelona Traction* case, the International Court of Justice said that obligations *erga omnes* are by their very nature "the concern of all States" and, "[i]n view of the importance of the rights involved, all States can be held to have a legal interest in their protection".[138] Similarly, the International Law Commission stated, in the Commentaries to its Articles on the Responsibility of States for Internationally Wrongful Acts, that there are certain rights in the protection of which, by reason of

---

135 *Ibid.*, Separate Opinion of Judge *ad hoc* Dugard, para. 10.
136 *Ibid.*, para. 12.
137 *Suresh* v. *Canada (Minister of Citizenship and Immigration)*, [2002] 1 SCR 3, 208 DLR (4th) 1, 37 Admin LR (3d) 159, 90 CRR (2d) 1, para. 65.
138 *Barcelona Traction, Light & Power Co. (Belgium* v. *Spain)*, [1970] ICJ Reports 3, para. 33. See also: *Legal Consequences of the Construction of a Wall in the Occupied Palestinian Territory, Advisory Opinion*, [2004] ICJ Reports 172, paras. 37-39.

THEORETICAL UNDERPINNINGS OF INTERNATIONAL LAW   77

their importance, "all States have a legal interest".[139] The International Court of Justice referred to "elementary considerations of humanity" that are "to be observed by all States whether or not they have ratified the conventions that contain them, because they constitute intransgressible principles of international customary law".[140] It has given, as an example of an *erga omnes* norm, the universal prohibition of genocide.[141]

2.1.2.3   Domestic Application of Customary International Law

Customary international law may be applied by Canadian courts without any need for an express legislative act, unless there is a clear conflict with statute law or common law.[142] According to Lord Denning, in *Trendtex Trading Corporation* v. *Central Bank of Nigeria*, customary norms of international law are incorporated into the common law automatically, and apply to the extent they are not incompatible with a statute.[143] Lord Denning rejected the "transformation" thesis, by which customary norms can only have legal effect if they have been made part of the law by judicial decision or statute. The incorporation view adopted by Lord Denning is more dynamic, because it allows the common law to evolve along with changes in customary international law. Lord Denning's thesis about customary law and its incorporation into domestic law is probably applicable in Canada as well.[144] However Canadian caselaw lacks any such clear statement of principle.[145]

---

139 UN Doc. A/56/10 at 278.

140 *Legality of the Threat or Use of Nuclear Weapons, Advisory Opinion,* [1996] ICJ Reports 257, para. 79. Also: *Legal Consequences of the Construction of a Wall, supra* note 138, para. 157.

141 *Application of the Convention on the Prevention and Punishment of the Crime of Genocide (Bosnia and Herzegovina* v. *Yugoslavia), Preliminary Objections,* [1996] ICJ Reports 616, para. 31).

142 Maxwell Cohen & Anne F. Bayefsky, "The Canadian Charter of Rights and Freedoms and International Law", (1983) 61 *Canadian Bar Review* 265, at 275.

143 *Trendtex Trading Corporation* v. *Central Bank of Nigeria,* [1977] 1 All ER 881 (HL).

144 Ronald St. J. MacDonald, "The Relationship Between International Law and Domestic Law in Canada", in Ronald St. J. MacDonald, Gerald L. Morris & Douglas J. Johnston, eds., *Canadian Perspectives on International Law and Organization,* Toronto: University of Toronto Press, 1974, pp. 88-136, at 111. Also: Anne F. Bayefsky, *International Human Rights Law, Use in Canadian Charter of Rights and Freedoms Litigation,* Toronto: Butterworths, 1992, at 22-66.

145 *Reference Re Powers of Municipalities to Levy Rates on Foreign Legations and High Commissioners' Residences,* [1943] SCR 208, [1943] 2 DLR 481; *Re Alberta Union of Provincial Employees and the Crown in Right of Alberta,* (1981) 120 DLR (3d) 590, 81 CLLC 14,089 (Alta QB), affirmed, (1981) 1981 CarswellAlta 553 (CA), leave to appeal refused, (1981) 130 DLR (3d) 191 (note) (SCC). See also: Stéphane Beaulac, "Customary International Law in Domestic Courts: Imbroglio, Lord Denning, *Stare Decisis*", in D.M. Waters, ed., *British and Canadian Perspectives on International Law,* Leiden &

The *Crimes Against Humanity and War Crimes Act* refers explicitly to "customary international law".[146] The *Act* gives jurisdiction to Canadian courts in cases of genocide, crimes against humanity and war crimes. It establishes a presumption that the crimes defined in the *Rome Statute of the International Criminal Court* constitute customary international law adding that "[t]his does not limit or prejudice in any way the application of existing or developing rules of international law". The legislation also establishes that crimes against humanity have been recognised as part of customary international law since 1945. The relevant provision states that

> For greater certainty, the offence of crime against humanity was part of customary international law or was criminal according to the general principles of law recognized by the community of nations before the coming into force of either of the following: (a) the Agreement for the prosecution and punishment of the major war criminals of the European Axis, signed at London on August 8, 1945; and (b) the Proclamation by the Supreme Commander for the Allied Powers, dated January 19, 1946.[147]

That Parliament felt the need to make a declaration that crimes against humanity were punishable under customary international law or general principles of law at the time of the post-Second World War prosecutions may seem surprising.

A close look at the 1994 *Finta* ruling of the Supreme Court of Canada may assist in understanding the rationale for this provision. Justice Peter Cory, who drafted the reasons of the majority, examined whether prosecution for crimes against humanity committed in 1944 violated the norm against retroactive prosecution. He noted that at the time, such eminent international lawyers as Georg Schwarzenberger and Hans Kelsen believed that the Nuremberg and Tokyo *Charters* were not in fact declarative of already existing international law.[148] Justice Cory endorsed these words of Kelsen:

> A retroactive law providing individual punishment for acts which were illegal though not criminal at the time they were committed, seems also to be an exception to the rule against ex post facto laws. The London Agreement is such a law. It is retroactive only in so far as it established individual criminal

---

Boston: Martinus Nijhoff, pp. 379-392; Francis Rigaldies & José Woehrling, "Le juge interne canadien et le droit international", (1980) 21 *Cahiers de Droit* 293, at 303; C. Vanek, "Is International Law a Part of the Law of Canada?", (1949-50) 8 *University of Toronto Law Journal* 251; Gérard V. La Forest, "May the Provinces Legislate in Violation of International Law?", (1961) 39 *Canadian Bar Review* 78.

146 *Crimes Against Humanity and War Crimes Act*, SC 2000, c. 24, ss. 4, 6. The provision is modelled on earlier legislation: *Criminal Code*, RSC, 1985, c. C-46, s. 7 (3.76).

147 *Ibid*, s. 4(5).

148 *R. v. Finta*, [1994] 1 SCR 701, 88 CCC (3d) 417, 112 DLR (4th) 513, 150 NR 370, p. 872 (SCR).

responsibility for acts which at the time they were committed constituted violations of existing international law, but for which this law has provided only collective responsibility. The rule against retroactive legislation is a principle of justice. Individual criminal responsibility represents certainly a higher degree of justice than collective responsibility, the typical technique of primitive law. Since the internationally illegal acts for which the London Agreement established individual criminal responsibility were certainly also morally most objectionable, and the persons who committed these acts were certainly aware of their immoral character, the retroactivity of the law applied to them can hardly be considered as absolutely incompatible with justice. Justice required the punishment of these men, in spite of the fact that under positive law they were not punishable at the time they performed the acts made punishable with retroactive force. In case two postulates of justice are in conflict with each other, the higher one prevails; and to punish those who were morally responsible for the international crime of the second World War may certainly be considered as more important than to comply with the rather relative rule against ex post facto laws, open to so many exceptions.[149]

Justice Cory said he found these remarks "eminently sound and reasonable", and used this as a basis to dismiss a constitutional challenge to the crimes against humanity provision that then applied in Canadian law.[150] The reference to the Nuremberg and Tokyo *Charters* in the new *Crimes Against Humanity and War Crimes Act* constitutes a legislative correction of Justice Cory's pronouncement in *Finta.*

Besides creating such a presumption, the *Crimes Against Humanity and War Crimes Act* establishes jurisdiction over crimes of customary international law as they evolve. For example, genocide is defined in the *Act* as

> . . .an act or omission committed with intent to destroy, in whole or in part, an identifiable group of persons, as such, that, at the time and in the place of its commission, constitutes genocide according to customary international law or conventional international law or by virtue of its being criminal according to the general principles of law recognized by the community of nations.[151]

Article II of the 1948 *Genocide Convention*, on which the definition of genocide is based, limits the scope of the crime to the intentional destruction of national, ethnic, racial and religious groups. The new Canadian statute seems to suggest that customary law might at some point in the future extend the concept of genocide to cover other groups, such as political, economic and social groups. Similarly, the definition of "war crime" in the Canadian legislation is "an act or omission committed during an armed conflict that,

---

149   *Ibid.*, p. 873, citing: Hans Kelsen, "Will the Judgment in the Nuremberg Trial Constitute a Precedent in International Law?", (1947) 1 *International Law Quarterly* 153, at 165.
150   *Ibid.*, p. 874.
151   *Crimes Against Humanity and War Crimes Act.*, *supra* note 146, ss. 4(3), 6(3).

at the time and in the place of its commission, constitutes a war crime according to customary international law or conventional international law applicable to armed conflicts".[152] Here the reference to customary international law is particularly *a propos*, given lacunae in the *Rome Statute's* enumeration of war crimes. For example, article 8 of the *Rome Statute* does not adequately cover the use of weapons that are unquestionably prohibited by customary international law.

In prosecutions under this provision, the Canadian courts are required to interpret and apply norms of customary international law. They have already had occasion to do this in prosecutions under the earlier legislation.[153] The *Deschênes Commission of Inquiry on War Criminals Report* considered that section 11(g) of the *Canadian Charter of Rights and Freedoms*, which prohibits retroactive criminal offences unless they constituted an offence under Canadian or international law or were "criminal according to the general principles of law recognized by the community of nations", actually adopted customary international law into Canadian law.[154]

Aside from the specific context of the *Criminal Code*, Canadian lawyers have only rarely attempted to invoke customary human rights norms before the courts.[155] Yet the common law suggests that they are directly applicable by the courts, even in the absence of any domestic legal provisions upon which to attach them. As a result, customary rules of international law, such as the guarantee of individuals belonging to ethnic, religious or linguistic minorities, in community with the other members of their group, to enjoy their own culture, to profess and practise their own religion, or to use their own language, or the right of peoples to self-determination, are part of the law of Canada and justiciable before our courts despite the fact that they are not incorporated in the *Charter* or in specific legislation.[156]

In *Re Canada Labour Code*, the Supreme Court of Canada studied "the international law doctrine of sovereign immunity",[157] that is, the customary law of sovereign immunity, to the extent that it was codified in the *State Immunity Act*.[158] Such a reference was made by the intervener Amnesty

---

152   *Ibid.*, ss. 4(3), 6(3).
153   See: *R.* v. *Finta, supra* note 148, at 731 (SCR); *Rudolph* v. *Canada (Minister of Employment and Immigration)*, (1992) 91 DLR (4th) 686 (Fed CA) at 690-692, leave to appeal refused, (1992) 93 DLR (4th) vii (note) (SCC).
154   *R.* v. *Finta, ibid.*, at 734 (SCR).
155   For examples (unsuccessful) see: *Re Alberta Union of Provincial Employees, supra* note 145, at 621 (DLR); *Orelien* v. *Canada*, [1992] 1 FC 592, 15 Imm LR (2d) 1 (CA), at 598-599, 607-608 (FC), *per* Mahoney J.
156   See: *Montana Band of Indians* v. *Canada*, [1990] 2 FC 198 (TD), reversed, (1991) 120 NR 200 (CA), leave to appeal refused, (1991) 136 NR 421n (SCC), at 203 (FC).
157   *Re Canada Labour Code*, (sub nom. *Code Canadien du Travail, Re*) [1992] 2 SCR 50, at para. 1.
158   SC 1980-81-82-83, c. 95 (now RSC 1985, c. S-18).

International in the recent case of *Schreiber v. Canada (Attorney General)*, also in the context of sovereign immunity. The Court summarily rejected the argument, because: "In the case at bar, there is no conflict between the principles of international law, at the present stage of their development, and those of the domestic legal order."[159] After resorting to an old *dicta* of Justice Pigeon's in *Daniels v. White*,[160] Justice Lebel wrote that the questions of sovereign immunity at issue: "fall within the purview of domestic legislation," and therefore "there would be little utility in examining international legal principles in detail".[161]

It is in the *Baker*[162] case that the Supreme Court missed a wonderful chance to apply customary law norms. It raised the issue of application of the "best interests of the child" principle to circumscribe the discretion exercised by immigration officials when making decisions on the basis of compassionate and humanitarian grounds.[163] The norm is set out in article 3 of the *Convention on the Rights of the Child*,[164] in force in Canada since 8 January 1992. The majority confirmed the application of article 3 in Canadian law, at least for the purposes of interpretation of Canadian statutes, but two minority justices charged the Court with usurping the role of Parliament. This unfortunate debate might have been avoided had the Court accepted that article 3 of the *Convention* simply codifies the customary norm of "best interest of the child". Arguably, all provisions of the *Convention* that have not been subject to any reservations, and article 3 is such a text, constitute customary law, given that only two States in the world have not ratified the *Convention*, and that one of them (the United States of America) has signed it, indicating its intent to abide by the *Convention*'s provisions.[165]

---

159 *Schreiber* v. *Canada (Attorney General)*, [2002] 3 SCR 269, (sub nom. *Schreiber* v. *Federal Republic of Germany*) 216 DLR (4th) 513, 167 CCC (3d) 51, 164 OAC 354, at para. 50.

160 *Daniels* v. *White*, [1968] SCR 517, at 541.

161 *Schreiber* v. *Canada (Attorney General)*, supra note 159, at para. 51.

162 *Baker* v. *Canada (Minister of Citizenship and Immigration)*, [1999] 2 SCR 817, 174 DLR (4th) 193, 14 Admin LR (3d) 173, 1 Imm LR (3d) 1, 243 NR 22, at paras 70-71 (*per* L'Heureux-Dubé J.).

163 *Immigration Regulations, 1978*, SOR/78-172, as amended by SOR/93-44, s. 2.1.

164 *Convention on the Rights of the Child*, GA Res. 44/25, Annex, [1992] CTS 3.

165 In accordance with article 18(a) of the *Vienna Convention on the Law of Treaties*, (1969) 1155 UNTS 331, [1980] CTS 37, 8 ILM 679. Somalia is the only State that has neither signed nor ratified the *Convention*, a situation attributable to domestic political disorder rather than any ideological disagreement.

2.1.3   General Principles of Law Recognized by Civilized Nations

"General principles of law recognized by civilized nations" are listed in the *Statute of the International Court of Justice* as one of the three principal sources of international law. The language is archaic, and a more acceptable and contemporary formulation of essentially the same concept appears in article 21(1)(c) of the *Rome Statute*: "general principles of law derived by the Court from national laws of legal systems of the world". In the statutes of the *ad hoc* international criminal tribunals for the former Yugoslavia and Rwanda, the judges are authorized to accord pardon or commutation based on the "interests of justice and the general principles of law".[166]

Although often confounded with customary international law,[167] evidence of general principles is not located primarily in international practice but rather in national legal systems. Classic examples of such general principles are the rule of *res judicata*,[168] the doctrine of estoppel,[169] the rule of good faith and equity,[170] and the obligation to make reparation for breach of an engagement.[171] As a Trial Chamber of the International Criminal Tribunal for the former Yugoslavia explained,

> The value of these sources is that they may disclose "general concepts and legal institutions" which, if common to a broad spectrum of national legal systems, disclose an international approach to a legal question which may be considered as an appropriate indicator of the international law on the subject. In considering these national legal systems the Trial Chamber does not conduct a survey of the major legal systems of the world in order to identify a specific legal provision which is adopted by a majority of legal systems but to consider, from an examination of national systems generally, whether it is possible to identify certain basic principles.[172]

---

166 *Statute of the International Criminal Tribunal for the former Yugoslavia*, UN Doc. S/RES/827 (1993), annex, art. 28; *Statute of the International Criminal Tribunal for Rwanda*, UN Doc. S/RES/955 (1994), annex, art. 27.

167 *Prosecutor* v. *Delalić* et al. (Case No. IT-96-21-T), Judgment, 16 November 1998, para. 321; *Prosecutor* v. *Hadžihasanović* et al. (Case No. IT-01-47-AR72), Decision on Interlocutory Appeal Challenging Jurisdiction in Relation to Command Responsibility, 16 July 2003, para. 93.

168 *Effect of Awards of U.N. Administrative Tribunal Case*, [1954] ICJ Reports 47, at 53.

169 *Canada* v. *United States*, [1984] ICJ Reports 246, paras. 129-148.

170 *Diversion of Water from the Meuse Case (Netherlands* v. *Belgium)*, [1937] PCIJ Reports, Series A/B, No. 70, pp. 76-77.

171 *Chorzow Factory Case (Merits)*, [1928] PCIJ Reports, Series A, No. 17, at 29.

172 *Prosecutor* v. *Kunarac* et al. (Case No. IT-96-23-T and IT-96-23/1-T), Judgment, 22 February 2001, para. 439.

In the words of Lord McNair, "it is never a question of importing into international law private law institutions 'lock, stock and barrel', ready made and fully equipped with a set of rules. It is rather a question of finding in the private law institutions indications of legal policy and principles appropriate to the solution of the international problem at hand."[173]

Because, by definition, such rules are derived from domestic law, most if not all of them are already recognized by Canadian courts. As a result, and in contrast with the situation that prevails with respect to treaty law and customary law, there is little practical interest in importing "general principles of law" from the body of international law into domestic law. They are there already.

There is a suggestion that certain criminal infractions form part of this body of international law. Section 11(g) of the *Charter* uses wording that is remarkably close to that of article 38 of the *Statute of the International Court of Justice* when it refers to "general principles of law recognized by the community of nations". Although the International Court of Justice has never looked at "general principles" from the perspective of substantive criminal law, it certainly seems arguable that the criminalization of murder or rape and other serious crimes belongs among general principles of law. Recent caselaw of the European Court of Human Rights has affirmed that States have a duty, under their human rights obligations, to ensure that serious crimes involving violence against the person are properly punished.[174] This has led the European Court deep into the realm of domestic criminal law. Indeed, through the vehicle of international human rights law, it seems that there may now be emerging a universal or cosmopolitan criminal law, to use the term of Emmanuel Kant.

The Deschênes Commission believed that prosecutions for war crimes could be taken before Canadian courts on the grounds that there had been a violation of such general principles of law.[175] In the end, however, the Commission did not adopt such an option, which it considered to be "too esoteric".[176] Justice La Forest of the Supreme Court of Canada considered that the Deschênes Commission's hypothesis of prosecution under general principles was "not self-evident" and "by no means clear".[177] Since the 1950s, Canadian law has disavowed so-called common law crimes, although they continue to exist in English law. In his opinion to Prime Minister Blair on the legality of the Iraq invasion, British Attorney-General Lord Gold-

---

173 *South-West Africa Case*, [1950] ICJ Reports 148.
174 *M.C.* v. *Bulgaria* (App. No. 39272/98), Judgment, 4 December 2003.
175 Jules Deschênes, *Commission of Inquiry on War Criminals, Part I*, Ottawa: Supply and Services Canada, 1986, at 132.
176 *Ibid*, at 133.
177 *R.* v. *Finta*, [1994] 1 SCR 701, 88 CCC (3d) 417, 112 DLR (4th) 513, 150 NR 370, at 734 (SCR).

smith cautioned that senior government officials might expose themselves to prosecution for the crime of aggression, although he described the possibility as "remote". According to Lord Goldsmith, "[a]ggression is a crime under customary international law which automatically forms part of domestic law. It might therefore be argued that international aggression is a crime recognized by the common law which can be prosecuted in the UK courts."[178]

2.2   International Law as an Aid to Interpretation

Chief Justice Brian Dickson, in his reasons in *Re Public Service Employee Relations Act*, rejected the "implementation by implication" thesis, and concluded that international human rights law was limited to the status of an important interpretative aid in *Charter* litigation:

> . . .the similarity between the policies and provisions of the *Charter* and those of international human rights documents attaches considerable relevance to interpretations of those documents by adjudicative bodies, in much the same way that decisions of the United States courts under the Bill of Rights, or decisions of the courts of other jurisdictions are relevant and may be persuasive. The relevance of these documents in *Charter* interpretation extends beyond the standards developed by adjudicative bodies under the documents to the documents themselves. As the Canadian judiciary approaches the often general and open textured language of the *Charter*, "the more detailed textual provisions of the treaties may aid in supplying content to such imprecise concepts as the right to life, freedom of association, and even the right to counsel." J. Claydon, "International Human Rights Law and the Interpretation of the Canadian Charter of Rights and Freedoms" (1982), 4 *Supreme Court L.R.* 287, at p. 293.
>
> Furthermore, Canada is a party to a number of international human rights Conventions which contain provisions similar or identical to those in the *Charter*. Canada has thus obliged itself internationally to ensure within its borders the protection of certain fundamental rights and freedoms which are also contained in the *Charter*. The general principles of constitutional interpretation require that these international obligations be a relevant and persuasive factor in *Charter* interpretation. As this Court stated in *R. v. Big M Drug Mart Ltd.*, [1984] 1 S.C.R. 295, at p. 344, interpretation of the *Charter* must be "aimed at fulfilling the purpose of the guarantee and securing for individuals the full benefit of the *Charter*'s protection". The content of Canada's international human rights obligations is, in my view, an important indicia of the meaning of the "full benefit of the *Charter*'s protection". I believe that the *Charter* should generally be presumed to provide protection at least as great as that afforded by similar provisions in international human rights documents which Canada has ratified.

---

178   Opinion of Lord Goldsmith, 23 March 2003.

In short, though I do not believe the judiciary is bound by the norms of international law in interpreting the *Charter*, these norms provide a relevant and persuasive source for interpretation of the provisions of the *Charter*, especially when they arise out of Canada's international obligations under human rights conventions.[179]

In this seminal passage, which appears in a dissenting opinion, Chief Justice Dickson drew a distinction between two categories of international law instruments, those that, while not necessarily binding upon Canada as a question of law, fit generally into the category of contemporary international human rights law, and those that actually bind Canada as a matter of international law. In the first category can be found such important treaties as the *European Convention on Human Rights* and the *American Convention on Human Rights*, as well as a range of declarations and other inherently non-binding norms,[180] such as the *Universal Declaration of Human Rights*,[181] the *Helsinki Final Act*[182] and the other documents of the Organization for Security and Cooperation in Europe, the *Standard Minimum Rules for the Treatment of Prisoners*,[183] the *Declaration on the Rights of Persons*

---

179   *Reference Re Public Service Employee Relations Act (Alberta)*, [1987] 1 RCS 313, 51 Alta LR (2d) 97, [1987] 3 WWR 577, (sub nom. *A.U.P.E.* v. *Alberta (Attorney General)*) 28 CRR 305, 38 DLR (4th) 161, (sub nom. *Reference re Compulsory Arbitration*) 74 NR 99, 78 AR 1, [1987] DLQ 225, 87 CLLC 14,021, at 348-350 (SCR).

180   On non-binding norms, see: Christine Chinkin, "The Challenge of Soft Law: Development and Change in International Law", (1989) 38 *International & Comparative Law Quarterly* 850; Anthony Aust, "The Theory and Practice of Informal International Instruments", (1986) 35 *International & Comparative Law Quarterly* 787; Oscar Schachter, "The Twilight Existence of Nonbinding International Agreements", (1977) 71 *American Journal of International Law* 296.

181   It can be argued that at least some of the norms contained in the *Universal Declaration* represent in reality codified provisions of customary human rights law: Richard B. Bilder, "The Status of International Human Rights Law: An Overview", (1978) *International Law & Practice* 1, at 8; John Humphrey, "The Canadian Charter of Rights and Freedoms and International Law", (1985-86) 50 *Saskatchewan Law Review* 13; John Humphrey, "The Universal Declaration of Human Rights: Its History, Impact and Judicial Character," in Bertrand G. Ramcharan, ed., *Human Rights: Thirty Years After the Universal Declaration*, The Hague: Martinus Nijhoff, 1984. The issue has been addressed by the courts: *Advisory Opinion on the continued presence of South Africa in Namibia (S.W. Africa)*, [1971] ICJ Reports 16, at 76 (*per* Ammoun J.); See also the dissent of Judge Tanaka in *South West Africa Cases, Second Phase*, [1966] ICJ Reports 6, 37 ILR 1, at 288-293 (ICJ); and *United States Diplomatic and Consular Staff in Tehran*, [1980] ICJ Reports 3, 61 ILR 530, at 42 (ICJ); *Fernandez* v. *Wilkinson*, 505 F. Supp. 787 (1980).

182   "Conference on Security and Cooperation in Europe, Final Act", 1 August 1975.

183   *Standard Minimum Rules for the Treatment of Prisoners*, ESC Res. 663 C, *amended by* ESC Res. 2076 (LXII). On the *Standard Minimum Rules*, see: Roger S. Clark, *The United Nations Crime Prevention and Criminal Justice Program*, Philadelphia: Pennsylvania University Press, 1994, at 145-179.

Belonging to National or Ethnic Religious and Linguistic Minorities[184] and the *Draft Declaration on the Rights of Indigenous Peoples*.[185] Such non-binding or "soft law" norms are above all relevant to *Charter* interpretation because they are sources of comparative law. Canadian courts have a long and quite exceptional tradition of referring to comparative law sources. Where fundamental rights are concerned, there has been a particular affinity for the caselaw of the United States courts with respect to that country's *Bill of Rights* that pre-dates the *Canadian Charter*. Chief Justice Dickson stressed the importance not only of the decisions of international tribunals and related bodies, but also of the texts of the instruments themselves, as these may assist in defining the content of the *Charter* norms.

In the second category are such instruments as the *International Covenant on Civil and Political Rights*, the *International Convention on the Elimination of All Forms of Racial Discrimination*, the *Convention on the Elimination of Discrimination Against Women*, the *Convention Against Torture and Other Cruel, Inhuman and Degrading Treatment or Punishment*, the *Convention on the Rights of the Child* and the *Rome Statute of the International Criminal Court*. The provisions of these instruments are often similar to those of the *Charter*, and they have been ratified or acceded to by Canada. According to Chief Justice Dickson, Canada is bound, at international law, to protect such rights within its borders. Interestingly, he did not specifically base his conclusion on the classic rule of interpretation by which domestic legislation is presumed to be consistent with international obligations. Rather, "general principles of constitutional interpretation require that these international obligations be a relevant and persuasive factor in *Charter* interpretation".

In his important declaration, Chief Justice Dickson did not cite precedents concerning statutory interpretation and international treaties, but rather he relied upon a *Charter* case, *R. v. Big M Drug Mart Ltd.*, which is an authority for purposive or teleological interpretation.[186] In identifying

---

184 *Declaration on the Rights of Persons Belonging to National or Ethnic Religious and Linguistic Minorities*, UN Doc. E/CN.4/1992/48 + Corr.1, UN Doc. A/RES/48/138, GA Res. 48/138. See: Alan Phillips & Allan Rosas, *The U.N. Minority Rights Declaration*, Abo: Abo Akademi University Institute for Human Rights, 1993; Natan Lerner, "The 1992 UN Declaration on Minorities", (1993) 23 *Israel Yearbook of Human Rights* 111.

185 "Draft Declaration on the Rights of Indigenous Peoples", UN Doc. E/CN.4/L.62.

186 *R. v. Big M Drug Mart Ltd.*, [1985] 1 SCR 295, 18 DLR (4th) 321, 18 CCC (3d) 385, [1985] 3 WWR 481, 37 Alta LR (2d) 97, 58 NR 81, 60 AR 161, 13 CRR 64, 85 CLLC 14,023, at 344 (SCR). On both the purposive interpretation and the role of international law in regard to the *Canadian Charter*, see: Stéphane Beaulac, "L'interprétation de la Charte: reconsidération de l'approche téléologique et réévaluation du rôle du droit international", in Gérald.-A. Beaudoin & Errol P. Mendes, eds., *Canadian Charter of*

the objective of the *Charter*'s provisions, he said that international obligations to which Canada is bound provide an "important indicia" to this effect.
He concluded that the *Charter* "should *generally* be presumed to provide
protection at least as great as that afforded by similar provisions in international human rights documents which Canada has ratified".[187] Even norms
that bind Canada, as a question of international law, do not bind the judiciary,
the Chief Justice insisted. Nevertheless, he clearly placed such binding
norms in a paramount category, at least in comparison with norms that do
not bind Canada. Both types of norm are, however, "a relevant and persuasive source" for *Charter* interpretation.

2.2.1   The "Relevant and Persuasive" Doctrine

In a 1988 speech to the Canadian Council on International Law, former
Justice of the Supreme Court of Canada Gérard La Forest said this of Chief
Justice Dickson's statement in *Re Public Service Employee Relations Act*:
"Though speaking in dissent, his comments on the use of international law
generally reflect what we all do".[188] More recently, in 2000, Justice Michel
Bastarache of the Supreme Court of Canada opined similarly: "While Chief
Justice Dickson rejected the implicit incorporation of international law
doctrine in a dissenting judgment, his opinion reflects the present state of
the law."[189]

The famous "relevant and persuasive" passage has been cited in subsequent Canadian cases. On the other hand, the distinction suggested by
Chief Justice Dickson between ratified and unratified instruments has generally been ignored. Canadian judges rarely, if ever, consider international
law sources by taking into account whether they have a legally binding
effect on Canada. Instead, they tend to consider all sources of international
human rights law as "relevant and persuasive". To be entirely accurate,
there continues to be some authority for distinguishing between binding and
non-binding instruments, but it is of little real significance. In *Mugesera*,
for example, the Supreme Court of Canada spoke of "the importance of
interpreting domestic law in a manner that accords with the principles of

---

Rights and Freedoms, 4th ed., Markham, Ont.: LexisNexis Butterworths, 2005, pp. 27-
69; reprinted in (2005) 27 *Supreme Court Law Review (2d)* 1.

187   *Reference Re Public Service Employee Relations Act, supra* note 179, at 350 (SCR,
emphasis added).

188   Gérard V. La Forest, "The Use of International and Foreign Material in the Supreme
Court of Canada", *Proceedings, XVIIth Annual Conference, Canadian Council on International Law*, 1988, pp. 230-241, at 232.

189   Michel Bastarache, "The Honourable G.V. La Forest's Use of Foreign Materials in the
Supreme Court of Canada and His Influence on Foreign Courts," in Rebecca Johnson
& John P. McEvoy, eds., *Gérard V. La Forest at the Supreme Court of Canada, 1985-
1997*, Winnipeg: Canadian Legal History Project, 2000, pp. 433-447, at 434.

customary international law and with Canada's treaty obligations".[190] The Court referred to *Baker*, which relied principally upon the *Convention on the Rights of the Child*, noting that it had been ratified by Canada.[191] But after acknowledging the fact of ratification, the majority in *Baker* conceded that: "International treaties and conventions are not part of Canadian law unless they have been implemented by statute." It proceeded with the observation that "the values reflected in international human rights law may help inform the contextual approach to statutory interpretation and judicial review". It also cited Driedger's work on statutory interpretation:

> [T]he legislature is presumed to respect the values and principles enshrined in international law, both customary and conventional. These constitute a part of the legal context in which legislation is enacted and read. *In so far as possible, therefore, interpretations that reflect these values and principles are preferred.*[192]

For the majority, Justice L'Heureux-Dubé then discussed two important instruments that are non-binding by their very nature, the *Universal Declaration of Human Rights* and the *Declaration on the Rights of the Child*. She concluded: "The principles of the Convention and other international instruments place special importance on protections for children and childhood, and on particular consideration of their interests, needs, and rights."[193] Thus, the majority in *Baker* did not in fact operate any distinction between binding and non-binding sources of international human rights law.

Similarly, in *R. v. Advance Cutting & Coring Ltd.*,[194] Justice Bastarache, dissenting, moved indifferently between binding and non-binding sources, without reference to the distinction proposed by Chief Justice Dickson. He cited the *International Covenant on Economic, Social and Cultural Rights*, to which Canada is bound at international law, alongside the *African Charter of Human and Peoples' Rights*,[195] to which, obviously, it is not.[196] Justice Bastarache even made specific reference to the dissent of Chief Justice Dickson, but without in any way addressing the bifurcated approach advo-

---

190 *Mugesera* v. *Canada (Minister of Citizenship and Immigration)*, [2005] 2 SCR 100, at para. 82.

191 *Baker* v. *Canada (Minister of Citizenship and Immigration)*, [1999] 2 SCR 817, 174 DLR (4th) 193, 14 Admin LR (3d) 173, 1 Imm LR (3d) 1, 243 NR 22, at para. 69.

192 *Ibid.*, at para. 70, citing Ruth Sullivan, *Driedger on the Construction of Statutes*, 3rd ed., Toronto & Vancouver: Butterworths, 1994, at 330 (emphasis added by the Supreme Court of Canada).

193 *Ibid.*, para. 71.

194 *R.* v. *Advance Cutting & Coring Ltd.*, [2001] 3 SCR 209, 205 DLR (4th) 385, 87 CRR (2d) 189.

195 *African Charter on Human and People's Rights*, OAU Doc. CAB/LEG/67/3 rev. 5, 4 EHRR 417, 21 *ILM* 58, arts. 8, 11.

196 *R.* v. *Advance Cutting & Coring Ltd.*, *supra* note 194, paras. 12-14.

cated therein.[197] Justice LeBel, writing for the majority, relied exclusively upon a non-binding instrument, the *European Convention on Human Rights*, distinguishing decisions of the European Court of Human Rights.[198]

The most recent affirmation of the "relevant and persuasive" approach appears in *Burns and Rafay*.[199] There, a unanimous Supreme Court of Canada cited Chief Justice Dickson's famous dictum, treating it as an authoritative statement of the applicable principles with respect to the use of international law in *Charter* interpretation. There was no reference to the distinction between binding and non-binding instruments. Of course, the issues did not lend themselves to such a distinction, given that at the time it had not been contended that Canada was bound as a matter of international law not to extradite to a country where the death penalty would be imposed.[200] The law has since changed with Canada's accession in November 2005 to the *Second Optional Protocol to the International Covenant on Civil and Political Rights Aiming at Abolition of the Death Penalty*.[201] Rather than speak of international legal obligations, in *Burns and Rafay* the Supreme Court of Canada hinged its argument on the suggestion that abolition of the death penalty had "emerged as a major Canadian initiative at the international level" and that it "reflects a concern increasingly shared by most of the world's democracies".[202] *Burns and Rafay* provides a good example of a situation where the distinction proposed by Chief Justice Dickson was in fact inconvenient, and did not encourage a result favourable to the protection of human rights. The Court effectively ignored it.

This practice may offend some public international law commentators, who find it to be legally unsophisticated and imprecise.[203] In fact, the distinction made by Chief Justice Dickson might be viewed as a half-baked version of the earlier thesis, advanced by Cohen and Bayefsky,[204] of the actual incorporation into Canadian law of ratified treaties. It does not, of course, go so far, and only creates an interpretative argument. Still, it tends

---

197   *Ibid.*, paras. 14, 30.

198   *Ibid.*, paras. 172, 249-251.

199   *United States* v. *Burns and Rafay*, [2001] 1 SCR 283, 195 DLR (4th) 1, [2001] 3 WWR 193, 151 CCC (3d) 97, 39 CR (5th) 205, 81 CRR (2d) 1, 85 BCLR (3d) 1.

200   Subsequent caselaw of the Human Rights Committee supports the argument that Canada would have been in breach of article 6(1) of the *International Covenant on Civil and Political Rights* had it proceeded with the extradition of Burns and Rafay. See: *Judge* v. *Canada* (No. 829/1998), UN Doc. CCPR/C/78/D/829/1998.

201   *Second Optional Protocol to the International Covenant on Civil and Political Rights Aimed at Abolition of the Death Penalty*, UN Doc. A/RES/44/128, annex.

202   *United States* v. *Burns and Rafay*, *supra* note 199, at para. 79 (heading).

203   In particular, see Gibran Van Ert, *Using International Law in Canadian Courts*, The Hague: Kluwer Law International, 2002.

204   Maxwell Cohen & Anne F. Bayefsky, "The Canadian Charter of Rights and Freedoms and International Law", (1983) 61 *Canadian Bar Review* 265.

to focus the attention on an initial distinction between two categories of international law, one which has direct impact on Canadian law by virtue of ratification, and the other which is really nothing more than a source of comparative law. It might also have been a stratagem to make resort to international law more palatable for conservative judges, who were resistant to foreign law but ready enough to cite international treaties if this could be rooted in a common law thesis about the relationship between domestic and international law.

Defenders of the binding versus non-binding dichotomy may see it as strengthening the role of international law in the interpretation of the *Charter*, by giving at least some sources of international human rights law a status that is higher than what might flow from their recognition as "relevant and persuasive" sources of interpretation.[205] Yet the opposite might well be the consequence, because while it enhances the legal importance of treaty norms, it might at the same time tend to weaken that of "soft law" sources. Strengthening the status of so-called binding norms has an unfortunate price, which is the marginalization of so-called non-binding norms. From the standpoint of the protection and promotion of human rights, the non-binding norms are often more advanced and more innovative.

But whatever the possible outcome, it bears repeating that Canadian courts have never really insisted upon the distinction made by Chief Justice Dickson. When a treaty norm has been ratified, they may draw attention to the fact. But in reality, they treat all sources of international human rights law as "relevant and persuasive".

2.2.2   Presumption of Intent Versus Contextual Argument

In the early years of *Charter* interpretation, there were frequent manifestations of attempts to justify the resort to international sources with reference to traditional principles of construction of statutes. Judges sometimes referred to principles or rules of interpretation as being applicable only where the legislation in question is ambiguous, as Justice Pigeon famously wrote in *Daniel v. White*.[206] This way of using international law in statutory interpretation falls within a broader approach to the construction of statutes, generally referred to as the "plain meaning rule" or the "literal rule", according to which "there is no need to resort to interpretation when the wording is clear".[207] Justice Pigeon was the champion of this method of

---

205   See: Jutta Brunnée & Stephen J. Toope, "A Hesitant Embrace: The Application of International Law by Canadian Courts", (2002) 40 *Canadian Yearbook of International Law* 3.

206   *Daniels* v. *White*, [1968] SCR 517, at 541.

207   *Ville de Montréal* v. *ILGWU Center Inc.*, (1971) [1974] SCR 59, 24 DLR (3d) 694, at 66 (SCR), *per* Fauteux J.).

statutory interpretation, which dates back to a time in the common law tradition when it was seriously believed that "Parliament changes the law for the worse"[208] and that a statute was an "alien intruder in the house of the common law".[209]

The "literal rule" is now generally considered obsolete in common law jurisdictions because courts have realised that the wording in legislation cannot be considered in isolation.[210] As Michael Zander explained: "The most fundamental objection to the rule is that is is based on a false premise, namely that words have plain, ordinary meanings apart from their context."[211] The House of Lords distanced itself some time ago from this restrictive approach to statutory interpretation:

> The days have long passed when the courts adopted a strict constructionist view of interpretation which required them to adopt the literal meaning of the language. The courts now adopt a purposive approach which seeks to give effect to the true purpose of legislation and are prepared to look at much extraneous material that bears upon the back ground against which the legislation was enacted.[212]

British author Francis Bennion has insisted upon the importance in all instances that when a judge interprets and applies legislation he or she should go beyond the letter of the law: "Without exception, statutory words require careful assessment of themselves and their context if they are to be construed correctly."[213]

In Canada, Justice L'Heureux-Dubé of the Supreme Court of Canada was one of the main proponents of a non-literalist approach to the interpretation of statutes. Already in *Hills v. Canada (Attorney General)*,[214] and most impressively in her minority opinion in *2747-3174 Québec Inc. v. Quebec (Régie des permis d'alcool)*,[215] she clearly favoured a construction of legislation that takes full account of the context and the purpose of an

---

208 Frederick Pollock, *Essays in Jurisprudence and Ethics*, London: Macmillan, 1882, at 85.
209 Harlan Stone, "The Common Law in the United States", (1936) 50 *Harvard Law Review* 4, at 15.
210 See: Stéphane Beaulac, "Le Code civil commande-t-il une interprétation distincte?", (1999) 22 *Dalhousie Law Journal* 236, at 251-252; and Stéphane Beaulac, "Parliamentary Debates in Statutory Interpretation: A Question of Admissibility of Weight?", (1998) 43 *McGill Law Journal* 287, at 310-312.
211 Michael Zander, *The Law-Making Process*, 4th ed., London: Butterworths, 1994, at 121.
212 *Pepper v. Hart*, [1993] AC 593 (HL), at 617.
213 Francis A.R. Bennion, *Statutory Interpretation A Code*, 4th ed., London: Butterworths, 2002, at 500.
214 *Hills v. Canada (Attorney General)*, [1988] 1 SCR 513.
215 *2747-3174 Québec Inc. v. Quebec (Régie des permis d'alcool)*, [1996] 3 SCR 919, 140 DLR (4th) 577, 42 Admin LR (2d) 1, 205 NR 1.

enactment, along with the statutory language used. In the latter case, L'Heureux-Dubé J. concluded thus her exhaustive historical and doctrinal review of the methodology of interpretation:

> What Bennion calls the "informed interpretation" approach is called the "modern interpretation rule" by Sullivan and "pragmatic dynamism" by Eskridge. All these approaches reject the former "plain meaning" approach. In view of the many terms now being used to refer to these approaches, I will here use the term "modern approach" to designate a synthesis of the contextual approaches that reject the "plain meaning" approach. According to this "modern approach," consideration must be given at the outset not only to the words themselves but also, *inter alia*, to the context, the statute's other provisions, provisions of other statutes *in pari materia* and the legislative history in order to correctly identify the legislature's objective.[216]

Nowadays, this approach to the construction of statutes has been endorsed, at least rhetorically, by the entire bench of the Supreme Court of Canada. It is articulated with the help of the so-called "modern principle" of statutory interpretation, as defined by Elmer Driedger in his book *The Construction of Statutes*.[217]

It must first be appreciated how this contemporary approach to legislation enjoys unquestionable authority at the Supreme Court of Canada and in the lower courts.[218] The excerpt where the "modern principle" is expressed comes from the second edition of *The Construction of Statutes* and reads as follows: "Today there is only one principle or approach, namely, the words of an Act are to be read in their entire context in their grammatical and ordinary sense harmoniously with the scheme of the Act, the object of the Act and the intention of Parliament."[219] From its very first use in 1984, with *Stubart Investments Ltd.* v. *R.*,[220] up to the end of 2005, there were no less than 59 decisions by the Supreme Court of Canada[221] making references to Driedger's words[222]; three other cases cited the third edition, *Driedger on*

---

216 *Ibid.*, at 1002.

217 Elmer A. Driedger, *Construction of* Statutes, Toronto: Butterworths, 1974.

218 This part borrows from Stéphane Beaulac & Pierre-André Côté, "Driedger's 'Modern Principle' at the Supreme Court of Canada: Interpretation, Justification, Legitimization", (2006) 40 *Revue juridique Thémis*, at 131.

219 Elmer A. Driedger, *Construction of Statutes*, 2nd ed., Toronto: Butterworths, 1983, at 87.

220 [1984] 1 SCR 536.

221 The fifty-nine cases are listed in Stéphane Beaulac & Pierre-André Côté, *supra* note 218, at 131.

222 Usually the cases referred to the relevant passage in a unanimous or majority set of reasons, although some references are in minority or dissenting opinions only; there are instances where more than one set of reasons quote Driedger. Finally, it is worth mentioning that in the large majority of cases, the Supreme Court judges actually used

the Construction of Statutes,[223] by Professor Ruth Sullivan, where the "modern principle" became the "modern rule" of statutory interpretation and was, in effect, recast in different terms.[224]

What is also worth emphasising is how Driedger's quote is used in all areas of the law and, in fact, in all facets of legal interpretation: from tax law to human rights law, from criminal law to family law, as well as to qualify legislation in constitutional challenges (*Charter* cases or division of powers cases), to interpret constitutional or quasi-constitutional texts, to construe delegated legislation like regulations and by-laws, to interpret transitional provisions in an enactment; it was extended to Quebec civil law in order to construe *Civil Code*[225] provisions and even once to help interpret a contract. Professions of faith over the years vis-à-vis the "modern principle" include that it is the "prevailing and preferred" or the "established" approach, that it is the "appropriate and proper" or the "traditional and correct" approach; Driedger's words would indeed be a "definitive formulation" which "best captures or encapsulates" the approach, even the "starting point" for statutory interpretation in Canada.

When extending the search to the country's lower courts, one finds unequivocal confirmation of Driedger's extraordinary influence. The grand total of references to Driedger's "modern principle" up to mid-2005, in federal courts and in superior courts of the provinces and territories – whatever edition of *The Construction of Statutes* and be it a direct quote, a reference to the passage, or an indirect endorsement via a Supreme Court of Canada case resorting to Driedger – is astonishing, some 724 citations.[226]

The "modern principle" is also referred to as the "word-in-total-context" approach to statutory interpretation, and justifiably so. Elmer Driedger himself pointed out: "Words, when read by *themselves* in the abstract can hardly be said to have meanings."[227] In the latest edition of *The Construction of Statutes*, Ruth Sullivan further develops this idea: "The meaning of a word depends on the context in which it is used. This basic principle of communication applies to all texts, including legislation."[228] What has become

---

an excerpt of the whole or part of the passage in question; only a few times did they refer to the author without quoting him.

223 Ruth Sullivan, *Driedger on the Construction of Statutes*, 3rd ed., Toronto & Vancouver: Butterworths, 1994, at 131-132.

224 For a defence and explanation of her reformulation, see Ruth Sullivan, "Statutory Interpretation in the Supreme Court of Canada", (1998-1999) 30 *Ottawa Law Review* 175.

225 *Civil Code of Quebec*, SQ 1991, c. 64.

226 For the references, see: Stéphane Beaulac & Pierre-André Côté, *supra* note 221.

227 Elmer A. Driedger, *supra* note 217, at 3 (emphasis in original).

228 Ruth Sullivan, *Sullivan and Driedger on the Construction of Statutes*, 4th ed., Markham, Ontario & Vancouver: Butterworths, 2002, at 161.

obvious in recent years is that the contextual element of statutory interpretation, within Driedger's "word-in-total-context" approach, include international law: "Under Driedger's modern principle, the words to be interpreted must be looked at in their total context. This includes not only the Act as a whole and the statute book as a whole but also the legal context, consisting of caselaw, common law and *international law*."[229] Sullivan's view is shared by most international law commentators, like Hugh Kindred, who writes that "where the context of the legislation includes a treaty or other international obligation, the statute should be interpreted in light of it."[230]

Undoubtedly, considering international law as an element of context within Driedger's approach is the better strategy to maximise the instances where these legal norms are used in the process of interpretation in Canada, including the construction of rights and freedoms in the *Charter*.[231] This way to resort to international law should be favoured over the presumption of conformity, according to which national legislation that is ambiguous should be read consistently with international law. This old common law canon of interpretation inherited from England was first formulated by Peter Maxwell as follows: "[E]very statute is to be so interpreted and applied, as far as its language admits, as not to be inconsistent with the comity of nations, or with the established rules of international law."[232] The presumption of conformity with international law is a type of presumption of intent, whose general function is "to attribute intentions to Parliament in certain circumstances, in the absence of an expression of a contrary intent",[233] as Elmer Driedger himself explained. Justice La Forest, writing extra-judicially, once associated the presumptions of legislative intent with the constitutional protection provided by the *Charter*, which "help to promote

---

229   *Ibid.*, at 262 (emphasis added). See also Ruth Sullivan, "Some Implications of Plain Language Drafting", (2001) 22 *Statute Law Review* 145, at 147-149.

230   Hugh Kindred, "Canadians as Citizens of the International Community: Asserting Unimplemented Treaty Rights in the Courts", in Stephen G. Coughlan & Dawn Russell, eds., *Citizenship and Citizen Participation in the Administration of Justice*, Montreal: Thémis, 2002, at 271.

231   This part borrows from Stéphane Beaulac, "International Law and Statutory Interpretation: Up with Context, Down with Presumption", in O. Fitzgerald, ed., *Globalized Rule of Law: Relationships Between International and Domestic Law*, Toronto: Irwin Law, pp. 331-365.

232   Peter B. Maxwell, *On the Interpretation of Statutes*, London: Sweet & Maxwell, 1896, at 122. For examples of application in England, see: *Salomon* v. *Commissioners of Customs and Excise*, [1967] 2 QB 116 (CA), and *Corocraft* v. *Pan American Airways*, [1968] 3 WLR 1273 (CA).

233   Elmer A. Driedger, *supra* note 217, at 137. See also: *Re Estabrooks Pontiac Buick Ltd.*, (1982) 44 NBR (2d) 201 (CA), at 211 (*per* La Forest JA).

second thought and public debate, a debate that all recognize as an essential safeguard in a parliamentary democracy".[234]

The main problem with the presumption of conformity with international law, as with any presumption of intent in statutory interpretation, is the preliminary requirement of ambiguity. Indeed, before courts can trigger the operation of this interpretative tool, there must be a finding that the legislative provision at issue is ambiguous, or is otherwise problematic. Short of fulfilling this precondition, the presumption of conformity with international law cannot become an argument of interpretation, which in turn means that the opportunity to resort to such legal norms is lost. This feature is highlighted in Pigeon J's remarks in *Daniels v. White*, which is often referred to as the accepted formulation in Canada of the presumption of conformity with international law:

> I wish to add that, in my view, this is a case for the application of the rule of construction that Parliament is not presumed to legislate in breach of a treaty or in any manner inconsistent with the comity of nations and the established rules of international law. It is a rule that is not often applied, because if a statute is unambiguous, its provisions must be followed even if they are contrary to international law.[235]

Pierre-André Côté has pointed out that this excerpt suggests that a legitimate utilisation of international law is possible if, and only if, there is a real interpretative difficulty with the legislative provision. Such reasoning involves the obsolete "literal rule" of construction.[236]

Even though Justice Gonthier attempted to set aside the ambiguity requirement in *National Corn Growers Assn.* v. *Canada (Import Tribunal)*,[237] the 2002 decision of the Supreme Court of Canada in *Schreiber v. Canada (Attorney General)* makes it clear that this fatal flaw associated with the presumption of conformity with international law still exists. It must be noted that LeBel J. endorsed Pigeon J.'s *dictum* in *Daniels v. White*, writing that it "sets out when international law is appropriately used to interpret domestic legislation." The last portion of the citation from Justice Pigeon was even underlined, emphasis that the presumption of conformity *"is not often applied, because if a statute is unambiguous, its provisions*

---

234   Gérard V. La Forest, "The Canadian Charter of Rights and Freedoms: An Overview", (1983) 61 *Canadian Bar Review* 19, at 20.

235   *Daniels* v. *While*, [1968] SCR 517, at 541.

236   Pierre-André Côté, *Interprétation des lois*, 3rd ed., Montreal: Thémis, 1999, at 466-467.

237   *National Corn Growers Assn.* v. *Canada (Import Tribunal)*, [1990] 2 SCR 1324, at 1371. This case is generally considered to have limited the authority of Estey J.'s statement in *Schavernoch* v. *Canada (Foreign Claims Commission)*, [1982] 1 SCR 1092, at 1098, about requiring a preliminary finding of ambiguity before proceeding to consider international law.

must be followed even if they are contrary to international law".[238] In the end, the international law argument was rejected: "The questions at stake fall within the purview of the domestic legislation." In order to dismiss the presumption of conformity and, with it, the influence of international legal norms, courts usually make a preliminary finding that the legislative provision at issue is clear, that is not ambiguous.[239] To put it another way, if the precondition of ambiguity is not met, the international law gate is shut tightly.

Furthermore, given that we are here concerned with the rights and freedoms protected by the *Charter*, and not with the interpretation of ordinary statutes, reasoning based on a presumption of intent is even more problematic. Generally, international law determines the rights and obligations of states, and not of individuals, who have only a secondary and very incidental role in litigation. Human rights law contemplates protection of the individual above all else. The rule of construction requiring that there be ambiguity ought to be tempered when human rights and freedoms are concerned. This view finds support in the numerous references to international law for the purpose of interpreting the *Charter* where there is no discussion of the ambiguity rule whatsoever, including the reasons of Chief Justice Dickson in *Re Public Service Alliance*.[240] Put another way, in human rights issues the burden ought to lie on the defendant or respondent to demonstrate that the legislation in question is unequivocal, unambiguous and an explicit derogation from Canada's international obligations.

In *Re Mitchell and the Queen*, Linden J., then of the Ontario High Court of Justice, expressed the view that the *International Covenant on Civil and Political Rights*:

> . . .may be used to assist a court to interpret ambiguous provisions of a domestic statute, notwithstanding the fact that the Covenant has not been incorporated into the law of Canada, provided that the domestic statute does not contain express provisions contrary to or inconsistent with the Covenant. If such contrary provisions exist, the Covenant cannot prevail.[241]

---

238 *Daniels* v. *White, supra* note 235, at 541 (emphasis by LeBel J. in *Schreiber*).

239 *Schreiber* v. *Canada (Attorney General)*, [2002] 3 SCR 269, (sub nom. *Schreiber* v. *Federal Republic of Germany*) 216 DLR (4th) 513, 167 CCC (3d) 51, 164 OAC 354, at 293-294.

240 *Reference Re Public Service Employee Relations Act (Alberta)*, [1987] 1 RCS 313, 51 Alta LR (2d) 97, [1987] 3 WWR 577, (sub nom. *A.U.P.E.* v. *Alberta (Attorney General)*) 28 CRR 305, 38 DLR (4th) 161, (sub nom. *Reference re Compulsory Arbitration*) 74 NR 99, 78 AR 1, [1987] DLQ 225, 87 CLLC 14,021, at 348 (SCR).

241 *Re Mitchell and R.*, [2002] 3 SCR 269, (sub nom. *Schreiber* v. *Federal Republic of Germany*) 216 DLR (4th) 513, 167 CCC (3d) 51, 164 OAC 354, at 493 (OR). In *Re R. and Warren*, (1983) 35 CR (3d) 173, 6 CRR 82 (Ont. HC), Linden J. concluded that because section 11(a) of the *Canadian Charter* was "not completely clear on its face",

Justice Linden was actually referring to the *Charter*, and no mere domestic statute. He concluded that sections 9 and 12 of the *Charter* are ambiguous, thereby permitting reference to the *International Covenant on Civil and Political Rights* as an aid in interpretation. But he found a clear conflict between section 11(i) of the *Charter* and article 15 of the *Covenant*. Justice Linden concluded "with some reluctance" that the *Covenant* could not be applied in the circumstances, although he did recognize "that in other cases it may be appropriate and desirable to have regard to the *International Covenant* when interpreting provisions of the *Charter*".

In *R. v. Rahey*, La Forest J. referred to the *European Convention on Human Rights* and the jurisprudence of the European Court of Human Rights in order to resolve ambiguity in section 11(b) of the *Charter*. After finding that ambiguity surrounding the term "to be tried. . ." was dispelled by reference to the French text which reads "d'être jugée. . .", he added:

> Some support for this conclusion may be found in the decision of the European Court of Human Rights in *Wemhoff*, judgement of 27 June 1968, Series A, No. 7. Article 5(3) of the *European Convention for the Protection of Human Rights and Fundamental Freedoms*, 213 UNTS 222, provides, in the English version, that "everyone arrested or detained. . .shall be entitled to trial within a reasonable time or to release pending trial". Like the Charter, the French version of the convention expresses this right by means of the word "jugée", which in *Wemhoff* the European Court interpreted as referring to the termination of the trial. It concluded, therefore, that the protection offered by the section extended to "the whole of the proceedings before the court, not just their beginning"(p. 23).[242]

The *European Convention on Human Rights*, cited by La Forest J., does not constitute an international obligation to which Canada is bound. However, the United Nations Human Rights Committee reached a similar conclusion in a Canadian case dealing with the issue of unreasonable delay.[243]

---

resort could be made to the *International Covenant on Civil and Political Rights* as "a tool of statutory interpretation". In *R. v. TR*, (1984) 28 Alta LR (2d) 383, 50 AR 56 (QB), Justice McDonald relied up article 14(7) of the *Covenant* to help resolve ambiguity about the meaning of section 11(h) of the *Charter*.

242 *R. v. Rahey*, [1987] 1 SCR 588, 33 CCC (3d) 289, 75 NR 81, 33 CRR 279, 57 CR (3d) 289, 78 NSR (2d) 183, 193 APR 183, 39 DLR (4th) 481, at 633 (SCR); Justice La Forest did not however rely on *Wemhoff* in the same fashion when the question arose as to whether the right "d'être jugée" includes the delay necessary for hearing of an appeal to a conviction. Such was the conclusion of the European Court, but on this point Canada's Supreme Court has not reached the same view: *R. v. Conway*, [1989] 1 SCR 1659, 49 CCC (3d) 289, 70 CR (3d) 209, 40 CRR 1, 96 NR 241, 34 OAC 165.

243 *Pinkney* v. *Canada* (No. 27/1978), UN Doc. CCPR/C/14/D/27/1977, UN Doc. CCPR/C/14/D/27/1977, UN Doc. CCPR/3/Add.1, Vol. II, p. 385, UN Doc. CCPR/C/OP/1, p. 95, 2 *Human Rights Law Journal* 344, [1983] *Canadian Human Rights Yearbook* 315.

On the other hand, whether it is the *Charter* or an ordinary piece of legislation that is being construed, resort to international law through the interpretative argument that consider such norms as an element of context does not run into any preliminary hurdle. There is no such preliminary requirement of ambiguity before international law may be considered in the process of construction. Rather, legal norms from the international order may always constitute an argument of construction, whether the case concerns an ordinary statute or *Charter*. In spite of the recent decision at the Supreme Court of Canada, *Canadian Foundation for Children, Youth and the Law v. Canada (Attorney General)*,[244] where the presumption of conformity with international law was invoked, it appears that the contextual argument of interpretation is the favoured means by which courts resort to international law.

In fact, the majority reasons of the Supreme Court of Canada in the *Baker* case actually signalled a tendency against the presumption and in favour of context. Justice L'Heureux-Dubé, writing for the majority, relied on an excerpt from the third edition of *Driedger on the Construction of Statutes*,[245] where Ruth Sullivan explained the two different ways in which international legal norms may be used:

> First, the legislature is presumed to comply with the obligations owed by Canada as a signatory of international instruments and more generally as a member of the international community. *In choosing among possible interpretations, therefore, the courts avoid interpretations that would put Canada in breach of any of its international obligations.* Second, the legislature is presumed to respect the values and principles enshrined in international law, both customary and conventional. *These constitute a part of the legal context in which legislation is enacted and read.* In so far as possible, therefore, interpretations that reflect these values and principles are preferred.[246]

The two highlighted sentences show that Ruth Sullivan refers, first, to the presumption of conformity with international law and its role in situations of ambiguity where an interpretation that is in line with the legal norms of the international order ought to be preferred and, second, to the argument

---

244 *Canadian Foundation for Children, Youth and the Law* v. *Canada (Attorney General)*, [2004] 1 SCR 76, 70 OR (3d) 95, 234 DLR (4th) 257, 180 CCC (3d) 353, 115 CRR (2d) 88, 16 CR (6th) 203, 46 RFL (5th) 1, 183 OAC 1. Other pre-*Baker* cases where the presumption was referred to include: *Ordon Estate* v. *Grail*, [1998] 3 SCR 437; *Pushpanathan* v. *Canada (Minister of Citizenship and Immigration)*, [1998] 1 SCR 982, amended, [1998] 1 SCR 1222; *Chan* v. *Canada (Minister of Employment & Immigration)*, [1995] 3 SCR 593; and *Canada (Attormney General)* v. *Ward*, (1990) 67 DLR (4th) 1, 10 Imm LR (2d) 199 (FCA), reversed, [1993] 2 SCR 689.
245 Ruth Sullivan, *supra* note 223.
246 *Ibid.*, at 541 (emphasis added).

of statutory interpretation pertaining to the context of adoption and of application in which international law falls.

Going back to L'Heureux-Dubé J. in *Baker*, what must be emphasised is that the quote from *Driedger on the Construction of Statutes* covers only the second way that international law may be used, namely the basic argument of international law as context. Her ladyship wrote:

> Nevertheless, the values reflected in international human rights law may help inform the contextual approach to statutory interpretation and judicial review. As stated in R. Sullivan, *Driedger on the Construction of Statutes* (3rd ed. 1994), at p. 33:
>
> > [T]he legislature is presumed to respect the values and principles enshrined in international law, both customary and conventional. These constitute a part of the legal context in which legislation is enacted and read. *In so far as possible, therefore, interpretations that reflect these values and principles are preferred.* [Emphasis added.]
>
> The important role of international human rights law as an aid in interpreting domestic law has also been emphasized in other common law countries.[247]

In other words, the majority of the Supreme Court of Canada in *Baker* reproduced and endorsed the views of Ruth Sullivan to the effect that international legal norms are part of the context of adoption and of application of domestic legislation, and that this contextual element should be considered relevant by courts where appropriate. On the other hand, it must be noted, and some significance ought to be attributed to the fact, that the first way in which international law may be utilised, as noted by Ruth Sullivan, namely through a presumption of legislative intent, was not referred to and therefore was not endorsed in the reasons for judgment by the majority in this case.

This aspect of *Baker* is highly meaningful, especially considering that Justice L'Heureux-Dubé wrote this opinion and that during her tenure at the Supreme Court of Canada she was one of the main proponents of a non-literalist approach to statutory interpretation, in accordance with Driedger's "modern principle". Thus, Justice L'Heureux-Dubé's endorsement of international law as context and her implicit rejection of the presumption of conformity with international law is consistent with her, and to a large extent the Court's, general approach to interpretation. A few years after *Baker*, in the unanimous decision in *114957 Canada Ltée (Spraytech, Société d'arrosage) v. Hudson (Town)*,[248] L'Heureux-Dubé J. had the opportunity to reiterate and confirm her views, that "the values reflected in inter-

---

247   *Baker v. Canada (Minister of Citizenship and Immigration)*, [1999] 2 SCR 817, 174 DLR (4th) 193, 14 Admin LR (3d) 173, 1 Imm LR (3d) 1, 243 NR 22, at 861.

248   *114957 Canada Ltée (Spraytech, Société d'arrosage) v. Hudson (Town)*, [2001] 2 SCR 241.

national human rights law may help inform the contextual approach to statutory interpretation and judicial review"[249] and to quote again the key passage (only the second portion, as in *Baker*) from *Driedger on the Construction of Statutes*.[250]

This reading of the *Baker* decision also finds support in the case of *Suresh v. Canada (Minister of Citizenship and Immigration)*.[251] It is a unanimous judgment in which the Supreme Court of Canada was asked to review a ministerial decision pursuant to immigration legislation that allows deportation to a country where a refugee faces serious risks of torture in exceptional cases of national security. Central to the case was whether such deportation was contrary to the principles of fundamental justice protected by section 7 of the *Canadian Charter of Rights and Freedoms*. To determine the scope of protection against torture in Canada, the Court first referred to section 12 of the *Charter* and its caselaw on cruel and unusual treatment or punishment,[252] including *United States v. Burns and Rafay*.[253] The Court then continued its analysis under the heading "The International Perspective", explaining:

> We have examined the argument that from the perspective of Canadian law to deport a Convention refugee to torture violates the principles of fundamental justice. However, that does not end the inquiry. The provisions of the *Immigration Act* dealing with deportation must be considered in their international context: *Pushpanathan, supra,* [*Pushpanathan v. Canada (Minister of Citizenship and Immigration)*, [1998] 1 SCR 982]. Similarly, the principles of fundamental justice expressed in s. 7 of the *Charter* and the limits on rights that may be justified under s. 1 of the *Charter* cannot be considered in isolation from the international norms which they reflect. A complete understanding of the Act and the *Charter* requires consideration of the international perspective.[254]

Such an "international perspective" involved considering (without deciding it, however) whether the international prohibition on torture was a peremptory norm of customary international law (that is, *jus cogens*), as well as examining the provisions of three international conventions, the *Interna-*

---

249   *Baker* v. *Canada, supra* note 247, at 861.
250   Ruth Sullivan, *Driedger on the Construction of Statutes*, 3rd ed., Toronto & Vancouver: Butterworths, 1994, at 330.
251   [2002] 1 SCR 3, 208 DLR (4th) 1, 37 Admin LR (3d) 159, 90 CRR (2d) 1.
252   *Kindler* v. *Canada (Minister of Justice)*, [1991] 2 SCR 779, 67 CCC (3d) 1, 84 DLR (4th) 438, 6 CRR (2d) 193, 129 NR 81; and *Canada* v. *Schmidt*, [1987] 1 SCR 500, 33 CCC (3d) 193, 39 DLR (4th) 18, 58 CR (3d) 1, 28 CRR 280, 76 NR 12, 61 OR (2d) 530.
253   *United States* v. *Burns and Rafay*, [2001] 1 SCR 283, 195 DLR (4th) 1, [2001] 3 WWR 193, 151 CCC (3d) 97, 39 CR (5th) 205, 81 CRR (2d) 1, 85 BCLR (3d) 1.
254   *Suresh* v. *Canada (Minister of Citizenship and Immigration), supra* note 251, at 37-38.

tional Covenant on Civil and Political Rights, the *Convention Against Torture and Other Cruel, Inhuman or Degrading Treatment or Punishment* and the *Convention Relating to the Status of Refugees.*

At the end of this part of its reasons, the Supreme Court of Canada held that international law prohibited any deportation to face torture, even in exceptional cases of national security. The Court explained that in interpreting section 7 of the *Charter* in its entire context, the total prohibition of deportation to face torture is the international legal norm that "best informs the content of the principles of fundamental justice".[255] Other statements in the decision show that international law was indeed used as a contextual argument of construction: "The Canadian and international perspective in turn inform our constitutional norms. . .[i]ndeed, both domestic and international jurisprudence suggest that torture is so abhorrent that it will almost always be disproportionate to interests on the other side of the balance, even security interests".[256] A final aspect of the *Suresh* case shows that international law was no more than legal context, and with no determinative weight; it is the very interpretation given in the end of the judgment that, according to Canadian domestic law, "in exceptional circumstances, deportation to face torture might be justified, either as a consequence of the balancing process mandated by s. 7 of the *Charter* or under s. 1".[257] Therefore, the legal norm against torture in this country was held to be different from that in the international legal order, less stringent in fact. This indicates without a doubt that the international law argument was given some weight by the Court, but not a presumption-type of weight, let alone a determinative one.

The *Baker* case, at first blush, may not seem to be an obvious authority for the proposition that international law should be used through the basic contextual argument of interpretation rather than by means of a presumption of intent. One must go further, however, looking at the details of L'Heureux-Dubé J.'s reasons in *Baker*, considering that her ladyship reiterated her position in the *Hudson* case, noting that a unanimous Supreme Court of Canada in the *Suresh* case agreed, going along with the idea that international law ought to be viewed as an element of context, and most importantly taking into account that this approach falls squarely within the Court's broader interpretative strategy articulated with the help of Driedger's "modern principle". Then the trend in Canadian law becomes clearer, with the triumph of the contextual argument over the presumption of conformity.[258]

---

255 *Ibid.*, at 45.
256 *Ibid.*
257 *Ibid.*, at 46.
258 See also: Stéphane Beaulac, "Le droit international comme élément contextuel en interprétation des lois", (2004) *Canadian International Lawyer* 1; Stéphane Beaulac, "International Treaty Norms and Driedger's 'Modern Principle' of Statutory Interpretation", in *Legitimacy and Accountability in International Law – Proceedings of the*

2.2.3   The International Law Context of Adoption

International law has often been referred to by the courts as part of the context of adoption of the *Canadian Charter of Rights and Freedoms.* Returning to the discussion of *Reference re Public Service Employee Relations Act,*[259] when Chief Justice Dickson introduced the "relevant and persuasive" approach to the use of international law in *Charter* interpretation, he echoed comments made by a number of scholars in the early years of *Charter* interpretation. Maxwell Cohen had noted that "it is evident that an international rights syntax and related word images. . .permeate this Canadian exercise in restating the 'rights of man'".[260] The parallels between the various international instruments and the *Charter* were conspicuous enough. Ann M. Hayward called this the "derivative theory" of the *Canadian Charter;*[261] Daniel Turp referred to it as the "contexte d'énonciation";[262] José Woehrling described it as the "contexte d'adoption".[263] The "legislative history" or context of the drafting of the *Charter* is rich with references to other models of human rights legislation, both domestic and international, extrinsic materials that may provide useful insight into the meaning of the *Charter* provisions. Thus, the diverse international instruments are part of the context of adoption of the *Charter* and form, to some extent, part of its legislative history.

The Special Joint Committee of the Senate and of the House of Commons on the Constitution of Canada (the Hays-Joyal Committee),[264] which

---

33rd Annual Conference of the Canadian Council on International Law, Ottawa: Canadian Council of International Law, 2005, pp. 141-163.

259 *Reference Re Public Service Employee Relations Act (Alberta),* [1987] 1 RCS 313, 51 Alta LR (2d) 97, [1987] 3 WWR 577, (sub nom. *A.U.P.E.* v. *Alberta (Attorney General))* 28 CRR 305, 38 DLR (4th) 161, (sub nom. *Reference re Compulsory Arbitration*) 74 NR 99, 78 AR 1, [1987] DLQ 225, 87 CLLC 14,021.

260 Maxwell Cohen, "Towards a Paradigm of Theory and Practice: The Canadian Charter of Rights and Freedoms – International Law Influences and Interactions", [1986] *Canadian Human Rights Yearbook* 47, at 65.

261 Ann M. Hayward, "International Law and the Interpretation of the Canadian Charter of Rights and Freedoms: Uses and Justifications", (1985) 23 *University of Western Ontario Law Review* 9; as opposed to what she calls the "implementation theory".

262 Daniel Turp, "Le recours au droit international aux fins de l'interprétation de la Charte canadienne des droits et libertés: un bilan jurisprudentiel", (1984) 18 *Revue juridique Thémis* 353.

263 José Woehrling, "Le rôle du droit comparé dans la jurisprudence des droits de la personne – rapport canadien", in Armand De Mestral et al., eds., *The Limitation of Human Rights in Comparative Constitutional Law,* Cowansville: Editions Yvon Blais, 1986, pp. 449-514.

264 Justice Lamer, as he then was, in *Reference Re British Columbia Motor Vehicle Act,* (1985) [1985] 2 SCR 486, 23 CCC (3d) 289, 63 NR 266, 24 DLR (4th) 536, 48 CR (3d) 289, [1986] 1 WWR 481, 69 BCLR 145, 36 MVR 240, 18 CRR 30, at 504-509 (SCR) stated that the minutes of the Hays-Joyal Committee are admissible in *Charter* litigation,

prepared the final version of the *Charter*, reviewed Canada's international obligations under the *International Covenant on Civil and Political Rights* in drafting a number of provisions, including sections 15(1)[265] and 24(1).[266] According to Justices Cory and Iacobucci in *R.* v. *Zundel*, the model for section 27 of the *Charter*, which recognizes the multicultural heritage of Canadians, is article 27 of the *International Covenant on Civil and Political Rights*.[267] In some cases, however, the Hays-Joyal Committee undoubtedly decided not to entrench rights otherwise guaranteed in international instruments, for example, the right to free legal assistance when charged with an offence where the interests of justice so require.[268]

Going still further back in the preparatory work of the *Charter*, we may look at the original published text of the Parliamentary version of the *Charter*, from which the Hays-Joyal Commission worked.[269] This text referred to the *International Covenant on Civil and Political Rights* and noted

---

but that they carry little weight. But for a more generous approach, see Justice Tarnopolsky's remarks in *R.* v. *Videoflicks Ltd.*, (1984) 14 DLR (4th) 10, 15 CCC (3d) 353, 34 RPR 97, 9 CRR 193, 48 OR (2d) 395, (sub nom. *Edwards Books & Art Ltd.* v. *R.*) 5 OAC 1 (CA), reversed, (1986) 1986 CarswellOnt 1012 (SCC), or the reasons of Justice O'Leary in *Service Employees' International Union Local 204* v. *Broadway Manor Nursing Home*, (1983) 4 DLR (4th) 231, 44 OR (2d) 392, 10 CRR 37 (Div Ct), reversed, (1984) 1984 CarswellOnt 829 (CA), leave to appeal refused, (1985), 8 OAC 320n (SCC); also, *R.* v. *Finta*, (1989) 50 CCC (3d) 236, 64 CR (3d) 223, 44 CRR 23 (Ont HC), additional reasons at, (1987) 50 CCC 236 (Ont HC).

265 Gordon Fairweather, Chairman, Canadian Human Rights Commission, 5:8; John P. Humphrey, President, Canadian Human Rights Foundation, 11:28. The protection accorded by section 15(1) of the *Charter* to unenumerated grounds of discrimination was added to the original draft after comparisons were made with article 26 of the *International Covenant on Civil and Political Rights*, (1976) 999 UNTS 171, [1976] CTS 47, which includes such open-endedness. For a discussion, see footnote 3 in John E. Claydon, "The Application of International Human Rights Law by the Canadian Courts", (1981) 30 *Buffalo Law Review* 727; John E. Claydon, "International Human Rights Law and the Interpretation of the Canadian Charter of Rights and Freedoms", (1982) 4 *Supreme Court Law Review* 287.

266 Hays-Joyal Committee, 15:20; the availability of an appropriate and just remedy for *Charter* violations was directly inspired by article 2(3) of the *International Covenant on Civil and Political Rights*, *ibid.*, and was added after the Canadian Bar Association noted that Canada's international obligations required that such a remedy exist.

267 *R.* v. *Zundel*, [1992] 2 SCR 731, 95 DLR (4th) 202, 16 CR (4th) 1, 75 CCC (3d) 449, at 815 (SCR).

268 See *Deutsch* v. *Law Society Legal Aid Fund*, (1985) 11 OAC 30, 48 CR (3d) 166, 16 CRR 349 (Div Ct); *R.* v. *Robinson*, (1990) 51 CCC (3d) 452, 70 Alta LR (2d) 31, 63 DLR (4th) 289, 100 AR 26, 73 CR (3d) 81 (CA), at 481 (CCC).

269 See: Robin Elliott, "Interpreting the Charter – Use of the Earlier Versions as an Aid", (1982) 16 *Charter Edition University of British Columbia Law Review* 11; *R.* v. *Konechny*, [1984] 2 WWR 481, 6 DLR (4th) 350, 10 CCC (3d) 233, 38 CR (3d) 69, 25 MVR 132 (BC CA), leave to appeal refused, (1984) 25 MVR 132, 55 NR 156 (SCC), at 490 (WWR).

that sections 11(a), (b), (e), (f) and (g) of the draft *Charter* were new rights drawn from the *Covenant*. The Ontario Court of Appeal has cited these sources on at least one occasion.[270] As for the section 1 limitation provision, it first emerged in a 1971 version of the *Charter* and was directly inspired by limitations provisions found in the *European Convention*.[271]

The contemporaneity of the international documents and the *Charter* is also germane. This common heritage is a powerful argument for the relevance of the international instruments in interpreting the *Canadian Charter*. Justice Belzil of the Alberta Court of Appeal, dissenting in *R.* v. *Big M Drug Mart*, stated: "...the Canadian Charter was not conceived and born in isolation. It is part of the universal human rights movement...Even the *Canadian Bill of Rights*, adopted before the *International Covenant*, was intended to link Canada with the world-wide movement for human rights."[272] Justice Belzil also expressed the view, in *Allman* v. *Commission of the Northwest Territories*, that the fundamental human rights declared in the *Charter* are derived from natural law, and not positive law.[273]

An important English decision is also cited as general authority for the international human rights background of the *Charter*. Lord Wilberforce, in *Minister of Home Affairs* v. *Fisher*,[274] referred to the influence of the *European Convention on Human Rights* and the *Universal Declaration of Human Rights* in the drafting of the Bermuda *Bill of Rights*, and comparisons with the Canadian situation have been drawn repeatedly by our courts.[275]

---

270 *Re Trumbley and Fleming*, (1986) (sub nom. *Trumbley* v. *Fleming*) 29 DLR (4th) 557, 55 OR (2d) 570, 15 OAC 279, 24 CRR 333, 21 Admin LR 232 (CA), affirmed, (1987) 1987 CarswellOnt 948 (SCC), affirmed, (1987) 1987 CarswellOnt 947 (SCC), affirmed, (1987) 1987 CarswellOnt 949 (SCC), at 585 (OR).
271 (1955) 213 UNTS 221, ETS 5, arts. 8(2), 9(2), 10(2), 11(2).
272 *R.* v. *Big M Drug Mart Ltd.*, [1984] 1 WWR 625, 5 DLR (4th) 121, 9 CCC (3d) 310, 28 Alta LR (2d) 289, 49 AR 194, 7 CRR 92 (CA), affirmed, [1985] 1 SCR 295, at 149 (DLR).
273 *Allman* v. *Commission of the Northwest Territories*, [1984] NWTR 65, 8 DLR (4th) 230, 50 AR 161 (CA) at 235 (DLR).
274 [1980] AC 319, [1979] 3 All ER 21.
275 *R.* v. *Therens*, [1983] 4 WWR 385, 148 DLR (3d) 672, 5 CCC (3d) 409, 33 CR (3d) 204, 20 MVR 8, 23 Sask R 81, 5 CRR 157 (CA), affirmed, [1985] 1 SCR 613; *R.* v. *Lace*, (1983) 3 CRR 48 (Ont. Co. Ct.); *Quebec Protestant School Boards* v. *A-G Quebec (No. 2)*, [1982] CS 273, 140 DLR (3d) 33, 3 CRR 114, affirmed, (1983) 1 DLR (4th) 573 (CA), affirmed, [1984] 2 SCR 66; *R.* v. *W.H. Smith Ltd.*, [1983] 5 WWR 235, (1983) 26 Alta LR 238 (Prov Ct); *R.* v. *Campbell* (1983) 28 Alta LR (2d) 20 (Prov Ct), reversed [1984] 2 WWR 594 (CA); *British Columbia* v. *Craig*, (1984) 4 DLR (4th) 746, 9 CCC (3d) 173, 36 CR (3d) 346 (BCSC), affirmed, (1984) 1984 CarswellBC 532 (CA), affirmed, (sub nom. *Carter* v. *R.*) [1986] 1 SCR 981; *Ville de Québec* v. *Commission des droits de la personne*, [1989] RJQ 831, 11 CHRR D/500 (CA), leave to appeal refused, (1989) 103 NR 160 (note) (SCC); *R.* v. *Bear*, [1986] AJ 848 (JCPC); *Thomson Newspapers Ltd.* v. *Director of Investigation and Research*, (1986) 54 OR (2d) 143

An analogous relationship between the international conventions and provincial legislation has also been noted in several judgments,[276] although one decision says that "[t]he non-Charter use of international human rights laws is less settled".[277] Judge Michèle Rivet, president of the Quebec Human Rights Tribunal, set out the role of international law in the interpretation of the Quebec *Charter of Human Rights and Freedoms* in terms that evoke those of Chief Justice Dickson:

> Le recours aux instruments internationaux aux fins d'interprétation des dispositions de la charte québécoise tire essentiellement sa pertinence de la similarité de langage entre ces documents, de l'inscription de la charte québécoise dans un contexte international d'affirmation, de promotion et de protection des droits et libertés de la personne, de la référence explicite faite aux formes internationales pertinentes lors des travaux préparatoires à l'adoption et à la

---

(HC), reversed, (1986) 1986 CarswellOnt 139 (CA), affirmed, (1990) 1990 CarswellOnt 991 (SCC) at 171 (OR); *Transpacific Tours Ltd.* v. *Director of Investigation and Research, Combines Investigation Act*, [1986] 2 WWR 34, 8 CPR (3d) 325, 25 DLR (4th) 202 (BC SC), at 48-49 (WWR). See also comments on this point in Daniel Turp, *supra* note 265, at 366-367.

276   *Ford* v. *A-G du Québec*, [1985] CS 147, 18 DLR (4th) 711, affirmed, (1986) 36 D.L.R. (4th) 374 (CA), affirmed, [1988] 2 SCR 712, 54 DLR (4th) 577, 19 QAC 69, 36 CRR 1, 90 NR 84, 10 CHRR D/5559: "We can certainly assume, at least as far as s. 3 is concerned, that the Quebec legislature did not create the *Charter* without external inspiration which must have included some, if not all, of the preceding texts." In *Devine* v. *P.-G. Québec*, [1982] CS 355, Justice Dugas of the Quebec Superior Court stated that the *Universal Declaration of Human Rights*, the *International Covenant on Civil and Political Rights* and the *European Convention on Human Rights* were all models for the Quebec *Charter of Rights and Freedoms*, RSQ, c. C-12 (at pp. 375-376). The explanatory notes accompanying the original draft articles of the Quebec *Charter*, proposed by F.R. Scott, Jean Beetz, G. LeDain and Jacques-Yvan Morin as amendments to the *Civil Code*, refer in a general way to the *Convention for the Prevention and Punishment of the Crime of Genocide*, the *Universal Declaration of Human Rights* and the *Charter* of the *United Nations* and indicate that section 5 of the Quebec *Charter* (the right to privacy) is directed inspired by article 12 of the *Universal Declaration*: Civil Code Revisions Office, *Report of the Civil Rights Committee*, Quebec City, 1966. In *Wong* v. *Hughes Petroleum Ltd* (1983), 28 Alta LR (2d) 155, 46 AR 276, 4 CHRR D/1488 (Q.B.), the Court noted similarities between section 10 of the Quebec *Charter* and article 1 of the *International Convention on the Elimination of All Forms of Racial Discrimination*. See also, on provincial codes and charters, *Canadian Odeon Theatres Ltd.* v. *Saskatchewan Human Rights Commission and Huck*, 18 DLR (4th) 93, (Sask CA), leave to appeal refused [1985] 1 SCR vi (note).

277   *Gould* v. *Yukon Order of Pioneers*, (1991) 87 DLR (4th) 618, 14 CHRR D/176 (YTSC), affirmed, (1993) 100 DLR (4th) 596 (YTCA), affirmed, [1996] 1 SCR 571, at D/188 [CHRR].

modification de la charte, et de la présomption de compatibilité du droit canadien à nos obligations.[278]

In a case respecting construction of section 10 of the Quebec *Charter of Human Rights and Freedoms*,[279] Justice Nichols of the Quebec Court of Appeal cited Marc Bossuyt's seminal study of discrimination in international human rights law[280] in defence of an approach based on "effects" rather than "intention". Justice Nichols observed that section 10, and the Quebec *Charter* more generally, were inspired by the international instruments: ". . .les articles 10 et 19 de la *Charte* [québécoise] nous viennent des instruments internationaux".[281] Justice Rousseau-Houle of the Quebec Court of Appeal described the Quebec *Charter* as a "prolongement" of international human rights law, although she took care to note that this did not constitute "la réception formelle, en droit interne" of international norms.[282]

In *Gosselin*, the Supreme Court of Canada debated the relationship between international human rights law and section 45 of the Quebec *Charter*, which states: "Every person in need has a right, for himself and his family, to measures of financial assistance and to social measures provided for by law, susceptible of ensuring such person an acceptable standard of living." In the Quebec Court of Appeal, Chief Justice Robert had written: "section 45 of the Quebec *Charter* thus bears a very close resemblance to article 11 of the *International Covenant on Economic, Social and Cultural Rights*" which mandates "a minimum core obligation to ensure the satisfaction of, at the very least, minimum essential levels [of subsistence needs and the provision of basic services]".[283] Justice L'Heureux-Dubé, dissenting, citing these remarks, wrote:

I am also in agreement that the Quebec *Charter* [TRANSLATION] "was intended to establish a domestic law regime that reflects Canada's international

278 *Dufour* v. *Centre hospitalier St-Joseph-de-la-Malbaie*, [1992] RJQ 825 (TDPQ), reversed (1998) 1998 CarswellQue 1013 (CA), leave to appeal refused (1999) 249 NR 391n (SCC), at 835. Also: *Commission des droits de la personne du Québec* c. *Commission scolaire de St-Jean-sur-Richelieu*, [1991] RJQ 3003 (TDPQ), varied, [1994] RJQ 227 (CA), at 3024.
279 RSQ, c. C-12.
280 Marc Bossuyt, *L'interdiction de la discrimination dans le droit international des droits de l'homme*, Brussels: Emile Bruylant, 1976. Also cited in: *Commission des droits de la personne du Québec* c. *Commission scolaire de Deux-Montagnes*, [1993] RJQ 1297 (TDPQ), at 1305.
281 *Ville de Québec* v. *Commission des droits de la personne*, *supra* note 275, at D/507, D/509 (CHRR).
282 *Commission scolaire St-Jean-sur-Richelieu* v. *Commission des droits de la personne du Québec*, [1994] RJQ 1227 (CA), at 1234.
283 *Gosselin* v. *Quebec (AG)*, [1999] RJQ 1033, [1999] QJ No 1365 (CA), affirmed, [2002] 4 SCR 429, 221 DLR (4th) 257, 100 CRR (2d) 1, 44 CHRR D/363, at 1092-1093 (English translation by the Supreme Court of Canada).

commitments" (p. 1099) and that (at p. 1101) [TRANSLATION] "the quasi-constitutional right guaranteed by section 45 to social and economic measures susceptible of ensuring an acceptable standard of living includes, at the very least, the right of every person in need to receive what Canadian society objectively considers sufficient means to provide the basic necessities of life."[284]

Justice LeBel, on the other hand, highlighted the distinctions between section 45 and the international text:

> The apparent similarity between s. 45 and Article 11(1) of the Covenant does not necessarily mean that the Quebec legislature intended to entrench the right to an acceptable standard of living in the *Quebec Charter*. In fact, the wording of s. 45 itself seems to negate that possibility. Section 45 does not guarantee the right to an acceptable standard of living, as Article 11(1) does; rather, it guarantees the right to social measures. In my view, that distinction supports the assertion that s. 45 protects a *right of access* to social measures for anyone in need. The fact that anyone in need is entitled not to measures to ensure him or her an acceptable standard of living, but to measures *susceptible* of ensuring him or her that standard of living, is also revealing. It seems to suggest that the legislature did not intend to give the courts the power to review the adequacy of the measures adopted, or to usurp the role of the legislature in that regard.[285]

The historical relationship between the international instruments and ordinary statutes has also won the attention of the courts. In *Bell Canada* v. *Quebec*, Justice Beetz of the Supreme Court of Canada observed that international treaties dealing with labour law "are the basis of contemporary legislation in occupational health and safety".[286] The United Nations Human Rights Committee itself, in its comments on an application from Canadian penitentiary inmates alleging deprivation of the right to vote, noted that Quebec's electoral legislation had been amended in 1979 in order to conform to the requirements of the *International Covenant on Civil and Political Rights*.[287]

While there is much commonality between the contextual approach proposed by Chief Justice Dickson and the historical approach of academic commentators and some judges, it is significant that the Chief Justice did

---

284 *Gosselin* v. *Quebec (Attorney General)*, [1999] RJQ 1033, [1999] QJ No. 1365 (CA), affirmed, [2002] 4 SCR 429, 221 DLR (4th) 257, 100 CRR (2d) 1, 44 CHRR D/363, at para. 148.

285 *Ibid.*, para. 418 (emphasis in the original).

286 *Bell Canada* v. *Québec* [1988] 1 SCR 749, 51 DLR (4th) 161, 85 NR 295, 21 CCEL 1, 15 QAC 217, at 806 (SCR). On the use of international instruments in statutory interpretation, see also *Stanley* v. *Royal Canadian Mounted Police*, (1987) 8 CHRR D/3799 (CHRT).

287 *C.F.* v. *Canada* (No. 113/1981) UN Doc. CCPR/C/OP/2, p. 13, 7 *Human Rights Law Journal* 300, [1986] *Canadian Human Rights Yearbook* 185.

not at all insist upon the role the international instruments played in the drafting of the *Charter*. This is highly important, because it does not fix *Charter* interpretation with respect to the state of international human rights law in 1982, when the *Charter* came into force. An undue emphasis on the specific role of international law in the drafting of the *Charter* may tend to focus the attention of judges on the state of international human rights law on the historic date of 17 April 1982. There have been many significant innovations since 1982, such as the *Second Optional Protocol to the International Covenant on Civil and Political Rights Aiming at Abolition of the Death Penalty*, the *Declaration on the Rights of Persons Belonging to National or Ethnic, Religious and Linguistic Minorities*, the *Convention Against Torture and Other Cruel, Inhuman and Degrading Treatment or Punishment* and the *Convention on the Rights of the Child*. Had Chief Justice Dickson insisted on the historical aspect, as scholars invited him to do, these new instruments might be condemned to insignificance.

Judges will sometimes recognize the "similarity of language" between various international instruments and the *Charter*,[288] or simply describe them as "useful".[289] Frequently the international instruments and cases are presented as a form of background material, like a volume of legal scholarship or *doctrine*, without any indication or suggestion as to whether or not they apply, and under what basis.[290] On the other hand, the courts have

---

288 *Canada v. Operation Dismantle Inc.*, [1983] 1 FC 745, 3 DLR (4th) 193, 49 NR 363, 39 CPC 120 (CA), affirmed, [1985] 1 SCR 441; *R. v. Videoflicks Ltd.*, (1984) 14 DLR (4th) 10, 15 CCC (3d) 353, 34 RPR 97, 9 CRR 193, 48 OR (2d) 395, (sub nom. *Edwards Books & Art Ltd. v. R.*) 5 OAC 1 (CA), reversed, (1986) 1986 CarswellOnt 1012 (SCC); *International Fund for Animal Welfare Inc., Best and Davies v. Canada*, [1989] 1 FC 335, 83 NR 303, 35 CRR 359 (CA); *Union of Bank Employees (Ont.), Loc. 2104 v. Bank of Montreal*, (1985) 10 CLRBR (NS) 129, 61 di 83 (Can LRB); *Reference Re Public Service Employee Relations Act (Alberta)*, [1987] 1 RCS 313, 51 Alta LR (2d) 97, [1987] 3 WWR 577, (sub nom. *A.U.P.E. v. Alberta (Attorney General)*) 28 CRR 305, 38 DLR (4th) 161, (sub nom. *Reference re Compulsory Arbitration*) 74 NR 99, 78 AR 1, [1987] DLQ 225, 87 CLLC 14,021; *R. v. Oakes*, (1983) 145 DLR (3d) 123, 40 OR (2d) 660, 2 CCC (3d) 339, 32 CR (3d) 193, 3 CRR 289 (CA), affirmed, [1986] 1 SCR 103, 24 CCC (3d) 321, 50 CR (3d) 1, 26 DLR (4th) 200, 53 OR (2d) 719n, 65 NR 87, 19 CRR 308, 14 OAC 335; *Service Employees' International Union, Local 204 v. Broadway Manor Nursing Home*, supra note 264; *Re Trumbley and Fleming*, supra note 270.
289 *Re Luscher and Deputy Minister, Revenue Canada, Customs and Excise*, [1985] 1 FC 85, (1985) 17 DLR (4th) 503, 45 CR (3d) 81, 57 NR 386, [1985] 1 CTC 246, (1985) 15 CRR 167, 9 CER 229 (CA).
290 *R. v. Stiopu*; *Mackay v. R.*, (1984) 8 CRR 216 (Alta QB), affirmed, (1984) 8 CRR 216 at 217n (CA); *R. v. Doucette*, (1985) 38 MVR 113, 33 CR (3d) 345 (NS Prov Ct), affirmed, (June 6, 1986) Doc C.H. 51934/86 (NS Co Ct), leave to appeal refused, (1987) 48 MVR 110 (NS CA), leave to appeal refused, (1987) 210 APR 450n (SCC); *Re Walton and Attorney-General of Canada*, (1984) [1985] 1 WWR 122, 13 DLR (4th) 379, (sub nom. *Walton v. Canada (Attorney General)*) 15 CCC (3d) 65, [1984] NWTR 353 (SC);

also dismissed the applicability of international agreements on the grounds of their process of adoption,[291] or because of textual differences, or simply for a lack of relevant authority on the question at issue,[292] and occasionally because they were not properly proven.[293] In the early years of the *Charter*, some judges have been frankly unimpressed by references to international law, but there is little sign of such sentiments in more recent judgments. Writing in 1986, Justice Jacques of the Quebec Court of Appeal declared that reference to international jurisprudence, and specifically the caselaw of the European Court of Human Rights, constituted a form of "tyranny".[294] In a case dealing with the interpretation of section 2(b) of the *Canadian Charter*, he wrote that it was inappropriate to compare the Canadian provisions with their counterparts in Europe and the United States:

> *[Translation]* Nor is it necessary to refer to the American jurisprudence and the jurisprudence of the European Court. These decisions are made in terms of legal systems which are different from ours, in terms of an historical evolution of law which is different from ours. . .The text of our constitution is clear and it is not necessary to explain it by means of foreign legal decisions based on a constitution different from our own, even if our philosophy and our scale of values is the same. . .
>
> As for what happens in other states, it may have some relevance, as the appellant suggests, but we must not beg the question: because it is done elsewhere, therefore it is reasonable. If that reasoning is valid in deciding whether a restriction which a government imposes here is reasonable, then the same is true for other countries: each one would consider the other's legislation reasonable.

R. v. *Cameron*, [1982] 6 WWR 270, 70 CCC (2d) 532, 29 CR (3d) 73, 39 AR 194, 22 Alta LR (2d) 1, 1 CRR 289 (QB), affirmed, [1983] 2 WWR 671 (CA); *Valente* v. *R.*, (1985) [1985] 2 SCR 673, 24 DLR (4th) 161, 23 CCC (3d) 193, 49 CR (3d) 97, 52 OR (2d) 779, 37 MVR 9, 64 NR 1, 19 CRR 354, 14 OAC 79, [1986] DLQ 85.

291 *R.* v. *Morgentaler*, (1984) 12 DLR (4th) 502, 14 CCC (3d) 258, 41 CR (3d) 193, 47 OR (2d) 353, 11 CRR 116 (HC), affirmed, (1984) 14 C.R.R. 107 (CA).

292 *R.* v. *Smith*, [1987] 1 SCR 1045, [1987] 5 WWR 1, 31 CRR 193, 75 NR 321, 15 BCLR (2d) 273, 58 CR (3d) 193, 34 CCC (3d) 97, 40 DLR (4th) 435.

293 *R.* v. *Keegstra*, (1985) 19 CCC (3d) 254 (Alta QB); *Re Boyd and Earl & Jennie Lohn Ltd.*, (1984) 11 DLR (4th) 265, 47 OR (2d) 111 (HC); *Taylor* v. *Canada Human Rights Commission*, [1987] 3 FC 593, 37 DLR (4th) 577, 78 NR 180, 29 CRR 222, 9 CHRR D/4929 (CA), affirmed, (1990) 1990 CarswellNat 742 (SCC).

294 *Irwin Toy Ltd.* v. *A.-G. Québec*, [1986] RJQ 2441, 32 DLR (4th) 641, 74 CPR (3d) 60, 26 CRR 193, 3 QAC 285 (CA), reversed, [1989] 1 SCR 927, 39 CRR 193, 25 CPR (3d) 417, 58 DLR (4th) 577, 94 NR 167, 24 QAC 2 at 2456 [RJQ]; also: *Asencios* v. *R.*, (1987) 56 CR (3d) 344 (Que CA), at 345.

> Our Charter of Rights and Freedoms has had the effect of liberating us from the "tyranny of the majority". We must not, in interpreting it, create another "tyranny of the majority", that of other states.[295]

These views are remarkably similar to those expressed quite recently, by Justice Antonin Scalia of the United States Supreme Court.[296] But these are marginal opinions.

The interpretative approach to international human rights sources that first espoused by Canadian courts in the early 1980s may have seemed anomalous to some observers at the time. Perhaps because they were already inured to foreign legal sources because of their colonial past, Canadian judges turned to others for guidance instead of looking for their own indigenous perspectives. But this could also be perceived as a reflection of a spirit of pluralism, of the open minds of jurists looking for the best and the fairest solutions to legal problems. Be that as it may, it has increasingly become clear that Canadian judges were at the lead of a worldwide movement within the judiciary. The phenomenon has been variously described as "transjudicial pluralism",[297] "transnational judicial dialogue",[298] "transnational legal process"[299] and "judicial globlization".[300] One important new tribunal to take the lead from the Canadian caselaw was the Constitutional Court of South Africa, created as part of the post-*apartheid* transition. In its very first decision, the South African Court borrowed from the constitutional analysis of the Supreme Court of Canada dealing with limitations on fun-

---

295 *Irwin Toy Ltd.* v. *A.-G. Québec, ibid.*, at 662-663 (DLR). See also: *Danielson* v. *Sterba*, [1985] 1 FC 821 (TD).

296 "I do not believe that approval by 'other nations and peoples' should buttress our commitment to American principles any more than, [. . .] disapproval by 'other nations and peoples' should weaken that commitment. What these foreign sources 'affirm', [. . .] is the justices' own notion of how the world ought to be, and their diktat that it shall be so henceforth in America," wrote Justice Scalia dissenting in *Roper* v. *Simmonds*, 125 SCt 1183, 1229 (2005).

297 Anne-Marie Slaughter, "A Typology of Transjudicial Communication", (1994) 29 *University of Richmond Law Review* 99.

298 Melissa A. Waters, "Mediating Norms and Identity: The Role of Transnational Judicial Dialogue in Creating and Enforcing International Law", (2005) 93 *Georgetown Law Journal* 487.

299 Harold Hongju Koh, "Transnational Legal Process", (1996) 75 *Nebraska Law Review* 181; Mary Ellen O'Connell, "New International Legal Process", (1999) 93 *American Journal of International Law* 334.

300 Claire L'Heureux-Dubé, "The Importance of Dialogue: Globalization and the International Impact of the Rehnquist Court", (1998) 34 *Tulsa Law Journal* 15; Anne-Marie Slaughter, "Judicial Globalization", (2000) 40 *Virginia Journal of International Law* 1103; Karen Knop, "Here and There: International Law in Domestic Courts", (2000) 32 *New York University Journal of International Law & Policy* 501; Paul Schiff Berman, "The Globalization of Jurisdiction", (2002) 151 *University of Pennsylvania Law Review* 311.

damental rights.[301] Justice Albie Sachs of the South African Constitutional Court, expressed this globalist philosophy with specific reference to United States decisions:

> I draw on statements by certain United States Supreme Court Justices [not because] I treat their decisions as precedents to be applied in our Courts, but because their *dicta* articulate in an elegant and helpful manner problems which face any modern court [. . .] Thus, though drawn from another legal culture they express values and dilemmas in a way which I find most helpful in elucidating the meaning of our own constitutional text.[302]

Indeed, Canadian jurisprudence under the *Charter* is now cited by courts around the world.[303] The so-called *Oakes* test for the analysis of section 1 of the *Charter*, itself derived from international caselaw, has been considered by foreign courts on numerous occasions.[304] Canadian judicial decisions have even been referred to in several judgments of the European Court of Human Rights, a generous gesture given that it was the Canadian courts that opened the eyes of many courts and judges to the relevance of European caselaw in the interpretation of their own national constitutions.[305]

---

301 *State* v. *Zuma and the Two Others*, Constitutional Court Case No. CCT/5/94 (5 April 1995), para. 15, citing *R.* v. *Big M Drug Mart Ltd*, [1985] 1 SCR 295, 18 DLR (4th) 321, 18 CCC (3d) 385, [1985] 3 WWR 481, 37 Alta LR (2d) 97, 58 NR 81, 60 AR 161, 13 CRR 64, 85 CLLC 14,023.

302 *State* v. *Lawrence*, 1997 (4) SALR 1176, at 1223.

303 For example: *Kartinyeri* v. *Commonwealth*, [1998] AILR 15; (1998) 3 AILR 180, 195 CLR 337 (HC Australia); *Re Chinamasa*, (2001) 9 BHRC 519 (Supreme Court, Zimbabwe); *Darmalingum* v *State*, (2000) 8 BHRC 662 (JCPC); *Banana* v. *State*, (2000) 8 BHRC 345 (Supreme Court, Zimbabwe); *Starrs* et al. v. *Procurator Fiscal (Linlithgow)*, (1999) 8 BHRC 1 (High Court of Justiciary, Scotland); *South African National Defence Union* v. *Minister of Defence* et al., (1999) 6 BHRC 574 (Constitutional Court, South Africa); *National Coalition for Gay and Lesbian Equality* et al. v. *Minister of Justice* et al., (1998) 6 BHRC 127 (Constitutional Court, South Africa); *Brown* et al. v. *Classification Review Board*, (1997) 5 BHRC 619 (Federal Court of Australia, Victorian District Registry); *Quilter* et al. v. *Attorney General of New Zealand*, (1997) 3 BHRC 461 (Court of Appeal, New Zealand); *Washington* et al. v. *Glucksberg* et al, (1997) 2 BHRC 539 (United States Supreme Court); *Abuki* v. *Attorney General of Uganda*, (1997) 3 BHRC 199 (Constitutional Court, Uganda); *Sookermany* v. *Director of Public Prosecutions of Trinidad and Tobago* et al., (1996) 1 BHRC 348 (Court of Appeal, Trinidad and Tobago); *Austin* v. *Commonwealth*, [2003] HCA 3.

304 *Re Employment Equality Bill 1996*, (1997) 4 BHRC 91 (Supreme Court, Ireland); *Case* et al. v. *Minister of Safety and Security* et al.; *Curtis* v. *Minister of Safety and Security* et al., (1996) 1 BHRC 541 (Constitutional Court, South Africa).

305 *Hirst* v. *United Kingdom* (No. 2) (App. No. 74025/01), 6 October 2005, paras. 35-37; *G.B.* v. *Bulgaria* (App. No. 42346/98), 11 March 2004, para. 62; *Iorgov* v. *Bulgaria* (App. No. 40653/98), 11 March 2004, para. 62; *Morris* v. *United Kingdom* (App. No. 38784/97), 26 February 2002, paras. 33-35; *Pretty* v. *United Kingdom* (App. No. 2346/02), 29 April 2002, para. 66; *Allan* v. *United Kingdom* (App. No. 48539/99), 5 November

Eventually, even the United States Supreme Court, which was one of the most resistant to this trend, began to refer to international authorities. In *Lawrence* v. *Texas*, which dealt with the right to engage in consensual homosexual conduct, Justice Kennedy, who wrote for the majority, referred to decisions of the European Court of Human Rights as evidence of its acceptance "as an integral part of human freedom in many other countries".[306] In the same case, dissenting Justice Antonin Scalia expressed shock at a contemporary ruling of the Ontario Court of Appeal authorising same-sex marriages, but the pioneering words of Justice Kennedy were echoed in subsequent decisions. In *Atkins*, the United States Supreme Court ruled that imposition of the death penalty on the mentally disabled was unconstitutional, referring to the views of "the world community".[307] Several international human rights treaties, including the *Convention on the Rights of the Child*, which the United States has yet to ratify, were invoked by the majority of the Court in support of its decision to prohibit execution of persons for crimes committed while under the age of eighteen.[308]

In its periodic reports to the Human Rights Committee, pursuant to article 40 of the *International Covenant on Civil and Political Rights*, Canada has explained the penchant of its judges for the use of international law in *Charter* interpretation:

> Since Canada's second and third reports on the Covenant there have been many cases relying upon the Covenant as an aid to interpreting the Canadian Charter of Rights and Freedoms, both for the purpose of determining ambit of Charter rights and freedoms, and whether limitations on them are acceptable within the terms of section 1 (reasonable limits) of the Charter. For example, in R. v. Brydges, the Supreme Court of Canada referred to article 14 (3) (d) of the Covenant in concluding that section 10 (b) of the Charter, which guarantees the right to retain and instruct counsel, includes the right to be informed of the availability of legal aid counsel (see annex 1 for case citations). In R. v. Keegstra, the Court referred to articles 19 and 20 to conclude that the prohibition against the wilful promotion of hatred in the Criminal Code was a reasonable limit on the Charter guarantee of freedom of expression. The Court pointed out that "a value enjoying status as an international human right is generally to be ascribed a high degree of importance under s. 1 of the Charter" (p. 750).[309]

2002, paras. 30-32, 51; *Appleby* et al. v. *United Kingdom* (App. No. 44306/98), 6 May 2003, para. 31.

306 *Lawrence* v. *Texas*, 539 US 558, 577 (2003), citing: *Dudgeon* v. *United Kingdom*, 23 September 1981, Series A, No. 45, 4 EHRR 149, 67 ILR 345; *Norris* v. *Ireland*, 26 October 1988, Series A, No. 142; *Modinos* v. *Cyprus*, 22 April 1993, Series A, No. 259.

307 *Atkins* v. *Virginia*, 536 US 304, 122 SCt 2242, 153 LEd2d 335 (2002).

308 *Roper* v. *Simmonds*, *supra* note 296.

309 "Fourth periodic report, Canada", UN Doc. CCPR/C/103/Add.5, paras. 8-9.

3

International Human Rights Law Sources

International law, according to *Black's Law Dictionary*, is "[t]he law which regulates the intercourse of nations; the law of nations. The Customary law which determines the rights and regulates the intercourse of independent nations in peace and war."[1] The definition, rooted in the history of nation states, might once have been appropriate but it is no longer entirely accurate. International law in the late twentieth century also determines the rights and freedoms of individuals and "peoples". It governs how States behave towards both citizens and aliens within their jurisdiction, and even, according to the most contemporary interpretations, how they act with respect to persons in territories that they occupy or in countries with which they are at war. It enables individuals to "appeal" from breaches of fundamental rights and freedoms to international "courts", some of which may impose sanctions and all of which enjoy a powerful moral authority. It even establishes crimes for which individuals who violate the human rights of others may be punished, by national as well as by international criminal courts.

Within the State's own jurisdiction, international human rights law also has an important influence on the interpretation and scope of domestic protections of human rights. In some cases, it has been directly incorporated or adopted into domestic law. More commonly, domestic courts are influenced in their construction of statutes and constitutional provisions by international instruments and jurisprudence. Moreover, the State may also be obliged to render account on human rights matters to international bodies, to justify the conformity of its legislation with international human rights law, to explain how individuals are protected from violations of their rights

---

1 *Black's Law Dictionary*, St. Paul, Minn: West Publishing, 1979, at 733.

and freedoms, and to report on what legislative changes have been made in response to international criticism. Canada is undoubtedly one of the world's best examples of this synergy between international and domestic law.

This legal transformation has taken place essentially since the Second World War. The *Charter of the United Nations*, adopted in June 1945 in the concluding days of the world's most devastating conflict, ascribed an important role in the protection of human rights to the fledgling organization.[2] Three years later, the General Assembly adopted the *Universal Declaration of Human Rights*,[3] and this in turn generated literally hundreds of treaties and declarations. At the same time of its adoption, the *Charter of the United Nations* also paid tribute to state sovereignty, affirming that the United Nations had no role to play in matters that were essentially of domestic jurisdiction.[4] This initial ambiguity defined the nascent human rights system. During the contemporaneous development of the International Military Tribunal, which was to sit in Nuremberg, the United States negotiator Robert Jackson explained: "It has been a general principle of foreign policy of our Government from time immemorial that the internal affairs of another government are not ordinarily our business; that is to say, the way Germany treats its inhabitants, or any other country treats its inhabitants is not our affair any more than it is the affair of some other government to interpose itself in our problems."[5] But in the six decades since 1945, international law has evolved dramatically. The international community has assumed an increasingly broad participation in matters that were previously considered to be the prerogative of sovereign States. The body of norms that has grown up to regulate this development is described as "international human rights law".

International human rights law is now studied in conjunction with two cognates, international humanitarian law and international criminal law. The term international humanitarian law is generally used to describe what were historically called the laws of armed conflict. According to the Appeals Chamber of the International Criminal Tribunal for the former Yugoslavia, the concept of international humanitarian law "emerged as a result of the

2 *Charter of the United Nations*, [1945] CTS 7, preamble, arts. 1(3), 13(1)(b) 55(c) 56, 68, 76(c). See: A. Petrenko, "The Human Rights Provisions of the United Nations Charter", (1978) 9 *Manitoba Law Journal* 53; Egon Schwelb, "The International Court of Justice and the Human Rights Clauses of the Charter", (1972) 66 *American Journal of International Law* 336.
3 *Universal Declaration of Human Rights*, GA Res. 217 A (III) UN Doc. A/810.
4 *Charter of the United Nations*, *supra* note 2, art. 2(7).
5 "Minutes of Conference Session of July 23, 1945", in *Jackson, United States Representative to the International Conference on Military Trials*, Washington: U.S. Government Printing Office, 1949, pp. 328-347, at 331.

influence of human rights doctrines on the law of armed conflict".[6] International criminal law governs the prosecution of serious violations of human rights, generally because the States where the crimes were committed have been unwilling or unable to bring the perpetrators to justice.

3.1   The League of Nations: First Steps Towards a Universal System

Our modern system of international human rights law begins with the close of the First World War. In his fourteen points, United States President Woodrow Wilson promoted a new world order, much of it a response to threats of socialist revolution coming from Russia and central Europe.[7] To the crumbling system of colonial empires, Wilson promoted the protection of minorities and the right of self-determination. When Lenin called for a worker's state, Wilson answered with a pledge of international norms governing labour and working conditions. As a result, the treaties that concluded the conflict contained provisions creating obligations not only among sovereign states but also of states towards individuals and, moreover, of individuals towards other individuals. Several important areas were addressed in these treaties, including the protection of minorities, the rights of labour and individual criminal liability for breaches of war crimes. Subsequently, the League of Nations began to explore new areas, such as the rights of the child.[8] The aftermath of the First World War also brought important strides towards an international protection regime for refugees.

The breakup of the Austro-Hungarian, German and Russian empires resulted in the creation of several new states, notably Poland, Czechoslovakia and Yugoslavia. Within these countries were significant national minorities, some of them associated with the former imperial states of Germany and Hungary, others, such as the Jews, having no such "kin state" within Europe. The treaties creating the new states contained elaborate provisions dealing with the protection of such minorities, including their rights to use their own language, to practice their own religion, to deal with the public administration in their own language and to educate their children in their mother tongue. According to the Permanent Court of International Justice, the minorities treaties were intended to "secure for certain elements incorporated in a State, the population of which differs from them in race, language or religion, the possibility of living peaceably alongside that pop-

---

6 *Prosecutor* v. *Tadić* (Case No. IT-94-1-AR72), Decision on the Defence Motion for Interlocutory Appeal on Jurisdiction, 2 October 1995, para. 87.

7 Anthony Whelan, "Wilsonian Self Determination and the Versailles Settlement", (1994) 43 *International and Comparative Law Quarterly* 99.

8 *Declaration on the Rights of the Child*, League of Nations OJ Spec. Supp. 21, p. 43, 26 September 1924.

ulation and co-operating amicably with it, while at the same time preserving the characteristics which distinguish them from the majority, and satisfying the ensuing special needs".[9] Hersh Lauterpacht said that "the system of Minorities Treaties failed to afford protection in many cases of flagrant violation and although it acquired a reputation for impotence, with the result that after a time the minorities often refrained from resorting to petitions in cases where a stronger faith in the effectiveness of the system would have prompted them to seek a remedy".[10]

For example, article 2 of the *Treaty of Peace Between the United States of America, the British Empire, France, Italy and Japan, and Poland* declares: "Poland undertakes to assure full and complete protection of life and liberty to all inhabitants of Poland without distinction of birth, nationality, language, race or religion."[11] Similar provisions appear in the post-war treaties governing Romania,[12] Czechoslovakia[13] and Yugoslavia.[14] The *Treaty of Saint-Germain-en-Laye* protects "life and liberty, without distinction of birth, nationality, language, race or religion".[15] Mechanisms were created by which aggrieved members of the minorities in central and eastern Europe could petition the League of Nations, and these eventually led to several important judgments of the Permanent Court of International Justice that address issues concerning minorities and that remain, to this day, extremely relevant.[16] The minority rights protection system was exploited, in the 1930s, by the Germans, and their association with irredentist movements eventually discredited the whole regime. Nevertheless, the treaty obligations appear to have hampered Hitler's racist schemes, at least in their early days, and arguably were responsible for the mitigation of some degree of human

---

9   *Minority Schools in Albania*, Advisory Opinion, 6 April 1935, PCIJ Series A/B, No. 64, p. 17.

10 Hersh Lauterpacht, *An International Bill of the Rights of Man*, New York: Columbia University Press, 1945, p. 219.

11 [1919] TS 8.

12 *Treaty between the Principal Allied and Associated Powers and Roumania*, (1921) 5 LNTS 336, art. 1.

13 *Treaty between the Principal Allied and Associated Powers and Czechoslovakia*, [1919] TS 20, art. 1.

14 *Treaty between the Principal Allied and Associated Powers and the Serb-Croat-Slovene State*, [1919] TS 17, art. 1.

15 [1919] TS 11, art. 63.

16 *Rights of Minorities in Upper Silesia (Minority Schools)* PCIJ, Series A, No. 15; *German Settlers in Poland*, PCIJ Series B, No. 6; *Acquisition of Polish Nationality*, PCIJ Series B., No. 7; *Access to German Minority Schools in Upper Silesia*, Series A-B, No. 40; *Minority Schools in Albania*, Advisory Opinion, 6 April 1935, PCIJ Series A/B, No. 64; *Advisory Opinion of 31 July 1930 on the Greco-Bulgarian Community*, PCIJ, Series B, No. 17. See: Nathan Feinberg, "La juridiction et la jurisprudence de la Cour permanente de Justice internationale en matière de mandats et de minorités", [1937] I *Receuil de cours de l'Academie de droit international* 592.

suffering for a time. In Upper Silesia, for example, the Nazis delayed introduction of racist laws because this would have violated the applicable international norms. Jews in the region, protected by a bilateral treaty between Poland and Germany, were sheltered from the Nuremberg laws and continued to enjoy equal rights, at least until the convention's expiry in 1937.[17] The minorities treaties are one of the forerunners of the modern international human rights legal system. The system collapsed prior to the outbreak of World War II. Minority rights, as a subject of concern for human rights, fell somewhat into abeyance as a result, and it was not until the 1980s and 1990s that their significance became firmly established within international human rights law.[18]

The *Treaty of Versailles*[19] created the International Labour Organization, and listed, in article 427, a series of important norms concerning the rights of labour:

> The High Contracting Parties, recognizing that the well-being, physical, moral and intellectual, of industrial wage-earners is of supreme international importance, have framed, in order to further this great end, the permanent machinery provided for in Section I associated with that of the League of Nations.
>
> They recognize that differences of climate, habits, and customs, of economic opportunity and industrial tradition, make strict uniformity in the conditions of

---

17 Jacob Robinson, *And the Crooked Shall be Made Straight*, New York: MacMillan, 1965, pp. 72-73.

18 On the minorities treaties generally, see: F. Capotorti, *Study on the Rights of Persons Belonging to Ethnic, Religious and Linguistic Minorities*, UN Doc. E/CN.4/Sub.2/384/ Add.1-7, U.N. Sales No. E.78.XIV.I; Patrick Thornberry, *International Law and the Rights of Minorities*, Oxford: Clarendon Press, 1991; P. de Azcarate, *League of Nations and National Minorities*, Washington: Carnegie Endowment for International Peace, 1945.

19 Canada signed the *Treaty of Versailles* on 28 June 1919, and it came into force the same day as a result of ratification by the United Kingdom, on behalf of Canada. Canada subsequently adopted implementing legislation: *Treaties of Peace Act, 1919*, SC 1919 (2nd sess.) v. 30. The *Treaty of Versailles* is cited in: *Re Legislative Jurisdiction Over Hours of Labour*, [1925] SCR 505, [1925] 3 DLR 1114; *Reference Re Weekly Rest in Industrial Undertakings Act*, [1936] SCR 461, [1936] 3 DLR 673, amended, (1937) 1937 CarswellNat 2 (Canada P.C.); *AG Canada* v. *AG Ontario Labour Conventions Case*, [1937] AC 326, [1937] 1 DLR 673, [1937] 1 WWR 299 (Canada P.C.); *Re Alberta Union of Provincial Employees and the Crown in Right of Alberta*, (1981) 120 DLR (3d) 590, 81 CLLC 14,089 (Alta QB), affirmed, (1981) 1981 CarswellAlta 553 (CA), leave to appeal refused, (1981) 130 DLR (3d) 191 (note) (SCC); *Cominco Ltd.*, (1980) 40 di 75 (CLRB); *Service Employees' International Union, Local 204* v. *Broadway Manor Nursing Home*, (1983) 4 DLR (4th) 231, 44 OR (2d) 392, 10 CRR 37 (Div Ct), reversed, (1984) 1984 CarswellOnt 829 (CA), leave to appeal refused, (1985), 8 OAC 320n (SCC); *R.* v. *Finta*, (1989) 50 CCC (3d) 236, 64 CR (3d) 223, 44 CRR 23 (Ont HC), additional reasons at, (1987) 50 CCC 236 (Ont HC); *R.* v. *Finta, (*1992) 92 DLR (4th) 1 (Ont CA), affirmed, [1994] 1 SCR 701, 88 CCC (3d) 417, 112 DLR (4th) 513, 150 NR 370.

labour difficult of immediate attainment. But, holding as they do, that labour should not be regarded merely as an article of commerce, they think that there are methods and principles for regulating labour conditions which all industrial communities should endeavour to apply, so far as their special circumstances will permit.

Among these methods and principles, the following seem to the High Contracting Parties to be of special and urgent importance:

First – The guiding principle above enunciated that labour should not be regarded merely as a commodity or article of commerce.

Second – The right of association for all lawful purposes by the employed as well as by the employers.

Third – The payment to the employed of a wage adequate to maintain a reasonable standard of life as this is understood in their time and country.

Fourth – The adoption of an eight hours day or a forty-eight hours week as the standard to be aimed at where it has not already been attained.

Fifth – The adoption of a weekly rest of at least twenty-four hours, which should include Sunday wherever practicable.

Sixth – The abolition of child labour and the imposition of such limitations on the labour of young persons as shall permit the continuation of their education and assure their proper physical development.

Seventh – The principle that men and women should receive equal remuneration for work of equal value.

Eighth – The standard set by law in each country with respect to the conditions of labour should have due regard to the equitable economic treatment of all workers lawfully resident therein.

Ninth – Each State should make provision for a system of inspection in which women should take part, in order to ensure the enforcement of the laws and regulations for the protection of the employed.

Without claiming that these methods and principles are either complete or final, the High Contracting Parties are of opinion that they are well fitted to guide the policy of the League of Nations; and that, if adopted by the industrial communities who are members of the League, and safeguard in practice by an adequate system of such inspection, they will confer lasting benefits upon the wage-earners of the world.[20]

The International Labour Organization survived the Second World War – it was housed temporarily at McGill University in Montreal during the conflict – and it continues to play a considerable role in the development of

---

20 Cited in: *Cominco Ltd.*, *ibid.*

international law. In a general sense, human rights considerations pervade the International Labour Organization conventions, including the *ILO Constitution*, which addresses the issues of equality, freedom of association and freedom of expression.[21] Several post-Second World War conventions directly concern themselves with human rights issues,[22] notably: *I.L.O Convention (No. 87) Concerning Freedom of Association and Protection of the Right to Organize*,[23] *ILO Convention (No. 98) Concerning the Application of the Principles of the Right to Organize and to Bargain Collectively*,[24] *ILO Convention (No. 100) Concerning Equal Remuneration for Men and Women Workers for Work of Equal Value*,[25] *ILO Convention (No. 105) Concerning the Abolition of Forced Labour*,[26] *ILO Convention (No. 111) Concerning Discrimination in Respect of Employment and Occupation*[27] and *ILO Convention (No. 182) Concerning the Prohibition and Immediate Action on the Elimination of the Worst Forms of Child Labour.*

Although Canada has only ratified thirty of the more than 180 International Labour Organization conventions, it is a party to all of the conventions mentioned above, with the exception of *ILO Convention No. 98*. In reply to a question from the United Nations Committee on Economic, Social and Cultural Rights, Canada explained its position with respect to *Convention No. 98*:

> There is a high level of conformity in Canada with the principles of Convention 98, particularly with respect to protections against unfair labour practices. The main obstacle to ratification is the ILO Committee of Experts interpretation that Convention 98 requires all workers, with the exception of the armed forces, the police and "public servants engaged in the administration of the State" to have access to statutory machinery providing for collective bargaining. This is the case for the vast majority of Canadian workers, however, in a number of jurisdictions some specific categories of workers, while entitled to engage in

---

21 *Constitution of the International Labour Organization*, [1946] CTS 48, which was adopted in Montreal on 9 October 1946. The preamble to the *Constitution* speaks of human rights, and the *Philadelphia Declaration* of 10 May 1944, which is annexed to the *Constitution*, deals with equality (art. 1(a)) freedom of expression (art. 1(d)) and freedom of association (art. 3(e)).

22 Wilfred C. Jenks, *Human Rights and International Labour Standards*, New York: Praeger, 1960; David A. Waugh, "The ILO and Human Rights", (1982) 5 *Comparative Labour Law* 186.

23 (1950) 68 UNTS 17, [1973] CTS 14, Cmd. 7628; ratified by Canada 23 March 1972, with entry into force for Canada on 23 March 1973.

24 (1950) 96 UNTS 257.

25 (1953) 165 UNTS 303, [1973] CTS 37.

26 (1959) 320 UNTS 291.

27 (1960) 362 UNTS 31.

collective bargaining with their employers on a voluntary basis, are excluded from industrial relations legislation.[28]

Canada has not ratified *Convention No. 138*, which deals with child labour. According to the government, Canada is not in full compliance with the provisions. In fact, many Canadian jurisdictions do not even have a minimum age below which employment is prohibited. According to Canada,

> Overall, the principles of Convention 138 are respected in all Canadian juris-
> dictions. There are numerous laws and regulations in place restricting the
> employment of children in work likely to be injurious to their life, health,
> education or welfare. Canadian legislation provides for mandatory school at-
> tendance until at least age 16 and limits or restricts the hours of work and the
> kinds of work for which children can be employed. There are also many
> programmes aimed specifically at protecting the health and safety of children.
> However, ratification is not presently being considered because legislation in
> most Canadian jurisdictions does not meet all the specific technical require-
> ments of Convention 138. For example, employment of school-age children is
> not prohibited to the extent required by Convention 138, and in most jurisdic-
> tions children under 13 years are not prohibited from engaging in light, age-
> appropriate work.[29]

Of particular interest is the activity of the ILO in the field of indigenous peoples. It has adopted a series of conventions dealing with the issue, of which the most significant is the *ILO Convention (No. 169) Concerning*

---

28 "List of issues to be taken up in connection with the consideration of the fifth periodic report of Canada concerning the rights referred to in articles 1-15 of the International Covenant on Economic, Social and Cultural Rights (E/C.12/CAN/5), Canada's Responses". See also the answer to a question in Parliament asked by MP Daniel Turp. The Minister of Labour said: "With respect to Convention 98, there is a high level of conformity in Canada to the convention's major principles, which include protection against acts of anti-union discrimination and workers' and employers' interference in each other's affairs, and the encouragement and promotion of voluntary collective bargaining. However, Canada has not ratified Convention 98 because there are some divergencies between the convention's requirements and the Canadian situation. The main obstacle to ratification is that, with the exception of the armed forces and the police and public servants engaged in the administration of the state, Convention 98 does not provide for any exclusions from collective bargaining rights. However, in Canada, a number of jurisdictions exclude some other types of workers, such as agricultural workers and certain professionals, from their collective bargaining legislation. This has been interpreted by the ILO as not being in compliance with Convention 98." HC Debates, 30 April 1999, p. 14949.

29 *Ibid.*

Indigenous and Tribal Peoples in Independent Countries.[30] Canada is not a party to this instrument, although it participated in the negotiations and voted in favour of its adoption by the International Labour Organization in 1989. According to the federal Government, consultations in 1991 between federal, provincial and territorial governments and with representatives of Aboriginal peoples in Canada did not result in a consensus on Canadian ratification. "In particular, there was uncertainty regarding the scope and meaning of the lands and resources provisions, as well as provisions on the administration of justice and education," said the Government in a statement to the United Nations Committee on Economic, Social and Cultural Rights. "Also, some Aboriginal representatives expressed concern that Convention No. 169 does not include recognition of the right to self-determination." Canada has no plans to ratify *Convention No. 169* at the present time.[31]

The Committee on Economic, Social and Cultural Rights has questioned Canada about other ILO conventions that have yet to be ratified by Canada, and has asked it to explain the situation.[32] With respect to the 1919 *Unemployment Convention*, Canada noted in reply that even the International Labour Organization did not consider it to be up to date. As for *Convention No. 29*, dealing with forced or compulsory labour, the government said these were "nonexistent or extremely rare in Canada and could be subject to prosecution under the *Criminal Code* of Canada". It was explained that in November 2005, the *Criminal Code* was amended to add new indictable offences that specifically address trafficking in persons, including for forced labour. Canada was said to be considering ratifying *Convention No. 29*. Concerning *Convention No. 81*, dealing with labour inspection, Canada answered that some jurisdictions may not be fully compliant with all of its specific technical requirements, in particular articles

---

30 ILO, *Official Bulletin*, vol. LXXII, 1989, Ser. A., no. 2, p. 63; entered into force 5 September 1991. Ratifications have been filed by Argentina, Bolivia, Brazil, Colombia, Costa Rica, Denmark, Dominica, Ecuador, Fiji, Guatemala, Honduras, Mexico, Netherlands, Norway, Paraguay, Peru and Venezuela. See: Michael Hudson, "La Convention no. 169 de l'O.I.T. – observation sur son importance et son actualité au Canada", (1989-90) 6 *Revue québecoise de droit international* 98; Lee Swepston, "A New Step in the International Law on Indigenous and Tribal Peoples: The ILO Convention 169 of 1989", (1990) 15 *Oklahoma City University Law Review* 677; Natan Lerner, "The 1989 ILO Convention on Indigenous Populations: New Standards?", (1990) 20 *Israel Yearbook on Human Rights* 223; Natan Lerner, "The 1989 ILO Convention on Indigenous Populations: New Standards?", in Yoram Dinstein & Mala Tabory, eds, *The Protection of Minorities in Human Rights*, Dordrecht: Nijhoff, 1992, p. 213; Russell Barsh, "An Advocate's Guide to the Convention on Indigenous and Tribal Peoples", (1990) 15 *Oklahoma City University Law Review* 209; S. James Anaya, "Indigenous Rights Norms in Contemporary International Law", (1991) 8 *Arizona Journal of International and Comparative Law* 1.

31 "List of issues . . .", *supra* note 28.

32 *Ibid.*, UN Doc. E/C.12/CAN/Q/5, para. 1.

12.1, 20 and 21. It said that ratification was therefore not being considered "at this time". Finally, as regards *Convention No. 102*, which concerns minimum standards for social security, Canada replied that it has a comprehensive social security system including employment insurance and income security programmes. According to Canada, "Convention 102 includes outdated gender stereotypes and is premised on the model of the male breadwinner and male-headed household. This does not reflect current social and labour market realities and is inconsistent with the *Canadian Charter of Rights and Freedoms* and Canadian human rights legislation generally."[33]

In 1998, the International Labour Conference adopted the International Labour Organization *Declaration on Fundamental Principles and Rights at Work*, affirming the principles with respect to fundamental rights that underpin the work of the organization: freedom of association and the effective recognition of the right to collective bargaining; the elimination of all forms of forced or compulsory labour; the effective abolition of child labour; and the elimination of discrimination in respect of employment and occupation.

Reference to the International Labour Organization conventions to which Canada has acceded has been made by Canadian courts, mainly where the interpretation of section 2(d) of the *Canadian Charter* has been at issue,[34] although in the leading case on freedom of association the justices of the Supreme Court of Canada did not mention International Labour Organization sources in their consideration of applicable international law.[35] The Quebec Human Rights Tribunal has cited *ILO Convention (No. 111) Concerning Discrimination in Respect of Employment and Occupation* on sev-

33 *Supra* note 31.
34 *Re Retail,Wholesale and Department Store Union Locals and Government of Saskatchewan*, [1984] 4 WWR 717, 12 DLR (4th) 10, 33 Sask R 219, 84 CLLC 14,061, 10 CRR 1 (QB), reversed, (1985) 1985 CarswellSask 193 (CA), reversed, (1987) 1987 CarswellSask 333 (SCC); *Service Employees' International Union Local 204* v. *Broadway Manor Nursing Home, supra* note 19; *Reference Re Public Service Employee Relations Act (Alberta); Labour Relations Act and Police Officers Collective Bargaining Act*, (1984) [1985] 2 WWR 289, 35 Alta LR (2d) 124, (sub nom. *Reference Re Compulsory Arbitration*) 57 AR 268, 85 CLLC 14,027, 16 DLR (4th) 359 (CA); *Reference Re Public Service Employee Relations Act (Alberta)*, [1987] 1 RCS 313, 51 Alta LR (2d) 97, [1987] 3 WWR 577, (sub nom. *A.U.P.E.* v. *Alberta (Attorney General)*) 28 CRR 305, 38 DLR (4th) 161, (sub nom. *Reference re Compulsory Arbitration*) 74 NR 99, 78 AR 1, [1987] DLQ 225, 87 CLLC 14,021; *RWDSU* v. *Saskatchewan*, [1987] 1 SCR 460, 38 DLR (4th) 277, [1987] 3 WWR 673, 87 CLLC 14,023, 74 NR 321, [1987] DLQ 233 (headnote), 56 Sask R 277; *Syndicat canadien de la fonction publique* v. *PG du Québec*, [1986] RJQ 2983 (SC); *Delisle* v. *Canada (Deputy Attorney General)*, [1999] 2 SCR 989, 176 DLR (4th) 513; *Dunmore* v. *Ontario (Attorney General)*, [2001] 3 SCR 1016, 207 DLR (4th) 193, 13 CCEL (3d) 1, 89 CRR (2d) 189, 154 OAC 201; *Syndicat de la fonction publique* v. *Procurer general du Québec*, [2004] RJQ 524 (SC).
35 *Reference Re Public Service Employee Relations Act, ibid.*

eral occasions.[36] Sometimes, Canadian courts refer to unratified International Labour Organization instruments in much the same way as they invoke other sources of international human rights law that do not bind Canada. For example, in *Dunmore*, the Supreme Court of Canada referred to International Labour Organizations concerning agricultural and rural workers.[37] Justice Bastarache noted that "although provincial jurisdiction has prevented Canada from ratifying Convention No. 11", it provides a "normative foundation for prohibiting *any* form of discrimination in the protection of trade union freedoms".[38]

A number of mechanisms exist within the framework of the International Labour Organization for the implementation of its norms and standards. Members of the organization are required to submit reports every two years on their compliance with the treaties that they have accepted.[39] These are examined by the Committee of Experts on the Application of Conventions and Recommendations. Where the Committee has serious concerns about a State's compliance, it may publish observations in its annual report to the International Labour Conference. In observations on Canada's lack of compliance with *ILO Convention (No. 1) Limiting the Hours of Work in Industrial Undertakings to 8 per Day and 48 per Week*,[40] which Canada ratified in 1935, the following appears:

> The information provided shows the absence of real progress in the implementation of the Convention, particularly at the level of the Provinces, and as regards the determination of the circumstances and limits within which exceptions to the normal hours of work may be allowed, in accordance with Article 6 of the Convention. These matters have been the subject of the Committee's repeated comments for many years, and a new request is being addressed directly to the Government.[41]

---

36 *Dufour* v. *Centre hospitalier St-Joseph-de-la-Malbaie*, [1992] RJQ 825 (TDPQ), reversed (1998) 1998 CarswellQue 1013 (CA), leave to appeal refused (1999) 249 NR 391n (SCC); *Commission des droits de la personne du Québec* v. *Immeubles Ni/Dia Inc.*, [1992] RJQ 2977 (TDPQ); *Commission des droits de la personne du Québec* v. *Commission scolaire Deux-Montagnes*, [1993] RJQ 1297 (TDPQ).

37 *Dunmore* v. *Ontario (Attorney General)*, [2001] 3 SCR 1016, 207 DLR (4th) 193, 13 CCEL (3d) 1, 89 CRR (2d) 189, 154 OAC 201, citing *ILO Convention (No. 11) concerning the Rights of Association and Combination of Agricultural Workers*, (1950) 38 UNTS 153, art. 1, and *ILO Convention (No. 141) concerning Organisations of Rural Workers and Their Role in Economic and Social Development*, ILO Official Bulletin, vol. LVIII, 1975, Series A, No. 1, p. 28, art. 2.

38 *Ibid.*, para. 27 (emphasis in the original).

39 *Constitution of the International Labour Organization*, *supra* note 21, arts. 22, 35.

40 (1949) 38 UNTS 18.

41 International Labour Organization, *Report of the Committee of Experts on the Application of Conventions and Recommendations, Report III (Part 4A)*, Geneva, ILO 1990, at 49.

Other important ILO bodies include the Fact-Finding and Conciliation Commission on Freedom of Association, and the Committee on Freedom of Association. Trade unions, but not individuals, may petition the Freedom of Association Committee. A number of such applications have been made by the Canadian labour movement.[42]

Follow-up on the work of the various committees is undertaken by the ILO Conference Committee on the Application of Conventions and Recommendations. In 1999, the Committee issued a significant comment on Canada's performance with respect to *ILO Convention (No. 87) Concerning Freedom of Association and Protection of the Right to Organize*:

> [T]he Committee observed that for a number of years the Committee of Experts and the Committee on Freedom of Association had been making comments on a number of issues relating to the application of the Convention. These issues included the excessive restrictions on the right of workers' organizations to formulate their programmes without undue interference from the public authorities resulting from federal and/or provincial legislation. The Committee further noted that labour relations legislation in some provinces (Alberta, New Brunswick, Ontario) excluded a number of workers from their coverage, including workers in agriculture and horticulture or domestic workers, thereby denying them the protection provided with regard to the right to organize and to negotiate collectively. The present Committee, like the Committee of Experts, stressed that the guarantees provided under the Convention applied to all workers without distinction whatsoever, and that all workers should enjoy the right to establish and join organizations of their own choosing to further and defend their occupational interests. The Committee further stressed that workers' organizations should enjoy the right to formulate their programmes without interference from the public authorities. The Committee expressed the firm hope that the Government would supply a detailed report to the Committee of Experts on the concrete measures taken to bring its legislation and practice into full conformity with the Convention.[43]

Canadian courts have occasionally referred to the caselaw of the Freedom of Association Committee.[44]

---

42 Brian W. Burkett, "Canada and the ILO: Freedom of Association since 1982", (2003) 10 *Canadian Labour and Employment Law Journal* 231; Michael Bendel, "The International Protection of Trade Union Rights: A Canadian Case Study", (1981) 13 *Ottawa Law Review* 169, at 189-190.

43 International Labour Organization, *Report of the* Committee on the Application of Conventions and Recommendations, Examination of individual case concerning Convention No. 87: Canada, Geneva, ILO 1999.

44 *Re Alberta Union of Provincial Employees and the Crown in Right of Alberta, supra* note 19; *Public Service Alliance of Canada* v. *R.*, [1984] 2 FC 580, 11 DLR (4th) 337, 9 CRR 248 (TD), affirmed, (1984) 11 D.L.R. (4th) 387 (CA), affirmed, [1987] 1 SCR 424; *S.A.C.* v. *Canada*, [1984] 2 FC 889 (CA), affirmed, [1987] 1 SCR 424; *Re Public Service Employee Relations Act, supra* note 34; *Canadian Broadcasting Corp.*, (1990) 83 di 102,

The *Treaty of Versailles* also proposed that a war crimes trial be held by an international tribunal. As part of the preliminary work on the *Versailles Treaty*, the victorious allies had created a Commission on Responsibilities, whose report used the expression "Violations of the Laws and Customs of War and of the Laws of Humanity".[45] Some of these breaches came close to the criminal behaviour now defined as genocide or crimes against humanity and involved the persecution of ethnic minorities or groups. At the Paris Peace Conference itself, Nicolas Politis, Greek Foreign Minister and a member of the Commission of Fifteen, proposed creating a new category of war crimes, designated "crimes against the laws of humanity", intended to cover the massacres of the Armenians.[46] Article 227 of the *Treaty of Versailles* stipulated that Kaiser Wilhelm II was to be tried "for a supreme offence against international morality and the sanctity of treaties". However, the Netherlands refused to extradite the German emperor, on the grounds that the prosecution would violate the principle against retroactive criminal law. Articles 228 to 230 recognized the right of the Allies to try Germans accused of war crimes before "military tribunals composed of members of the military tribunals of the Powers". This was, in effect, the first recognition in international law of an international criminal tribunal.[47] According to the *Treaty of Sèvres*, which was the corresponding treaty concerning the war in Asia Minor, Turkey undertook "to hand over to the Allied Powers the persons whose surrender may be required by the latter as being responsible for the massacres committed during the continuance of the state of war on territory which formed part of the Turkish Empire on the 1st August, 1914", a reference to what we now call the Armenian genocide.

These international military tribunals were to try persons accused of violating the laws and customs of war. The new German government voted to accept the treaty, but conditionally, and it refused the war criminals clauses, noting that the country's penal code prevented the surrender of

---

91 CLLC 16,007 (Can LRB), reconsideration refused, (1991) 1991 CarswellNat 1022 (Can LRB), affirmed, (1992) 1992 CarswellNat 105 (Fed CA), affirmed, (1995) 1995 CarswellNat 265 (SCC).

45 *Violations of the Laws and Customs of War, Reports of Majority and Dissenting Reports of America and Japanese Members of the Commission of Responsibilities, Conference of Paris, 1919*, Oxford: Clarendon Press, 1919, p. 23.

46 Vahakn N. Dadrian, *The History of the Armenian Genocide: Ethnic Conflict from the Balkans to Anatolia to the Caucasus*, 6th ed., New York & Oxford: Berghahn Books, 2003, p. 278.

47 *Treaty of Peace between the Allied and Associated Power and Germany* ("Treaty of Versailles"), [1919] TS 4. There were similar penal provisions in the related peace treaties: *Treaty of St. Germain-en-Laye*, [1919] TS 11, art. 173; *Treaty of Neuilly-sur-Seine*, [1920] TS 5, art. 118; *Treaty of Trianon*, (1919) 6 LNTS 187, art. 15.

Germans to a foreign government for prosecution and punishment.[48] A compromise deemed compatible with article 228 of the *Versailles Treaty* allowed that the Supreme Court of the Empire in Leipzig would judge those charged by the Allies. Germany opposed arraignment of most of those chosen for prosecution by the Allies, arguing that the trial of its military and naval elite could imperil the government's existence.[49] In the end, only a handful of German soldiers were tried, for atrocities in prisoner of war camps and sinking of hospital ships.[50] A Commission of Allied jurists set up to examine the results at Leipzig concluded "that in the case of those condemned the sentences were not adequate".[51] As for the Armenian genocide, the *Treaty of Sèvres* was never ratified by Turkey.[52] It was subsequently replaced by the *Treaty of Lausanne* of 24 July 1923.[53] It included a "Declaration of Amnesty" for all offences committed between 1 August 1914 and 20 November 1922.

It was all a very unsatisfying first venture in international criminal justice. Yet, as Georges Clemenceau reminded his allies when they were initially considering the proposal, "[t]he first tribunal must have been summary and brutal; it was nevertheless the beginning of a great thing".[54]

These initial efforts at international criminal justice were the forerunners of the Nuremberg and Tokyo trials, at the conclusion of the Second World War, and, more recently, of the international criminal tribunals for the former Yugoslavia and Rwanda, and the International Criminal Court. The prosecutions did leave a small legacy in the form of caselaw clarifying important legal issues involved in prosecutions, such as the admissibility of a defense of superior orders. In *Finta*, the majority of the Supreme Court of Canada cited two of the Leipzig decisions as authority for the customary

---

48 George Goldberg, *The Peace to End Peace, The Paris Peace Conference of 1919*, New York: Harcourt, Brace & World: 1969, p. 151.

49 *German War Trials, Report of Proceedings before the Supreme Court in Leipzig*, London: His Majesty's Stationery Office, 1921, p. 19. Also: "Question of International Criminal Jurisdiction, Report by Ricardo J. Alfaro, Special Rapporteur", UN Doc. A/CN.4/15 and Corr. 1, para. 9.

50 James F. Willis, *Prologue to Nuremberg: The Politics and Diplomacy of Punishing War Criminals of the First World War*, Westport, Connecticut: Greenwood Press, 1982; Sheldon Glueck, *War Criminals. Their Prosecution and Punishment*, New York: Knopf, 1944.

51 United Nations War Crimes Commission, *History of the United Nations War Crimes Commission and the Development of the Laws of War*, London: His Majesty's Stationery Office, 1948, p. 48.

52 *Treaty of Sèvres*, [1920] TS 11.

53 *Treaty of Lausanne Between Principal Allied and Associated Powers and Turkey*, (1923) 28 LNTS 11.

54 Arthur S. Link, ed., *The Papers of Woodrow Wilson*, Vol. 56, Princeton: Princeton University Press, 1987, p. 534.

law governing superior orders.[55] The development of international criminal law and its institutions is discussed in greater detail later in this chapter.

The post-First World War period also gave birth to international legal efforts directed at the protection of refugees. In 1921, the League of Nations appointed the Norwegian humanitarian, Fridtjof Nansen, as the first High Commissioner for Refugees. The League was responding to the immediate needs of an estimated one million Russian refugees. In 1923, he undertook a major effort to resettle refugees from the 1922 war between Greece and Turkey. He was also involved in assisting Armenian refugees. Nansen created what was known as the "Nansen passport", a document that enabled thousands of refugees to travel so that they could find a place to reside on a more or less permanent basis. He also negotiated "arrangements" with various countries that led, after his death in 1930, to the adoption of the Refugee Convention of 1933. From 1931, activities were coordinated by the Nansen International Office. In 1939, the League of Nations created the Office of the High Commissioner for Refugees, which was headquartered in London.

With the rise of Nazism, interest soon shifted from the refugees of the previous war to the needs of European Jews fleeing Hitler. Like other Western democracies, Canada showed itself to be indifferent to the needs of those who were fleeing persecution in Europe. In 1939, the ship St. Louis, carrying some 900 Jewish refugees, was denied entry to various Atlantic ports, including those of Canada. It returned to Germany, and most passengers perished in concentration camps.

After the Second World War, the United Nations Relief and Rehabilitation Administration assumed responsibility for an estimated eight million displaced persons, many of whom had been taken prisoner or put to work as slave labourers. It was later replaced by the International Refugee Organization and, in December 1950, the United Nations High Commissioner for Refugees. The mandate of the UNHCR has expanded over the years to include persons who are described as being "of concern", including "internally displaced persons" or IDPs. The latter are often colloquially described as "refugees", but because they are still within the borders of their country of origin they do not meet the legal definition.

---

55 *R.* v. *Finta*, [1994] 1 SCR 701, 88 CCC (3d) 417, 112 DLR (4th) 513, 150 NR 370, citing *Empire* v. *Neumann* (Hospital Ship "Dover Castle") (1921) 21 ILR 429, 16 *American Journal of International Law* 704; *Empire* v. *Dithmar and Boldt* (Hospital Ship "Llandovery Castle"), (1921) 2 ILR 437, 16 *American Journal of International Law* 708.

Canada ratified the the *Convention Relating to the Status of Refugees*[56] on 4 June 1969. According to Justice La Forest,

Underlying the Convention is the international community's commitment to the assurance of basic human rights without discrimination. This is indicated in the preamble to the treaty as follows: Considering that the Charter of the United Nations and the Universal Declaration of Human Rights approved on 10 December 1948 by the General Assembly have affirmed the principle that human beings shall enjoy fundamental rights and freedoms without discrimination.[57]

In *Pushpanathan*, the Supreme Court of Canada said that "[t]he human rights character of the Convention" was further confirmed by section 3 of the *Immigration Act*, which declares that Canadian immigration policy must fulfil Canada's international legal obligations with respect to refugees and uphold its humanitarian tradition with respect to the displaced and the persecuted.[58] At the time of ratification of the *Refugee Convention*, Canada formulated reservations to articles 23 and 24. The withdrawal of these reservations is currently being considered by the Canadian government. A *Protocol* to the *Convention*, adopted in 1967,[59] extended the application of the *Convention* to cases subsequent to those resulting from the Second World War. Canada has also ratified the *Protocol*. Provisions of the *Convention*, and specifically its definition of the term "refugee", have been incorporated into the *Immigration and Refugee Protection Act*.[60] Canada is also a party to the *Constitution of the International Refugee Organization*,[61] and to the *Statute of the Office of the United Nations High Commissioner for Refugees*.[62] One "non-binding" source that has been frequently cited by Canadian courts is the Handbook of the United Nations High Commissioner

56 (1954) 189 UNTS 137, [1969] CTS 7. See: James C. Hathaway, *The Rights of Refugees Under International Law*, Cambridge: Cambridge University Press, 2005; Guy Goodwin-Gill, *The Refugee in International Law*, Oxford: Oxford University Press, 1983; Atle Grahl-Madsen, *The Status of Refugees in International Law*, Leyden: Sijthoff, 1966; S. Aga Khan, "Legal Problems Relating to Refugees and Displaced Persons", (1976) 149 *Recueil de cours de l'Academie de droit international* 287; James C. Hathaway, *The Law of Refugee Status*, Toronto: Butterworths, 1991; Julius H. Grey, *Immigration Law in Canada*, Toronto: Butterworths, 1984; Hélène Lambert, *Seeking Asylum: Comparative Law and Practice in Selected European Countries*, Dordrecht: Kluwer, 1995; François Crépeau, *Droit d'asile, de l'hospitalité aux contrôles migratoires*, Brussels: Éditions Bruylant, 1995.
57 *Canada (AG)* v. *Ward*, [1993] 2 SCR 689, p. 733.
58 *Pushpanathan* v. *Canada (Minister of Citizenship and Immigration)*, [1998] 1 SCR 982, para. 57.
59 (1967) 606 UNTS 267, [1969] CTS 6.
60 SC 2001, c. 27, ss. 2(1), 3(2)(b), 3(3)(f).
61 (1946) 18 UNTS 3, [1946] CTS 47.
62 GA Res. 428(V), [1969] CTS 7.

for Refugees, which provides interpretative guidelines for the *Refugee Convention*.[63] Justice La Forest of the Supreme Court of Canada has stated:

> [W]hile not formally binding upon signatory states such as Canada, the UNHCR Handbook has been formed from the cumulative knowledge available concerning the refugee admission procedures and criteria of signatory states. This much-cited guide has been endorsed by the Executive Committee of the UNHCR, including Canada, and has been relied upon for guidance by the courts of signatory nations. Accordingly, the UNHCR Handbook must be treated as a highly relevant authority in considering refugee admission practices. This, of course, applied not only to the Board but also to a reviewing Court.[64]

But early attempts by Canadian lawyers to argue that domestic tribunals are bound by the terms of the *Convention Relating to the Status of Refugees* have been, with rare exceptions, unsuccessful.[65] Two other treaties dealing with the rights and the protection of stateless persons: the *Convention Relating to the Status of Stateless Persons*,[66] which Canada has not ratified, codifies the rights and obligations of stateless persons, while the *Convention on the Reduction of Statatelessness*[67] requires States parties to confer citizenship on stateless persons in specific cases.

As early as the eighteenth century, international law turned its attention to the scourge of slavery and the slave trade. The campaign against slavery led to the formation of the first great international human rights non-governmental organization, the Anti-Slavery Society, which operates to this day. The first Canadian measures on the subject are a statute enacted by the

---

63   *Handbook on Procedures and Criteria for Determining Refugee Status*, Geneva: Office of the United Nations High Commissioner for Refugees, 1988. Cited in, *e.g.*: *Canada (AG) v. Ward*, *supra* note 57, at 713-714; *Chan v. Canada (Minister of Employment and Immigration)*, [1995] 3 SCR 593, at 620; *Mileva v. Canada*, [1991] 3 FC 398 (CA), at 410-411; *Canada v. Mehmet*, [1992] 2 FC 598, at 608, 611-614, 618; *Ramirez v. Canada*, [1992] 2 FC 306 (CA), at 312-313; *Hailu v. Canada (Minister of Employment and Immigration)*, [1994] FCJ 207 (TD); *Maslova v. Canada (Minister of Citizenship and Immigration)*, (1994) 86 FTR 34; *Orelien v. Canada*, [1992] 1 FC 592, 15 ILR (2d) 1 (CA), at 601-602, 604-605 (CA); *Pushpanathan v. Canada*, *supra* note 58, at para. 53.

64   *Chan v. Canada*, *ibid.*, at 620 (*per* La Forest J.) and at 658-659 (*per* Major J.).

65   *Hurt v. MEI*, [1978] 2 FC 340, 21 NR 525 (CA); *In Re Immigration Act, 1976 and in re Miroslavs*, [1979] 2 FC 82 (TD); *Re Minister of Employment and Hudnik*, [1980] 1 FC 180, 103 DLR (3d) 308 (CA); *Ernewein v. Minister of Employment and Immigration*, [1980] 1 SCR 639, 103 DLR (3d) 1, 14 CPC 264, 30 NR 316; *Dolack v. MMI*, [1982] 1 FC 396 (TD), affirmed [1983] 1 FC 194, 140 DLR (3d) 767, 45 NR 146 (CA); *Vincent v. Minister of Employment and Immigration*, [1983] 1 FC 1057, 148 DLR (3d) 385, 48 NR 214 (CA); *Singh v. Minister of Employment and Immigration*, [1985] 1 SCR 177, 17 DLR (4th) 422, 58 NR 1, 14 CRR 13, 12 Admin LR 137; *Hayer v. Minister of Employment and Immigration*, (1987) 10 FTR 203, 2 Imm LR (2d) 187, 25 Admin LR 136.

66   (1960) 360 UNTS 131.

67   (1975) 989 UNTS 175, [1978] CTS 32.

first legislative assembly of the Province of Upper Canada entitled *An Act to Prevent the further introduction of slaves and to limit the term of Contracts for Servitude within this Province.*[68] The legislation confirmed that it was legal to own slaves but said that the children of slaves, upon reaching the age of twenty-five years, would be liberated. Many freed slaves had come north following the American revolution, having fought with the British in exchange for promises of freedom. They were disappointed with what they found, and large numbers left for Africa to found what is today the state of Sierra Leone. Some of their ancestors still live in Nova Scotia. Slavery was abolished in Canada as a result of British imperial legislation, enacted in 1833.[69] There is no reference to the prohibition of slavery in either the *Canadian Bill of Rights* or the *Canadian Charter*, despite relevant provisions in the *Universal Declaration of Human Rights*[70] and the *International Covenant on Civil and Political Rights.*[71] Probably it was considered superfluous.

Although several nineteenth century treaties contained clauses concerning the slave trade,[72] the first universal instrument on the subject only dates to 1928. The *Slavery Convention* was adopted by the Assembly of the League of Nations on 25 September 1926. It was signed by Canada the same day, and ratified two years later.[73] There are regular claims that slavery continues to be practiced, although no state allows it as a question of policy or law. In recent years, human rights law has turned its attention to what are called "contemporary forms of slavery", which include such practices as trafficking in persons. In 2003, Canada ratified a modern instrument dealing with such "contemporary forms of slavery", the *Protocol to Prevent, Suppress and Punish Trafficking in Persons, Especially Women and Children, Supplementing the United Nations Convention Against Transnational Organized Crime.*[74]

3.2   Human Rights Law and the United Nations

The ideological underpinning of the Allied cause in the Second World War rested on human rights. In his 1941 "state of the union" address, United

---

68   1793 SUC (2nd session), c. 7.
69   *Emancipation Act*, 3 & 4 Wm. IV, c. 73.
70   *Universal Declaration of Human Rights*, GA Res. 217 A (III) UN Doc. A/810, art. 4.
71   *International Covenant on Civil and Political Rights*, (1976) 999 UNTS 171, [1976] CTS 47, art. 8.
72   *e.g., General Act of the Berlin Conference on Central Africa.*
73   *Slavery Convention (1926)*, (1926) 60 LNTS 253, [1928] CTS 5.
74   UN Doc. A/55/383. See: Michael Leir, ed., "Protocol to Prevent, Suppress, and Punish Trafficking in Persons, Especially Women and Children", (2000) 38 *Canadian Yearbook of International Law* 332-334.

States President Franklin D. Roosevelt proclaimed the four freedoms: freedom of opinion, freedom of expression, freedom from fear and freedom from want. His speech is remarkable in that it contains not only the classic liberal political freedoms but also an important economic and social element. The *Charter of the United Nations*, adopted by the Allies in San Francisco in the closing days of the Second World War, inaugurated the system of international human rights law which now comprises both general treaties and declarations and several specialized thematic agreements dealing with such matters as racial discrimination, discrimination against women, torture and the rights of the child. The *Charter* states that one of the purposes of the United Nations is "to achieve international cooperation. . .in promoting and encouraging respect for human rights and fundamental freedoms for all. . ."[75] In the *Secession* Reference, the Supreme Court of Canada cited part of article 1(2) of the *Charter of the United Nations*, noting that one of the purposes of the United Nations was "to develop friendly relations among nations based on respect for the principle of equal rights and self-determination of peoples, and to take other appropriate measures to strengthen universal peace".[76] The Court added: "Article 55 of the U.N. Charter further states that the U.N. shall promote goals such as higher standards of living, full employment and human rights '[w]ith a view to the creation of conditions of stability and well-being which are necessary for

---

75 *Charter of the United Nations*, [1945] CTS 7, art. 1(3).

76 *Reference re Secession of Quebec*, [1998] 2 SCR 217, 161 DLR (4th) 385, 55 CRR (2d) 1, para. 115. The *Charter of the United Nations* has often been cited by Canadian courts: *Re Drummond Wren*, [1945] 4 DLR 674, [1945] OR 778 (HC); *Re Noble and Wolf*, [1948] 4 DLR 123, [1948] OR 579 (HC); *Re Noble and Wolf*, [1949] 4 DLR 375, [1949] OR 503 (CA); *Bhadauria* v. *Board of Governors of Seneca College*, (1980) 105 DLR (3d) 707, 27 OR (2d) 142, 11 CCLT 121, 9 BLR 117, 81 CLLC 14,003 (CA), reversed, [1981] 2 SCR 181, 124 DLR (3d) 193, 2 CHRR D/468, 17 CCLT 106, 81 CLLC 14,117, 22 CPC 130, 14 BLR 157, 37 NR 455; *Board of Governors of Seneca College of Applied Arts and Technology* v. *Bhadauria*, [1981] 2 SCR 181, 124 DLR (3d) 193, 2 CHRR D/ 486, 17 CCLT 106, 81 CLLC ¶14,117, 22 CPC 130, 14 BLR 157, 37 NR 455; *Cameron* v. *Nel-Gor Castle Nursing Home*, (1984) 5 CHRR D/2170, 84 CLLC ¶17,008 (Ont. Comm. Inquiry); *Bancroft* v. *University of Toronto*, (1986) 24 DLR (4th) 620, 53 OR (2d) 460, 21 CRR 269 (HC); *Committee for the Commonwealth of Canada* v. *Canada*, [1991] 1 SCR 139, 77 DLR (4th) 385, 4 CRR 260, 120 NR 241, 40 FTRn, 25 ACWS (3d) 40; *Canada (AG)* v. *Ward*, [1993] 2 SCR 689; *R.* v. *Finta*, *supra* note 55; *Basyony* v. *Canada (Minister of Employment and Immigration)*, (1994) 75 FTR 225, 27 Imm LR (2d) 303; *Thamotharampillai* v. *Minister of Employment and Immigration*, (1994) 77 FTR 114; *Commission des droits de la personne du Québec* v. *Brzozowski*, [1994] RJQ 1447 (HRT); *Commission scolaire St-Jean-sur-Richelieu* v. *Commission des droits de la personne du Québec*, [1994] RJQ 1227 (CA); *Maslova* v. *Canada (Minister of Citizenship and Immigration)*, (1994) 86 FTR 34; *Narvaez* v. *Canada (Minister of Citizenship and Immigration)*, (1995) 89 FTR 94; *Pushpanathan* v. *Canada (Minister of Citizenship and Immigration)*, [1996] 2 FC 49, 191 NR 247 (CA).

peaceful and friendly relations among nations based on respect for the principle of equal rights and self-determination of peoples'."[77] According to article 55 of the *Charter of the United Nations*, members of the United Nations pledge "universal respect for, and observance of, human rights and fundamental freedoms for all".[78] However, the drafters of the *Charter of the United Nations* stopped short of a proposal to include a declaration of human rights, reflecting the tension between those States that sought an active role for the new organization in the protection of human rights and those that hoped to protect their internal policies from prying international eyes.[79]

The human rights activities of the various organs of the United Nations, notably the Human Rights Council (and its forerunner, the Commission on Human Rights) and the Office of the High Commissioner for Human Rights, but also bodies such as the General Assembly, the Security Council and the International Court of Justice, are rooted in the provisions of the *Charter of the United Nations*. For this reason, these mechanisms are often described as being "*Charter*-based", in contrast with other human rights systems that are "treaty-based". These two concepts may seem a bit odd, because the *Charter* is also a treaty. The point here is to distinguish between those aspects of United Nations human rights activity that flow as a natural consequence from membership in the organization, and those human rights obligations that result from the ratification of a particular treaty or convention. Many important human rights conventions have been adopted within the context of the United Nations, usually the result of a drafting process that began in the Commission on Human Rights and proceeded to the General Assembly. Once adopted in the General Assembly, the treaty has then been held out to States for signature, ratification and accession, as they have seen fit. The General Assembly or the Commission on Human Rights might have attempted to incite States to accept the treaty, but they have been under no obligation to do so.

3.2.1   *Charter*-Based Protection of Human Rights

Over the sixty years since the *Charter of the United Nations* was adopted, human rights has moved from the periphery of the organization's activities to its very centre. Although the references to human rights in the *Charter* are important, no fair reading of the original document suggests anything like the important role of human rights that features today in the work of the United Nations. In the *Charter*, specific responsibility for human rights is assigned to the Commission on Human Rights, a specialized organ

---

77   *Reference re Secession of Quebec, ibid.*, para. 116.

78   *Charter of the United Nations, supra* note 75, art. 55.

79   Paul Gorden Lauren, *The Evolution of International Human Rights, Visions Seen*, 2nd ed., Philadelphia: University of Pennsylvania Press, 2003.

of the United Nations subordinate to the Economic and Social Council (or "ECOSOC").[80] The ECOSOC is listed in the *Charter* as one of the principal organs of the United Nations. In practice, however, its role has been greatly overshadowed by that of the other principal organs, the Security Council, the General Assembly, the Secretariat and the International Court of Justice.

In 2005, the Secretary-General of the United Nations proposed a restructuring of the organization in which the Commission on Human Rights would be replaced by a Human Rights Council, and he implied that the appropriate position for such a Council was as a principal organ of the United Nations. States were still unwilling to go so far, however, and in March 2006 the General Assembly agreed to establish a Human Rights Council that is a subsidiary organ, subordinate to the General Assembly.[81]

With the 2006 reform, there are two focal points for human rights activity within the United Nations, the Human Rights Council and the Office of the High Commissioner for Human Rights. Both institutions are based in Geneva. As the organ that replaces the Commission on Human Rights, which played such a crucial role historically in the field of human rights within the United Nations, the Human Rights Council takes on many of its existing functions. The Council is composed of forty-seven Member States who are elected by the General Assembly. In May 2006, Canada was elected as a member of the first Human Rights Council. Members are required to demonstrate a relatively credible profile in respect of human rights, although given the highly politicized nature of the elections in the General Assembly it has proved impossible to ensure full respect for such a criterion in practice. In the first elections, it appears that some states with especially egregious records simply decided not to present themselves as candidates. The Council is to hold a minimum of three sessions each year, in contrast with the Commission on Human Rights, which met once every year for a six-week session and then, very occasionally, in special session.[82]

The General Assembly Resolution that mandates the establishment of the Human Rights Council sets out its responsibilities and functions. The Council is to promote human rights training and education, including technical assistance and capacity-building. It shall serve as a forum for dialogue on thematic issues on all human rights. The Council is empowered to make recommendations to the General Assembly for the further development of international law in the field of human rights. It is also charged with pro-

---

80 *Charter of the United Nations, supra* note 75, art. 68. See: Jean-Bernard Marie, *La Commission des droits de l'homme de l'O.N.U.*, Paris: Pedone, 1975.

81 UN Doc. A/RES/60/251.

82 For a few years in the 1940s, the Commission held two annual sessions. The first special session of the Commission was convened in 1992 in order to address the war on the territory of the former Yugoslavia.

moting the full implementation of human rights obligations undertaken by States and ensuring follow-up to the goals and commitments related to the promotion and protection of human rights emanating from United Nations conferences and summits. Much of this was already within the scope of the work of the Commission. But the Council is also required to

> [u]ndertake a universal periodic review, based on objective and reliable infor-
> mation, of the fulfilment by each State of its human rights obligations and
> commitments in a manner which ensures universality of coverage and equal
> treatment with respect to all States; the review shall be a cooperative mecha-
> nism, based on an interactive dialogue, with the full involvement of the country
> concerned and with consideration given to its capacity-building needs.

The Resolution insists that the new mechanism "shall complement and not duplicate the work of treaty bodies", but it would seem quite possible that over time the reporting procedure to the Council will largely overshadow similar processes that take place pursuant to various treaties. The beauty of periodic review before the Council is that it covers all Member States, and not only those that have accepted specific treaty obligations.[83]

Like its predecessor, the Human Rights Council will generate a body of "soft law" instruments, generally in the form of resolutions and presidential statements, on a range of thematic issues. Some may also be targeted at specific countries, following the practice of the Commission on Human Rights. For example, since 1997 the Commission on Human Rights has adopted an annual resolution on capital punishment. In *Burns and Rafay*, the Supreme Court of Canada referred to these resolutions, and more specifically one of the operative paragraphs stating that the Commission "[r]equests States that have received a request for extradition on a capital charge to reserve explicitly the right to refuse extradition in the absence of effective assurances from relevant authorities of the requesting State that capital punishment will not be carried out".[84] The Court noted Canada's support for the resolution, adding "it is difficult to avoid the conclusion that in the Canadian view of fundamental justice, capital punishment is unjust and it should be stopped".[85]

In the first decades of the United Nations, the Commission on Human Rights was largely concerned with standard setting. Its work focussed on the drafting of the core human rights instruments, namely the *Universal Declaration of Human Rights* and the treaties that were to follow. The Commission would debate and then agree upon the text of a treaty. Upon adoption by the Commission, the draft would subsequently be sent to the

---

83   UN Doc. A/RES/60/251
84   *United States* v. *Burns and Rafay*, [2001] 1 SCR 283, 195 DLR (4th) 1, [2001] 3 WWR 193, 151 CCC (3d) 97, 39 CR (5th) 205, 81 CRR (2d) 1, 85 BCLR (3d) 1, para. 84.
85   *Ibid.*

General Assembly for final approval, and then held out to States for signature and ratification or accession. Although new treaties continue to be adopted, the standard-setting role of the Commission (and now the Council) has become somewhat less central to its activity. Nevertheless, efforts continue in the preparation of new standard-setting instruments, in areas such as the rights of the disabled and forced disappearance.

In the late 1940s, the Sub-Commission on Prevention of Discrimination and Protection of Minorities was established as a subsidiary body to the Commission. Unlike the Commission, which was composed of country delegations, the Sub-Commission was properly described as an expert body, whose members were elected in their individual capacity. The Sub-Commission operated as the "think tank" of the Commission, generating studies, reports and resolutions on a range of issues that were often too sensitive for the broader and more political forum of the Commission, such as the rights of indigenous or aboriginal peoples. Eventually, the name of the Sub-Commission was changed to the Sub-Commission on Protection and Promotion of Human Rights, better reflecting the broader mandate that it had taken on over the years. In the 1980s, Canadian jurist Jules Deschênes was elected to the Sub-Commission. The definition of minorities that he proposed continues to be cited as authoritative.[86]

As States gradually became less uncomfortable with international supervision of their own human rights records, the Commission on Human Rights invented a number of innovative mechanisms. Known as "special procedures", these consist of an assortment of special rapporteurs, experts and working groups that address thematic or geographic issues. The first to be created was the special rapporteur on extrajudicial, summary or arbitrary executions. Others have addressed such important issues as torture, violence against women, impunity and the protection of human rights defenders. One of the special procedures, the Working Group on Arbitrary Detenion, makes frequent "country visits". In 2005, the Group made a two-week tour of Canada, leading to recommendations concerning the overrepresentation of Aboriginals in the prisons, the excessive use of pretrial detention with regard to accused belonging to vulnerable social groups, and unmet needs for legal aid. The Working Group recommended changes to immigration law and policy. Expressing great concern about the process of issuing security certificates, the Group said that terrorism suspects be detained in the criminal process, with the attached safeguards, and not under immigration laws.[87]

---

86 Jules Deschênes, "Proposal Concerning a Definition of the Term 'Minority'", UN Doc. E/CN.4/Sub.2/1985/31, para. 181.

87 "Report of the Working Group on Arbitrary Detention, Addendum, Visit to Canada (1-15 June 2005)", UN Doc. E/CN.4/2006/7/Add.2.

Several Canadians have served on the special procedures.[88] The special procedures can be especially dynamic, given the personal nature of the position. The experts who comprise them are often human rights activists with a distinguished record in non-governmental organizations. Special rapporteurs and the other mechanisms provide the United Nations with a substantial written record, mainly in the form of annual reports to the Commission (and now, the Council). Canadian courts have referred only very occasionally to the work of the special procedures.[89]

Each year since its establishment, the Commission on Human Rights has presented an annual report to the Economic and Social Council, which in turn reports to the General Assembly. The intermediate and largely superfluous step of reporting to the Economic and Social Council disappeared in 2006 with the establishment of the Human Rights Council, which reports directly to the General Assembly. Within the General Assembly, human rights matters are usually examined within its Third Committee. The records of the Third Committee provide considerable insight into the debates surrounding various General Assembly resolutions. There have been many references to other General Assembly resolutions in Canadian caselaw.[90]

---

88   For example, Maurice Copithorne, who was Special Representative of the Commission on Human Rights on the situation of human rights in the Islamic Republic of Iran, Stephen Toope, who has served as member and chairman of the Working Group on Enforced or Involuntary Disappearances, and Peter Leuprecht, who has served as Special Representative of the Secretary General for Human Rights in Cambodia.

89   *United States* v. *Burns and Rafay*, *supra* note 84, para. 85; *Mugesera* v. *Minister of Citizenship and Immigration*, [2004] 1 FCR 3, 232 DLR (4th) 75, 309 NR 14, 31 Imm LR (3d) 159 (CA), paras. 75-76; *Criminal Lawyers' Association* v. *Ontario (Ministry of Public Safety and Security)*, (2004) 70 OR (3d) 332 (SCJ, DC), para. 79.

90   For example: "Declaration on Principles of International Law Concerning Friendly Relations and Co-operation Among States in Accordance with the Charter of the United Nations", GA Res. 2625 (XXV), cited in *Reference re Secession of Quebec*, *supra* note 76; "Declaration on the Occasion of the Fiftieth Anniversary of the United Nations", GA Res. 50/6, cited in *Reference re Secession of Quebec*, *supra* note 76; "Questions of the Elderly and the Aged", GA Res. 3137 (XXVIII), cited in *McKinney* v. *University of Guelph*, [1990] 3 SCR 229, 76 DLR (4th) 545, 91 CLLC ¶17,004, 13 CHRR D/171, 45 OAC 1, 118 NR 1, 2 OR (3d) 319n; "Declaration on the Protection of All Persons from Enforced Disappearance", GA Res. 47/133, cited in *Pushpanathan* v. *Canada (Minister of Citizenship and Immigration)*, [1998] 1 SCR 982; "Declaration on the Elimination of Discrimination Against Women", GA Res. 2263 (XXII), cited in *Schachter* v. *Canada*, [1988] 3 FC 515, 52 DLR (4th) 525, 18 FTR 199, 88 CLLC ¶14,021, 20 CCEL 301, 9 CHRR D/5320 (TD); "Declaration on the Elimination of Violence Against Women", GA Res. 48/104, cited in *R.* v. *Ewanchuk*, [1999] 1 SCR 330; "Declaration on Measures to Eliminate International Terrorism", GA Res. 51/210, cited in *Pushpanathan* v. *Canada*, *ibid.* this note; "World Programme of Action concerning Disabled Persons", UN Doc. A/RES/37/52, cited in *Granovsky* v. *Canada (Minister of Employment and Immigration)*, [2000] 1 SCR 703, 186 DLR (4th) 1, 50 CCEL (2d) 177, 253 NR 329; "Declaration on the Rights of the Child", GA Res. 1384 (XIV), cited in *Hélène G.* v. *Centre I.*, [1976]

The most important General Assembly resolution in the area of human rights is the *Universal Declaration of Human* Rights, adopted in the early

---

CBES 2001; *Transpacific Tours Ltd.* v. *Director of Investigation and Research, Combines Investigation Act*, [1986] 2 WWR 34, 8 CPR (3d) 325, 25 DLR (4th) 202 (BCSC); *Thompson Newspapers Ltd.* v. *Director of Investigation and Research*, (1986) 26 DLR (4th) 507, 54 OR (2d) 143 (HCJ); *Commission scolaire St-Jean sur-Richelieu* v. *Commission des droits de la personne du Québec*, [1994] RJQ 1227 (CA); *Charran* v. *Canada (Minister of Citizenship and Immigration)* (1995), 89 FTR 113, 28 Imm LR (2d) 282; *Gordon* v. *Goertz*, [1996] 2 SCR 27, 196 NR 321, 141 Sask R 241, 114 WAC 241, [1996] 5 WWR 457, 19 RFL (4th) 177, 134 DLR (4th) 321; "Affirmation of the Principles of International Law Recognized by the Charter of the Nürnberg Tribunal", GA Res. 95 (I), cited in *R.* v. *Finta*, (1989) 50 CCC (3d) 236, 64 CR (3d) 223, 44 CRR 23, 69 OR (2d) 557, 61 DLR (4th) 85 (HC); *Rudolph* v. *Canada (Minister of Employment and Immigration)*, (1992) 91 DLR (4th) 686 (Fed CA), leave to appeal refused, (1992) 93 DLR (4th) vii (note) (SCC); *R.* v. *Finta*, [1994] 1 SCR 701, 88 CCC (3d) 417, 112 DLR (4th) 513, 150 NR 370; "Basic Principles on the Independence of the Judiciary", GA Res. 40/32, cited in *Southam Inc.* v. *Québec (P.-G.)*, [1993] RJQ 2374 (SC); "Declaration on the Elimination of All Forms of Intolerance and of Discrimination based on Religion or Belief", GA Res. 36/55, cited in *Commission des droits de la personne du Québec* v. *Autobus Legault*, [1994] RJQ 3027 (HRT); "United Nations Principles for Older Persons", GA Res. 46/91, cited in *Commission des droits de la personne du Québec* v. *Brzozowski*, *supra* note 76; "Extradition and Punishment of War Criminals", GA Res. 3 (I), cited in *Décision relative à la preuve étrangère*, [1986] DLQ 40 (Comm. Inquiry); *R.* v. *Finta*, (HC) *ibid.*, this note; "Surrender of War Criminals and Traitors", GA Res. 170 (II), cited in *Décision relative à la preuve étrangère*, [1986] DLQ 40 (Comm. Inquiry); "Declaration on the Protection of All Persons from Being Subjected to Torture and Other Cruel, Inhuman or Degrading Treatment or Punishment", GA Res. 3452 (XXX), UN Doc. A/ 10034 (1975), cited in *Pushpanathan* v. *Canada*, *ibid.* this note; *Suresh* v. *Canada (Minister of Citizenship and Immigration)*, [2002] 1 SCR 3, 208 DLR (4th) 1, 37 Admin LR (3d) 159, 90 CRR (2d) 1; "Recommendation on Consent to Marriage and Minimum Age for Marriage", GA Res. 2018 (XX), cited in *B. (L.Y.) (Re)*, [1995] CRDD 78; "Declaration on Social Progress and Development", GA Res. 2542 (XXIV), cited in *Commission des droits de la personne du Québec* v. *Brzozowski*, *supra* note 76; "Declaration on the Rights of Mentally Retarded Persons", GA Res. 2856 (XXVI), cited in *Commission des droits de la personne du Québec* v. *Commission scolaire de St-Jean-sur-Richelieu*, [1991] RJQ 3003 (HRT); *Commission des droits de la personne du Québec* v. *Brzozowski*, *supra* note 76; *Commission scolaire St-Jean sur-Richelieu* v. *Commission des droits de la personne du Québec*, *ibid*, this note; *Lisenko* v. *Commission scolaire Saint-Hyacinthe Val-Monts*, JE 96-787 (HRT); "Declaration on the Rights of Disabled Persons", GA Res. 3448 (XXX), cited in *Re Saskatchewan Human Rights Commission and Canadian Odeon Theatres Ltd*, [1985] 3 WWR 717, 18 DLR (4th) 93, 6 CHRR D/ 2682, 39 Sask R 81 (CA), *C.P. Ltd.* v. *Canada (Cdn. Human Rights Commission)*, (1986), 7 CHRR D/3278 (C.HRT), *Commission des droits de la personne du Québec* v. *Commission scolaire de St-Jean-sur-Richelieu*, *ibid.* this note, *Commission des droits de la personne du Québec* v. *Brzozowski*, *supra* note 76, *Commission scolaire St-Jean sur-Richelieu* v. *Commission des droits de la personne du Québec*, *ibid.*, this note, *Mooring* v. *Canada (National Parole Board)*, [1996] 1 SCR 75, 104 CCC (3d) 97, *Lisenko* v. *Commission scolaire Saint-Hyacinthe Val-Monts*, *ibid.* this note; "Declaration on the Elimination of All Forms of Intolerance and of Discrimination based on Religion or

hours of the morning on 10 December 1948. Drafts were initially debated within the Commission on Human Rights, which adopted a text in June 1948 for consideration by the General Assembly. Over two months in late 1948, the Third Committee of the General Assembly worked on the draft, finally agreeing upon a text on 7 December 1948. Canada abstained in the vote to adopt the draft *Universal Declaration* taken in the Third Committee of the General Assembly a few days prior to final adoption, but voted in favour in the plenary session three days later.[91] Since then, however, the *Universal Declaration* has played an important role in Canadian domestic law, and was an important source for the drafters of the *Canadian Bill of Rights* of 1960,[92] the *Canadian Charter of Rights and Freedoms*[93] and of the various provincial human rights codes and charters.[94] The *Universal Declaration of Human Rights* was first cited by the Quebec Court of Appeal in a case resulting from the 1970 October crisis. Two imprisoned political leaders challenged the creation of a retroactive offense, arguing that this was forbidden by article 11 of the *Universal Declaration of Human Rights*. The Quebec Court of Appeal dismissed the challenge, declaring that the *Universal Declaration of Human Rights* had no binding authority in Canadian law and could not trump duly enacted federal law.[95] A decade later, the *Canadian Charter* established a constitutional protection against retroactive offences. Since that first case, in 1971, the *Universal Declaration of Human Rights* has been cited by Canadian courts in literally hundreds of

---

Belief", GA Res. 36/55, cited in *Commission des droits de la personne du Québec* v. *Autobus Legault, ibid.* this note; "Statement of Basic Principles for the Treatment of Prisoners", GA Res. 45/111, cited in *X. (Z.H.) (Re)*, [1992] CRDD 368, *L. (O.Q.) (Re)*, [1993] CRDD 136.

91   See Chapter 1 for an account of the Canadian difficulties with the draft *Universal Declaration of Human Rights*.

92   RSC 1985, Appendix III.

93   RSC 1985, Appendix II, No. 44.

94   For the Quebec *Charter of Human Rights and Freedoms*, RSQ, c. C-12, see: André Morel, "La Charte québécoise: un document unique dans l'histoire législative canadienne", (1987) 21 *Revue juridique Thémis* 1, at 17. The *Universal Declaration* is referred to directly in the preamble of the *Ontario Human Rights Code, 1981*, RSO 1990, c. H.19, and its importance was stressed by Peter A. Cumming in the first decision rendered under the Ontario *Code: Cameron* v. *Nel-Gor Castle Nursing Home, supra* note 76. See also the comments of Justice Marcel Nichols of the Quebec Court of Appeal in *Ville de Québec* v. *Commission des droits de la personne*, [1989] RJQ 831, 11 CHRR D/500 (CA), at D/507-508 (CHRR).

95   *Gagnon and Vallières* v. *R.*, [1971] Que. CA 454, 14 CR ns 321.

cases, generally to more positive effect than in that first judgment of the Quebec Court of Appeal.[96]

Canadian law professor John Peters Humphrey, who headed the secretariat of the Commission on Human Rights at the time, prepared the initial draft of the *Universal Declaration* by cataloguing the human rights provisions in domestic constitutions.[97] From this comparative law analysis, a text consisting of thirty articles and covering a broad range of civil and political but also economic, social and cultural rights was compiled. Besides providing thorough and comprehensive descriptions of fundamental rights and freedoms, the *Universal Declaration* introduced the concept of a limitation clause,[98] an approach which has been followed in most subsequent human rights instruments, including section 1 of the *Canadian Charter of Rights and Freedoms*. Article 29(2) of the *Universal Declaration* declares: "In the exercise of his rights and freedoms, everyone shall be subject only to such limitations as are determined by law solely for the purpose of securing due recognition and respect for the rights and freedoms of others and of meeting the just requirements of morality, public order and the general welfare in a democratic society." The *Universal Declaration of Human Rights* is not a treaty and it is not, at least theoretically, a source of binding norms at international law. It is a mistake to speak of "signatories" or "parties" to the *Declaration*, as some do, or of its "ratification". Reference to the *Universal Declaration of Human Rights* in subsequent instruments, in particular the *Helsinki Final Act* of 1975,[99] has enhanced its significance. There is some authority for the position that the *Universal Declaration* is a codification of

---

96   The *Universal Declaration of Human Rights* was cited for the first time by the Supreme Court of Canada in *Bhadauria* v. *Board of Governors of Seneca College*, *supra* note 76. Recent examples of reference to the *Universal Declaration of Human Rights* by the Supreme Court of Canada include: *Pushpanathan* v. *Canada*, *supra* note 90; *Suresh* v. *Canada*, *supra* note 90; *R.* v. *Advance Cutting & Coring Ltd.*, (1998) 1998 CarswellQue 302, (sub nom. *Thériault c. R.*) [1998] RJQ 911 (CS), affirmed, [2001] 3 SCR 209, 205 DLR (4th) 385, 87 CRR (2d) 189; *Baker* v. *Canada (Minister of Citizenship and Immigration)*, [1999] 2 SCR 817, 174 DLR (4th) 193, 14 Admin LR (3d) 173, 1 Imm LR (3d) 1, 243 NR 22; *Gosselin* v. *Quebec (Attorney General)*, [2002] 4 SCR 429, 221 DLR (4th) 257, 100 CRR (2d) 1, 44 CHRR D/363; *R.* v. *Sharpe*, [2001] 1 SCR 45, 194 DLR (4th) 1, [2001] 6 WWR 1, 150 CCC (3d) 321, 39 CR (5th) 72, 86 CRR (2d) 1, 88 BCLR (3d) 1.

97   UN Doc. E/CN.4/W.4.

98   *Universal Declaration of Human Rights*, GA Res. 217 A (III) UN Doc. A/810, art. 29(2).

99   "Conference on Security and Cooperation in Europe, Final Act", 1 August 1975, Part 1, para. VII: "In the field of human rights and fundamental freedoms, the participating States will act in conformity with the purposes and principles of the Charter of the United Nations and with the Universal Declaration of Human Rights."

customary law.[100] In 1995, a Canadian government minister said that "Canada regards the principles of the Universal Declaration of Human Rights as entrenched in customary international law binding on all governemnts".[101] Alternatively, others have argued that the *Universal Declaration of Human Rights* provides an authoritative interpretation of the human rights clauses of the *Charter of the United Nations*, thereby rooting its authority in treaty law rather than in customary law.

In an opinion on the possibility of amending the *Universal Declaration of Human Rights*, the Legal Bureau of the Canadian Department of Foreign Affairs recalled that when the instrument was being adopted, Eleanor Roosevelt had insisted that it was "not a treaty or international agreement and did not impose legal obligations; it was rather a statement of basic principles of inalienable human rights setting up a common standard of achievement for all peoples and all nations". Accordingly, said the Legal Bureau:

> As the Declaration is a statement of general principles and was not initially legally binding, there is no evidence that its drafters intended it to be subject to amendment. This is supported by the fact that there have been no amendments to the Declaration since its adoption in 1948. Although the Declaration, when adopted, was not meant to be legally binding, it has over the years gained binding character as customary law and has been effectively relied on worldwide.[102]

The Legal Bureau warned that "[e]ven if it were possible to amend the Declaration, it would not be advisable as the process would be extremely divisive with the possible result of a regression rather than advancement of human rights".[103]

---

100 *Advisory Opinion on the Continued Presence of South Africa in Namibia (S.W. Africa)*, [1971] ICJ Reports 16, at 76 (*per* Ammoun J.); See also the dissent of Judge Tanaka in *South West Africa Cases, Second Phase*, [1966] ICJ Reports 16, 37 ILR 1, at 288-293 (ICJ); and *United States Diplomatic and Consular Staff in Tehran*, [1980] ICJ Reports 3, 61 ILR 530, at 42 (ICJ); *Fernandez* v. *Wilkinson*, 505 F. Supp. 787 (1980). Also: R. Bilder, "The Status of International Human Rights Law: An Overview", (1978) *International Law and Practice* 1, at 8; John P. Humphrey, "The Canadian Charter of Rights and Freedoms and International Law", (1985-86) 50 *Saskatchewan Law Review* 13; John P. Humphrey, "The Universal Declaration of Human Rights: Its History, Impact and Judicial Character", in Bertrand G. Ramcharan, ed., *Human Rights: Thirty Years After the Universal Declaration*, The Hague: Martinus Nijhoff, 1984.

101 "Notes for an Address by the Honourable Christine Stewart, Secretary of State (Latin America and Africa) at the10th Annual Consultation Between Non-Governemntal Organizations and the Department of Foreign Affairs and International Trade", Ottawa, 17 January 1995.

102 Michael Leir, ed., "Amendments to the Universal Declaration of Human Rights", (1999) 37 *Canadian Yearbook of International Law* 331-332.

103 *Ibid.*

The *Charter of the United Nations* suggests that the principal organ responsible for human rights is the Economic and Social Council.[104] In practice, its role has been very secondary, generally consisting of perfunctory endorsement of initiatives taken within the Commission on Human Rights. In his 2005 report, *In Larger Freedom*, Secretary-General Kofi Annan said that "the Economic and Social Council has been too often relegated to the margins of global economic and social governance",[105] and he called for it to be revitalized, although with a focus on development issues rather than human rights.[106] The Council is the source of some important documents concerning human rights, notably in the area of criminal law, that have occasionally attracted the attention of the Canadian courts. These include one of the important efforts to codify norms for the treatment of prisoners[107] and statements dealing with the death penalty.[108]

The other major institution within the United Nations system that is addressed specifically to the protection and promotion of human rights is the Office of the High Commissioner for Human Rights. John Humphrey was one of the strong voices favouring establishment of a high commissioner for human rights, and the proposal to create the position circulated for many years, but to no avail.[109] It only managed to achieve sufficient consensus at the 1993 Vienna Conference on Human Rights. The text adopted at the conclusion of the conference called upon the General Assembly to consider establishing such a position, something it did with due dispatch.[110] In December 1993, the General Assembly agreed to proceed, mandating the Secretary-General to appoint the individual who would hold this post. A

104 *Charter of the United Nations*, [1945] CTS 7, art. 60.
105 "In Larger Freedom", UN Doc. A/59/2005, para. 165.
106 *Ibid.*, paras. 171-180.
107 *Standard Minimum Rules for Treatment of Prisoners*, approved by ESC Res. 663C (XXIV) and 2076 (LXII). Cited in: *Collin* v. *Kaplan*, [1983] 1 FC 496, 143 DLR (3d) 121, 1 CCC (3d) 309, 2 CRR 352 (TD); *Stanley* v. *Royal Canadian Mounted Police*, (1987) 8 CHRR D/3799 (Can Human Rights Trib).
108 *Capital Punishment*, ESC Res. 1574 (L). Cited in: *Kindler* v. *Canada*, [1991] 2 SCR 779, 67 CCC (3d) 1, 84 DLR (4th) 438, 6 CRR (2d) 193, 129 NR 81.
109 Alan John Hobbins, "Humphrey and the High Commissioners: The Genesis of the Office of the High Commissioner for Human Rights", (2001) 3 *Journal of the History of International Law* 37.
110 UN Doc. A/RES/48/141. On the position of High Commissioner, see: Andrew Clapham, "The High Commissioner of Human Rights", in P. Alston, ed., *The United Nations and Human Rights*, Oxford: Clarendon Press, 2004; Andrew Clapham, "Creating the High Commissioner for Human Rights: The Outside Story", (1994) 5 *European Journal of International Law* 556; Philip Alston, "Neither Fish nor Fowl: The Quest to Define the Role of the UN High Commissioner for Human Rights", (1997) 8 *European Journal of International Law* 321; Bertrand Ramcharan, *The United Nations High Commissioner for Human Rights: The Challenges of International Protection*, The Hague: Kluwer Academic, 2002.

lacklustre Peruvian diplomat was the first to hold the job, José Ayala-Lasso, taking office only days before the beginning of the Rwandan genocide. He was succeeded by the dynamic former president of Ireland, Mary Robinson, who brought great credibility and enthusiasm to the position.[111] Her successor, Sergio Vieira de Mello, was killed shortly after his appointment by a terrorist bomb in Baghdad, with the interregnum assured by his deputy, Bertrand Ramcharan. In mid-2004, the Secretary-General appointed Canadian Supreme Court Justice Louise Arbour to a five-year term as High Commissioner for Human Rights.

The High Commissioner for Human Rights promotes the study and development of positions on a range of issues. She is described as "the United Nations official with principal responsibility for United Nations human rights activities under the direction and authority of the Secretary-General".[112] The High Commissioner oversees an office with a staff of more than 500, located in Geneva but with regional outposts in many of the hot spots of the globe. The Office of the High Commissioner is very much the lynch pin in the entire United Nations human rights system. The Office has also been involved in managing important international initiatives with a significant United Nations presence, such as the Sierra Leone Truth and Reconciliation Commission.

Certainly, the Human Rights Council (formerly the Commission on Human Rights) and the High Commissioner for Human Rights lie at the centre of human rights work within the United Nations. The progressive expansion of the activities and mandates of both bodies attests to the increasing significance of human rights within the United Nations as a whole. But this process is also manifested in the work of other parts of the United Nations, notably in the Security Council. Franklin D. Roosevelt famously described the General Assembly as the place where small countries would "let off steam", while the real work of the organization was conducted by the Security Council. The *Charter of the United Nations* gives the Security Council authority in matters concerning international peace and security. Beginning in the early 1990s, the Security Council began to justify various initiatives it was undertaking in the name of the protection of human rights. The starting point was probably Security Council Resolution 688, adopted in April 1991. It authorised intervention in Iraq so as to protect vulnerable minorities within the country's borders. Since then, the Council has often ordered a variety of measures, including sanctions and the establishment of peace support missions, using the protection of human rights as justification for intervention. And when it has not acted promptly and decisively to

---

111   Mary Robinson, *A Voice for Human Rights*, Philadelphia: University of Pennsylvania Press, 2006.
112   UN Doc. A/RES/48/141, para. 4.

protect human rights, for example when confronted with the genocide in Rwanda in April and May 1994, there was widespread condemnation. The Security Council was responsible for the establishment of the *ad hoc* tribunals for the former Yugoslavia, Rwanda and Sierra Leone. Meeting in September 2005, the World Summit of Heads of State and Government affirmed the responsibility to protect populations from serious human rights abuses, declaring:

> . . . we are prepared to take collective action, in a timely and decisive manner, through the Security Council, in accordance with the UN Charter, including Chapter VII, on a case by case basis and in cooperation with relevant regional organizations as appropriate, should peaceful means be inadequate and national authorities manifestly failing to protect their populations from genocide, war crimes, ethnic cleansing and crimes against humanity.[113]

Finally, the contribution to the protection and promotion of human rights by the International Court of Justice, which is the principal judicial organ of the United Nations, should not be overlooked. Like the Security Council, it seems to have taken on human rights as an important priority in recent years. The Court, of course, can only consider cases that are submitted to it, either by States in the context of a contentious procedure, or by the Security Council or the General Assembly, in a request for an advisory opinion. During the late-1990s and into the first years of the twenty-first century, the International Court of Justice considered several cases concerning capital punishment.[114] It also addressed issues relating to the protection of vulnerable minorities, and the consequences of armed conflict on respect for human rights. In December 2005, it actually condemned a State for violating the *International Covenant on Civil and Political Rights* within the territory of another State, the first time that the *Covenant* has been successfully invoked in inter-State litigation before any international tribunal.[115] As this book went to press, it was deliberating on a lengthy case filed by Bosnia and Herzegovina against Serbia and Montenegro based on the charge that genocide had been committed during the 1992-1995 war. A judgment is expected in 2007. In *Pushpanathan*, the Supreme Court of Canada cited judgments of the International Court of Justice as authority

---

113 "Outcome Document of the World Summit of Heads of State and Government", 13 September 2005, UN Doc. A/RES/60/1, para. 139.

114 *LaGrand (Germany* v. *United States of America), Provisional Measures, Order of 3 March 1999,* [1999] ICJ Reports 1; *Case Concerning Avena and Other Mexican Nationals (Mexico v. United States of Mexico),* 31 March 2003.

115 *Case Concerning Armed Activities on the Territory of the Congo (Democratic Republic of the Congo v. Uganda),* 19 December 2005.

for the concept of "fundamental principles enunciated in the Universal Declaration of Human Rights".[116]

3.2.2   Treaty-Based Protection of Human Rights

The United Nations human rights system has a universal dimension, through the "*Charter*-based" mechanisms, but it also has an asymmetric component, resulting from a network of generalized and specialized treaties.[117] Because of the number of treaties, and a rather widespread practice of reservations, it is probably accurate to say that no two Member States are subject to entirely identical obligations under these treaties. Canada, for example, is a rather enthusiastic participant in the treaty-based system, but it has not ratified all of the relevant instruments. As a result, any analysis of a State's specific legal obligations resulting from United Nations human rights treaties requires rather meticulous analysis, and the application of sophisticated concepts of treaty law. Nevertheless, over the years, ratification of the human rights treaties has increased dramatically. In many cases it is now possible to speak of near-universal ratification. For example, the *Convention on the Rights of the Child* has been ratified by every Member State of the United Nations, with the exception of the United States and Somalia. But given the large number of reservations to specific provisions of the *Convention*, it would be unwise to claim that the treaty as a whole enjoys universal acceptance.

3.2.2.1   *Drafting of the Covenants*

At the centre of the United Nations treaty-based human rights systems are two instruments, the *International Covenant on Civil and Political Rights* and the *International Covenant on Economic, Social and Cultural Rights*.[118] These treaties are meant to give binding effect at international law to the norms set out in the *Universal Declaration of Human Rights*. In the case of the *International Covenant on Civil and Political Rights*, there are two optional supplementary treaties or "protocols", the first providing a

---

116 *Pushpanathan* v. *Canada (Minister of Citizenship and Immigration)*, [1998] 1 SCR 982, citing: *United States Diplomatic and Consular Staff in Tehran*, [1980] ICJ Reports 3, 61 ILR 530 and *Legal Consequences for States of the Continued Presence of South Africa in Namibia (South West Africa) notwithstanding Security Council Resolution 276 (1970)*, [197] ICJ Reports 4.

117 See, generally: Anne F. Bayefsky, ed., *The UN Human Rights Treaty System in the 21st Century*, The Hague/London/Boston: Kluwer Academic, 2000.

118 *International Covenant on Economic, Social and Cultural Rights*, (1976) 993 UNTS 3, [1976] CTS 46.

right of individual recourse to the Human Rights Committee,[119] the second amending article 6 of the *Covenant* and totally prohibiting the death penalty.[120] These five documents are sometimes referred to collectively as the "International Bill of Rights".[121] The Canadian legislation creating the International Centre for Human Rights and Democratic Development refers to the "international bill of rights", stating that

> The objects of the Centre are to initiate, encourage and support cooperation between Canada and other countries in the promotion, development and strengthening of democratic and human rights institutions and programmes that give effect to the rights and freedoms enshrined in the *International Bill of Rights*, including, among those rights, (a) the right to an adequate standard of living; (b) the rights of persons not to be subject to torture or to cruel, inhuman or degrading treatment or punishment; (c) the rights of freedom of opinion and expression; and (d) the right to vote and be elected at periodic, genuine elections in pluralistic political systems.[122]

There has also been judicial reference to the concept of an "international bill of rights".[123]

Even prior to adoption of the *Universal Declaration of Human Rights*, it was understood that at least one other instrument would be required. It was to be a formal treaty that would be subject to ratification and that would bind States parties, in contrast with the *Universal Declaration of Human Rights*, whose role was essentially hortatory. Because of its legally binding nature, the treaty was expected to be considerably more detailed than the *Universal Declaration of Human Rights.* As a result, its drafting was much more complicated and arduous. During 1947 and 1948, the Untied Nations Commission on Human Rights worked on both the *Universal Declaration* and the draft treaty in parallel, initially hoping that they could be completed simultaneously. In mid-1948, it became apparent that although the *Universal Declaration of Human Rights* was nearing completion, drafting of what was being called the "covenant" would take considerably longer. The Commission on Human Rights decided to proceed with immediate adoption of

---

119 *Optional Protocol on the International Covenant on Civil and Political Rights*, (1976) 999 UNTS 171, [1976] CTS 47

120 *Second Optional Protocol to the International Covenant on Civil and Political Rights Aimed at Abolition of the Death Penalty*, UN Doc. A/RES/44/128, annex.

121 Louis Henkin, ed., *The International Bill of Rights: The Covenant on Civil and Political Rights*, New York: Columbia University Press, 1981; Walter S. Tarnopolsky, "Human Rights, International Law and the International Bill of Rights", (1986) 50 *Saskatchewan Law Review* 21.

122 *Centre for Human Rights and Democratic Development* Act, RS v. 54 (4th Supp.), s. 4.

123 *Gosselin* v. *Québec (AG)*, [1999] RJQ 1033 (CA), affirmed, [2002] 4 SCR 429, 221 DLR (4th) 257, 100 CRR (2d) 1, 44 CHRR D/363.

the *Universal Declaration*, and to continue work on the "Covenant" in its subsequent sessions.

But after the *Universal Declaration of Human Rights* was adopted, some States took the position that not all of the rights listed therein actually belonged in a binding treaty. Conditioned by the cold war climate, the United States and the United Kingdom, in particular, argued that the economic, social and cultural rights set out in articles 22 to 27 of the *Universal Declaration* were not justiciable and therefore could not be included in a binding treaty. These States made the distinction with the civil and political rights, many of which had been present in national constitutions since the eighteenth century. Courts had long been familiar with litigation concerning such rights as freedom of expression or the right to a fair trial, it was explained, whereas there was no comparable practice with respect to the right to housing or to medical care. Whereas an individual might litigate issues relating to freedom of expression, which appeared to impose no other obligation on the State than that it abstain from interfering, the same individual could not insist before the courts upon respect of his right to social benefits, as this would require the State to make financial commitments. Western States suggested that attempts to include economic, social and cultural rights in the covenant was merely a communist ruse. The socialist States, supported by allies in the emerging underdeveloped world, refused to abandon recognition of such rights. In reply, they argued that the so-called liberal freedoms were an antiquated concept, and of little significance to those suffering from malnutrition, illiteracy and unemployment. A compromise was reached. The General Assembly decided to divide the covenant into two distinct instruments,[124] the *International Covenant on Civil and Political Rights* and the *International Covenant on Economic, Social and Cultural Rights*.

The division is not without its problems. Some rights, such as those concerning labour and trade unions, can be found in both instruments.[125] An identical text, known as "common article 1", recognizing the right of peoples to self-determination, appears in the two treaties. On the other hand, the drafters could not agree on how to define and where to put the right to property, which is article 17 of the *Universal Declaration of Human Rights*, and they eventually left this important right out.[126] Perhaps the most important distinction between the two *Covenants* is in the texts concerning the

---

124   GA Res. 543 (VI).

125   *International Covenant on Civil and Political Rights, International Covenant on Civil and Political Rights*, (1976) 999 UNTS 171, [1976] CTS 47, art. 22; *International Covenant on Economic, Social and Cultural Rights, supra* note 118, art. 8.

126   William A. Schabas, "The Omission of the Right to Property in the International Covenants", in (1991) 4 *Hague Yearbook of International Law* 135.

nature of the obligations they impose. In the case of the *International Covenant on Civil and Political Rights*, a State is bound immediately "to ensure to all individuals within its territory and subject to its jurisdiction the rights recognized" in the instrument.[127] In the case of the *International Covenant on Economic, Social and Cultural Rights*, a State is bound "to take steps, individually and through international assistance and co-operation, especially economic and technical, to the maximum of its available resources, with a view to achieving progressively the full realization of the rights recognized" in the instrument.[128] Another indication of the relatively secondary importance that the drafters attached to the *International Covenant on Economic, Social and Cultural Rights* is the failure to create a treaty body or committee having responsibility for implementation, like the Human Rights Committee which was established under the *International Covenant on Civil and Political Rights*.

The distinction between the obligations imposed under the two Covenants has not escaped the attention of the Canadian courts. Justice Paul Reeves of the Quebec Superior Court, in a case involving social welfare benefits where lawyers invoked the *International Covenant on Economic, Social and Cultural Rights*, wrote that

> Il y a une différence de nature entre, d'une part, les droits économiques et sociaux qui exigent une intervention active et l'engagement de ressources importantes de l'État pour leur mise en œuvre et, d'autre part, les droits civils et politiques, qui n'exigent généralement que des aménagements aux institutions politiques et juridiques et sont ainsi susceptibles de mise en œuvre immédiate par les États, quel que soit leur niveau de développement".[129]

This unfortunate division between the two categories of rights, betraying an initial unity that can be found in the *Universal Declaration on Human Rights* as well as in the "four freedoms" speech of Roosevelt, has been the subject of continuing controversy. The dichotomy has tended to discredit international human rights in general, particularly in the underdeveloped world. The answer has been to insist upon the indivisibility of human rights, and the equal, inseparable importance of both categories. At the Vienna Conference on Human Rights, held in June 1993, the indivisibility of human rights was formally recognized. According to the *Vienna Declaration*, "[a]ll human rights are universal, indivisible and interdependent and interre-

---

127   *International Covenant on Civil and Political Rights*, *supra* note 125, art. 2(1).

128   *International Covenant on Economic, Social and Cultural Rights*, *supra* note 118, art. 2(1).

129   *Gosselin* v. *Québec (Procureur général)*, [1992] RJQ 1647 (SC), affirmed, [1999] RJQ 1033 (CA), affirmed, [2002] 4 SCR 429, 221 DLR (4th) 257, 100 CRR (2d) 1, 44 CHRR D/363, at 1669.

lated."[130] The concept of indivisibility has been reaffirmed on numerous occasions since then, most recently in the General Assembly resolution establishing the Human Rights Council.

The process of adoption of the two *Covenants* by the United Nations General Assembly was not completed until 1966,[131] when the treaties became open for signature. The text was annexed to a single resolution, which was adopted unanimously.[132] A third treaty had also been prepared, the *Optional Protocol to the International Covenant on Civil and Political Rights*, creating an individual petition mechanism in the case of violations of the *International Covenant on Civil and Political Rights*. This took the form of an "optional protocol" so those States that were prepared to subscribe to the norms in the *Covenant* but reluctant to accept an individual petition mechanism would not be totally excluded. The two *Covenants* and the *Optional Protocol* came into force early in 1976. Each of the *Covenants* required thirty-five ratifications, the *Protocol* only ten. Canada ratified all three instruments in 1976, although it did so a few months after their entry into force.

The two *Covenants* now have in excess of 150 States parties, whereas the *Optional Protocol* has slightly more than 100. Most States, with a few exceptions, ratify both Covenants at the same time, and this is itself a manifestation of the "indivisibility" of the two instruments. Because the *International Covenant on Civil and Political Rights* allows the death penalty as an exception to the right to life, in States that have not abolished it, during the 1980s there were efforts to correct this anachronism, which is now out of step with contemporary human rights law. In 1989, a *Second Optional Protocol* was adopted by the General Assembly, aiming at abolition of the death penalty.[133] It came into force in 1991, and has obtained

---

130   *Vienna Declaration and Programme of Action*, UN Doc. A/CONF.157/24, (1993) 14 *Human Rights Law Journal* 352, para. 5.

131   The *travaux préparatoires* of the *International Covenant on Civil and Political Rights* are readily available and have been analysed in an exhaustive volume: Marc J. Bossuyt, *Guide to the "travaux préparatoires' of the International Covenant on Civil and Political Rights*, Dordrecht: Martinus Nijhoff, 1987. Because it is an international treaty, according to article 32 of the *Vienna Convention on the Law of Treaties*, (1969) 1155 UNTS 331, [1980] CTS 37, 8 ILM 679, the *travaux préparatoires* are a "supplementary means of interpretation". The Human Rights Committee has frequently used the *travaux préparatoires* in construing provisions of the *International Covenant on Civil and Political Rights*.

132   GA Res. 2200/A (XXI).

133   *Second Optional Protocol, supra* note 120. The *Second Optional Protocol* was cited in *Kindler* v. *Canada, supra* note 108; *United States* v. *Burns and Rafay*, [2001] 1 SCR 283, 195 DLR (4th) 1, [2001] 3 WWR 193, 151 CCC (3d) 97, 39 CR (5th) 205, 81 CRR (2d) 1, 85 BCLR (3d) 1. On the *Second Optional Protocol*, see: William A. Schabas, *The Abolition of the Death Penalty in International Law*, 3rd. ed., Cambridge: Cambridge University Press, 2003.

more than fifty ratifications. Canada acceded to the *Second Optional Protocol* on 15 November 2005. A few years earlier, in *Burns and Rafay*, the Supreme Court of Canada invoked the *Second Optional Protocol* as evidence of the international trend towards abolition, noting that "Canada's position is still being given 'careful consideration'".[134]

3.2.2.2 *The* International Covenant on Civil and Political Rights

The *International Covenant on Civil and Political Rights*, in articles 6 through 27, repeats, but in greater detail, many of the rights found in the *Universal Declaration of Human Rights*.[135] For example, article 6 of the *Covenant* proclaims the right to life. But rather than simply affirm its existence, as in article 3 of the *Universal Declaration* ("Everyone has the right to life. . ."), six distinct paragraphs of the *Covenant* set out in detail the scope of the right to life, including its principal exception, capital punishment:

Article 6

1. Every human being has the inherent right to life. This right shall be protected by law. No one shall be arbitrarily deprived of his life.

2. In countries which have not abolished the death penalty, sentence of death may be imposed only for the most serious crimes in accordance with the law in force at the time of the commission of the crime and not contrary to the provisions of the present Covenant and to the Convention on the Prevention and Punishment of the Crime of Genocide. This penalty can only be carried out pursuant to a final judgment rendered by a competent court.

3. When deprivation of life constitutes the crime of genocide, it is understood that nothing in this article shall authorize any State Party to the present Covenant to derogate in any way from any obligation assumed under the provisions of the Convention on the Prevention and Punishment of the Crime of Genocide.

4. Anyone sentenced to death shall have the right to seek pardon or commutation of the sentence. Amnesty, pardon or commutation of the sentence of death may be granted in all cases.

5. Sentence of death shall not be imposed for crimes committed by persons below eighteen years of age and shall not be carried out on pregnant women.

---

134 *United States* v. *Burns and Rafay, ibid.*, at para. 87.

135 On the *Covenant* generally, see: Manfred Nowak, *Covenant on Civil and Political Rights: CCPR Commentary*, 2nd ed., Kehl: Engel, 2005; Dominic McGoldrick, *The Human Rights Committee, Its Role in the Development of the International Covenant on Civil and Political Rights*, 2nd ed., Oxford: Clarendon Press, 2000; Sarah Joseph, Jenny Schultz and Melissa Castan, *The International Covenant on Civil and Political Rights – Cases, Materials, and Commentary*, 2nd ed., Oxford: Oxford University Press, 2005.

6. Nothing in this article shall be invoked to delay or to prevent the abolition of capital punishment by any State Party to the present Covenant.

But despite its specificity, article 6 of the *International Covenant on Civil and Political Rights* provides no guidance as to the status of abortion or euthanasia, for example, or on the principles applicable to the taking of life in armed conflict.

Several of the provisions of the *Covenant* are accompanied by limitations clauses, broadly similar in effect to section 1 of the *Canadian Charter of Rights and Freedoms*. For example, article 19 of the *International Covenant on Civil and Political Rights* ensures freedom of expression, but subject to certain restrictions. Departing from the simple formulation of the *Universal Declaration of Human Rights*, the *Covenant* presents a complex series of provisions that allow for exceptions on limitations on that freedom, including protection of the reputation of others, and the prohibition of hate propaganda and propaganda for war.

Article 19

1. Everyone shall have the right to hold opinions without interference.

2. Everyone shall have the right to freedom of expression; this right shall include freedom to seek, receive and impart information and ideas of all kinds, regardless of frontiers, either orally, in writing or in print, in the form of art, or through any other media of his choice.

3. The exercise of the rights provided for in paragraph 2 of this article carries with it special duties and responsibilities. It may therefore be subject to certain restrictions, but these shall only be such as are provided by law and are necessary:

(a)   For respect of the rights or reputations of others;
(b)   For the protection of national security or of public order (ordre public), or of public health or morals.

Article 20

1. Any propaganda for war shall be prohibited by law.

2. Any advocacy of national, racial or religious hatred that constitutes incitement to discrimination, hostility or violence shall be prohibited by law.

Similar detailed limitations clauses appear in the provisions of the *International Covenant on Civil and Political Rights* concerning freedom of movement, freedom of religion, freedom of association and freedom of peaceful assembly.

The *International Covenant on Civil and Political Rights* also innovates, including rights that do not appear in the *Universal Declaration of Human Rights*, such as the right of persons belonging to ethnic, religious or linguistic minorities to use their language, to enjoy their own culture and to practice their religion.[136]

Article 27

In those States in which ethnic, religious or linguistic minorities exist, persons belonging to such minorities shall not be denied the right, in community with the other members of their group, to enjoy their own culture, to profess and practise their own religion, or to use their own language.

The drafters of the *Universal Declaration of Human Rights* had considered but ultimately dropped a draft provision on the rights of national minorities.[137]

In addition to its declaratory articles which set out the protected rights and freedoms, the *International Covenant on Civil and Political Rights* also creates the Human Rights Committee, which is a panel of eighteen experts "of high moral character and recognized competence in the field of human rights".[138] Pursuant to the *Covenant*, the Committee has two principal functions: to receive and study reports from States Parties "on the measures they have adopted which give effect to the rights recognized herein and on the progress made in the enjoyment of those rights",[139] and to receive communications from one State party alleging a breach of the *Covenant* by another State party.[140] For the interstate communications procedure to apply, States must make a supplementary declaration. Canada,[141] as well as more than fifty other States party to the *Covenant*, has taken such a step. However, since there has never yet been an interstate communication to the Human Rights Committee under the *Covenant* nor, for that matter, any similar

---

136 Albert Verdoodt, "Influence des structures ethniques et linguistiques des pays membres des Nations Unies sur la rédaction de la Déclaration universelle des droits de l'homme", in *Liber Amicorum Discipulorumque René Cassin*, Paris: Pedone, 1969, pp. 403-416.

137 William A. Schabas, "Les droits des minorités: Une déclaration inachevée", in *Déclaration universelle des droits de l'homme 1948-98, Avenir d'un idéal commun*, Paris: La Documentation française, 1999, pp. 223-242.

138 *Supra* note 125, art. 28(2). Three Canadians have served on the Committee, Walter S. Tarnopolsky (1977-1983), Gisèle Côté-Harper (1983-1984) and Maxwell Yalden (1997-2004).

139 The obligation to submit periodic reports on the *International Covenant on Civil and Political Rights* was mentioned by Justice Tallis in *Scowby* v. *Chairman of the Board of Inquiry*, [1983] 4 WWR 97, 148 DLR (3d) 55, 5 CCC (3d) 117, 23 Sask R 16, 4 CHRR D/1355 (CA), reversed, (1986) 1986 CarswellSask 249 (SCC) and by Justice Linden in *Re Mitchell and R.* (1983) 150 DLR (3d) 449, 6 CCC (3d) 193, 35 CR (3d) 225, 42 OR (2d) 481 (HC)

140 *Supra* note 125, art. 40.

141 (1979) 1147 UNTS 316. Canada's declaration is subject to a condition of reciprocity, whereby Canada will only accept petitions directed against it if the petitioning State has made a similar declaration at least twelve months earlier.

application under the equivalent interstate communications procedures in the other United Nations treaties.

It is of course also possible for one State to take a claim against another for breach of the *Covenant*, or another treaty, before the International Court of Justice, to the extent that both States have accepted the jurisdiction of the Court in accordance with article 36 of its *Statute*. In December 2005, the International Court of Justice ruled in the first claim of this type. In a suit filed by the Democratic Republic of Congo, it found that Uganda was in violation of several international human rights treaties, including the *International Covenant on Civil and Political Rights*, the *International Covenant on Economic, Social and Cultural Rights*, and the *Convention on the Rights of the Child.*

3.2.2.3   *Reporting to the Human Rights Committee*

The periodic reporting procedure has proven to be an extremely important function of the Committee, and an effective method of monitoring compliance with the *Covenant*. States must prepare a detailed report within one year of ratification, and subsequently at intervals determined by the Committee, "on the measures they have adopted which give effect to the rights recognized herein and on the progress made in the enjoyment of those rights".[142] The reports are published and distributed to United Nations depository libraries found throughout the world and, of course, posted on the web site of the Office of the High Commissioner for Human Rights. They are presented by representatives of the State party during a public session of the Human Rights Committee that normally takes one or two days. Members of the Committee question representatives of the State party, often criticizing aspects of the report or pointing to its omissions. Although the Committee does not have any real independent research facility in order to conduct an independent review of the reports, its members invariably receive considerable documentation from representatives of non-governmental organizations who attend the sessions and, informally, lobby the members of the Committee. The deliberations of the Committee, when it is examining the periodic reports, are public. A précis of these sessions is printed as a United Nations document, and a summary later appears in the annual report of the Committee, which is available in most reference libraries and on the Internet.[143] At the conclusion of the reporting procedure,

---

142   *International Covenant on Civil and Political Rights, supra* note 125, art. 40(1).

143   On the system of periodic reports, see: Ineke Boerefijn, *The Reporting Procedure under the Covenant on Civil and Political Rights: Practice and Procedure of the Human Rights Committee*, Antwerp/Groningen/Oxford: Hart, 1999; Agnès Dormenval, *Procédures onusiennes de mise en oeuvre des droits de l'homme: limites ou défauts*, Geneva: Presses universitaires de France, 1991, at 13-32; Dana D. Fisher, "Reporting Under the

according to a practice in effect since 1997, the Committee issues "concluding observations".[144] These are usually a balanced mixture of praise and polite criticism, reflecting the climate of dialogue and exchange that generally prevails in the Committee's meetings with States. In 2002, the Committee decided to name a Special Rapporteur for Follow-Up on Concluding Observations. It appointed Maxwell Yalden, a Canadian member, to the position.[145] The Special Rapporteur's task is to "establish, maintain or restore a dialogue with the State party",[146] to examine the follow-up information submitted by governments and to make recommendations to the Committee that may include reconsideration of the date when the next periodic report is to be presented.[147]

Since acceding to the *International Covenant on Civil and Political Rights* in 1976, Canada has presented six reports to the Human Rights Committee: an initial report in 1979,[148] a supplementary report in 1984 (to take account of developments since entry into force of the *Canadian Charter*),[149] a second[150] and third[151] report, which were examined jointly on 23-24 October 1990,[152] the fourth report presented in 1999[153] and the fifth report

---

Covenant on Civil and Political Rights: the First Five Years of the H.R.C.", (1982) 76 *American Journal of International Law* 142; J.L. Gomez del Prado, "United Nations Conventions on Human Rights: The Practice of the Human Rights Committee and the Committee on the Elimination of Racial Discrimination in Dealing with Reporting Obligations of States Parties", (1985) 7 *Human Rights Quarterly* 492; Farrock Jhabvala, "The Practice of the Covenant's Human Rights Committee, 1976-82: Review of State Party Reports", (1984) 6 *Human Rights Quarterly* 81; Sarah Joseph, "New Procedures Concerning the Human Rights Committee's Examination of State Reports", (1995) 13 *Netherlands Quarterly of Human Rights* 5; T. Opsahl, "The Human Rights Committee", in P. Alston, ed., *The United Nations and Human Rights*, Oxford: Clarendon Press, 1992, pp. 369-443.

144   Michael O'Flaherty, "The Concluding Observations of the United Nations Treaty Bodies", (2006) 6 *Human Rights Law Review* 27.

145   UN Doc. A/57/40, Vol. I, para 55.

146   "General Comment No. 30 (75), Reporting Obligations of States parties under article 40 of the Covenant", UN Doc. CCPR/C/21/Rev.2/Add.12, para. 5.

147   *Ibid.*, para. 6. The procedure was confirmed in Rule 70A, adopted by the Committee on 21 March 2002: UN Doc. A/57/40, Vol. I, Annex III.A, para. 5.

148   UN Doc. CCPR/C/1/Add.43, examined 25, 26 and 28 March 1980 (UN Doc. CCPR/C/SR.205 to 208 and 211).

149   UN Doc. CCPR/C/1/Add.62, examined 31 October, 1-2 November 1984 (UN Doc. CCPR/C/SR.558 to 560 and 562).

150   UN Doc. CCPR/C/51/Add.1.

151   UN Doc. CCPR/C/64/Add.1.

152   UN Doc. CCPR/C/SR.1010 to 1013.

153   UN Doc. CCPR/C/103/Add.5, examined 26 March 1999 (UN Doc. CCPR/SR.1737-1738).

presented in 2005.[154] The periodic reports are prepared jointly by the federal, provincial and territorial governments, each responsible for questions subject to its jurisdiction.[155] When presenting the initial report in March 1980, Canadian ambassador McPhail told the Committee that

> . . . in his country's opinion, the Committee's questions and comments, whether in the context of the Covenant or of its Optional Protocol, could have a significant impact and help to increase the understanding of the States parties of their obligations under the Covenant. The dialogue between the Committee and States parties was potentially one of the most important factors in the long-term development of international protection of human rights.[156]

In its fourth periodic report to the Human Rights Committee, the Government of Canada explained:

> 17. The question of ensuring implementation of international human rights treaties and, in particular, that there is adequate follow-up to the concluding observations of United Nations committees on Canada's reports on implementation of such treaties, is increasingly a matter of attention and priority in Canada.

> 18. Copies of the concluding observations of the Human Rights Committee on Canada's second and third reports were provided to all relevant federal departments after they were received. The summary records and a summary of the questions raised by the Committee were provided to all officials participating in the preparation of the present report, at the federal, provincial and territorial levels, with a request that questions and concerns of the Committee be taken into account in preparing the present report.

> 19. The Continuing Committee of Officials on Human Rights, which is the federal-provincial-territorial committee responsible for maintaining collaboration and consultation among governments in Canada with respect to implementation of international human rights instruments that Canada has ratified, is currently considering how better to achieve adequate follow-up to the concluding observations of United Nations committees on human rights matters, and has agreed that the question of implementation of human rights treaties should be a standing item on the agenda for its meetings.[157]

---

154   UN Doc. CCPR/C/CAN/2004/5, examined 17-18 October 2005 (UN Doc. CCPR/C/SR.2312-2313).

155   UN Doc. CCPR/C/SR.559, para. 19. See: Marie-France Major, "Reporting to the Human Rights Committee: The Canadian Experience", (2000) 38 *Canadian Yearbook of International Law* 261; Daniel Turp, "La préparation des rapports périodiques du Canada en application des traités relatifs aux droits et libertés", (1986) 23 *Canadian Yearbook of International Law* 161.

156   UN Doc. CCPR/C/SR.205.

157   UN Doc. CCPR/C/103/Add.5, paras. 17-19.

The lack of direct implementing legislation, making the *Covenant* directly applicable before the Canadian courts, is an ongoing sore point with some members of the Committee. On various occasions, Canadian representatives have explained to the Committee that Canadian law does not allow for direct application of the *Covenant*.[158] Canadian representative Martin Low told the Committee, during presentation of the supplementary report in 1984, that "[t]he courts could employ international standards only by construing them through a provision of domestic law, but they might refer to the Covenant, as part of international law, in coming to an interpretation of domestic laws that were ambiguous".[159] But Canadian officials have also told the Committee that "[t]he Charter gave effect to a number of substantive provisions of the Covenant."[160] In its fourth periodic report, Canda explained:

> The Canadian Charter of Rights and Freedoms, which is part of the Constitution of Canada and applies to all governments in Canada, is not a direct incorporation of the Covenant into domestic Canadian law. There are differences in both structure and substance between the two documents. However, the rights recognized in the Covenant are protected in Canada by a combination of constitutional, legislative and other measures. As Canada is a federal State, different aspects of human rights fall within the jurisdiction of the different levels of government (federal, provincial, territorial). There are a number of mechanisms that promote coordination and consistency between jurisdictions.[161]

Although the *Canadian Charter* and the *International Covenant on Civil and Political Rights* are not identical in all respects, government representatives have said that the differences between the two texts should not conceal their great similarity and their complementarity.[162] On occasion, members of the Committee have seemed perplexed by the relationship between Canadian law and the *Covenant*.[163] One member, Sir Vincent Evans, proposed the creation of a remedy within Canadian law based on the *Covenant* itself,[164] but this does not appear to have been taken seriously by Canadian officials or legislators.

Canada's most recent report, filed in November 2004, presents a somewhat streamlined approach, focussing on key measures adopted by Canadian jurisdictions over the previous decade that strengthen the country's compliance with the *International Covenant on Civil and Political Rights*.[165]

---

158 UN Doc. CCPR/C/SR.205, para. 4.
159 UN Doc. CCPR/C/SR.559, para. 23.
160 UN Doc. CCPR/C/SR.558, para. 5.
161 UN Doc. CCPR/C/103/Add.5, para. 22.
162 UN Doc. CCPR/C/SR.558, para. 12; also: UN Doc. CCPR/C/SR.559, para. 13.
163 UN Doc. CCPR/C/SR.558, paras. 36-37.
164 UN Doc. CCPR/C/SR.206, para. 44.
165 "Fifth periodic report, Canada", UN Doc. CCPR/C/CAN/2004/5.

The report contains separate subheadings for the federal government, each of the ten provisions and the three territories. It notes that non-governmental organizations have been consulted with respect to the federal portion of the report. It directly addresses concerns previously expressed by the Human Rights Committee.

Periodic reports provide interesting information about Canadian policies and legislation, but they are also of some significance from a strictly legal standpoint, because they indicate the interpretation that Canada gives to specific provisions of the *Covenant*. This aspect of the periodic report may be relevant in future human rights litigation before the Canadian courts, where the interpretation expressed therein might be invoked to challenge a position being taken by the Canadian government. For example, in the fifth periodic report of 2004 the Canadian government addressed the issue of homelessness within the context of article 6 of the *Covenant*, which protects the right to life.[166] This suggests an expansive interpretation of the right to life as expressed within Canadian law, for example in section 7 of the *Canadian Charter*. With respect to article 22 of the *Covenant*, which concerns protection of the family, the right to marriage and equality between spouses, Canada indicated that same-sex couples fall within the general scope of this provision.[167] In the federal section of the report, each specific provision in the *International Covenant* is accompanied by a subheading concerning caselaw and interpretation of the *Canadian Charter*, evidence of the relationship between these two instruments.

Subsequent to filing of the report, and in order to focus the presentation of the report in public session, the Human Rights Committee transmits a "list of issues" to a State party.[168] In its list of issues concerning the fifth periodic report, the Committee concentrated on such matters as Aboriginal land claims and related questions, the status of human rights commissions and counter-terrorism measures. After presentation of the report in October 2005, the Committee issued its "concluding observations". Several of the Committee's comments dealt with the rights and the treatment of Aboriginal peoples, as well as legislative measures adopted in response to threatened terrorism. It expressed great concern that under Canadian law it was possible to deport someone to a country where he or she might face torture or cruel, inhuman or degrading treatment of punishment. According to the Committee:

> The State party should recognize the absolute nature of the prohibition of torture, cruel, inhuman or degrading treatment, which in no circumstances can

166 *Ibid.*, paras. 35-40.
167 *Ibid.*, para. 138.
168 *e.g.*, "List of issues to be taken up in connection with the consideration of the fifth periodic report of Canada", UN Doc. CCPR/C/85/L/CAN.

be derogated from. Such treatments can never be justified on the basis of a balance to be found between society's interest and the individual's rights under article 7 of the Covenant. No person, without any exception, even those suspected of presenting a danger to national security or the safety of any person, and even during a state of emergency, may be deported to a country where he/ she runs the risk of being subjected to torture or cruel, inhuman or degrading treatment. The State party should clearly enact this principle into its law.[169]

The Human Rights Committee added that "[w]hile appreciating the firm denial by the delegation, the Committee is concerned by allegations that Canada may have cooperated with agencies known to resort to torture with the aim of extracting information from individuals detained in foreign countries".[170]

The Committee also drew attention to shortcomings in the jurisdiction of human rights commissions:

> It is concerned that human rights commissions still have the power to refuse referral of a human rights complaint for adjudication and that legal aid for access to courts may not be available. The State party should ensure that the relevant human rights legislation is amended at federal, provincial and territorial level and its legal system enhanced, so that all victims of discrimination have full and effective access to a competent tribunal and to an effective remedy.[171]

3.2.2.4   Petitions to the Human Rights Committee

When the two covenants were adopted, the idea that an individual petition might ensure some measure of enforcement of the obligations they set out was highly controversial.[172] The General Assembly agreed that only one mechanism would be created, for the *International Covenant on Civil and Political Rights* but not for the *International Covenant on Economic, Social and Cultural Rights*, and that it would be optional. Canada was among the first countries to subscribe to the *Optional Protocol*. Within months, petitions from aggrieved Canadians were being filed at the Geneva or the

---

169 "Concluding Observations of the Human Rights Committee, Canada", UN Doc. CCPR/ C/CAN/CO/5, para. 15.

170 *Ibid.*, para. 16.

171 *Ibid.*, para. 11.

172 On individual petitions, see, generally: Alfred de Zayas, "The Examination of Individual Complaints by the United Nations Human Rights Committee under the Optional Protocol to the International Covenant on Civil and Political Rights", in Gudmundur Alfredsson, Jonas Grimhelden, Bertrand Ramcharan & Alfred de Zayas, *International Human Rights Monitoring Mechanisms: Essays in Honour of Jakob Th. Möller*, The Hague/Boston/London: Kluwer Academic, 2001.

New York offices of the Human Rights Committee.[173] Many countries were initially wary of this petition procedure and its encroachment on their national sovereignty, but as the prestige and authority of the Human Rights Committee has spread, so the list of States parties to the *Optional Protocol* has grown. They now comprise a substantial majority of States parties to the *International Covenant on Civil and Political Rights*. The petition mechanism was an important innovation because previously individuals had been for all intents and purposes without standing at international law. The protection of their fundamental rights had been viewed as an internal matter for each state, of only marginal concern to international courts or other bodies. The *Optional Protocol* in effect creates a form of international court of appeal in the field of civil and political rights of individuals, albeit without enforcement powers, but nevertheless of considerable persuasive authority.

The language used in the *Optional Protocol* eschews suggestions that the Human Rights Committee might constitute some kind of international "tribunal". In a general sense, the terminology employed in the *Optional Protocol* avoids judicial jargon, although the reality is somewhat different. Petitions or applications are called "communications", and the final judgments of the Committee are described as "views". This reflects unease at the time the Covenants were being adopted that the Committee might turn into some kind of international court. In fact, that development was more or less inevitable. Over the years, while the official nomenclature in the *Optional Protocol* has remained unchanged, colloquial references to the procedure increasingly reflect its quasi-judicial nature. It is now common to speak of the caselaw or jurisprudence of the Human Rights Committee.

In principle, like many other United Nations bodies, the Committee operates by consensus, and this has meant that its decisions are often extremely general and quite summary in scope. Because of the traditions of the Committee, which were born in the consensus culture of the Cold War, members compromise on quite summary findings, often little more than a sentence or two. Its decisions can be contrasted with judgments of the European Court of Human Rights or the Inter-American Court of Human Rights, which often undertake substantial and detailed legal developments. This creates a problem when lawyers attempt to invoke decisions of the

---

173 Probably the first was *L.P.* v. *Canada* (No. 2/1976) UN Doc. CCPR/C/OP/1, p. 21, [1984-85] *Canadian Human Rights Yearbook* 341, a complaint from an American detained in a British Columbia penitentiary. Following the practice of the Human Rights Committee, once the application of "L.P." was declared admissible, his full name appeared in the style of cause. The case was re-registered, and the final views of the Committee are reported as *Pinkney* v. *Canada* (No. 27/1978), UN Doc. CCPR/C/14/D/27/1977, UN Doc. CCPR/3/Add.1, Vol. II, p. 385, UN Doc. CCPR/C/OP/1, p. 95, 2 *Human Rights Law Journal* 344, [1983] *Canadian Human Rights Yearbook* 315. Since 1976, more than 100 petitions have been filed against Canada.

Human Rights Committee before national judges. Although the latter recognize rulings of the European Court of Human Rights or the Inter-American Court of Human Rights, because they seem to resemble their own judgments, the laconic decisions of the Human Rights Committee are quite unfamiliar. This impacts negatively on the persuasive dimension of views of the Human Rights Committee when they are produced in domestic jurisdictions. There has been a tendency for individual members to draft their own views, some of them concurring, some of them dissenting, and this has considerably enriched the jurisprudence of the Committee. In a Canadian case involving extradition for a capital crime to the United States, *Cox* v. *Canada*, a majority of the Committee's eighteen members signed individual concurring or dissenting opinions.[174]

Despite their officially non-binding character, decisions of the Human Rights Committee often result in legislative and policy changes, the result of political initiatives rather than national judicial intervention. Canada provides some of the best examples of this compliance with Committee "judgments". One of the first Canadian cases before the Committee, *Lovelace* v. *Canada*,[175] involved a woman from the Maliseet Indian band. She invoked section 12(1)(b) of the *Indian Act*,[176] a provision that deprived Aboriginal women who married non-Aboriginal men of their Indian status; although it did not do the same for Aboriginal men who married non-Aboriginal women. In the early 1970s, the Supreme Court of Canada dismissed a challenge to the provision based on the *Canadian Bill of Rights* in the *Lavell* case,[177] setting the stage for one of the first "communications" to the Human Rights Committee. In its views, issued in 1981, the Committee held that the impugned provision of the *Indian Act* violated Ms Lovelace's right to enjoy her own culture as a member of an ethnic minority, as set out in article 27 of the *Covenant*, although the Committee did not consider that she was a victim of discrimination within the meaning of article 26 of the *Covenant*.[178] Canada reacted to the Committee's conclusions by amending the *Indian Act* and repealing the provision.[179] When Canada presented its subsequent periodic report to the Committee, it proudly announced the measures it had taken to comply with the Committee's views.[180] The amend-

---

174 *Cox* v. *Canada* (No. 539/1993), UN Doc. CCPR/C/52/D/539/1993, (1995) 15 *Human Rights Law Journal* 410.

175 *Lovelace* v. *Canada* (No. 24/1977), UN Doc. CCPR/C/13/D/24/1977, UN Doc. CCPR/3/Add.1, Vol. II, p. 320, UN Doc. CCPR/C/OP/1, p. 83, [1983] *Canadian Human Rights Yearbook* 306, 68 ILR 17.

176 RSC 1970, c. I-6.

177 *Canada (Attorney General)* v. *Lavell*, [1974] SCR 1349.

178 But see: UN Doc. CCPR/C/SR.206, para. 27 (Graefrath).

179 *An Act to amend the Indian Act*, SC 1985, c. 27, s. 4.

180 UN Doc. CCPR/C/OP/2, p. 224, [1984-85] *Canadian Human Rights Yearbook* 373.

ments to the *Indian Act* that were adopted following the *Lovelace* decision where themselves challenged by an Aboriginal band, mainly on the grounds that they violated the right of peoples to self-determination. The petition was dismissed at the admissibility stage as being incompatible *ratione materiae* with the right of petition under the *Optional Protocol*.[181]

Another excellent example of compliance with the Committee's views is provided by the Quebec government's behaviour in the case involving provisions of the *Charter of the French Language*[182] prohibiting signs in English as one of many measures aimed at protecting the French language. The legislation had been declared contrary to the constitutional protection of freedom of expression by the Supreme Court of Canada in *Ford* v. *Quebec*,[183] but the Quebec government reacted by invoking section 33 of the *Canadian Charter* and re-enacting the same provision "notwithstanding" the *Canadian Charter*.[184] This meant that the legislation was unattackable before the courts, at least pursuant to domestic law. However, the *Covenant*'s notwithstanding or "derogation" clause requires proof of a national emergency,[185] of which there was obviously no suggestion, and as a result, if the Committee were to take the same view of freedom of expression as that of the Supreme Court, there would be a violation of the *Covenant*.

Students of the Committee had known for many years that its members had already expressed astonishment at the scope of section 33 of the *Charter*.[186] One member of the Committee once said that section 33 was in breach of article 4 of the *Covenant*, which authorizes derogation or suspension of certain human rights, including freedom of expression, but only "[i]n time of public emergency which threatens the life of the nation and the existence of which is officially proclaimed".[187] Canadian representatives had valiantly attempted to justify section 33 with references to the British parliamentary tradition.[188] According to Martin Low, who presented Canada's supplementary report to the Committee in 1984:

> In the view of the Federal Government, any resort to section 33 would have to be compatible with Canada's international obligations, which would be invoked if there were any real derogation from the rights and freedoms set out in the Canadian Charter. Canada was obliged to report to the Human Rights Com-

181 *R.L.* et al. v. *Canada* (No. 358/1989), UN Doc. CCPR/C/43/D/358/1989, para. 6.4.
182 LRQ, c. C-11.
183 *Ford* v. *Québec (AG)*, [1988] 2 SCR 712, 54 DLR (4th) 577, 19 QAC 69, 36 CRR 1, 90 NR 84, 10 CHRR D/5559.
184 *An Act to Amend the Charter of the French Language*, SQ 1988, c. 54, s. 10.
185 *International Covenant on Civil and Political Rights*, (1976) 999 UNTS 171, [1976] CTS 47, art. 4(1).
186 UN Doc. CCPR/C/SR.558, para. 48; UN Doc. CCPR/C/SR.559, para. 11.
187 UN Doc. CCPR/C/SR.559, para. 9.
188 UN Doc. CCPR/C/SR.558, para. 18; UN Doc. CCPR/C/SR.559, para. 27.

mittee and was a party to the Optional Protocol so that anyone seeking to assert a right would be able to have recourse to the Committee if deprived of a remedy under section 33.[189]

This is exactly what happened following the Quebec National Assembly's adoption of legislation in 1988 aimed at neutralizing the effects of the Supreme Court's judgment in *Ford*. Three Quebec merchants petitioned the Committee, arguing that the legislation violated their freedom of expression as well as their rights, as members of a linguistic minority, to use their own language. When Canada presented its second and third periodic reports, in October 1990, these communications were already pending. Members of the Committee renewed their criticism of section 33.[190] The Committee's views were a foregone conclusion. In effect endorsing the reasoning of the Supreme Court of Canada, it declared that the contested provisions of the *Charter of the French Language* breached article 19 of the *International Covenant on Civil and Political Rights*, which protects freedom of expression.[191] The Committee did not, however, conclude that article 27, which guarantees minority rights, had been breached. The Committee said that English-speaking Quebeckers could not be considered a minority, because they in fact enjoyed a majority position within Canada. In the weeks that followed publication of the Committee's views, the Quebec government amended its legislation in order to eliminate the offending provisions. Thus, the Quebec provincial government complied with the views of the Human Rights Committee, although it had defied the same opinion when this emanated from the Supreme Court of Canada, as well as from the Quebec Court of Appeal.

Gauthier v. *Canada* concerned eligibility for full membership in the Canadian Press Gallery, a private association of journalists whose members had a monopoly over the media facilities of Parliament. This included access to the press gallery in Parliament, the only place where the public can take notes during parliamentary proceedings. Canada argued that such a measure was a restriction on freedom of expression that was justified in order to balance the need to ensure the effective and dignified operation of Parliament and the safety and security of its members. The Human Rights Committee did not disagree with the proposition that the protection of parliamentary procedure could be seen as a legitimate goal of public order and that an accreditation system could be a justified means of achieving that goal. But it said that because the accreditation system operated as a restric-

---

189   UN Doc. CCPR/C/SR.559, para. 28.

190   UN Doc. CCPR/C/SR.1010, paras. 54, 67; UN Doc. CCPR/C/SR.1013, paras. 13, 36.

191   *Ballantyne and Davidson, and McIntyre* v. *Canada* (Nos. 359/1989 and 385/1989), UN Doc. CCPR/C/47/D/385/1989, UN Doc. A/48/40, Vol. II, p. 91, 14 *Human Rights Law Journal* 171, 11 *Netherlands Quarterly of Human Rights* 469.

tion on freedom of expression, enshrined in article 19 of the *Covenant*, its operation and application must be shown as necessary and proportionate to the goal in question and not arbitrary. "In the instant case, the State party has allowed a private organization to control access to the parliamentary press facilities, without intervention", wrote the Committee. "The scheme does not ensure that there will be no arbitrary exclusion from access to the parliamentary media facilities."[192] Six members of the Committee also considered that there had been a violation of article 22, which protects freedom of association.[193]

Gauthier was issued in April 1999. By October that year the Government of Canada had reported back to the Committee that it had appointed an independent expert to review the Press Gallery's criteria for accreditation, as well as Gauthier's application for accreditation. The Government said it had also taken measures to allow visitors to Parliament to take notes. In order to address the Committee's concern that there should be a possibility of recourse for individuals who are denied membership of the Press Gallery, Canada said that in the future the Speaker of the House would be competent to receive complaints and appoint an independent expert to report to him about the validity of the complaints. In March 2000, Canada provided the Committee with a copy of the expert report on the Press Gallery's criteria for accreditation and their application in Gauthier's case. Following the issuance of the report, Gauthier was invited to apply again for accreditation with the Press Gallery.[194] But Gauthier subsequently complained that the Human Rights Committee's decision had not been implemented.[195] He told the Committee he had been granted a temporary six-month pass, which he had accepted "for economic reasons". He said the review by the independent expert was summary and superficial.[196]

The second edition of this book, published in 1996, stated: "In practice, the Committee's 'views' are quite analogous to judgments, because States act in response to them. Canada provides some of the best examples of this compliance with Committee 'judgments'."[197] But Gauthier's difficulties seemed to herald a new phase in Canada's relationship with the Committee

---

192 *Gauthier* v. *Canada* (No. 633/1995), UN Doc. CCPR/C/65/D/633/1995, para. 13.6.
193 *Ibid.*, Individual opinion by Lord Colville, Elizabeth Evatt, Cecilia Medina Quiroga and Hipólito Solari Yrigoyen (partly dissenting); Individual opinion by David Kretzmer *(partly dissenting)*; Individual opinion by Prafullachandra N. Bhagwati *(partly dissenting)*.
194 UN Doc. A/55/40, para. 607.
195 UN Doc. A/56/40 (Vol. I), para. 186.
196 UN Doc. A/57/40 (Vol. I), para. 234.
197 William A. Schabas, *International Human Rights Law and the Canadian Charter*, 2nd ed., Toronto: Carswell, 1996, p. 72.

characterized by difficulties in implementing the Committee's views. Two recent cases exemplify the change.

In *Waldman*, the Human Rights Committee held that the failure to provide Jewish parents with parochial schools for their children constituted discrimination prohibited by article 26 of the *International Covenant on Civil and Political Rights*. According to the Committee, "the Covenant does not oblige States parties to fund schools which are established on a religious basis. However, if a State party chooses to provide public funding to religious schools, it should make this funding available without discrimination."[198] The petitioner had complained that public funding was being provided for "separate schools" for Catholic children, but similar support was not available for other religious groups. Acknowledging the differential treatment, Canada argued that the separate schools resulted from a constitutional imperative with deep historical roots. The Committee explained:

> The Committee begins by noting that the fact that a distinction is enshrined in the Constitution does not render it reasonable and objective. In the instant case, the distinction was made in 1867 to protect the Roman Catholics in Ontario The material before the Committee does not show that members of the Roman Catholic community or any identifiable section of that community are now in a disadvantaged position compared to those members of the Jewish community that wish to secure the education of their children in religious schools. Accordingly, the Committee rejects the State party's argument that the preferential treatment of Roman Catholic schools is nondiscriminatory because of its Constitutional obligation.[199]

The case had come to the Committee following an unsuccessful challenge in the Supreme Court of Canada.[200] Shortly after the views in *Waldman* issued, Canada informed the Committee that the Government of Ontario had said it had no plans to extend funding to private religious schools or to the parents of children that attend such schools, and that it intends to adhere fully to its constitutional obligation to fund Roman Catholic schools.[201] A representative of the Committee met with Canadian officials to discuss follow-up but nothing productive seems to have come of it. Waldman himself complained about Canada's non-compliance, telling the Committee that Ontario's Minister of Education had said that the Government of Ontario was not prepared to adopt its proposals.[202] Ontario has not responded to the views of the Human Rights Committee, and was silent on the subject

---

198 *Waldman* v. *Canada* (No. 694/1996), UN Doc. CCPR/C/67/D/694/1996, para. 10.6.

199 *Ibid.*, para. 10.4.

200 *Adler* v. *Ontario*, [1996] 3 SCR 609, 30 OR (3d) 642n, 140 DLR (4th) 385, 40 CRR (2d) 1, 95 OAC 1.

201 UN Doc. A/55/40, para. 608.

202 UN Doc. A/56/40 (Vol. I), para. 187; UN Doc. A/57/40 (Vol. I), para. 237.

in its submission to Canada's fifth periodic report. In its concluding observations on the fifth periodic report, the Committee chided Canada on the
subject, saying it "should adopt steps in order to eliminate discrimination
on the basis of religion in the funding of schools in Ontario".[203] A companion
case to *Waldman* was dismissed at the admissibility stage because the
petitioners did not seek public funds for religious schools for their own
children but rather the removal of the benefit accorded to Catholic schools.
The Committee held that they were not "victims" within the meaning of the
Optional Protocol.[204]

Even more recently, Canada has been openly obstinate in refusing to
accept the findings of the Human Rights Committee. In *Ahani*, the Committee held that there had been a violation of article 9(4) of the *International
Covenant on Civil and Political Rights* when Mansour Ahani was deported
to Iran, after being detained for several months on the basis of a security
certificate. The Committee said that he had been denied the procedural
protections to which a detained person is entitled.[205] It also chastised Canada
because it had returned Ahani to Iran despite a provisional measures request
from the Committee that it keep him in Canada pending the determination
of the communication. Canada replied to the Committee:

> The State party contests the Committee's Views and submits that it has not
> violated its obligations under the Covenant. There has been no violation of its
> obligations in deporting the author while the case is under consideration by the
> Committee, as neither interim measures requests or indeed the Committee's
> views are binding on the State party. As there was no substantial risk of
> irreparable harm upon removal, and because the author posed a threat to the
> security of Canada, removal could not be delayed pending the Committee's
> decision. Despite the non-binding nature of interim measure requests the State
> party ensures the Committee that it always gives, as it did in this case, careful
> consideration to them, and will accept them wherever possible. This approach
> should not in any way be construed as a diminution of Canada's commitment
> to human rights or its ongoing collaboration with the Committee.
>
> Decisions on interim measure requests will be made on a case-by-case
> basis. As to the finding of a violation of article 9, paragraph 4, as the period of
> nine and a half months after the final resolution of the constitutionality of the
> security certificate procedure was too long, the State party reiterates the points
> made in its submission prior to consideration, that the delay of nine and a half
> months was attributable to the author. It submits that the reasonableness hearing
> was prolonged between July 1997 and April 1998 to accommodate the author's

203 "Concluding Observations of the Human Rights Committee, Canada", UN Doc. CCPR/
    C/CAN/CO/5, para. 21.
204 *Tadman* et al. v. *Canada* (No. 816/1998), UN Doc. CCPR/C/67/D/816/1998, para. 6.2.
205 *Ahani* v. *Canada* (No. 1051/2002), UN Doc. CCPR/C/80/D/1051/2002, paras. 10.3-
    10.4.

counsel of choice. Neither the author nor his counsel expressed any concern with the delay and never requested the Court to expedite the hearing.

Equally, the State party contests the finding of a violation of article 13, submitting that the expulsion decision was confirmed to be in accordance with law by the Supreme Court and that the author did not argue otherwise. The author was permitted to submit reasons against his expulsion and these submissions were considered by the Minister prior to concluding that he constituted a danger to the security of Canada and that he faced only a minimal risk of harm upon deportation. The author was aware that the information used in the determination of the reasonableness of the security certificate process was to be the basis of the assessment of the danger he represented to the security of Canada. In the State party's view, article 13 does not require that he be given all the information available to the State and, considering it was a national security case, the process was fair. However, in order to simplify the process with respect to whether a person who is a danger to the security of Canada may be removed from Canada, the State party confirms that it now affords to all persons the same "enhanced procedural guarantees". In particular, all documents used to form the danger opinion are now provided to the person redacted for security concerns and they are entitled to make submissions.

The State party submits that its determination that the author did not face a substantial risk of torture upon removal has been confirmed by subsequent events, including a conversation between a Canadian representative and the author's mother, the latter of whom confirmed that the author was in good health, and a visit by the author to the Canadian embassy in Tehran on 1 October 2002, during which he did not complain of being ill-treated.

For the aforementioned reasons, the State party disagrees that it should make any reparation to the author or that it has any obligations to take further steps in this case. Nevertheless, in October 2002, Canada indicated to Iran that it expects it to comply with its international human rights obligations, including with respect to the author.

In its reply to the list of issues of the Committee against Torture, the State party submitted that it was in full compliance with its international obligations in this case and that it did not violate its obligations under article 13 Covenant. The Supreme Court of Canada concluded that the process accorded to the author was consistent with the principles of fundamental justice guaranteed by the Canadian Charter of Rights and Freedoms. The Court was satisfied that Ahani was fully informed of the Minister's case against him and given a full opportunity to respond. It also concluded that the procedures followed did not prejudice the author.

The decision to remove was confirmed to be in accordance with law by the Supreme Court of Canada. Canada, on the basis of all of the evidence available to it, including Ahani's testimony and extensive submissions made by his counsel, concluded that the risk that the author would face upon return to Iran was only "minimal". Indeed, Canada's decision in this regard was upheld at all levels of judicial review and appeal. The Supreme Court of Canada held that the Minister's decision that the author did not face a substantial risk of torture on deportation was "unassailable."

The author was able to submit reasons against his removal. The decision to remove Ahani was the result of the balancing between the danger the author represented to the security of Canada and the risk he would face if returned to his country. This process culminated in the opinion issued by the Minister that Ahani constitutes a danger to the security of Canada and that he faced only a minimal risk of harm upon deportation. In order to simplify the process with respect to whether a person who is a danger to the security of Canada may be removed from Canada, the Canadian government now affords all such persons the same enhanced procedural guarantees. In particular, all documents used to form the danger opinion are now provided to the person redacted for security concerns and they are entitled to make submissions.[206]

In its fifth periodic report to the Human Rights Committee, Canada expressed its position on interim measures orders more generally:

> Canada is of the view that interim measures requests are non-binding. Article 39(2) of the *Covenant* provides that the Committee shall establish its own rules of procedure. Rule 86 of the Committee's Rules of Procedure provides that the Committee may inform the State of its views as to whether interim measures may be desirable to avoid irreparable damage to the victim of the alleged violation. The language of Rule 86 is consistent with the non-binding nature of the Committee's views. Neither the Covenant nor the Optional Protocol provides for Committee to make orders binding on States. Nevertheless, the Government of Canada always gives careful consideration to interim measures requests from the Committee, and will respect them where it is possible to do so. Canada notes that it usually acts in accordance with the interim measures requests issued by human rights bodies. It is committed to do so in the future, although the decision whether or not to act in accordance with an interim measures request must necessarily be made on a case-by-case basis. This should not in any way be construed as a diminution of Canada's commitment to human rights or its ongoing collaboration with the Committee.[207]

The response is quite unprecedented, in that for the first time Canada has simply rejected the Committee's conclusions. It is a rather sobering reminder of the fact that Committee decisions are at best only persuasive, and not only before the courts but also for the governments themselves.

The Human Rights Committee reacted to the Canadian position in its views on the *Ahani* petition:

> Interim measures pursuant to rule 86 of the Committee's rules adopted in conformity with article 39 of the Covenant, are essential to the Committee's role under the Protocol. Flouting of the rule, especially by irreversible measures such as the execution of the alleged victim or his/her deportation from a State

---

206   "Report of the Human Rights Committee", UN Doc. A/60/40 (Vol. II), pp. 499-501.
207   "Fifth periodic report, Canada", UN Doc. CCPR/C/CAN/2004/5, paras. 47-48.

party to face torture or death in another country, undermines the protection of Covenant rights through the Optional Protocol.[208]

Later, in its Concluding Observations on Canada's Fifth Periodic Report, it returned to the subject:

> The Committee notes with concern the State party's reluctance to consider that it is under an obligation to implement the Committee's requests for interim measures of protection. The Committee recalls that in acceding to the Optional Protocol, the State party recognized the Committee's competence to receive and examine complaints from individuals under the State party's jurisdiction. Disregard of the Committee's requests for interim measures is inconsistent with the State party's obligations under the Covenant and the Optional Protocol. The State party should adhere to its obligations under the Covenant and the Optional Protocol, in accordance with the principle of *pacta sunt servanda*, and take the necessary measures to avoid similar violations in future.[209]

Canada's position weakens the entire regime, and will provide comfort to many States parties who tend to be dismissive of the significance and the findings of the Human Rights Committee.

There have been ten findings of violation by the Committee. Besides the *Lovelace*, *Gauthier*, *Ballantyne*, *Waldman* and *Ahani* cases, discussed above, the Committee has found Canada to be in breach of the *Covenant* in cases dealing with procedural guarantees in a criminal appeal,[210] Aboriginal land claims,[211] two cases involving extradition or deportation where capital punishment may be imposed[212] and a second case concerning Quebec language legislation.[213]

---

208 *Ahani* v. *Canada, supra* note 205, para. 8.2.
209 "Concluding Observations of the Human Rights Committee, Canada", UN Doc. CCPR/C/CAN/CO/5, para. 7; see also: "Concluding Observations of the Human Rights Committee, Canada", UN Doc. CCPR/C/79/Add.105, para. 14
210 *Pinkney* v. *Canada* (No. 27/1978), UN Doc. CCPR/C/14/D/27/1977, UN Doc. CCPR/3/Add.1, Vol. II, p. 385, UN Doc. CCPR/C/OP/1.
211 *Lubicon Lake Band (Bernard Ominayak)* v. *Canada* (No. 167/1984) UN Doc. CCPR/C/38/D/167/1984, UN Doc. A/45/40, Vol. II, p. 1, 11 *Human Rights Law Journal* 305, [1991-92] *Canadian Human Rights Yearbook* 221. In another case, involving fishing rights, the Committee found no violation of the *Covenant*: *Howard* v. *Canada* (No. 879/1999), UN Doc. CCPR/C/84/D/879/1999.
212 *Ng* v. *Canada* (No. 469/1991), UN Doc. CCPR/C/49/D/469/1991, UN Doc. A/49/40, Vol. II, p. 189, 15 *Human Rights Law Journal* 149; *Judge* v. *Canada* (No. 829/1998), UN Doc. CCPR/C/78/D/829/1998. In the 2005 Annual Report of the Committee, UN Doc. A/60/40 (Vol. II), at 499, Canada stated, with respect to the Judge case: "Following the Special Rapporteur's request to the State party to provide an update from the United States authorities on the author's situation, the State party reiterated its response outlined in the Follow-up Report (CCPR/C/80/FU1) and the Annual Report (CCPR/C/81/CRP.1/

Canadian petitions have accounted for a substantial percentage of the Committee's caseload although, as the former Director of Communications for the Committee, Jakob Möller, pointed out some years ago:

> This does certainly not mean that human rights violations are more widespread in Canada than in other countries. It would be wiser to conclude that the Covenant and the Optional Protocol are better known instruments to the public in Canada than in most other countries.[214]

Because Canada was among the first States to accept the *Optional Protocol*, it attracted what may appear to have been disproportionate attention from the Human Rights Committee. In fact, most Canadian applications to the Committee have been declared inadmissible for failure to exhaust domestic remedies.[215] In order for communications to be admissible, the Committee must be satisfied that local remedies have been exhausted, and that similar proceedings are not pending before another international tribunal or body.

There is no requirement that petitions be filed within a particular period of time following the alleged violation, although they must concern events subsequent to the coming into force of the *Optional Protocol*.[216] A portion of one application was dismissed for lack of jurisdiction *ratione temporis* on this basis, given that it concerned facts that arose before the entry into force of the *International Covenant on Civil and Political Rights*.[217] Increas-

---

Add.6). It added that a stay of execution was issued by the United States District Court for Eastern Pennsylvania in October 2002, and no date has been set for his execution."

213   *Singer* v. *Canada* (No. 455/1991), UN Doc. A/49/40, Vol. II, p. 155. Another case concerning Quebec's language legislation was dismissed for failure to exhaust domestic remedies: *Hoffmann* et al. v. *Canada* (No. 1220/2003), UN Doc. CCPR/C/84/D/1220/2003.

214   Jakob Th. Möller, "Recent Jurisprudence of the Human Rights Committee", [1991-92] *Canadian Human Rights Yearbook* 79.

215   *Adu* v. *Canada* (No. 654/1995), UN Doc. CCPR/C/60/D/654/1995, para. 6.2; *Atkinson* et al. v. *Canada* (No. 573/1994), UN Doc. CCPR/C/55/D/573/1994, para. 8.3; *Cziklin* v. *Canada* (No. 741/1997), UN Doc. CCPR/C/66/D/741/1997; *Dupuy* v. *Canada* (No. 939/2000), UN Doc. CCPR/C/83/D/939/2000, para. 7.5; *G.T.* v. *Canada* (No. 420/1990), UN Doc. CCPR/C/46/D/420/1990; *Hoffmann* et al. v. *Canada*, *supra* note 213; *Zundel* v. *Canada* (No. 953/2000), UN Doc. CCPR/C/78/D/953/2000, para. 8.6; *K.C.* v. *Canada* (No. 86/1992), UN Doc. CCPR/C/45/D/486/1992; *Nartey* v. *Canada* (No. 604/1994), UN Doc. CCPR/C/60/D/604/1994; *Romans* v. *Canada* (No. 1040/2001), UN Doc. CCPR/C/81/D/1040/2001; *R.L.* et al. v. *Canada* (No. 358/1989), UN Doc. CCPR/C/43/D/358/1989, para. 6.4; *N.S.* v. *Canada* (No. 26/1978), UN Doc. CCPR/C/4/D/26/1978; *E.H.P.* v. *Canada* (No. 67/1980), UN Doc. CCPR/C/17/D/67/1980; *J.S.* v. *Canada* (No. 130/1982), UN Doc. CCPR/C/18/D/130/1982; *S.H.B.* v. *Canada* (No. 192/1985), UN Doc. CCPR/C/29/D/192/1985; *R.L.* v. *Canada* (No. 342/1988), UN Doc. CCPR/C/35/D/342/1988.

216   *C.E.* v. *Canada* (No. 13/1977), UN Doc. CCPR/C/2/D/13/1977; *J.K.* v. *Canada* (No. 174/1984), UN Doc. CCPR/C/23/D/174/1984.

217   *Atkinson* et al. v. *Canada* (No. 573/1994), UN Doc. CCPR/C/55/D/573/1994, para. 8.2.

ingly, the Committee considers the admissibility and the merits of communications in the same decision.

The Committee requires that petitions be submitted by specific and identifiable victims. The Committee has ruled that a case claiming a violation of the right to freedom of expression because a press conference was not allowed in the Parliamentary press gallery was simply incompatible *ratione materiae* with article 19 of the *International Covenant on Civil and Political Rights.*

> Although the right to freedom of expression, as enshrined in article 19, paragraph 2, of the Covenant, extends to the choice of medium, it does not amount to an unfettered right of any individual or group to hold press conferences within the parliamentary precincts, or to have such press conferences broadcast by others. While it is true that the author had obtained a booking with the Press Gallery for the Charles Lynch Press Conference Room and that this booking was made inapplicable through the motion passed unanimously by Parliament to exclude the author's access to the parliamentary precincts, the Committee notes that the author remained at liberty to hold a press conference elsewhere. The Committee therefore takes the position, after a careful examination of the material before it, that the author's claim, based on the inability to hold a press conference in the Charles Lynch Press Conference Room, falls outside the scope of the right to freedom of expression, as protected under article 19, paragraph 2, of the Covenant.[218]

In another case, it denied the application of an Aboriginal band based on article 1 of the *Covenant*, which establishes the right of peoples to self-determination, on the basis that this fell outside the scope of the individual petition mechanism.[219]

Several cases have been declared admissible, but then dismissed on the merits. The Committee has rejected applications concerning expulsion of Canadian residents for criminal activity,[220] discrimination based on an obligation to wear a hard hat at work,[221] fishing rights of Aboriginal peoples[222] and political participation of Aboriginal peoples in constitutional negotiations.[223] In the *Ross* case, which addressed disciplinary sanctions on a teacher for expression of anti-Semitic views, the Committee essentially upheld the

---

218 *Zundel* v. *Canada, supra* note 215, para. 8.5.

219 *R.L.* et al. v. *Canada, supra* note 215, para. 6.2.

220 *Stewart* v. *Canada* (No. 538/1993), UN Doc. CCPR/C/58/D/538/1993; *Canepa* v. *Canada* (No. 558/1993), UN Doc. CCPR/C/59/D/558/1993.

221 *Bhinder* v. *Canada* (No. 208/1986), UN Doc. CCPR/C/37/D/208/1986, UN Doc. A/45/40, Vol. II, p. 50, [1989-90] *Canadian Human Rights Yearbook* 306. *Bhinder* is discussed in some detail in Chapter 4, at 414-415.

222 *Howard* v. *Canada, supra* note 211.

223 *Marshall* et al. *(Micmaq Tribal Society)* v. *Canada* (No. 205/1986), UN Doc. CCPR/C/43/D/205/1986, UN Doc. A/47/40, p. 213.

findings of the Supreme Court of Canada,[224] and concluded that the measures taken were justifiable under article 19(3) of the *International Covenant on Civil and Political Rights*.[225] In one of its first cases, the Committee considered whether changes in Canadian law affecting parole eligibility violated the prohibition of retroactive penalties set out in article 15(1) of the *Covenant*:

> The Committee further notes that its interpretation and application of the International Covenant on Civil and Political Rights has to be based on the principle that the terms and concepts of the Covenant are independent of any particular national system or law and of all dictionary definitions. Although the terms of the Covenant are derived from long traditions within many nations, the Committee must now regard them as having an autonomous meaning. The parties have made extensive submissions, in particular as regards the meaning of the word "penalty" and as regards relevant Canadian law and practice. The Committee appreciates their relevance for the light they shed on the nature of the issue in dispute. On the other hand, the meaning of the word "penalty" in Canadian law is not, as such, decisive. Whether the word "penalty" in article 15 (1) should be interpreted narrowly or widely, and whether it applies to different kinds of penalties, "criminal" and "administrative", under the Covenant, must depend on other factors. Apart from the text of article 15 (1), regard must be had, inter alia, to its object and purpose.[226]

The Committee declined to rule on this interesting question, however, because it found that by the time the application was considered, the petitioner had already been released, and that therefore he had obtained the benefit that he had sought. In a case concerning the right of penitentiary inmates to vote, it declared the application admissible, but then reconsidered the question and ruled that a declaratory judgment was an available remedy. The Committee ruled the case inadmissible, but noted as "follow up", that the Canadian Government had subsequently informed the Committee of a Federal Court of Canada ruling upholding the right of penitentiary prisoners in Quebec to vote in provincial elections and ordering the Federal Minister of Justice and the Solicitor General to make the necessary arrangements to put this into effect.[227]

---

224 *Ross* v. *New Brunswick School District No. 15*, (sub nom. *Attis* v. *New Brunswick School District No. 15*) [1996] 1 SCR 825.
225 *Ross* v. *Canada* (No. 736/1997), UN Doc. CCPR/C/70/D/736/1997.
226 *Van Duzen* v. *Canada* (No. 50/1979), UN Doc. CCPR/C/15/D/50/1979, UN Doc. CCPR/3/Add.1, Vol. II, p. 402, UN Doc. CCPR/C/OP/1, p. 118, [1983] *Canadian Human Rights Yearbook* 330, 3 *Human Rights Law Journal* 181, 70 ILR 235. See also: *MacIsaac* v. *Canada* (No. 55/1979), UN Doc. CCPR/C/17/D/55/1979.
227 *C.F.* v. *Canada* (No. 113/1981), UN Doc. CCPR/C/24/D/113/1981, UN Doc. CCPR/C/OP/1, p. 13, 7 *Human Rights Law Journal* 300, [1986] *Canadian Human Rights Yearbook* 185. The Federal Court decision is reported: *Lévesque* v. *Canada (AG)*, [1986]

Sometimes, cases have been rejected at the admissibility stage for insufficiently substantiating a claim, hinting at a finding on the merits rather than just a procedural basis for the dismissal. Examples include matters concerning lack of impartiality of a refugee tribunal[228] and of a civil court,[229] tax provisions that discriminate against mothers having custody of children,[230] parole elibility,[231] double jeopardy with respect to a compensation order in a criminal trial,[232] denial of immigration sponsorship,[233] detention during refugee proceedings,[234] procedural abuse during criminal trials,[235] denial of medical treatment to prisoners,[236] discrimination in employment matters,[237] legal provisions that violate the presumption of innocence,[238] expulsion to a country where there is a threat of torture,[239] administrative review of availability for military pensions[240] and failure to provide for discrimination on grounds of political belief in the *Ontario Human Rights Code*.[241] Very occasionally, in rejecting an application on procedural grounds, the Committee has indicated its interest in considering the matter on the merits. In a communication concerning environmental degradation resulting associated with the Port Hope nuclear refinery, the Committee said it "raise[d] serious issues, with regard to the obligation of States parties to protect human life (article 6 (1))".[242]

The Committee has consistently refused to consider cases that amount to an *actio popularis*, that is, where the individual has not demonstrated

---

2 FC 287, 25 DLR (4th) 184, 7 CHRR D/3617, 20 CRR 15 (TD). The litigation is discussed in more detail in Chapter 4, at 330-332.

228 *Adu* v. *Canada, supra* note 215, para. 6.3.
229 *Lacika* v. *Canada* (No. 638/1995), UN Doc. CCPR/C/55/D/638/1995; *R.L.* v. *Canada, supra* note 215.
230 *Byrne* et al. v. *Canada* (No. 742/1997), UN Doc. CCPR/C/65/D/742/1997, paras., 6.3-6.4.
231 *A.R.S.* v. *Canada* (No. 91/1981), UN Doc. CCPR/C/14/D/91/1981.
232 *Devgan* v. *Canada* (No. 948/2000), UN Doc. CCPR/C/70/D/948/2000.
233 *A.S.* v. *Canada* (No. 68/1980), UN Doc. CCPR/C/12/D/68/1980.
234 *V.M.R.B.* v. *Canada* (No. 236/1987) UN Doc. CCPR/C/33/D/236/1987.
235 *Dupuy* v. *Canada, supra* note 215; *Z.Z.* v. *Canada* (No. 17/1977, UN Doc. CCPR/C/4/D/17/1977.
236 *Fabrikant* v. *Canada* (No. 970/2001), UN Doc. CCPR/C/79/D/970/2001.
237 *Keshavjee* v. *Canada* (No. 949/2000), UN Doc. CCPR/C/70/D/949/2000; *J.M.* v. *Canada* (No. 559/1993), UN Doc. CCPR/C/50/D/559/1993; *G.* v. *Canada* (No. 934/2000), UN Doc. CCPR/C/69/D/934/2000; *Riley* et al. v. *Canada* (No. 1379/2005), UN Doc. CCPR/C/84/D/1379/2005; *Singh* v. *Canada* (No. 761/1997), UN Doc. CCPR/C/60/D/761/1997; *Tadman* et al. v. *Canada* (No. 816/1998), UN Doc. CCPR/C/67/D/816/1998.
238 *Gillan* v. *Canada* (No. 936/2000), UN Doc. CCPR/C/69/D/936/2000.
239 *Singh* v. *Canada* (No. 1315/2004), UN Doc. CCPR/C/86/D/1315/2004.
240 *Landry* v. *Canada* (No. 25/112), UN Doc. CCPR/C/27/D/R.25/112.
241 *Jazairi* v. *Canada* (No. 958/2000), UN Doc. CCPR/C/82/D/958/2000, para. 7.4.
242 *E.H.P.* v. *Canada* (No. 67/1980), UN Doc. CCPR/C/17/D/67/1980, para. 8.

sufficient personal interest and is simply litigating an issue of general public interest.[243] Unlike some other international human rights instruments, which authorize applications by organizations, the *Optional Protocol* confines the right of petition to individuals (in the French version, *particuliers*).[244] A political party, for example, has no standing to petition the Committee.[245] In an early Canadian case, a Grand Captain of the Mikmaq tribal society petitioned the Committee alleging a violation of the right of self-determination by Canada. The Committee was not satisfied that the petitioner was authorized to act on behalf of the Mikmaq tribal society.[246] It seemed implicit in its reasoning that the Mikmaq tribal society was entitled to assert a violation of its collective right of self-determination.[247] Subsequently, however, the Committee clarified the matter in *Lubicon Lake Band* v. *Canada*, ruling that only an individual may submit a communications under the *Optional Protocol*.[248]

In exceptionally clear cases, the Committee has dismissed cases for "abuse of process"[249] or "abuse of the right of submission",[250] acting pursuant to article 3 of the *Optional Protocol*. Occasionally, it will refer to article 3 of the *Optional Protocol*, which says it "shall consider inadmissible any communication under the present Protocol which is anonymous, or which it considers to be an abuse of the right of submission of such communications or to be incompatible with the provisions of the Covenant", but without specifying precisely on what basis the petition is declared inadmissible.[251]

---

243 *Jazairi* v. *Canada, supra* note 241, para. 7.6; *Queenan* v. *Canada* (No. 1379/2005), UN Doc. CCPR/C/84/D/1379/2005, para. 4.
244 *Optional Protocol to the International Covenant on Civil and Political Rights*, (1976) 999 UNTS 171, [1976] CTS 47, art. 1.
245 *J.R.T. and W.G.P.* v. *Canada* (No. 104/1981), UN Doc. CCPR/C/OP/2, p. 25, [1984-85] *Canadian Human Rights Yearbook* 357, 5 CHRR D/2097, 4 *Human Rights Law Journal* 193, para. 8(a).
246 *A.D.* v. *Canada* (No. 78/1980) UN Doc. CCPR/C/22/D/78/1980, para. 8.2.
247 Manfred Nowak, *Covenant on Civil and Political Rights: CCPR Commentary*, 2nd ed., Kehl: Engel, 2005, at 831.
248 *Lubicon Lake Band (Bernard Ominayak)* v. *Canada*, (No. 167/1984) UN Doc. CCPR/C/38/D/167/1984, UN Doc. A/45/40, Vol. II, p. 1, 11 *Human Rights Law Journal* 305, [1991-92] *Canadian Human Rights Yearbook* 221, para. 32.1.
249 *Jazairi* v. *Canada, supra* note 241, para. 7.2.
250 *M.A.B.* et al. v. *Canada* (No. 570/1993), UN Doc. CCPR/C/50/D/570/1993, para. 4.3; *Z.P.* v. *Canada* (No. 341/1988), UN Doc. CCPR/C/41/D/341/1988, para. 5.5.
251 *H.R.B.* v. *Canada* (No. 534/1993), UN Doc. CCPR/C/49/D/534/1993.

Reference has been made on several occasions by Canadian tribunals to the jurisprudence or "views" of the Human Rights Committee.[252] In one case, the Canadian Human Rights Tribunal actually relied on a finding by the Human Rights Committee that section 13(1) of the *Canadian Human Rights Act* was consistent with Canada's international obligations under the *International Covenant on Civil and Political Rights.*[253]

---

252 *Commission des droits de la personne du Québec* c. *Immeubles Ni/Dia Inc.*, [1992] RJQ
2977 (TDPQ) and *Kelly* v. *Canada (Minister of Employment and Immigration)*, [1993]
IADD No 739 (Imm & Ref Bd (App Div)), citing *Aumeeruddy-Cziffra* v. *Mauritius*
(No. 35/1978), UN Doc. A/36/40, pp. 144-153, 62 ILR 285; *Québec (Procureur général)*
v. *Cour du Québec*, JE 92-1592 (SC) and *Immeubles Claude Dupont Inc.* v. *Québec
(PG)*, [1994] RJQ 1973 (SC), citing *Ballantyne and Davidson, and McIntyre* v. *Canada*,
(Nos. 359/1989 and 385/1989), UN Doc. CCPR/C/47/D/385/1989, UN Doc. A/48/40,
Vol. II, p. 91, 14 *Human Rights Law Journal* 171, 11 *Netherlands Quarterly of Human
Rights* 469; *Lévesque* v. *Canada (AG)*, [1986] 2 FC 287, 25 DLR (4th) 184, 7 CHRR
D/3617, 20 CRR 15 (TD), citing *C.F.* v. *Canada*, (No. 113/1981), UN Doc. CCPR/C/
24/D/113/1981, UN Doc. CCPR/C/OP/1, p. 13, 7 *Human Rights Law Journal* 300,
[1986] *Canadian Human Rights Yearbook* 185; *Commission des droits de la personne
du Québec* c. *Immeubles Ni/Dia Inc.*, *ibid.*, citing *Danning* v. *Netherlands* (No. 180/
1984), UN Doc. CCPR/C/OP/2, p. 205, 9 *Human Rights Law Journal* 259 and *Sprenger*
v. *Netherlands* (No. 395/1990), UN Doc. A/47/40, p. 319 *Bailey* v. *Minister of National
Revenue*, (1980) 1 CHRR D/193 (CHRT), *Cameron* v. *Nel-Gor Castle Nursing Home*,
(1984) 5 CHRR D/2170, 84 CLLC ¶17,008 (Ont. Comm. Inquiry), *Twinn* v. *R.*, (1986)
[1987] 2 FC 450, 6 FTR 138 (TD), *Batchewana Indian Band* v. *Batchewana Indian
Band* [1994] 1 FC 394 (TD), varied, [1997] 1 FC 689 (CA), leave to appeal allowed,
(1997) 215 NR 239n, [1999] 2 SCR 203, reconsideration refused, (2000) 2000
CarswellNat 2393 (SCC) and *Kelly* v. *Canada (Minister of Employment and Immigration)*, *ibid.*, citing *Lovelace* v. *Canada*, (No. 24/1977), UN Doc. CCPR/C/13/D/24/1977,
UN Doc. CCPR/3/Add.1, Vol. II, p. 320, UN Doc. CCPR/C/OP/1, p. 83, [1983] *Canadian Human Rights Yearbook* 306, 68 ILR 17; *Taylor* v. *Canadian Human Rights
Commission*, [1987] 3 FC 593, 37 DLR (4th) 577, 78 NR 180, 29 CRR 222, 9 CHRR
D/4929 (CA), affirmed, (1990) 1990 CarswellNat 742 (SCC), *Nealy* v. *Johnston*, (1989)
10 CHRR D/6450 (CHRT), 317, *R.* v. *Keegstra*, [1990] 3 SCR 697, 61 CCC (3d) 1,
[1991] 2 WWR 1, 1 CR (4th) 129, 3 CRR (2d) 193, 77 Alta LR (2d) 193, 114 AR 81,
117 NR 1, and *Canada* v. *Taylor*, [1990] 3 SCR 892, 75 DLR (4th) 577, 13 CHRR 435,
3 CRR (2d) 116, citing *J.R.T. and W.G.P.* v. *Canada*, *supra* note 245; *Re Mitchell and
R.* (Case No. 790/01), Admissibility, Report No. 74/03, 22 October 2003, para. 30,
citing *Van Duzen* v. *Canada*, (No. 50/1979), UN Doc. CCPR/C/15/D/50/1979, UN Doc.
CCPR/3/Add.1, Vol. II, p. 402, UN Doc. CCPR/C/OP/1, p. 118, [1983] *Canadian
Human Rights Yearbook* 330, 3 *Human Rights Law Journal* 181, 70 ILR 235; *Charkaoui
(Re)*, [2005] 2 FCR 299 (CA), leave to appeal allowed, (2005) 346 NR 393n (S.C.C.),
citing *Ahani* v. *Canada*, (No. 1051/2002), UN Doc. CCPR/C/80/D/1051/2002. In *British
Columbia (AG)* v. *Craig*, (1984) (sub nom. *R.* v. *Carter*) 4 DLR (4th) 746, 9 CCC (3d)
173, 36 CR (3d) 346 (BC SC), affirmed, (1984) 1984 CarswellBC 532 (CA), affirmed,
(1986) 1986 CarswellBC 706 (SCC), at 753 (DLR), the absence of decisions of the
Human Rights Committee on the matter of "pre-charge delay" was noted.

253 *Nealy* v. *Johnston, ibid.*

The procedure for individual petitions is simple and devoid of formalism. Usually, applicants are represented by counsel, although the proceedings are entirely written and there is no opportunity for oral argument. In some Canadian jurisdictions, legal aid has been accorded for proceedings before the Human Rights Committee.[254] Sessions of the Committee are not open to the public when it is considering individual communications.[255] The final "views" of the Committee as well as the admissibility decisions, where communications are declared inadmissible, are published as individual United Nations documents and appear in the annual reports of the Committee. A selection of the views is also published in specialized periodicals like the *Human Rights Law Journal*, the *Revue universelle des droits de l'homme*, the *International Human Rights Reports* and the *International Law Reports*. They are also readily available on the web site of the Office of the High Commissioner for Human Rights.

Only two of the five permanent members of the United Nations Security Council, France and the Russian Federation, are parties to the *Optional Protocol to the International Covenant on Civil and Political Rights*. The United States of America ratified the *International Covenant on Civil and Political Rights* in 1992, but not the *Optional Protocol*. Thus, although the United States is bound at international law to ensure respect of the *Covenant*'s provisions, the principal international remedy in the case of its violation is not available. The United Kingdom has also declined to subject itself to the individual petition mechanism created by the *Protocol*, although it is an enthusiastic participant in the regional human rights petition system created under the auspices of the Council of Europe.[256] China was the last permanent member of the Security Council to accept international human rights law instruments, signing the *International Covenant on Civil and Political Rights* in 1998. It is working towards ratification, but considerably more slowly than many had hoped.

3.2.2.5   *General Comments*

The Committee has issued more than thirty "General Comments". These are general interpretative guidelines as to the meaning and construc-

---

254 Unreported decision of a Comité de révision created pursuant to the Quebec *Legal Aid Act*, No. 20670 (Joseph Kindler), 11 March 1992.

255 A Canadian journalist has succeeded in obtaining copies of the government files using access to information legislation. See: *Héroux* v. *Ministère de la Justice*, [1991] CAI. 68.

256 See: Council of Europe, *European Court of Human Rights, Survey of Activities, 1959-1994*, Strasbourg, 1995.

tion of specific articles of the *Covenant*.[257] Arguably, the reference to "comments" in article 40 of the *Covenant* was intended to apply to observations by the Committee on State party reports. But there was much opposition to such an idea when the *Covenant* was being adopted. When an amendment was proposed to add the adjective "general" before "comments",[258] Canada called for a separate vote on the word "general", insisting that the addition represented a substantive change.[259] Canada's intervention has strengthened arguments that the drafters did not intend that "comments" would apply to the reports of States parties, but rather that they would be "general comments" on interpretative issues. And this is how the Human Rights Committee has interpreted the provision. Eventually, when the Committee considered that it had the authority to issues observations on State party reports, it decided to label them "concluding observations", a term that is unknown in the text of the *Covenant*.[260]

General Comments have been issued concerning many of the substantive provisions of the *Covenant*, such as the right to life, the prohibition of torture, the right to a fair trial, freedom of expression and the rights of minorities. Some of them also address particular legal problems, such as states of emergency and the jurisdictional scope of the *Covenant*. An early "general comment" on the right to life declared that nuclear weapons were contrary to the right to life, protected by article 6 of the *Covenant*. In 1994, the Committee issued a particularly controversial general comment on reservations.[261] The Committee has stated that its general comments are "not strictly binding" although it hopes that the comments carry "a certain weight and authority. In the Committee's experience, States parties often wished to give careful consideration to them for that reason."[262] The Canadian government has declared that it does not consider "General Comments" to be

> authoritative interpretations of *Covenant* obligations, legal or otherwise. Rather the General Comments merely represent the views or interpretations of Com-

---

257 General Comments are adopted pursuant to article 40(4) of the *Covenant*: "The Committee shall study the reports submitted by the States Parties to the present Covenant. It shall transmit its reports, and such general comments as it may consider appropriate, to the States Parties. . ."

258 UN Doc. A/C.3/SR.1426, para. 14.

259 UN Doc. A/C.3/SR.1427, para. 61.

260 In accordance with UN Doc. CCPR/C/3/Rev.6 and Corr.1, UN Doc. A/56/40, Vol. I, Annex III.B.

261 "General Comment No. 24 (52), Issues relating to reservations made upon ratification or accession to the Covenant or the Optional Protocols thereto, or in relation to declarations under article 41 of the Covenant", UN Doc. CCPR/C/21/Rev.1/Add.6. See: William A. Schabas, "Reservations to International Human Rights Treaties", (1995) 32 *Canadian Yearbook of International Law* 39.

262 UN Doc. CCPR/C/SR.1406, (3).

mittee members in their independent capacities. The General Comments have not been endorsed by Canada or other States Parties to the *Covenant* and they do not enjoy any status in law.[263]

Some substantive provisions of the *Covenant* have not yet been the subject of a General Comment,[264] and there would seem to be no great initiative within the Committee to provide a comprehensive collection. Nor do the general comments address all of the outstanding issues. The general comments on the right to life, for example, do not speak of the issue of abortion, although an early draft attempted to address the matter. It simply proved to be too divisive for the members of the Committee. Given that the general comments are adopted by consensus, the more difficult issues tend to be avoided, as they cannot be resolved. According to Manfred Nowak, author of the main commentary on the Covenant, "that General Comments are adopted by consensus among all Committee members and thus among the various cultures, ideologies, religions, traditions and legal systems underscores the 'authoritative and universal character of these interpretations'".[265]

The Committee's General Comments have been considered on occasion by Canadian courts[266] For example, in *Suresh*, the Supreme Court of Canada cited General Comment 20, which affirms that "States parties must not expose individuals to the danger of torture [. . .] upon return to another country by way of their extradition, expulsion or refoulement".[267] Justice Robertson of the Federal Court of Appeal had written that General Comment

---

263 The statement was made by a Canadian delegation in the context of the *International Covenant on Economic, Social and Cultural Rights*, but clearly applies to General Comments issued under the other treaties too. Colleen Swords, ed., "Legal Status of 'General Comments of the Committee on Economic Social and Cultural Rights'", (2003) 41 *Canadian Yearbook of International Law* 467.

264 Articles 8 (prohibition of slavery), 11 (imprisonment for debt), 15 (non-retroactivity of criminal offences), 16 (recognition as a person before the law), 21 (freedom of peaceful assembly) and 22 (freedom of association).

265 Manfred Nowak, *supra* note 247, at 749.

266 "General Comment No. 16 (32), The right to respect of privacy, family, home and correspondence, and protection of honour and reputation (Article 17)", UN Doc. CCPR/8/Add.1, Vol. II, p. 301, is cited in *Kelly* v. *Canada, supra* note 252; "General Comment No. 22 (48), The right to freedom of thought, conscience and religion (Article 18)", UN Doc. CCPR/C/21/Rev.1/Add.4, (1993) 15 *Human Rights Law Journal* 233, is cited in *Commision des droits de la personne du Québec* v. *Autobus Legault*, [1994] RJQ 3027 (HRT); "General Comment No. 25 (57), The right to participate in public affairs, voting rights and the right of equal access to public service", UN Doc. CCPR/C/21/Rev.1/Add.7, cited in *Sauvé* v. *Canada (Chief Electoral Officer)*, [2002] 3 SCR 519, 218 DLR (4th) 577, 168 CCC (3d) 449, 5 CR (6th) 203, 98 CRR (2d) 1.

267 "General Comment No. 20 (44), Replaces general comment 7 concerning prohibition of torture and cruel treatment or punishment (Article 7)", UN Doc. HRI/GEN/1/Rev. 1, para. 9.

20 should be disregarded because he felt it contradicted the language of article 7 of the *Covenant*.[268] According to the Supreme Court of Canada,

> *General Comment 20* does not run counter to Article 7; rather, it explains it. Nothing would prevent a state from adhering both to Article 7 and to *General Comment 20*, and *General Comment 20* does not detract from rights preserved or provided by Article 7. The clear import of the ICCPR, read together with the *General Comment 20*, is to foreclose a state from expelling a person to face torture elsewhere.[269]

The general comments are published in the annual reports of the Committee, and in private publications such as the *Human Rights Law Journal*, the *Revue universelle des droits de l'homme* and the *European Human Rights Reports*. A complete set appears as an appendix to the major academic study on the *Covenant*.[270] They are also available on the web site of the Office of the High Commissioner for Human Rights.

3.2.2.6   *The* International Covenant on Economic, Social and Cultural Rights

The *International Covenant on Economic, Social and Cultural Rights* deals with such matters as the rights of labour and trade unions, social insurance, protection of the family, education and cultural life. The treaty did not initially provide for creation of a committee that would operate in a similar manner to the Human Rights Committee, although it did require States to submit periodic reports to the Secretary General. A Committee on Economic, Social and Cultural Rights was established by the Economic and Social Council of the United Nations in 1985,[271] and it has taken on an increasingly vigorous role.[272]

---

268   *Suresh* v. *Canada (Minister of Citizenship and Immigration)*, [2000] 2 FC 592, 183 DLR (4th) 629, 252 NR 1, 18 Admin L.R. (3d) 159, 5 Imm LR (3d) 1 (CA), leave to appeal allowed, (2000) 2000 CarswellNat 879 (SCC), reversed, (2002) 2002 CarswellNat 7 (SCC). But the same General Comment was cited approvingly in *Thamotharampillai* v. *Canada (Minister of Citizenship and Immigration)*, (2001) 84 CRR (2d) 346, 14 Imm LR (3d) 201 (FCA), para. 27.

269   *Suresh* v. *Canada (Minister of Citizenship and Immigration)*, [2002] 1 SCR 3, 208 DLR (4th) 1, 37 Admin LR (3d) 159, 90 CRR (2d) 1, para. 67.

270   Manfred Nowak, *supra* note 247, at 1089-1157.

271   ESC Res. 1985/17.

272   Raphaël Sodini, *Le Comité des droits économiques, sociaux et culturels*, Paris: Montchrestien, 2000; P. Alston and B. Simma, "First Session of the U.N. Committee on Economic, Social and Cultural Rights", (1987) 81 *American Journal of International Law* 747; Daniel Turp, "Le contrôle du respect du Pacte international relatif aux droits économiques, sociaux et culturels", in *Le droit au service de la justice, de la paix et du développement: Mélanges Michel Virally*, Paris: Pedone, 1991, p. 465; Habib Gherari, "Le Comité des droits économiques, sociaux et culturels", (1992) 96 *Revue générale de droit international public* 75.

The Committee receives periodic reports from States parties, in much the same way as the Human Rights Committee. Canada ratified the *International Covenant on Economic, Social and Cultural Rights* in 1976, at the same time as it ratified the *International Covenant on Civil and Political Rights* and the *Optional Protocol*. Canada has presented seven periodic reports to the Committee on Economic, Social and Cultural Rights.[273] Initially, the Committee requested reports on specific provisions of the *Covenant*. Canada submitted two reports dealing with articles 6 to 9,[274] two with articles 10 to 12,[275] and two with articles 13 to 15.[276] Subsequently, States parties have been called upon to submit a single comprehensive report. Canada prepared a third,[277] fourth[278] and fifth[279] report on this basis.

The obligation to submit periodic reports on the *International Covenant on Economic, Social and Cultural Rights* was mentioned by Chief Justice Dickson in *Re Public Service Employee Relations Act (Alberta)*.[280] In *Gosselin c. Québec (Procureur général)*, Chief Justice Robert of the Quebec Court of Appeal took note of the importance of the reporting process, and of the Concluding Observations of the Committee on Economic, Social and Cultural Rights:

> A la lumière de ce qui précède, il est intéressant de prendre connaissance de diverses conclusions adoptées par le Comité des droits économiques, sociaux et culturels concernant le second rapport périodique que le Canada lui à soumis au sujet des droits visés aux articles 10 a 15 du Pacte. Elles font suite aux rapports soumis, aux termes des articles 16 et 17 du Pacte, et indiquant les mesures de caractère legislatif, judiciaire, politique et autre prises par un Etat partie pour assurer la jouissance des droits énoncés dans le Pacte. Présentables, à l'origine, en trois étapes biennales et par catégories d'articles, les rapports des Etats concernent désormais l'ensemble des droits protégés et sont dûs tous les cinq ans. Le Comité y félicite d'abord le Canada pour la qualité de son rapport et pour le renforcement de la protection générale des droits de la

---

273   Daniel Turp, "L'examen des rapports périodiques du Canada en application du Pacte international relatif aux droits économiques, sociaux et culturels", (1991) 28 *Canadian Yearbook of International Law* 330.

274   UN Doc. E/1978/8/Add.32, examined: UN Doc. E/1982/WG.1/SR.1-2; UN Doc. E/1984/7/Add.28, examined UN Doc. E/C.12/1989/SR.8 and 11.

275   UN Doc. E/1980/6/Add.32, examined: UN Doc. E/1985/WG1/SR.4 and 6; UN Doc. E/1990/6/Add.13. examined UN Doc. E/C.12/1993/SR.5 and 6.

276   UN Doc. E/1982/3/Add.34, examined: UN Doc. E/1986/WG1/SR.113, 115 and 116; UN Doc. E/1990/6/Add.13. examined UN Doc. E/C.12/1993/SR.5 and 6.

277   UN Doc. E/1994/104/Add.17, examined: UN Doc. E/C.12/1998/SR.46-48.

278   UN Doc. E/C.12/4/Add.15.

279   UN Doc. E/C.12/CAN/5.

280   *Reference re Public Service Employee Relations Act (Alberta)*, [1987] 1 RCS 313, 51 Alta LR (2d) 97, [1987] 3 WWR 577, (sub nom. *A.U.P.E.* v. *Alberta (Attorney General)*) 28 CRR 305, 38 DLR (4th) 161, (sub nom. *Reference re Compulsory Arbitration*) 74 NR 99, 78 AR 1, [1987] DLQ 225, 87 CLLC 14,021, at 185 (DLR).

personne à travers, notamment, l'adoption de la Charte canadienne des droits et libertés , la portée de quelques jugements et la réalisation de certains progrès dans les domaines de la famille et de la santé. Cependant, le Comité exprime une préoccupation toute particuliere à l'endroit de la persistance de la pauvreté et ce, à la lumière de l'obligation du Canada, pays doté d'une situation enviable au plan économique, de consacrer le maximum des ressources disponibles à la mise en oeuvre progressive des droits énoncés dans le Pacte. Après avoir souligné la situation précaire des mères célibataires et de leurs enfants, le Comité note ce qui suit:

> 104. The Committee is concerned that there seems to exist no procedure to ensure that those who must depend entirely on welfare payments do not thereby derive an income which is at or above the poverty line.
>
> 105. A further subject of concern for the Committee is the evidence of hunger in Canada and the reliance on food banks operated by charitable organizations [. . .]
>
> 107. The Committee has learned from non-governmental organizations of widespread discrimination in housing against people with children, people on social assistance, people with low incomes, and people who are in-debted [. . .]
>
> 109. Given the evidence of homelessness and inadequate living conditions, the Committee is surprised that expenditures on social housing are as low as 1.3 per cent of Government expenditures.

Fort éloquentes sont également, à notre avis, les observations du Comité par rapport aux difficultés d'application que connaissent, devant les tribunaux cette fois, les droits prévus au Pacte:

> 110. The Committee is concerned that, in some court decisions and in recent constitutional discussions, social and economic rights have been described as mere "policy objectives" of Governments rather than as fundamental human rights. The Committee is also concerned to receive evidence that some provincial governments in Canada appear to take the position in courts that the rights in article 11 of the Covenant are not protected, or only minimally protected, by the Charter of Rights and Freedoms. The Committee would wish to have heard of some measures being undertaken by provincial governments in Canada to provide for more effective legal remedies against violations of each of the rights contained in the Covenant.
>
> 113. The Committee is concerned that provincial human rights legislation has not always been applied in a manner which would provide improved remedies against violations of social and economic rights, particularly concerning the rights of families with children, and the right to an adequate standard of living, including food and housing.

Compte tenu de ces conclusions, il n'est pas surprenant de retrouver les suggestions et recommandations suivantes faites par le Comité:

118. In recognition of the increasingly important role played by the courts in ordering remedial action against violations of social and economic rights, the Committee recommends that the Canadian judiciary be provided with training courses on Canada's obligations under the Covenant and on their effect of the interpretation and application of Canadian law.

119. The Committee encourages the Canadian courts to continue to adopt a broad and purposive approach to the interpretation of the Charter of Rights and Freedoms and of human rights legislation so as to provide appropriate remedies against violations of social and economic rights in Canada.

Notons que si les conclusions et recommandations du Comité n'ont pas de caractère contraignant, elles n'en reflètent pas moins l'opinion du seul organe d'experts chargé de faire des déclarations de cette nature.[281]

Canada's fourth and fifth reports pursuant to the *International Covenant on Economic, Social and Cultural Rights* were considered by the Committee on Economic, Social and Cultural Rights on 5 and 8 May 2006.[282] Many Canadian NGOs made submissions to the Committee, including the Assembly of First Nations, the Canadian Bar Assocation, the Canadian Council for Refugees, the Canadian Human Rights Commission and the Ligue des droits et libertés. In its Concluding Observations, the Committee noted its ongoing concern with Canada's "restrictive interpretation of its obligations under the Covenant, in particular its position that the Covenant sets forth principles and programmatic objectives rather than legal obligations, and the consequent lack of awareness, in the Provinces and Territories" of Canada's legal obligations under the Covenant.[283] The Committee signaled a number of specific problems, including lack of adequate legal aid for enforcement of economic and social rights, relatively high levels of poverty considering the country's overall prosperity, discrimination against First Nations women and their children, the absence of a provision in the *Criminal Code* to address domestic violence, failure to recognize the right to water as an entitlement, and inadequate measures for the protection of Aboriginal languages and recognition of intellectual property rights for the protection and promotion of ancestral rights and traditional knowledge of Aboriginal peoples.[284] The Committee reminded Canada

. . . that although trade liberalization has a wealth generating potential, such liberalization does not necessarily create and lead to a favorable environ-

---

281 *Gosselin* v. *Québec (AG)*, [1999] RJQ 1033 (CA), affirmed, [2002] 4 SCR 429, 221 DLR (4th) 257, 100 CRR (2d) 1, 44 CHRR D/363

282 UN Doc. E/C.12/2006/SR.9-12.

283 Concluding Observations of the Committee on Economic, Social and Cultural Rights, Canada, UN Doc. E/C.12/CAN/CO/5, para. 11(a).

284 *Ibid.*, paras. 11-33.

ment for the realization of economic, social and cultural rights. In this regard, the Committee recommends the State party to consider ways in which the primacy of Covenant rights may be ensured in trade and investment agreements, and in particular in the adjudication of investor-state disputes under Chapter XI of NAFTA.[285]

No individual petition mechanism exists under the *International Covenant on Economic, Social and Cultural Rights* as yet, although negotiations are underway to prepare an optional protocol to the *Covenant* that will create one. The idea has been around since the beginning of the 1990s,[286] and was endorsed by the Vienna Conference on Human Rights in 1993.[287] In 1996, the Committee on Economic, Social and Cultural Rights prepared a proposal to this effect.[288] Answering a request from the Secretary-General to comment on the proposed optional protocol to the *Covenant*, on 6 February 1998, Canada set out its views. While conceding that "[a]ll human rights are universal", Canada said that "it does not necessarily follow that all rights are easily amenable to or best implemented by an adjudicative-type process. The creation of an optional protocol to the International Covenant on Economic, Social and Cultural Rights may be premature where the core requirements of those rights have yet to be defined with precision."[289] Canada contrasted economic, social and cultural rights with civil and political rights, arguing that the parameters of the latter were more certain and well-established. "Moreover, the difficulty of determining the core requirements of the rights in the Covenant is greatly exacerbated by the obligation in article 2 to achieve 'progressively the full realization of the rights recognized in the ... Covenant'. Progressive realization is not a concept which easily lends itself to adjudication, in that standards will vary according to circumstances."[290] The absence of such a mechanism was Quebec Court of Appeal: "La pleine application des droits énoncés dans le Pacte dépend d'autant plus de l'existence, au niveau national, de lois et de voies de recours appropriées qu'il n'existe toujours aucune procédure de plainte individuelle prévue au

285 *Ibid.*, para. 68.
286 UN Doc. E/1992/23, paras. 360-366; UN Doc. E/CN.4/Sub.2/1992/16, para. 211. For a review of the question, see: "Annual Report of the Committee on Economic, Social and Cultural Rights on its 14th and 15th Sessions, 30 April-17 May 1996 and 18 November-6 December 1996", UN Doc. E/1997/22, Annex IV.
287 *Vienna Declaration and Programme of Action*, UN Doc. A/CONF.157/24, (1993) 14 *Human Rights Law Journal* 352, para. 75. The *Vienna Declaration* was cited by the Supreme Court of Canada in *Reference re Secession of Quebec*, [1998] 2 SCR 217, 161 DLR (4th) 385, 55 CRR (2d) 1, para. 119. Also: *Gosselin* v. *Québec (AG)*, *supra* note 281.
288 "Draft Optional Protocol to the International Covenant on Economic, Social and Cultural Rights. Note by the Secretary-General", UN Doc. E/CN.4/1997/105.
289 UN Doc. E/CN.4/1998/84/Add.1, para. 1.
290 *Ibid.*, para. 3.

titre de cet instrument. Cette dernière est cependant l'objet d'études sérieuses. . .."[291]

Canada also focussed on the reference in article 2 of the *Covenant* to each State taking steps "to the maximum of its available resources". How is the "maximum" to be determined, asked Canada, and by whom? "Different systems of government have radically different approaches to resource allocation and management of their economies, which would make it difficult to apply a common standard."[292] For example, Canada asked whether the right to work in article 6 of the Covenant obliges States to eliminate all unemployment. "[W]ill the Committee find a violation whenever unemployment exists in a State or, alternatively, would the Committee be prepared to tell an individual complainant that his or her inability to obtain a job is consistent with the Covenant?", questioned Canada. "Is the right to adequate food in article 11 of the Covenant satisfied by a State party's support for food banks or must there by government assistance equivalent to the cost of an adequate and nutritional diet?"[293] Canada suggested that "a more appropriate path may be for the Committee to delineate, with some precision, the scope and content of the rights in the Covenant, perhaps through the use of general comments. A better assessment could then be made of whether an adjudicative-type system is an effective mechanism for addressing such rights and, if so, how it should be structured. . ."[294]

International adjudication was never meant to be a substitute for domestic solutions. In keeping with the general approach to such matters, such a new petition mechanism will require litigants to exhaust local remedies before taking their case to the international body. The problem, at least for Canada, is in the existence of local remedies for the enforcement of economic, social and cultural rights. As the Committee on Economic, Social and Cultural rights has noted:

> [I]n some court decisions and in recent constitutional discussions, social and economic rights have been described as mere "policy objectives" of governments rather than as fundamental human rights. The Committee was also concerned to receive evidence that some provincial governments in Canada appear to take the position in courts that the rights in article 11 of the Covenant are not protected, or only minimally protected, by the Charter of Rights and Freedoms. The Committee would like to have heard of some measures being undertaken by provincial governments in Canada to provide for more effective legal remedies against violations of each of the rights contained in the Covenant.[295]

---

291 *Gosselin* v. *Québec (AG)*, *supra* note 281, para. 450.
292 UN Doc. E/CN.4/1998/84/Add.1, para. 4.
293 *Ibid.*, para. 5.
294 *Ibid.*, para. 6.
295 *Ibid.*, para. 21.

The proposed optional protocol and various other options have been studied in recent years by an open-ended working group of the Commission on Human Rights.[296]

Like the Human Rights Committee, the Committee on Economic, Social and Cultural Rights has adopted several general comments addressing a range of important issues with regard to economic, social and cultural rights, including the right to adequate housing, evictions, persons with disabilities, the economic, social and cultural rights of older persons, economic sanctions, the right to adequate food and the right to the highest attainable standard of health.[297]

3.2.3   Other United Nations Treaties in the Field of Human Rights

Five other instruments within the United Nations system deal with specific problems or areas in the protection of human rights make up, with the two covenants, the core treaties. Four of them have been ratified by Canada: the *International Convention on the Elimination of All Forms of Racial Discrimination*;[298] the *Convention on the Elimination of Discrimination Against Women*;[299] the *Convention Against Torture and Cruel, Inhuman or Degrading Treatment or Punishment*;[300] and the *Convention on the Rights of the Child*.[301] The fifth and most recent of the treaties, the *International Convention on the Protection of the Rights of All Migrant Workers and Members of Their Families*, has not yet been signed or ratified by Canada. This treaty, which entered into force on 1 July 2003, has been welcomed by countries of emigration but greeted with indifference by countries of immigration upon whom, as a general rule, the obligations fall.[302] Two additional treaties are currently being prepared, dealing with forced disappearance[303] and with the rights of the disabled.

All five treaties autorise the establishment of a committee or treaty body.[304] The jurisdiction and responsibilities of the five committees are broadly similar to those of the Human Rights Committee and the Committee

---

296 "Report of the Open-Ended Working Group to Consider Options Regarding the Elaboration of an Optional Protocol", UN Doc. E/CN.4/2005/52.

297 UN Doc. HRI/GEN/1/Rev.6.

298 (1969) 660 UNTS 195, [1976] CTS 47.

299 (1981) 1249 UNTS 13, [1982] CTS 31.

300 UN Doc.A/39/51, p. 197 (1984), [1987] CTS 36.

301 GA Res. 44/25, Annex, [1992] CTS 3.

302 UN Doc. A/RES/45/158, annex.

303 "International Convention for the Protection of All Persons from Enforced Disappearance", UN Doc. E/CN.4/2005/WG.22/WP.1/Rev.4.

304 See Michael O'Flaherty, *Human Rights and the United Nations: Practice Before the Treaty Bodies*, The Hague: Kluwer Academic, 2002.

on Economic, Social and Cultural Rights, which monitor implementation of the two covenants.

The first of the five specialized treaties to be adopted was the *International Convention on the Elimination of All Forms of Racial Discrimination*. It predates slightly the two covenants, having been drafted by the General Assembly in 1965,[305] following the adoption, two years earlier, of a declaration on the same subject.[306] The *Convention* establishes a range of obligations, including a duty to punish the dissemination of ideas based on racial superiority or hatred, and to prohibit organizations that promote and incite racial discrimination.

Canada signed the *Convention* on 24 August 1966, and ratified it on 14 October 1970. On 10 May 1978, Quebec filed a "ratification" of the *Convention*.[307] When Yemen formulated a reservation to certain provisions of the *Convention*, Canada registered an objection:

> The effect of these reservations would be to allow racial discrimination in respect of certain of the rights enumerated in Article 5. Since the objective of the International Convention on the Elimination of All Forms of Racial Discrimination, as stated in its Preamble, is to eliminate racial discrimination in all its forms and manifestations, the Government of Canada believes that the reservations made by the Yemen Arab Republic are incompatible with the object and purpose of the International Convention. Moreover, the Government

---

305 (1969) 660 UNTS 195, [1976] CTS 47. See: Patrick Thornberry, "Confronting Racial Discrimination: A CERD Perspective", (2005) 5 *Human Rights Law Review* 239; Linos-Alexandre Sicilianos, "L'actualité et les potentialités de la Convention sur l'élimination de la discrimination raciale", (2005) 16 *Revue trimestrielle des droits de l'homme* 861; Michael Banton, *International Action Against Racial Discrimination*, Oxford: Clarendon Press, 1996; Natan Lerner, *The U.N. Convention on the Elimination of all Forms of Racial Discrimination*, Alphen den Rijn: Sitjhoff and Noordhoof, 1989; Georges Ténékidès, "L'action des Nations Unies contre la discrimination raciale", (1989) 180 *Receuil de cours de l'Académie de droit international* 269; Patricia J. Myhall, "Canada's Unjustified Ratification of the Race Convention", (1972) 30 *University of Toronto Faculty of Law Review* 31; Theodor Meron, "The Meaning and Reach of the International Convention on the Elimination of All Forms of Racial Discrimination", (1985) 79 *American Journal of International Law* 283; Egon Schwelb, "The U.N. Convention on the Elimination of All Forms of Racial Discrimination", (1966) 15 *International and Comparative Law Quarterly* 996.

306 *Declaration on the Elimination of All Forms of Racial Discrimination*, GA Res. 1904 (XVIII), cited in: *Taylor v. Canadian Human Rights Commission*, [1990] 3 SCR 892, 75 DLR (4th) 577, 13 CHRR 435, 3 CRR (2d) 116.

307 REIQ (1984-89) no. 1978 (8) p. 836. Quebec has "ratified" several of the international human rights instruments. No mention is made of this in the United Nations documents, however. Nevertheless, while essentially symbolic these acts of ratification are not without legal consequences. In one case, the Quebec Court of Appeal took note of Quebec's adhesion to the *International Covenant on Economic, Social and Cultural Rights*: *Gosselin* v. *Québec (AG)*, *supra* note 281.

of Canada believes that the principle of non-discrimination is generally accepted and recognized in international law and therefore is binding on all states.

There is an explicit reference to the *Convention* in the preamble of the *Multiculturalism Act*.[308] Section 318 of the *Criminal Code*, prohibiting hate propaganda, constitutes domestic implementation of an obligation imposed by the *Convention*. The *International Convention on the Elimination of All Forms of Racial Discrimination* has been cited by Canadian courts on many occasions.[309]

The Committee on the Elimination of Racial Discrimination (CERD) considers periodic reports of States parties. Canada has been submitting the report to CERD since the beginning of the 1970s.[310] In recent years, its

---

308 SC 1988, preamble. See also: *Canadian Race Relations Foundation Act,* SC 1991, c. 8, preamble.

309 *R.* v. *Therens,* [1983] 4 WWR 385, 148 DLR (3d) 672, 5 CCC (3d) 409, 33 CR (3d) 204, 20 MVR 8, 23 Sask R 81, 5 CRR 157 (CA), affirmed, [1985] 1 SCR 613; *Wong* v. *Hughes Petroleum Ltd* (1983), 28 Alta LR (2d) 155, 46 AR 276, 4 CHRR D/1488 (Q.B.); *R.* v. *Keegstra,* (1985) 19 CCC (3d) 254 (Alta QB), reversed, [1988] 5 WWR 211, 43 CCC (3d) 150, 65 CR (3d) 289, 60 Alta LR (2d) 1, 87 AR 177, 39 CRR 5 (CA), additional reasons at, [1991] 4 WWR 136 (CA), reversed, [1990] 3 SCR 697, 61 CCC (3d) 1, [1991] 2 WWR 1, 1 CR (4th) 129, 3 CRR (2d) 193, 77 Alta LR (2d) 193, 114 AR 81, 117 NR 1; *Taylor* v. *Canadian Human Rights Commission, supra* note 306; *R.* v. *Andrews,* (1989) 43 CCC (3d) 193, 65 OR (2d) 161, 28 OAC 161, 65 CR (3d) 320, 39 CRR 36 (CA), affirmed, (1990) 75 OR (2d) 481n (SCC); *Nealy* v. *Johnston,* (1989) 10 CHRR D/6450 (CHRT) 317; *R.* v. *Keegstra,* [1990] 3 SCR 697, 61 CCC (3d) 1, [1991] 2 WWR 1, 1 CR (4th) 129, 3 CRR (2d) 193, 77 Alta LR (2d) 193, 114 AR 81, 117 NR 1; *R.* v. *Zundel,* [1992] 2 SCR 731, 95 DLR (4th) 202, 16 CR (4th) 1, 75 CCC (3d) 449; *Commission des droits de la personne du Québec* c. *Commission scolaire Deux-Montagnes,* [1993] RJQ 1297 (TDPQ); *Gagnon et Commission des droits de la personne et des droits de la jeunesse du Québec* v. *Quévillon,* [1999] TDPQ 6 (HRT); *Bia-Domingo et Québec (Commission des droits de la personne et des droits de la jeunesse)* v. *Sinatra,* (1999) 1999 CarswellQue 3292 , [1999] JTDPQ no 19 (TDPQ); *Délicieux et Québec (Commission des droits de la personne et des droits de la jeunesse)* v. *Yazbeck,* (2001) 2001 CarswellQue 2220, [2001] TDPQ 12 (TDPQ); *Commission des droits de la personne et des droits de la jeunesse* v. *Collège Montmorency,* [2004] RJQ 1381 (TDPQ); *Commission des droits de la personne et des droits de la jeunesse* v. *Pettas,* (2005) 2005 CarswellQue 3317, [2005] JTDPQ no 7 (TDPQ).

310 "Initial report, Canada", UN Doc. CERD/C/R.25/Add. 5, examined 24-25 February 1972 (UN Doc. CERD/C/SR.97 and 98); "Second report, Canada", UN Doc. CERD/C/R.53/Add.6, examined 4 April 1974 (UN Doc. CERD/C/SR. 188); "Third report, Canada", UN Doc. CERD/C/R.78, Add.6, examined 4 August 1976 (UN Doc. CERD/C/R/SR.297 and 298); "Fourth report, Canada", UN Doc. CERD/C/52, examined 6 April 1979 (UN Doc. CERD/C/SR.425 and 426); "Fifth report, Canada", UN Doc. CERD/C/50/Add.6 and 7, examined 7 April 1981 (UN Doc. CERD/C/SR.522); "Sixth report, Canada", UN Doc. CERD/C/76/Add.6, examined 15 July 1983 (UN Doc. CERD/C/R.25/SR.633 and 634); "Seventh report, Canada", UN Doc. CERD/C/107/Add. 8, and "Eighth report", UN Doc. CERD/C/132/Add. 3, examined together 3-4 March 1987 (UN Doc. CERD/C/SR.778 and 781); "Ninth report, Canada", UN Doc. CERD/C/159/

reports to the Committee have been produced several years after they were due, rather uncharacteristic for Canada which is normally fairly diligent in this respect. When its thirteenth and fourteenth reports were considered in August 2002, the Committee noted that principal responsibility for implementing the *Convention* lay with the federal government, and expressed its concern that Ottawa could not compel provincial and territorial governments to align their laws with the requirements of the *Convention*.[311] The Committee also expressed concern about references to "visible minorities" in Canadian anti-discrimination policy, "since this term, which basically refers to non-white persons, does not appear to cover fully the scope of article 1 of the Convention".[312] It also complained that the process of implementing the recommendations adopted in 1996 by the Royal Commission on Aboriginal Peoples had not yet been completed.[313] The Committee also said it was concerned that some aspects of the *Indian Act*[314] may not be in conformity with the *Convention*, in particular the right to marry and to choose one's spouse, the right to own property and the right to inherit, with a specific impact on Aboriginal women and children.[315]

As with the Human Rights Committee, it is possible for States to accept jurisdiction over both individual and interstate petition mechanisms. However, Canada has not made the additional declarations required for these to take effect. There is a relatively limited body of caselaw resulting from the individual petition mechanism, most of it dealing with the prohibition of hate propaganda. In recent years, the Committee has also developed an urgent procedure allowing it to provide early warning and to respond promptly to emergencies involving racial discrimination, ethnic cleansing and genocide. The Committee on the Elimination of Racial Discrimination has adopted several General Recommendations, which are broadly equivalent to the General Comments adopted by other treaty bodies. These deal with such issues as measures to eradicate incitement to or acts of discrimination, membership of racial or ethnic groups based on self-identification, non-citizens, training of law enforcement officials, racial segregation and

---

Add.3, and "Tenth report, Canada", UN Doc. CERD/C/185/Add. 3, examined together 15 March 1991 (UN Doc. CERD/C/SR.905 and 906); "Eleventh report, Canada", UN Doc. CERD/C/210/Add.2, and "Twelfth report, Canada", UN Doc. CERD/C/240/Add.1, examined together 2-3 August 1994; "Thirteenth report, Canada", UN Doc. CERD/C/320/Add.5, and "Fourteenth report, Canada", UN Doc. CERD/C/320/Add.5, examined together 5-6 August 2002 (UN Doc. CERD/C/SR.1524 and 1525); "Fifteenth and sixteenth report, Canada", UN Doc. CERD/C/409/Add.4, not yet examined; "Seventeenth and eighteenth report, Canada", UN Doc. CERD/C/CAN/18, not yet examined.

311   UN Doc. A/57/18, para. 326.
312   *Ibid.*, para. 328.
313   *Ibid.*, para. 329.
314   *Indian Act*, SRC 1985, c. I-5.
315   UN Doc. A/57/18, para. 332.

apartheid, the right to self-determination, refugees and displaced persons, indigenous peoples, gender-related dimensions of racial discrimination and descent-based discrimination.[316]

The second of the specialized treaties is the *Convention on the Elimination of Discrimination Against Women.*[317] After the *Convention on the Rights of the Child, the Convention on the Elimination of Discrimination Against Women* is the most widely-ratified of the principal human rights conventions, with approximately 180 States parties. Nevertheless, many States have diluted their obligations under the *Convention* by formulating reservations, some of them very broad in scope.[318] Similar in some respects to its predecessor concerning racial discrimination, it is noteworthy for its intrusion deep into the private sphere. The obligations are imposed upon States parties, of course, but they largely concern what are known as "horizontal obligations", that is, the obligation of a State party to ensure that individuals respect the rights enshrined therein. Although the idea that individuals owe duties to others in the respect of human rights is well entrenched in international human rights law, it has taken a very secondary role in the international instruments. The *Universal Declaration of Human Rights* affirms that "every individual and every organ of society, keeping this Declaration constantly in mind, shall strive by teaching and education to promote respect for these rights and freedoms",[319] and declares that "[e]veryone has duties to the community".[320] The idea is also present in the preamble of the international covenants, which state that "the individual, having duties to other individuals and to the community to which he belongs is under a responsibility to strive for the promotion and observance of the rights recognized in the present Covenant".

The *Convention on the Elimination of Discrimination Against Women* was adopted by the United Nations General Assembly in 1979. Canada signed the *Convention* on 17 July 1980, and ratified it on 10 December

---

316 UN Doc. HRI/GEN/1/Rev.6.

317 (1981) 1249 UNTS 13, [1982] CTS 31. See: Catherine Tinker, "Human Rights for Women: the U.N. Convention on the Elimination of Discrimination Against Women", (1981) 3 *Human Rights Quarterly* 32; Marie Caron, "Les travaux du Comité pour l'élimination de la discrimination à l'égard des femmes", (1985) 2 *Revue québecoise de droit international* 295.

318 Rebecca Cook, "Reservations to the Convention on the Elimination of Discrimination Against Women", (1990) 30 *Virginia Journal of International Law* 643.

319 *Universal Declaration of Human Rights*, GA Res. 217 A (III) UN Doc. A/810, preamble.

320 *Ibid.*, art. 29(1).

1981.[321] On 20 October 1981, Quebec "ratified" the *Convention*.[322] At the time of ratification, Canada made the following declaration:

> The Government of Canada states that the competent legislative authorities within Canada have addressed the concept of equal pay referred to in article 11(1)(d) by legislation which requires the establishment of rates of remuneration without discrimination on the basis of sex. The competent legislative authorities within Canada will continue to implement the object and purpose of article 11(1)(d) and to that end have developed, and where appropriate will continue to develop, additional legislative and other measures.

On 28 May 1992, the Government of Canada notified the Secretary-General of the United Nations of its decision to withdraw the declaration respecting article 11(1)(d) of the *Convention*. Canada has objected to reservations made by Maldives. The *Convention* has been cited by Canadian courts on a number of occasions.[323]

In accordance with the *Convention*, the Committee on the Elimination of Discrimination Against Women (CEDAW) considers periodic reports of

321   Canada is also a party to two other United Nations treaties concerning the rights of women: the *Convention on the Political Rights of Women*, (1954) 193 UNTS 135, [1957] CTS 3, cited in *S. (K.L.) (Re)*, (September 13, 1993) No M92-13594, [1993] C.R.D.D. No. 185 (Imm. & Ref. Bd (Ref Div)), and the *Convention on the Nationality of Married Women*, (1958) 309 UNTS 65, [1960] CTS 2.

322   REIQ (1984-89) no. (1981) (12) p. 850.

323   *Attorney-General of Canada* v. *Stuart*, [1983] 1 FC 651, 137 DLR (3d) 740, 44 NR 320 (CA); *R.* v. *Morgentaler*, (1986) 22 DLR (4th) 641, 22 CCC (3d) 353, 48 CR (3d) 1, 52 OR (2d) 353, 11 OAC 81, 17 CRR 223 (CA), reversed, [1988] 1 SCR 30, (1988) 31 CRR 1, 37 CCC (3d) 449, 44 DLR (4th) 365, 62 CR (3d) 1, 82 NR 1; *Andrews* v. *Law Society of British Columbia*, [1986] 4 WWR 242, 27 DLR (4th) 600, 91 NR 255 (BC CA), affirmed, [1989] 1 SCR 143, 56 DLR (4th) 1, [1989] 2 WWR 289, 36 CRR 193, 25 CCEL 255, 10 CHRR D/5719, 34 BCLR (2d) 273, 91 NR 255; *Reference re Use of French in Criminal Proceedings in the Courts of Saskatchewan*, [1987] 5 WWR 577, 44 DLR (4th) 16, 43 CRR 189, 36 CCC (3d) 353 (Sask CA); *Ville de Québec* v. *Commission des droits de la personne*, [1989] RJQ 831, 11 CHRR D/500 (CA), leave to appeal refused, (1989) 103 NR 160 (note) (SCC); *Roberts* v. *Ontario (Ministry of Health)*, (1989) 10 CHRR D/6353 (Ont Bd of Inquiry), affirmed, (1990) 1990 CarswellOnt 2783 (Div Ct), reversed, (1994) 1994 CarswellOnt 2209 (CA); *Leroux* v. *Co-operators General Insurance Co.*, (1990) 65 DLR (4th) 702 (Ont HC), reversed, (1991) 83 DLR (4th) 694 (Ont CA); *Canada Trust Co.* v. *Ontario Human Rights Commission*, (sub nom. *Leonard Foundation Trust, Re*) (1990) 37 OAC 191, 69 DLR (4th) 321 (CA); *Gould* v. *Yukon Order of Pioneers*, (1991) 87 DLR (4th) 618, 14 CHRR D/176 (YTSC), affirmed, (1993) 100 DLR (4th) 596 (YTCA), affirmed, [1996] 1 SCR 571; *Commission des droits de la personne du Québec* v. *Immeubles Ni/Dia Inc.*, [1992] RJQ 2977 (TDPQ); *Chan* v. *Canada (Minister of Employment and Immigration)*, [1995] 3 SCR 593; *Canadian Foundation for Children, Youth and the Law* v. *Canada (Attorney General)*, [2004] 1 SCR 76, 70 OR (3d) 95, 234 DLR (4th) 257, 180 CCC (3d) 353, 115 CRR (2d) 88, 16 CR (6th) 203, 46 RFL (5th) 1, 183 OAC 1.

States parties. Canada's first report was examined in 1985.[324] In the "Concluding Comments" on Canada's fifth periodic report, which was examined in 2003, CEDAW urged Canada to accelerate its efforts to eliminate *de jure* and *de facto* discrimination against aboriginal women both in society at large and in their communities, particularly with respect to the remaining discriminatory legal provisions and the equal enjoyment of their human rights to education, employment and physical and psychological well-being.[325] The Committee said it was concerned that caregivers were allowed into Canada only as temporary residents, without adequate social security and having to live in the homes of their employers, exposing them to exploitation and abuse.[326] Other issues raised by the Committee included participation of women in political life, and a continuing lack of *de facto* equality in the labour market.[327]

An *Optional Protocol* to the *Convention* adopted by the United Nations General Assembly in 1999 allows for individual petitions to be filed.[328] Canada acceded to the *Optional Protocol* in 2002. The first decisions by the Committee pursuant to the *Optional Protocol* were issued in 2005, and dealt with violence against women.[329] The Committee on the Elimination of Discrimination Against Women also issues General Recommendations. These have addressed such issues as temporary special measures (affirmative action), the opportunity of women to represent their governments in international affairs, statistical data concerning the situation of women, violence against women, equal remuneration for work of equal value, female circumcision, non-discrimination of women in national strategies for the prevention and control of AIDS, unpaid female workers in rural and urban family enterprises, measurement of the domestic activities of women and their recognition in the economy, disabled women, equality in marriage and family relations, political and public life and women and health.[330]

---

324 Canada has presented five reports: "Initial report, Canada", UN Doc. CEDAW/C/5/Add.16, examined 22 and 25 January 1985 (UN Doc. CEDAW/C/SR.48 and 54); "Second report, Canada", UN Doc. CEDAW/C/13/Add.11, examined 1 February 1990 (UN Doc. CEDAW/C/SR.167); "Third report, Canada", UN Doc. CEDAW/C/CAN/3, and "Fourth report, Canada", UN Doc. CEDAW/C/CAN/4, examined 28 January 1997 (UN Doc. CEDAW/C/SR.329 and 330); "Fifth report, Canada", UN Doc. CEDAW/C/CAN/5 and Add. 1, examined 23 January 2003 (UN Doc. CEDAW/C/SR.603 and 604).

325 UN Doc. A/58/38, para. 362.

326 *Ibid.*, para. 365.

327 *Ibid.*, paras. 371-374.

328 *Optional Protocol to the Convention on the Elimination of Discrimination Against Women*, UN Doc. A/RES/54/4.

329 *A.T.* v. *Hungary* (No. 2/2003), UN Doc. A/60/38 (Part I), pp. 27-39. See: Bal Sokyi-Bulley, "The Optional Protocol to CEDAW: First Steps", (2006) 6 *Human Rights Law Review* 143.

330 UN Doc. HRI/GEN/1/Rev.6.

The Committee on the Elimination of Discrimination Against Women has issued several General Recommendations, which are similar in nature to the General Comments of the Human Rights Committee and some of the other treaty bodies. In *R. v. Ewanchuk,*[331] Justices L'Heureux-Dubé and Gonthier referred to General Recommendation No. 19 of the Committee, adopted at its eleventh session in 1992, which deals with violence against women.[332]

The *Convention Against Torture and Cruel, Inhuman or Degrading Treatment or Punishment* is the third of the specialized treaties.[333] It provides a definition of torture, and imposes obligations upon States with respect to the investigation, prosecution and punishment of the crime of torture. It establishes the Committee Against Torture with responsibility for monitoring the obligations under the *Convention.* The *Convention* was adopted by the United Nations General Assembly in 1984, following a General Assembly Resolution of a decade earlier.[334] Canada signed the *Convention* on 23 August 1985 and ratified it on 24 June 1987. Canada has recognized the individual petition procedure in the *Convention Against Torture*, as well as the interstate petition procedure provided by article 21 of the same instru-

331 *R.* v. *Ewanchuk,* [1999] 1 SCR 330.

332 "General Recommendation No. 19, Violence against women", UN Doc. A/47/38.

333 UN Doc.A/39/51, p. 197 (1984), [1987] CTS 36. See: Ahcene Boulesbaa, *The UN Convention on Torture and the Prospects for Enforcement,* The Hague: Martinus Nijhoff, 1999; Nigel Rodley, *The Treatment of Prisoners under International Law,* Oxford: Clarendon Press, 1999; Ahcene Boulesbaa, "An Analysis of the 1984 Draft Convention Against Torture and Other Cruel, Inhuman or Degrading Treatment or Punishment", (1986) 4 *Dickinson Journal of International Law* 185; Jean-François Bonin, "La protection contre la torture et les traitements cruels, inhumains et dégradants: l'affirmation d'une norme et l'évolution d'une définition en droit international", (1986) 3 *Revue québécoise de droit international* 169; J.H. Burgers & Hans Danelius, *The United Nations Convention Against Torture: A Handbook of the Convention Against Torture and Other Cruel, Inhuman or Degrading Treatment or Punishment,* Dordrecht: Martinus Nijhoff, 1988; Hans Danelius, "The International Protection Against Torture and Inhuman or Degrading Treatment or Punishment", (1991) 2:2 *Collected Courses of the Academy of European Law* 151; Z. Haquani, "La Convention des Nations Unies contre la torture", (1986) *Revue générale de droit international public* 127; Christine Chanet, "Le Comité contre la torture", (1991) 37 *Annuaire français de droit international* 553.

334 *Declaration on the Protection of All Persons from being subjected to Torture and Other Cruel, Inhuman or Degrading Treatment or Punishment,* GA Res. 3453 (XXX). Cited in: *R.* v. *McC. (T.),* (1991) 4 OR (3d) 203 (Prov Div); *Kindler* v. *Canada,* [1991] 2 SCR 779, 67 CCC (3d) 1, 84 DLR (4th) 438, 6 CRR (2d) 193, 129 NR 81. In *R.* v. *McC. (T.),* Judge King of the Ontario Court (Provincial Division), referring to the *Declaration,* said "Canada is a signatory to this treaty", which is of course incorrect, because there are no signatories to General Assembly resolutions. Human rights treaties developed within the United Nations system are, however, generally adopted as resolutions by the General Assembly prior to them being open for signature, ratification or accession.

ment.[335] Canada has objected to reservations made by the German Democratic Republic and Chile. Quebec "ratified" the *Convention* on 10 June 1987.[336] Canadian law professor Peter Burns was a member of the Committee from 1995 to 2003, and served as its president for several years.

An *Optional Protocol* to the *Convention*, allowing the Committee Against Torture to make inspection visits at detention facilities, even without prior warning, was adopted by the General Assembly on 18 December 2002.[337] Canada has neither signed nor ratified the *Optional Protocol*.

At the time of ratification of the *Convention*, Canada amended the *Criminal Code* in order to create a specific offence of torture.[338] Acts of torture would be subject to prosecution under the ordinary provisions of the *Code*, such as assault. But in order to comply with obligations under the *Convention*, it was necessary to give Canadian courts jurisdiction over the offence of torture where the offender is present in Canada even if the crime was committed elsewhere, where the crime was committed on a Canadian ship, and where either the offender or the victim are Canadian citizens. There are a few references to the *Convention Against Torture* in Canadian caselaw.[339]

---

335 The declarations state: "The Government of Canada declares that it recognizes the competence of the Committee Against Torture, pursuant to article 21 of the said Convention, to receive and consider communications to the effect that a state party claims that another state party is not fulfilling its obligations under this Convention. The Government of Canada also declares that it recognizes the competence of the Committee Against Torture, pursuant to article 22 of the said Convention, to receive and consider communications from or on behalf of individuals subject to its jurisdiction who claim to be victims of a violation by a state party of the provisions of the Convention." In the case of the *Torture Convention*, Quebec did not adopt a decree, similar to the one it adopted in the case of article 41 of the *International Covenant on Civil and Political Rights*; however, its Department of International Affairs sent a letter to the Secretary of State for Foreign Affairs of Canada expressing agreement with the declaration made by Canada.

336 REIQ (1984-89) no. 1987 (16) p. 870.

337 GA Res. 57/199.

338 SC 1987, c. 13 (currently s. 269.1).

339 *Kindler* v. *Canada, supra* note 334; *Basyony* v. *Canada (Minister of Employment and Immigration)*, (1994) 75 FTR 225, 27 Imm LR (2d) 303; *Suresh* v. *Canada (Minister of Citizenship and Immigration)*, [2000] 2 FC 592, 183 DLR (4th) 629, 252 NR 1, 18 Admin L.R. (3d) 159, 5 Imm LR (3d) 1 (CA), leave to appeal allowed, (2000) 2000 CarswellNat 879 (SCC), reversed, (2002) 2002 CarswellNat 7 (SCC); *Suresh* v. *Canada (Minister of Citizenship and Immigration)*, [2002] 1 SCR 3, 208 DLR (4th) 1, 37 Admin LR (3d) 159, 90 CRR (2d) 1; *L. (O.Q.) (Re)*, (June 3, 1993) Doc M91-09406, M91-09407, M91-12573, M91-12574, [1993] CRDD No 136 (Imm & Ref Bd (Ref Div)); *X. (Z.H.) (Re)*, (January 27, 1992) No M91-08125, [1992] CRDD No 368 (Imm & Ref Bd (Ref Div)); *B. (L.Y.) (Re)*, (April 11, 1995), Doc T94-04946, T94-04947, T94-04948, T94-04949 and T94-04950, [1995] CRDD No 78 (Imm & Ref Bd (Ref Div)); *G. (T.O.) (Re)*, (July 6, 1994) Doc U93-08203, U93-08205, U93-08206, U93-08207, U93-08208,

Five Canadian reports have been presented to the Committee.[340] The Committee expressed several concerns when it examined the third periodic report, in November 2000, including inappropriate use of pepper spray and force by police authorities to break up demonstrations and restore order, failure to implement many of the recommendations of the Arbour report on the Prison for Women,[341] undue force and involuntary sedation in the removal of rejected asylum-seekers and the over-representation of Aboriginal people in prison throughout the criminal justice system.[342] Among its recommendations, the Committee said Canada should repeal legislation that could provide a torturer with a defense of immunity.[343] The Supreme Court of Canada referred approvingly to the Conclusions and Recommendations of the Committee directed towards Canada with respect to its third periodic report.[344]

When Canada presented its fourth and fifth reports in 2005, it was questioned about compliance with article 14, which imposes an obligation to ensure that the victim of an act of torture obtains redress and has an enforceable right to fair and adequate compensation including the means for as full rehabilitation as possible. A member of the delegation said that Canada took the view that article 14 established an obligation to ensure redress where an act of torture took place within the State's own jurisdiction but did not modify the well-established principles of State immunity. "[I]t was implicit in the article that it intended to refer only to acts of torture committed by the State in question. It did not require States to assert jurisdiction in their domestic courts over acts occurring outside the forum State", she said.[345] In its "Conclusions and Recommendations" the Committee lamented "[t]he failure of the Supreme Court of Canada, in *Suresh v. Minister of Citizenship and Immigration*, to recognize at the level of domestic law the absolute nature of the protection of article 3 of the Convention,

---

[1994] CRDD No 183 (Imm & Ref Bd (Ref Div)); *S. (K.L.) (Re)*, (September 13, 1993) No M92-13594, [1993] CRDD No 185 (Imm. & Ref. Bd (Ref Div)); *L. (W.I.) (Re)*, (February 25, 1991) Doc C90-00364, [1991] CRDD No 70 (Imm & Ref Bd (Ref Div)).

340 Canada has presented five reports: "Initial report, Canada", UN Doc. CAT/C/5/Add.15, examined 17 November 1989 (UN Doc.CAT/C/SR.32 and 33); "Second report, Canada", UN Doc.CAT/C/17/Add.5, examined 10 April 1993 (UN Doc. CAT/C/SR.139 and 140); "Third report, Canada", UN Doc. CAT/C/34/Add.13, examined 17, 20 and 22 November 2000 (UN Doc. CAT/C/SR.446, 449 and 453); "Fourth report, Canada", UN Doc. CAT/C/55/Add.8, and "Fifth report, Canada", UN Doc. CAT/C/81/Add.3, examined together on 4 and 6 May 2005 (UN Doc. CAT/C/SR.643 and 646/Add.1).

341 Louise Arbour, *Commission of Inquiry into Certain Events at the Prison for Women at Kingston*, Canada, 1996.

342 UN Doc. A/56/44, para. 58.

343 *Ibid.*, para. 59.

344 *Suresh* v. *Canada, supra* note 339, para. 73.

345 UN Doc. CAT/C/SR.646/Add.1, paras. 41-42.

which is not subject to any exception whatsoever". It also condemned the role of Canadian authorites in expulsion of Maher Arar from the United States to Syria, where torture was reported. The Committee criticized Canada's "willingness, in the light of the low number of prosecutions for terrorism and torture offences, to resort in the first instance to immigration processes to remove or expel individuals from its territory, thus implicating issues of article 3 of the Convention more readily, rather than subject him or her to the criminal process".[346]

Several individual communications or petitions have been directed against Canada, generally concerning expulsion of failed refugee claimants. In *Khan* v. *Canada*, the Committee Against Torture ruled that removal of an unsuccessful refugee claimant to Pakistan by Canada would breach the *Convention*.[347] It has reached similar conclusions concerning expulsion to Iran[348] and Mexico.[349] In other cases, concerning Sri Lanka,[350] Afghanistan,[351] Iran,[352] Honduras[353] and India,[354] the Committee has dismissed the petition against Canada. In one application concerning deportation to China, the Committee said it was "aware of the seriousness of the human rights situation in China", but based on the evidence submitted and the representations of Canada it concluded that the petitioner had not substantiated his claim that he would be personally at risk of being subject to torture if he were returned to China.[355] Some applications have also been rejected for failure to exhaust domestic remedies,[356] or because there was a pending application before another international adjudicative body such as the Inter-American Commission for Human Rights,[357] or simply because they were

---

346   UN Doc. CAT/C/CR/34/CAN, para. 4.
347   *Khan* v. *Canada* (No. 15/1994), UN Doc. CAT/C/13/D/15/1994, (1995) 15 *Human Rights Law Journal* 426.
348   *Dadar* v. *Canada* (No. 258/2004), UN Doc. CAT/C/35/D/258/2004.
349   *Rios* v. *Canada* (No. 33/1999), UN Doc. CAT/C/33/D/133/1999.
350   *S.V.* et al. v. *Canada* (No. 49/1996), UN Doc. CAT/C/26/D/49/1996.
351   *Z.Z.* v. *Canada* (No. 123/1998), UN Doc. CAT/C/26/D/123/1998.
352   *B.S.* v. *Canada* (No. 166/2000), UN Doc. CAT/C/27/D/166/2000.
353   *V.N.I.M.* v. *Canada* (No. 204/2002), UN Doc. CAT/C/29/D/119/1998.
354   *T.P.S.* v. *Canada* (No. 99/1997), UN Doc. CAT/C/24/D/99/1997; *B.S.S.* v. *Canada* (No. 196/2002), UN Doc. CAT/C/32/D/183/2001; *S.S.S.* v. *Canada* (No. 245/2004), UN Doc. CAT/C/35/D/245/2004.
355   *P.Q.L.* v. *Canada* (No. 57/1996), UN Doc. CAT/C/19/D/57/1996.
356   *M.A.* v. *Canada* (No. 22/1995), UN Doc. CAT/C/14/D/22/1995; *K.K.H.* v. *Canada* (No. 35/1995), UN Doc. CAT/C/15/D/35/1995; *R.K.* v. *Canada* (No. 42/1996), UN Doc. CAT/C/19/D/42/1996; *V.V.* v. *Canada* (No. 47/1996), UN Doc. CAT/C/20/D/47/1996; *P.S.S.* v. *Canada* (No. 66/1997), UN Doc. CAT/C/21/D/66/1997; *Akhidenor* et al. v. *Canada* (No. 67/1997), UN Doc. CAT/C/21/D/67/1997; *P.S.* v. *Canada* (No. 86/1997), UN Doc. CAT/C/23/D/86/1997; *L.O.* v. *Canada* (No. 95/1997), UN Doc. CAT/C/24/D/95/1997.
357   *X.* v. *Canada* (No. 26/1995), UN Doc. CAT/C/15/D/26/1995.

"manifestly unfounded".[358] The Committee has often issued interim measures requests to Canada to ensure that petitioners are not expelled until after it has pronounced itself on the application. Canada's "reluctance" to comply with all requests for interim measures was a "subject of concern" listed by the Committee Against Torture following presentation of Canada's periodic report in 2005.[359] Decisions of the Committee Against Torture have been cited on several occasions by Canadian courts.[360]

The Committee Against Torture has issued three general comments. One of them, concerning guidelines for the individual petition mechanism, has been cited on several occasions by Canadian courts.[361]

The most recent of the major human rights treaties to which Canada subscribes, the *Convention on the Rights of the Child*,[362] is also the most

---

358 *Villamar* et al. v. *Canada* (No. 163/2000), UN Doc. CAT/C/33/D/163/2000/Rev.1.

359 UN Doc. CAT/C/CR/34/CAN, para. 4.

360 *Dadar* v. *Minister of Citizenship and Immigration*, 2006 FC 382, para. 10, citing *Dadar* v. *Canada, supra* note 348; *Thamotharampillai* v. *Canada (Minister of Citizenship and Immigration)*, (2001) 84 CRR (2d) 346, 14 Imm LR (3d) 201 (FCA), para. 29, *Khaliq* v. *Solicitor General of Canada,* 2004 FC 1561, paras. 15-16, and *Bouaouni* v. *Canada (Minister of Citizenship and Immigration)*, 2003 FC 1211, para. 36, citing *Khan* v. *Canada, supra* note 347; *Re Charkaoui*, 2005 FC 1670, at para. 33, citing *Agiza* v. *Sweden* (No. 233/2003), UN Doc. CAT/C/34/D/233/2003, at para. 13.4: para. 33; *Bouaouni* v. Canada *(Minister of Citizenship and Immigration)*, 2003 FC 1211, para. 40, citing *Tala* v. *Sweden* (No. 43/1996, UN Doc. CAT/C/17/D/43/1996; *Nadjat* v. *Canada (Minister of Citizenship and Immigration)*, 2006 FC 302, citing *G.R.B.* v. *Sweden (No.* 83/1997, UN Doc. CAT/C/20/D/83/1997, and, *B.S.S.* v. *Canada* (No. 196/2002), UN Doc. CAT/C/32/D/183/2001; *Mutombo* v. *Switzerland* (No. 13/1993), UN Doc. A/49/44, p. 45, cited in *Yi Mei Li* v. *Canada (Minister of Citizenship and Immigration)*, 2003 FC 1514, affirmed, (2005) 2005 CarswellNat 30 (FCA), leave to appeal refused, (2005) 2005 CarswellNat 1112 (SCC), para. 39.

361 "General Comment No. 1, Implementation of article 3 of the Convention in the context of article 22", UN Doc. A/53/44, annex IX, cited in *Suresh* v. *Canada (Minister of Citizenship and Immigration)*, (1999) 173 FTR 1, 50 Imm LR (2d) 183, 65 CRR (3d) 344 (TD), affirmed, (2000) 2000 CarswellNat 25 (CA), leave to appeal allowed, (2000) 2000 CarswellNat 879 (SCC), reversed, (2002) 2002 CarswellNat 7 (SCC); *Yi Mei Li* v. Canada *(Minister of Citizenship and Immigration), ibid.*

362 GA Res. 44/25, Annex, [1992] CTS 3. See: Sharon Detric *et al., The United Nations Convention on the Rights of the Child: A Guide to the "Travaux préparatoires"*, Dordrecht, Martinus Nijhoff, 1992; Philip E. Veerman, *The Rights of the Child and the Changing Image of Childhood*, Dordrecht, Martinus Nijhoff, 1992; Michael Freeman & Philip Veerman, *The Ideologies of Children's Rights*, Dordrecht, Martinus Nijhoff, 1992; Marc Bossuyt, "La Convention des Nations Unies sur les droits de l'enfant", (1990) 2 *Revue universelle des droits de l'homme* 141; Renée Joyal, "La notion d'intérêt supérieur de l'enfant: sa place dans la Convention des Nations Unies sur les droits de l'enfant", (1991) 62 *Revue international de droit public* 785; Adam Lopatka, "Convention relative aux droits de l'enfant", (1991) 62 *Revue international de droit public* 765; Dominic McGoldrick, "The United Nations Convention on the Rights of the Child", (1991) 5 *International Journal of the Law of the Family* 132; Marta Santos Pais, "La

successful in terms of its rapid and quite unprecedented acceptance. Although it was only adopted by the General Assembly in 1989, it now counts 191 States parties, which is near-universal ratification. The only real exceptions are the United States of America, which has signed the treaty, and Somalia, which does not have an operational foreign ministry. The *Convention* establishes the Committee on the Rights of the Child, which has responsibility for monitoring compliance, principally by means of examining the periodic reports of States. In 2005, Canadian David Brent Parfitt was elected to the Committee on the Rights of the Child. There are no individual or interstate petition mechanisms under the *Convention*.

Children's rights surfaced as an international law issue in the early days of the League of Nations, when the *Declaration on the Rights of the Child* was adopted, following an initiative from Save the Children International Union.[363] A similar initiative was taken by the United Nations General Assembly in 1959.[364] The *Convention on the Rights of the Child* was adopted by the United Nations General Assembly in 1989.[365] Canada worked actively

---

Convention sur les droits de l'enfant", in Institut canadien d'études juridiques supérieures, *Droits de la personne: l'émergence des droits nouveaux, aspects canadiens et européens, Actes des Journées strasbourgeoises de 1992*, Cowansville, Éditions Yvon Blais, 1992, p. 665; Cynthia Price Cohen, "The U.N. Convention on the Rights of the Child: Developing an Information Model to Computerize the Monitoring of Treaty Compliance", (1992) 14 *Human Rights Law Journal* 216; Eugen Verhellen, ed., *Monitoring Children's Rights*, Dordrecht: Martinus Nijhoff, 1996.

363 *Declaration on the Rights of the Child*, League of Nations OJ Spec. Supp. 21, p. 43, 26 September 1924. Cited in: *Gordon* v. *Goertz*, [1996] 2 SCR 27, 196 NR 321, 141 Sask R 241, 114 WAC 241, [1996] 5 WWR 457, 19 RFL (4th) 177, 134 DLR (4th) 321.

364 *Declaration on the Rights of the Child*, GA Res. 1386 (XIV). The *Declaration* has been cited by the Canadian courts on many occasions, perhaps most notably by Justice L'Heureux-Dubé in *Baker* v. *Canada (Minister of Citizenship and Immigration)*, [1999] 2 SCR 817, 174 DLR (4th) 193, 14 Admin LR (3d) 173, 1 Imm LR (3d) 1, 243 NR 22, at para. 71. See also: *Hélène G.* v. *Centre I.*, [1976] CBES 2001, *M. et Mme A.* v. *M. et Mme D.*, [1976] CBES 2023, *R.* v. *M. (J.G.)*, (1985) 24 CCC (3d) 288 (Ont Prov Ct); *Transpacific Tours Ltd.* v. *Director of Investigation and Research, Combines Investigation Act*, (1985) [1986] 2 WWR 34, 8 CPR (3d) 325, 25 DLR (4th) 202 (BC SC); *Thomson Newspapers Ltd.* v. *Director of Investigation and Research*, (1986) 26 DLR (4th) 507, 54 OR (2d) 143 (HC), reversed, (1986) 1986 CarswellOnt 139 (CA), affirmed, (1990) 1990 CarswellOnt 991 (SCC); *Kelly* v. *Canada (Minister of Employment and Immigration)*, (1 December 1993) Doc T93-04542 [1993] IADD No 739 (Imm & Ref Bd (App Div)); *Commission scolaire St-Jean-sur-Richelieu* v. *Commission des droits de la personne du Québec*, [1994] RJQ 227 (CA); *Charran* v. *Canada (Minister of Citizenship and Immigration)*, (1995) 89 FTR 113, 28 Imm LR (2d) 282; *Lisenko* c. *Commission scolaire St-Hyacinthe Val-Monts*, JE 96-787 (TDPQ); *Gordon* v. *Goertz*, *supra* note 363.

365 UN Doc. GA Res. 44/25, annex.

during the drafting process, the first time it had taken such a prominent role in the creation of human rights treaty law.[366]

Canada signed the *Convention* on 28 May 1990 and ratified it on 12 December 1991. On 9 December 1991, Quebec "ratified" the *Convention*.[367] Canada accompanied its ratification with two reservations. The first concerns article 21, which establishes an obligation on States that permit adoption to ensure that this takes place in the best interest of the child. Canada reserved "the right not to apply the provisions of article 21 to the extent that they may be inconsistent with customary forms of care among aboriginal peoples in Canada". The second relates to article 37(c), requiring the separation of children from adults when they are detained as part of the criminal justice process: "The Government of Canada accepts the general principles of article 37(c) of the Convention, but reserves the right not to detain children separately from adults where this is not appropriate or feasible." Canada also formulated a declaration, known as an understanding, to article 30 of the *Convention*, which concerns the rights of minorities:

> It is the understanding of the Government of Canada that, in matters relating to aboriginal peoples of Canada, the fulfillment of its responsibilities under article 4 of the Convention must take into account the provisions of article 30. In particular, in assessing what measures are appropriate to implement the rights recognized in the Convention for aboriginal children, due regard must be paid to not denying their right, in community with other members of their group, to enjoy their own culture, to profess and practice their own religion and to use their own language.

A number of references have been made to the *Convention on the Rights of the Child* in Canadian caselaw.[368]

---

366 Standing Senate Committee on Human Rights, *Who's in Charge Here? Effective Implementation of Canada's International Obligations with Respect to the Rights of Children*, Ottawa, November 2005, p. 36.

367 REIQ (1990-92) 1992 (4) p. 361.

368 *Commission des droits de la personne du Québec* v. *Commission scolaire St-Jean-sur-Richelieu*, [1991] RJQ 3003 (TDPQ), varied, [1994] RJQ 227 (CA); *Commission des droits de la personne du Québec* v. *Commission scolaire régionale Chauveau*, (1993) 18 CHRR D/433, [1993] RJQ 929 (TDPQ); *R.* v. *L. (D.O.)*, (1991) 73 Man R (2d) 238, 6 CR (4th) 277, 65 CCC (3d) 465 (CA), reversed, [1993] 4 SCR 419; *Young* v. *Young*, [1993] 4 SCR 3, 108 DLR (4th) 193, 160 NR 1; *Kelly* v. *Canada (Minister of Employment and Immigration)*, (1 December 1993) Doc T93-04542 [1993] IADD No 739 (Imm & Ref Bd (App Div)); *Commission scolaire St-Jean-sur-Richelieu* v. *Commission des droits de la personne du Québec*, supra note 364; *G. (B.B.) (Re)*, [1994] CRDD No 397; *Charran* v. *Canada (Minister of Citizenship and Immigration)*, (1995) 89 FTR 113, 28 Imm LR (2d) 282; *Langner* v. *Canada (Minister of Employment and Immigration)*, (1995) 1995 CarswellNat 1337, [1995] FCJ No 469 (CA), leave to appeal refused, [1995] 3 SCR vii (SCC); *U. (N.X.) (Re)*, (July 25, 1995) No T93-12579, [1995] CRDD No 74 (Imm & Ref Bd (Ref Div)); *Baker* v. *Canada (Minister of Citizenship and*

There are two optional protocols to the *Convention on the Rights of the Child*, dealing with child soldiers and sexual abuse of children, both of them ratified by Canada. The *Optional Protocol to the Convention on the Rights of the Child on the Involvement of Children in Armed Conflict*[369] prevents conscription of persons under eighteen and requires states to "take all feasible measures to ensure that members of their armed forces who have not attained the age of 18 years do not take a direct part in hostilities". Ratification was accompanied by a declaration, noting that the Canadian Armed Forces permit voluntary recruitment of children as young as sixteen, but that recruitment of persons under eighteen requires the consent of a parent or guardian. A curious portion of the declaration states that Canada requires persons under eighteen to prove their age by means of a certificate. Presumably persons over eighteen must also prove their age! In its fifth periodic report to the Human Rights Committee, Canada said: "Canada has signed the *Optional Protocol to the Convention on the Rights of the Child on the Sale of Children, Child Prostitution and Child Pornography*[370] on 10 November 2001 and has undertaken measures to facilitate its ratification in the near future."[371] The *Optional Protocol* was ratified by Canada on 14 September 2005. It was cited by the Supreme Court of Canada in the challenge to the child pornography provisions of the *Criminal Code*.[372]

Canadian reports to the Committee on the Rights of the Child have been studied on two occasions, in 1995 and 2003.[373] In its "Concluding Observations", concerning the Second Periodic Report, the Committee has focussed on the high level of child poverty in Canada, issues concerning children in migration and Aboriginal children, and the continued tolerance of corporal punishment in Canadian criminal law.[374] Canada is also required to submit periodic reports pursuant to the two protocols. In 2005, Canada presented its initial report on children in armed conflict.[375]

The Committee on the Rights of the Child has issued several General Comments, dealing with such issues as the aims of education, HIV/AIDS

Immigration), (1995) 101 FTR 110, 31 Imm LR (2d) 150, affirmed, [1997] 2 FC 127, reversed, [1999] 2 SCR 817, 174 DLR (4th) 193, 14 Admin LR (3d) 173, 1 Imm LR (3d) 1, 243 NR 22; *Baker* v. *Canada (Minister of Citizenship and Immigration), supra* note 363; *Canadian Foundation for Children, Youth and the Law* v. *Canada (Attorney General)*, [2004] 1 SCR 76, 70 OR (3d) 95, 234 DLR (4th) 257, 180 CCC (3d) 353, 115 CRR (2d) 88, 16 CR (6th) 203, 46 RFL (5th) 1, 183 OAC 1.

369 UN Doc. A/RES/54/263, [2002] CTS 5.
370 UN Doc. A/RES/54/263.
371 "Fifth periodic report, Canada", UN Doc. CCPR/C/CAN/2004/5, para. 57.
372 *R.* v. *Sharpe*, [2001] 1 SCR 45, para. 178.
373 Initial report (UN Doc. CRC/C/11/Add.3), examined in 1995; second report (UN Doc. CRC/C/83/Add.6), examined 17 September 2003 (UN Doc. CRC/C/SR.894 and 895).
374 UN Doc. CRC/C/15/Add.215.
375 UN Doc. CRC/C/OPAC/CAN/1.

and the rights of the child, and the treatment of unaccompanied and separated children outside of their country of origin.[376]

Human rights treaties have also been adopted by specialized agencies of the United Nations, specifically the International Labour Organization (discussed above), the United Nations Educational, Scientific and Cultural Organization (UNESCO) and the World Health Assembly.[377] The UNESCO *Constitution* states that its purpose is the promotion of "collaboration among nations through education, science and culture in order to further. . .human rights and fundamental freedoms". It is responsible for several conventions and recommendations dealing with human rights in the field of education, science and culture, as well as racial discrimination.[378] There is a little known and little used petition mechanism, authorizing UNESCO to receive communications from individuals or groups who allege "violations of human rights falling within UNESCO's competence in the fields of education, science, culture and information [that are] not motivated exclusively by other considerations".[379] Within this context, UNESCO has dealt with such matters as teachers' strikes, the detention of teachers, expulsion of university students and the education of nomadic gypsies.[380]

3.3   The Organization of American States

States in the Western hemisphere had contemplated the preparation of international instruments to protect human rights as early as 1902, and an international declaration on civil and political rights was considered, although not adopted, in 1916.[381] The *American Declaration of the Rights*

---

376   UN Doc. HRI/GEN/1/Rev.6.
377   World Health Assembly resolutions dealing with the campaign against tobacco consumption were cited in: *RJR-Macdonald Inc.* v. *Canada*, [1995] 3 SCR 199, 127 DLR (4th) 1 (*per* La Forest J.).
378   Such as the *Convention against Discrimination in Education and its related Protocol*, (1960) 429 UNTS 93 (not ratified by Canada); *Unesco Declaration on Race and Racial Prejudice*, UNESCO Doc. 14 C/3/1.2, 1978; *Convention for the Protection of Cultural Property in the Event of Armed Conflict*, (1954) 249 UNTS 240. See: P. Mertens, "L'application de la Convention and de la Recommandation de l'UNESCO concernant la lutte contre la discrimination dans le domaine de l'enseignement, Un bilan provisoire", (1968) 1 *Revue des droits de l'homme* 91.
379   *Evaluation of the procedures adopted by the Executive Board for the examination of communications concerning violations of human rights falling within Unesco's fields of competence: Report by the Executive Board and the Director-General*, UNESCO Doc. 23 C/17, 8 October 1985.
380   *Ibid.*, at 15, 17.
381   Francisco José Aguilar-Urbina, "A Comparison Between the Covenant and the American Convention as Regards the Procedure", [1991] *Canadian Human Rights Yearbook* 127; A.H. Robertson, *Human Rights in the World*, Manchester: Manchester University Press, 1972, at 111.

and Duties of Man was adopted in April 1948 at the Chapultepec conference of the Organization of American States.[382] It comprises an enumeration of rights that is comparable to although not identical with that of the *Universal Declaration of Human Rights*.[383] Perhaps the most significant distinction is the greater emphasis placed by the *American Declaration*, as its name suggests, on duties. Ten of its thirty-eight articles deal with duties, including those of children and parents, a duty to educate oneself, to vote, to respect the law, to pay taxes, a duty to work and to abstain from political activity in a foreign country. The *Universal Declaration of Human Rights* devotes only one of its thirty articles, and only in a very general sense, to the issue of duties.[384]

Both declarations – the *Universal Declaration* of the United Nations and the *American Declaration* of the Organization of American States – were conceived of as non-binding instruments that would merely set "a common standard of achievement". However, in 1967 the Organization of American States decided to modify the vocation of the *American Declaration*, making it binding on all States party to the *Charter of the Organi-*

---

382 *American Declaration of the Rights and Duties of Man*, OAS Doc. OEA/Ser. L./V/II.23, doc. 21, rev. 6. Cited in: *Commission des droits de la personne du Québec* c. *Immeubles Ni/Dia Inc.*, [1992] RJQ 2977 (TDPQ); *B. (R.)* v. *Children's Aid Society of Metropolitan Toronto*, [1995] 1 SCR 315, 122 DLR (4th) 1, 176 NR 161; *R.* v. *Demers*, (1999) 176 DLR (4th) 741, 137 CCC (3d) 297 (BC SC), affirmed, (2003) 102 CRR (2d) 367 (BC CA), leave to appeal refused, (2003) 321 NR 399n (SCC). See: Stephen Livingstone & David J. Harris, *The Inter-American System of Human Rights*, Oxford: Oxford University Press, 1998; Scott Davidson, *The Inter-American Human Rights System*, Aldershot: Dartmouth, 1997; Thomas Buergenthal, Robert Norris & Dinah Shelton, *Protecting Human Rights in the Americas: Selected Problems*, 4th ed., Kehl: N.P. Engel, 1996; Hector Gros-Espiell, "L'O.É.A.", *in* Karel Vasak, ed., *Les dimensions internationales des droits de l'Homme*, Paris, Unesco, 1978, p. 600; Hector Gros-Espiell, "Le système interaméricain comme régime régional de protection internationale des droits de l'Homme", (1975) 145 *Receuil de cours de l'Académie de droit international* 1; Thomas Buergenthal, "The Inter-American System for the Protection of Human Rights", in Theodor Meron, ed., *Human Rights and International Law Legal and Political Issues*, Oxford, Oxford University Press, 1985, p. 439; Robert Norris, "The Individual Petition Procedure of the Inter-American System for the Protection of Human Rights", in Hurst Hannum, ed., *Guide to International Human Rights Law Practice*, Philadelphia, University of Pennsylvania Press, 1984, p. 104.

383 For the influence of the *American Declaration of the Rights and Duties of Man* in the drafting of the *Universal Declaration of Human Rights*, see for example: UN Doc. E/CN.4/122; UN Doc. A/C.3/224; UN Doc. A/C.3/SR.104/Corr.1; UN Doc. A/C.3/SR.107.

384 *Universal Declaration of Human Rights*, GA Res. 217 A (III) UN Doc. A/810, art. 29(1): "Everyone has duties to the community in which alone the free and full development of his personality is possible."

zation of American States.[385] Furthermore, all such States are also bound by the *Statute*[386] and *Regulations*[387] of the Inter-American Commission of Human Rights. Taken together, these instruments create an individual petition procedure that exists by virtue of membership in the Organization of American States, without the requirement of any additional declaration or undertaking. The individual petition procedure under the *Declaration* is applicable to Canada and to other Member States that have not ratified the *American Convention on Human Rights*, which is a treaty similar in content to the *International Covenant on Civil and Political Rights* and the *European Convention on Human Rights*, and which has its own petition procedure to the Inter-American Commission on Human Rights.

Pursuant to article 20(b) of the *Statute of the Inter-American Commission of Human Rights*, the Inter-American Commission has jurisdiction "to examine communications submitted to it and any other available information, to address the government of any Member State not a Party to the Convention for information deemed pertinent by this Commission, and to make recommendations to it, when it finds this appropriate, in order to bring about more effective observance of fundamental human rights."[388] According to article 51 of its *Regulations*, the Commission is competent, with respect to the Member States of the Organization of American States, to "receive and examine any petition that contains a denunciation of alleged violations of the human rights set forth in the American Declaration of the Rights and Duties of Man, concerning the members states of the Organization that are not parties to the American Convention on Human Rights".[389]

Therefore, as the Inter-American Commission has noted:

> The State is a member State of the Organization of American States but is not a party to the American Convention on Human Rights. Consequently the State is subject to the Commission's jurisdiction as regards the American Declaration of the Rights and Duties of Man, as provided for in Article 49 of the Commis-

---

385 *Charter of the Organization of American States*, (1952) 119 UNTS 4, 46 *American Journal of International Law* Supp. 43, as amended by *Protocol of Buenos Aires*, (1970) 721 UNTS 324, [1990] CTS 23, arts. 3j, 16, 51e, 112 and 150.

386 *Statute of the Inter-American Commission of Human Rights, Basic Documents Pertaining to Human Rights in the Inter-American System*, OAS Doc. OEA/Ser.L.V/II.71, Doc. 6 rev. 1, p. 65.

387 *Regulations of the Inter-American Commission of Human Rights, Basic Documents Pertaining to Human Rights in the Inter-American System*, OAS Doc. OEA/Ser.L.V/ II.71, Doc. 6 rev. 1, p. 75.

388 *Statute of the Inter-American Commission of Human Rights*, *supra* note 386.

389 *Regulations of the Inter-American Commission of Human Rights*, *supra* note 387.

sion's Rules of Procedure. Canada deposited its instrument of ratification of the OAS Charter on January 8, 1990.[390]

Canada does not seem to have contested the jurisdiction of the Commission to rule on petitions to the Inter-American Commission on Human Rights alleging breaches of the *American Declaration of the Rights and Duties of Man*.[391] There has been modest interest in the procedure among Canadian human rights lawyers, and a few applications have been filed with the Commission. According to the rules of the Commission, such petitions remain confidential as long as they are pending, and are only made public once a final decision is taken. The first of the handful of reported cases was filed by Cheryl Monica Joseph, a Trinidadian citizen, who had lived in Canada with her husband and their five children for five years. They had applied for refugee status and their claim was rejected. They sought "precautionary measures" under article 29 of the Commission *Regulations*, which would allow her to remain in Canada while the case was being decided. Canada agreed to this. Joseph alleged breaches of articles XVIII (fair trial), XXVI (due process), V (honour, personal reputation and private and family life), VI (family), VII (mothers and children). The Commission concluded that the domestic remedies had not been exhausted, and the petition was declared inadmissible. But the Commission asked "the Government of Canada to give favourable consideration to the possibility of permitting Ms Joseph to remain in Canada until the completion of the court's action in connection with the estate of her late husband".[392]

In 2002, the Inter-American Commission considered aspects of the *Suresh* case, after the matter had been addressed in the Supreme Court of Canada.[393] As the Commission explained, the issue before it was not whether Suresh could be deported to Sri Lanka, where it was alleged he would face a risk of torture, because the Supreme Court had held he was entitled to a

---

390 *Mitchell* v. *Canada* (Case No. 790/01), Admissibility, Report No. 74/03, 22 October 2003, para. 30. Also: *Suresh* v. *Canada* (Case No. 11.661), Admissibility, Report No. 7/02, 27 February 2002, para. 21.

391 In contrast with the United States, which bitterly contested the Commission's right to consider such petitions: *White and Potter* v. *United States* (Case no. 2141), Resolution No. 23/81, OAS Doc. A/Ser.L/V/II.52 doc. 48, OAS Doc. A/Ser.L/V/II.54 doc. 9 rev. 1, at 25-54, Inter-American Commission on Human Rights, *Ten Years of Activities, 1971-1981*, Washington, D.C.: Organization of American States, 1982, at 186-209, (1981) 1 *Human Rights Law Journal* 110.

392 *Joseph* v. *Canada* (Case 11.092), Decision of the Commission as to the Admissibility, Report No. 27/93, 6 October 1993, in *Annual Report of the Inter-American Commission on Human Rights, 1993*, OAS Doc. OEA/SER.L/V/II.85 Doc. 9 rev. (1994). For a discussion of the case, see Cecilia Medina, "Inter-American System", (1994) 12 *Netherlands Quarterly of Human Rights* 327, at 327-328.

393 *Suresh* v. *Canada (Minister of Citizenship and Immigration)*, [2002] 1 SCR 3, 208 DLR (4th) 1, 37 Admin LR (3d) 159, 90 CRR (2d) 1.

new deportation hearing and therefore his domestic remedies had not been exhausted on that issue. Suresh argued, however, that he had been denied the right to have the legality of his detention ascertained without delay, by a simple, brief procedure before a court, as required by article XVIII of the *American Declaration of the Rights and Duties of Man*, and whether his detention for two years and five months as a non-resident alien violated articles II and XXVI of *Declaration*. "The larger issue presented", explained the Commission, "is whether international human rights law requires states to grant not only citizens, but also aliens, the right to habeas corpus, to determine the legality of their detention in status proceedings."[394] The Commission ruled the case admissible.[395]

A Canadian case dealing with claims by Aboriginal peoples to be free of import duties on cigarettes was judged admissible by the Inter-American Commission. Without ruling on the merits, the Commission considered that an argument based on the "right to culture", which is set out in article XIII of the *Declaration*, deserved "a further in-depth substantive briefing". The Commission noted that it was not bound by the definition of the "right to culture" as determined by the Canadian courts, or the *Van der Peet* test,[396] and acknowledged that the analysis and interpretation of Canadian courts might "provide certain useful insights for the Commission's interpretation of the substantive content of Article XIII of the American Declaration".[397] Another reported case in an immigration matter was declared inadmissible because the applicant had "inexcusably" failed to exhaust his domestic remedies.[398]

In specific cases, some litigants may prefer the Inter-American Commission as opposed to the Human Rights Committee and the Committee Against Torture because of its perceived willingness to request a provisional stay, pending determination on the merits of the petition. Because the Human Rights Committee has no rule of *res judicata*, there is nothing to stop an individual going first to the Inter-American Commission and subsequently to the Human Rights Committee. There are also substantive differences between the applicable instruments that may argue in favour of the *American Declaration* rather than the *International Covenant on Civil and Political Rights*. For example, the *American Declaration* recognizes a right to property, something that was omitted from the *International Covenant*, as well as from the *Canadian Charter of Rights and Freedoms*. The guar-

---

394 *Suresh* v. *Canada, supra* note 390, para. 25.
395 *Ibid.*, para. 31.
396 Referring to the test set out in *R.* v. *Van der Peet*, [1996] 2 SCR 507, [1996] 4 CNLR 177 (SCC), reconsideration refused, (January 16, 1997) Doc 23803 (SCC).
397 *Mitchell* v. *Canada, supra* note 390, para. 37.
398 *Harte* et al. v. *Canada* (Case No. 11.862), Inadmissibility, Report No. 81/05, 24 October 2005, para. 89.

antees of economic and social rights within the *American Declaration* are also of considerable interest.

In addition to its contentious procedure, the Inter-American Commission regularly prepares reports on human rights issues that concern the hemisphere. Often, these are the result of on-site visits by the Commission. In 1997, at the invitation of the government, the Inter-American Commission conducted an on-site visit in Canada to investigate the situation of asylum seekers within the Canadian refugee determination system.[399] The Commission described the Canadian system as "humanitarian in spirit and highly generous in terms of its results".[400] But it also observed that

> [w]ith certain important exceptions, the Commission noted a surprising lack of information or understanding on the part of administration and judicial officials at both the federal and provincial levels of Canada's regional and international human rights obligations in the refugee context. The Commission also noted a perception on the part of some officials that international human rights law was a question falling within the sphere of foreign affairs rather than one pertaining to the implementation of domestic law.[401]

The Commission made a number of quite detailed and specific recommendations with respect to the process.

Like the United Nations system, it has its own "special procedures" in the form of special rapporteurs designated by the Inter-American Commission. There are special rapporteurs dealing with the rights of women, of migrant workers and their families and with freedom of expression. In 2005, Eduardo Bertoni, the Special Rapporteur for Freedom of Expression of the Inter-American Commission of Human Rights, testified before the Standing Senate Committee on Human Rights.[402]

The *American Convention on Human Rights* was adopted by the Organization of American States at San Jose, Costa Rica, in 1969, in order to bring its human rights system up to date with that of the Council of Europe and the United Nations.[403] The Commission had already been operational

399 "Report on the Situation of Human Rights of Asylum Seekers Within the Canadian Refugee Determination System", OAS Co. OEA/Ser.L/V/II.106, Doc. 40 rev.
400 *Ibid.*, para. 167.
401 *Ibid.*, para. 168.
402 Proceedings of the Standing Senate Committee on Human Rights, First Session, Thirty-eighth Parliament, 2004, 16 May 2005.
403 *American Convention on Human Rights*, (1979) 1144 UNTS 123, OASTS 36. See: Thomas Buergenthal, "The Inter-American Court of Human Rights", (1982) 76 *American Journal of International Law* 23; Thomas Buergenthal, "The Advisory Practice of the Inter-American Court of Human Rights", (1985) 79 *American Journal of International Law* 11; Christina M. Cerna, "La Cour interaméricaine des droits de l'homme, ses premières affaires", (1983) 29 *Annuaire français de droit international* 300; Christina M. Cerna, "La Cour interaméricaine des droits de l'Homme: les affaires récentes", (1987) 33 *Annuaire français de droit international* 351.

since the late 1950s, but unlike the European system, there was no court. In addition, it was considered important to give the fundamental norms more legal clarity, in keeping with the approach of the other two systems. The *Convention* comprises an enumeration of norms that are both more detailed and somewhat different than those in the *American Declaration*. It also creates the Inter-American Court of Human Rights. There are currently twenty-four States party to the *American Convention*, almost all of them from Latin America. The United States of America has signed but not ratified the *Convention*. Canada has neither signed nor ratified the *Convention*.

The *American Convention* improves upon the *Covenant* and the *European Convention* in certain respects. For example, it explicitly recognizes economic, social and cultural rights. Article 26 of the *Convention* states:

> The States Parties undertake to adopt measures, both internally and through international cooperation, especially those of an economic and technical nature, with a view to achieving progressively, by legislation or other appropriate means, the full realization of the rights implicit in the economic, social, educational, scientific, and cultural standards set forth in the Charter of the Organization of American States as amended by the Protocol of Buenos Aires.

A *Protocol to the American Convention of Human Rights dealing with Economic, Social and Cultural Rights (Protocol of San Salvador)*, which entered into force in 1999, endeavours to flesh out this rather summary affirmation with a complete and rather innovative enumeration.[404] A second protocol concerns capital punishment, and amends article 4 of the *Convention* so as to prohibit the death penalty in time of peace and in wartime.[405]

In terms of implementation, the *Convention* imposes upon all States Parties a petition mechanism to the Inter-American Commission, with the prospect of a subsequent hearing by the Inter-American Court of Human Rights. The Inter-American Court has developed an important body of jurisprudence in contentious cases, and was the first international human rights body to recognize the notion that States may be held responsible even for acts committed by non-State actors, such as "death squads", thereby giving a kind of horizontal effect to the international norms.[406] The Inter-American Court of Human Rights assumes jurisdiction in cases of individual petitions only if the State party to the *Convention* has made a supplementary

---

404 OASTS 69, 28 ILM 161. See: A.A. Cançado Trindade, "La protection des droits économiques, sociaux et culturels: évolutions et tendances particulièrement à l'échelle régionale", (1990) 94 *Revue générale de droit international public* 913.

405 *Additional Protocol to the American Convention on Human Rights to Abolish the Death Penalty*, OASTS 73.

406 *Velasquez Rodriguez* v. *Honduras*, Series C, No. 4.

declaration recognizing its jurisdiction.[407] All petitions are initially considered by the Commission, which operates as a kind of court of first instance, in a manner similar to that of the European Commission of Human Rights prior to its abolition in 1998. The early caselaw of the Inter-American Court of Human Rights featured a large number of "advisory opinions". These were sometimes disguised attempts to question the human rights profile of an Organization of American States Member State. These advisory opinions have addressed such matters as the suspension of human rights in emergency situations,[408] the death penalty,[409] rights of journalists,[410] rights to citizenship,[411] equality of men and women[412] and matters dealing more generally with the interpretation of international human rights instruments.[413] In the *Secession Reference*, the Supreme Court of Canada noted the authority of the Inter-American Court of Human Rights to render advisory opinions.[414] Occasional reference to the *American Convention* has been made by Canadian courts.[415] There do not appear to have been any references to the jurisprudence of the Inter-American Court or the Inter-American Commission, however. In comparison with the European Court of Human Rights

---

407 *American Convention on Human Rights, supra* note 403, art. 62.

408 *Habeas corpus in Emergency Situations (Non Derogeable Guarantee)* Advisory Opinion OC-8/87, Series A No. 8, 9 *Human Rights Law Journal* 94, 27 *ILM* 1588, 11 EHRR 33; *Judicial Guarantees in States of Emergency*, Advisory Opinion OC-9/87, Series A No. 9, 9 *Human Rights Law Journal* 204.

409 *Restrictions to the Death Penalty*, Advisory Opinion OC-3/83, Series A No. 3, 4 *Human Rights Law Journal* 352, 70 ILR 449.

410 *Compulsory Membership in an Association Prescribed by Law for the Practice of Journalism (Arts. 13 and 29 American Convention on Human Rights)* Advisory Opinion OC-5/85, Series A No. 5, 7 *Human Rights Law Journal* 88, 75 ILR 30.

411 *Proposed Amendments to the Naturalization Provisions of the Political Constitution of Costa Rica,* Advisory Opinion OC-4/84, Series A No. 4, 5 *Human Rights Law Journal* 161, 79 ILR 282.

412 *Ibid.*

413 *The Word "Laws" in Article 30 of the American Convention on Human Rights*, Advisory Opinion OC-6/86, Series A No. 6, 7 *Human Rights Law Journal* 231, 79 ILR 325; *"Other Treaties" Subject to the Consultative Jurisdiction of the Court (Art. 64 American Convention of Human Rights)* Advisory Opinion OC-1/82, Series A No. 1, 3 *Human Rights Law Journal* 146, 67 ILR 594.

414 *Reference re Secession of Quebec*, [1998] 2 SCR 217, 161 DLR (4th) 385, 55 CRR (2d) 1, para. 115, para. 14.

415 *R. v. Big M Drug Mart Ltd.*, [1984] 1 WWR 625, 5 DLR (4th) 121, 9 CCC (3d) 310, 28 Alta LR (2d) 289, 49 AR 194, 7 CRR 92 (CA), affirmed, [1985] 1 SCR 295; *Allman v. Commissioner of the Northwest Territories , [1984] NWTR 65, 8 DLR (4th) 230, 50 AR 161 (CA); R. v. Morgentaler*, (1986) 22 DLR (4th) 641, 22 CCC (3d) 353, 48 CR (3d) 1, 52 OR (2d) 353, 11 OAC 81, 17 CRR 223 (CA), reversed, [1988] 1 SCR 30, (1988) 31 CRR 1, 37 CCC (3d) 449, 44 DLR (4th) 365, 62 CR (3d) 1, 82 NR 1; *R. v. Demers*, (1999) 176 DLR (4th) 741, 137 CCC (3d) 297 (BC SC), affirmed, (2003) 102 CRR (2d) 367 (BC CA), leave to appeal refused, (2003) 321 NR 399n (SCC).

and the *European Convention on Human Rights*, the Inter-American system has barely registered with Canadian judges.

When Canada joined the Organization of American States it was widely believed that ratification of the *Convention* would follow shortly.[416] The Secretary of State for External Affairs announced this would occur in the spring of 1992.[417] Ratification of the human rights instruments of the Organization of American States system, including the *American Convention*, was first discussed at a federal/provincial consultation on 22 November, 1990.[418] Curiously, there does not appear to have been any meaningful consultation with the provinces prior to ratification of the *Organization of American States Charter*, in January 1990, despite the fact that this involved assuming obligations in the field of human rights that clearly concerned areas of provincial competence.

In 1991, Canada sent a signal to other Organization of American States members of its intention to be a full player in the system, including not only ratification of the *Convention* but also acceptance of the jurisdiction of the Court, when it nominated retired Supreme Court Justice Bertha Wilson for a seat on the seven-member tribunal. Judges of the Court are "elected in an individual capacity from among jurists of the highest moral authority and of recognized competence in the field of human rights",[419] criteria that Bertha Wilson's record in her rulings in *Charter* cases when she was sitting on the Supreme Court of Canada had clearly established. Canada did not vote in the election, which is limited to States party to the *Convention*.[420] Bertha Wilson fell one short of the required number of votes. In her place was elected a former foreign minister in the Somoza government of Nicaragua, Dr. Alejandro Montiel Arguello, a man whose commitment to human

---

416 See: Carol Hilling, "La participation canadienne au système interaméricain de protection des droits and libertés: les obligations immédiates and les perspectives d'avenir", in Canadian Council for International Law, *Canada and the Americas: Proceedings of the 1991 Annual Meeting of the Canadian Council of International Law*, Ottawa: Canadian Council of Inernational Law, 1992, p. 223; Norman P. Farrell, "The American Convention on Human Rights: Canada's Present Law and the Effect of Ratification", (1992) 30 *Canadian Yearbook of International Law* 233; William A. Schabas, "Substantive and Procedural Issues in the Ratification by Canada of the *American Convention on Human Rights*", (1991) 12 *Human Rights Law Journal* 405; William A. Schabas, "Canadian Ratification of the American Convention on Human Rights", (1998) 16 *Netherlands Quarterly of Human Rights* 315.

417 James C. Hathaway, "Canada and the Inter-American Rights System: What Contribution to Expect?", October, 1991.

418 "Canada's First Year in the Organization of American States: Implementing the Strategy for Latin America", Brochure published by the Department of External Affairs and International Trade Canada, January 1991, p. 14.

419 *American Convention on Human Rights*, *supra* note 403, art. 52(1).

420 *Ibid.*, art. 53.

rights is dubious.[421] The Canadian Ambassador to the Organization of American States at the time, Jean-Paul Hubert, suggested that Justice Wilson's defeat may have been because Canada had not yet ratified the *Convention*. But the reason may also have been more banal, a confusion of the delegates about the nominating procedure.[422] On the election of Judge Montiel, one observer wrote:

> [M]any of the twenty-three voting governments view seats on the Court more as privileges than as responsibilities. The nomination process is, *de facto*, relatively closed. So far as I am aware, neither the Organization of American States nor any government publicized the nominees or sought the views of human rights non-governmental organizations (NGOs) on the candidates. Nor, apparently, did they investigate Dr. Montiel's record, particularly his public defense of Somoza's human rights record.
>
> Likewise, the vote turned more on horse-trading than on human rights; the Central American nations had reportedly agreed in advance of the General Assembly meeting to vote as a bloc in support of all Central American candidates for all Organization of American States posts. Even so, Dr. Montiel won by only one vote.
>
> NGOs were caught off guard by his election. Few had followed the nomination process at all; others had been under the impression that a Canadian judge with a good human rights record was expected to fill the vacancy to be created by the expiration of the second term of Judge Thomas Buergenthal (a United States jurist and leading human rights expert nominated to the Court by Costa Rica).[423]

Following the defeat of Justice Wilson's candidacy for the Inter-American Court, Canada's enthusiasm for ratification of the *Convention* seemed to run out of steam. On 7 June 1993 in Managua, at the XXIIIrd General Assembly of the Organization of American States, Foreign Minister Barbara McDougall spoke of Canada being a "fervent defender" of the Inter-American Commission on Human Rights, but made no mention whatsoever of either the Court or of Canada's position on ratification of the *Convention*, matters which ought to have been at the top of the agenda. In the mid-1990s, Harold Hickman, Counsellor and Alternate Permanent Representative to the Canadian Mission to the Organization of American States, was quoted as saying Canada's delay is due to matters concerning the division of powers and consultation with the provinces and the territories.[424] Later in the decade,

---

421 Douglass W. Cassel, Jr., "Somoza's Revenge: A New Judge for the Inter-American Court of Human Rights", (1992) 13 *Human Rights Law Journal* 137.

422 Canada-Caribbean-Central America Policy Alternatives, *Report on Canada's Second Year in the OAS*, April, 1992, p. 7 note 17.

423 Douglass W. Cassel, Jr., *supra* note 421, at 139.

424 Brian Tittemore, "Canada and the OAS – The First Five Years", *Human Rights Brief*, Vol. 2, No. 1, p. 3.

officials explained to the Inter-American Commission on Human Rights that "Canada has reservations concerning the Convention regarding the exact scope of its obligations [there]under . . . and, therefore, with its ability to ensure full compliance". Canada referred to

> some apparent inconsistencies between provisions of the Convention and other international human rights norms and trends in international human rights law. The State referred to specific concerns relative to certain Convention provisions, observing that ratification would accordingly require a series of reservations and statements of understanding, a result contrary to its position that reservations to human rights treaties should be few and limited in scope. Canada indicated that, while it "does not adhere to the Convention, this does not undermine our commitment to its fundamental principles".[425]

It may well be true that Ottawa is prepared to ratify the *Convention*, and that it is being stymied by provincial resistance. Perhaps some of the provinces have been irritated in recent years when the federal government apparently short-circuited the consultation procedure. The lack of full consultation at the time of ratification of the *Organization of American States Charter* in 1990 is one example. Another may be the prompt ratification of the *Convention on the Rights of the Child* in September 1991, less than two years after its adoption by the United Nations General Assembly. Yet these examples also show that where there is federal determination and impatience, provincial foot-dragging has not been a serious obstacle to ratification. This is not to suggest that there are not legal and political problems concerned with ratification of the *Convention*, notably with respect to article 4(1), which proclaims the right to life "in general, from the moment of conception". Since the *Morgentaler* decision of the Supreme Court of Canada,[426] there has been no federal legislation whatsoever dealing with abortion, and it might be argued before the Court that Canada does not respect that provision of the *Convention*. Although Canada could comfortably argue that the spirit of article 4(1) is respected within Canada, it may be wise to formulate a reservation on this point.

In a letter dated 13 September 1999, the Legal Bureau of the Department of Foreign Affairs discussed the issue of ratification:

> Before Canada can ratify a human rights convention, it must ensure that it is in a position to live up to the commitments it would undertake by ratifying the convention.
>
> Problems identified by all levels of government relate to the vague, imprecise and outdated language used in the American Convention on Human Rights (ACHR), as well as the ambiguity of many of its provisions. Certain

---

425 "Report on the Situation of Human Rights of Asylum Seekers Within the Canadian Refugee Determination System", *supra* note 399, para. 183.
426 *R.* v. *Morgentaler*, *supra* note 415.

concepts used in the Convention are unknown or problematic in Canadian law. More importantly, numerous provisions are inconsistent with other international human rights norms.

The problematic provisions include Article 4 of the Convention which sets out a "right to life [. . .] from the moment of conception" that is incompatible with the state of Canadian legislation and jurisprudence. As well, Canada's protection of vulnerable groups through legislation prohibiting hate propaganda and child pornography would be contrary to Article 13 of the Convention which prohibits prior censorship. The concept of a "right to reply" referred to in Article 14 of the Convention is unknown in Canadian legislation. Article 22 of the Convention prohibits a state from expelling its nationals. This provision would run counter to Canada's obligations under extradition treaties, as well as its commitments to international tribunals, including under the Statute of the International Criminal Court. Also, the equality provisions of the Convention, Articles 1, 23 and 24, do not contemplate affirmative action. Affirmative action programmes, fundamental to Canadian human rights law, could be considered in contravention of the Convention's equality provisions.[427]

This view seems overly pedantic. There are many provisions in the United Nations treaties that, on a strict and literal construction, might be just as objectionable to Canadian government officials. Canadian ratification of the *American Convention* might not be of great significance for the protection of human rights in Canada, given the already existing obligations and mechanisms under the treaties of the United Nations system, but it would help to reinforce the human rights system of the Organization of American States.

Of particular interest is the focus of the inter-American system upon the rights of women. Shortly after Canada joined the Organization, it ratified the *Inter-American Convention on the Granting of Civil Rights to Women*,[428] the *Inter-American Convention on the Granting of Political Rights to Women*[429] and the *Convention on the Nationality of Women*.[430] The rights enshrined in these treaties are also protected by United Nations treaties to which Canada has been a party for many years,[431] so the move was rather more of a symbolic gesture than a substantive new commitment. Of greater legal significance is the *Inter-American Convention on the Prevention, Punishment and Eradication of Violence against Women*, the first treaty of its type. In 1991, Canada joined the organization's body that deals with women's rights, the Inter-American Commission of Women, and began

---

427 Michael Leir, ed., "Ratification of the American Convention on Human Rights", (1999) 37 *Canadian Yearbook of International Law* 327.

428 OASTS No. 23.

429 OASTS No. 3.

430 OASTS No. 4.

431 *Convention on Political Rights of Women* (1954) 193 UNTS 135, [1957] CTS 3; *Convention on the Nationality of Married Women* (1958) 309 UNTS 65, [1960] CTS 2.

encouraging adoption of a treaty dealing with violence against women. The principle of drafting such an instrument was accepted by the Organization of American States General Assembly in 1991,[432] and the Canadian International Development Agency provided the Commission with a quarter of a million dollars to encourage the work.[433] The treaty entered into force in 1995.[434]

The Organization of American States has also adopted specialized treaties dealing with the prevention of torture,[435] discrimination again persons with disabilities[436] and forced disappearance.[437] None of the specialized human rights treaties of the Inter-American system has been either signed or ratified by Canada. When the Inter-American Commission encouraged Canada to consider accepting the specialized instruments concerning violence against women and the prevention of torture, it replied that because the *American Convention on Human Rights* was the fundamental instrument of the system, "it would be difficult for it, as a non-Party, to ratify these two treaties. It also noted several content-related concerns while stressing its strong commitment to gender equality and the prevention and punishment of torture under national and international law."[438]

3.4   The European Regional Systems

Three distinct European systems are concerned with human rights, the Council of Europe, the European Union and the Organization for Security and Cooperation in Europe. The Council of Europe, based in Strasbourg, is responsible for more than one hundred treaties dealing with such issues as human rights, cultural matters, education, social issues and criminal law. Foremost among them is the *European Convention on Human Rights*, and the judicial organ charged with its implementation, the European Court of Human Rights. The European Union (formerly the European Communities), based in Brussels, had economic integration as its historic function. But

---

432   OAS Doc. AG/Res. 1128 (XXI-O91) (2).

433   OAS Doc. OEA/Ser.L/II.7.4 (1991) at 2.

434   *Inter-American Convention on the Prevention, Punishment and Eradication of Violence Against Women*, OAS Doc. OEA/Ser.P AG/doc.3090/94.

435   *Inter-American Convention to Prevent and Punish Torture*, OASTS 87.

436   *Inter-American Convention on the Elimination of All Forms of Discrimination Against Persons with Disabilities*, adopted at Guatemala City, Guatemala at the twenty-ninth regular session of the General Assembly of the OAS, held on 7 June 1999, and in force since 14 September 2001.

437   *Inter-American Convention on Forced Disappearance of Persons*, adopted at Belém do Pará, on 9 June 1994, at the twenty-fourth regular session of the General Assembly, and in force since 28 March 1996.

438   "Report on the Situation of Human Rights of Asylum Seekers Within the Canadian Refugee Determination System", OAS Co. OEA/Ser.L/V/II.106, Doc. 40 rev, para. 184.

early in its work, issues of human rights became significant with respect to labour standards, discrimination and mobility issues. More recently, the European Union has developed its own foreign policy which has the protection of human rights as a central theme. Finally, the Organization for Security and Cooperation in Europe (formerly the Conference on Security and Cooperation in Europe) is also concerned with a wide range of human rights issues, but with a particular focus on democratic development, electoral reform and the treatment of national minorities.

The three bodies concern somewhat different territories. The OSCE has the largest scope, covering all of Europe but also northern Asia (Siberia) as well as Canada and the United States. The OSCE has fifty-five "participating states".[439] Slightly smaller than the OSCE, the Council of Europe will only admit States that meet its demanding standards in terms of democratic development and human rights. Five States, including Canada, have observer status with the Council of Europe.[440] During the 1990s it underwent a dramatic expansion, welcoming as members the new democracies that emerged following the end of the Cold War in central and eastern Europe. Its membership stands at fifty-five, and it is described as the largest regional security organization in existence. The European Union is the most narrow of the three institutions. Its membership consisted of fifteen prosperous States in western and southern Europe until 2004, when ten new Member States, mainly from Central and Eastern Europe, were admitted. Further expansion is anticipated. Adherence to relatively strict human rights standards is a *sine qua non* for membership in the European Union.

3.4.1   Council of Europe

The Council of Europe was established in London on 5 May 1949. The purpose was to provide an institutional framework and normative basis for a post-war Europe founded on principles of democracy, peace and human rights. The first major task of the Council was the adoption of a human rights treaty, in November 1950, whose official name is the *Convention for the Protection of Human Rights and Fundamental Freedoms* but which has always been called the "European Convention on Human Rights".[441] The

---

439 The terminology dates from the 1970s, and reflects the unique concept of the body, which was described as a "conference" and not an "organization" until it changed its name in the mid-1990s.

440 The others are the United States of America, Mexico, Japan and the Holy See.

441 (1955) 213 UNTS 221, ETS 5. See: Clare Ovey & Robin C.A. White, *Jacobs & White, The European Convention on Human Rights*, Oxford: Clarendon Press, 2002; Mark W. Janis, Richard S. Kay & Anthony W. Bradley, *European Human Rights Law*, Oxford: Oxford University Press, 2000; David J. Harris, M. O'Boyle & Colin Warbrick, *Law of the European Convention on Human Rights*, London: Butterworths, 1995; Emmanuel Decaux, Pierre-Henri Imbert & Louis E. Pettiti, eds., *La Convention européenne des*

Convention was strongly influenced by the *Universal Declaration of Human Rights*, to which reference is made in its preamble, and by an early draft of the *International Covenant on Civil and Political Rights*.

The *European Convention* is considerably narrower in focus than the *Universal Declaration of Human Rights*, confining itself mainly to the core civil rights that had long been recognized in many national constitutions. Over the years, fourteen protocols have been added to the *Convention* addressing a variety of special issues, including procedural matters, and six of which recognize substantive rights not covered by the original instrument.[442] They include property rights, political rights, the right to education,

---

droits de l'Homme: commentaire article par article, Paris: Economica, 1999; Ronald St. J. MacDonald, F. Matscher & Hubert Petzold, eds. *The European System for the Protection of Human Rights*, Dordrecht, Martinus Nijhoff, 1994; Francis G. Jacobs, *The European Convention on Human Rights*, Oxford: Clarendon Press, 1975; J.E.S. Fawcett, *The Application of the European Convention on Human Rights*, 2nd ed., Oxford: Clarendon Press, 1987; Daniel Turp & Gérald-A. Beaudoin, eds. *Perspectives canadiennes et européennes des droits de la personne*, Cowansville: Éditions Yvon Blais, 1986; Gérald-A. Beaudoin, ed., *Vues canadiennes et européennes des droits de and libertés,* Cowansville: Éditions Yvon Blais, 1989; William A. Schabas, "Le rôle du droit européen dans la jurisprudence des tribunaux canadiens", (1991-92) 7 *Revue québecoise de droit international* 235; Guillaume Cliche, "L'utilisation de la Convention européenne des droits de l'Homme pour l'interprétation de la Charte canadienne", (1993) 7 *Revue juridique des étudiants de l'Université Laval* 93; Frédéric Sudre, *La Convention européenne des droits de l'homme*, Paris: Presses universitaires de France ("Que sais-je?") 1990; Frédéric Sudre, *Droit international et européen des droits de l'homme*, 2nd. ed., Paris: Presses universitaires de France, 1994; Gérard Cohen-Jonathan, *La Convention européenne des droits de l'homme*, Paris: Economica, 1989; Jacques Velu & Rusen Ergec, *La Convention européenne des droits de l'Homme*, Brussels: Bruylant, 1990.

442   Three of which have attracted Canadian attention: *Protocol [No. 1] to the Convention for the Protection of Human Rights and Fundamental Freedoms*, (1955) 213 UNTS 262, ETS 9, cited in: *Bureau métropolitain des écoles protestantes de Montréal v. Ministre de l'Education du Québec*, [1976] CS 430, *R. v. Jones*, [1986] 2 SCR 284, 31 DLR (4th) 569, 28 CCC (3d) 513, 69 NR 241, [1986] 6 WWR 577, 47 Alta LR (2d) 97, 73 AR 133 and *Sauvé v. Canada (Chief Electoral Officer)*, [2002] 3 SCR 519, 218 DLR (4th) 577, 168 CCC (3d) 449, 5 CR (6th) 203, 98 CRR (2d) 1; *Protocol No. 4 to the Convention for the Protection of Human Rights and Fundamental Freedoms*, ETS 46, cited in: *Federal Republic of Germany v. Rauca*, (1983) 145 DLR (3d) 638, 4 CCC (3d) 385, 41 OR (2d) 223, 4 CRR 42, 34 CR (3d) 97 (CA) and *United States of America v. Cotroni; United States of America v. El Zein*, (sub nom. *El Zein c. Centre de Prévention de Montréal*) [1989] 1 SCR 1469, (sub nom. *United States v. Cotroni*) 48 CCC (3d) 193, (sub nom. *United States v. El Zein*) 96 NR 321, (sub nom. *El Zein c. Centre de Prévention de Montréal*) 42 CRR 101, (sub nom. *El Zein c. Centre de Prévention de Montréal*) 23 QAC 182; *Protocol No. 6 to the Convention for the Protection of Human Rights and Fundamental Freedoms Concerning the Abolition of the Death Penalty*, ETS 114, cited in: *Kindler v. Canada (Minister of Justice)*, [1991] 2 SCR 779, 67 CCC (3d) 1, 84 DLR (4th) 438, 6 CRR (2d) 193, 129 NR 81; *United States v. Burns and Rafay*, [2001] 1 SCR 283, 195 DLR (4th) 1, [2001] 3 WWR 193, 151 CCC (3d) 97, 39 CR (5th) 205, 81 CRR (2d) 1, 85 BCLR (3d) 1.

freedom of movement, the right to remain in one's country of nationality, abolition of the death penalty, the right to appeal criminal convictions protection against double jeopardy, rights of the family and discrimination.

The European Court of Human Rights sits in Strasbourg and hears applications from individuals who are "within the jurisdiction" of Contracting States.[443] Recent caselaw has held that this may extend to territories under occupation by European powers, such as Cyprus, part of which has been occupied by Turkey since the 1974 invasion,[444] and even Iraq,[445] but only where they exercise effective control.[446] Under the original scheme of the *Convention*, cases were first presented to a body known as the European Commission on Human Rights. The decisions and reports of the Commission have been cited on numerous occasions by Canadian courts, especially in the early days of *Charter* interpretation.[447] In 1998, an amendment to the

---

443 *European Convention on Human Rights*, (1955) 213 UNTS 221, ETS 5, art. 1.

444 *Loizidou* v. *Turkey* (App. No. 15318/89), Merits, 18 December 1996, Reports 1996-VI, 23 EHRR 513; *Loizidou* v. *Turkey*, Preliminary Objections, 23 March 1995, Series A, No. 310, 20 EHRR 99.

445 *R. (on the application of Al-Skeini and others)* v. *Secretary of State for Defence*, [2004] All ER 197 (QB Div'l Ct); *Issa* v. *Turkey* (App. No. 31821/96), 16 November 2004.

446 *Bankovic* et al. v. *Belgium* et al. (App. No. 52207/99), 12 December 2001.

447 *R.* v. *Oakes*, (1983) 145 DLR (3d) 123, 40 OR (2d) 660, 2 CCC (3d) 339, 32 CR (3d) 193, 3 CRR 289 (CA), affirmed, [1986] 1 SCR 103, 24 CCC (3d) 321, 50 CR (3d) 1, 26 DLR (4th) 200, 53 OR (2d) 719n, 65 NR 87, 19 CRR 308, 14 OAC 335; *R.* v. *King*, [1984] 4 WWR 531, 31 Alta LR 253, 27 MVR 212 (QB); *Re Rowland and R.*, (1984) 10 DLR (4th) 724, 13 CCC (3d) 367, 33 Alta LR (2d) 252, 56 AR 10, 28 MVR 239 (QB); *Re Lazarenko and Law Society of Alberta*, (1983) [1984] 2 WWR 24, (sub nom. *Lazarenko* v. *Law Society (Alberta)*) 4 DLR (4th) 389, 29 Alta LR (2d) 28, 50 AR 337 (QB); *Borowski* v. *AG Canada*, [1984] 1 WWR 15, 4 DLR (4th) 112, 8 CCC (3d) 392, 36 CR (3d) 259, 29 Sask R 16 (QB); *Re Education Act (Ontario) and Minority Language Education Rights*, (1984) 47 OR (2d) 1, 10 DLR (4th) 491 (CA); *R.* v. *Morgentaler*, (1984) 12 DLR (4th) 502, 14 CCC (3d) 258, 41 CR (3d) 193, 47 OR (2d) 353, 11 CRR 116 (HC), affirmed, (1984) 14 C.R.R. 107 (CA); *Ford* v. *Attorney General of Québec*, [1985] CS 147, 18 DLR (4th) 711, affirmed, (1986) 36 D.L.R. (4th) 374 (CA), affirmed, [1988] 2 SCR 712, 54 DLR (4th) 577, 19 QAC 69, 36 CRR 1, 90 NR 84, 10 CHRR D/ 5559; *R.* v. *Punch*, [1985] NWTR 373, 22 CCC (3d) 289, 46 CR (3d) 374, [1986] 1 WWR 592, [1986] 2 CNLR 114, 18 CRR 74 (SC); *R.* v. *Oakes*, [1986] 1 SCR 103, 24 CCC (3d) 321, 50 CR (3d) 1, 26 DLR (4th) 200, 53 OR (2d) 719n, 65 NR 87, 19 CRR 308, 14 OAC 335; *Association des détaillants en alimentation du Québec* v. *Ferme Carnaval Inc.*, [1986] RJQ 2513, [1987] DLQ 42 (CS); *Black* v. *Law Society of Alberta*, [1986] 3 WWR 591, 27 DLR (4th) 527, Alta LR (2d) 1, 68 AR 259, 20 Admin LR 140, 20 CRR 177 (CA), affirmed, [1989] 1 SCR 591, 58 DLR (4th) 317, 37 Admin LR 161, 38 CRR 193, [1989] 4 WWR 1, 66 Alta LR (2d) 97, 96 AR 352, 93 NR 266; *Ford* v. *Québec (AG)*, [1988] 2 SCR 712, 54 DLR (4th) 577, 19 QAC 69, 36 CRR 1, 90 NR 84, 10 CHRR D/5559; *Borowski* v. *AG Canada*, [1987] 4 WWR 385, 33 CCC (3d) 402, 29 CRR 244, 56 Sask R 129, 59 CR (3d) 223, 39 DLR (4th) 731 (Sask CA), affirmed, [1989] 1 SCR 342; *Canada* v. *Schmidt*, [1987] 1 SCR 500, 33 CCC (3d) 193, 39 DLR (4th) 18, 58 CR (3d) 1, 28 CRR 280, 76 NR 12, 61 OR (2d) 530; *R.* v. *Morgentaler*,

Convention abolishing the Commission entered into force.[448] The primary objective of the reform was to streamline the system, but with the enormous expansion in membership the Court has found itself overwhelmed with applications. Yet another reform is planned, but the amending protocol has not entered into force.[449]

The Court may dismiss a petition as inadmissible for failure to exhaust local remedies or where it is "manifestly unfounded", a course of action it adopts in the large majority of cases. If it declares a case admissible, it will proceed to render judgment on the merits. Judgments are issued by Chambers of seven judges. Sometimes, where a case pending before a Chamber raises a serious question affecting the interpretation of the *Convention* or the protocols thereto, or where the resolution of a question before the

---

(1986) 22 DLR (4th) 641, 22 CCC (3d) 353, 48 CR (3d) 1, 52 OR (2d) 353, 11 OAC 81, 17 CRR 223 (CA), reversed, [1988] 1 SCR 30, (1988) 31 CRR 1, 37 CCC (3d) 449, 44 DLR (4th) 365, 62 CR (3d) 1, 82 NR 1; *Kindler* v. *Canada (Minister of Justice)*, [1989] 2 FC 492, 46 CCC (3d) 257, 91 NR 359, 42 CRR 262, 69 CR (3d) 38, 25 FTR 240n (CA), leave to appeal allowed, (1989) 102 NR 158n (S.C.C.), affirmed, [1991] 2 SCR 779, 67 CCC (3d) 1, 84 DLR (4th) 438, 6 CRR (2d) 193, 129 NR 81; *United States of America* v. *Cotroni; United States of America* v. *El Zein*, (sub nom. *El Zein c. Centre de Prévention de Montrél)*, *supra* note 442; *Tremblay* v. *Daigle*, [1989] 2 SCR 530, 11 CHRR D/165, 102 NR 81, 62 DLR (4th) 634; *R.* v. *Pearson*, [1990] RJQ 2438, 59 CCC (3d) 406, 79 CR (3d) 90, 5 CRR (2d) 164 (CA), reversed [1992] 3 SCR 665; *Québec (P.G.)* v. *Lippé*, [1990] RJQ 2200, 60 CCC (3d) 34, 80 CR (3d) 1 (CA), reversed, (sub nom. *R. c. Lippé)* [1991] 2 SCR 114, (sub nom. *R. v. Lippé)* 64 CCC (3d) 513, (sub nom. *Lippé* v. *Québec (Procureur général))* 128 NR 1, 5 CRR (2d) 31, 39 QAC 241; *R.* v. *Keegstra*, [1990] 3 SCR 697, 61 CCC (3d) 1, [1991] 2 WWR 1, 1 CR (4th) 129, 3 CRR (2d) 193, 77 Alta LR (2d) 193, 114 AR 81, 117 NR 1; *Taylor* v. *Canadian Human Rights Commission*, [1987] 3 FC 593, 37 DLR (4th) 577, 78 NR 180, 29 CRR 222, 9 CHRR D/4929 (CA), affirmed, (1990) 1990 CarswellNat 742 (SCC); *Lavigne* v. *Ontario Public Service Employees Union*, [1991] 2 SCR 211, 81 DLR (4th) 545, 4 CRR 193, 91 CLLC 14,029, 3 OR (3d) 511, 126 NR 161, 48 OAC 241, reconsideration refused, (1991) 4 OR (3d) xii (SCC); *Kindler* v. *Canada*, *supra* note 442; *Tavares* v. *Canada*, (1992) 17 Imm LR (2d) 135 (Imm & Ref Bd (App Div)); *United States of America* v. *Doyer*, (1992) (sub nom. *United States of America* v. *Doyer)* 77 CCC (3d) 203 (Que. CA), reversed, (1993) 1993 CarswellQue 169 (SCC); *Commission des droits de la personne du Québec* v. *Immeubles Ni/Dia Inc.*, [1992] RJQ 2977 (TDPQ); *Commission des droits de la personne du Québec* v. *Commission scolaire Deux-Montagnes*, [1993] RJQ 1297 (TDPQ); *R.* v. *Stevens*, (1993) 82 CCC (3d) 97, [1993] 7 WWR 38 (Man Prov Ct), affirmed, (1995) 96 CCC (3d) 238 (Man CA); *Beck* v. *Edmonton (City)*, [1994] 1 WWR 248 (Alta QB); *Thomson Newspapers Co.* v. *Canada (Attorney General)*, [1998] 1 SCR 877; *Sauvé* v. *Canada*, *supra* note 442.

448 *Protocol No. 11 to the Convention for the Protection of Human Rights and Fundamental Freedoms, restructuring the control machinery established thereby*, ETS No. 155. At the same time, *Protocol No. 9*, ETS No. 140, which entered into force on 1 October 1994, was repealed, and *Protocol No. 10*, ETS No. 146, lost its purpose.

449 *Protocol No. 14 to the Convention for the Protection of Human Rights and Fundamental Freedoms, amending the control system of the Convention*, ETS No. 194.

Chamber might have a result inconsistent with a judgment previously delivered by the Court, a Chamber may relinquish jurisdiction to a Grand Chamber, which is composed of seventeen judges.[450] A Grand Chamber may also sit in what amounts to an appeal of a ruling of a Chamber, provided leave is granted.[451] Judgments of the European Court are available in published collections, such as the *European Human Rights Reports*, the *Human Rights Law Journal* and the *Revue universelle des droits de l'homme*, and on the web site of the Council of Europe.

Although Canada is not and cannot be a party to the *European Convention*,[452] the instrument has been abundantly cited by Canadian courts in *Charter* interpretation.[453] Perhaps the greatest interest of the *European Con-*

---

450 *European Convention on Human Rights*, as amended, *supra* note 443, art. 30.

451 *Ibid.*, art. 43.

452 In 1981 a Canadian national, Ronald St.J. MacDonald, was elected a judge of the Court representing Liechtenstein; he was re-elected to a second nine-year term. Judge MacDonald died in September 2006. In *R.* v. *Robinson*, (1990) 51 CCC (3d) 452, 70 Alta LR (2d) 31, 63 DLR (4th) 289, 100 AR 26, 73 CR (3d) 81 (CA), the Alberta Court of Appeal erroneously stated that Canada was a party to the *European Convention*.

453 European Court of Human Rights decisions have been cited more than fifty times by Canadian Courts. The Supreme Court of Canada has cited judgments of the European Court in more than twenty cases: *R.* v. *Mills*, [1986] 1 SCR 863, 58 OR (2d) 544*n*, 16 OAC 81, 29 DLR (4th) 161, 26 CCC (3d) 481, 52 CR (3d) 1, 67 NR 241; *R.* v. *Rahey*, [1987] 1 SCR 588, 33 CCC (3d) 289, 75 NR 81, 33 CRR 279, 57 CR (3d) 289, 78 NSR (2d) 183, 193 APR 183, 39 DLR (4th) 481; *BCGEU* v. *Attorney-General of British Columbia*, [1988] 2 SCR 214, 53 DLR (4th) 1, 44 CCC (3d) 289, [1988] 6 WWR 577, 71 Nfld & PEIR 93, 22 APR 93, 30 CPC (2d) 221, 88 CLLC 14,047, 87 NR 241, 31 BCLR (2d) 273; *Ford* v. *Québec (AG)*, *supra* note 447; *Andrews* v. *Law Society of British Columbia*, [1989] 1 SCR 143, 56 DLR (4th) 1, [1989] 2 WWR 289, 36 CRR 193, 25 CCEL 255, 10 CHRR D/3719, 34 BCLR (2d) 273, 91 NR 255; *Irwin Toy* v. *Québec (AG)*, [1989] 1 SCR 927, 39 CRR 193, 25 CPR (3d) 417, 58 DLR (4th) 577, 94 NR 167, 24 QAC 2; *R.* v. *Conway*, [1989] 1 SCR 1659, 49 CCC (3d) 289, 70 CR (3d) 209, 40 CRR 1, 96 NR 241, 34 OAC 165; *Edmonton Journal* v. *Alberta (AG)*, (1989) [1989] 2 SCR 1326, 64 DLR (4th) 577, [1990] 1 WWR 557, 41 CPC (2) 109, 45 CRR 1, 103 AR 321, 71 Alta LR (2d) 273, 102 NR 321; *R.* v. *Keegstra*, *supra* note 447; *Committee for the Commonwealth of Canada* v. *Canada*, [1991] 1 SCR 139, 77 DLR (4th) 385, 4 CRR (2d) 260, 120 NR 241, 40 FTRn, reconsideration refused, (May 8, 1991) Doc. 20334 (S.C.C.); *R.* v. *Lippé*, (1990) (sub nom. *R.* c. *Lippé*) [1991] 2 SCR 114, 64 CCC (3d) 513, 128 NR 1, 5 CRR (2d) 31, 39 QAC 241; *Lavigne* v. *Ontario Public Service Employees Union*, [1991] 2 SCR 211, 81 DLR (4th) 545, 4 CRR (2d) 193, 22 CLLC 12,257, 3 OR (3d) 511, 126 NR 161, 48 OAC 241, reconsideration refused, (1991) 4 O.R. (3d) xii (S.C.C.); *Kindler* v. *Canada*, *supra* note 442; *Reference re Ng Extradition (Canada)* [1991] 2 SCR 858, 67 CCC (3d) 61, 84 DLR (4th) 498; *R.* v. *Butler*, [1992] 1 SCR 452, 70 CCC (3d) 129, 89 DLR (4th) 449, 11 CR (4th) 137, 8 CRR (2d) 1, [1992] 2 WWR 577, 78 Man R (2d) 1, 134 NR 81, 15 WCB (2d) 159, reconsideration refused, [1993] 2 W.W.R. lxi (S.C.C.); *R.* v. *Nova Scotia Pharmaceutical Society*, [1992] 2 SCR 606, 93 DLR (4th) 36, 15 CR (4th) 1, 74 CCC (3d) 289, 139 NR 241; *R.* v. *Potvin*, [1993] 2 SCR 880, 105 DLR (4th) 214, 155 NR 241, 23 CR (4th) 10, 83 CCC (3d) 97; *Dagenais* v. *Canadian Broadcasting Corporation*, [1994] 3

vention on Human Rights is that it has already produced a much more substantial corpus of judicial interpretation than the Human Rights Committee. The judgments are relatively detailed and contain sophisticated legal analysis, a feature often lacking in the views of the United Nations Committee. Canadian judges find that European Court decisions are more familiar in form to their own. Furthermore, litigants before the European Court of Human Rights raise issues relating to fundamental rights and freedoms within a modern developed country comparable in many ways to that of Canada. The analogies between European and Canadian law are often more fertile than those that often preoccupy the Human Rights Committee or the organs of the Organization of American States, countries where dictatorship, disappearance and torture have been a more frequent preoccupation. Canadian courts find the comments and observations of European jurists, whose training and outlook is not unlike their own, to be compelling. According to Justice La Forest, writing extra-judicially:

> The Convention decisions are obviously not directly applicable to the Canadian context, reflecting as they do the compromises necessary for a multinational agreement in Post-war Europe. However, given that the Commission has had the opportunity to consider many of the issues that are coming before our courts, the more frequent citation of these materials would assist us as we develop a Canadian approach to these common issues.[454]

They are not alone. The caselaw of the European Court of Human Rights has had an impact on many domestic courts outside of Europe. Its landmark decision on the "death row phenomenon",[455] for example, has been cited not only by the Supreme Court of Canada,[456] but also by the United States Supreme Court,[457] the Supreme Court of Zimbabwe,[458] the South African

---

SCR 835, 94 CCC (3d) 289, 120 DLR (4th) 12, 34 CR (4th) 269, 25 CRR (2d) 1, 76 OAC 81, 175 NR 1; *Thomson Newspapers Co.* v. *Canada (Attorney General)*, [1998] 1 SCR 877; *R.* v. *Lucas*, [1998] 1 SCR 439; *R.* v. *Advance Cutting & Coring Ltd.*, (1998) 1998 CarswellQue 302, (sub nom. *Thériault c. R.*) [1998] RJQ 911 (CS), affirmed, [2001] 3 SCR 209, 205 DLR (4th) 385, 87 CRR (2d) 189; *Sauvé* v. *Canada, supra* note 442; *Canadian Foundation for Children, Youth and the Law* v. *Canada (Attorney General)*, [2004] 1 SCR 76, 70 OR (3d) 95, 234 DLR (4th) 257, 180 CCC (3d) 353, 115 CRR (2d) 88, 16 CR (6th) 203, 46 RFL (5th) 1, 183 OAC 1.

454   G.V. La Forest, "The Use of International and Foreign Material in the Supreme Court of Canada", *Proceedings, XVIIth Annual Conference, Canadian Council on International Law*, 1988, pp. 230-241.

455   *Soering* v. *United Kingdom and Germany*, 7 July 1989, Series A, Vol. 161, 11 EHRR 439.

456   *Kindler* v. *Canada, supra* note 442.

457   *Lackey* v. *Texas*, 115 SCt 1421, 63 LW 3705, 131 LEd2d 304 (1995).

458   *Catholic Commission for Justice and Peace in Zimbabwe* v. *Attorney-General et al.*, (1993) 1 ZLR 242 (S), 4 SA 239), 14 *Human Rights Law Journal* 323 (ZSC).

Constitutional Court,[459] the High Court of Tanzania[460] and the Judicial Committee of the Privy Council, sitting in review of the Jamaican Court of Appeal.[461]

Economic and social rights were not included in the *European Convention on Human Rights* but found their place in a subsequent instrument of the Council of Europe, the *European Social Charter*, which was adopted in 1961 and came into force in February 1965.[462] The *European Social Charter* has a relationship to the *European Convention on Human Rights* that is analogous to that of the *International Covenant on Economic, Social and Cultural Rights* vis à vis the *International Covenant on Civil and Political Rights*. It enumerates nineteen rights and principles, dealing with such matters as labour and trade union rights, the rights of children and young people to protection, mobility rights, and family rights. The control mechanism is less effective than that of the *Convention*. No individual petition procedure exists. Rather, States parties must submit biennial reports to the Council of Europe, which are examined by the European Committee of Social Rights. The *European Social Charter* allows for "recommendations" to States parties following study of these reports, though none has ever been made.[463] Defenders of the *European Social Charter*, however, answer its critics by pointing to an impressive list of changes to legislation and practice within States Parties as a result of its influence.[464] In May 1988, several members of the Council of Europe signed a protocol to the *European Social Charter* which guarantees four additional rights: the right to equal opportunities and treatment in occupational and employment matters with-

---

459 *S.* v. *Makwanyane*, 1995 (3) SA 391, (1995) 16 *Human Rights Law Journal* 154.

460 *Republic* v. *Mbushuu et al.*, [1994] 2 LRC 335.

461 *Pratt* v. *Attorney General for Jamaica*, [1993] 4 All ER 769, [1993] 2 LRC 349, [1994] 2 AC 1, [1993] 3 WLR 995, 43 WIR 340 (Jamaica P.C.), 14 *Human Rights Law Journal* 338, 33 ILM 364 (JCPC).

462 (1965) 529 UNTS 89, ETS 25. Cited in: *C.G.A.* v. *Pinkerton's of Canada Ltd.*, (1990) 8 CLRBR (2d) 79 (Ont LRB); *R.* v. *Keegstra, supra* note 447; *Dufour* v. *Centre hospitalier St-Joseph-de-la-Malbaie*, [1992] RJQ 825 (TDPQ), reversed (1998) 1998 CarswellQue 1013 (CA), leave to appeal refused (1999) 249 N.R. 391n (S.C.C.). See: Graine de Burca & Bruno de Witte, eds., *Social Rights in* Europe, Oxford: Oxford University Press, 2005; H. Wiebringhaus, "La Charte sociale européenne: vingt ans après la conclusion du Traité", (1982) 86 *Annuaire français de droit international* 934; Alexandre Berenstein & David Harris, *The European Social Charter,* Charlottesville: University of Virginia Press, 1985; L. Betten, "The European Social Charter", (1988) 6 *Netherlands Quarterly of Human Rights* 82; Alexandre Berenstein, "Les droits économiques et sociaux garantis par la Charte sociale européenne", in Daniel Turp & Gérald-A. Beaudoin, eds., *Perspectives canadiennes et européennes des droits de la personne*, Cowansville, Éditions Yvon Blais, 1986, p. 405.

463 A.Ph.C.M. Jaspers & L. Betten, eds., *25 Years, European Social Charter*, Deventer: Kluwer, 1988, at 3.

464 *Ibid.*, at 20-22; Alexandre Berenstein & David Harris, *supra* note 462, at 308-311.

out discrimination on grounds of sex; the right of workers to information and consultation; the right of workers to take part in the determination and improvement of working conditions and environment; and the right of the elderly to social protection.[465] A further protocol to the *Charter*, adopted in 1994, entered into force in 1999.[466] A protocol creating a system of collective complaints was adopted in 1995 and entered into force the following year.[467]

Like the United Nations system, the Council of Europe also has a certain number of specialized instruments. The *European Convention for the Prevention of Torture and Inhuman or Degrading Treatment or Punishment* was opened for signature on 26 November 1987 and came into force in February 1989.[468] It creates a committee with powers to visit *carceral* institutions, to meet in private with detainees and, after consultation with the State party, to make a public statement where the State Party fails to co-operate or refuses to improve the situation. In 1994, the Council of Europe adopted the *Framework Convention for the Protection of National Minorities*,[469] which constitutes the first multilateral human rights treaty dealing with minority rights since the time of the League of Nations.[470] The *Framework Convention* may be signed and ratified by non-members of the Council of Europe, if they are invited to do so. Among the many other treaties in the Council of Europe system are the *Convention on Human Rights and Biomedicine*,[471] the *European Convention on State Immunity*[472] and the *European Charter for Regional or Minority Languages*.[473]

---

465 *Additional Protocol to the European Social Charter*, ETS 128. See: L. Betten, "The Protocol to the European Social Charter: More Rights, A Better Impact?", (1988) 6 *Netherlands Quarterly of Human Rights* 9. The *Protocol* has been cited in: *Dufour* v. *Centre hospitalier St-Joseph-de-la-Malbaie*, *supra* note 462; *Commission des droits de la personne du Québec* v. *Brzozowski*, [1994] RJQ 1447 (HRT).

466 *Protocol Amending the European Social Charter*, ETS 142.

467 *Additional Protocol to the European Social Charter Providing for a system of Collective Complaints*, ETS 158.

468 (1988) 27 ILM 1164.

469 C of E Doc. H(94) 10, [1995] *ICJ Review* 105.

470 See: European Commission for Democracy through Law, *The Protection of Minorities*, Strasbourg: Council of Europe Press, 1994; Jacques Robert, "La Commission européenne pour la démocratie par le droit, dite Commission de Venise", in Alexandre-Linos Sicilianos & Emmanuel Decaux, *La CSCE: Dimension humaine et règlement des différends*, Paris: Montchrestien, 1993, p. 255; Giorgio Malinverni, "Le projet de Convention pour la protection des minorités élaboré par la Commission européenne pour la démocratie par le droit", (1991) 3 *Revue universelle des droits de l'homme* 157.

471 ETS No. 164.

472 *European Convention on State Immunity*, (1972) ETS 74, 11 ILM 470, cited in *Schreiber* v. *Canada (Attorney General)*, [2002] 3 SCR 269, (sub nom. *Schreiber* v. *Federal Republic of Germany*) 216 DLR (4th) 513, 167 CCC (3d) 51, 164 OAC 354.

473 ETS No. 148.

The European Commission for Democracy through Law (the "Venice Commission") was established in 1990 to provide expertise in constitutional law and policy during the political transformations in central and eastern Europe. Since then, it has become the "think tank" of the Council of Europe, providing expert opinions in such areas as elections and minority rights. According to article 2 of its Statute, the Commission is composed of "independent experts who have achieved eminence through their experience in democratic institutions or by their contribution to the enhancement of law and political science". In March 2006, it issued an opinion on the legal obligations of States with respect to illegal detention centres and what have been called "extraordinary renditions".[474] In its opinion on self-determination in constitutional law, the Commission analysed the *Secession Reference* of the Supreme Court of Canada.[475] Canada is one of ten non-European states with observer status at the Commission. Judge Yves de Montigny of the Federal Court of Canada is a member of the Commission; Senator Gérald-A. Beaudoin serves as his alternate.

In 1999, the Council of Europe established its own Commissioner for Human Rights, which is a position established by the Parliamentary Assembly of the Council. The first Commissioner, Alvaro Gil Robles, served until 2005, and was succeeded by Thomas Hammarberg. The Commissioner is elected by the Council of Europe's Parliamentary Assembly. The role of the Commissioner is defined as "a non-judicial institution to promote education in, awareness of and respect for human rights, as embodied in the human rights instruments of the Council of Europe".[476] The Commissioner has produced useful documents in such areas as the situation of elderly persons in retirement homes or institutions, the role of monotheist religions in armed conflict, human rights in the armed forces and the protection of persons with mental disabilities. The Commissioner has also issued "Opinions" on specific issues, such as procedural safeguards for pretrial detention, derogation from human rights obligations and the establishment of national institutions to counter discrimination.

---

474 "Opinion on the International legal obligations of Council of Europe member States in respect of secret detention facilities and inter-State transport of Prisoners adopted by the Venice Commission at its 66th Plenary Session, (Venice, 17-18 March 2006)", Opinion no. 363 / 2005, C of E Doc. CDL-AD(2006)009.

475 "Self-determination and secession in constitutional law, Report adopted by the Commission at its 41th meeting, (Venice, 10-11 December 1999)", C of E Doc. CDL-INF (2000) 2. Also: "Interim Report on the Constitutional situation of the Federal Republic of Yugoslavia, Adopted by the Venice Commission at its 48th Plenary Meeting, (Venice, 19-20 October 2001)", C of E Doc. CDL-INF (2001) 23.

476 Resolution (99)50 on the Council of Europe's Commissioner for Human Rights, 7 May 1999, para. 1.

3.4.2   European Union

The European Union traces its origins to efforts at economic integration that began in the early 1950s with the creation of the European Coal and Steel Community. The European Union was formally established in 1992, by the Treaty of Maastricht. It has expanded to encompass twenty-five Member States, with further enlargement under consideration. Over the years, its economic focus has evolved and the European Union now has a very significant role in international human rights.[477] Much of the foreign policy initiative of the European Member States in the area of human rights, especially within international bodies like the Commission on International Law and the Third Committee of the General Assembly, is now handled collectively. As a general rule, the State that holds the rotating semestrial presidency speaks on behalf of the Member States.

The Amsterdam Treaty, which was adopted on 2 October 1997 and came into force on 1 May 1999, states that "[t]he Union is founded on the principles of liberty, democracy, respect for human rights and fundamental freedoms, and the rule of law, principles which are common to the Member States".[478] The Amsterdam Treaty and a declaration on capital punishment in the Final Act was the impetus for the General Affairs Council of the European Union to adopt, on 29 June 1998, the "Guidelines to EU Policy Towards Third Countries on the Death Penalty".[479] European Union activities in this area have included a range of initiatives within countries that retain the death penalty, such as China and Indonesia. The European Union has submitted *amicus curiae* briefs to the United States Supreme Court in death penalty cases.

The *Charter of Fundamental Rights of the European Union* was adopted at Nice in December 2000, following a decision to prepare such an instrument taken at the European Council of Cologne, in June 1999.[480] The *Charter* was intended to reflect the fundamental rights guaranteed by the *European Convention on Human Rights*, as well as those derived from constitutional traditions common to Member States and general principles of community law. It is in many ways the product of a long-standing debate about whether or not the European Union should itself ratify the *European*

---

477   See, generally, Philip Alston, ed., *The EU and Human Rights*, Oxford: Oxford University Press, 1999.

478   *Treaty of Amsterdam amending the Treaty on European Union, the Treaties establishing the European Communities and Certain Related Acts*, OJ C 340, 10 November 1997, art. F(a)(1).

479   "Guidelines for EU Policy Towards Third Countries on the Death Penalty", in European Union Annual Report on Human Rights, 11317/00, p. 87.

480   *Charter of Fundamental Rights*, [2000] OJ C364. See: Laurence Burgorgue-Larsen, Anne Levade & Fabrice Picod, *Traité établissant une Constitution pour l'Europe, Commentaire article par article*, Vol. II, Brussels: Bruylant, 2005.

Convention on Human Rights. The *Charter* is not a treaty and is without binding effect, although there would be little quarrel among Member States with a claim that it codifies European human rights norms.

The European Court of Justice and Court of First Instance, which sit in Luxembourg, and which are often confused with the European Court of Human Rights, deal with litigation arising within the European Union.[481] In *Law Society of British Columbia* v. *Andrews*, Justice La Forest found the caselaw of the European Court of Justice to be helpful in studying whether a citizenship requirement for attorneys was a "reasonable limit".[482]

There are many other normative provisions adopted within the European Union that address human rights concerns. Judge Michèle Rivet of the Quebec Human Rights Tribunal has cited a number of these that deal with sexual harassment, insisting upon their relevance, after concluding that there were no international norms binding upon Canada on the subject.[483] She even found that the terms used in the European Union texts were "plus élégant peut-être" than those recognized in Canadian law.[484] In the *Secession Reference*, the Supreme Court cited the guidelines developed by the European Community (forerunner of the European Union) for the recognition of new states following the breakup of Yugoslavia and the Soviet Union. It said this was evidence that "[t]he process of recognition, once considered to be an exercise of pure sovereign discretion, has come to be associated with legal norms".[485] Decisions have also cited European texts in such areas as tobacco advertising,[486] electronic commerce,[487] intellectual property,[488] cannabis,[489] enforcement of judgments[490] and anti-corruption measures.[491]

---

481   The European Court of Justice will draw upon the *European Convention on Human Rights* "and other human rights instruments" as a source of "guidelines" for the construction of European law: *J. Nold* v. *Commission of the EC*, Case 4/73, [1974] 2 CMLR 354, at 355.

482   *Law Society of British Columbia* v. *Andrews*, [1989] 1 SCR 143, 56 DLR (4th) 1, [1989] 2 WWR 289, 36 CRR 193, 25 CCEL 255, 10 CHRR D/3719, 34 BCLR (2d) 273, 91 NR 255; see also *Black* v. *Law Society of Alberta*, [1986] 3 WWR 591, 27 DLR (4th) 527, Alta LR (2d) 1, 68 AR 259, 20 Admin LR 140, 20 CRR 177 (CA), affirmed, [1989] 1 SCR 591, 58 DLR (4th) 317, 37 Admin LR 161, 38 CRR 193, [1989] 4 WWR 1, 66 Alta LR (2d) 97, 96 AR 352, 93 NR 266.

483   *Commission des droits de la personne du Québec* v *Habachi*, [1992] RJQ 1439 (T.D.P.Q.), reversed, (1999) 1999 CarswellQue 3076 (Que. C.A.), at 1445-1446. See also: *Jackson* v *Bousquet*, [1996] TDPQ No. 1, 27 CHRR D/343 (TDPQ).

484   *Ibid.*, at 1453.

485   "Guidelines on the Recognition of New States in Eastern Europe and in the Soviet Union", 16 December 1991, (1992) 31 *ILM* 1486, cited in *Reference re Secession of Quebec*, [1998] 2 SCR 217, 161 DLR (4th) 385, 55 CRR (2d) 1, para. 115, para. 143.

486   *RJR-Macdonald Inc.* v *Canada*, [1995] 3 SCR 199, 127 DLR (4th) 1 (*per* La Forest J.).

487   *Society of Composers, Authors and Music Publishers of Canada* v. *Canadian Assn. of Internet Providers*, [2004] 2 SCR 427.

488   *Harvard College* v. *Canada (Commissioner of Patents)*, [2002] 4 SCR 45; *Monsanto*

3.4.3   Organization for Security and Cooperation in Europe

The Organization for Security and Cooperation in Europe (OSCE) is the successor of the Conference on Security and Cooperation in Europe, which came into being in the 1970s. The basic instrument of the OSCE is the *Helsinki Final Act*, signed 1 August 1975 by thirty-three European nations, and by the United States and Canada.[492] The *Helsinki Final Act* is not a treaty, but rather an expression of what Gérard Cohen-Jonathan calls an "accord des volontés", a kind of *sui generis* international instrument that the "participating states" refer to as "commitment".[493] An ongoing dialogue more than a formal structure, at least in its early years, the CSCE met on several occasions throughout the 1970s and 1980s, and adopted concluding documents at the end of these lengthy meetings. In 1989, at the close of the cold war, the CSCE undertook a new focus on what it called the "human dimension", a term that corresponds in a general sense to human rights. The human dimension undertakings were set out in a series of instruments, of which the most important are the *Charter of Paris*[494] and the *Concluding Document of the Copenhagen Conference*.[495] Canada was very actively invovled in the Copenhagen Conference and contributed in an important way to the drafting of the *Concluding Document*, particularly with respect to the language concerning human rights issues. The OSCE's "Moscow mechanism", named for a procedure developed at its Moscow meeting in 1991, led to the creation of the International Criminal Tribunal for the former Yugoslavia.[496]

Besides general statements of principle on human rights, many of which are comparable to those in the other major instruments, the OSCE instruments provide extremely detailed provisions covering the rights of journalists, transborder information flow, protection of minorities, reunification of

Canada Inc. v. *Schmeiser*, [2004] 1 SCR 902; *Kirkbi AG* v. *Ritvik Holdings Inc.*, [2005] 3 SCR 302; *Veuve Clicquot Ponsardin* v. *Boutiques Cliquot Ltée*, 2006 SCC 23.
489   *R.* v. *Clay*, [2003] 3 SCR 735.
490   *Spar Aerospace Ltd.* v. *American Mobile Satellite Corp.*, [2002] 4 SCR 205.
491   *Merk* v. *International Association of Bridge, Structural, Ornamental and Reinforcing Iron Workers, Local 771*, [2005] 3 SCR 425.
492   "Conference on Security and Cooperation in Europe, Final Act", 1 August 1975.
493   Gérard Cohen-Jonathan & Jean-Paul Jacqué, "Obligations Assumed by the Helsinki Signatories", in Thomas Buergenthal, ed., *Human Rights, International Law and the Helsinki Accord*, Montclair, New Jersey: Allenheld, Osman, 1975, pp. 43-70.
494   "Charter of Paris for a New Europe", 19-21 November 1990.
495   "Document of the Copenhagen Meeting of the Conference on the Human Dimension of the CSCE", 1989.
496   Discussed below, at 239-241.

families and the right of national self-determination.[497] The primary OSCE institution for the human dimension is the Warsaw-based Organization for Democratic Institutions and Human Rights (ODIHR). As its name suggests, ODIHR is directly involved in human rights work, but it is also engaged in related areas, such as election observation, democratic development, tolerance and non-discrimination, and promotion of the rule of law.

Issues concerning self-determination and the rights of minorities have always been very much at the heart of the work of the OSCE. It was deeply involved in the political transformations within Central and Eastern Europe during the late 1980s and early 1990s, and developed a sophisticated approach to secession and the establishment of new states. Not surprisingly, the Supreme Court of Canada turned to the legal instruments of the OSCE in addressing the issues of independence for Quebec. In the 1998 *Secession Reference*, the Supreme Court cited the *Helsinki Final Act* as authority for the proposition that "international law expects that the right to self-determination will be exercised by peoples within the framework of existing sovereign states and consistently with the maintenance of the territorial integrity of those states", but that "[w]here this is not possible. . .a right of secession may arise".[498] It also turned to the concluding document of the 1989 Vienna Meeting of the CSCE, which referred to the right of peoples to determine "their internal and external political status".[499] Lest this be taken as an unqualified right to secede, the Supreme Court noted that "the participating states will at all times act, as stated in the Helsinki Final Act, 'in conformity with the purposes and principles of the Charter of the United Nations and with the relevant norms of international law, *including those relating to territorial integrity of state*'".[500] The Court went on to observe that

> Principle 5 of the concluding document states that the participating states (including Canada): ". . .confirm their commitment strictly and effectively to observe the principle of the territorial integrity of States. They will refrain from any violation of this principle and thus from any action aimed by direct or indirect means, in contravention of the purposes and principles of the Charter of the United Nations, other obligations under international law or the provisions of the [Helsinki] Final Act, at violating the territorial integrity, political

---

497   Jochen Abr. Frowein, "The Interrelationship between the Helsinki Final Act, the International Covenants on Human Rights, and the European Convention on Human Rights", in Thomas Buergenthal, *supra* note 493, pp. 71-82; Mary Frances Dominick, *Human Rights and the Helsinki Accord*, Nashville: William S. Hein, 1981.

498   *Reference re Secession of Quebec*, *supra* note 485, paras. 121-122.

499   "Concluding Document of the Vienna Meeting of the Conference on Security and Cooperation in Europe", 19 January 1989.

500   *Ibid.*, para. 129 (emphasis added by the Supreme Court of Canada).

independence or the unity of a State. *No actions or situations in contravention of this principle will be recognized as legal by the participating States.*"[501]

Thus, for the Supreme Court of Canada, "the reference in the Helsinki Final Act to a people determining its external political status is interpreted to mean the expression of a people's external political status through the government of the existing state", save in exceptional circumstances.[502] The Court took special note of the "history and textual structure of this document".[503] Canadian courts have also referred to the Concluding Document of the 1983 Madrid meeting.[504]

In the 1990s, the OSCE developed a special interest in the rights of national, ethnic, linguistic and religious minorities.[505] Work in this area is led by its High Commissioner on National Minorities.[506] The first High Commissioner, Max van der Stoel, was appointed in 1993. His successor, Rolf Ekéus, took office in 2001. The job of the High Commissioner is to identify and seek early resolution of tensions involving national minorities which in his view might endanger peace, stability or friendly relations. His focus is on tensions that have security implications, and the position is described "an instrument of conflict prevention, not a human rights om-

---

501 *Ibid.* (emphasis added by the Supreme Court of Canada).

502 *Ibid.*

503 *Ibid.*

504 "Concluding Document of the Conference on Security and Cooperation in Europe, Madrid, 7-9 September 1983", (1983) 22 *ILM* 1398; *S.E.I.U., Local 204* v. *Broadway Manor Nursing Home*, (1983) 4 DLR (4th) 231, 44 OR (2d) 392, 10 CRR 37 (Div Ct), reversed, (1984) 1984 CarswellOnt 829 (CA), leave to appeal refused, (1985), 8 OAC 320n (SCC), and *Delisle c. Canada (Sous-procureur général)*, [1999] 2 SCR 989, 176 DLR (4th) 513.

505 Arie Bloed, "The CSCE and the Protection of National Minorities", in Alan Phillips, Allan Rosas, *The U.N. Minority Rights Declaration*, Abo: Abo Akademi University Institute for Human Rights, 1993, pp. 95-101; Arie Bloed, "The CSCE and the Protection of National Minorities", (1993) 1:3 *CSCE ODHIR Bulletin* 1; Felix Ermacora, "Rights of Minorities and Self-determination in the Framework of the CSCE", in A. Bloed & Pieter Van Dijk, *The Human Dimension of the Helsinki Process*, Dordrecht: Nijhoff, 1991, p. 205; Mala Tabory, "Minority Rights in the CSCE Context", (1990) 20 *Israel Yearbook of Human Rights* 197; Mala Tabory, "Minority Rights in the CSCE Context", in Yoram Dinstein & Mala Tabory, *The Protection of Minorities in Human Rights*, Dordrecht: Nijhoff, 1992, pp. 187-212; Jan Helgesen, "Protection of Minorities in the Conference on Security and Co-operation in Europe (CSCE) Process", in A. Rosas & J. Helgesen, *The Strength of Diversity: Human Rights and Pluralist Democracy*, Dordrecht: Nijhoff, 1992, pp. 159-186; Emmanuel Decaux, "Vers un nouveau droit des minorités nationales", *Gazette du palais*, 16-17 December 1994, p. 2; S.J. Roth, "Comments on the Geneva CSCE Meeting of Experts on National Minorities", (1991) 12 *Human Rights Law Journal* 330.

506 Emmanuel Decaux, "Le Haut Commissaire de la CSCE pour les minorités nationales", in Linos-Alexandre Sicilianos, ed., *New Forms of Discrimination*, Paris: Pedone, 1995, pp. 269-280.

budsman". He does not address individual cases. Recently, the High Commissioner has turned his attention to so-called "new minorities", and to issues relating to policing in multi-ethnic societies. The High Commissioner has prepared "Recommendations" concerning such issues as the linguistic and educational rights of minorities.

The OSCE is also extremely active in the provision of technical assistance for elections, and their observance.

3.5   African Union

The third regional system of human rights protection is part of the African Union, founded in 2002 and successor to the earlier Organization of African Union. The principal human rights instrument is the *African Charter on Human and Peoples' Rights*, adopted at Nairobi on 28 June 1981, and entered in force on 21 October 1986.[507] The *African Charter* is considerably less oriented towards the rights of the individual *vis-à-vis* the State than its counterparts such as the *European Convention*, and insists not only on the individual's rights but also his or her duties.

The *African Charter* establishes the African Commission on Human and Peoples' Rights. Although no corresponding judicial body was contemplated at the time the *Charter* was adopted, on 25 January 2004 a protocol to the *Charter* entered into force providing for establishment of the African Court of Human and Peoples' Rights. In January 2006, eleven judges were

---

507 *African Charter on Human and Peoples' Rights*, OAU Doc. CAB/LEG/67/3 rev. 5, 4 EHRR 417, 21 *ILM* 58. The *African Charter* has been referred to only rarely by Canadian courts: *Basyony* v. *Canada (Minister of Employment and Immigration)*, (1994) 75 FTR 225, 27 Imm LR (2d) 303; *B. (R.)* v. *Children's Aid Society of Metropolitan Toronto*, [1995] 1 SCR 315, 122 DLR (4th) 1, (sub nom. *Sheena B., Re*)176 NR 161; *R.* v. *Advance Cutting & Coring Ltd.*, (1998) 1998 CarswellQue 302, (sub nom. *Thériault* c. *R.*) [1998] RJQ 911 (CS), affirmed, [2001] 3 SCR 209, 205 DLR (4th) 385, 87 CRR (2d) 189; *Suresh* v. *Canada (Minister of Citizenship and Immigration)*, [2002] 1 SCR 3, 208 DLR (4th) 1, 37 Admin LR (3d) 159, 90 CRR (2d) 1. See: Rachel Murray, *Human Rights in Africa: From the OAU to the African Union*, Cambridge: Cambridge University Press, 2004; Manfred Nowak, "The African Charter on Human and Peoples' Rights", (1986) 7 *Human Rights Law Journal* 399; Richard Gittleman, "The African Charter on Human and Peoples' Rights: A Legal Analysis", (1982) 22 *Virginia Journal of International Law* 667; Olusolo Ojo & Amadu Sesay, "The OAU and Human Rights: Prospects for the 1980s and Beyond", (1986) 8 *Human Rights Quarterly* 89; Emmanuel G. Bello, "The African Charter on Human and People's Rights. A Legal Analysis", (1985) 194 *Receuil de cours de l'Académie de droit international* 91; O.U. Omozurike, "The African Charter of Human Rights", (1983) 77 *American Journal of International Law* 511; Tunguru Huaraka, "The African Charter on Human and Peoples' Rights: A Significant Contribution to the Development of International Human Rights Law", in Daniel Prémont, ed., *Essais sur le concept de "droit de vivre" en mémoire de Yougindra Khushalani*, Brussels: Bruylant, 1988, pp. 193-211.

elected at the Eighth Ordinary Session of the Executive Council of the African Union. Discussions are now underway regarding a proposal to fuse the new human rights court with the proposed African Court of Justice, which would consider legal issues arising from other obligations within the African Union.

After an initial period during which its caselaw was confidential, the African Commission began disseminating its decisions, like its counterparts in Europe and the Americas. Recent cases have provided interesting and original perspectives on such matters as the right to equality within the context of electoral law,[508] environmental degradation resulting from the development of natural resources[509] and the differential application of Islamic cultural rules to girls and boys.[510]

The African Union also has specialized instruments dealing with refugees,[511] children[512] and women.[513]

3.6   Other International Human Rights Systems

Several other international organizations, some of them in which Canada participates, may engage with human rights to a greater or lesser extent.

For example, within the context of the North American Free Trade Organization, the Commission for Labour Cooperation promotes labour cooperation pursuant to the *North American Agreement on Labour Cooperation*.[514] The *Agreement* identifies eleven core labour principles, divided into three categories: freedom of association, collective bargaining and the right to strike; forced labour, pay equity, employment discrimination, compensation for injury or illness and protection of migrant labour; and child labour minimum wage and occupational safety. There is a mechanism that allows one Member State to complain that another Member State is not observing specific labour principles and, theoretically at least, it can lead to sanctions.[515]

---

508 *Legal Resources Foundation* v. *Zambia*, May 2001.
509 *The Social and Economic Rights Action Center and the Center for Economic and Social Rights* v. *Nigeria*, October 2001.
510 *Doebbler* v. *Sudan*, May 2003.
511 *Convention Governing the Specific Aspects of Refugee Problems in Africa*, (1974) 1001 UNTS 45.
512 *African Charter on the Rights and Welfare of the Child*, (1999) OAU Doc. CAB/LEG/ 24.9/49.
513 *Protocol to the African Charter on the Rights of Women in Africa*.
514 [1994] CTS 2.
515 N. Keresztezi, "Mexican Labour Laws and Practices Come to Canada: A Comment on the First Case Brought to Canada Under the North American Agreement on Labour Cooperation", (2000) 8 *Canadian Labour and Employment Law Journal* 411.

Canada is one of the founding members of the Commonwealth, which was formed as a result of the *Statute of Westminster* in 1931. Its membership essentially consists of former British colonies, although exceptionally a former Portuguese colony in southern African, Mozambique, was admitted in recognition of its contribution to the struggle against *apartheid* in South Africa. Human rights were declared to be among the core principles of the Commonwealth in its 1991 Harare Declaration. Through its Ministerial Action Group, the Commonwealth will investigate "serious and persistent violations" of human rights. In the case of egregious human rights abuses, Member States of the Commonwealth have been suspended. Rhodesia was suspended in 1964, under its white supremicist government. It became a full member again in 1980, as Zimbabwe, only to be suspended again in 2002. Zimbabwe withdrew from the organisation in 2003. Fiji, Pakistan and Nigeria have also been suspended in the past.

Reflecting the growing importance of human rights in the work of the Commonwealth, in 2002 the institution revised the mandate of its Human Rights Unit to give it greater autonomy. The Unit is responsible for developing programmes with a specific emphasis on the indivisibility of civil, political, economic and social rights. Expert groups have been convened to develop a Commonwealth "best practice", focussing on such issues as as human trafficking, victims of crime, freedom of expression and freedom of assembly and association.

Canada also participates actively in the *Francophonie*, an organization of States having French as a common language. Quebec, New Brunswick and Ontario also participate in an autonomous manner within the body. Like the Commonwealth, the *Francophonie* promotes human rights among its Member States, especially those undergoing major crises and conflicts. In 2000, a specialized meeting adopted the *Déclaration de Bamako*, confirming the commitment of the *Francophonie* to basic principles of human rights, democratization and the rule of law.

3.7   International Humanitarian Law

Humanitarian law is a close relative of human rights law, although the two fields should not be confused. Humanitarian law is another expression for the law of armed conflict. It can trace its origins back to customary rules governing the conduct of soldiers and concerning such matters as attacking undefended towns, treatment of prisoners and the prohibition of perfidious acts such as deceptive flying of the white flag. As the Supreme Court of Canada explained, in *Finta*, there were customary legal rules on the conduct of war and individual responsibility for them "found in Christian codes of conduct, in rules of chivalry and in the writing of the great international law writers such as Grotius".[516] Efforts to codify this law began in the mid-nineteenth century. A Columbia University law professor, Francis Lieber, prepared a code of the laws of war that President Lincoln proclaimed to govern the conduct of government troops during the United States Civil War.[517] A few years earlier, Swiss businessman Henry Dunant published *Un souvenir de Solférino*, a book whose influence prompted the creation of the International Committee of the Red Cross. Under its auspices, a diplomatic conference was convened at Geneva in 1864 that resulted in a convention protecting the activities of medical personnel during armed conflict. The ICRC, based in Geneva, continues to play a central role in the development of humanitarian law.[518]

The St. Petersburg Declaration of 1868 outlawed the use of expanding bullets, and was a specific expression of the general customary prohibition of weapons that cause superfluous harm or unnecessary suffering. More comprehensive attempts at international codification followed with the *Hague Conventions* of 1899 and 1907.[519] The *Hague Conventions* were invoked by the Nuremberg Tribunal and the other post-war military courts as evidence of customary law, applicable even when the Conventions themselves did not, strictly speaking, apply and this has been confirmed in recent years in rulings of the International Court of Justice.[520] Only in the twentieth century did humanitarian law shift its focus from the methods and materials of warfare to the victims of armed conflict, initially wounded combatants and prisoners of war and, later, civilians. The four *Geneva Conventions* of

---

516 *R. v. Finta*, [1994] 1 SCR 701, 88 CCC (3d) 417, 112 DLR (4th) 513, 150 NR 370, at 782 (SCR).

517 Instructions for the Government of Armies of the United States in the Field, prepared by Francis Lieber, LL.D., originally Issued as General Orders No. 100, Adjutant General's Office, 1863, Washington 1898: Government Printing Office.

518 On the International Committee of the Red Cross, see David Forsythe, *The Humanitarians*, Cambridge: Cambridge University Press, 2005.

519 *International Convention with respect to the Laws and Customs of War by Land*, [1942] CTS 6, which came into force for Canada on September 1900, with ratification by the United Kingdom; *International Convention Concerning the Laws and Customs of War by Land*, [1910] TS 9, which came into force for Canada on 27 November 1909, with ratification by the United Kingdom. The *Hague Conventions* have been cited on several occasions by Canadian courts: *R. v. Kaehler and Stolski*, [1945] 3 DLR 272, [1945] 1 WWR 566 83 CCC 353 (Alta CA); *R. v. Finta*, (1989) 50 CCC (3d) 236, 64 CR (3d) 223, 44 CRR 23 (Ont HC), additional reasons at, (1989) 1989 CarswellOnt 997 (Ont. H.C.); *Rudolph v. Canada (Minister of Employment & Immigration)*, (1992) 91 DLR (4th) 686 (Fed CA), leave to appeal refused (1992), 93 D.L.R. (4th) vii (note) (S.C.C.); *R. v. Finta, supra* note 516.

520 *Legal Consequences of the Construction of a Wall in the Occupied Palestinian Territory, Advisory Opinion*, [2004] ICJ Reports 172, para. 89; *Case Concerning Armed Activities on the Territory of the Congo (Democratic Republic of the Congo v. Uganda)*, 19 December 2005, para. 217.

1949, complemented by two additional *Protocols* of 1977, now form the core of international humanitarian law.

Canada adhered to these humanitarian law conventions virtually from their entry into force. The United Kingdom acceded to the first Geneva Convention, of 1864, on behalf of Canada, and it entered into force for Canada on 18 February 1865.[521] Similarly, London ratified the 1907 *Hague Convention* on behalf of Canada on 27 November 1909.[522] The two 1929 *Geneva Conventions*, which are the ancestors of the four *Geneva Conventions* that now apply, were ratified by Canada in 1933.[523] The 1929 *Geneva Convention* concerning prisoners of war was actually applied by Canadian courts during the Second World War, in cases concerning escaped German prisoners.[524] The four *Geneva Conventions*, adopted at a diplomatic conference in 1949,[525] have all been ratified by Canada and are incorporated by statute into domestic legislation.[526] The two *Protocols* of 1977[527] were ratified by Canada in late 1990, and they too are now incorporated into Ca-

---

521   *Convention for the Amelioration of the Condition of the Wounded and Sick in Armies in the Field*, [1942] CTS 6. Also: *Convention for the Revision of the Geneva Convention of 1864*, [1916] TS 1; *Convention for Adapting to Maritime Warfare the Principles of the Geneva Convention of 1864 (Convention no 3)*, [1942] CTS 6.

522   *International Convention Concerning the Laws and Customs of War by Land*, [1910] BTS 9.

523   *International Convention Relative to the Treatment of Prisoners of War*, (1931-32) 118 LNTS 343, [1942] CTS 6; *International Convention for the Amelioration of the Condition of the Wounded and Sick in Armies in the Field*, (1931-32) 118 LNTS 303, [1933] CTS 6, [1942] CTS 6. Both of these were ratified by Canada on 20 February 1933, and came into force for Canada on 20 August 1933.

524   *R. v. Shindler*, [1944] 3 WWR 125, 82 CCC 206 (Alta Pol Ct); *R. v. Brosig*, [1945] 2 DLR 232, 83 CCC 199, [1945] OR 240, [1945] OWN 225 (CA); *R. v. Kaehler and Stolski, supra* note 519.

525   *Geneva Convention for the Amelioration of the Condition of the Wounded and Sick in Armed Forces in the Field*, (1950) 75 UNTS 31, [1965] CTS 20; *Geneva Convention for the Amelioration of the Condition of the Wounded, Sick and Shipwrecked Members of the Armed Forces at Sea*, (1950) 75 UNTS 85, [1965] CTS 20; *Geneva Convention Relative to the Protection of Civilian Persons in Time of War*, (1950) 75 UNTS 287, [1965] CTS 20; *Geneva Convention Relative to the Treatment of Prisoners of War*, (1950) 75 UNTS 135, [1965] CTS 20.

526   *Geneva Conventions Act*, RSC 1985, c. G-3.

527   *Protocol Additional I to the 1949 Geneva Conventions and Relating to The Protection of Victims of International Armed Conflicts*, (1979) 1125 UNTS 3, [1991] CTS 2, cited in: *R. v. Brocklebank*, (1996) 106 CCC (3d) 234 (Can. Ct. Martial App. Ct.), *Sumaida v. Canada (Minister of Citizenship and Immigration)*, [2000] 3 FC 66 (Fed CA); *Protocol Additional II to the 1949 Geneva Conventions and Relating to The Protection of Victims of Non-International Armed Conflicts*, (1979) 1125 UNTS 609, [1991] CTS 2, cited in: *Orelien* v. *Canada*, (1991) [1992] 1 FC 592, 15 Imm LR (2d) 1 (CA), *Sumaida v. Canada (Minister of Citizenship and Immigration), ibid., R. v. Brocklebank, ibid.*

nadian law,[528] as well as the *Convention for the Protection of Cultural Property in the Event of Armed Conflict*.[529] Canada has also ratified a number of important treaties concerning the prohibition of various categories of weapons, including the convention on anti-personnel mines, commonly referred to as the "Ottawa Convention".[530] A third additional protocol to the Geneva Conventions was adopted in December 2005. Not yet in force, it creates a new humanitarian emblem, the red crystal.

Many of the core provisions of international humanitarian law are largely similar to those of human rights law. In what is known as the Martens Clause, in honour of its author, who was the legal advisor to the Russian Emperor, the preambles of the 1899 and 1907 *Hague Conventions* declare that

> [u]ntil a more complete code of the laws of war is issued, the High Contracting Parties think it right to declare that in cases not included in the Regulations adopted by them, populations and belligerents remain under the protection and empire of the principles of international law, as they result from the usages established between civilized nations, from the laws of humanity, and the requirements of the public conscience.

Subsequent treaties provide a more general idea of what these "laws of humanity" might be. Accordingly, common article 3 of the 1949 Geneva Conventions, says that non-combattants should "in all circumstances be treated humanely, without any adverse distinction founded on race, colour, religion or faith, sex, birth or wealth, or any other similar criteria". Other prohibited acts include violence to life and person, murder of all kinds, mutilation, cruel treatment and torture, "outrages upon personal dignity",

---

528 *Act to Amend the Geneva Conventions Act, the National Defence Act and the Trade-Marks Act*, RS 1990, c. 14; *Prisoner-of-War Status Determination Regulations*, DORS/ 91-134, G.C.II, 13/2/91, 843.

529 [1999] 4 CTS 52.

530 *Protocol for the Prohibition of the Use of Asphyxiating, Poisonous or Other Gases, and of Bacteriological Methods of Warfare; Convention on Prohibitions or Restrictions on the Use of Certain Conventional Weapons which may be deemed to be Excessively Injurious or to have Indiscriminate Effects*, (1983) 1342 UNTS 7; *Protocol on Prohibitions or Restrictions on the Use of Incendiary Weapons*, (1983) 1342 UNTS 7; *Protocol on Blinding Laser Weapons*, (1983) 1342 UNTS 7; *Protocol on Non-Detectable Fragments*, (1983) 1342 UNTS 7; *Convention on the Prohibition of the Use, Stockpiling, Production and Transfer of Anti-Personnel Mines and on their Destruction*, [1999] CTS 4; *Protocol on Prohibitions or Restrictions on the Use of Mines, Booby-Traps and Other Devices*, [1998] CTS 41; *Convention on the Prohibition of the Development, Production, Stockpiling and Use of Chemical Weapons and on their Destruction (with Annexes); Additional Protocol to the Convention on Prohibitions or Restrictions on the Use of Certain Conventional Weapons Which May be Deemed to be Excessively Injurious or to Have Indiscriminate Effects done at Geneva on October 10, 1980 (Protocol IV)*.

in particular humiliating and degrading treatment, and "the passing of sentences and the carrying out of executions without previous judgment pronounced by a regularly constituted court, affording all the judicial guarantees which are recognized as indispensable by civilized peoples".[531] Still more detailed texts appear in the two protocols of 1977.[532] In a case concerning the execution of juvenile offenders in the United States, the Inter-American Commission on Human Rights referred to the prohibition on capital punishment for crimes committed by persons under the age of eighteen found in the fourth *Geneva Convention* of 1949.[533] The Commission said that it could "identify no appropriate justification for applying a more restrictive standard for the application of the death penalty to juveniles in times of occupation than in times of peace, relating as this protection does to the most basic and non-derogable protections for human life and dignity of adolescents that are common to both regimes of international law".[534]

Some human rights treaties encroach upon areas that would logically fall within international humanitarian law. The *Convention on the Rights of the Child*, for example, says that States are to "undertake to respect and to ensure respect for rules of international humanitarian law applicable to them in armed conflicts which are relevant to the child". The *Convention* specifically addresses the issue of recruitment of child soldiers, requiring them to "take all feasible measures to ensure that persons who have not attained the age of fifteen years do not take a direct part in hostilities".[535] Many States were dissatisfied with this provision, and in 2000 a protocol to the *Convention* was adopted raising the age to eighteen.[536] Canada ratified the *Protocol*

---

531 *Geneva Convention for the Amelioration of the Condition of the Wounded and Sick in Armed Forces in the Field, supra* note 525, art. 3; *Geneva Convention for the Amelioration of the Condition of the Wounded, Sick and Shipwrecked Members of the Armed Forces at Sea, supra* note 525, art. 3; *Geneva Convention Relative to the Protection of Civilian Persons in Time of War, supra* note 525, art. 3; *Geneva Convention Relative to the Treatment of Prisoners of War, supra* note 525, art. 3.

532 *Protocol Additional I to the 1949 Geneva Conventions and Relating to The Protection of Victims of International Armed Conflicts, supra* note 527, art. 75; *Protocol Additional II to the 1949 Geneva Conventions and Relating to The Protection of Victims of Non-International Armed Conflicts, supra* note 527, art. 6.

533 *Geneva Convention Relative to the Treatment of Prisoners of War, supra* note 525, art. 68(4). Also: *Protocol Additional I to the 1949 Geneva Conventions and Relating to The Protection of Victims of International Armed Conflicts, ibid.*, art. 77(5); *Protocol Additional II to the 1949 Geneva Conventions and Relating to The Protection of Victims of Non-International Armed Conflicts, ibid.*, art. 6(4).

534 *Domingues* v. *United States*, Report No. 62/02, Merits, Case 12.285, 22 October 2002, para. 67.

535 *Convention on the Rights of the Child*, GA Res. 44/25, Annex, [1992] CTS 3, art. 38.

536 *Optional Protocol to the Convention on the Rights of the Child on the Involvement of Children in Armed Conflict*, UN Doc. A/RES/54/263, [2002] CTS 5.

in 2002, but with a declaration noting that the Canadian Armed Forces permit voluntary recruitment from the age of sixteen. The declaration does not explicitly state that Canada will prevent soldiers who are under the age of eighteen from participating actively in armed conflict.[537]

The relationship between human rights law and humanitarian law is an area of legal uncertainty.[538] In a recent advisory opinion, the International Court of Justice described it as follows:

> [T]he Court considers that the protection offered by human rights conventions does not cease in case of armed conflict, save through the effect of provisions for derogation of the kind to be found in Article 4 of the International Covenant on Civil and Political Rights. As regards the relationship between international humanitarian law and human rights law, there are thus three possible situations: some rights may be exclusively matters of international humanitarian law; others may be exclusively matters of human rights law; yet others may be matters of both these branches of international law. In order to answer the question put to it, the Court will have to take into consideration both these branches of international law, namely human rights law and, as *lex specialis*, international humanitarian law.[539]

The Human Rights Committee, in a General Comment, has explained that

> [d]uring armed conflict, whether international or non-international, rules of international humanitarian law become applicable and help, in addition to the provisions in article 4 and article 5, paragraph 1, of the Covenant, to prevent the abuse of a State's emergency powers. The Covenant requires that even during an armed conflict measures derogating from the Covenant are allowed only if and to the extent that the situation constitutes a threat to the life of the nation.[540]

The approaches of the International Court of Justice and the Human Rights Committee may not be perfectly reconcilable. The Court seems to consider that human rights norms will be informed by principles of humanitarian law, whereas the Committee approaches the two bodies of law as distinct and additive in effect. The potential conflict becomes particularly acute with

---

537 The text of the declaration is reproduced in the Appendix to this volume, at 441.

538 See, *e.g.*, "Working paper on the relationship between human rights law and international humanitarian law by Françoise Hampson and Ibrahim Salama", UN Doc. E/CN.4/Sub.2/2005/14; Robert Kolb, "Aspects historique de la relation entre le droit international humanitaire et les droits de l'homme", (1999) 37 *Canadian Yearbook of International Law* 57; Noam Lubell, "Challenges in Applying Human Rights Law to Armed Conflict", (2005) 87 *International Review of the Red Cross* 737; René Provost, *International Human Rights and Humanitarian Law*, Cambridge: Cambridge University Press, 2002.

539 *Legal Consequences of the Construction of a Wall in the Occupied Palestinian Territory*, *supra* note 520, para. 106.

540 "General Comment No. 29, States of Emergency (Article 4)", UN Doc. CCPR/C/21/Rev.1/Add.11, para. 3.

respect to the right to life. Article 6(1) of the *International Covenant on Civil and Political Rights* protects the right not to be "arbitrarily" deprived of life. In its advisory opinion on nuclear weapons, the International Court of Justice said that "whether a particular loss of life, through the use of a certain weapon in warfare, is to be considered an arbitrary deprivation of life contrary to Article 6 of the Covenant, can only be decided by reference to the law applicable in armed conflict and not deduced from the terms of the Covenant itself".[541] The loss of life of civilians, when it is characterized as "collateral damage", does not necessarily violate international humanitarian law.[542] Similarly, the rights of prisoners of war do not correspond perfectly with those of persons detained under the regime of article 9 of the *International Covenant on Civil and Political Rights.*

The International Court of Justice has left no doubt, however, about the application of international human rights treaties to an occupied territory. In its advisory opinion on the so-called "wall" or "separation fence" that Israel has constructed around communities in the territories that it occupies in Palestine, the Court said that "the International Covenant on Civil and Political Rights is applicable in respect of acts done by a State in the exercise of its jurisdiction outside its own territory", and made similar findings with respect to the *International Covenant on Economic, Social and Cultural Rights* and the *Convention on the Rights of the Child.*[543] In December 2005, in a contentious case between the Democratic Republic of Congo and Uganda, the Court held that Uganda was responsible for violations of various human rights treaties committed during its occupation of certain areas in the neighbouring territory of Congo.[544]

An important difficulty that attempts to relate the two bodies of law arises with respect to the lawfulness of the war itself. International humanitarian law proclaims an indifference to the *jus ad bellum*, that is, the legality of the conflict. It applies without distinction to both aggressor and victim. But human rights law is not based upon the same premise. In its first General Comment on the right to life, the Human Rights Committee wrote:

> The Committee observes that war and other acts of mass violence continue to be a scourge of humanity and take the lives of thousands of innocent human beings every year. Under the Charter of the United Nations the threat or use of force by any State against another State, except in exercise of the inherent right

---

541 *Legality of the Threat or Use of Nuclear Weapons, Advisory Opinion,* [1996] ICJ Reports 257, para. 25.

542 *Protocol Additional I to the 1949 Geneva Conventions and Relating to The Protection of Victims of International Armed Conflicts, supra* note 527, arts. 51-52.

543 *Legal Consequences of the Construction of a Wall in the Occupied Palestinian Territory, supra* note 520, paras. 111-113.

544 *Case Concerning Armed Activities on the Territory of the Congo (Democratic Republic of the Congo* v. *Uganda),* 19 December 2005, para. 219.

of self-defence, is already prohibited. The Committee considers that States have the supreme duty to prevent wars, acts of genocide and other acts of mass violence causing arbitrary loss of life. Every effort they make to avert the danger of war, especially thermonuclear war, and to strengthen international peace and security would constitute the most important condition and guarantee for the safeguarding of the right to life.[545]

The Committee noted the connection between the right to life, protected by article 6 of the *Covenant*, and the obligation on States to prohibit any propaganda for war, which is found in article 20(1). As a consequence, loss of life resulting from aggressive war should be treated as "arbitrary" deprivation of the right to life and a violation of article 6(1) of the *Covenant*.

3.8   International Criminal Law

Closely related to human rights law, but also to international humanitarian law, is the field of international criminal law. Long before the *Universal Declaration of Human Rights*, international law had declared acts such as piracy and trade in women, children, drugs and obscene publications to be "international crimes". In a very general sense, they were described as such because international cooperation was required for their suppression. Often they were committed outside the jurisdiction of any state, for example on the high seas. Special rules were therefore required because they escaped the traditional jurisdictional scope of national justice systems. Aside from these exceptions, jurisdiction over criminal law was confined to the territory of a given state and to its own nationals. This itself was a matter of international law, because to attempt to exercise criminal law jurisdiction in the territory of another state was considered to be a breach of its sovereignty.[546]

Several international treaties within the field of human rights and humanitarian law contain provisions that concern the prosecution of individuals for breaches of their provisions, among them the *Convention for the Prevention and Punishment of the Crime of Genocide*,[547] the *Convention*

---

545   "General Comment No. 6 (16), The Right to Life (Article 6)", UN Doc CCPR/C/21/ Add.1, UN Doc A/37/40, Annex V, pp. 382-383, para. 2.

546   The general principles of international law in this area were set out in a famous case of the Permanent Court of International Justice: *SS Lotus (France v. Turkey)*, PCIJ, 1927, Series A, No. 10.

547   *Convention on the Prevention and Punishment of the Crime of Genocide*, (1951) 78 UNTS 277, [1949] CTS 27. Referred to in: *Ramirez* v. *Canada (M.E.I.)*, [1992] 2 FC 306, 89 DLR (4th) 173, 135 NR 390 (CA); *I. (L.G.) (Re)*, [1995] CRDD 60; *R.* v. *Gottfriedson*, [1995] BCJ No. 1791 (B.C. P.C.); *R.* v. *Williams*, (1993) [1993] BCJ No. 2296, 1993 CarswellBC 901 (SC), affirmed, (1994) 1994 CarswellBC 1731 (CA), leave to appeal refused, (1995) 193 N.R. 239 (note) (SCC); *Y. (F.B.) (Re)*, [1991] CRDD 321; *Mugesera* v. *Canada (Minister of Citizenship and Immigration)*, [2005] 2 SCR 100; *Mugesera* v. *Minister of Citizenship and Immigration*, QML-95-00171, Immigration

Against Torture and Other Cruel, Inhuman or Degrading Treatment or Punishment,[548] the *International Convention on the Suppression and Punishment of the Crime of Apartheid*[549] and the four *Geneva Conventions*.[550] Essentially, these treaties declare certain or all of their norms to require that all States parties undertake to either prosecute offenders or extradite them to another State that is ready to do so (*aut dedere aut judicare*).[551] Implicit in this rule is the notion of "universal jurisdiction", which is an exception to the general principle by which States may only exercise criminal law jurisdiction where there is a significant link, either territorial or personal, with the crime.[552]

International criminal law began its association with international human rights law at the time of the First World War. Atrocities committed

---

and Refugee Board, Appeal Division, 11 July 1996; *Mugesera* v. *Minister of Citizenship and Immigration*, (2003) [2004] 1 FCR 3, 232 DLR (4th) 75, 309 NR 14, 31 Imm LR (3d) 159 (Fed CA), additional reasons at, (2004) 2004 CarswellNat 2750 (FCA), leave to appeal allowed, (2004) 2004 CarswellNat 376 (SCC), reversed, (2005) 2005 CarswellNat 1740 (SCC); *Mugesera* v. *Minister of Citizenship and Immigration*, [2001] 4 FC 421, 205 FTR 29 (TD), reversed, (2003) 2003 CarswellNat 2663 (Fed CA), additional reasons at, (2004) 2004 CarswellNat 2750 (FCA), leave to appeal allowed, (2004) 2004 CarswellNat 376 (SCC), reversed, (2005) 2005 CarswellNat 1740 (SCC). On the *Genocide Convention*, see: William A. Schabas, *Genocide in International Law*, Cambridge: Cambridge University Press, 2000.

548   UN Doc. A/39/51, p. 197, REIQ (1984-89) no (1987) (16) p. 870.

549   *International Convention on the Suppression and Punishment of the Crime of Apartheid*, (1976) 1015 UNTS 244. Cited in *Bancroft* v. *University of Toronto*, (1986) 24 DLR (4th) 620, 53 OR (2d) 460, 21 CRR 269 (HC); *O. (B.R.) (Re)*, [1991] CRDD 154. Canada has neither signed nor ratified the *Apartheid Convention*.

550   *Convention for the Amelioration of the Condition of the Wounded and Sick in Armed Forces in the Field*, (1949) 75 UNTS 31, art. 50; *Convention for the Amelioration of the Condition of Wounded, Sick and Shipwrecked Members of Armed Forces at Sea*, (1950) 75 UNTS 85, art. 51; *Convention Relative to the Treatment of Prisoners of War*, (1950) 75 UNTS 135, art. 130; *Convention Relative to the Protection of Civilian Persons in Time of War*, (1950) 75 UNTS 287, art. 147.

551   The *Genocide Convention* is an exception to this principle, in that it does not authorize prosecution in a State other than the one where the crime was committed. However, it is now generally agreed that genocide not only may but should be prosecuted, wherever the offender is to be found: *Attorney-General of the Government of Israel* v. *Eichmann*, (1961) 36 ILR 5. See also: *Case Concerning the Arrest Warrant of 11 April 2000 (Democratic Republic of the Congo v. Belgium)*, 14 February 2002, Joint Separate Opinion of Judges Higgins, Kooijmans and Buergenthal, and Dissenting Opinion of Judge Van den Wyngaert. This issue is discussed by Justice La Forest of the Supreme Court of Canada in *R.* v. *Finta*, [1994] 1 SCR 701, 88 CCC (3d) 417, 112 DLR (4th) 513, 150 NR 370, at 731-733 (SCR).

552   Section 6(2) of the *Criminal Code*, RSC 1985, c. C-46, specifies that "no person shall be convicted. . .of an offence committed outside Canada". In exceptional circumstances, the *Code* allows for prosecution where the crime is committed outside Canada: s. 7. See: *R.* v. *Stratton*, (1978) 90 DLR (3d) 420 (Ont. CA), at 426-427.

against the Armenian population in the Ottoman Empire[553] had been met with a joint declaration from the governments of France, Great Britain and Russia, dated 24 May 1915, asserting that "[i]n the presence of these new crimes of Turkey against humanity and civilization, the allied Governments publicly inform the Sublime Porte that they will hold personally responsible for the said crimes all members of the Ottoman Government as well as those of its agents who are found to be involved in such massacres".[554] It has been suggested that this constitutes the first use, at least within an international law context, of the term "crimes against humanity".[555] At the Paris Peace Conference, the Allies debated the wisdom and the legality of holding international war crimes trials. Generally hostile to the idea, the United States argued that responsibility for breach of international conventions, and above all for crimes against the "laws of humanity" – a reference to civilian atrocities within a state's own borders – was a question of morality. The drafters of the *Treaty of Versailles* ultimately dropped the concept of "laws of humanity", but promised prosecution of Kaiser Wilhelm II "for a supreme offence against international morality and the sanctity of treaties".[556] Pursuant to articles 228-230 of the *Treaty*, a series of internationalized war crimes trials, known as the Leipzig Trials, took place. In *Finta*, Justice Peter Cory referred to two of the more celebrated decisions of the Leipzig court as authority for the definition of the defense of superior orders under public international law.[557] He did not mention the Canadian connection with one of the cases. The *Llandovery Castle* was a hospital ship, used to transport sick and wounded soldiers from Europe back home to Halifax. She was marked accordingly, in conformity with the tenth Hague Convention of 1907, and was therefore immune from attack. In the evening of 27 June 1919, the ship was torpedoed and sunk off the coast of Ireland by U-

---

553   Richard G. Hovannisian, ed., *The Armenian Genocide, History, Politics, Ethics*, New York: St. Martin's Press, 1991; R. Melson, *Revolution and Genocide: on the Origin of the Armenian Genocide and of the Holocaust*, Chicago: University of Chicago Press, 1992.

554   English translation quoted in: United Nations War Crimes Commission, *History of the United Nations War Crimes Commission and the Development of the Laws of War*, London: His Majesty's Stationery Office, 1948, p. 35.

555   The concept, however, had been in existence for many years. During debates in the National Assembly, French revolutionary Robespierre described the King, Louis XVI, as a "[c]riminal against humanity": Maximilien Robespierre, *Œuvres, IX*, Paris: Presses universitaires de France, 1952, p. 130. In 1890, an American observer, George Washington Williams, wrote to the United States Secretary of State that King Leopold's regime in Congo was responsible for "crimes against humanity": Adam Hochschild, *King Leopold's Ghost*, Boston & New York: Houghton Mifflin, 1998, p. 112.

556   *Treaty of Peace between the Allied and Associated Powers and Germany*, 1919 TS 4, art. 227.

557   *R. v. Finta, supra* note 551, p. 832 (SCR).

boat 86. Some 234 Canadians lost their lives in the illegal attack. The Germans then attempted to destroy the traces of the crime by firing on the lifeboats containing the few survivors. The first and second officers of the watch, Dithmar and Boldt, were prosecuted for war crimes. In defence, they argued that they were acting under superior orders. Noting that the firing on the lifeboats was "an offence against the law of nations", the court said that while soldiers and sailors were under no obligation to question the order of a superior officer, this could not excuse their criminal behaviour "if such an order is universally known to everybody, including also the accused, to be without any doubt whatever against the law".[558] The same position on international law with respect to superior orders was confirmed by the Supreme Court of Canada, in *Finta*,[559] and is reflected most recently in article 33 of the *Rome Statute of the International Criminal Court.*

The human rights dimension of international criminal law really emerged with the Second World War prosecutions, of which the trial held by the International Military Tribunal at Nuremberg was the main event. The Canadian High Commission in London sent an observer to the wartime meetings of the United Nations War Crimes Commission, which was set up in late 1943 to prepare the post-war trials. Initially, British and American lawyers resisted expanding the scope of war crimes prosecutions so as to cover atrocities committed against the civilian population of Germany itself, arguing that this fell outside the scope of international law. At the London Conference of June-August 1945, which set up the legal basis for the Nuremberg trial, the American delegate, Robert Jackson, explained his government's reticence to recognize what were already being described as "crimes against humanity":

> [O]rdinarily we do not consider that the acts of a government toward its own citizens warrant our interference. We have some regrettable circumstances at times in our own country in which minorities are unfairly treated. We think it is justifiable that we interfere or attempt to bring retribution to individuals or to states only because the concentration camps and the deportations were in pursuance of a common plan or enterprise of making an unjust or illegal war in which we became involved. We see no other basis on which we are justified in reaching the atrocities which were committed inside Germany, under German law, or even in violation of German law, by authorities of the German state.[560]

Although drafted by the four great powers, the *Agreement for the Prosecution and Punishment of Major War Criminals of the European Axis, and*

---

558   *Empire* v. *Dithmar and Boldt* (Hospital Ship "Llandovery Castle"), (1921) 2 ILR 437, 16 *American Journal of International Law* 708.

559   *R.* v. *Finta, supra* note 551, p. 842.

560   *Ibid.*, p. 833.

Establishing the Charter of the International Military Tribunal (I.M.T.) was adhered to by nineteen other States, though not, for reasons which are unknown, by Canada.[561] Canada held a few of its own war crimes trials.[562] The prosecutor at one of the more famous ones was Clarence Campbell, who would later direct the National Hockey League.[563] But the war crimes trial programme soon lost steam. Meanwhile, Canadian immigration authorities were rather relaxed about admitting those who had fought with the Nazis, including many suspected of participating in atrocities, to settle in the country.[564]

Only in the 1980s, responding to pressure from Jewish NGOs, was a Royal Commission established to examine the question of war criminals within Canada. Presided by Justice Jules Deschênes, the Commission prepared a list of suspects, and recommended that the *Criminal Code* be amended in order to authorize Canadian courts to exercise jurisdiction over war crimes and crimes against humanity committed abroad and lacking any particular nexus with the country.[565] His move had been somewhat anticipated by the drafters of the *Canadian Charter of Rights and Freedoms*, who in section 11(g) had allowed for the prospect of prosecution of war criminals despite the general prohibition on retroactive criminal liability. Deschênes proposed that Canada authorise "universal jurisdiction", an exception to the general principle by which States may only exercise criminal law jurisdiction where there is a significant link, either territorial or personal, with the crime. Acting pursuant to amendments to the *Criminal Code* resulting from the recommendation of the Deschênes Commission,[566] the federal Department of Justice undertook a series of unsuccessful prosecutions, culminating in the acquittal of a Hungarian gendarme, Imre Finta. The accused did not

---

561 *Agreement for the Prosecution and Punishment of Major War Criminals of the European Axis, and Establishing the Charter of the International Military Tribunal (I.M.T.)*, annex, (1951) 82 UNTS 279. See: Arieh J. Kochavi, *Prelude to Nuremberg, Allied War Crimes Policy and the Question of Punishment*, Chapel Hill and London: University of North Carolina Press, 1998; *Report of Robert H. Jackson, United States Representative to the International Conference on Military Trials*, Washington: U.S. Government Printing Office, 1949.

562 Patrick Brode, *Casual Slaughters and Accidental Judgments, Canadian War Crimes Prosecutions, 1944-1948*, Toronto: University of Toronto Press, 1997.

563 *Canada* v. *Meyer*, (1948) 4 LRTWC 98 (Canadian Military Court). See: Howard Margolian, *Conduct Unbecoming: The Story of the Murder of Canadian Prisoners of War in Normandy*, Toronto: University of Toronto Press, 1998.

564 Howard Margolian, *Unauthorized Entry: The Truth about Nazi War Criminals in Canada, 1946-1956*, Toronto: University of Toronto Press, 2000.

565 Jules Deschênes, *Commission of Inquiry on War Criminals Report*, Ottawa: Minister of Supply and Services, 1986.

566 RSC, 1985, c. 30 (3rd Supp.), s. 3.71-2.76. The *Code* definition of crimes against humanity varied slightly from the definitions proposed by international law: *Canada* v. *Mehmet*, [1992] 2 FC 598 (CA), at 618.

even testify to deny charges that he participated in the persecution of thousands of Jews and their transport to Nazi death camps. The majority of the Supreme Court of Canada upheld the majority of the Ontario Court of Appeal[567] on two important points concerning the trial judge's jury instructions that had the effect of imposing an almost impossibly high standard on the Crown. A decade later, the Supreme Court of Canada revisited the issue of crimes against humanity in *Mugesera*, adjusting the law slightly to facilitate prosecution.[568] Within a few months of the Supreme Court's decision, the Department of Justice revived its programme of prosecutions, announcing the arrest of a Désiré Munyaneza for genocide, crimes against humanity and war crimes committed in Rwanda in 1994.[569]

The 1987 amendments to the *Criminal Code* and the subsequent launch of Canada's war crimes prosecutions were one of the early manifestations of an international trend towards accountability for human rights abuses. On the international level, this can be traced to one of the first judgments of the Inter-American Court of Human Rights, which held that states were under a duty to ensure that individual perpetrators of serious violations of human rights be brought to justice.[570] Within the United Nations human rights institutions there was a growing interest in the rights of victims of crime, and in questions concerning reparation and restitution. At its 1989 session, the United Nations General Assembly revived the project of creating an international criminal court.[571] The idea had been recognized in article VI of the 1948 *Genocide Convention*, but after a few years of consideration it had lain dormant, mainly because Cold War tension made the concept unviable.

While the United Nations International Law Commission worked on a draft statute for the proposed court, proof that this was an idea whose time had come soon emerged in the form of calls for international prosecutions and the establishment of *ad hoc* tribunals. In 1990, British Prime Minister Margaret Thatcher and United States President George Bush, both evoking the precedent of the Nuremberg trials, broached the idea of an international tribunal to deal with the Iraqi invasion of Kuwait, one that might address

---

567 *R. v. Finta,* (1992) 92 DLR (4th) 1 (Ont CA), affirmed, (1994) 1994 CarswellOnt 61 (SCC), reconsideration refused, (June 23, 1994) Doc. 23023, 23097 (SCC).

568 *Mugesera* v. *Canada (Minister of Citizenship and Immigration), supra* note 547 (SCC).

569 Terry Weber, "Mounties charge Rwandan with war crimes", *Globe and Mail,* 19 October 2005.

570 *Velasquez Rodriguez* v. *Honduras,* Series C, No. 4.

571 GA Res. 44/89.

such crimes as aggression and hostage-taking.[572] Nothing came of the proposal, but within a few years later, as war raged in the Balkans, the United Nations Security Council decided to establish the International Criminal Tribunal for the former Yugoslavia.[573] Eighteen months later it created a second *ad hoc* Tribunal to deal with the Rwandan genocide.[574] Canadian jurist Jules Deschênes was elected by the General Assembly as one of the first judges of the International Criminal Tribunal for the former Yugoslavia. He served on the Appeals Chamber of both tribunals, and signed one of the classic judgments of modern international criminal law, the *Tadić Jurisdictional Decision* of 2 October 1995.[575] In mid-1996, the Security Council designated another Canadian, Louise Arbour, as Prosecutor of the two tribunals. She held office for three years, stepping down to take up an appointment to the Supreme Court of Canada. Professor Sharon Williams, of Osgoode Hall Law School, served as an *ad litem* judge at the International Criminal Tribunal for the former Yugoslavia from 2001 to 2003, sitting principally as a trial judge in a case concerning ethnic cleansing of Bosnian Croats and Muslims in northwestern Bosnia and Herzegovina during 1992 and 1993.[576] In 2005, another Canadian, Kimberley Prost, was elected an *ad litem* judge of the International Criminal Tribunal for the former Yugoslavia. Canada has adopted legislation to facilitate its cooperation with the International Criminal Tribunals, in accordance with the *United Nations Act*.[577] In July 1999, following the arrest warrant and freezing order issued with respect to Slobodan Milosevic, Canada promulgated regulations to ensure that any assets of Milosevic and his four alleged accomplices would

---

572 For Thatcher, see her television interview of 1 September 1990: (1990) 61 *British Yearbook of International Law* 602; Marc Weller, "When Saddam is brought to court . . .", *The Times*, 3 September 1990. For Bush, see: *US Department of State Dispatch*, 22 October 1990, Vol. I(8), p. 205; *US Department of State Dispatch*, 12 November 1990, Vol. I(11), p. 260. Also: Louis Rene Beres, "Iraqi Crimes and International Law: The Imperative to Punish", (1993) 21 *Denver Journal of International Law & Policy* 335; Louis Rene Beres, "Prosecuting Iraqi Crimes: Fulfilling the Expectations of International Law After the Gulf War", (1992) 10 *Dickinson Journal of International Law* 425.

573 UN Doc. S/RES/827 (1993).

574 UN Doc. S/RES/955 (1994).

575 *Prosecutor* v. *Tadić* (Case No. IT-94-1-AR72), Decision on the Defence Motion for Interlocutory Appeal on Jurisdiction, 2 October 1995. Judge Deschênes also penned an individual opinion complaining of the failure to issue the decision in French as well as English: *Prosecutor* v. *Tadić* (Case No. IT-94-1-AR72), Separate Declaration of Judge J. Deschênes on the Defence Motion for Interlocutory Appeal on Jurisdiction, 2 October 1995.

576 *Prosecutor* v. *Simić, Tadić and Zarić* (Case No. IT-95-9-T), Judgment, 17 October 2003.

577 *United Nations Act*, RS 1985, c. U-2.

be frozen.[578] Caselaw of the international criminal tribunals has been referred to on various occasions by the Canadian courts.[579]

As the two *ad hoc* tribunals heard their first cases, work proceeded more rapidly than most had expected on the proposed permanent international criminal court. When the International Law Commission completed its draft in 1994, the General Assembly authorized a series of meetings aimed at producing a text that would be broadly acceptable. Canada participated actively in the process, chairing a group of states known as the "like minded" who sought a court with greater independence from the United Nations Security Council than what had originally been proposed. During June and July 1998, a diplomatic conference chaired by Canadian international lawyer Philippe Kirsch, who was ably assisted by a team of skilled Canadian diplomats and criminal law experts, succeeded in adopting a definitive text.[580] The *Rome Statute of the International Criminal Court* was opened for signature, ratification and accession at the close of the conference, on 17 July 1998.[581] Following the sixtieth ratification, the *Rome Statute*

---

578 *United Nations International Criminal Tribunal for the Former Yugoslavia Regulations*, SOR/99-304. The Regulations were repealed in 2004: *Regulations Repealing the United Nations International Criminal Tribunal for the Former Yugoslavia Regulations*, SOR/2004-13.

579 In *Mugesera* v. *Canada*, *supra* note 547 (SCC), the Supreme Court of Canada cited several decisions of the International Criminal Tribunal for the former Yugoslavia and the International Criminal Tribunal for Rwanda. See also: *Suresh* v. *Canada (Minister of Citizenship and Immigration)*, [2002] 1 SCR 3, 208 DLR (4th) 1, 37 Admin LR (3d) 159, 90 CRR (2d) 1; *Mugesera* v. *Minister of Citizenship and Immigration)*, *supra* note 547 (FCA); *Zazai* v. *Canada (Minister of Citizenship and Immigration)*, 2005 FCA 303; *Bukumba* v. *Canada (Minister of Citizenship and Immigration)*, 2004 FC 93; *Fabela* v. *Canada (Minister of Citizenship and Immigration)*, 2005 FC 1028; *M.* v. *Canada (Minister of Citizenship and Immigration)*, 2002 FCT 833 (TD); *Nagamany* v. *Canada (Minister of Citizenship and Immigration)*, 2005 FC 1554; *Ali* v. *Canada (Solicitor General)*, 2005 FC 1306.

580 Philippe Kirsch & John T. Holmes, "The Birth of the International Criminal Court: The 1998 Rome Conference", (1998) 36 *Canadian Yearbook of International Law* 3-39.

581 *Rome Statute of the International Criminal Court*, UN Doc. A/CONF.183/9. There are already a few references to the *Rome Statute* in Canadian caselaw: *United States* v. *Burns and Rafay*, [2001] 1 SCR 283, 195 DLR (4th) 1, [2001] 3 WWR 193, 151 CCC (3d) 97, 39 CR (5th) 205, 81 CRR (2d) 1, 85 BCLR (3d) 1; *Mugesera* v. *Canada*, *supra* note 568; *Zrig* v. *Canada (Minister of Citizenship and Immigration)*, [2003] 3 FC 761 (CA); *Harb* v. *Canada (Minister of Citizenship and Immigration)*, 2003 FCA 39; *Fabela* v. *Canada (Minister of Citizenship and Immigration)*, 2005 FC 1028; *M.* v. *Canada (Minister of Citizenship and Immigration)*, (2002) 221 FTR 195 (TD); *Zazai* v. *Canada (Minister of Citizenship and Immigration)*, [2005] 2 FCR 78 (FC), affirmed, (2005) 2005 CarswellNat 2933 (FCA); *Ali* v. *Canada (Solicitor General)*, 2005 FC 1306; *Ruiz Blanco* v. *Canada (Minister of Citizenship and Immigration)*, 2006 FC 623; *Kathiravel* v. *Canada (Minister of Citizenship and Immigration)*, 2003 FCT 680 (TD); *Fuentes* v. *Canada (Minister of Citizenship and Immigration)*, [2003] 4 FC 249, 231 FTR 172 (TD). In *Pushpanathan* v. *Canada (Minister of Citizenship and Immigration)*, [1998] 1

entered into force on 1 July 2002.[582] Kirsch was elected judge of the Court the following year. His colleagues agreed that he would be the Court's first president. He was re-elected to a second term as President in March 2006.

After Canada had signed the *Rome Statute*, on 18 December 1998, Parliament enacted the *Crimes Against Humanity and War Crimes Act*.[583] The legislation received Royal Assent on 29 June 2000. Canada deposited its instrument of ratification of the *Rome Statute* a week later, on 7 July 2000, becoming the fourteenth State party. The *Crimes Against Humanity and War Crimes Act* repealed the 1987 legislation that had been the basis of the *Finta* prosecution, incorporating into Canadian criminal law the definitions of genocide, crimes against humanity and war crimes that were set out in the *Rome Statute*. In fact, the *Crimes Against Humanity and War Crimes Act* declares that the three crimes, genocide, crimes against humanity and war crimes, are defined by customary law. As guidance for the courts, the *Act* makes two attempts to determine the state of customary law. A general provision, applicable to crimes committed both inside and outside Canada, states: "For greater certainty, crimes described in Articles 6 and 7

SCR 982, at para. 70, Justice Bastarache cited an early version of the draft statute of the International Criminal Court.

582 On the International Criminal Court generally, see: Roy Lee, ed., *The International Criminal Court, The Making of the Rome Statute, Issues, Negotiations, Results*, The Hague: Kluwer Law International, 1999; Otto Triffterer, ed., *Commentary on the Rome Statute of the International Criminal Court, Observers' Notes, Article by Article*, Baden-Baden: Nomos, 1999 (a second edition will appear in 2007); Herman von Hebel, Johan G. Lammers & Jolien Schukking, eds., *Reflections on the International Criminal Court: Essays in Honour of Adriaan Bos*, The Hague: T.M.C. Asser, 1999; Flavia Lattanzi & William A. Schabas, eds., *Essays on the Rome Statute of the ICC*, Rome: Editrice il Sirente, 2000; Dinah Shelton, ed., *International Crimes, Peace, and Human Rights: The Role of the International Criminal Court*, Ardsley, New York: Transnational Publishers, 2000; Roy Lee, ed., *The International Criminal Court, Elements of Crimes and Rules of Procedure and Evidence*, Ardsley, New York: Transnational Publishers, 2001; Mauro Politi & Giuseppe Nesi, eds., *The Rome Statute of the International Criminal Court, A Challenge to Impunity*, Aldershot: Ashgate, 2001; Antonio Cassese, Paola Gaeta & John R.W.D. Jones, *The Rome Statute of the International Criminal Court, A Commentary*, Oxford: Oxford University Press, 2002; William A. Schabas, *Introduction to the International Criminal Court*, 2nd ed., Cambridge: Cambridge University Press, 2004.

583 *Crimes Against Humanity and War Crimes Act*, SC 2000, c. 24. Also: *International Criminal Court Privileges and Immunities Order*, SOR/2004-156. See: William A. Schabas, "Canada", in Ben Brandon & Max Du Plessis, eds., *The Prosecution of International Crimes, A Guide to Prosecuting ICC Crimes in Commonwealth States*, London: Commonwealth Secretariat, 2005, pp. 153-172; William A. Schabas, "Canadian Implementing Legislation for the Rome Statute", (2000) 3 *Yearbook of International Humanitarian Law* 337; William A. Schabas, "Canadian Implementing Legislation for the Rome Statute: Jurisdiction and Defences", in M. Neuner, ed., *National Legislation Incorporating International Crimes*, Berlin: Berliner Wissenschafts-Verlag/Wolf Legal Publishers, 2003, pp. 35-43.

and paragraph 2 of Article 8 of the Rome Statute are, as of July 17, 1998, crimes according to customary international law."[584] The second provision establishes that crimes against humanity have been recognised as part of customary international law since 1945. It is applicable only to crimes committed outside Canada (the legislation does not authorise retrospective application of crimes committed inside Canada). The provision states that

> [f]or greater certainty, the offence of crime against humanity was part of customary international law or was criminal according to the general principles of law recognized by the community of nations before the coming into force of either of the following: (a) the Agreement for the prosecution and punishment of the major war criminals of the European Axis, signed at London on August 8, 1945; and (b) the Proclamation by the Supreme Commander for the Allied Powers, dated January 19, 1946.[585]

That Parliament felt the need to make a declaration that crimes against humanity were punishable under customary international law or general principles of law at the time of the post-Second World War prosecutions may seem surprising. A close look at the 1994 *Finta* ruling of the Supreme Court of Canada may assist in understanding the rationale for this provision. Justice Peter Cory, who drafted the reasons of the majority, examined whether prosecution for crimes against humanity committed in 1944 violated the norm against retroactive prosecution. He noted that at the time, such eminent international lawyers as Georg Schwarzenberger and Hans Kelsen believed that the Nuremberg and Tokyo Charters were not in fact declarative of already existing international law.[586] As for the other two categories, genocide and war crimes, they too may be prosecuted under the *Act* when they have been committed outside Canada prior to its entry into force, but Parliament has declined to provide any legislative direction to the courts as to where they may seek guidance in this area.

The declaration that the offences of genocide, crimes against humanity and war crimes as they are defined in the *Rome Statute* constitute customary law at the time of their adoption, on 17 July 1998, is a technique that is not without potential difficulties. Customary law will continue to evolve; indeed, in a provision based on article 10 of the *Rome Statute*, the Canadian legislation specifically contemplates this eventuality: "This does not limit or prejudice in any way the application of existing or developing rules of international law."[587] The presumption seems to be that international law will become increasingly broad, although evolution in the other direction is

---

584   *Ibid.*, ss. 4(4), 6(4).

585   *Ibid*, art. 4(5).

586   *R.* v. *Finta*, [1994] 1 SCR 701, 88 CCC (3d) 417, 112 DLR (4th) 513, 150 NR 370, p. 872 (SCR).

587   *Ibid.*

not inconceivable, in which case Canada might find its courts applying definitions that are narrower than those in the *Rome Statute*.

The caselaw of the International Criminal Tribunal for the former Yugoslavia already provides some evidence of divergence between customary international law and the applicable law of the International Criminal Court. The Appeals Chamber of the Tribunal would probably quarrel with the claim in the Canadian legislation that the *Rome Statute* is consistent with customary international law. For example, article 7 of the *Rome Statute* states that crimes against humanity must be committed "pursuant to or in furtherance of a State or organizational policy to commit such attack".[588] But in a 2002 case, the Appeals Chamber held that "no such requirement exists under customary international law" that "a policy or plan constitutes an element of the definition of crimes against humanity".[589] In *Mugesera*, the Supreme Court of Canada considered the issue of whether there was a State plan or policy element. It noted the position requiring this element with considerable deference,[590] but also acknowledged that the Appeals Chamber of the Yugoslavia Tribunal was taking the law in a different direction. "It seems that there is currently no requirement in customary international law that a policy underlie the attack, though we do not discount the possibility that customary international law may evolve over time so as to incorporate a policy requirement", said the Supreme Court of Canada.[591] The International Criminal Tribunal for the former Yugoslavia has also held that some of the *Elements of Crimes*[592] adopted pursuant to the *Rome Statute* are inconsistent with customary international law.[593] However, because the Canadian legislation only declares that the *Rome Statute* is compatible with customary law, and does not refer to its subordinate legislation, such as the *Elements of Crimes*, Canadian judges could reason in the same way as the Appeals Chamber and disregard the *Elements* as being in some way a reflection of customary international law.

For each of the three crimes defined in the *Crimes Against Humanity and War Crimes Act*, there are in fact two distinct definitional provisions, one for crimes committed within Canada, the other for crimes committed outside Canada. The two sets of provisions resemble each other closely. The provisions concerning crimes committed within Canada[594] are only

---

588 *Rome Statute, supra* note 581, art. 7(2)a).
589 *Prosecutor* v. *Kunarac* et al. (Case No. IT-96-23 & IT-96-23/1-A), Judgment, 12 June 2002, footnote 114. Also: *Prosecutor* v. *Krstic* (Case No: IT-98-33-A), Judgment, 19 April 2004, para. 225.
590 *Mugesera* v. *Canada*, [2005] 2 SCR 100 (SCC).
591 *Ibid.*, para. 158.
592 ICC-ASP/1/3, pp. 108-155.
593 *Prosecutor* v. *Krstic, supra* note 589, para. 224.
594 *Crimes Against Humanity and War Crimes Act*, SC 2000, c. 24, s. 4.

prospective in effect. They will enable Canada to prosecute crimes within the temporal jurisdiction of the International Criminal Court, and thereby ensure that Canada, in the terms of the *Rome Statute*, is "willing and able genuinely"[595] to investigate and prosecute atrocities. The preamble to the *Rome Statute* recognises "that it is the duty of every State to exercise its criminal jurisdiction over those responsible for international crimes".

The part concerning crimes committed outside Canada is intended to update the earlier war crimes legislation. It authorises Canadian courts to exercise universal jurisdiction in the case of genocide, crimes against humanity and war crimes, and operates retrospectively. Consistent with article 15 of the *International Covenant on Civil and Political Rights*, the *Canadian Charter of Rights and Freedoms* does not prohibit retrospective criminal law provisions to the extent that the offences were recognised under international law at the time of their commission.[596] The new *Crimes Against Humanity and War Crimes Act* applies the definitions of the three core crimes as they are set out in the *Rome Statute*, although it is careful to limit these, in the case of offences committed prior to adoption of the *Statute*, to such crimes only insofar as they correspond to the state of customary law at the time of their commission.[597]

The Canadian legislation states that

> . . . "genocide" means an act or omission committed with intent to destroy, in whole or in part, an identifiable group of persons, as such, that, at the time and in the place of its commission, constitutes genocide according to customary international law or conventional international law or by virtue of its being criminal according to the general principles of law recognized by the community of nations, whether or not it constitutes a contravention of the law in force at the time and in the place of its commission.[598]

The text is not the same as the definition of the crime of genocide presented in article 6 of the *Rome Statute*, which is essentially identical with that of the 1948 *Convention on the Prevention and Punishment of the Crime of Genocide*.[599]

The Canadian definition contemplates the expansion of the *Convention* definition of genocide in two respects. In article 6 of the *Rome Statute* (and

---

595 *Rome Statute, supra* note 581, art. 17.

596 *Canadian Charter of Rights and Freedoms*, RSC 1985, Appendix II, No. 44, s. 11(g).

597 *Crimes Against Humanity and War Crimes Act, supra* note 594, s. 6.

598 *Ibid.*, ss. 4(3), 6(3). Note that some of the provinces have also enacted legislation referring to "genocide": *An Act to Proclaim Armenian Genocide Memorial Day*, RSQ, c. J-0.2; *Holocaust Memorial Day and Genocide Remebrance Act*, RSA, c. H-10. These provincial statutes do not provide a definition of the crime or make reference to its source in international law.

599 (1951) 78 UNTS 277, [1949] CTS 27. Canada signed the *Convention* on 28 November 1949, and ratified it on 3 September 1952.

article 2 of the 1948 *Genocide Convention*), there is an exhaustive list of five punishable acts. The Canadian enactment anticipates the development of customary law so as to include other punishable acts. At the time the *Genocide Convention* was being drafted, a lengthy list of punishable acts was considered, broadly grouped into three main categories, defined by the adjectives physical, biological and cultural. Ultimately, the *Convention*'s scope was confined to physical and biological genocide, with the exception of the last punishable act, forcibly transferring children from one group to another, which is an act of cultural genocide. But there was no doubt of the reluctance of States, in 1948, to recognise international criminal liability for acts such as prohibition of language and religion that might be intended to destroy a group.

Ironically, in 1948 Canada was one of a group of States who felt strongly that cultural genocide should be excluded from the *Convention*. In the Sixth Committee of the General Assembly, the representative of Canada declared that if the Committee were to retain the cultural genocide provision, the Canadian government would have to make certain reservations.[600] Speaking in the Sixth Committee of the General Assembly, the Canadian representative said that "the people of his country were deeply attached to their heritage, which was made up mainly of a combination of Anglo-Saxon and French elements and they would strongly oppose any attempt to undermine the influence of those two cultures in Canada. . .[His delegation] felt that the idea of genocide should be limited to the mass physical destruction of human groups."[601]

Documents in the National Archives of Canda show how sensitive and important this issue really was:

> The Canadian delegation to the seventh session of Economic and Social Council was instructed to support or initiate any move for the deletion of Article III on "cultural" genocide (see document E/794) and, if this move were not successful, it should vote against Article III and, if necessary, against the whole convention. The delegation was instructed that the convention as a whole, less Article III, was acceptable though legislation will naturally be required in Canada to implement the convention.[602]

The delegation's report to Ottawa at the conclusion of the debate states:

> According to instructions from External Affairs, the Canadian delegate had only one important task, namely to eliminate the concept of "cultural genocide"

---

600 UN Doc. A/C.6/SR.83 (Lapointe, Canada).
601 *Ibid*. See, generally, Johannes Morsink, "Cultural Genocide, the Universal Declaration, and Minority Rights", (1999) 21 *Human Rights Quarterly* 1009.
602 "Commentary for the Use of the Canadian Delegation", National Archives of Canada RG 25, Vol. 3699, File 5475-DG-3-40"2" (this text is also in nac RG 25, Vol. 3699, File 5475-DG-1-40).

from the Convention. He took a leading part in the debate on this point and succeeded in having his viewpoints accepted by the Committee. The remaining articles are of no particular concern for Canada.[603]

There is in fact some evidence of an evolution in the interpretation of the crime of genocide so as to encompass a broader range of punishable acts that might be characterised as cultural genocide, with the concept of "ethnic cleansing" first and foremost among them. The German courts have extended the definition of genocide in this way,[604] although the International Criminal Tribunal for the former Yugoslavia has been reluctant to follow out of fear of breaching the norm *nullum crimen sine lege*.[605] There is also a dissenting opinion of the Appeals Chamber of the International Criminal Tribunal for the former Yugoslavia to the same effect.[606]

At the core of international criminal prosecution for atrocities that amount to gross and systematic violations of human rights is the concept of crimes against humanity. Justice La Forest, in *R.* v. *Finta*, said that "crimes against humanity are aimed at giving protection to the basic human rights of all individuals throughout the world".[607] Crimes against humanity are defined in the Canadian legislation as

> . . .murder, extermination, enslavement, deportation, imprisonment, torture, sexual violence, persecution or any other inhumane act or omission that is committed against any civilian population or any identifiable group and that, at the time and in the place of its commission, constitutes a crime against humanity according to customary international law or conventional international law or by virtue of its being criminal according to the general principles of law recognized by the community of nations, whether or not it constitutes a contravention of the law in force at the time and in the place of its commission.

The definition is inspired by its predecessor in the 1987 legislation, although the acts of torture and sexual violence have been added to the list, drawing

---

603 "Progress reports on work of Canadian delegation, in Paris, November 1, 1948", National Archives of Canda RG 25, Vol. 3699, File 5475-DG-2-40.

604 *Nikolai Jorgic, Bundesverfassungsgericht,* [Federal Constitutional Court], Fourth Chamber, Second Senate, 12 December 2000, 2 BvR 1290/99, para. 23; *Novislav Djajic, Bayerisches Oberstes Landesgericht,* 23 May 1997, 3 St 20/96, excerpted in 1998 Neue Juristische Wochenschrift 392. See: Christoph J.M. Safferling, "Public Prosecutor v. Djajic", (1998) 92 *American Journal of International Law* 528.

605 *Prosecutor* v. *Krstic* (Case No: IT-98-33-T), Judgment, 2 August 2001, para. 580.

606 *Prosecutor* v. *Krstić* (Case No. IT-98-33-A), Partial Dissenting Opinion of Judge Shahabuddeen, 19 April 2004, paras. 45-54. Also: *Prosecutor* v. *Blagojević* (Case No. IT-02-60-T) Judgment, 17 January 2005, para. 666.

607 *R.* v. *Finta, supra* note 586, at 735 (SCR). For a discussion of the definition of crimes against humanity, see, *e.g., Sivakumar v. Canada,* (1993) [1994] 1 FC 433 (CA), leave to appeal refused, (1994) 175 NR 324n (SCC) at 442-444 [FC]. Also: *Moreno v. Canada,* (1993) [1994] 1 FC 298 (CA).

upon the new codification in the *Rome Statute*.[608] Nevertheless, the list in the new Canadian legislation is striking for its omission of certain punishable acts of crimes against humanity listed in article 7 of the *Rome Statute*, specifically enforced disappearance of persons and apartheid. Canada never signed or ratified the *International Convention on the Suppression and Punishment of the Crime of Apartheid*,[609] perhaps out of unease with the grievances of the country's Aboriginal population. The *Act* refers to "sexual violence" rather than "rape"; Canadian criminal law no longer defines the crime of "rape", having opted, instead, for the unquestionably gender-neutral concept of "sexual assault".[610]

The definition of "war crime" is the simplest, in that it is really no definition. It simply declares as an offence "an act or omission committed during an armed conflict that, at the time and in the place of its commission, constitutes a war crime according to customary international law or conventional international law applicable to armed conflicts, whether or not it constitutes a contravention of the law in force at the time and in the place of its commission". Similar issues as those referred to with respect to crimes against humanity arise. It is probably in the area of war crimes where the disconnect between the *Rome Statute* and customary law may raise the greatest difficulty, because in some respects the *Rome Statute* studiously avoided customary law. For example, the *Rome Statute* prohibits the employment of "material and methods of warfare which are of a nature to cause superfluous injury or unnecessary suffering or which are inherently indiscriminate" but only to the extent they are part of a comprehensive prohibition included in an annex to the *Statute*, which does not as yet exist.[611] But article 23(e) of the 1907 *Hague Regulations*, to which Canada is a party,[612] prohibits the employment of "arms, projectiles, or material calculated to cause unnecessary suffering" as a general principle.[613] Might a

---

608   Canadian courts have previously noted the inconsistencies of the definition with the recognised models derived from international law: *Canada v. Mehmet*, [1992] 2 FC 598 (CA), at 618.

609   *International Convention on the Suppression and Punishment of the Crime of Apartheid*, (1976) 1015 UNTS 244.

610   SC 1980-81-82-83, c. 125. See: Christine Boyle, *Sexual Assault*, Toronto, Carswell, 1984; David Watt, *The New Offences Against the Person: The Provisions of Bill C-127*, Toronto: Butterworths, 1984; G. Parker, "The 'New' Sexual Offences", (1983) 31 CR (3d) 317.

611   *Rome Statute of the International Criminal Court*, UN Doc. A/CONF.183/9, art. 8(b)(xx).

612   *International Convention Concerning the Laws and Customs of War by Land*, [1910] TS 9. The *Hague Convention* came into force for Canada on 27 November 1909 as a consequence of ratification by the United Kingdom.

613   Similarly, see *Legality of the Threat or Use of Nuclear Weapons, Advisory Opinion*, [1996] ICJ Reports 257.

Canadian judge consider that the use, or even the possession, of anti-personal mines falls within this prohibition, either by a creative application of conventional law or an innovative reading of customary law?

In addition to the definition of the international crimes themselves, the *Rome Statute* also provides for various other substantive criminal law issues, such as defences and modes of participation. The provisions have already attracted some interest from Canadian courts. For example, in an expulsion case, the applicant argued that he had committed crimes against humanity under duress. Justice Lemieux of the Federal Court, Trial Division, noted that the applicable defense of duress was reflected in article 31(d) of the *Rome Statute*.[614] But Justice Décary of the Federal Court of Appeal, applying article 1(F) of the *Refugee Convention*, said "it is the rules of complicity in Canadian criminal law that must be applied in the event of disparities between these rules and those set out in paragraph 3 of article 25 of the Rome Statute".[615]

In addition to Canadian criminal law, the *Immigration Act* addresses crimes against humanity and war crimes in the case of refugee determination. An individual who would otherwise meet the criteria for refugee status may be denied this, pursuant to the so-called "exclusion clauses" of Article F of the *Refugee Convention*,[616] which are set out in the Schedule to the *Immigration Act*[617] and are therefore directly incorporated into Canadian law. Section F reads:

F. The provisions of this Convention shall not apply to any person with respect to whom there are serious reasons for considering that:

(a) he has committed a crime against peace, a war crime, or a crime against humanity, as defined in the international instruments drawn up to make provision in respect of such crimes;

(b) he has committed a serious non-political crime outside the country of refuge prior to his admission to that country as a refugee;

(c) he has been guilty of acts contrary to the purposes and principles of the United Nations.

Canadian tribunals, and particularly the Refugee Determination Division of the Immigration and Refugee Board, make frequent use of international criminal law in the application and interpretation of this provision.[618]

---

614 *Kathiravel* v. *Canada (Minister of Citizenship and Immigration)*, 2003 FCT 680 (T.D.), para. 46.
615 *Zrig* v. *Canada (Minister of Citizenship and Immigration)*, [2003] 3 FC 761 (CA), para. 146.
616 *Convention Relating to the Status of Refugees*, (1954) 189 UNTS 137, [1969] CTS 29.
617 *Immigration and Refugee Protection Act*, SC 2001, c. 27.
618 See, for example, *Pushpanathan* v. *Canada (Minister of Citizenship and Immigration)*, [1998] 1 SCR 982.

The *Crimes Against Humanity and War Crimes Act* establishes a form of universal jurisdiction that is sometimes called custodial jurisdiction, to distinguish it from universal jurisdiction *in absentia*.[619] In other words, there must be some *nexus* with the prosecuting State, even if the only link with the offender is presence within Canada. Section 8 of the *Act* gives jurisdiction to Canadian courts where the offence was committed outside Canada if "after the time the offence is alleged to have been committed, the person is present in Canada". The legislation also allows for jurisdiction if, at the time the offence was committed: the alleged offender was a Canadian citizen, or was employed by Canada in a civilian or military capacity; the person was a citizen of a state that was engaged in an armed conflict against Canada, or was employed in a civilian or military capacity by such a state; or the victim was a Canadian citizen or a citizen of a state that was allied with Canada in an armed conflict.

There is a lingering ambiguity with respect to so-called *in absentia* jurisdiction. In the case of alleged offenders with no other personal link to Canada, in other words universal jurisdiction as opposed to a form of active or passive personal jurisdiction, the text of the *Act* says they must have been "present in Canada [. . .] after the time the offence is alleged to have been committed". It does not say that they must be present in Canada at the time prosecution is initiated, however, or even during trial. Several scenarios can be imagined. An investigation might be carried out with respect to a suspect in Canada, but by the time it was completed and an indictment issued, the person might have fled the jurisdiction. Would this make the entire proceedings illegal or void? In Canada it is not possible for a trial to begin without the presence of the accused, but the *Criminal Code* will allow one to proceed in the absence of the accused when he or she absconds.

This seems to suggest that it is possible, at least theoretically, for Canadian courts to attempt to exercise jurisdiction over an individual who is not physically present in Canada for crimes not committed in Canada and where there is no other personal *nexus* with the country. If this interpretation seems far-fetched, the contrary construction appears to be even more unreasonable. Why should a prosecutor, at the time of issuance of an indictment, be required to ensure that the suspect is in Canada? Given the availability of air travel and the possibility of fleeing the jurisdiction within hours, a suspect might easily evade arrest by leaving Canada? Could this void the proceedings, or make them illegal under Canadian or international law? On a practical level, it might be unlikely that the authorities would

---

619 On the ongoing debate in public international law about these concepts see: *Arrest Warrant of 11 April 2000 (Democratic Republic of the Congo v. Belgium)*, Judgment, 15 February 2002, *Separate Opinion of President Guillaume*; *Joint Separate Opinion of Judges Higgins, Buergenthal and Kooijmans*.

want to devote the significant resources involved in a universal jurisdiction prosecution if they did not have physical custody of the offender. But in law, the prospect cannot be ruled out. The fact that the exceptions to presence of the accused at trial apply to proceedings under the *Crimes Against Humanity and War Crimes Act* is in fact specified by a distinct provision: "For greater certainty, in a proceeding commenced in any territorial division under subsection (1), the provisions of the *Criminal Code* relating to requirements that an accused appear at and be present during proceedings *and any exceptions to those requirements* apply".[620]

With respect to defenses to genocide, crimes against humanity and war crimes, section 11 of the *Crimes Against Humanity and War Crimes Act* sets out a general rule "In proceedings for an offence under any of sections 4 to 7, the accused may, subject to sections 12 to 14 and to subsection 607(6) of the *Criminal Code*, rely on any justification, excuse or defence available under the laws of Canada or under international law at the time of the alleged offence or at the time of the proceedings." This is an exception to the ordinary rule by which an accused may only invoke defences that were available at the time the alleged acts were committed. Defences under Canadian law consist of a combination of statutory provisions, set out in the *Criminal Code*, and common law rules, elaborated by Canadian judges and, to a certain extent, those of other common law jurisdictions.[621] As for international law, a number of defences are set out in articles 31 to 33 of the *Rome Statute* itself. But the *Statute* recognises that the list is not exhaustive, and allows other defences "derived from applicable law as set forth in article 21". These might include, for example, military necessity and reprisal.[622] Still other defences seem to be implicit in the nature of the crimes, and exist despite the silence of the *Rome Statute*. An example is consent, which can be a defence to such crimes as rape, enforced prostitution and enforced sterilisation. Some have argued that aspects of the defence of self-defence, set out in article 31(1)(c) of the *Rome Statute*, are in fact contrary to international law and in violation of norms of *jus cogens*.[623]

Because there is considerable overlap between the available defences under Canadian law and those offered by international law, conflicts may arise. The *Crimes Against Humanity and War Crimes Act* seems quite clear that in such cases, the accused is entitled to the more favourable provision.

---

620 *Crimes Against Humanity and War Crimes Act*, SC 2000, c. 24, s. 9(2) (emphasis added).

621 *Criminal Code*, RSC 1985, c. C-46, s. 8(3).

622 See: Albin Eser, "'Defences' in War Crime Trials", in Yoram Dinstein, Mala Tabory, eds., *War Crimes in International Law*, The Hague/Boston/London: Kluwer Law International, 1996, pp. 251-273, at 268-269.

623 Éric David, *Principes de droit des conflits armés*, 2nd ed., Brussels: Bruylant, 1999, p. 694, para. 4.184c.

For example, Canadian law explicitly excludes the defence of mistake of law,[624] something that appears to be contemplated by article 32 of the *Rome Statute*. In a prosecution for one of the core crimes, a defendant would therefore be entitled to invoke a defence of mistake of law (this may give Canadian prosecutors a good reason to prefer to charge the traditional underlying offences of murder, theft and rape rather than the international offences of genocide, crimes against humanity and war crimes).

The defence of insanity is set out in section 16 of the *Criminal Code* and in article 31(1)(b) of the *Rome Statute* in terms that are similar but not identical.[625] There would appear to be a fundamental difference, however, respecting the burden of proof. Under Canadian law, a defendant must establish the defence of insanity on a preponderance of evidence.[626] But under the *Rome Statute*, the overriding presumption of innocence seems only to impose upon the defendant the need to raise a reasonable doubt; anything more would conflict with article 67(1)(i) which protects an accused against "any reversal of the burden of proof or any onus of rebuttal".[627] The *Crimes Against Humanity and War Crimes Act* says nothing about the burden of proof of defences, however, and judges may eventually have to decide whether section 11 of the *Act* applies not only to the substantive defences but also to the evidentiary onus.

An aspect of what international law knows as the defence of *ne bis in idem*, and what common law calls the defence of "double jeopardy", is considered in section 12 of the *Act*, as well as in section 607(6) of the *Criminal Code*. Canadian law takes a larger view of the *ne bis in idem* defence than many other jurisdictions. Thus, an acquittal or conviction in a foreign jurisdiction may be set up as an obstacle to prosecution before Canadian courts. Section 607(6) of the *Criminal Code* allows for a special plea of "previously convicted" (*autrefois convict*), "previously acquitted" (*autrefois acquit*) or pardon in the case of international offences that have been tried outside of Canada, where the proceedings have been held *in absentia* or where the offender has not been punished in accordance with the sentence imposed. The provision is a codification of principles of common law.[628] The *Crimes Against Humanity and War Crimes Act* suspends

---

624 *Criminal Code*, supra note 621, s. 19. But see the remarks of Chief Justice Lamer in *R. v. Jorgensen*, [1995] 4 SCR 55.

625 The common law basis of the test in the two instruments is the same, however: *M'Naghten's Case*, (1843) 10 Cl. & Fin 200, 8 ER 718.

626 *Criminal Code*, supra note 621, s. 16(3).

627 But contrast this with the caselaw of the International Criminal Tribunal for the Former Yugoslavia: *Prosecutor v. Delalic* et al. (Case No. IT-96-21-A), Judgment, 20 February 2001, paras. 575-576.

628 *R. v. Riddle*, (1979) [1980] 1 WWR 592, 48 CCC (2d) 365 (SCC).

the effect of section 607(6) and applies a special rule, which is set out in section 12.

Section 13 of the *Act* declares the defence of obedience to law, set out in section 15 of the *Criminal Code*, to be unavailable to prosecution for the three core crimes.[629] According to section 15 of the *Code,* no one shall be convicted of an offence in respect of conduct that was in obedience to laws made by authorities in *de facto* possession of the sovereign power over the place where the conduct occurred. The 1987 amendments to the *Code* had attempted to exclude the defence of section 15, but the wording of the provision gave rise to some ambiguity, and it was argued that judges had a degree of discretion as to the admissibility of the defence of obedience to law.[630] Section 13 of the *Act* endeavours to correct the situation.

The *Crimes Against Humanity and War Crimes Act* offers the limited defence of superior orders as it is codified in article 33 of the *Rome Statute*.[631] Section 14(3) of the *Act* addresses an issue raised by the *Finta* decision,[632] and in effect overrules one of the findings of the Supreme Court of Canada. The majority of the Court, in perhaps the more disturbing aspect of the decision, considered evidence of Nazi propaganda claiming Jews were disloyal to be relevant to the existence of an honest but mistaken belief that orders calling for deportation of Jewish civilians were lawful.[633] Accordingly, the 2000 *Act* declares that "[a]n accused cannot base their [*sic*] defence under subsection (1) on a belief that an order was lawful if the belief was based on information about a civilian population or an identifiable group of persons that encouraged, was likely to encourage or attempted to justify the commission of inhumane acts or omissions against the population or group".[634]

---

629 *Crimes Against Humanity and War Crimes Act, supra* note 620, s. 13.
630 *R. v. Finta,* [1994] 1 SCR 701, 88 CCC (3d) 417, 112 DLR (4th) 513, 150 NR 370, p. 829 (SCR, per Cory J.). Also: M. Cherif Bassiouni, *Crimes Against Humanity in International Law,* 2nd ed., The Hague: Kluwer Law International, 1999, p. 450.
631 *Crimes Against Humanity and War Crimes Act, supra* note 620, c. 24, s. 14.
632 See: Irwin Cotler, "R. v. Finta", (1996) 90 *American Journal of International Law* 460.
633 *R. v. Finta, supra* note 630, pp. 816-817 and 847-848 (SCR, *per* Cory J.).
634 *Crimes Against Humanity and War Crimes Act, supra* note 620, s. 14(3).

4

International Human Rights Law and Canadian Caselaw Under the *Charter*

From their earliest decisions under the *Canadian Charter*, Canadian courts have drawn upon international human rights law as an aid in interpretation. Despite some predictions to the contrary,[1] the enthusiasm was not short-lived, with the superior and the appellate courts continuing to make ample reference to an increasing range of international instruments as well as to the caselaw of the European Commission and Court of Human Rights, the Human Rights Committee, and other international adjudicative bodies. This chapter reviews the references to international human rights law in Canadian cases on the *Charter*, taking a section-by-section approach. References to the relevant provisions of the international instruments are provided for each *Charter* section.

4.1 Limitations and Section 1

Section 1 of the *Canadian Charter* provides that protected rights and freedoms are subject to ". . . such reasonable limits prescribed by law as can be demonstrably justified in a free and democratic society". *Charter* rights are therefore not absolute, something repeated on countless occasions in the decisions. It follows that their scope is defined not only when interpreting the relevant provisions on their own, but also in evaluating their

---

1 Such a prognosis was the minority view however. See: Berend Hovius & Robert Martin, "The Canadian Charter of Rights and Freedoms in the Supreme Court of Canada", (1983) 61 *Canadian Bar Review* 354.

limits within the framework established by section 1.[2] There is nothing comparable to this limitation provision in the *Canadian Bill of Rights*[3] or, for that matter, in the United States *Bill of Rights*. The *Charter*'s limitation section is inspired directly from international human rights instruments that contain similar provisions. Section 1 stands as a prominent and pervasive reminder of the contribution of international human rights law to the application of Canadian legislation and the work of national courts.

The original model of limitations clauses is the *Universal Declaration of Human Rights*.[4] The *Universal Declaration* contains a single limitations clause of general scope, one that is applicable to all of the rights and freedoms set out in that document:

> 29. (2) In the exercise of his rights and freedoms, everyone shall be subject only to such limitations as are determined by law solely for the purpose of securing due recognition and respect for the rights and freedoms of others and of meeting the just requirements of morality, public order and the general welfare in a democratic society.

It should be borne in mind that the *Universal Declaration of Human Rights* was not intended to be a mandatory legal instrument but rather, as its preamble sets out, "a common standard of achievement".[5] When human rights lawmakers sought to create genuinely binding obligations, in the form of international treaties, they opted for a more specific approach to the notion of limitations.

The first to do this were the drafters of the *European Convention on Human Rights*.[6] The acceptable limitations on rights in the *European Convention* vary, depending on the right or freedom in question, and this gives further precision to the extent to which rights and freedoms may be restrained. The *European Convention on Human Rights* contains four quite specific limitation clauses, each of which is appended to the provision

---

2 See: Sidney R. Peck, "An Analytical Framework for the Application of the Canadian Charter of Rights and Freedoms", (1987) 25 *Osgoode Hall Law Journal* 1.

3 RSC 1985, Appendix III. See: Michael Bothe, "La protection des droits fondementaux au Canada", *Jahrbuch des öffentlichen Rechts der Gegenwart*, 1986, at 292-294. Canadian courts did, however, use the somewhat analogous concept of "valid federal objective" to impose a form of limitation on the *Canadian Bill of Rights*: *R. v. Burnshine*, (1974) [1975] 1 SCR 693, 44 DLR (3d) 584, 15 CCC (2d) 505, 25 CRNS 270, [1974] 4 WWR 49. Justice Wilson, in *R. v. Turpin*, [1989] 1 SCR 1296, at 1326-1328, stated that the *Burnshine* approach was inapplicable to the *Charter*.

4 *Universal Declaration of Human Rights*, GA Res. 217 A (III), UN Doc. A/810. See also article 28 of the *American Declaration of the Rights and Duties of Man*, OAS Doc. OEA/Ser. L./V/II.23, doc. 21, rev. 6.

5 See generally: Johannes Morsink, *The Universal Declaration of Human Rights: Origins, Drafting, and Intent*, Philadelphia: University of Pennsylvania Press, 1999.

6 (1955) 213 UNTS 221, ETS 5.

guaranteeing a specific right or freedom. For example, article 8 of the *European Convention* protects the right to respect for private and family life, home and correspondence. This right is subject to limitations that are "in accordance with the law and is necessary in a democratic society", a phrasing that resembles that of section 1 of the *Charter*, with the significant distinction being the *European Convention*'s requirement that the limitation be "necessary" whereas the *Canadian Charter* requires only that it be "reasonable". However, the *European Convention* then goes on to specify the grounds upon which a limitation on this right may be allowed: "in the interests of national security, public safety or the economic well-being of the country, for the prevention of disorder or crime, for the protection of health or morals, or for the protection of the rights and freedoms of others". Article 9 of the *Convention* enshrines the right to freedom of thought, conscience and religion. It permits limitations only to the "freedom to manifest one's religion or beliefs". Although it adopts the same general wording as article 8, it does not refer to national security, the economic well-being of the country, or the prevention of disorder or crime, replacing these criteria with "the protection of public order". Article 10 concerns freedom of expression, which the *European Convention* recalls "carries with it duties and responsibilities". Limitations on this freedom may be justified "in the interests of national security, territorial integrity or public safety, for the prevention of disorder or crime, for the protection of health or morals, for the protection of the reputation or rights of others, for preventing the disclosure of information received in confidence, or for maintaining the authority and impartiality of the judiciary". Finally, article 11 of the *European Convention*, which concerns freedom of assembly and association, including the right to form and join trade unions, allows limitations "in the interests of national security or public safety, for the prevention of disorder or crime, for the protection of health or morals or for the protection of the rights and freedoms of others".

The *International Covenant on Civil and Political Rights*,[7] the *American Convention on Human Rights*[8] and the *African Charter of Human and People' Rights*[9] all contain similar limitations clauses. Besides specific clauses limiting the classic "freedoms", these international instruments also contain limitations clauses in the case of mobility rights,[10] the right to

---

7 (1976) 999 UNTS 171, [1976] CTS 47, arts. 12(3), 18(2), 19(3), 21, 22.

8 *American Convention on Human Rights*, (1979) 1144 UNTS 123, OASTS 36, arts. 15, 16(2), 16(3), 22(3), 23(2), 30.

9 *African Charter on Human and People's Rights*, OAU Doc. CAB/LEG/67/3 rev. 5, 4 EHRR 417, 21 *ILM* 58, arts. 8, 11.

10 *International Covenant on Civil and Political Rights*, *supra* note 7, art. 12(3).

asylum[11], the right to a public trial,[12] the right to property[13] and political rights.[14] Human rights law also provides for specific limitations to particular rights, although not following the same model. For example, the right to life may be limited by capital punishment,[15] and the prohibition on slavery does not include forced labour as part of a prison sentence or alternative service for conscientious objectors.[16] Finally, some limitations are implicit, even in the absence of a specific clause. The *International Covenant on Civil and Political Rights* does not recognize explicitly the right to self defence as a limitation on the right to life, although this most surely exists.[17] Similarly, the presumption of innocence, which is recognized in the fair trial provisions of all of the major instruments, does not appear subject to any limitations. Yet caselaw has acknowledged that in certain cases the burden of proof in criminal proceedings may be reversed, and an onus of presentation imposed upon the defendant.[18]

The ancestor of section 1 of the *Canadian Charter* made its appearance in the Statement of Conclusions at the Third Constitutional Conference, 8-9 February 1971:

> It was agreed to entrench in the Constitution the following basic political rights:
>
> (a) universal suffrage and free, democratic elections at least every five years;
> (b) freedom of thought, conscience and religion;
> (c) freedom of peaceful assembly and association.
>
> The exercise of these freedoms may be subject only to such limitations as are prescribed by law and as are reasonably justifiable in a democratic society in

---

11 *Ibid.*, art. 13.

12 *Ibid.*, art. 14(1).

13 *American Convention on Human Rights, supra* note 8, art. 21(2); *African Charter of Human and Peoples' Rights, supra* note 9, art. 14.

14 *American Convention on Human Rights, supra* note 8, art. 23(2).

15 *International Covenant on Civil and Political Rights, supra* note 7, art. 6(2); *European Convention on Human Rights, supra* note 6, art. 2(1); *American Convention on Human Rights, supra* note 8, art. 4(2).

16 *International Covenant on Civil and Political Rights, supra* note 7, art. 8(3)(*b*); *European Convention on Human Rights, supra* note 6, art. 4(3); *American Convention on Human Rights, supra* note 8, art. 6(3).

17 It is, however, explicitly set out in the *European Convention on Human Rights, supra* note 6, art. 2(2).

18 See: Nihal Jayawickrama, *The Judicial Application of Human Rights Law – National, Regional and International Jurisprudence*, Cambridge, Cambridge University Press, 2002, at 535-550.

the interests of national security, public safety, health or morals or the fundamental rights and freedoms of others.[19]

But after this initial proposal, the drafters of the *Charter* set aside the idea
of a general limitation clause, like that in the *Universal Declaration*, and
contemplated instead the use of specific limitations clauses, similar to those
found in the *European Convention on Human Rights*,[20] the *International
Covenant on Civil and Political Rights*[21] and the *American Convention on
Human Rights*.[22] Such an approach was followed in a July 1980 draft of the
Charter. Subsequent versions, notably the one presented to Parliament in
October 1980, provided once again for a single clause along the lines of the
eventual section 1 that appears in the finished document.[23] Canada's single
limitations clause has since provided a prototype for other constitutions,
notably that of the Republic of South Africa.[24]

---

19 *Debates*, HC, 1971, Appendix "A", 3268. See: Errol P. Mendes, "The Crucible of the
Charter: Judicial Principles v. Judicial Deference in the Context of Section 1", in Gerald-
A. Beaudoin & Errol P. Mendes, eds., *Canadian Charter of Rights and Freedoms*, 4th
ed., Markham, Ont., LexisNexis Butterworths, 2005, pp. 163-214, at 168-169; Janet L.
Hiebert, "The Evolution of the Limitation Clause", (1990), 28 *Osgoode Hall Law Journal*
103, and Robin Elliott, "Interpreting the Charter – Use of the Earlier Versions as an Aid",
(1982) 16 *Charter Edition University of British Columbia Law Review* 11.

20 *Supra* note 6, arts. 8(2), 9(2), 10(2), 11(2).

21 *Supra* note 7, arts. 12(3), 18(2), 19(3), 21, 22.

22 *Supra* note 8, arts. 15, 16(2), 16(3), 22(3), 23(2), 30.

23 André Morel, "La recherche d'un équilibre entre les pouvoirs législatif et judiciaire –
essai de psychologie judiciaire," in Armand De Mestral *et al.*, eds., *The Limitation of
Human Rights in Comparative Constitutional Law*, Cowansville: Editions Yvon Blais,
1986, pp 115-135, at 116.

24 See: Peter W. Hogg, "Canadian Law in the Constitutional Court of South Africa", (1998),
13 *South African Publiekreg/Public Law* 1. The South African limitation clause appears
in section 39(1) of the *Constitution of the Republic of South Africa (Act No. 108 of 1996)*,
which reads:

> 1. The rights in the Bill of Rights may be limited only in terms of law of general
> application to the extent that the limitation is reasonable and justifiable in an open
> and democratic society based on human dignity, equality and freedom, taking into
> account all relevant factors, including
> a. the nature of the right;
> b. the importance of the purpose of the limitation;
> c. the nature and extent of the limitation;
> d. the relation between the limitation and its purpose; and
> e. less restrictive means to achieve the purpose.

See: Jeremy Sarkin, "The Drafting of South Africa's Final Constitution from a Human-
Rights Perspective", (1999) 47 *American Journal of Comparative Law* 67; Lourens M.
Du Plessis, "The Bill of Rights in the Working Draft of the New Constitution: An
Evaluation of Aspects of a Constitutional Text *Sui Generis*", (1995) 6 *Stellenbosch Law
Review* 3.

The drafters of the *Charter* were aware of limitations clauses not only because of their place in the international authorities but also because, by ricochet, such provisions had found their way into a number of constitutions of Commonwealth countries. In effect, the British ensured that at the time of decolonisation most of their former territories were provided with constitutional instruments patterned on the *European Convention on Human Rights*, which already applied to the territory in question.[25] One consequence of this was that limitations clauses had already been considered by the Judicial Committee of the Privy Council, sitting as a Commonwealth court of last instance. This may well have made Canadian lawyers and lawmakers more comfortable with the whole concept. According to the late Justice Walter Tarnopolsky of the Ontario Court of Appeal:

> Section 1 of the *Charter* was designed pursuant to scrutiny of Commonwealth and international bills of rights. . . In formulating a limitation provision, the Charter's drafters had one eye on the American constitutional experience, where courts were left to fashion limitations upon rights that had been guaranteed in absolutist language, and the other on several post-war conventions, which contain explicit restrictions on the ambit of civil and political rights.[26]

Yet, as Justice Tarnopolsky observed, the influence of United States law cannot be gainsaid. Nevertheless, if the drafters of the *Canadian Charter* had one eye on the United States approach and another on the international approach, they clearly favoured the latter.[27] The Ontario Court of Appeal noted, in *McKinney* v. *University of Guelph*, that because "post-war Charters" such as the *International Covenant on Civil and Political Rights* and the *European Convention on Human Rights* include limitations clauses, they are therefore quite different from the United States *Bill of Rights*, where rights and freedoms are proclaimed in an absolute fashion and their limitation left to the total discretion of the courts. According to the Ontario

---

25 See: A.W. Brian Simpson, *Human Rights and the End of Empire: Britain and the Genesis of the European Convention*, Oxford, New York: Oxford University Press, 2001.

26 *R.* v. *Squires*, (1992) 78 CCC (3d) 97 (Ont. CA), leave to appeal refused, (1993) 25 CR (4th) 103n (S.C.C.), at 124 (CCC). See also: Walter S. Tarnopolsky, *The Canadian Bill of Rights*, Toronto: McClelland and Stewart, 1975, at 18.

27 On the two options, see: Robert Wai, "Justice Gérard La Forest and the Internationalist Turn in Canadian Jurisprudence", in R. Johnson *et al.*, *Gérard V. La Forest at the Supreme Court of Canada, 1985-1997*, Winnipeg: Faculty of Law: University of Manitoba, 2000, at 471; Jamie Cameron, "The First Amendment and Section 1 of the Charter", (1990) 1 *Media & Communication Law Review* 59; Berend Hovius, "The Limitation Clauses of the European Convention on Human Rights and Freedoms", (1986) 6 *Yearbook of European Law* 1; Berend Hovius, "The Limitation Clauses of the European Convention of Human Rights: A Guide for the Application of Section 1 of the Charter?", (1985) 17 *Ottawa Law Review* 213; and Paul Bender, "The Canadian Charter and the U.S. Bill of Rights", (1983) 28 *McGill Law Journal* 811.

Court of Appeal, the *Canadian Charter* is therefore "more like" the international instruments than it is like the United States *Bill of Rights*.[28] The Court of Appeal added: "The *Canadian Charter* carries the pattern of post war charters one step further by providing only one limitation clause in s. 1 which applies to all rights and freedoms guaranteed by the Charter."[29] In *Committee for the Commonwealth of Canada*, Justice Hugessen of the Federal Court of Appeal spoke of the "overly absolute formulation of certain rights" in the United States *Bill of Rights*, something he said that the *Canadian Charter*'s limitations clause, with its international models, had sought to avoid.[30] In *R. v. Keegstra*, the majority of the Supreme Court of Canada rejected the more "absolutist" approach of the United States *Bill of Rights* to freedom of expression in favour of the more nuanced view that flows from the international models.[31]

In its fourth periodic report to the Human Rights Committee, the Government of Canada commented on the relationship between the limitations clauses of the *Covenant* and the *Canadian Charter*:

> Indeed, on occasion, the courts have referred to the limitation clauses in the Covenant as an aid in assessing whether a limitation on a Charter right or freedom was acceptable. For example, in Ontario (Attorney-General) v. Dieleman, the Ontario Court (General Division) referred to the objective of protecting public health included in the limitation clauses in articles 18, 19, 21 and 22 of the Covenant in concluding that protecting the health of women seeking abortions was an objective of sufficient importance to justify limiting the freedom of expression of anti-abortion activists outside abortion clinics.[32]

Not all Canadian judges have been enthusiastic about the use of the international models in the construction of section 1 of the *Charter*. In her dissenting judgment in *R. v. Keegstra*, Justice McLachlin, as she then was, considered the analogy between section 1 of the *Charter* and article 10(2)

---

28 *McKinney* v. *University of Guelph*, (1987) 46 DLR (4th) 193, 29 Admin LR 227, 24 OAC 241 (CA), affirmed, (1990) 1990 CarswellOnt 1019 (SCC), at 221 (DLR); the Ontario Court of Appeal referred to Peter W. Hogg, *Constitutional Law of Canada*, 2nd ed., Toronto: Carswell, 1985, at 680; see also Peter W. Hogg, "Section one of the Canadian Charter of Rights and Freedoms", in Armand De Mestral *et al.*, *supra* note 23, pp. 3-40, at 6. The Canada Labour Relations Board has also noted that section 1 of the *Charter* has "wording roughly similar" to the *European Convention*, except that the *European Convention* specifies limits for each specific right: *Union of Bank Employees (Ontario), Local 2104* v. *Bank of Montreal*, (1985) 10 CLRBR (ns) 129, 61 di 83.

29 *McKinney* v. *University of Guelph, ibid.*, at 222 (DLR).

30 *Committee for the Commonwealth of Canada v. Canada*, [1987] 2 FC 68, 36 DLR (4th) 501, 76 NR 338 (CA), affirmed, (1991) 1991 CarswellNat 827 (SCC), reconsideration refused, (May 8, 1991) Doc. 20334 (SCC), at 511 (DLR).

31 *R. v. Keegstra*, (1990) [1990] 3 SCR 697, 61 CCC (3d) 1, [1991] 2 WWR (2d) 193, 1 CR (4th) 129, 3 CRR (2d) 193, 77 Alta LR (2d) 193 114 AR 81, 117 NR 1.

32 UN Doc. CCPR/C/103/Add.5, para. 12.

of the *European Convention on Human Rights*, providing for limits on freedom of expression, to be inappropriate. She noted that the European Commission on Human Rights "had little difficulty in holding that prosecutions for dissemination of racist ideas and literature are permitted" under article 10(2) of the *Convention*. She added:

> In view of the breadth of the limitations clause, which specifically mentions the protection of "health or morals" and "the reputation or rights of others", this is unsurprising. In other contexts, protection for free expression under this article has at times been decidedly lukewarm, as befits an international instrument which is designed to limit as little as possible the sovereignty of the nations that signed it.[33]

She referred critically to the famous *Handyside* judgment of the European Court of Human Rights,[34] which dismissed the petition of a Northern Irish bookseller who had been prosecuted for selling an educational book on sexuality aimed at adolescents on grounds of "the protection of health or morals".[35] Justice McLachlin continued, comparing the approach of the international instruments with that of the American courts pursuant to the first amendment to the United States *Constitution*.

> These international instruments embody quite a different conception of freedom of expression than the caselaw under the U.S. First Amendment. The international decisions reflect the much more explicit priorities of the relevant documents regarding the relationship between freedom of expression and the objective of eradicating speech which advocates racial and cultural hatred. The approach seems to be to read down freedom of expression to the extent necessary to accommodate the legislation prohibiting the speech in question.
>
> Both the American and international approach recognize that freedom of expression is not absolute, and must yield in some circumstances to other values. The divergence lies in the way the limits are determined. On the international approach, the objective of suppressing hatred appears to be sufficient to override freedom of expression. In the United States, it is necessary to go much further and show clear and present danger before free speech can be overriden.[36]

In her view, the *Canadian Charter* "follows the American approach in method. . . This in keeping with the strong liberal tradition favouring free speech in this country. . ."[37] Justice McLachlin's views were rejected by the

---

33 *R.* v. *Keegstra, supra* note 31, at 820 (SCR).

34 *Handyside* v. *United Kingdom*, 7 December 1976, Series A, No. 24, 1 EHRR 737, 59 ILR 150.

35 *R.* v. *Keegstra, supra* note 31, at 820 (SCR).

36 *Ibid.*, at 822 (SCR). See also: *Canada (HRC)* v. *Taylor*, [1990] 3 SCR 892, 75 DLR (4th) 577, 13 CHRR 435, 3 CRR (2d) 116, at 952 (SCR).

37 *R.* v. *Keegstra, ibid.*, at 822 (SCR).

majority, which opted for an approach to freedom of expression and its limits that is more closely aligned with the international models.[38] In *R. v. Butler*, which was decided the following year, Justices Gonthier and L'Heureux-Dubé cited article 10(2) of the *European Convention* and the *Handyside* case, noting that the validity of prohibitions of obscene materials was well accepted as a limitation on freedom of expression in European human rights law.[39]

Justice McLachlin's observation that the *European Convention*'s limitations clause is extremely broad because it is an international instrument designed to limit as little as possible the sovereignty of the States parties is of some interest. This point should certainly be borne in mind by Canadian courts when they transpose European caselaw to the section 1 analysis. Perhaps even more important is an understanding of the European Court's "margin of appreciation" doctrine, which is a form of deference based on respect for different cultural and judicial traditions in the States parties to the *European Convention on Human Rights*.[40] Until the beginning of the 1990s, the *Convention* was confined principally to Western European States, and the "margin of appreciation" was thus applied in a relatively homogeneous context. But the application of the *European Convention* has since considerably expanded in jurisdictional and cultural terms, covering virtually all of Central and Eastern Europe, and in fact extending deep into Asia with the admission of the Russian Federation to the Council of Europe in 1996. In a recent ruling, for example, the European Court of Human Rights invoked the "margin of appreciation" and refused to condemn Turkish legislation that prohibited university students from wearing Islamic headscarves out of deference to the country's secular policies despite the rather flagrant incompatibility of such measures with the protection of freedom of religion.[41]

Some of the initial enthusiasm for the use of international models in the interpretation of section 1 seems to have worn off. Since 1996 there has

---

38 On the *Keegstra* case and its impact on the role of international human rights law in *Charter* interpretation, see: William A. Schabas & Daniel Turp, "La *Charte canadienne des droits et libertés* et le droit international: les enseignements de la Cour suprême dans les affaires *Keegstra, Andrews* et *Taylor*", (1989-90) 6 *Revue québécoise de droit international* 12; and Anne W. La Forest, "Domestic Application of International Law in *Charter* Cases: Are We There Yet?", (2004) 37 *University of British Columbia Law Review* 157.

39 *R. v. Butler*, [1992] 1 SCR 452, 70 CCC (3d) 129, 89 DLR (4th) 449, 11 CR (4th) 137, 8 CRR (2d) 1, [1992] 2 WWR 577, 78 Man R (2d) 1, 134 NR 81, reconsideration refused, [1993] 2 WWR lxi (SCC), at 533 (SCR).

40 See, generally: Howard Charles Yourow, *The Margin of Appreciation Doctrine in the Dynamics of European Human Rights Jurisprudence*, The Hague: Martinus Nijhoff, 1996.

41 *Şahin v. Turkey* (App. No. 44774/98), 10 November 2005, paras. 110, 111, 122.

been only one reference in a majority opinion at the Supreme Court of Canada to the *European Convention* in a section 1 analysis.[42] It is noteworthy that, albeit in the context of defining freedom of association at section 2(d) of the *Charter*, the majority made the following remarks in *R. c. Advance Cutting & Coring Ltd.*:[43] "Thus, interesting as it may be, the consideration of European jurisprudence is not determinative."[44] In *Advance Cutting*, Justice LeBel, referring to a specific right rather than its limitations clause, made remarks that are most apposite in relation to section 1:

> It must be understood, as well, that the European Convention is applied in a legal environment that reflects a different history of labour relations than in Canada or Quebec, in particular. The structures and methods of collective bargaining, the patterns of union organization and their status within the enterprise all differ deeply from the Canadian experience in the development of labour law and the management of labour relations. These labour systems may reject the principle of monopoly representation by a particular union or forms of union security like the union shop and the compulsory check off of union dues. On the other hand, the right to strike may be affirmed by the constitution itself, as in France. (See A. Mazeaud, *Droit du travail* (2nd ed. 2000), at pp. 204-5.) Many European nations recognize the broad societal role which unions play, and have entrenched union rights to participate in the management of private commercial and industrial enterprises. (See M. Weiss, "Workers" Participation in the European Union", in P. Davies et al., eds., *European Community Labour Law: Principles and Perspectives* (1996), 213; B. Bercusson, *European Labour Law* (1997), at pp. 248-61.) The labour laws of a country

---

42   *R.* v. *Lucas*, [1998] 1 SCR 439, at para. 50, *per* Cory J. for the majority. The reference was to article 10 of the *European Convention on Human Rights*, along with other international and regional human rights instruments protecting freedom of expression, in support of the following broad proposition: "The existence of these provisions reflects a consensus within the international community that the protection of reputation is an objective sufficiently important to warrant placing some restrictions upon freedom of expression."

43   *R.* v. *Advance Cutting & Coring Ltd.*, [2001] 3 SCR 209, 205 DLR (4th) 385, 87 CRR (2d) 189.

44   *Ibid.*, at para. 251. These words are reminiscent of those expressed in 1991 by Justice Wilson in *Lavigne v. Ontario Public Service Employees Union*, [1991] 2 SCR 211, 81 DLR (4th) 545, 4 CRR (2d) 193, 22 CLLC 12,257, 3 OR 511, 126 NR 161, 48 OAC 241, reconsideration refused, (1991) (1991), 4 OR (3d) xii (SCC), at 256-257 (SCR):

> [T]his Court must exercise caution in adopting any decision, however compelling, of a foreign jurisdiction. This Court has consistently stated that even although it may undoubtedly benefit from the experience of American and other courts in adjudicating constitutional issues, it is by no means bound by that experience or the jurisprudence it generated. The uniqueness of the *Canadian Charter of Rights and Freedoms* flows not only from the distinctive structure of the *Charter* as compared to the American Bill of Rights but also from the special features of the Canadian cultural, historical, and social and political tradition.

evidence a social and political compromise about the place of unions in that society and the proper balance between unions and employers.[45]

This caveat goes a long way in qualifying the role of the European human rights experience in *Charter* caselaw and in alleviating the concerns identified above with respect to the influence of the "margin of appreciation" on section 1.

Since the mid-1990s, there has been a very measureable decline in reference by the Canadian courts, including the Supreme Court of Canada, to European caselaw. Perhaps the more distant approach to European law in the application of section 1 in recent years simply results from the fact that the Canadian courts now have their own well-established methodology, and may feel they have little to learn from the European Court of Human Rights and similar bodies in this area. Interestingly, the Supreme Court of Canada has developed its own ways to promote deference vis-à-vis government measures within the framework of the *Charter* limitation clause. First, *RJR-MacDonald Inc. v. Canada (Attorney General)*[46] confirmed that legislatures ought to enjoy a certain degree of latitude in adopting measures, especially where there are competing social, political or economic claims from different sectors of society.[47] "While deference is appropriate", Justice Iacobucci stated in *Little Sisters Book and Art Emporium v. Canada (Minister of Justice)*, "our Court cannot abdicate its duty to demand that the government justify legislation limiting Charter rights".[48] Second, the 1998 decision in *Vriend v. Alberta*[49] saw Canadian constitutional law adopt a new metaphor, that of the "dialogue" among the branches of government.[50] It is

---

45 *R. v. Advance Cutting & Coring Ltd.*, *supra* note 43, at para. 251.

46 *RJR-Macdonald Inc.* v. *Canada*, [1995] 3 SCR 199, 127 DLR (4th) 1, *per* McLachlin J., at para. 135-136.

47 This idea was first set out in *Irwin Toy* v. *Québec (AG)*, [1989] 1 SCR 927, 39 CRR 193, 25 CPR (3d) 417, 58 DLR (4th) 577, 94 NR 167, 24 QAC 2, at 993-994 (SCR). A recent manifestation appears in the remarks of Justice Deschamps in *Chaoulli* v. *Québec (Attorney General)*, [2005] 1 SCR 791, at paras. 85-95.

48 *Little Sisters Book and Art Emporium* v. *Canada (Minister of Justice)*, [2000] 2 SCR 1120, at para. 221. See also: Janice Benedet, "Little Sisters Book and Art Emporium v. Minister of Justice: Sex Equality and the Attack on R. v. Butler", (2001) 39 *Osgoode Hall Law Journal* 187; and Brenda Cossman, "Disciplining the Unruly Sexual Outlaws, *Little Sisters* and the Legacy of *Butler*", (2003) 36 *University of British Columbia Law Review* 77.

49 *Vriend* v. *Alberta*, [1998] 1 SCR 493, at 565-566. See also *R.* v. *Mills*, [1999] 3 SCR 668, at 711-713.

50 See: Peter W. Hogg & Allison A. Bushell, "The *Charter* Dialogue Between Courts and Legislatures", (1997) 35 *Osgoode Hall Law Journal* 75. See also: Kent Roach, "Constitutional and Common Law Dialogues Between the Supreme Court and Canadian Legislatures", (2001) 81 *Canadian Bar Review* 481; Kent Roach, "Dialogic Judicial Review and its Critics", (2004) 23 *Supreme Court Law Review* (2d) 49; and Luc B. Tremblay,

not yet clear what impact this latest doctrine will have on the limitation clause, but the fact that it prompted the following comment by Justice Gonthier, dissenting in *Sauvé v. Canada (Chief Electoral Officer)*, is not insignificant: "Importantly, the dialogue metaphor *does not signal a lowering of the s. 1 justification standard.*"[51] But that is exactly what it seems to call for, especially when associated with a deferential approach, just as the idea of "margin of appreciation" does for the *European Convention on Human Rights*.

4.1.1   Specific International Models for "Reasonable Limits"

The *Canadian Charter* departs from the approach in international human rights treaties in its use of a general limitations clause of universal application, rather than employing detailed limitations clauses for individual rights. Despite this distinction, the more elaborate limitations provisions in the *International Covenant on Civil and Political Rights* and the *European Convention on Human Rights* have frequently been employed by Canadian courts to assist in defining the scope of section 1. In effect, the individually tailored limitations clauses of the international treaties provide guidance on the relevant particularities to be considered in addressing specific rights and freedoms. Limitations on freedom of expression may be somewhat different than those on freedom of religion, for example, and the clauses in the international treaties are helpful in making the distinctions.

According to Justice Macfarlane of the British Columbia Court of Appeal, the quite specific limitations clauses of the *European Convention* and the *International Covenant on Civil and Political Rights* ". . .demonstrate the type of reasonable limit which may be justified in a free and democratic society".[52] In *International Fund for Animal Welfare Inc* v. *Canada*,[53] Justice MacGuigan of the Federal Court of Appeal seemed to accept the argument that article 19(3) of the *International Covenant on Civil*

"Legitimacy of Judicial Review: The Limits of Dialogue Between Courts and Legislatures", (2005) 3 *International Journal of Constitutional Law* 617.

51   *Sauvé* v. *Canada (Chief Electoral Officer)*, [2002] 3 SCR 519, 218 DLR (4th) 577, 168 CCC (3d) 449, 5 CR (6th) 203, 98 CRR (2d) 1, at para. 104 (emphasis in the original).

52   *Hirt* v. *College of Physicians & Surgeons*, (1985) 17 DLR (4th) 472, 60 BCLR 273 (CA); see also *R.* v. *Hothi*, [1985] 3 WWR 256, 33 Man R (2d) 180, (sub nom. *Singh v. R.*) 14 CRR 85 (QB), affirmed, [1986] 3 WWR 671 (CA), leave to appeal refused, (1986) 70 N.R. 397n (SCC); *R.* v. *Kopyto*, (1988) 47 DLR (4th) 213, 39 CCC (3d) 1, 61 CR (3d) 109, 62 OR (2d) 449 (CA) (*per* Houlden JA); *Association des membres de la Division "C"* v. *G.R.C. (Ottawa)* (1987) 14 CLRBR (NS) 46, [1986] DLQ 450n.

53   *International Fund for Animal Welfare Inc., Best and Davies* v. *Canada*, (1988) [1989] 1 FC 335, 83 NR 303, 35 CRR 359 (CA).

and Political Rights,[54] the limitations clause of that instrument's freedom of expression provision, helped define objectives to be considered in determining the scope of section 1's "reasonable limits". In *R.* v. *Big M Drug Mart Ltd.*,[55] Chief Justice Dickson used language similar to that of article 9(2) of the *European Convention*, although he made no direct reference to the instrument in his reasons.[56] Justice Adams of the Ontario Court, General Division, referred to the limitations clauses in the *International Covenant on Civil and Political Rights* dealing with the freedoms of religion, expression, assembly and association, showing that they are subordinated to concerns for health.[57]

In a British Columbia Court of Appeal case, *Hirt* v. *College of Physicians*,[58] the *Vancouver Sun* had invoked section 2(b) of the *Charter* in support of a motion to quash an *in camera* order imposed during a disciplinary inquiry into a doctor's alleged sexual activities with his patients. The *in camera* order had been made to protect the privacy of the complainants, who were testifying at the hearing. But nothing in the *Canadian Charter* guarantees expressly the right to privacy, and Canadian courts had already expressed their eagerness to ensure that justice be done in public and that the freedom of the press be guaranteed.[59] Justice Macfarlane upheld the *in camera* order in the interests of the privacy of the witnesses. He relied on article 14(1) of the *International Covenant on Civil and Political Rights* and article 10 of the *European Convention*. In effect, both documents, using wording that is relatively similar, explain that courts may proceed *in camera* "when the interest of the private lives of the parties so requires". According to the learned judge, "those instruments demonstrate the type of reasonable

---

54 *International Covenant on Civil and Political Rights,* (1976) 999 UNTS 171, [1976] CTS 47:

> (3) The exercise of the rights provided for in paragraph 2 of this article carries with it special duties and responsibilities. It may therefore be subject to certain restrictions, but these shall only be such as are provided by law and are necessary:
> a) For respect of the rights or reputations of others;
> b) For the protection of national security or of public order (*ordre public*), or of public health or morals.

For a recent application by the United Nations Human Rights Committee, see: *Lovell* v. *Australia* (No. 920/2000), UN Doc. CCPR/C/80/D/920/2000.

55 [1984] 1 WWR 625, 5 DLR (4th) 121, 9 CCC (3d) 310, 28 Alta LR (2d) 289, 49 AR 194, 7 CRR 92 (CA), affirmed, [1985] 1 SCR 295.

56 *Union of Bank Employees (Ont.), Loc. 2104* v. *Bank of Montreal,* (1985) 10 CLRBR (NS) 129, 61 di 83 (Can LRB).

57 *Ontario (Attorney General)* v. *Dieleman,* (1994) 20 OR (3d) 229 (Ont Gen Div), at 281-282 [OR], additional reasons at, (1995) 22 OR (3d) 785, 22 OR (3d) 785 at 794.

58 *Supra* note 52.

59 *Re Southam Inc. and R. (No. 1),* (1983) 146 DLR (3d) 408, 3 CCC (3d) 515, 41 OR (2d) 113, 33 RFL (2d) 279, 34 CR (3d) 27 (CA).

limit which may be justified in a free and democratic society".[60] He continued: ". . .a court order which achieves the purpose of protecting the innocent by non-disclosure of their identities, or any information which could disclose their identities, is a reasonable limit prescribed by law as can be demonstrably justified in a free and democratic society."[61]

In his dissent in *Edmonton Journal* v. *Alta (AG)*, Justice La Forest referred to article 19(3) of the *International Covenant on Civil and Political Rights* and article 10(2) of the *European Convention on Human Rights* for assistance in determining the nature of limits that would be permissible on the right to freedom of expression and, as in *Hirt*, he expressly referred to the right to privacy.[62] In *R.* v. *Kopyto*, Justice Cory, then of the Ontario Court of Appeal, cited article 10(2) of the *European Convention* (limiting freedom of speech), and noted that: ". . .like other courts in other jurisdictions, the European Court of Human Rights has stressed the paramount importance of freedom of expression in a free and democratic society, and has limited the scope of the restriction imposed on the freedom."[63]

4.1.2   "Prescribed by Law"

The term "prescribed by law" in section 1 of the *Canadian Charter* finds its equivalent in the limitations clauses of the *Universal Declaration of Human Rights* ("determined by law"), the *European Convention on*

---

60 *Hirt* v. *College of Physicians, supra* note 52, at 282 (BCLR). But it is interesting to note that the French Cour de cassation has considered similar provisions in that country's professional law to be contrary to art. 6(1) of the *European Convention on Human Rights*: Cour de cassation (1re ch. civ.), 10 January 1984, JCP. 84, II, 20210, concl. avoc. gén. Gulphe; Rev. dr. civ. 1984, 771, observ. Perrot. The European Court of Human Rights has also held that professional disciplinary proceedings be held in public, at least in the absence of a request to the contrary from the subject of the inquiry: *H.* v. *Belgium*, 30 November 1987, Series A, No. 127, 10 EHRR 339; see also *Albert and Le Compte* v. *Belgium*, 10 February 1983, Series A, No. 58; *Le Compte, van Leuven and de Meyere* v. *Belgium*, 23 June 1981, Series A, No. 43, 4 EHRR 1.

61 *Hirt* v. *College of Physicians, ibid.*, at 285-286 (BCLR).

62 *Edmonton Journal* v. *Alberta (AG)*, [1989] 2 SCR 1326, 64 DLR (4th) 577, [1990] 1 WWR 557, 41 CPC (2) 109, 45 CRR 1, 103 AR 321, 71 Alta LR (2d) 273, 102 NR 321, at 1374 (SCR). Prior to proclamation of the *Charter*, the Supreme Court of Canada had dismissed the "privacy argument" as a basis for judicial secrecy: *AG (Nova Scotia)* v. *MacIntyre* , [1982] 1 SCR 175, at 185. Michael Bothe reviews the fact that the right to privacy was included in the 1980 draft of the *Charter*, and then left out of the final version, an omission he says was "de toute apparence, voulue": Michael Bothe, "La protection des droits fondementaux au Canada", *Jahrbuch des öffentlichen Rechts der Gegenwart*, 1986. The Supreme Court of Canada has also considered that section 8 of the *Charter* serves to protect privacy: *Hunter* v. *Southam*, [1984] 6 WWR 577, 41 CR (3d) 97, 33 Alta LR (2d) 193, 27 BLR 297, 84 DTC 6467, [1984] 2 SCR 145, (1984) 11 DLR (4th) 641, 14 CCC (3d) 97, 2 CPR (3d) 1, 55 AR 291, 9 CRR 355, 55 NR 241.

63 *R.* v. *Kopyto, supra* note 52, at 238 (DLR, *per* Cory JA).

Human Rights[64] and the *International Covenant on Civil and Political Rights.*[65] According to Manfred Nowak, author of the authoritative work on the *International Covenant*, a systematic interpretation of the differences in formulation leads to the conclusion that there is no distinction intended between the terms "prescribed by law", "provided by law", "established by law" and "prévues par la loi". He has suggested, however, that the limitations clauses concerning protection of aliens against arbitrary expulsion ("in accordance with law"/"conformément à la loi") and freedom of assembly ("in conformity with the law"/"conformément à la loi") should be interpreted less strictly.[66]

The European Court of Human Rights has interpreted the meaning of "prescribed by law" in several decisions.[67] In the celebrated *Sunday Times* case it held that the law must be accessible and formulated in such a precise way as to enable the citizen to regulate and control his behaviour.[68] The

64 The English version of article 8(2) of the *European Convention on Human Rights*, uses the term "in accordance with the law" as do provisions in *Protocol No. 4* and *Protocol No. 7*; articles 9(2), 10(2) and 11(2) use the term "prescribed by law". With a few exceptions, the French version of similar provisions in the *European Convention on Human Rights* uses "prévues par la loi".

65 Articles 18(3) and 22(2) use the term "prescribed by law", article 9 says "established by law", article 13 uses "in accordance with the law", articles 12(3) and 19(3) say "provided by law", article 21 says "in conformity with the law"; the French version uses "prévues par la loi" (arts. 9, 12, 18 and 22), "fixées par la loi" (art. 19) and "conformément à la loi" (arts. 13 and 21)

66 Mandred Nowak, *Covenant on Civil and Political Rights, CCPR Commentary*, 2nd ed., Kehl, Strasbourg, Arlington: N.P. Engel, 2005, pp. 287-289.

67 *Sunday Times* v. *United Kingdom*, 26 April 1979, Series A, No. 30, 2 EHRR 245, 58 ILR 491; *Larissi* et al. v. *Greece* (App. No. 23372/94), Reports 1998-I, p. 378, para. 40; *Hashman and Harrup* v. *United Kingdom* (App. No. 25594/94), 25 November 1999, Reports 1999-VIII, para. 31; and *Rotaru* v. *Romania* (App. No. 28341/950), 4 May 2000, Reports 2000-V, para. 52.

68 Justice MacGuigan of the Federal Court of Appeal, referring to *Sunday Times* v. *United Kingdom, ibid.,* called this the "forseeability rule": *Committee for the Commonwealth of Canada* v. *Canada*, [1987] 2 FC 68, 36 DLR (4th) 501, 76 NR 338 (CA), affirmed, (1991) 1991 CarswellNat 827 (SCC), reconsideration refused, (May 8, 1991) Doc. 20334 (SCC). See the discussion of the *Sunday Times* case in Clare Beckton, "Freedom of expression", in Walter S. Tarnopolsky & Gérald-A. Beaudoin, eds., *The Canadian Charter of Rights and Freedoms: Commentary*, Toronto: Carswell, 1982; L.Neville Brown, "Thalidomide, the 'Sunday Times' and the Reform of the English Law of Contempt of Court", in Daniel Turp & Gérald-A. Beaudoin, eds., *Perspectives canadiennes et européennes des droits de la personne*, Cowansville: Editions Yvon Blais, 1986, pp. 527-541; Vincent Berger, *Jurisprudence de la Cour européenne des droits de l'homme*, Paris: Sirey, 1994, pp. 342-346; Christine Gray, "European Convention on Human Rights. Freedom of Expression and the Thalidomide Case", (1979) 38 *Commonwealth Law Journal* 242; Francis Mann, "Contempt of Court in the House of Lords and the European Court of Human Rights", (1979) 95 *Law Quarterly Review* 348.

finding overturned a judgment of the English House of Lords upholding a conviction for contempt of court.[69] The European Court declared:

> 49. In the Court's opinion, the following are two of the requirements that flow from the expression "prescribed by law". First, the last must be adequately accessible: the citizen must be able to have an indication that is adequate in the circumstances of the legal rules applicable to a given case. Secondly, a norm cannot be regarded as a "law" unless it is formulated with sufficient precision to enable the citizen to regulate his conduct: he must be able – if need be with appropriate advice – to foresee, to a degree that is reasonable in the circumstances, the consequences which a given action may entail. . .[70]

More recently, the European Court has held that legislation that was "arbitrary" and that was "based on legal provisions which allowed an unfettered discretion to the executive and did not meet the required standards of clarity and foreseeability" failed to meet the "prescribed by law" criterion.[71] According to the Court:

> For domestic law to meet these requirements it must afford a measure of legal protection against arbitrary interferences by public authorities with the rights safeguarded by the Convention. In matters affecting fundamental rights it would be contrary to the rule of law, one of the basic principles of a democratic society enshrined in the Convention, for a legal discretion granted to the executive to be expressed in terms of an unfettered power. Consequently, the law must indicate with sufficient clarity the scope of any such discretion conferred on the competent authorities and the manner of its exercise.[72]

The caselaw of the European Court was analysed in some detail by Justice Gonthier of the Supreme Court of Canada in the context of a discussion of the "void for vagueness" doctrine in *R. v. Nova Scotia Pharmaceutical Society*.[73] He noted that *Sunday Times* gave the notion of "prescribed by law" a substantive content. For the European Court, legislation must be both "accessible" and "foreseeable". In a subsequent judgment, noted Justice Gonthier, the European Court "added the limitation of enforcement discretion to the range of interests underpinning its interpretation of 'prescribed by law'".[74] The European Court stated: "The phrase [prescribed

---

69 *A.G.* v. *Times Newspapers Ltd.*, [1974] AC 273 (HL).

70 *Sunday Times* v. *United Kingdom*, *supra* note 67.

71 *Hasan and Chaush* v. *Bulgaria* (App. No. 30985/96), 26 October 2000, para. 86.

72 *Ibid.*, para. 84.

73 15 CR (4th) 1, (sub nom. *R. v. Nova Scotia Pharmaceutical Society*) [1992] 2 SCR 606, (sub nom. *R. v. Nova Scotia Pharmaceutical Society*) 93 DLR (4th) 36, (sub nom. *R. v. Nova Scotia Pharmaceutical Society*) 74 CCC (3d) 289, (sub nom. *R. v. Nova Scotia Pharmaceutical Society*) 139 NR 241. On the void for vagueness doctrine, see: Stéphane Beaulac, "Les bases constitutionnelles de la théorie de l'imprécision: partie d'un précaire dynamique globale de la Charte", (1995) 55 *Revue du Barreau* 257.

74 *R. v. Nova Scotia Pharmaceutical Society*, *ibid.*, at 637.

by law] thus implies. . .that there must be a measure of legal protection domestic law against arbitrary interferences by public authorities with rights protected by the *European Convention*."[75] "In my opinion", wrote Justice Gonthier, "the caselaw of the European Court of Human Rights is a very valuable guide on this issue."[76] Furthermore, Justice Gonthier looked to European caselaw for indications on what the scope of precision should be. He noted that the European Court of Human Rights had frequently warned against "a quest for certainty" and had preferred an "area of risk" approach.[77] He also approved of the European Court's comments to the effect that "laws that are framed in general terms may be better suited to the achievement of their objectives, inasmuch as in fields governed by public policy circumstances may vary widely in time and from one case to another".[78] He noted, finally, that the European Court of Human Rights had also insisted upon the establishment of proper legislative guidelines for the exercise of discretion.[79]

In another case dealing with the vagueness argument, *Young* v. *Young*,[80] Justice L'Heureux-Dubé held that the "best interests of the child standard" was not unconstitutionally vague because it was specifically recognized in international human rights instruments, notably the *Convention on the*

---

75 *Malone* v. *United Kingdom*, 2 August 1984, Series A, No. 82, 7 EHRR 14, at 32. Justice Gonthier also cited: *Kruslin* v. *France*, 24 April 1990, Series A, No. 176-A, 12 EHRR 547, at 24-25; *Huvig* v. *France*, 24 April 1990, Series A, No. 176-B, 12 EHRR 528, at 56. See: Alexandre Kiss, "Le problème de l'interception des communictions téléphoniques devant la Cour européene des droits de l'homme: l'affaire Malone", [1986] *Canadian Human Rights Yearbook* 77; Gérard Cohen-Jonathan, "La Cour européenne et les écoutes téléphoniques. Les arrêts Kruslin et Huvig du 24 avril 1990", (1990) 2 *Revue universelle des droits de l'homme* 185.

76 *R.* v. *Nova Scotia Pharmaceutical Society*, *supra* note 73, at 637.

77 *Ibid.*, at 639. Justice Gonthier cited: *Sunday Times* v. *United Kingdom*, *supra* note 67; *Silver* v. *United Kingdom*, 25 March 1983, Series A, No. 61, 5 EHRR 347, at 33-34; *Malone* v. *United Kingdom*, 2 August 1984, Series A, No. 82, 7 EHRR 14, at 32-33.

78 *Nova Scotia* v. *Pharmaceutical Society* , *supra* note 73, at 641-642. On this point, Justice Gonthier cited: *Sunday Times* v. *United Kingdom*, *supra* note 67; *Barthold* v. *Federal Republic of Germany*, 25 March 1985, Series A. No. 90, 7 EHRR 383, at 22; *Müller* v. *Switzerland*, 24 May 1988, Series A, No. 133, at 20.

79 *R.* v. *Nova Scotia Pharmaceutical Society*, *ibid.*, at 642. On this point, Justice Gonthier referred to: *Malone* v. *United Kingdom*, *supra* note 77, at 32-33; *Leander* v. *Sweden*, 26 March 1987, Series A, No. 116, at 23.

80 *Young* v. *Young*, [1993] 4 SCR 3, 108 DLR (4th) 193, 160 NR 1, at 75. See also *R.* v. *M. (S.)*, (1996) 1996 CarswellBC 2501, [1996] BCJ No 2302 (CA), leave to appeal refused, [1997] 1 SCR ix, at para. 67, where the majority referred *inter alia* to definitions in international conventions (in general) to hold that "child" in section 155 of the *Criminal Code*, RSC 1985, c. C-46, was not unconstitutionally vague.

Rights of the Child.[81] The latest case at the Supreme Court of Canada to examine the void for vagueness doctrine is the so-called "spanking case", *Canadian Foundation for Children, Youth and the Law v. Canada (Attorney General).*[82] Writing for the majority, Chief Justice McLachlin concluded that the exemption for parents and teachers from criminal sanctions in the use of corrective force on children or pupils that is "reasonable under the circumstances", as provided for by section 43 of the *Criminal Code,*[83] was not unconstitutionally vague. She resorted to the interpretative guidance provided by the *Convention on the Rights of the Child*[84] and the *International Covenant on Civil and Political Rights,*[85] as well as by the *European Convention on Human Rights*[86] and its caselaw.[87] Justice Arbour's dissent also addressed the issue of vagueness, and relied on the same international instruments to support the opposite conclusion.[88] The same approach was adopted by Justice Hill of the Ontario Superior Court in *R. v. Campbell,*[89] where reference was made to decisions of the European Court of Human Rights[90] as well as those of the International Criminal Tribunal for the former Yugoslavia[91] to assist in deciding that the word "brutality" in section 753(1)(a)(iii) of the *Criminal Code*[92] was not unconstitutionally vague.

The term "prescribed by law" has also been examined in the context of the *International Covenant on Civil and Political Rights.* According to the Siracusa Principles, adopted in the 1980s by a group of international human

---

81 *Convention on the Rights of the Child,* GA Res. 44/25, Annex, [1992] CTS 3, art. 3(1): "In all actions concerning children, whether undertaken by public or private social welfare institutions, courts of law, administrative authorities or legislative bodies, the best interests of the child shall be a primary consideration." Also, arts. 9(1), 9(3), 18(1), 20(1), 21, 37(c), 40(2)(b)(iii).

82 *Canadian Foundation for Children, Youth and the Law* v. *Canada (Attorney General),* [2004] 1 SCR 76, 70 OR (3d) 95, 234 DLR (4th) 257, 180 CCC (3d) 353, 115 CRR (2d) 88, 16 CR (6th) 203, 46 RFL (5th) 1, 183 OAC 1.

83 *Criminal Code,* RSC 1985, c. C-46.

84 *Convention on the Rights of the Child, supra* note 81, arts. 5, 19(1) and 37(a).

85 *International Covenant on Civil and Political Rights,* (1976) 999 UNTS 171, [1976] CTS 47, preamble and art. 7. The majority of the Court also referred to comments by the United Nations Human Rights Committee: UN Doc. A/50/40, paras. 426 and 434; UN Doc. A/54/40, para. 358; UN Doc. A/55/40, paras. 306 and 429.

86 *European Convention on Human Rights,* (1955) 213 UNTS 221, ETS 5, art. 3.

87 Chief Justice McLachlin cited: *A.* v. *United Kingdom,* (App. No. 25599/94), 23 September 1998, Reports 1998-VI.

88 *Canadian Foundation for Children, Youth and the Law* v. *Canada (Attorney General), supra* note 82.

89 *R.* v. *Campbell,* (2004) 120 CRR (2d) 231 (Ont SCJ), at para. 62.

90 *Kucera* v. *Austria,* (App. No. 40072/98), 3 October 2002.

91 *Prosecutor* v. *Plavšić* (Case No. IT-00-39&40/1), Sentencing Judgment, 27 February 2003.

92 *Criminal Code,* supra note 83.

rights experts to assist in applying limitations clauses, for a provision to be "prescribed by law" it must be in force (principle no. 15), it must not be arbitrary or unreasonable (principle no. 16), and it must be clear and accessible to everyone (principle no. 17).[93] The Human Rights Committee has interpreted the expression "prescribed by law" in a Canadian case, *Pinkney* v. *Canada*, holding that it provides a safeguard against arbitrariness.[94] In another case, the Committee concluded that the phrase "in accordance with law", which appears in article 13 of the *Covenant*, requires a State to apply the relevant provisions of its domestic law "in good faith and in a reasonable manner".[95]

The *American Convention on Human Rights* adopts a slightly different formulation in its article 30, using the expressing "in accordance with laws". In its advisory opinion on the interpretation of this phrase, the Inter-American Court held that laws must be "normative acts directed towards the general welfare, passed by a democratically elected legislature, and promulgated by the Executive Branch".[96] The Inter-American Court declared: "Law in a democratic State is not merely a mandate of authority cloaked with certain necessary formal elements. It denotes a content and is directed towards a specific goal."[97] In other words, where a limitation is "prescribed by law", the test is substantive and not merely formal. A "law" which is arbitrary, illegitimate or incompatible with "the general welfare" could not be saved by section 1.

According to the European Court of Human Rights, "law" includes common law as well as statute law,[98] an approach that is of course shared by the Supreme Court of Canada in the interpretation of section 1 of the

---

93 Alexandre Kiss, "Commentary on Limitations Provisions", (1985) 7 *Human Rights Quarterly* 15.

94 *Pinkney* v. *Canada* (No. 27/1978), UN Doc. CCPR/C/14/D/27/1977, UN Doc. CCPR/3/Add.1, Vol. II, p. 385, UN Doc. CCPR/C/OP/1, p. 95, 2 *Human Rights Law Journal* 344, [1983] *Canadian Human Rights Yearbook* 315.

95 *Maroufidou* v. *Sweden* (No. 58/1979), UN Doc. CCPR/3/Add.1, Vol. II, p. 318, UN Doc. CCPR/C/OP/1, p. 80.

96 *The Word "Laws" in Article 30 of the American Convention on Human Rights*, Advisory Opinion OC-6/86, Series A No. 6, 7 *Human Rights Law Journal* 231, 79 ILR 325, at 335 (ILR).

97 *Ibid.*, p. 334. For a recent example, see *Baena-Ricardo* et al. v. *Panama*, [2003] IACHR 7, at paras. 168-170.

98 *Sunday Times* v. *United Kingdom*, 26 April 1979, Series A, No. 30, 2 EHRR 245, 58 ILR 491, a view echoed by the comments of Justice Lamer in *Reference re the Motor Vehicle Act British Columbia*, (1985) [1985] 2 SCR 486, 23 CCC (3d) 289, 63 NR 266, 24 DLR (4th) 536, 48 CR (3d) 289, [1986] 1 WWR 481, 69 BCLR 145, 36 MVR 240, 18 CRR 30, at 309 (CCC). See also: *S.W.* v. *United Kingdom*, 22 November 1995, Series A, No. 335-B, paras. 35-36; *C.R.* v. *United Kingdom*, 22 November 1995, Series A, No. 335-B, paras. 33-34.

*Canadian Charter.*⁹⁹ In *R.* v. *Keegstra,* Justice Kerans of the Alberta Court
of Appeal questioned whether international law is also included, but determined that he did "not need to address that difficult issue" in order to resolve
the case at bar.¹⁰⁰ That question was answered, at least indirectly, by Justice
Cory of the Ontario Court of Appeal, as he then was, addressing the same
issue as Justice Kerans. He ruled that although section 319 (then section
281.2) of the *Criminal Code,*¹⁰¹ dealing with hate propaganda, was contrary
to section 2(b) of the *Charter,* it met the section 1 test precisely because it
was justified under international law in free and democratic societies. Indeed, the provision had been enacted so that Canada could conform to its
international obligations under the *International Convention on the Elimination of All Forms of Racial Discrimination.*¹⁰² Justice Cory did not specifically address the issue in the context of a "prescribed by law" discussion,
but rather in consideration of the phrase "justified in a free and democratic
society". His ruling in *Andrews* constitutes an important innovation, to the
extent that Canada's international commitments and international law more
generally may be invoked as justification for reasonable limits on *Charter*
rights and freedoms.¹⁰³ It should be noted, however, that Justice Cory did
not attempt to apply international law to any of the specific elements of the
test for application of section 1 proposed by the Supreme Court of Canada
in *R.* v. *Oakes.*¹⁰⁴ Rather, the relevance of the international authorities is
explained as indicating that the impugned legislation "was demonstrably
justified in free and democratic societies",¹⁰⁵ that "to promote hatred against
an identifiable group is contrary to and is the antithesis of the underlying
values and principles of a democratic society"¹⁰⁶ and that "the international

99 *R.* v. *Chaulk,* [1990] 3 SCR 1303, 62 CCC (3d) 193, 119 NR 161, [1991] 2 WWR 385,
    2 CR (4th) 1.
100 *R.* v. *Keegstra,* (1985) 19 CCC (3d) 254 (Alta QB), reversed, [1988] 5 WWR 211, 43
    CCC (3d) 150, 65 CR (3d) 289, 60 Alta LR (2d) 1, 87 AR 177, 39 CRR 5 (CA),
    additional reasons at, [1991] 4 WWR 136 (CA), reversed, [1990] 3 SCR 697, 61 CCC
    (3d) 1, [1991] 2 WWR 1, 1 CR (4th) 129, 3 CRR (2d) 193, 77 Alta LR (2d) 193, 114
    AR 81, 117 NR 1; see also *Black* v. *Law Society of Alberta,* [1986] 3 WWR 591, 27
    DLR (4th) 527, Alta LR (2d) 1, 68 AR 259, 20 Admin LR 140, 20 CRR 177 (CA),
    affirmed, [1989] 1 SCR 591, at 543 (DLR).
101 *Supra* note 83.
102 (1969) 660 UNTS 195, [1976] CTS 47.
103 *R.* v. *Andrews,* (1989) 43 CCC (3d) 193, 65 OR (2d) 161, 28 OAC 161, 65 CR (3d) 320,
    39 CRR 36 (CA), affirmed, (1990) 75 OR (2d) 481n (SCC); Rosalie S. Abella, "Limi-
    tations on the Right to Equality Before the Law", in Armand de Mestral et al., eds, *The
    Limitation of Human Rights in Comparative Constitutional Law,* Cowansville: Editions
    Yvon Blais, 1986, pp 223-236, at 235.
104 *R.* v. *Oakes,* [1986] 1 SCR 103, 24 CCC (3d) 321, 50 CR (3d) 1, 26 DLR (4th) 200, 53
    OR (2d) 719n, 65 NR 87, 19 CRR 308, 14 OAC 335.
105 *R.* v. *Andrews, supra* note 103, at 182 (OR).
106 *Ibid.,* at 183-184.

commitments of Canada. . .demonstrate that [the impugned provisions of the *Criminal Code*] are consistent with freedom and democracy".[107]

In *R. v Oakes*, both the Ontario Court of Appeal[108] and the Supreme Court of Canada[109] referred to European cases and examples in defining the reasonable limits which might be imposed on the presumption of innocence in "reverse onus" provisions. In *Germany (Federal Republic) v. Rauca*,[110] the Ontario Court of Appeal cited both the *International Covenant on Civil and Political Rights* and the *European Convention on Human Rights* in determining whether extradition constitutes a reasonable limit on the rights conferred by section 6(1) of the *Canadian Charter*. On two occasions in the *Borowski* cases,[111] where the issue was the "reasonableness" of limits on the right to life in the case of abortion, reference was made to the *Paton* case,[112] in which the European Commission on Human Rights considered that to benefit from the "right to life" provisions of article 2(1) of the *European Convention* it was necessary to be born alive. The European Commission had concluded that the English courts had not violated the *Convention* in refusing an injunction to a father seeking to prevent his wife from obtaining an abortion.[113]

---

107 *Ibid.*, at 188.

108 *R. v. Oakes*, (1983) 145 DLR (3d) 123, 40 OR (2d) 660, 2 CCC (3d) 339, 32 CR (3d) 193, 3 CRR 289 (CA), affirmed, [1986] 1 SCR 103, 24 CCC (3d) 321, 50 CR (3d) 1, 26 DLR (4th) 200, 53 OR (2d) 719n, 65 NR 87, 19 CRR 308, 14 OAC 335.

109 *R. v. Oakes, supra* note 104.

110 *Re Federal Republic of Germany v. Rauca*, (1983) 145 DLR (3d) 638, 4 CCC (3d) 385, 41 OR (2d) 223, 4 CRR 42, 34 CR (3d) 97 (CA).

111 *Borowski v. AG Canada* , [1984] 1 WWR 15, 4 DLR (4th) 112, 8 CCC (3d) 392, 36 CR (3d) 259, 29 Sask R 16 (QB), affirmed, [1987] 4 WWR 385, 33 CCC (3d) 402, 29 CRR 244, 56 Sask R 129, 59 CR (3d) 223, 39 DLR (4th) 731 (Sask CA), affirmed, [1989] 1 S.C.R. 342.

112 *Paton v. United Kingdom* (App. No. 8416/78), (1980) 22 DR 27, 3 EHRR 408. *Paton* has been cited twice by the Supreme Court of Canada, in *R. v. Morgentaler*, (1986) 22 DLR (4th) 641, 22 CCC (3d) 353, 48 CR (3d) 1, 52 OR (2d) 353, 11 OAC 81, 17 CRR 223 (CA), reversed, [1988] 1 SCR 30, (1988) 31 CRR 1, 37 CCC (3d) 449, 44 DLR (4th) 365, 62 CR (3d) 1, 82 NR 1, and in *Tremblay v. Daigle*, [1989] 2 SCR 530, 11 CHRR D/165, 102 NR 81, 62 DLR (4th) 634.

113 None of the Canadian judgments dealing with abortion has referred to *White and Potter v. United States* (Case no. 2141), Resolution No. 23/81, OAS Doc. A/Ser.L/V/II.52 doc. 48, OAS Doc. A/Ser.L/V/II.54 doc. 9 rev. 1, at 25-54, Inter-American Commission on Human Rights, *Ten Years of Activities, 1971-1981*, Washington, D.C.: Organization of American States, 1982, at 186-209, (1981) 1 *Human Rights Law Journal* 110, a decision of the Inter-American Commission of Human Rights. The Commission held that by permitting abortion in Massachusetts hospitals, the United States had not violated article I of the *American Declaration of the Rights and Duties of Man*, OAS Doc. OEA/Ser. L./V/II.23, doc. 21, rev. 6, which protects the right to life. The Commission rejected arguments urging it to read in the term "from the moment of conception". Article 4(1) of the *American Convention of Human Rights*, (1979) 1144 UNTS 123, OASTS 36,

In *Black v. Law Society of Alberta*, Justice Kerans referred frequently to international documents on mobility rights, including the interpretation given by the European Court of Justice and national courts within the European Community, as it was then known, to the mobility provisions of the *Treaty of Rome*.[114] In *Andrews v. Law Society of British Columbia*,[115] Justice La Forest cited a European case in determining whether the British Columbia bar's citizenship requirement constituted a reasonable limit: ". . .a requirement of citizenship would be acceptable if limited to crown Attorneys or lawyers directly employed by government and, therefore, involved in policy-making or administration, so that it could be said that the lawyer was an architect or instrumentality of government policy."[116]

Most interestingly, a *dicta* in the recent case of *R. v. Malmo-Levine*[117] suggests a reason why international law is relevant in the application of the limitation clause of the *Canadian Charter* and, arguably, in the interpretation of the rights and freedoms therein generally. Dissenting on one of the two appeals heard together by the Supreme Court of Canada, Justice Arbour concluded that the prohibition of simple possession of cannabis (marijuana) for personal use pursuant to the *Narcotic Control Act*[118] was unconstitutional because it infringed section 7 and was not saved by section 1 of the *Canadian Charter*. Exceptionally, in this case, her Ladyship was of the view that international law had no role to play because the relevant conventional norms are explicitly submitted to Canada's constitutional law.[119] *A contra-*

---

provides that the right to life be protected "generally, from the moment of conception". Justice McIntyre in his dissent in *R. v. Morgentaler, ibid.*, referred to article 4(1) of the *Convention*. See: Dinah Shelton, "Abortion and Right to Life in the Inter-American System: The Case of Baby Boy", (1981) 2 *Human Rights Law Journal* 309.

114   *Black v. Law Society of Alberta*, [1986] 3 WWR 591, 27 DLR (4th) 527, Alta LR (2d) 1, 68 AR 259, 20 Admin LR 140, 20 CRR 177 (CA), affirmed, [1989] 1 SCR 591: *Van Binsbergen v. Bestuur van Bedrijfsverenging voor de Metalnijverheid*, [1975] 1 CMLR 298; *Coenen v. Social-Economische Raad*, [1976] 1 CMLR 30. In *Black v. Law Society of Alberta*, [1989] 1 SCR 591, 58 DLR (4th) 317, 37 Admin LR 161, 38 CRR 193, [1989] 4 WWR 1, 66 Alta LR (2d) 97, 96 AR 352, 93 NR 266, the Supreme Court of Canada referred to another European Court of Justice case, *Ordre des Avocats au Barreau de Paris v. Klopp*, [1985] 2 WLR 1058.

115   *Andrews v. Law Society of British Columbia*, [1989] 1 SCR 143.

116   *Rayners v. The Belgian State*, [1974] 2 CMLR 305, [1974] 1 CMLR 397, (1974) CMR ¶8256.

117   *R. v. Malmo-Levine*, [2003] 3 SCR 571, 233 DLR (4th) 415, [2004] 4 W.W.R. 407, 179 CCC (3d) 417, 114 CRR (2d) 189, 16 CR (6th) 1, 23 BCLR (4th) 1.

118   *Narcotic Control Act*, RSC 1985, c. N-1, substance included in s. 3 of the Schedule to the Act (now section 1, Schedule II, *Controlled Drugs and Substances Act*, SC 1996, c. 19).

119   The two international treaties are: *Single Convention on Narcotic Drugs, 1961*, [1964] CTS 30, art. 36; and *Convention against Illicit Traffic in Narcotic Drugs and Psychotropic Substances*, [1990] CTS 42, art. 3(2).

rio, she was in effect suggesting that in normal circumstances international law should play a role in *Charter* interpretation. From an international point of view, the reason is straightforward: "The general approach in international law is that a state may not invoke its internal law as justification for its failure to perform a treaty",[120] a rule codified in section 27 of the *Vienna Convention on the Law of Treaties*,[121] as Justice Arbour noted.[122]

4.1.3   International Origins of the *Oakes* Test

The test to be applied in the section 1 analysis was elaborated by Chief Justice Dickson in *R. v. Oakes*,[123] and has been refined in subsequent judgments.[124] According to the *Oakes* test, any violation of the *Charter* must be sufficiently important to justify the limitation, it must be proportional, and its deleterious effects must not be overly severe keeping in mind the objective of the limitation. Though the test itself is to some extent an original one, many of its elements and much of its philosophy derive from international sources and, more specifically, from the jurisprudence of the European Court and Commission of Human Rights.[125] Justice Martin of the Ontario Court of Appeal, in his reasons in *R. v. Oakes*, observed the similarities between the relevant provisions of the *European Convention on Human Rights* and the impugned provision of the *Canadian Charter*. He reviewed the test used in the European jurisprudence in determining whether a reverse onus clause would meet the test of section 1.[126] Reference was made to English legislation dealing with procuring, which had met the test applied by the European Commission of Human Rights.[127] In *Alberta (Attorney General)* v. *Interwest Publications Ltd.*, Justice Berger of the Alberta Court of Queen's Bench (could he have been unaware that it was the Strasbourg organs that inspired the Canadian test and not the other way around?) observed that the European Court of Human Rights had used an

---

120 *R. v. Malmo-Levine, supra* note 117, at para. 271.
121 *Vienna Convention on the Law of Treaties*, (1969) 1155 UNTS 331, [1980] CTS 37, 8 ILM 679.
122 *R. v. Malmo-Levine, supra* note 117, at para. 271.
123 *R. v. Oakes, supra* note 104.
124 Notably: *R. v. Chaulk, supra* note 99; *Dagenais* v. *Canadian Broadcasting Corporation*, [1994] 3 SCR 835, 94 CCC (3d) 289, 120 DLR (4th) 12, 34 CR (4th) 269, 25 CRR (2d) 1, 76 OAC 81, 175 NR 1; *Thomson Newspapers Co.* v. *Canada (Attorney General)*, [1998] 1 SCR 877; and *Sauvé* v. *Canada (Chief Electoral Officer)*, [2002] 3 SCR 519, 218 DLR (4th) 577, 168 CCC (3d) 449, 5 CR (6th) 203, 98 CRR (2d) 1.
125 An oft-cited formulation of the test applied by the Strasbourg organs appears in a report of the European Commission on Human Rights: *Arrowsmith* v. *United Kingdom* (App. No. 7050/75), (1979) 22 European Convention on Human Rights Yearbook 446, 19 DR 5, 3 EHRR 218.
126 *R. v. Oakes, supra* note 108.
127 *X.* v. *United Kingdom* (App. No. 5124/71), (1973) 42 Coll. 135.

analysis similar to that set out in *R.* v. *Oakes.* Justice Berger concluded that "the analysis undertaken by the European Court, including the balancing of interests in view of the factual underpinnings of the specific case, is consistent with the contextual approach enunciated by Wilson J. in the *Edmonton Journal* case, *supra*, and which, I have held, is applicable to the case at bar".[128]

4.1.3.1   Objective

The Strasbourg organs assess the acceptability of limitations under the *European Convention* by initially considering whether the legislation in question responds to a "pressing social need".[129] The first leg of the *Oakes* test is comparable. It requires that "[t]he objective of the impugned provision must be of sufficient importance to warrant overriding a constitutionally protected right or freedom; it must relate to concerns which are pressing and substantial in a free and democratic society before it can be characterized as sufficiently important".[130] In *Black* v. *Law Society of Alberta*,[131] where the Alberta Court of Appeal dealt with a challenge to the bylaws of the provincial bar association that prevented inter-provincial law partnerships, Justice Kerans referred to the "pressing social need" test as set forth in several European cases, including *Handyside* v. *United Kingdom*,[132] *Lingens* v. *Austria*,[133] *Dudgeon* v. *United Kingdom*,[134] and *Young, Jones and Webster* v. *United Kingdom*,[135] in applying section 1 of the *Charter*.

In *Slaight Communications Inc.* v. *Davidson*, Chief Justice Dickson wrote the following about the role of international law in regard to the limitations clause: "Canada's international human rights obligations should inform not only the interpretation of the content of the rights guaranteed by the *Charter* but also the interpretation of what can constitute pressing and substantial s. 1 objectives which may justify restrictions upon those

---

128   *Alberta (Attorney General)* v. *Interwest Publications Ltd.*, [1990] 5 WWR 498, 74 Alta LR (2d) 372, 108 AR 173, 73 DLR (4th) 83, 58 CCC (3d) 114 (QB), at 511 (WWR).

129   *Sunday Times* v. *United Kingdom, supra* note 98; *Olsson* v. *Sweden*, Series A, No. 130. For a recent case, see: *Fressoz and Roire* v. *France* (App. No. 29183/95), 21 January 1999; *Şahin* v. *Turkey* (App. No. 44774/98), 10 November 2005, Dissenting Opinion of Judge Tulkens, para. 5.

130   *R.* v. *Chaulk, supra* note 99, at 216-217 (CCC).

131   *Black* v. *Law Society of Alberta, supra* note 114.

132   *Handyside* v. *United Kingdom*, 7 December 1976, Series A, No. 24, 1 EHRR 737, 59 ILR 150.

133   *Lingens* v. *Austria* (App. No. 9815/82), (1984) 34 DR 180, 6 EHRR 550.

134   *Dudgeon* v. *United Kingdom*, 23 September 1981, Series A, No. 45, 4 EHRR 149, 67 ILR 345.

135   *Young, James & Webster* v. *United Kingdom*, 26 June 1981, Series A, No. 55, 5 EHRR 201, 70 ILR 324.

rights."[136] He further suggested that there is some kind of presumption that a human right recognised internationally help meet the first branch of the *Oakes* test: "Furthermore, for purposes of this stage of the proportionality inquiry, the fact that a value has the status of an international human right, either in customary international law or under a treaty to which Canada is a State Party, should generally be indicative of a high degree of importance attached to that objective."[137] The Chief Justice's encouragement to consult international law has only resonated modestly at the level of the lower courts.[138]

In *Keegstra*, Chief Justice Dickson again invoked international human rights principles "for guidance with respect to assessing the legislative objective". He observed that "[n]o aspect of international human rights has been given attention greater than that focussed upon discrimination".[139] Chief Justice Dickson noted the obligations imposed upon States to take positive measures, including the adoption of criminal law provisions, in order to suppress racist propaganda. These are found specifically in article 4(a) of the *International Convention on the Elimination of All Forms of Racial Discrimination* and article 20(2) of the *International Covenant on Civil and Political Rights*. Chief Justice Dickson also referred to the fact that a communication directed against Canada before the Human Rights Committee, attacking hate propaganda legislation had been declared incompatible with the provisions of the *Covenant*.[140] Finally, he referred to the *European Convention on Human Rights* and decisions of the European

---

136 *Slaight Communications Inc.* v. *Davidson*, [1989] 1 SCR 1038, 59 DLR (4th) 416, 93 NR 183, 89 CLLC 14,031, 26 CCEL 85, 40 CRR 100, at 1056-1057 (SCR).

137 *Ibid.*, at 1057.

138 See: *Saskatchewan (Human Rights Commission)* v. *Bell*, (1991) [1992] 2 WWR 1, 88 DLR (4th) 71, 96 Sask R 296 (QB), reversed, (1994) 1994 CarswellSask 196 (CA), at 92 (DLR); *R.* v. *Sharpe*, (1999) 175 DLR (4th) 1 (BC CA), reversed, [2001] 1 SCR 45, 194 DLR (4th) 1, [2001] 6 WWR 1, 150 CCC (3d) 321, 39 CR (5th) 72, 86 CRR (2d) 1, 88 BCLR (3d) 1, at paras. 145-146; *Rasa* v. *Canada (Minister of Citizenship and Immigration)*, (2000), 191 FTR 129, 75 CRR (2d) 105, 6 Imm LR (3d) 52 (TD), at para. 56; and *Auton (Guardian* ad litem *of)* v. *British Columbia (Attorney General)*, (2003) 220 DLR (4th) 411 (BCCA), reversed, [2004] 3 SCR 657, at paras. 63-64.

139 *R.* v. *Keegstra*, (1990) [1990] 3 SCR 697, 61 CCC (3d) 1, [1991] 2 WWR (2d) 193, 1 CR (4th) 129, 3 CRR (2d) 193, 77 Alta LR (2d) 193 114 AR 81, 117 NR 1, at 750 (SCR).

140 *J.R.T. and W.G.P.* v. *Canada* (No. 104/1981), UN Doc. CCPR/C/OP/2, p. 25, [1984-85] *Canadian Human Rights Yearbook* 357, 5 CHRR D/2097, 4 *Human Rights Law Journal* 193. See also: *Canada (HRC)* v. *Taylor*, [1990] 3 SCR 892, 75 DLR (4th) 577, 13 CHRR 435, 3 CRR (2d) 116, at 920 (SCR).

Commission on Human Rights[141] upholding the notion that prohibition of racist communication was a valid exception to the protection of freedom of expression.[142] The Chief Justice made the same argument for the majority in *Canada (HRC)* v. *Taylor*,[143] one of the companion judgments to *Keegstra*, which dealt with section 13(1) of the *Canadian Human Rights Act*.[144] These statements were picked up and relied upon some years later by La Forest J. in the unanimous decision, *Ross* v. *New Brunswick School District No. 15*.[145]

In *Zundel*, Justice McLachlin contrasted the clear legislative purpose of the hate propaganda provisions in the *Code*, which were upheld by the Court in *Keegstra*. She noted that "the evil addressed was hate-mongering, particularly in the racial context. No similar purpose could be demonstrated for section 181, the relatively archaic provision dealing with 'false news'." She continued:

> It is noteworthy that no suggestion has been made before this Court that Canada's obligations under the international human rights conventions to which it is a signatory require the enactment of any provision(s) other than that section which was under review in *Keegstra*: s. 319. The retention of s. 181 is not therefore necessary to fulfil any international obligation undertaken by Parliament. Can it be said in these circumstances that the Crown has discharge the burden upon it of establishing that the objection of the legislation is pressing and substantial, in short, of sufficient importance to justify overriding the constitutional guarantee of freedom of expression? I think not.[146]

Justices Cory and Iacobucci, in their dissent in *Zundel*, challenged Justice McLachlin's view, noting that two international instruments to which Canada is a party, the *International Covenant on Civil and Political Rights* and the *International Convention on the Elimination of All Forms of Racial Discrimination*, provide that advocacy of national, racial or religious discrimination, hostility or violence shall be prohibited by law. Addressing the objectives issue, they wrote: "These instruments serve to emphasize the important objective of s. 181 in preventing the harm caused by calculated falsehoods which are likely to injure the public interest in racial and social

---

141   *Felderer* v. *Sweden* (App. No. 11001/84), (1986) 8 EHRR 91; *X.* v. *Federal Republic of Germany* (App. No. 9235/81), (1982) 29 DR 194; *Lowes* v. *United Kingdom* (App. No. 133214/87), unreported decision of 9 December 1988; *Glimmerveen* v. *Netherlands* (App. Nos. 8348/78 and 8406/78), (1979) 18 DR 187.

142   *R.* v. *Keegstra, supra* note 139, at 750-755, 758 (SCR).

143   *Canada (HRC)* v. *Taylor, supra* note 140, at 919-920 (SCR).

144   SC 1976-77, c. 33.

145   *Ross* v. *New Brunswick School District No. 15*, (sub nom. *Attis* v. *New Brunswick School District No. 15*) [1996] 1 SCR 825, at para. 97-98.

146   *R.* v. *Zundel*, [1992] 2 SCR 731, 95 DLR (4th) 202, 16 CR (4th) 1, 75 CCC (3d) 449, at 764-765 (SCR).

tolerance."[147] In their view, section 319 was a specific response to the obligations, but that Parliament had also decided to further the same objectives by retaining section 181.[148]

The 1992 decision in *R*. v. *Butler*[149] saw Justice Sopinka for the majority of the Supreme Court of Canada examine whether the obscenity provisions of the *Criminal Code* pursued a "pressing and substantial" objective. He noted that the enactment of the impugned provision was consistent with Canada's international obligations and, in support, referred to the *Agreement for the Suppression of the Circulation of Obscene Publications* and the *Convention for the Suppression of the Circulation of and Traffic in Obscene Publications*.[150] In his concurring reasons, Justice Gonthier wrote that the State could legitimately intervene in the area of morality.[151] He cited article 10 of the *European Convention*, and referred to two judgments of the European Court, *Handyside*[152] and *Müller*.[153]

For the majority in *R*. v. *Lucas*,[154] Justice Cory resorted to international conventions to show the importance of the objective of protecting reputation through the defamatory libel provisions of the *Criminal Code*.[155] They included the *International Covenant on Civil and Political Rights*[156] and the *Universal Declaration of Human Rights*.[157] "That a number of international conventions, ratified by Canada, contain explicit limitations of freedom of expression in order to protect the rights and reputations of individuals", wrote Cory J, "further supports the conclusion that this constitutes a pressing and substantial objective."[158] He also referred to other regional human rights instruments, namely the *European Convention of Human Rights*[159] and the *American Convention on Human Rights*.[160]

---

147 *Ibid.*, at 811.
148 *Ibid.*, at 812.
149 *R*. v. *Butler*, [1992] 1 SCR 452, 70 CCC (3d) 129, 89 DLR (4th) 449, 11 CR (4th) 137, 8 CRR (2d) 1, [1992] 2 WWR 577, 78 Man R (2d) 1, 134 NR 81, reconsideration refused, [1993] 2 WWR lxi (SCC). See also: *Ontario (Attorney General)* v. *Langer*, (1995) 123 DLR (4th) 289 (Ont Gen Div), leave to appeal refused, (1995) 42 C.R. (4th) 410n (SCC).
150 *Ibid.*, at 498 (SCR).
151 *Ibid.*, at 522 (SCR).
152 *Handyside* v. *United Kingdom*, 7 December 1976, Series A, No. 24, 1 EHRR 737, 59 ILR 150.
153 *Müller* v. *Switzerland*, 24 May 1988, Series A, No. 133.
154 *R*. v. *Lucas*, [1998] 1 SCR 439.
155 RSC 1985, c. C-46, ss. 298, 299 and 300.
156 (1976) 999 UNTS 171, [1976] CTS 47, art. 17.
157 GA Res. 217 A (III), UN Doc. A/810, art. 12.
158 *R*. v. *Lucas*, *supra* note 154, at para. 50. See also *Lavoie* v. *Canada*, [2002] 1 SCR 769, at para. 56.
159 (1955) 213 UNTS 221, ETS 5, art. 10.
160 (1979) 1144 UNTS 123, OASTS 36, art. 13.

After explaining how unfortunate it was that the Crown had conceded that section 163.1(4) of the *Criminal Code* criminalising the possession of child pornography violated freedom of expression in section 2(b) of the *Canadian Charter*, L'Heureux-Dubé, Gonthier and Bastarache JJ, in their concurring reasons in *R. v. Sharpe*,[161] resorted to international law in their section 1 analysis. The compelling nature of the underlying objective of the provision, pertaining to the protection of children, was indeed highlighted by the one-hundred-and-ninety-one ratifications or accessions to the *Convention on the Rights of the Child*,[162] as of 19 January 2001, "making it the most universally accepted human rights instrument in history".[163] In further support to their conclusion are numerous international instruments:

> Article 25(2) of the *Universal Declaration of Human Rights*, G.A. Res. 217 A (III), U.N. Doc A/810, at p. 71 (1948), recognizes that "childhood [is] entitled to special care and assistance". The United Nations *Declaration of the Rights of the Child*, G.A. Res. 1386 (XIV) (1959), in its preamble, states that the child "needs special safeguards and care". In 1992, the United Nations Commission on Human Rights adopted the *Programme of Action for the Prevention of the Sale of Children, Child Prostitution and Child Pornography*, 55th Mtg., 1992/74. Additional instruments such as the *International Covenant on Economic, Social and Cultural Rights*, 993 UNTS 3, art. 10(3), and the *International Covenant on Civil and Political Rights*, 999 UNTS 171, art. 24, also emphasize the protection of children. The recent *Optional Protocol to the Convention on the Rights of the Child on the sale of children, child prostitution and child pornography*, A/RES/54/263 (2000), which prohibits, *inter alia*, child pornography, has already been signed by 69 states;[164]

Before continuing their analysis of the objective underlying section 163.1(4) of the *Criminal Code* with a comparative law perspective, L'Heureux-Dubé, Gonthier and Bastarache JJ examined the works of certain international bodies, which show a growing trend in favour of criminalising the possession of child pornography. Their reasons made reference to various international documents, including *Child Pornography: Note by the Secretary-General*,[165] *Programme of Action for the Prevention of the Sale of Children, Child Prostitution and Child Pornography*,[166] *Draft Joint Action to Combat*

---

161   *R. v. Sharpe*, [2001] 1 SCR 45, 194 DLR (4th) 1, [2001] 6 WWR 1, 150 CCC (3d) 321, 39 CR (5th) 72, 86 CRR (2d) 1, 88 BCLR (3d) 1. See also: Robert Martin, "*R. v. Sharpe*", (2001) 39 *Alberta Law Review* 585; Janice Benedet, "Children in Pornography after *Sharpe*", (2002) 43 *Cahiers de Droit* 327.
162   GA Res. 44/25.
163   *R. v. Sharpe*, *supra* note 161, at para. 177.
164   *Ibid.*, at para. 178.
165   "Sale of Children, Child Prostitution and Child Pornography: Note by the Secretary-General", UN Doc. A/49/478, at paras. 196-197.
166   "Programme of Action for the Prevention of the Sale of Children, Child Prostitution and Child Pornography", UN Doc. E/CN.4/1992/74, at para. 53.

Child Pornography on the Internet[167] and *International Traffic in Child Pornography.*[168]

In *United States v. Burns and Rafay,*[169] recourse to international law was mainly in regard to the issue of whether or not the order to extradite fugitives without obtaining assurances from the United States authorities that the death penalty would not be imposed violated section 7 of the *Canadian Charter.* A brief excursion on the international plane was also made by the Supreme Court of Canada in order to assess whether the infringement could be justified under section 1 of the *Charter.* It was done when the argument on international comity was considered and rejected because "[t]here is no suggestion in the evidence that asking for assurances would undermine Canada's international obligations or good relations with neighbouring states".[170] The Court also referred to the decision of the European Court of Human Rights in the *Soering* case,[171] dealing with the extradition of a West German national from the United Kingdom to the United States where he might have faced possible execution.[172]

4.1.3.2 *Proportionality*

If the first part of the test is met, the European Court (and formerly the Commission) will proceed to examine the proportionality of the measure, which is, in general terms, the second portion of the *Oakes* test.[173] The Court will consider whether the limitation is "necessary in a free and democratic society".[174] The European Court of Human Rights has held that "necessity"

---

167   "Draft Joint Action to Combat Child Pornography on the Internet", [1999] OJC 219/68, article 1.
168   "International Traffic in Child Pornography", ICPO-Interpol AGN/65/RES/9 (1996).
169   *United States* v. *Burns and Rafay,* [2001] 1 SCR 283, 195 DLR (4th) 1, [2001] 3 WWR 193, 151 CCC (3d) 97, 39 CR (5th) 205, 81 CRR (2d) 1, 85 BCLR (3d) 1.
170   *Ibid.,* at para. 136.
171   *Soering* v. *United Kingdom,* 7 July 1989, Series A, No. 161, 11 EHRR 439.
172   *United States* v. *Burns and Rafay, supra* note 169, at para. 137.
173   *Moustaquim* v. *Belgium,* 18 February 1991, Series A, No. 193; *Funke* v. *France,* 25 February 1993, Series A, No. 256-A; *Silver* v. *United Kingdom,* 25 March 1983, Series A, No. 61, 5 EHRR 347; *Lingens* v. *Austria,* 8 April 1986, Series A, No. 103; *Informationsverein Lentia et al.* v. *Austria,* 24 November 1993, Series A, No. 178; *Niemietz* v. *Germany,* 16 December 1992, Series A, No. 251-B; *Fuentes Bobo* v. *Spain* (App. No. 39293/98), 29 February 2000; and *Murphy* v. *Ireland* (App. No. 44179/98), 10 July 2003.
174   *Handyside* v. *United Kingdom, supra* note 152; *Olsson* v. *Sweden,* Series A, No. 130; *Leander* v. *Sweden,* 26 March 1987, Series A, No. 116; *Gillow* v. *United Kingdom,* 24 November 1986, Series A, No. 109; *Silver* v. *United Kingdom,* 25 March 1983, Series A, No. 61, 5 EHRR 347; *Kokkinakis* v. *Greece,* Series A, No. 260-A; *Sunday Times* v. *United Kingdom,* 26 April 1979, Series A, No. 30, 2 EHRR 245, 58 ILR 491; *Castells* v. *Spain,* Series A, No. 236; *Autronic AC* v. *Switzerland,* 22 May 1990, Series A, No. 178; *Müller* v. *Switzerland,* 24 May 1988, Series A, No. 133; *Open Door and Dublin*

is not so demanding as to require that a measure be "indispensable", "inadmissible", "useful", *"reasonable"* or "desirable".[175] But the *Canadian Charter*, unlike the *European Convention*, and for that matter the *International Covenant on Civil and Political Rights*, requires only that limitations on fundamental rights be "reasonable". In *Luscher* v. *Deputy Minister of National Revenue*, Justice Hugessen of the Federal Court of Appeal noted that although "the experience of others is very helpful", and although article 10 of the *European Convention* uses wording similar to that in the *Charter*, unlike the *Charter* it does not require that restrictions be "necessary", only that they be "reasonable".[176]

In *Reich* v. *College of Physicians and Surgeons of Alberta (No. 2)*, Justice McDonald of the Alberta Court of Queen's Bench noted the distinction between the standard of "reasonableness" found in section 1 of the *Canadian Charter* and the standard of "necessity" which is required in the *European Convention*. He said that "the standard to be met by the State, in order that a limit or a guaranteed right be protected, is therefore lower than would have been required if the notion of 'necessity' had been employed, as in those articles of the European Convention". The same comments apply to the *International Covenant on Civil and Political Rights*, which also uses the word "necessary" in articles 18(3) (freedom of thought, conscience and religion), 19(3) (freedom of expression), 21 (freedom of peaceful assembly) and 22(2) (freedom of association and trade unions). Therefore, wrote Justice McDonald in *Reich*, "[i]t cannot be without significance that the drafters of the Charter, in drafting s. 1, did not choose to employ the words 'necessary in a democratic society', which are found in articles 21 and 22 of the International Covenant".[177] The argument is interesting, but there is no evidence in the drafting history of the *Charter* to suggest that this compar-

---

Well Woman Clinic v. *Ireland*, 29 October 1992, Series A, No. 246-A; *Grigoriades* v. *Greece* (App. No. 24348/94), 25 November 1997, Reports 1997-VII; *Sener* v. *Turkey* (App. No. 26680/95), 18 July 2000; and *Krone Verlag GmbH & CoKG (No. 2)* v. *Austria* (App. No. 40284/98), 6 November 2003.

175 *Handyside* v. *United Kingdom, ibid.*, para. 48; *Sunday Times* v. *United Kingdom, ibid.*, para. 59. See also Graham Zellick, "The European Convention on Human Rights: Its Significance for Charter Litigation", in R.J. Sharpe, ed., *Charter Litigation*, Toronto: Butterworths, 1987, pp. 102-103; André Morel, "La clause limitative de l'article 1 de la Charte canadienne des droits et libertés; une assurance contre le gouvernement des juges", (1983) 61 *Canadian Bar Review* 81, at 93-94.

176 *Re Luscher and Deputy Minister, Revenue Canada, Customs and Excise*, [1985] 1 FC 85, (1985) 17 DLR (4th) 503, 45 CR (3d) 81, 57 NR 386, [1985] 1 CTC 246, (1985) 15 CRR 167, 9 CER 229 (CA).

177 *Reich* v. *College of Physicians and Surgeons of the Province of Alberta (No. 2)*, (1984), 8 DLR (4th) 696, 31 Alta LR (2d) 205, 53 AR 325 (QB), at 711 (DLR). See also: *R.* v. *Professional Technology of Canada Ltd.*, (1986) 1986 CarswellAlta 852, [1986] AJ No 85 (Prov Ct).

ison ever crossed the minds of its authors. In one of the earliest *Charter* decisions, Justice Jules Deschênes of the Quebec Superior Court alluded to the jurisprudence of the European Court in interpreting the word "reasonable"[178] in section 1 of the *Charter*. Referring to the *Handyside Case*[179] of the European Court, he determined that any violation of protected rights and freedoms must be "proportionate" to the public interest being invoked in defense of such a breach.

In construing the *Canadian Bill of Rights*, in *MacKay* v. *The Queen*, the Supreme Court of Canada in fact adopted a form of "necessity" test.[180] In *Reference Re Use of French in Criminal Proceedings in Saskatchewan*, Justice Cameron of the Saskatchewan Court of Appeal compared the test of the Supreme Court of Canada in *MacKay* with the provisions of article 14 of the *European Convention on Human Rights*, and found both approaches to be "relevant".[181]

To meet the proportionality test, the impugned legislation must be rationally connected to the objective and must not be arbitrary, unfair or based on irrational considerations. In *R.* v. *L.(D.O.)*, Justice L'Heureux-Dubé concluded that section 715.1 of the *Criminal Code* was not arbitrary and that "it was perfectly legitimate for Parliament to draw the line where it did". Section 715.1 concerns admissibility of videotaped statements by young victims of sexual abuse, with the age of the victim being set at under eighteen years of age. In support, she cited the *Convention on the Rights of the Child*: "This international convention, to which Canada is a signatory, demands that children under the age of eighteen be protected as a class (Articles 19 and 34)."[182]

Chief Justice Dickson examined the constitutionality of section 319 of the *Criminal Code*, which proscribes hate propaganda, under the "rational connection" arm of the proportionality component of the *Oakes* test with reference to international law. Referring to his earlier discussion, which was placed under the rubric of the legislative objective, he wrote: "Nor, as has been discussed, has the international community regarded the promulgation

178 *Quebec Protestant School Boards* v. *A.G. Quebec (No. 2)*, [1982] CS 273, 140 DLR (3d) 33, 3 CRR 114, affirmed, (1983) 1 DLR (4th) 573 (CA), affirmed, [1984] 2 SCR 66, at 697-698 (CS).
179 *Handyside* v. *United Kingdom, supra* note 174.
180 *MacKay* v. *R.*, [1980] 2 SCR 370, 114 DLR (3d) 393, 54 CCC (2d) 129.
181 *Reference re Use of French in Criminal Proceedings in Saskatchewan*, [1987] 5 WWR 577, 44 DLR (4th) 16, 43 CRR 189, 36 CCC (3d) 353 (Sask CA).
182 *R.* v. *L. (D.O.)*, [1993] 4 SCR 419, at 465. Note that Justice L'Heureux-Dubé made her comments in the context of a section 7 analysis, although they have been included here because of their relevance to the "minimal impairment" component of the section 1 analysis.

of laws suppressing hate propaganda as futile or counter-productive."[183] The Chief Justice cited a study by the United Nations on the implementation of article 4 of the *International Convention on the Elimination of All Forms of Racial Discrimination.*[184]

Minimal impairment is also an important part of the proportionality analysis. In a case challenging section 16(4)(c) of *Public Service Employment Act,*[185] which gives Canadian citizens preferred status in competition for public service jobs, the plaintiffs argued that "a more appropriate and less intrusive means of achieving Parliament's ends would be to adopt the 'political function test' as applied by the European Court of Justice in interpreting European Community Law".[186] The European Court of Justice has adopted a narrow definition of public service in order to facilitate mobility of workers within the European Union, and thus foster European integration.

Writing concurring reasons in *R. v. Sharpe,*[187] L'Heureux-Dubé, Gonthier and Bastarache JJ not only referred to international human rights law with respect to the first branch of the *Oakes* test, they also examined it in the context of the minimal impairment stage of the proportionality inquiry. They opined that the *Criminal Code* prohibition of possession of child pornography set out in section 163.1(4), in combination with the definition of child pornography in section 163.1(1), minimally impaired freedom of expression guaranteed in section 2(b) of the *Canadian Charter*. It is justified to define "child" as "a person under the age of eighteen years" in view of the objective pursued in several provisions of the *Criminal Code,*[188] namely the prevention of sexual exploitation of adolescents between 14 and 17 years of age. The definition, noted the minority, is consistent with the one found in the *Convention on the Rights of the Child.*[189] "This international convention requires that Canadian children under the age of 18 be protected as a class," they wrote.[190]

---

183   *R. v. Keegstra,* (1990) [1990] 3 SCR 697, 61 CCC (3d) 1, [1991] 2 WWR (2d) 193, 1 CR (4th) 129, 3 CRR (2d) 193, 77 Alta LR (2d) 193 114 AR 81, 117 NR 1, at 770 (SCR). Also: *Canada (HRC) v. Taylor,* [1990] 3 SCR 892, 75 DLR (4th) 577, 13 CHRR 435, 3 CRR (2d) 116, at 924 (SCR).

184   (1969) 660 UNTS 195, [1976] CTS 47.

185   RSC 1985, c. P-33.

186   *Lavoie v. Canada,* (1995) 95 FTR 1 (TD), affirmed, [2000] 1 FC 3 (CA), leave to appeal allowed, [2000] 1 SCR xiv, affirmed, [2002] 1 SCR 769, 210 DLR (4th) 193, 15 CCEL (3d) 159, 92 CRR (2d) 1, at 27-28 (FTR).

187   *R. v. Sharpe, supra* note 161.

188   Their Lordships mentioned section 153, on sexual contacts between adolescents and people in a position of trust, and section 212(4), on obtaining sexual services by adolescents for consideration; *ibid.,* at para. 226.

189   GA Res. 44/25, art. 1.

190   *R. v. Sharpe, supra* note 161, at para. 226.

4.1.4 "Free and Democratic Societies"

Section 1 of the *Canadian Charter* is a broad invitation to examine the law in effect in other "free and democratic societies". No more complicated legal justification is required for employing international sources in such an analysis than the observation that the *International Covenant on Civil and Political Rights*, the *Universal Declaration of Human Rights*, the *American Declaration of the Rights and Duties of Man*, the *American Convention on Human Rights* and the *European Convention of Human Rights* represent judicial norms and standards that should prevail in the free and democratic societies to which section 1 refers.[191] As José Woehrling has observed, a major advantage of this approach is that it provides a dynamic, evolving treatment of the *Charter*, allowing reference to international instruments as well as national legislation and constitutions irrespective of whether they were "contemplated" by the drafters of the *Charter*, or of whether they were even in existence on 17 April 1982.[192] International instruments and jurisprudence have been cited by Canadian courts on several occasions on this basis.[193]

A recent case on point is *United States v. Burns and Rafay*,[194] where the Supreme Court of Canada had to decide whether or not an extradition order against a fugitive given without assurances from the United States that the death penalty would not be imposed was unconstitutional under the *Charter*, a question answered in the negative some ten years earlier in

---

191 See José Woehrling, "Le rôle du droit comparé dans la jurisprudence des droits de la personne – rapport canadien", in Armand De Mestral *et al.*, eds., *The Limitation of Human Rights in Comparative Constitutional Law*, Cowansville: Editions Yvon Blais, 1986, pp. 449-514, at 460; Guy Tremblay, "La Charte canadienne des droits et libertés et quelques leçons tirées de la Convention européenne des droits de l'homme", (1982) 23 *Cahiers de Droit* 795, at 806; Daniel J. Arbess, "Limitations on Legislative Override Under the Canadian Charter of Rights and Freedoms: A Matter of Balancing Values", (1983) 21 *Osgoode Hall Law Journal* 113, at 123; Timothy Christian, "The Limitation of Liberty: A Consideration of Section 1 of the Charter of Rights and Freedoms", [1982] *Charter Edition University of British Columbia Law Review* 105.

192 José Woehrling, *ibid.*

193 *Hirt v. College of Physicians and Surgeons*, (1985) 17 DLR (4th) 472, 60 BCLR 273 (CA); *Black v. Law Society of Alberta*, [1986] 3 WWR 591, 27 DLR (4th) 527, Alta LR (2d) 1, 68 AR 259, 20 Admin LR 140, 20 CRR 177 (CA), affirmed, [1989] 1 SCR 591; *R. v. Oakes*, (1983) 145 DLR (3d) 123, 40 OR (2d) 660, 2 CCC (3d) 339, 32 CR (3d) 193, 3 CRR 289 (CA), affirmed, [1986] 1 SCR 103, 24 CCC (3d) 321, 50 CR (3d) 1, 26 DLR (4th) 200, 53 OR (2d) 719n, 65 NR 87, 19 CRR 308, 14 OAC 335, *R. v. Oakes*, [1986] 1 SCR 103, 24 CCC (3d) 321, 50 CR (3d) 1, 26 DLR (4th) 200, 53 OR (2d) 719n, 65 NR 87, 19 CRR 308, 14 OAC 335; *R. v. Andrews*, (1989) 43 CCC (3d) 193, 65 OR (2d) 161, 28 OAC 161, 65 CR (3d) 320, 39 CRR 36 (CA), affirmed, (1990) 75 OR (2d) 481n (SCC).

194 *United States v. Burns and Rafay, supra* note 169.

Kindler v. Canada (Minister of Justice)[195] and *Reference re Ng Extradition (Can.)*.[196] In reversing its position, which revolved mainly around the interpretation of the self-limiting rights to liberty and security of the person and the principles of fundamental justice under section 7, the Court relied extensively on the latest developments on the international plane as well as in foreign jurisdictions.[197] In the final analysis, the Court opined:

> The outcome of this appeal turns on an appreciation of the principles of fundamental justice, which in turn are derived from the basic tenets of our legal system. These basic tenets have not changed since 1991 when *Kindler* and *Ng* were decided, but their application in particular cases (the "balancing process") must take note of factual developments in Canada and in relevant foreign jurisdictions. When principles of fundamental justice as established and understood in Canada are applied to these factual developments, many of which are of far-reaching important in death penalty cases, a balance which tilted in favour of extradition without assurance in *Kindler* and *Ng* now tilts against the constitutionality of such an outcome.[198]

In the so-called "balancing process", therefore, which was part and parcel of the section 7 analysis in this case as it is inherent to section 1 and the *Oakes* test in general, the way in which "free and democratic societies" address difficult issues like the death penalty is not only relevant, but is also by definition a dynamic and evolving feature.

In 1984, a group of international jurists, including the Canadian human rights lawyer John Humphrey, reached agreement on what are called the Siracusa Principles. They examined the meaning of the term "in a democratic society", which appears in article 29 of the *Universal Declaration* and in several provisions of the *International Covenant on Civil and Political Rights*.[199] The group considered that a state "which recognizes and respects the United Nations Charter and the Universal Declaration of Human Rights" would meet the definition of "democratic society".[200] It is difficult to imagine Canadian courts devoting much effort to assessing whether or

---

195 *Kindler* v. *Canada*, [1991] 2 SCR 779, 67 CCC (3d) 1, 84 DLR (4th) 438, 6 CRR (2d) 193, 129 NR 81.

196 *Reference re: Ng Extradition (Can.)*, [1991] 2 SCR 858, 67 CCC (3d) 61, 84 DLR (4th) 498.

197 The Court said it did not reverse its opinion, it simply nuanced it. But when the European Court of Human Rights took note of *Burns and Rafay*, it understood that the earlier precedent in *Kindler* had been overturned: *G.B.* v. *Bulgaria* (App. No. 42346/98), 11 March 2004, para. 62; *Iorgov* v. *Bulgaria* (App. No. 40653/98), 11 March 2004, para. 62.

198 *United States* v. *Burns and Rafay*, *supra* note 169, at para. 144.

199 "The Siracusa Principles in the Limitation and Derogation Principles in the International Covenant on Civil and Political Rights", (1985) 7 *Human Rights Quarterly* 3.

200 Alexandre Kiss, "Commentary on Limitations Provisions", (1985) 7 *Human Rights Quarterly* 15, at 19.

not a particular country meets the "free and democratic society" test, or whether it indeed respects the *Charter of the United Nations* and the *Universal Declaration of Human Rights*. But there is no question that the limits imposed on rights and freedoms protected by the *International Covenant on Civil and Political Rights* and the *European Convention on Human Rights*, and delineated by the caselaw of the Human Rights Committee and the European Court of Human Rights, are also "reasonable limits. . .in a free and democratic society" within the meaning of section 1 of the *Charter*.

In the United States of America, there is a long overdue opening to the consideration of international human rights law in interpreting the *Bill of Rights*, which, however, provokes strong opposition both inside the judiciary and outside.[201] Although references to foreign experiences (that is, presumably, to other "free and democratic societies") go back nearly half a century,[202] it is really only with the decision in the so-called "sodomy case", *Lawrence v. Texas*,[203] that a majority or plurality judgment of the United States Supreme Court has cited the product of an international human rights legal regime, namely decisions of the European Court of Human Rights.[204] Of course, having no general limitation clause, it is through definitional balancing of the constitutional guarantee that justifiable limits to rights or freedoms are considered, including those which are influenced by foreign and international law.

The most recent example is the 2005 judgement in *Roper v. Simmons*,[205] where the United States Supreme Court reversed a fifteen-year-old precedent in *Stanford v. Kentucky*[206] and held that the Eighth and Fourteenth Amendments forbid the imposition of the death penalty on offenders who were under the age of eighteen at the time the crimes were committed. In

---

201 See: Joan L. Larsen, "Importing Constitutional Norms from a 'Wider Civilization': Lawrence and the Rehnquist Court's Use of Foreign and International Law in Domestic Constitutional Interpretation", (2004) 65 *Ohio State Law Journal* 1283. See also, from a wider media perspective: Thomas Sowell, "Who Needs Europe?", *Wall Street Journal*, 26 August 2003.

202 See: *Trop* v. *Dulles*, 356 US 86, 78 SCt 590, 2 LEd2d 630 (1958); *Coker* v. *Georgia*, 433 US 584, 97 SCt 2861, 53 LEd2d 982 (1977); *Enmund* v. *Florida*, 458 US 782, 102 SCt 3368, 73 LEd2d 1140 (1982); *Thompson* v. *Oklahoma*, 487 US 815, 108 SCt 2687, 101 LEd2d 702 (1988); and *Atkins* v. *Virginia*, 536 US 304, 122 SCt 2242, 153 LEd2d 335 (2002).

203 *Lawrence* v. *Texas*, 539 US 558, 123 SCt 2472, 156 LEd2d 508 (2003), at 573 and 576 (US).

204 *Dudgeon* v. *United Kingdom*, 23 September 1981, Series A, No. 45, 4 EHRR 149, 67 ILR 345; *Norris* v. *Ireland*, 26 October 1988, Series A, No. 142; *Modinos* v. *Cyprus*, 22 April 1993, Series A, No. 259; and *P.G. and J.H.* v. *United Kingdom* (App. No. 44787/98), 25 September 2001.

205 *Roper* v. *Simmons*, 125 SCt 1183 (2005).

206 *Stanford* v. *Kentucky*, 492 U.S. 361, 109 SCt 2969, 106 LEd2d 306 (1989).

interpreting the "cruel and unusual punishment" clause in the Eighth Amendment, the majority *per* Justice Kennedy referred to several international law instruments, including the *Convention on the Rights of the Child*,[207] the *Covenant on Civil and Political Rights*,[208] the *American Convention on Human Rights*,[209] and the *African Charter on the Rights and Welfare of the Child*.[210] References were also made to the way in which the United Kingdom has dealt with these issues, emphasising that: "It is proper that we acknowledge the overwhelming weight of international opinion against the juvenile death penalty, resting in large part on the understanding that the instability and emotional imbalance of young people may often be a factor in the crime."[211]

Knowing that the use of international law in the construction of the American Constitution meets with some resistance, Justice Kennedy considered it necessary to add the following remarks: "The opinion of the world community, while not controlling our outcome, does provide respected and significant confirmation for our own conclusions." Put another way, the international law experience obviously does not govern the interpretation of the American *Bill of Rights*, any more than it does the *Canadian Charter*, but it may be useful in defining the scope and the limits of guaranteed rights and freedoms. Justice O'Connor, dissenting on other grounds (thus making it a majority of six *versus* three on this issue), elaborated as follows:

> But this Nation's evolving understanding of human dignity certainly is neither wholly isolated from, nor inherently at odds with, the values prevailing in other countries. On the contrary, we should not be surprised to find congruence between domestic and international values, especially where the international community has reached clear agreement – expressed in international law or in the domestic laws of individual countries – that a particular form of punishment is inconsistent with fundamental human rights.[212]

Justices Scalia was the main dissenting voice on the bench as regards the domestic role of international law. In *Roper*, he vehemently condemned the "centre stage" in the reasons of the majority given to the views of other countries and the international community. Confusing the persuasive role of international law with a kind of binding effect, he wrote: "[T]he basic premise of the Court's argument – that American law should conform to

---

207   *Supra* note 189, art. 37.
208   (1976) 999 UNTS 171, [1976] CTS 47, art. 6(5).
209   (1979) 1144 UNTS 123, OASTS 36, art. 4(5).
210   *African Charter on the Rights and Welfare of the Child*, (1999) OAU Doc. CAB/LEG/ 24.9/49, art. 5(3).
211   *Roper* v. *Simmons, supra* note 205, at 1200 (SCt).
212   *Ibid.*, at 1215-1216 (SCt).

the laws of the rest of the world – ought to be rejected out of hand."[213] In spite of these comments, there are reasons to rejoice, given that the Courts of the United States have, at last, firmly joined the contemporary trend shown by national and international adjudicative bodies in favour of cross-fertilisation among human rights experiences, including those found in international law, to help define the scope and limits of guaranteed rights and freedoms.

4.2   Fundamental Freedoms

Section 2 of the *Canadian Charter* sets out the four "fundamental freedoms", religion, expression, assembly and association.

2. Everyone has the following fundamental freedoms:

a)   freedom of conscience and religion;
b)   freedom of thought, belief, opinion and expression, including freedom of the press and other media of communication;
c)   freedom of peaceful assembly; and
d)   freedom of association.

The Canadian text is strikingly succinct compared with the extensive description of these freedoms found in the international instruments. Not only are the rights themselves expressed in greater detail in the international models, so are the specific terms applicable to their limitation. Canada's courts have found these more extensive texts to be of particular use in analysing the scope of section 2 of the *Charter*. Interestingly, because the international models focus on the limitations on the fundamental freedoms, they are often invoked to restrict rather than to expand the protection accorded by the *Charter*.

4.2.1   Freedom of Conscience and Religion

Section 2(a) of the *Canadian Charter* declares that everyone has the "fundamental freedom" of "conscience and religion". International law ascribes to freedom of conscience and religion a kind of pre-eminence within the enumeration of fundamental freedoms.[214] Freedom of belief was one of the "four freedoms" listed by President Franklin D. Roosevelt in his famous wartime speech, and it is repeated in the preamble to the *Universal Declaration of Human Rights*. Article 18 of the *Universal Declaration* states:

---

213   *Ibid.*, at 1226 (SCt).
214   Irwin Cotler, "Freedom of Conscience and Religion (Section 2(a))", in Gérald-A. Beaudoin & Ed Ratushny, eds., *The Canadian Charter of Rights and Freedoms*, 2nd ed., Toronto: Carswell, 1989, pp. 165-193, at 190; the author supports his affirmation with reference to the Siracusa Principles.

"Everyone has the right to freedom of thought, conscience and religion; this right includes freedom to change his religion or belief, and freedom, either alone or in community with others and in public or private, to manifest his religion or belief in teaching, practice, worship and observance."[215]

The *International Covenant on Civil and Political Rights* takes the text of the *Universal Declaration*, and adds a protection against coercion that would impair religious affiliation, freedom to manifest religion, and the right of parents to ensure moral and religious teachings for their children that are in accordance with their own beliefs.[216] The *Covenant* also enshrines the right of persons belonging to religious minorities, "in community with the other members of their group,. . .to profess and practise their own religion".[217] The *European Convention on Human Rights* is comparable to the *International Covenant on Civil and Political Rights*, except that it does not provide for either the protection against coercion or the right to parochial instruction.[218] The *American Convention on Human Rights* adds the right to "disseminate one's religion or beliefs".[219]

---

215 *Universal Declaration of Human Rights*, GA Res. 217 A (III), UN Doc. A/810. For a recent example where a Canadian court referred to this instrument in the context of freedom of conscience and religion, see: *Maurice* v. *Canada (Attorney General)*, (2002) 210 DLR (4th) 186 (Fed TD).

216 *International Covenant on Civil and Political Rights*, *supra* note 208, art. 18. For a recent example where a Canadian court referred to this instrument in the context of freedom of conscience and religion, see: *R.* v. *Poulin*, (2002) 7 CR (6th) 369, 169 CCC (3d) 378 (PEI TD).

217 *International Covenant on Civil and Political Rights*, *supra* note 208, art. 27.

218 *European Convention on Human Rights*, (1955) 213 UNTS 221, ETS 5, art. 9; see also: *Protocol* [No. 1] *to the Convention for the Protection of Human Rights and Fundamental Freedoms*, (1955) 213 UNTS 262, ETS 9, art. 2. It was not until 1993 that the European Court of Human Rights issued its first significant decision concerning article 9 of the *Convention*: *Kokkinakis* v. *Greece*, Series A, No. 260-A. See: Vincent Berger, *Jurisprudence de la Cour européenne des droits de l'homme*, Paris: Sirey, 1994, pp. 335–337, 507; F. Rigaux, "L'incrimination du prosélytisme face à la liberté d'expression", [1994] *Revue trimestrielle des droits de l'homme* 144; Frédéric Sudre *et al.*, "Chronique de la jurisprudence de la Cour européenne des droits de l'homme. Première partie: janvier-mai 1993" (1993) 4 *Revue universelle des droits de l'homme* 217. Many aspects of the right have since been examined by the Strasbourg organs; see: *Otto-Preminger-Institut* v. *Austria*, 20 September 1994, Series A, No. 295-A; *Manoussaki* et al. v. *Greece* (App. No. 18748/91), 26 September 1996, Reports 1996-IV; *Kalac* v. *Turkey* (App. No. 20704/92), 1 July 1997, Reports 1997-IV; *Larissi* et al. v. *Greece* (App. No. 23372/94), 24 February 1998, Reports 1998-I, p. 378; *Buscarini* et al. v. *San Marino* (App. No. 24645/94), 18 February 1999; *Serif* v. *Greece* (App. No. 38178/97), 14 December 1999; and *Şahin* v. *Turkey* (App. No. 44774/98), 29 June 2004.

219 *Supra* note 209, art. 12. See also: *American Declaration of the Rights and Duties of Man*, *supra* note 215, art. III; *African Charter of Human and Peoples' Rights*, OAU Doc. CAB/LEG/67/3 rev. 5, 4 EHRR 417, 21 *ILM* 58, art. 8; *Convention on the Rights of the Child*, GA Res. 44/25, art. 14; *International Convention on the Elimination of All Forms of Racial Discrimination*, (1969) 660 UNTS 195, [1976] CTS 47, art. 5(d)(vii).

All three international instruments contain specific limitation clauses that are similar in content. The *International Covenant on Civil and Political Rights* states, for example, that "[f]reedom to manifest one's religion or beliefs may be subject only to such limitations as are prescribed by law and are necessary to protect public safety, order, health, or morals or the fundamental right and freedoms of others".[220] Although not directly cited by the Supreme Court of Canada, Justice Dickson used the same terms as those found in article 18(3) of the *International Covenant on Civil and Political Rights* in determining the limits that section 1 may place on section 2(a) of the *Charter*.[221] Freedom of religion is frequently deemed a non-derogable provision, and may never be suspended, even in time of war or other national emergency.[222]

In 1981, the United Nations General Assembly, with Canada's support, adopted the *Declaration on the Elimination of All Forms of Intolerance and Discrimination based on Religion and Belief*.[223] It was originally intended for there to be a Convention that would mirror the *International Convention on the Elimination of All Forms of Racial Discrimination*, but there has been no real progress on this. Issues relating to freedom of religion and the struggle against intolerance have been the subject of several declarations within the forum of the Organization on Security and Cooperation in Europe.

The generous approach to freedom of religion in section 2(a) of the *Charter* has been justified in part by reference to international law, including detailed definitions of the right found in international instruments such as

---

220 *Supra* note 208, art. 18(3). See also: "Document of the Copenhagen Meeting of the Conference on the Human Dimension of the CSCE", 1989, para. 9.4.

221 *R.* v. *Big M Drug Mart*, [1985] 1 SCR 295, 18 DLR (4th) 321, 18 CCC (3d) 385, [1985] 3 WWR 481, 37 Alta LR (2d) 97, 58 NR 81, 60 AR 161, 13 CRR 64, 85 CLLC 14,023, at 346 (SCR). In *R.* v. *Hothi*, [1985] 3 WWR 256, 33 Man R (2d) 180, (sub nom. *Singh v. R.*) 14 CRR 85 (QB), affirmed, [1986] 3 WWR 671 (CA), leave to appeal refused, (1986) 70 N.R. 397n (SCC), Justice Dewar of the Manitoba Court of Queen's Bench referred to the limits on freedom of religion permissible under article 18(3) of the *International Covenant on Civil and Political Rights* in determining that a ban on the wearing of ceremonial daggers by Sikhs during a trial did not infringe the *Charter*. On a similar issue, this time on the wearing of such daggers in a school setting under certain conditions, see: *Multani v. Commission scolaire Marguerite-Bourgeoys*, 2006 SCC 6.

222 *International Covenant on Civil and Political Rights, supra* note 208, art. 4(2); *American Convention on Human Rights, supra* note 209, art. 27(2). But: *European Convention on Human Rights, supra* note 218, art. 15(2).

223 *Declaration on the Elimination of All Forms of Intolerance and Discrimination based on Religion and Belief*, GA Res. 35/55. See: Natan Lerner, "Toward a Draft Declaration Against Religious Intolerance and Discrimination", (1981) 11 *Israel Yearbook of Human Rights* 82.

in article 18 of the *International Covenant on Civil and Political Rights*.[224] Justice Tarnopolsky of the Ontario Court of Appeal, in one of the first Sunday closing cases under the *Charter*, drew particular attention to the reference in the international models to the right to "manifest" religion.[225] He also referred to the multiculturalism provisions of section 27 of the *Canadian Charter* in determining the scope of freedom of religion within the meaning of section 2(a). In support of his view, he cited not only article 18 but also article 27 of the *International Covenant on Civil and Political Rights*, which protects the rights of religious minorities. Also in the context of Sunday closing laws, Justice Charles D. Gonthier, then of the Quebec Superior Court, referred to a European Commission on Human Rights case[226] in which the applicant had argued that in being forced to resign from his teaching job because he was required to attend Friday prayers at his mosque he was denied freedom of religion.[227]

Many decisions invoking article 18 of the *Covenant* have used the international law limitations provisions in order to restrain the scope of freedom of religion.[228] In an early *Charter* decision, *R. v. Big M Drug Mart*, Justice Belzil of the Alberta Court of Appeal considered that the majority has a right to impose practices and customs, such as Sunday closing.[229] He said that "[f]reedom of religion in the *Charter* has the same meaning as freedom of religion in the *International Covenant on Civil and Political Rights* and in the other documents on human rights to which I have referred, including the *Canadian Bill of Rights*".[230] He concluded that freedom of religion was aimed at protecting religious groups from oppression and repression, and that it had nothing to do with a guarantee of equal treatment for all religious groups within a given jurisdiction. The General Division of the Ontario Court made reference to article 18(3) of the *Covenant* in support of the notion that "freedom of conscience does not include either acts of

---

224 See: Brad A. Elberg & Mark C. Power, "Freedom of Conscience and Religion", in Gérald-A. Beaudoin & Errol P. Mendes, eds., *Canadian Charter of Rights and Freedoms*, 4th ed., Markham, Ont., LexisNexis Butterworths, 2005, pp. 217-256, at 222.

225 *Re R. and Videoflicks*, (1984) 14 DLR (4th) 10, 15 CCC (3d) 353, 34 RPR 97, 9 CRR 193, 48 OR (2d) 395, (sub nom. *Edwards Books & Art Ltd. v. R.*) 5 OAC 1 (CA), reversed, (1986) 1986 CarswellOnt 1012 (SCC).

226 *Ahmad v. United Kingdom* (App. No. 8160/78) (1981), 4 EHRR 106.

227 *Association des détaillants en alimentation du Québec v. Ferme Carnaval Inc.*, [1986] RJQ 2513, [1987] DLQ 42 (CS). On Sunday closing, see also: *R. v. W.H. Smith*, [1983] 5 WWR 235, (1983) 26 Alta LR 238 (Prov Ct).

228 See, for example: *Bediako v. Canada (Solicitor General)*, 1995 CarswellNat 2196, [1995] FCJ No 292 (TD).

229 *R. v. Big M Drug Mart Ltd.*, [1984] 1 WWR 625, 5 DLR (4th) 121, 9 CCC (3d) 310, 28 Alta LR (2d) 289, 49 AR 194, 7 CRR 92 (CA), affirmed, [1985] 1 SCR 295, at 156 (DLR).

230 *Ibid.*, at 149 (DLR).

disapproval of the beliefs of others or 'day to day' decisions to act other ways".[231] The Federal Court of Canada has referred to the caselaw of the Human Rights Committee dismissing an argument that article 18 of the *International Covenant* entitles an individual to refuse to pay taxes where the use of government revenues went contrary to his or her religious principles. The Court noted that in the case at bar, the applicant's own communication to the Committee had already been dismissed.[232]

Proselytizing by religious groups has provoked considerable debate within human rights circles, particularly when attempts are made to distinguish the activities of "cults" from those of "legitimate" religious groups.[233] In a refugee determination decision, which was affirmed by the Federal Court,[234] reference was made to the *International Covenant on Civil and Political Rights*. Although article 18 does not explicitly deal with the matter, proselytizing may be considered a substantial part of a person's religious beliefs; such practices, however, may be subject to limitations when they impinge upon other people's freedoms.

Canadian courts have also referred to international law provisions protecting the rights of parents in the case of parochial education.[235] Justice Wilson of the Supreme Court of Canada, in her dissenting opinion in *R.* v. *Jones*, held that the *Charter* protects the right to educate children in accordance with their parents" religious and philosophical convictions. She relied on article 8(1) of the *European Convention* as well as article 2 of its *First Protocol*[236] in concluding that this right is "widely recognized":

> No person shall be denied the right to education. In the exercise of any functions which it assumes in relation to education and to teaching, the State shall respect the right of parents to ensure such education and teaching in conformity with their own religious and philosophical convictions.[237]

---

231 *Ontario (Attorney General)* v. *Dieleman*, (1994) 20 OR (3d) 229 (Ont Gen Div), at 252-253, 281, additional reasons at, (1995) 22 OR (3d) 785, 22 OR (3d) 785.

232 *Petrini* v. *R.*, (1994) 1994 CarswellNat 1131, [1994] FCJ No 1451 (CA), leave to appeal refused, (1995) 188 NR 238n (SCC).

233 See, for example: *Kokkinakis* v. *Greece*, Series A, No. 260-A; and, more recently, *Larissi* et al. v. *Greece* (App. No. 23372/94), 24 February 1998, Reports 1998-I, p. 378.

234 *Selvadurai* v. *Canada (Minister of Citizenship and Immigration)*, (1994) [1994] FCJ No 1395, 1994 CarswellNat 404 (TD).

235 See: Geraldine Van Bueren, *The International Law on the Rights of the Child*, Dordrecht, Boston & London: Martinus Nijhoff Publishers, 1995, at 152-159.

236 *Protocol No. 1, supra* note 218. Section 41 of the Quebec *Charter of Human Rights and Freedoms*, RSQ, c. C-12, is similar, but it specifies that such a right is exercised "within the framework of the curricula provided for by law".

237 *R.* v. *Jones*, [1986] 2 SCR 284, 31 DLR (4th) 569, 28 CCC (3d) 513, 69 NR 241, [1986] 6 WWR 577, 47 Alta LR (2d) 97, 73 AR 133.

However, the basis for such protection under the *Canadian Charter*, according to Justice Wilson, would appear to be the "liberty interest" of section 7 rather than section 2(a). In a case involving a status Indian, Justice Muldoon of the Federal Court (Trial Division) noted that a government policy permitting Catholic children to attend parochial schools, even at added expense, was consonant with the *International Covenant on Civil and Political Rights*, "whether intentionally or not".[238]

The recent case of *Chamberlain v. Surrey School District No. 36* saw an attempt to bring back the argument relating to the role of parents in the education of children within the purview of freedom of religion under section 2(a) *Charter*. At issue was whether or not the resolution adopted by a school board declining to approve books depicting same-sex parented families for a kindergarten curriculum was valid. The British Columbia Court of Appeal overturned the decision of the chambers judge, who held that the resolution was contrary to the secular principles prescribed by the enabling statute. In addition to aspects of discrimination, the rights of parents, vis-à-vis their children's education, was considered important by Mackenzie JA,[239] who referred to article 18(4) of the *International Covenant on Civil and Political Rights* providing for the "liberty of parents [. . .] to ensure the religious and moral education of their children in conformity with their own convictions".

On appeal at the Supreme Court of Canada, the majority held that the school board stepped outside its statutory mandate because the resolution violated *inter alia* the principles of secularism and tolerance. For the majority, McLachlin CJ wrote: "Moreover, although parental involvement is important, it cannot come at the expense of respect for the values and practices of all members of the school community."[240] Justice Gonthier, in dissent, wrote that the role of parents was paramount in the education of their children: "[P]arents clearly have the right, whether protected by s. 7 or s. 2(a) of the *Charter*, to nurture, educate and make decisions for their children, as long as these decisions are in the children's 'best interests'."[241] The reference to international human rights law in support of this conclusion included not only article 8(1) of the *European Convention of Human Rights*,

---

238 *Canada Human Rights Commission v. Canada (Department of Indian Affairs and Northern Development) and Prince*, (1994) 89 FTR 249, at 258.
239 *Chamberlain v. Surrey School District No. 36*, (2000) 191 DLR (4th) 128 (BC CA), additional reasons at, (2001) 2001 CarswellBC 2146 (CA), leave to appeal allowed, (2001) 283 N.R. 396n (SCC), reversed, [2002] 4 SCR 710, at para. 60.
240 *Chamberlain v. Surrey School District No. 36*, [2002] 4 SCR 710, at para. 33.
241 *Ibid.*, at para. 108.

as in *R. v. Jones*,[242] but also article 18(4) of the *International Covenant*, as in the decision at the Court of Appeal in the case at hand.[243]

4.2.2   Freedom of Thought, Belief, Opinion and Expression

Freedom of "thought, belief, opinion and expression, including freedom of the press and other media of communication" is protected by section 2(b) of the *Canadian Charter*. With respect to the international models it is a bit of a hybrid, because although they make the same general distinction as the *Canadian Charter* between "freedom of religion" (s. 2(a)) and "freedom of expression" (s. 2(b)), the former generally include "thought" and "belief" within their "freedom of religion" and not their "freedom of expression" provisions.[244] In *R. v. Myrrmidon*, Justice Twaddle of the Manitoba Court of Appeal mused as to why "thought" and "belief" are coupled with "opinion and expression" in the *Canadian Charter*, rather than with "conscience" and "religion", as in the *Universal Declaration of Human Rights*, although he drew no particular conclusions.[245]

The international provisions supply considerable detail as to the scope of the protection of freedom of expression. Article 19 of the *Universal Declaration of Human Rights*, for example, reads: "Everyone has the right to freedom of opinion and expression; this right includes freedom to hold opinions without interference and to seek, receive and impart information and ideas through any media and regardless of frontiers." Even more explicit is article 19 of the *International Covenant on Civil and Political Rights*, which states that freedom of expression "shall include freedom to seek, receive and impart information and ideas of all kinds, regardless of frontiers, either orally, in writing or in print, in the form of art, or through any other media of his choice".[246] International norms concerning freedom of the press

---

242 *Supra* note 237.

243 *Chamberlain* v. *Surrey School District No. 36, supra* note 240, at paras. 107 and 109.

244 See, for example, article 18 of the *Universal Declaration of Human Rights*, GA Res. 217 A (III), UN Doc. A/810, which states that "[e]veryone has the right to freedom of thought, conscience and religion. . ." Also: *International Covenant on Civil and Political Rights*, (1976) 999 UNTS 171, [1976] CTS 47, art. 18; *European Convention on Human Rights*, (1955) 213 UNTS 221, ETS 5, art. 10; *African Charter of Human and People's Rights*, OAU Doc. CAB/LEG/67/3 rev. 5, 4 EHRR 417, 21 *ILM* 58, art. 8. However, the *American Convention on Human Rights*, (1979) 1144 UNTS 123, OASTS 36, includes freedom of "thought" in its "freedom of expression" clause, art. 13.

245 *R.* v. *Myrrmidon Inc.*, [1988] 5 WWR 385, 43 CCC (3d) 137, 52 Man R (2d) 303 (CA), at 312 (Man R).

246 *International Covenant on Civil and Political Rights, supra* note 244.

also appear in the documents of the Organization for Security and Cooperation in Europe.[247]

The *Canadian Charter* is silent about "freedom of information", although in *Ford* v. *Quebec (Attorney General)*, the Supreme Court of Canada held that freedom of expression "protects listeners as well as speakers".[248] The *Universal Declaration* and the *International Covenant on Civil and Political Rights*, as well as the *European Convention on Human Rights* and the *American Convention on Human Rights*, explicitly include the right to receive and impart information within the scope of freedom of expression;[249] the *African Charter*, for its part, actually places the right to receive information ahead of the right to freedom of expression.[250] In *International Fund for Animal Welfare*, Justice MacGuigan of the Federal Court of Appeal, making reference to article 19(2) of the *International Covenant on Civil and Political Rights*,[251] appeared to welcome the argument that section 2(b) of the *Charter* includes "freedom of information". Justice McNair, hearing the case in first instance, had accepted the usefulness of the *International Covenant on Civil and Political Rights* in circumscribing the interpretation of section 2(b),[252] and Justice MacGuigan endorsed his reasoning.

The ramifications of freedom of expression pertaining to the right to receive information was considered by the Supreme Court of Canada in *Harper v. Canada (Attorney General)*.[253] The issue was whether or not the statutory regime[254] dealing with third party election advertising, including the blackout on polling day, was in violation of the right to vote in section

---

247 "Document of the Copenhagen Meeting of the Conference on the Human Dimension of the CSCE", 1989, para. 10; "Document of the Moscow Meeting of the Conference on the Human Dimension of the CSCE", 1991, para. 26.

248 *Ford* v. *Québec (AG)*, [1988] 2 SCR 712, 54 DLR (4th) 577, 19 QAC 69, 36 CRR 1, 90 NR 84, 10 CHRR D/5559. According to section 44 of the Quebec *Charter of Human Rights and Freedoms*, RSQ, c. C-12, "[e]very person has a right to information to the extent provided by law".

249 For the latter two, *European Convention on Human Rights, supra* note 244, art. 10(1), and *American Convention on Human Rights, supra,* note 244, art. 13(1). See also: *Compulsory Membership in an Association Prescribed by Law for the Practice of Journalism (Arts. 13 and 29 American Convention on Human Rights)* Advisory Opinion OC-5/85, Series A No. 5, 7 *Human Rights Law Journal* 88, 75 ILR 30, para. 30.

250 *African Charter of Human and People's Rights, supra* note 244, art. 9(1).

251 *International Fund for Animal Welfare Inc. v. Canada (Minister of Fisheries & Oceans)*, (1988) [1989] 1 FC 335, 83 NR 303, 35 CRR 359 (CA), at 309, 312 (FC).

252 *International Fund for Animal Welfare Inc. v. Canada (Minister of Fisheries & Oceans)*, (1986) [1987] 1 FC 244, 30 CCC (3d) 80, 5 FTR 193 (TD), reversed, (1988) 1988 CarswellNat 143 (Fed CA).

253 *Harper* v. *Canada (Attorney General)*, [2004] 1 SCR 827.

254 *Canada Elections Act*, SC 2000, c. 9. On election spending and freedom of expression with respect to section 2(b) of the *Charter*, see also: *Libman* v. *Québec (Attorney General)*, [1997] 3 SCR 569.

3 of the *Charter* or the right to freedom of expression in section 2(b). Both the majority and the dissent agreed that freedom of political expression was infringed; they disagreed on the outcome of the section 1 analysis. In concluding that the limits were unjustifiable, Chief Justice McLachlin and Justice Major insisted that "[f]reedom of expression protects not only the individual who speaks the message, but also the recipient. Members of the public – as viewers, listeners and readers – have a right to information on public governance, absent which they cannot cast an informed vote."[255] Such protection to both speakers and listeners finds support, they noted,[256] in the *Universal Declaration of Human Rights*[257] and the *International Covenant on Civil and Political Rights.*[258]

In *Irwin Toy*, the European Court of Human Rights was cited in support of the notion that freedom of expression should receive a very large ambit, and that limitations are to be imposed by means of the limitations clause (article 10(2) of the *European Convention*, section 1 of the *Canadian Charter*).[259] The Supreme Court referred to the *Handyside* case, where the European Court referred to freedom of expression as ". . .applicable not only to 'information' or 'ideas' that are favourably received or regarded as inoffensive or as a matter of indifference, but also to those that offend, shock or disturb the State or any sector of the population. Such are the demands of pluralism, tolerance and broadmindedness without which there is 'no democratic society'."[260] Richard Handyside had published and attempted to distribute the English translation of "The Little Red Schoolbook" until references to sexual activity provoked English authorities to seize the unsold copies. The European Court, by thirteen votes to one, ruled that the measures

---

255 *Harper* v. *Canada (Attorney General), supra* note 253, at para. 17.

256 *Ibid.,* at para. 18. On this aspect, see also: *Ruby* v. *Canada (Solicitor General),* [2002] 4 SCR 3, 219 DLR (4th) 385, 22 CPR (4th) 289, 49 Admin LR (3d) 1, 7 CR (6th) 88, 99 CRR (2d) 324, at para. 52.

257 *Universal Declaration of Human Rights, supra* note 244, art. 19.

258 *International Covenant on Civil and Political Rights, supra* note 244, art. 19(2).

259 *Irwin Toy* v. *Québec (AG),* [1989] 1 SCR 927, 39 CRR 193, 25 CPR (3d) 417, 58 DLR (4th) 577, 94 NR 167, 24 QAC 2. See also: *R.* v. *Butler,* [1989] 6 WWR 35, 72 CR (3d) 18, 60 Man R (2d) 82, 50 CCC (3d) 97 (QB), affirmed, [1991] 1 WWR 97, 5 CRR (2d) 68 (CA), reversed, [1992] 1 SCR 452, 70 CCC (3d) 129, 89 DLR (4th) 449, 11 CR (4th) 137, 8 CRR (2d) 1, [1992] 2 WWR 577, 78 Man R (2d) 1, 134 NR 81, 15 WCB (2d) 159, at 55 (WWR).

260 *Handyside* v. *United Kingdom,* 7 December 1976, Series A, No. 24, 1 EHRR 737, 59 ILR 150. On *Handyside,* see: Cora Feingold, "The Little Red Schoolbook and the European Court of Human Rights", (1978) 11 *Revue des droits de l'homme* 21; David J. Harris, "Decisions on the European Convention on Human Rights during 1976-1977", (1976-77) 48 *British Yearbook of International Law* 381.

were in fact "necessary" in a free and democratic society and dismissed the application.[261]

International law has also been invoked to delineate whether or not section 2(b) covers commercial speech, and whether it extends to the language itself. Justice Boudreault of the Quebec Superior Court relied on the jurisprudence of the European Commission on Human Rights[262] in concluding that "commercial speech" was encompassed by "the fundamental freedom of expression".[263] Although the reference to international law is less extensive, Justice Dugas of the Quebec Superior Court, in a judgment dealing with the same provisions of the *Charter of the French Language*,[264] reached the opposite conclusion. In effect, he failed to find any protection for the language in which the message is conveyed, only protection for the message itself.[265] Indeed, as a general rule, the courts have been extremely cautious in applying international authorities to the language issue. In *Chaussures Brown's*, Justice Bisson of the Quebec Court of Appeal wrote:

> Devrions-nous, en matière linguistique, comme on nous a invité à le faire, avoir recours aux rapports de la Commission européenne des droits de l'homme ou encore aux arrêts de la Cour européenne des droits de l'homme faits et prononcés en conformité de la Convention de sauvegarde des droits de l'homme et des libertés fondamentales adoptée par le Conseil de l'Europe, en 1950? Le problème des langues, au Canada, est tellement spécifique à notre histoire et au contexte de notre pays que j'estime qu'il faut y apporter une solution qui soit propre à ce contexte.[266]

The Supreme Court of Canada confirmed Justice Bisson's caveat that the European human rights jurisprudence on the language issue is "all distinguishable". And yet, taking considerable pains to analyse the reasoning of the European authorities, the Supreme Court also suggested that these could

---

261 The Court reached a similar conclusion in another obscenity case, this time involving allegedly obscene paintings: *Müller* v. *Switzerland*, 24 May 1988, Series A, No. 133.

262 For example: *Pastor X and Church of Scientology* v. *Sweden* (App. No. 7805/77), (1978) 16 DR 68, 22 European Convention on Human Rights Yearbook 244. Since that decision, there have been others: *Markt Intern and Beeman* v. *Federal Republic of Germany* (App. No. 10572/83), (1989) 11 EHRR 212.

263 *Ford* v. *P.-G. du Québec*, [1985] CS 147, 18 DLR (4th) 711, at 727 (DLR), affirmed, (1986) 36 D.L.R. (4th) 374 (CA), affirmed, [1988] 2 SCR 712, 54 DLR (4th) 577, 19 QAC 69, 36 CRR 1, 90 NR 84, 10 CHRR D/5559.

264 LRQ, c. C-11, s. 58.

265 *Devine* v. *P.-G. Québec*, [1982] CS 355, at 375-376.

266 *Québec* v. *Chaussures Brown's Inc.*, [1987] RJQ 80, 36 DLR (4th) 374, (sub nom. *Chaussure Brown's Inc. c. Québec (P.G.)*) 5 QAC 119, [1987] DLQ 82 (CA), affirmed, [1988] 2 SCR 712, at 90 (RJQ).

have "persuasive authority", echoing the dictum of Chief Justice Dickson with respect to the use of international authorities in general.[267]

In *Ballantyne and Davidson, and McIntyre v. Canada*,[268] the United Nations Human Rights Committee adopted essentially the same view of language and freedom of expression as the Supreme Court of Canada. Following the decision of the Human Rights Committee, in 1993 the Quebec National Assembly modified the *Charter of the French Language*,[269] making the provisions consistent with the view expressed by the Committee that the use of another language beside French in commercial signs be allowed so long as the latter be clearly predominant.[270] A new challenge to the legal regime governing language in Quebec arose in *Entreprises W.F.H. Ltée v. Québec (Procureure Générale)*. At the Court of Appeal, the appellant argued that the statute had to be interpreted in light of the *International Covenant on Civil and Political Rights* so that the rights of the people living in Quebec not be restricted more than those living in other Canadian provinces. Justice Biron wrote:

> Il y a lieu de signaler qu'aucune loi n'est venue mettre en oeuvre, en droit interne, le pacte de 1976 [*International Covenant on Civil and Political Rights*]. Les juges ne sont donc pas liés par les normes du droit international quand ils interprètent la charte, mais ces normes constituent une norme pertinente et persuasive d'interprétation des dispositions de cette dernière, tel que l'affirment le juge en chef Dickson dans le *Renvoi relatif à la* Public Service Employee

---

267 *Ford v. Québec (AG)*, *supra* note 248. On commercial signs and freedom of expression with respect to section 2(*b*) of the *Charter* in general, see also: *R. v. Guignard*, [2002] 1 SCR 472; Maya Hertig Randall, "Commercial Speech under the European Convention on Human Rights: Subordinate or Equal", (2006) 6 *Human Rights Law Review* 53.

268 *Ballantyne and Davidson, and McIntyre v. Canada* (Nos. 359/1989 and 385/1989), UN Doc. CCPR/C/47/D/385/1989, UN Doc. A/48/40, Vol. II, p. 91, 14 *Human Rights Law Journal* 171, 11 *Netherlands Quarterly of Human Rights* 469. See also *Singer v. Canada*, (No. 455/1991), UN Doc. A/49/40, Vol. II, p. 155.

269 *Supra* note 264, amended by the *Act to Amend the Charter of the French Language*, SQ 1993, c. 40, section 18. The new section 58 reads:

> Public signs and posters and commercial advertising must be in French. They may also be both in French and in another language provided that French is markedly predominant. However, the Government may determine, by regulation, the places, cases, conditions or circumstances where public signs and posters and commercial advertising must be in French only, where French need not be predominant or where such signs, posters and advertising may be in another language only.

See: Kent Roach & David Schneiderman, "Freedom of Expression in Canada", in Gérald-A. Beaudoin & Errol P. Mendes, eds., *Canadian Charter of Rights and Freedoms*, 4th ed., Markham, Ont., LexisNexis Butterworths, 2005, pp. 257-323, at 269-270.

270 See: *Immeubles Claude Dupont Inc. v. Québec (PG)*, [1994] RJQ 1968 (SC).

Relations Act *(Alb.)* et la juge L'Heureux-Dubé dans *Baker* v. *Ministre de la Citoyenneté et de l'Immigration du Canada.*[271]

Interestingly, one can notice in this passage the same hesitation of previous decisions. Courts seem very reluctant to rely on international legal norms when it comes to the interpretation and application of our language laws.

Like freedom of religion, freedom of expression is subject to limitations, and these are set out in detail in the international instruments.[272] The *International Covenant on Civil and Political Rights* recalls that freedom of expression "carries with it special duties and responsibilities", and that it is subject "to certain restrictions" that "are provided by law and are necessary: (a) For respect of the rights or reputations of others; (b) For the protection of national security or of public order (*ordre public*), or of public health or morals".[273] The limitation clause in the *European Convention on Human Rights* goes into even greater detail, stating that these may be justified "in the interests of national security, territorial integrity or public safety, for the prevention of disorder or crime, for the protection of health or morals, for the protection of the reputation or rights of others, for preventing the disclosure of information received in confidence, or for maintaining the authority and impartiality of the judiciary".[274] The *American Convention on Human Rights*, while broadly patterned on the *Covenant* with respect to limitations, adds that freedom of expression "shall not be subject to prior censorship but shall be subject to subsequent imposition of liability," a reflection of the constitutional law jurisprudence of the United States.[275]

Criminal legislation dealing with defamatory libel has been upheld with reference to the limitation clauses specific to freedom of expression in

---

271   *Entreprises W.F.H. Ltée* v. *Québec (Procureur général)*, [2001] RJQ 2557 (CA), leave to appeal refused, 307 N.R. 189n, [2002] 4 SCR VI (SCC), at 2569 [RJQ] (references omitted), confirming [2000] RJQ 1222 (SC). See also *Gosselin (tuteur de)* v. *Québec (Procureur général)*, [2000] RJQ 2973 (SC), affirmed, [2002] RJQ 1298 (CA), affirmed, [2005] 1 SCR 238.

272   For a judicial endorsement of this observation, made in the second edition of the present work, see: *Lafferty, Harwood & Partners* v. *Parizeau & Bouchard*, [2003] RJQ 2758 (CA), leave to appeal allowed, (2004) (sub nom. *Lafferty, Harwood & Partners Ltd. v. Parizeau*) 330 N.R. 395n (SCC), affirmed, (2000) 2000 CarswellQue 472 (SCC), at 2777 [RJQ], *per* Nuss JA; leave to appeal at the Supreme Court of Canada granted on 6 May 2004, but appeal discontinued because of settlement out of court, 1 February 2005.

273   *International Covenant on Civil and Political Rights, supra* note 244, art. 19(3). For a recent case of application by the United Nations Human Rights Committee, see *Hak-Chul Shin* v. *Republic of Korea* (No. 926/2000), UN Doc. CCPR/C/80/D/926/2000).

274   *European Convention on Human Rights, supra* note 244, art. 10(2).

275   *American Convention on Human Rights, supra* note 244, art. 13(2). But article 13(4) makes an exception to this rule, stating that "public entertainments may be subject by law to prior censorship for the sole purpose of regulating access to them for the moral protection of childhood and adolescence".

international instruments, including that in article 19(3)(a) of the *International Covenant*, which makes explicit reference to the importance of "respect of the rights or reputations of others".[276] A Manitoba court referred to the *Covenant* provision as well as decisions of the European Commission on Human Rights applying article 10(2) of the *European Convention*.[277] According to the Court, "[t]his recognition by the international community of the fundamental value of reputation and the inherent dignity of all persons emphasizes the importance of the objective behind s. 300 [of the *Criminal Code*]".[278] The conclusion was upheld by the Manitoba Court of Appeal, which referred to a judgment rendered by a Grand Chamber (at the time, nineteen judges) of the European Court of Human Rights.[279]

The issue was considered at the Supreme Court of Canada in *R. v. Lucas*[280] where, following the usual approach to section 2(b) of the *Charter*, the decision centred on whether the limits to freedom of expression broadly defined could be justified in a free and democratic society. Under the *Oakes* test, the objective of the *Criminal Code*[281] provisions dealing with defamatory libel, namely to protect an individual's reputation from wilful and false attack, was considered pressing and substantial. In his reasons for the majority, Justice Cory referred to the provisions limiting freedom of expression for the purpose of protecting the reputation of individuals found in the international instruments to which Canada consented, such as article 17 of the *International Covenant on Civil and Political Rights* and article 12

---

276 *International Covenant on Civil and Political Rights*, (1976) 999 UNTS 171, [1976] CTS 47, art. 19(3)(a).

277 *R. v. Stevens*, (1993) 82 CCC (3d) 97, [1993] 7 WWR 38 (Man Prov Ct), at 124 (CCC), affirmed, (1995) 96 CCC (3d) 238 (Man CA). The Court referred to: *X. v. Federal Republic of Germany* (App. No. 9235/81), (1982) 29 DR 194; *Lingens v. Austria* (App. No. 9815/82), (1984) 34 DR 180, 6 EHRR 550; *Gay News Ltd. and Lemon v. United Kingdom* (App. No. 8710/79), (1982) 5 EHRR 125. On defamatory libel, see also: *Busuioc v. Moldova* (App. No. 61513/00), 21 December 2004; *Constantinescu v. Romania* (App No. 28871/95), ECHR 351; *De Haes and Gijsels v. Belgium* (App. No. 19983/92), [1997] ECHR 7; *Lingens v. Austria*, 8 April 1986, Series A, No. 103; *Castells v. Spain*, 23 April 1992, Series A, No. 236; *Thorgeirson v. Iceland*, 25 June 1992, Series A, No. 239; *Demicoli v. Malta*, 27 August 1991, Series A, No. 210; J. Andrews, "Freedom of Speech and Politicians", (1986) 11 *European Law Reports* 491; J.J. Cremona, "The Thick Hide of Politicians and Article 10 of the European Convention on Human Rights", in *Présence du droit public et des droits de l'homme. Mélanges offerts à Jacques Vélu*, Vol. III, Brussels: Bruylant, 1992, pp. 1799-1811; Ronald St.J. Macdonald, "Politicians and the Press", in *Protecting Human Rights: The European Dimension*, Cologne: Carl Heymanns, 1988, pp. 361-372.

278 *R. v. Stevens*, *ibid.*

279 *R. v. Stevens*, (1995) 96 CCC (3d) 238 (Man CA), referring to *Jersild v. Denmark*, 23 September 1994, Series A, No. 298, 15 *Human Rights Law Journal* 361.

280 *R. v. Lucas*, [1998] 1 SCR 439.

281 RSC, 1985, c. C-46, ss. 298, 299 and 300.

of the *Universal Declaration of Human Rights*, as well as to those found in other international conventions, such as article 10 of the *European Convention on Human Rights* and article 13 of the *American Convention on Human Rights*.

Canadian courts have made frequent reference to a celebrated judgment of the European Court of Human Rights, *Sunday Times* v. *United Kingdom*, which held that an injunction upon a publication dealing with thalidomide and its effects issued by the courts of the United Kingdom violated article 10 of the *European Convention on Human Rights* and could not be saved as an acceptable limitation pursuant to article 10(2).[282] In *Ford et al.* v. *P.G. Québec*, a case applying the "freedom of expression" provisions of both the Canadian and the Quebec *Charters*,[283] Justice Pierre Boudreault of the Quebec Superior Court referred to article 19 of the *Universal Declaration of Human Rights*, article 10 of the *European Convention on Human Rights*, and the *Sunday Times Case* of the European Court of Human Rights. He observed that "[t]he European Court of Human Rights, in *Sunday Times* v. *United Kingdom*, [1979] 2 E.H.R.R. 245 (Strasbourg, April 26, 1979), concluded that there was a corollary between the function of the media in communicating information and ideas and the right of the public to receive them."[284]

Similarly, Justice James Hugessen of the Federal Court of Appeal, in *Re Luscher and Deputy Minister, Revenue Canada, Customs and Excise*, held that article 10 of the *European Convention* and the *Sunday Times Case* were "very helpful" in the construction of section 2(b) of the *Canadian Charter*.[285] However, in *Dagenais* v. *Canadian Broadcasting Corp.*, Justice Gonthier of the Supreme Court of Canada warned against misinterpreting the scope of *Sunday Times*:

> In the United Kingdom, as in Canada, the power to order a publication ban was historically seen as part of the ability of the courts to deal with *ex facie* criminal contempt. Reference to the position and tradition in the United Kingdom may strike some as odd in the face of the condemnation of that country by the European Court of Human Rights in the *Sunday Times* case [. . .] The condemnation in the *Sunday Times* case, however, has been viewed as being based only on differing opinions as to whether an interference with freedom of expression was necessary in the circumstances of the particular case [references omitted]. In fact, the majority of the European Court made it clear that it was

---

282 *Sunday Times* v. *United Kingdom*, 26 April 1979, Series A, No. 30, 2 EHRR 245, 58 ILR 491.

283 Section 3 of the Quebec *Charter of Human Rights and Freedoms*, RSQ, c. C-12.

284 *Ford* v. *AG Québec*, *supra* note 263, at 723 (DLR, translation).

285 *Re Luscher and Deputy Minister, Revenue Canada, Customs and Excise*, [1985] 1 FC 85, (1985) 17 DLR (4th) 503, 45 CR (3d) 81, 57 NR 386, [1985] 1 CTC 246, (1985) 15 CRR 167, 9 CER 229 (CA).

not condemning the English law of contempt and that there would be cases where restraint would be necessary to avoid "trial by newspaper".[286]

In *R.* v. *Kopyto*, the European Court's ruling in the *Sunday Times Case* was cited in the separate reasons of Justices Cory and Houlden, and in the dissent of Justice Dubin. Justice Cory discussed the limits on freedom of expression found in the *European Convention on Human Rights*, but observed that the European Court had confined them to the minimum: "Thus, like other courts in other jurisdictions, the European Court of Human Rights has stressed the paramount importance of freedom of expression in a free and democratic society, and has limited the scope of the restriction imposed on the freedom."[287] In *R.* v. *Kopyto*, the Ontario Court of Appeal found that the common law offense of scandalizing the court was not a permissible limit on freedom of expression. Justice Dubin, in his dissenting opinion, observed that the European Court of Human Rights had not, however, declared that contempt of court proceedings were in themselves a violation of the *Convention.*[288]

The Manitoba Court of Appeal noted, in a criminal case, that sometimes the fair trial provision respecting penal and criminal proceedings[289] and the rights enshrined in section 2(b) may collide.[290] Comparisons with the *European Convention*[291] and the *International Covenant on Civil and Political Rights*[292] may be helpful, the Court said, because these instruments delineate acceptable restrictions on press or public access to judicial and quasi-judicial proceedings. The relevant provisions were also referred to indirectly by the British Columbia Court of Appeal in *Hirt* v. *College of Physicians and Surgeons.*[293] In other words, limits on freedom of expression, in the context of media access to hearings, have already been envisaged by the international authorities. Justice La Forest's dissent in *Edmonton Journal* v. *Alta (AG)*, a case concerning press access to family court proceedings, referred to article 19(3) of the *International Covenant on Civil and Political Rights*

---

286 *Dagenais* v. *Canadian Broadcasting Corp.*, [1994] 3 SCR 835, 94 CCC (3d) 289, 120 DLR (4th) 12, 34 CR (4th) 269, 25 CRR (2d) 1, 76 OAC 81, 175 NR 1, at 926 (SCR).

287 *R.* v. *Kopyto*, (1988) 47 DLR (4th) 213, 39 CCC (3d) 1, 61 CR (3d) 109, 62 OR (2d) 449 (CA), at 238 (DLR).

288 *Ibid.*, at 286.

289 Section 11(*d*) of the *Canadian Charter*; this would arise, for example, where the press contests a publication ban on proceedings at a bail hearing or preliminary inquiry. Such temporary bans are intended to confine publication of evidence that might be admissible in preliminary proceedings but would later be found inadmissible at trial.

290 *R.* v. *Sophonow (No. 2)*, (1983) 150 DLR (3d) 590, 6 CCC (3d) 396, 34 CR (3d) 287, 21 Man R (2d) 110, 5 CRR 331 (CA), affirmed, (1984) 31 Man R (2d) 8 (SCC).

291 (1955) 213 UNTS 221, ETS 5, art. 6(1). See, for example: *Ekbatani* v. *Sweden*, 26 May 1988, Series A, No. 134.

292 *Supra* note 276, art. 14(1).

293 (1985) 17 DLR (4th) 472, 60 BCLR 273 (CA).

and article 10(2) of the *European Convention on Human Rights* for this purpose.[294]

The scope of protection provided by section 2(b) of the *Canadian Charter* with respect to access to information was considered in *Criminal Lawyers' Association* v. *Ontario (Ministry of Public Safety and Security)*.[295] At issue were provisions of the Ontario *Freedom of Information and Protection of Privacy Act*.[296] It was argued that the fact that the public interest override exemption does not apply to law enforcement records and to matters protected by solicitor-client privilege constitutes an impermissible violation of freedom of expression. The Court refused to recognise a general constitutional right of access to information in the possession or under the control of the government.[297] Although the open court principle falls within the purview of section 2(b) of the *Charter*, "its application has been limited to assuring public access to judicial and quasi-judicial proceedings; it does not apply to investigations by non-adjudicative bodies".[298] In fact, the principle has been restricted to the parts of the criminal justice system that are considered within the public arena, which is not the case for law enforcement investigations and documents protected by solicitor-client privilege. The international argument does not show otherwise because, the Court pointed out,[299] the protection provided by article 19(3) of the *International Covenant on Civil and Political Rights*, including the "freedom to seek, receive and impart information and ideas of all kinds", may be limited by laws necessary "for the protection of national security or of public order, or of public health

---

294 *Supra* note 291, at 1374 (SCR). Except in *Dagenais* v. *Canadian Broadcasting Corp.*, *supra* note 286, the recent caselaw at the Supreme Court of Canada on publication bans and public access to information in judicial proceedings has not referred to international human rights law. See: *Canadian Broadcasting Corp.* v. *New Brunswick (Attorney General)*, [1996] 3 SCR 480; *Lac d'Amiante du Québec Ltée* v. *2858-0702 Québec Inc.*, [2001] 2 SCR 743; *R.* v. *Mentuck*, [2001] 3 SCR 442; and *Sierra Club of Canada* v. *Canada (Minister of Finance)*, [2002] 2 SCR 522. See also Sébastien Grammond, "La justice secrète: information confidentielle et procès civil", (1996) 56 *Cahiers de Droit* 437.

295 *Criminal Lawyers' Association* v. *Ontario (Ministry of Public Safety and Security)*, (2004) 70 OR (3d) 332 (SCJ, DC).

296 RSO 1990, c. F.31, ss. 14, 19, 23.

297 See: *Travers* v. *Canada (Board of Inquiry on the Activities of the Canadian Airborne Regiment Battle Group in Somalia)*, [1993] 3 FC 528 (TD), affirmed [1994] 171 NR 158 (FCA); *Ontario (Attorney General)* v. *Finebert*, (1994) 19 OR (3d) 197, 116 DLR (4th) 498 (SCJ, DC); and *Yeager* v. *Canada (Correctional Service)*, (2003) 223 DLR (4th) 234 (FC).

298 *Criminal Lawyers' Association* v. *Ontario (Ministry of Public Safety and Security)*, *supra* note 295, at para. 75.

299 *Ibid.*, at para. 79.

or morals".[300] Finally, the various United Nations publications,[301] a white paper from the United Kingdom Cabinet Office,[302] as well as judicial decisions by international[303] and foreign[304] courts, all submitted by the applicant, were held not to support such a positive duty to disclose information as part of freedom of expression.[305]

By virtue of the *International Convention on the Elimination of All Forms of Racial Discrimination*, Canada has bound itself to ". . .declare an offence punishable by law all dissemination of ideas based on racial superiority or hatred".[306] The *Convention for the Prevention and Punishment of the Crime of Genocide* declares "[d]irect and public incitement to commit genocide" to be punishable as an international crime.[307] And under article 20 of the *International Covenant on Civil and Political Rights*:

> 20. (1) Any propaganda for war shall be prohibited by law.
>
> (2) Any advocacy of national, racial or religious hatred that constitutes incitement to discrimination, hostility or violence shall be prohibited by law.

The *Criminal Code* has prohibited the advocacy of genocide and the incitement of hatred against "any identifiable group".[308] A certain number of

---

300 *International Covenant on Civil and Political Rights*, *supra* note 276, article 19(3)(b).

301 See: "Report of the Special Rapporteur, Mr. Abid Hussain, Promotion and Protection of the Right to Freedom of Opinion and Expression", UN Doc. E/CN.4/1995/32; "Right to Freedom of Opinion and Expression", UN Doc. E/CN.4/1999/167; and "Report of the Special Rapporteur, Mr. Abid Hussain, Protection and Promotion of the Right to Freedom of Opinion and Expression" UN Doc. E/CN.4/1999/64.

302 United Kingdom, Cabinet Office (Office for Public Service), *Your Right to Know: The Government's Proposals for a Freedom of Information Act (White Paper) by Chancellor of the Duchy of Lancaster*, London: Her Majesty's Stationary Office, 1997, c. 1-3.

303 From the European Court of Human Rights: *Guerra* et al. v. *Italy* (App. No. 14967/89), 19 February 1998, Reports 1998-I; and from the Court of Justice of the European Communities: *Netherlands* v. *Council*, C-58/94, [1996] ECR I-2169.

304 From the United States of America: *Houchins* v. *KQED, Inc.*, 438 US 1 (1978); and from India: *S.P. Gupta* v. *President of India* et al., [1982] AIR (SC) 149.

305 *Criminal Lawyers' Association* v. *Ontario (Ministry of Public Safety and Security)*, *supra* note 295, at para. 78-88.

306 *International Convention on the Elimination of All Forms of Racial Discrimination*, (1969) 660 UNTS 195, [1976] CTS 47, art. 4(a). See also: *American Convention on Human Rights*, (1979) 1144 UNTS 123, OASTS 36, art. 13(5).

307 *Convention for the Prevention and Punishment of the Crime of Genocide*, (1951) 78 UNTS 277, [1949] CTS 27, art. 3(c). Also: *Statute of the International Criminal Tribunal for the former Yugoslavia*, UN Doc. S/RES/827 (1993), annex, art. 2(3)(c); *Statute of the International Criminal Tribunal for Rwanda*, UN Doc. S/RES/955 (1994), annex, art. 2(3)(c); *Rome Statute of the International Criminal Court*, UN Doc. A/CONF.183/9, art. 25(3)(e).

308 RSC 1985, c. C-46, ss. 318, 319. It is noteworthy that war propaganda has not been criminalised in Canada, as required by article 20(1) of the *International Covenant on Civil and Political Rights*, a shortcoming that has been noted by the Human Rights

professional bigots have attacked these provisions on the grounds that they conflict with section 2(b) of the *Charter*. These challenges have led to disparate decisions in the higher courts and conflicting uses of international law.

The Alberta Court of Appeal upheld the constitutionality of section 281.2 (now s. 318) of the *Criminal Code*,[309] overturning the judgment at first instance.[310] Justice Kerans of the Court of Appeal ruled that the *Criminal Code* provision was overly broad, and that it could not meet the section 1 test. In defense of his reasoning, he pointed out that the *Canadian Charter* had no provision comparable to article 17 of the *European Convention on Human Rights*, which reads: "Nothing in this Convention may be interpreted as implying for any State, group or person any right to engage in any activity or perform any act aimed at the destruction of any of the rights and freedoms set forth herein or at their limitation to a greater extent than is provided for in the Convention." Justice Kerans said that the issue of whether the provisions of the *International Convention on the Elimination of All Forms of Racial Discrimination* constitute a reasonable limit pursuant to section 1 of the *Charter* need not be decided.[311] He added that section 2(b) even includes the freedom "to hate and despise the Charter".[312]

The Ontario Court of Appeal reached the opposite conclusion in *R.* v. *Andrews*, and expressly disagreed with the approach of the Alberta Court of Appeal. Justice Cory, as he then was, referred to Canada's international commitments, and specifically the *International Convention on the Elimination of All Forms of Racial Discrimination*. He stated:

> By that convention Canada undertook to adopt immediate and positive measures designed to eradicate all incitement to acts of discrimination and undertook to declare an offence punishable by law all dissemination of ideas based on racial superiority or hatred as well as all acts of violence or incitement to such acts of violence against any race or group of persons of another colour or ethnic origin.
>
> That commitment by Canada as well as other countries would seem to indicate that section 281.2 [now 319] was demonstrably justified in free and democratic societies. The convention is designed to eradicate the promotion of

---

Committee: UN Doc. A/35/40, para. 171. Many Western States, but not Canada, made reservations to article 20(1) at the time of ratification or accession. See: Michael Kearney, "The Prohibition of Propaganda for War in the International Covenant on Civil and Political Rights", (2005) 23 *Netherlands Quarterly of Human Rights* 551.

309 *R.* v. *Keegstra*, (1990) [1990] 3 SCR 697, 61 CCC (3d) 1, [1991] 2 WWR (2d) 193, 1 CR (4th) 129, 3 CRR (2d) 193, 77 Alta LR (2d) 193 114 AR 81, 117 NR 1.

310 *R.* v. *Keegstra*, (1985) 19 CCC 254 (Alta QB).

311 *R.* v. *Keegstra*, *supra* note 309, at 167 (CCC).

312 *Ibid.*, at 161 (CCC).

hatred against identifiable groups, an evil which has been recognized by the international community.[313]

Noting that Canada "is not unique in having legislation prohibiting the promotion of hatred", Justice Cory cited legislative policy in other countries, such as France and India: "The international commitments of Canada and the similar legislation enacted by other nations demonstrate that its provisions are consistent with freedom and democracy."[314]

The suggestion that there is some fundamental right to promote race hatred has also arisen in the context of contempt of court proceedings. John Ross Taylor was ordered by the Canada Human Rights Commission to cease transmitting a racist telephone message,[315] in accordance with section 13(1) of the *Canadian Human Rights Act*:

> 13. (1) [Hate messages] It is a discriminatory practice for a person or a group of persons acting in concert to communicate telephonically or to cause to be so communicated, repeatedly, in whole or in part by means of the facilities of a telecommunication undertaking within the legislative authority of Parliament, any matter that is likely to expose a person or persons to hatred or contempt by reason of the fact that that person or those persons are identifiable on the basis of a prohibited ground of discrimination.[316]

Taylor refused to comply, and was held to be in contempt of court. He challenged the order of the Canadian Human Rights Commission before the Human Rights Committee of the United Nations, pursuant to the *Optional Protocol to the International Covenant on Civil and Political Rights*, as a violation of his rights under article 19 of the *Covenant*. The Committee found Taylor's communication to be inadmissible for failure to exhaust local remedies, but so as the decision would be more than merely technical, it added:

> . . . the opinions which Mr T[aylor] seeks to disseminate through the telephone system clearly constitute the advocacy of racial or religious hatred which Canada has an obligation under article 20(2) of the Covenant to prohibit. In the Committee's opinion, therefore, the communication is, in respect of this claim, incompatible with the provisions of the Covenant.[317]

---

313 *R.* v. *Andrews*, (1989) 43 CCC (3d) 193, 65 OR (2d) 161, 28 OAC 161, 65 CR (3d) 320, 39 CRR 36 (CA), affirmed, (1990) 75 OR (2d) 481n (SCC), at 182.

314 *Ibid.*, at 188.

315 *CHRC et al.* v. *Western Guard Party et al*, unreported, Canada Human Rights Commission, 20 July 1979 (Leddy, Lederman, Volpini).

316 RSC 1985, c. H-6.

317 *J.R.T. and W.G.P.* v. *Canada* (No. 104/1981), UN Doc. CCPR/C/OP/2, p. 25, [1984-85] *Canadian Human Rights Yearbook* 357, 5 CHRR D/2097, 4 *Human Rights Law Journal* 193, at 28 (UN Doc. CCPR/C/OP/2).

Taylor's case had arisen prior to proclamation of the *Canadian Charter*. Subsequently, and after serving a prison term for contempt of court, he renewed his telephone message campaign and was again cited by the Canadian Human Rights Commission. The Federal Court of Appeal dismissed his argument that his section 2(b) rights had been violated, referring to the provisions of the *International Convention on the Elimination of All Forms of Racial Discrimination* and to the earlier Human Rights Committee decision.[318]

At the Supreme Court of Canada,[319] the constitutionality of the provision of the *Canada Human Rights Act* was upheld in *Canadian (Human Rights Commission) v. Taylor*,[320] which had become a companion case to *R. v. Keegstra*.[321] In those cases, however, the Supreme Court did not consider the debate from the standpoint of section 2(b), conceding that there was a violation of freedom of expression, and that it could only be saved by operation of section 1.[322] Essentially, the debate in the divided Court was between the view of freedom of expression adopted by international human rights law, which readily accepts and even requires limits concerning hate propaganda, and the more absolute view of the United States Supreme Court in its judgments dealing with the First Amendment to the *Constitution*. Referring to the *International Convention on the Elimination of All Forms of Racial Discrimination* and the *International Covenant on Civil and Political Rights*, Chief Justice Dickson wrote for the majority:

> *CERD [International Convention on the Elimination of All Forms of Racial Discrimination]* and *ICCPR [International Covenant on Civil and Political Rights]* demonstrate that the prohibition of hate-promoting expression is con-

---

318 *Taylor* v. *Canadian Human Rights Commission*, (1987) 78 NR 180, 37 DLR (4th) 572, 29 CRR 223 (FCA). In its periodic reports pursuant to the *International Convention on the Elimination of All Forms of Racial Discrimination*, under the heading "Article 4. Prosecution of Racist Propaganda Activities", Canada provided the Committee for the Elimination of Racial Discrimination with "progress reports" on the prosecutions of Taylor, Keegstra and Andrews: UN Doc. CERD/C/132/Add. 3, paras. 39-41 and 181; UN Doc. CERD/C/159/Add.3, paras. 40-44; UN Doc. CERD/C/185/Add. 3, para. 24.

319 See: Irwin Cotler, "Hate Speech, Equality, and Harm under the Charter: Towards a Jurisprudence of Respect for a 'Free and Democratic Society,'" in Gérald-A. Beaudoin & Errol P. Mendes, eds., *Canadian Charter of Rights and Freedoms*, 4th ed., Markham, Ont., LexisNexis Butterworths, 2005, pp. 1399-1490; and Sanjeev Anand, "Beyond *Keegstra*: The Constitutionality of the Wilful Promotion of Hatred Revisited", (1997-1998) 9 *National Journal of Constitutional Law* 117.

320 *Canada (HRC) v. Taylor*, [1990] 3 SCR 892, 75 DLR (4th) 577, 13 CHRR 435, 3 CRR (2d) 116.

321 *R.* v. *Keegstra, supra* note 309.

322 *Ibid.*, at 732-734 (SCR, *per* Dickson CJ). This ruling is in keeping with its decision in *Toy* v. *Québec (AG)*, [1989] 1 SCR 927, 39 CRR 193, 25 CPR (3d) 417, 58 DLR (4th) 577, 94 NR 167, 24 QAC 2.

sidered to be not only compatible with a signatory nation's guarantee of human rights, but is as well an obligatory aspect of this guarantee. Decisions under the *European Convention for the Protection of Human Rights and Fundamental Freedoms* are also of aid in illustrating the tenor the international community's approach to hate propaganda and free expression. This is not to deny that finding the correct balance between prohibiting hate propaganda and ensuring freedom of expression has been a source of debate internationally [references omitted]. But despite debate Canada, along with other members of the international community, has indicated a commitment to prohibiting hate propaganda, and in my opinion this Court must have regard to that commitment in investigating the nature of the government objective behind s. 319(2) of the *Criminal Code*. That the international community has collectively acted to condemn hate propaganda, and to oblige State Parties to *CERD* and *ICCPR* to prohibit such expression, thus emphasizes the importance of the objective behind s. 319(2) and the principles of equality and the inherent dignity of all persons that infuse both international human rights and the *Charter*.[323]

Justice McLachlin wrote for the minority, arguing that the freedom of expression provision of the *Charter* was not essentially based on the international models. She referred to the freedom of expression provisions of the *International Covenant* and the *European Convention*, noting that these were "internally limited" by their limitations clauses, unlike the *Canadian Charter*:

> The guarantees of free expression in those documents explicitly permit a wide variety of limitations on free expression – limitations which the person asserting the right of free expression must observe. By contrast, the Canadian guarantee of free expression is more comprehensive.[324]

This argument overlooks the drafting history of the *Charter*, which demonstrates that section 1 of the *Charter* was directly inspired by provisions such as article 19(3) of the *International Covenant* and article 10(2) of the *European Convention*. Moreover, it appears to contradict the Dickson dictum, in *Public Service Alliance*, which insists on an interpretation of the *Charter* that essentially conforms to Canada's international obligations under the *Covenant*.[325]

The approach adopted by the majority in those cases with regard to the relevance of international human rights instruments was endorsed by a unanimous Court in *Ross v. New Brunswick School District No. 15*. At issue was whether or not the decision ordering a school board to remove a teacher

323 *R.* v. *Keegstra, ibid.*, at 754-755 (SCR).
324 *Ibid.*, at 807 (SCR).
325 *Reference re Public Service Employee Relations Act (Alberta)*, [1987] 1 RCS 313, 51 Alta LR (2d) 97, [1987] 3 WWR 577, (sub nom. *A.U.P.E.* v. *Alberta (Attorney General)*) 28 CRR 305, 38 DLR (4th) 161, (sub nom. *Reference re Compulsory Arbitration*) 74 NR 99, 78 AR 1, [1987] DLQ 225, 87 CLLC 14,021.

from his teaching position based on a discriminatory statement made publicly during his off-duty time and to terminate his employment if he continued to write and publish anti-Semitic materials was in breach of the teacher's fundamental freedoms. In allowing the appeal in part and restoring the order concerning the appointment to a non-teaching position, Justice La Forest gave a broad interpretation to section 2 of the *Charter* and left competing rights to be reconciled in the section 1 analysis. It is in the first prong of the *Oakes* test that Chief Justice Dickson remarks in *Canada (Human Rights Commission) v. Taylor*[326] were recalled and that the Court concluded that "[b]ased upon the jurisprudence, Canada's international obligations and the values constitutionally entrenched, the objective of the impugned order is clearly 'pressing and substantial'."[327]

4.2.3   Freedom of Peaceful Assembly

Freedom of assembly and association were treated together in the *Canadian Bill of Rights*.[328] This is also the approach of the *Universal Declaration of Human Rights*, which declares: "Everyone has the right to freedom of peaceful assembly and association."[329] The distinction between sections 2(c) ("freedom of peaceful assembly") and 2(d) ("freedom of association") in the *Canadian Charter of Rights and Freedoms* was apparently inspired by the *International Covenant on Civil and Political Rights*.[330] The *Covenant* affirms that "[t]he right of peaceful assembly shall be recognized" and goes on to define its limitations: "No restrictions may be placed on the exercise of this right other than those imposed in conformity with the law and which are necessary in a democratic society in the interests of national security or public safety, public order (ordre public), the protection of public health or morals or the protection of the rights and freedoms of others."[331]

---

326 *Canada (Human Rights Commission)* v. *Taylor*, *supra* note 320.

327 *Attis* v. *New Brunswick District No. 15 Board of Education*, (sub nom. *Ross* v. *New Brunswick School District No. 15*) [1996] 1 SCR 825, at para. 98.

328 *Canadian Bill of Rights*, RSC 1985, Appendix III, s. 1(e).

329 *Universal Declaration of Human Rights*, GA Res. 217 A (III), UN Doc. A/810, art. 20(1). See also: *European Convention on Human Rights*, (1955) 213 UNTS 221, ETS 5, art. 11(1); *International Convention on the Elimination of All Forms of Racial Discrimination*, *supra* note 306, art. 5(d)(ix); *Convention on the Rights of the Child*, GA Res. 44/25, art. 15.

330 Robin Elliott, "Interpreting the Charter — Use of the Earlier Versions as an Aid", (1982) 16 *Charter Edition University of British Columbia Law Review* 11.

331 *International Covenant on Civil and Political Rights*, (1976) 999 UNTS 171, [1976] CTS 47, art. 21. See also: *American Convention on Human Rights*, *supra* note 306, art. 15, which adds that the right of peaceful assembly must be "without arms": art. 15. Also on freedom of assembly, see: *American Declaration of the Rights and Duties of Man*, OAS Doc. OEA/Ser.L./V/II.23, doc. 21, rev. 6, art. XXI; *African Charter of Human*

In a case heard by the European Court of Human Rights, a lawyer in Guadeloupe challenged a disciplinary measure taken against him because of his participation in a public demonstration. The Court concluded that the measure was provided by law, and that it had a legitimate objective. However, passing to the proportionality component of its analysis, the Court concluded that the protection of public order should not be used to discourage lawyers from taking part in public expressions of their political views. France was found to have breached article 11 of the *European Convention on Human Rights*, which protects freedom of assembly.[332]

International law has not been applied by Canadian courts in any reported judicial interpretation of section 2(c) to date.

4.2.4 Freedom of Association

Section 2(d) of the *Charter* refers succinctly to the protection of "freedom of association". The *Universal Declaration of Human Rights* makes a similar brief reference to freedom of association: "Everyone has the right to freedom of peaceful assembly and association;"[333] but it adds that "[n]o one may be compelled to belong to an association".[334] The *Declaration* also provides for "the right to form and to join trade unions", but in a distinct provision presented as part of the "right to work", and thus an economic and social right rather than a civil and political right.[335]

According to article 22(1) of the *International Covenant on Civil and Political Rights*, "[e]veryone shall have the right to freedom of association with others, including the right to form and join trade unions for the protection of his interests". In paragraph 3 of the same provision, the *Covenant* states: "Nothing in this article shall authorize States Parties to the International Labour Organization Convention of 1948 concerning Freedom of Association and Protection of the Right to Organize to take legislative measures which would prejudice, or to apply the law in such a manner as to prejudice the guarantees provided for in that Convention." The *Convention* in question, often identified as "ILO Convention 87" is the principal international treaty dealing with the right to organize unions and employer's organizations, and it has been ratified by Canada.[336] Although less prolix, the *European Convention on Human Rights* provision also explicitly links

---

and Peoples' Rights, OAU Doc. CAB/LEG/67/3 rev. 5, 4 EHRR 417, 21 *ILM* 58, art. 11.

332 *Ezelin* v. *France*, 26 April 1991, Series A, No. 202.

333 *Universal Declaration of Human Rights, supra* note 329, art. 20(1).

334 *Ibid.*, art. 20(2).

335 *Ibid.*, art. 23(4).

336 *ILO Convention (No. 87) Concerning Freedom of Association and Protection of the Right to Organize*, (1950) 68 UNTS 17, [1973] CTS 14.

freedom of association with "the right to form and to join trade unions for the protection of his interests".[337] The labour organization slant of the *Covenant*'s provision is far less obvious in the freedom of association provision of the *American Convention on Human Rights*. It states, at article 16(1), that "[e]veryone has the right to associate freely for ideological, religious, political, economic, labor, social, cultural, sports, or other purposes".[338]

The international models also provide detailed limitations clauses, applicable to freedom of association. According to the *International Covenant on Civil and Political Rights*, the right may be limited "in the interests of national security or public safety, public order (*ordre public*), the protection of public health or morals or the protection of the rights and freedoms of others".[339] The *Covenant* adds that the provision shall not prevent the imposition of lawful restrictions on members of the armed forces and of the police.

The principal difficulty in interpretation arises because the dichotomy in the *Universal Declaration of Human Rights* between freedom of association (article 20) and the right to form and join trade unions (article 23(4)) was maintained when the *Covenants* were drafted. It should be recalled that the original intention was to prepare a single *Covenant*, one that would give legally binding effect to the common standards set out in the *Declaration*. But cold war politics resulted in a split, and it was decided to prepare not one but two covenants. In principle, the civil and political rights listed in the *Declaration*, including freedom of association, were assigned to one instrument, while the economic and social rights listed in the *Declaration*, including trade union rights, were assigned to the other.[340] But the division was not as rigorous as first suggested, and it proved impossible to make a clean distinction between the two categories of rights. Indeed, in recent years, human rights law has increasingly insisted upon the "indivisibility"

---

337 *European Convention on Human Rights, supra* note 329, art. 11(1). However, the European Court of Human Rights has interpreted that provision broadly enough to include a general right to form an association. See: *Sidiropoulos* et al. v. *Greece* (App. No. 26695/95), 10 July 1998, Reports 1998-IV.

338 *American Convention on Human Rights*, (1979) 1144 UNTS 123, OASTS 36, art. 16. See also: *African Charter of Human and Peoples' Rights, supra* note 331, art. 10; *American Declaration of the Rights and Duties of Man, supra* note 331, art. XXII; *International Convention on the Elimination of All Forms of Racial Discrimination*, (1969) 660 UNTS 195, [1976] CTS 47, art. 5(d)(ix); *Convention on the Rights of the Child, supra* note 329, art. 15. Also "Document of the Copenhagen Meeting of the Conference on the Human Dimension of the CSCE", 1989, para. 7.6.

339 *International Covenant on Civil and Political Rights, supra* note 331, art. 22(2). See also: *American Convention on Human Rights, supra* note 338, art. 16(2) and (3); *European Convention on Human Rights, supra* note 329, art. 11(2).

340 This is discussed in Chapter 3, *supra*, at 145-148.

of human rights, affirming that the two *Covenants* are interrelated and indissociable.[341]

As we have seen, there are explicit references to trade union rights in the *International Covenant on Civil and Political Rights* provision dealing with freedom of association. Moreover, the *International Covenant on Economic, Social and Cultural Rights* provides for the right to form unions, including with it a limitation clause similar to that in the other *Covenant*.[342] Furthermore, the *International Covenant on Economic, Social and Cultural Rights* affirms "[t]he right to strike, provided that it is exercised in conformity with the laws of the particular country".[343] A right to strike is also implied from certain of the International Labour Organizations conventions, notably *ILO Convention (No. 87) Concerning Freedom of Association and Protection of the Right to Organize*.[344]

International law has been cited on numerous occasions by Canadian courts in an attempt to determine whether the right to strike is included in the freedom of association provisions of section 2(d).[345] The question has arisen with respect to legislation enacted to prevent strikes within the public service. Prior to entry into force of the *Canadian Charter* in 1982, labour unions representing public sector employees had attempted to rely on these international law provisions in challenging anti-strike legislation, but without any success.[346] Lawyers had attempted to argue that a right to strike was part of customary international law, but this contention was rejected. "It is

---

341   *Vienna Declaration and Programme of Action*, UN Doc. A/CONF.157/24, (1993) 14 *Human Rights Law Journal* 352, para. 5.

342   *International Covenant on Economic, Social and Cultural Rights*, (1976) 993 UNTS 3, [1976] CTS 46, art. 8(a), (c).

343   *Ibid.*, art. 8(d).

344   (1950) 68 UNTS 17, [1973] CTS 14.

345   See: Michael Bendel, "The International Protection of Trade Union Rights: A Canadian Case Study", (1981) 13 *Ottawa Law Review* 169; Paul J.J. Cavaluzzo, "Freedom of Association and the Right to Bargain Collectively", in Paul Weiler & Robin Elliott, eds., *Litigating the Values of a Nation: The Canadian Charter of Rights and Freedoms*, Toronto: Carswell, 1986, p. 195, at 197; Brian W. Burkett, John D.R Craig & S. Jodi Gallagher, "Canada and the ILO: Freedom of Association since 1982", (2003) 10 *Canadian Labour & Employment Law Journal* 231; and Ken Norman, "Freedom of Association (Section (d))", in Gérald-A. Beaudoin & Errol P. Mendes, eds., *Canadian Charter of Rights and Freedoms*, 4th ed., Markham, Ont., LexisNexis Butterworths, 2005, pp. 325-359, at 330-334 & 340-341.

346   *Re Alberta Union of Public Employees and the Crown in Right of Alberta*, (1981) 120 DLR (3d) 590, 81 CLLC 14,089 (Alta QB), affirmed, (1981) 1981 CarswellAlta 553 (CA), leave to appeal refused, (1981) 130 DLR (3d) 191 (note) (SCC). A communication was also submitted to the Human Rights Committee, where a majority, accompanied by a strong and well-reasoned dissent, concluded that the right to strike was not included in article 22: *JB et al. v. Canada* (No. 118/1982), UN Doc. CCPR/C/OP/2, p. 34, [1987] *Canadian Human Rights Yearbook* 213, 235, 5 *DJI* 641.

not, and has never been, part of the customary international law that public servants have the right to strike", wrote Justice Sinclair of the Alberta Court of Queen's Bench,[347] in a judgment that "presents a serious consideration of the requirements of international law, clearly acknowledging their potential relevance in the interpretation of domestic law".[348]

Upon proclamation of the *Charter*, trade union lawyers renewed their efforts, this time claiming that section 2(d) of the *Charter* incorporated the international law guarantees of the right to strike. In one of the first cases, Justice Reed of the Federal Court, Trial Division declared that a "right to strike" was not protected by the *International Covenant on Civil and Political Rights*, the *European Convention on Human Rights*, or the *Universal Declaration of Human Rights*, but that the ILO Conventions and the *International Covenant on Economic, Social and Cultural Rights* went further. She dismissed the argument that freedom of association included a right to strike, stating that "the fact that Canada has acceded to international conventions which provide for a right to strike does not mean that the Charter of Rights [. . .] intended to incorporate all rights contained in those international conventions".[349]

But in the *Broadway Manor case*, Justice O'Leary of the Ontario Divisional Court took the opposite view, concluding that freedom of association included a right to strike. He referred to article 8(1)(d) of the *International Covenant on Economic, Social and Cultural Rights*, as well as *ILO Convention No. 87*. "The right to organize and bargain collectively is only an illusion if the right to strike does not go with it", he concluded.[350] Justice Kerans, in *Reference Re Public Service Employee Relations Act*, recognized the ambiguity of the *International Covenant on Civil and Political Rights* provisions: "I accept that these two provisions might be open to the interpretation that freedom of association includes the right to strike, although a

---

347   *Re Alberta Union of Public Employees and the Crown in Right of Alberta, ibid.*, at 621 (DLR).

348   Maxwell Cohen & Anne F. Bayefsky, "The Canadian Charter of Rights and Freedoms and International Law", (1983) 61 *Canadian Bar Review* 265, at 300.

349   *Public Service Alliance of Canada* v. *Canada*, [1984] 2 FC 580, 11 DLR (4th) 337, 9 CRR 248 (TD), affirmed, (1984) [1984] 21 FC 889 (CA), affirmed, [1987] 1 SCR 424, at 354 (DLR).

350   *Service Employees' International Union Local 204* v. *Broadway Manor Nursing Home*, (1983) 4 DLR (4th) 231, 44 OR (2d) 392, 10 CRR 37 (Div. Ct.), reversed, (1984) 1984 CarswellOnt 829 (CA), leave to appeal refused, (1985), 8 OAC 320 (note) (SCC). The same view was adopted by Justice Croteau of the Quebec Superior Court, in *Syndicat canadien de la fonction publique* v. *PG du Québec*, [1986] RJQ 2983 (SC).

contrary interpretation is also arguable."[351] And Justice Esson of the British Columbia Court of Appeal found that even the *International Covenant on Economic, Social and Cultural Right* was not totally unequivocal on the subject, and that it "contemplates laws restricting the right to strike".[352]

Eventually, the Supreme Court of Canada, in *Re Public Service Employee Relations Act*,[353] concluded that the *Charter* does not protect the right to strike. The opinions of the Court are rich in international law references. Chief Justice Dickson, in his dissenting reasons, took up the arguments of Justice O'Leary in *Broadway Manor*, drawing extensively not only on the international instruments themselves but also on the jurisprudence of the International Labour Organization's Freedom of Association Committee. He focussed on article 8 of the *International Covenant on Economic, Social and Cultural Rights* which not only protects the right of trade unions "to function freely" but which, moreover, explicitly refers to "[t]he right to strike, provided that it is exercised in conformity with the laws of the particular country". He added, however, that "[t]his qualification that the right must be exercised in conformity with domestic law does not, in my view, allow for legislative abrogation of the right though it would appear to allow for regulation of the right".[354] He noted that article 8(2) allowed limitation on trade union rights in the case of members of the armed forces, the police and the State administration, but that article 8(3) (which he inaccurately called the "non-derogation clause") affirmed that the *Covenant* was without prejudice to the provisions of *ILO Convention No. 87*. Chief Justice Dickson also pointed out that article 22 of the *International Covenant on Civil and Political Rights*, while it did not explicitly protect the right to strike, had a similar without prejudice clause "mak[ing] it clear that the article is not to be interpreted as authorizing legislative measures that would prejudice the guarantees of International Labour Organization Convention No. 87".[355]

ILO Convention No. 87 does not make any explicit reference to a right to strike. However, as Chief Justice Dickson observed, it has been inter-

351 *Reference re Public Service Employee Relations Act, Labour Relations Act and Police Officers Collective Bargaining Act*, (1984) [1985] 2 WWR 289, 35 Alta LR (2d) 124, (sub nom. *Reference re Compulsory Arbitration*) 57 AR 268, 85 CLLC 14,027, 16 DLR (4th) 359 (CA), at 372 (DLR).

352 *Dolphin Delivery Ltd. v. Retail, Wholesale & Department Store Union, Local 580*, [1984] 3 WWR 481, 52 BCLR 1, 84 CLLC 14,036, 10 DLR (4th) 198 (CA), affirmed, [1986] 2 SCR 573.

353 *Reference re Public Service Employee Relations Act (Alberta)*, [1987] 1 RCS 313, 51 Alta LR (2d) 97, [1987] 3 WWR 577, (sub nom. *A.U.P.E.* v. *Alberta (Attorney General)*) 28 CRR 305, 38 DLR (4th) 161, (sub nom. *Reference re Compulsory Arbitration*) 74 NR 99, 78 AR 1, [1987] DLQ 225, 87 CLLC 14,021.

354 *Ibid.*, at 351 (SCR).

355 *Ibid.*, at 352 (SCR).

preted by decision-making bodies within the International Labour Organization, specifically the Committees of Experts, Commissions of Inquiry and the Freedom of Association Committee, as implicitly encompassing a right to strike, even in the public sector.[356] Chief Justice Dickson then turned to the Freedom of Association Committee's treatment of a series of Canadian cases, some of which were the subject of reference before the Supreme Court. In its conclusions with respect to legislation adopted by Alberta, the Committee stated:

> The Committee recalls that it has been called to examine the strike ban in a previous case submitted against the Government of Canada/Alberta [. . .] In that case the Committee recalled that the right to strike, recognized as deriving from Article 3 of the Convention, is an essential means by which workers may defend their occupational interests. It also recalled that, if limitations on strike action are to be applied by legislation, a distinction should be made between publicly-owned undertakings which are genuinely essential, i.e. those which supply services whose interruption would endanger the life, personal safety or health of the whole or part of the population, and those which are not essential in the strict sense of the term. The Governing Body, on the Committee's recommendation, drew the attention of Government to this principle and suggested to the Government that it consider the possibility of introducing an amendment to the Public Service Employee Relations Act in order to confine the prohibition of strikes to services which are essential in the strict sense of the term.[357]

In conclusion, Chief Justice Dickson wrote:

> The most salient feature of the human rights documents discussed above in the context of this case is the close relationship in each of them between the concept of freedom of association and the organization and activities of labour unions. As a party to these human rights documents, Canada is cognizant of the importance of freedom of association to trade unionism, and has undertaken as a binding international obligation to protect to some extent the associational freedoms of workers within Canada. Both of the U.N. human rights Covenants contain explicit protection of the formation and activities of trade unions subject to reasonable limits. Moreover, there is a clear consensus amongst the ILO adjudicative bodies that Convention No. 87 goes beyond merely protecting the formation of labour unions and provides protection of their essential activities – that is of collective bargaining and the freedom to strike.[358]

His dissent includes an affirmation of the importance of international law that has been uncontested. The argument was not, of course, about the

---

356 *Ibid.*, at 355-356 (SCR).
357 *Ibid.*, at 357-358 (SCR). The Chief Justice cited *Canadian Labour Congress (Confederation of University Teachers of Alberta)* v. *Canada (Alberta)*, Case No. 1247, (1985) 68 *Official Bulletin* (Series B.) 29, pp. 34-35.
358 *Ibid.*, at 358-359 (SCR).

relevance of international authorities, but about their interpretation. Chief Justice Dickson won the argument in principle about the "pertinence" of international law, but he was only able to convince Justice Wilson, who signed his dissenting reasons, that section 2(d) protected the right to strike.

Justice Le Dain, with Beetz and La Forest JJ., drafted brief reasons that make no reference to the international law arguments. Essentially, he argued that the approach of the Chief Justice was too restrictive in that it confined the scope of freedom of association to trade union matters. He said that freedom of association was actually a much broader right, one that impacted upon other fundamental freedoms, such as freedom of expression and freedom of religion.[359] Justice McIntyre, in his individual concurring judgment, completely ignored the international authorities, although he noted that a right to strike is recognized in certain foreign constitutions. "The omission of similar provisions in the *Charter*, taken with the fact that the overwhelming preoccupation of the *Charter* is with individual, political and democratic rights with conspicuous inattention to economic and property rights, speaks strongly against any implication of a right to strike."[360] The silence of the majority on the subject of the international law debate is a great disappointment, and sits poorly with the observation that in subsequent cases, the majority of the Supreme Court has appeared to have no quarrel with the Dickson dictum holding international law to be "relevant and persuasive" in *Charter* interpretation.

In a companion case, *RWDSU* v. *Saskatchewan*, Chief Justice Dickson upheld the challenged back-to-work legislation because he concluded it was a reasonable limit allowed by section 1 of the *Charter*. In *Public Service Alliance*, he had invoked international law and specifically the opinions of the ILO Freedom of Association Committee in concluding that the legislation in question was "over-inclusive" and that it could not be saved by section 1. Justice Wilson, the lone dissenter in *RWDSU*, felt that the Chief Justice was contradicting himself. How, she asked, could the Freedom of Association Committee's definition of "essential service" be used to save legislation prohibiting strikes by workers in the dairy sector. As Justice Wilson pointed out, the Freedom of Association Committee has consistently defined an essential service as a service "whose interruption would endanger the life, personal safety or health of the whole or part of the population".[361]

Attempts to revive the issue since the Supreme Court's pronouncements have been unsuccessful. Justice Pierre Viau of the Quebec Superior Court

---

359   *Ibid.*, at 390-391 (SCR).
360   *Ibid.*, at 413 (SCR).
361   *RWDSU* v. *Saskatchewan*, [1987] 1 SCR 460, 38 DLR (4th) 277, [1987] 3 WWR 673, 87 CLLC 14,023, 74 NR 321, [1987] DLQ 233 (headnote), 56 Sask R 277, at 486 (SCR); also, at 489 (SCR).

wrote, in a case raising the issue of freedom of association under both the
Canadian Charter and the Quebec *Charter of Human Rights and Freedoms*:

> Les deux éléments principaux de la liberté syndicale (le droit de négocier et
> celui de faire la grève) ne sont pas inclus dans les catégories énumérées à
> l'article 2 [of the *Canadian Charter*] et ces droits ne sont pas semblables aux
> libertés citées à l'article 3 [of the *Quebec Charter*]. Quant aux documents
> internationaux, ils ne reconnaissent comme fondamentaux ni le droit de né-
> gocier ni celui de faire la grève qui ne s'apparentent pas d'ailleurs aux notions
> de liberté de pensée, de conscience ou de religion apparaissant dans les pactes
> et les traités. On sait que la liberté d'association est protégée par les chartes,
> mais il est clair qu'elle ne comprend pas les droits constituant la liberté synd-
> icale telle que définie par les parties demanderesses. D'ailleurs, lorsqu'un
> document international en parle, il réfère à la même notion que celle de liberté
> d'association connue dans notre droit.[362]

As for the more general right of establishment and membership to a
labour union, the Supreme Court of Canada, in a split decision, gave another
restrictive interpretation of section 2(d) of the *Charter* in *Professional Institute of the Public Service of Canada v. Northwest Territories (Commissioner)*.[363] The set of reasons forming the majority opinion in this case agreed
that the exclusion of certain workers from a statutory labour relations regime
does not violate freedom of association because it leaves them free to
establish and be part of another union outside this regime. A similar issue
arose in *Delisle v. Canada (Deputy Attorney General)*,[364] where it was
argued that the definition of "employee" in section 2(e) of the *Public Service
Staff Relations Act*,[365] which expressly excludes members of the Royal
Canadian Mounted Police from the application of the legal regime created
by the Act, constituted an infringement of section 2(d) *Charter*. The majority
reiterated that freedom of association is not violated when groups of workers
are excluded from a statutory regime because it does not affect their right
to form an independent union and carry on labour activities outside the
regime.

Dissenting in *Delisle c. Canada (Sous-procureur général)*, Justices
Cory and Iacobucci were of the view that the very purpose of the exclusion
at hand was to ensure that these employees remain unassociated and thus
vulnerable to management, which is sufficient in itself to constitute an

---

362 *Fédération des infirmières et infirmiers du Québec* v. *Québec (Procureur général)*,
     [1991] RJQ 2607 (CS) at 2621 (RJQ), reversed, (sub nom. *Centrale de l'enseignement
     du Québec c. Québec (procureur général)*) [1998] RJQ 2897 (CA), leave to appeal
     refused, (1998) 245 NR 199n (SCC).

363 *Professional Institute of the Public Service of Canada* v. *Northwest Territories (Com-
     missioner)*, [1990] 2 SCR 367. Justices Wilson, Gonthier and Cory dissenting.

364 *Delisle* v. *Canada (Deputy Attorney General)*, [1999] 2 SCR 989, 176 DLR (4th) 513.

365 RSC 1985, c. P-35.

infringement of their freedom of association.[366] It is in support of the basic right to form and join a labour union that they resorted to international instruments,[367] namely the *Universal Declaration of Human Rights*,[368] the *International Covenant on Civil and Political Rights*,[369] the *International Covenant on Economic, Social and Cultural Rights*,[370] the International Labour Organization's *Convention (No. 87) Concerning Freedom of Association and Protection of the Right to Organize*,[371] and the *Concluding Document* of the Madrid Meeting of the Conference on Security and Co-operation in Europe.[372] "All of these instruments," noted Justices Cory and Iacobucci, "protect the fundamental freedom of employees to associate together in pursuit of their common interests as employees."[373] The possibility of lawful restrictions of this right for armed forces and police, if necessary to protect national security or public safety, is recognized by several of these instruments but, in the context of the *Canadian Charter*, such considerations are relevant to the section 1 analysis rather than at the definition stage in section 2(d), the dissenters opined.[374]

The argument that freedom of association is infringed if the purpose or effect of the exclusion of groups of workers from a labour relations legal regime is to prevent unionisation was considered again in *Dunmore* v. *Ontario (Attorney General)*. Justice Bastarache began his opinion: "This discussion will include a purposive analysis of s. 2(d), one which aims to protect the full range of associational activity contemplated by the *Charter* and to honour Canada's obligation under international human rights law."[375] The case bore many similarities with *Delisle*. It concerned agricultural workers who were excluded from the Ontario *Labour Relations Act, 1996*,[376] without however expressly or intentionally prohibiting them from associating. The issue turned in part on the notion of underinclusion and whether

---

366 *Delisle* v. *Canada, supra* note 364, at para. 107. Dissenting at the Court of Appeal; Baudouin J. was of the same view; see: [1997] RJQ 386 (CA), affirmed, (1999) 1999 CarswellQue 2840 (SCC).

367 *Delisle* v. *Canada, ibid.*, at para. 71.

368 GA Res. 217 A (III), UN Doc. A/810, art. 23(4).

369 (1976) 999 UNTS 171, [1976] CTS 47, art. 22.

370 (1976) 993 UNTS 3, [1976] CTS 46, art. 8.

371 (1950) 68 UNTS 17, [1973] CTS 14, arts. 2 and 3.

372 "Concluding Document of the Conference on Security and Cooperation in Europe, Madrid, 7-9 September 1983", (1983) 22 *ILM* 1398.

373 *Delisle* v. *Canada, supra* note 364, at para. 71.

374 *Ibid.*

375 *Dunmore* v. *Ontario (Attorney General)*, [2001] 3 SCR 1016, 207 DLR (4th) 193, 13 CCEL (3d) 1, 89 CRR (2d) 189, 154 OAC 201, at para. 13. See also: Diane Pothier, "Twenty Years of Labour Law and the Charter", (2002) 40 *Osgoode Hall Law Journal* 369.

376 *Labour Relations Act, 1995*, SO 1995, c. 1, Schedule A, section 3(b).

or not it can be the basis for freedom of association infringement. It is to help answer this question in the affirmative that Justice Bastarache resorted extensively to international human rights law:

> Article 2 of *Convention (No. 87) concerning Freedom of Association and Protection of the Right to Organize*, 67 UNTS 17, provides that "[w]orkers and employers, *without distinction whatsoever*, shall have the right to establish and ... to join organisations of their own choosing" (emphasis added), and that only members of the armed forces and the police may be excluded (Article 9). In addition, Article 10 of Convention No. 87 defines an "organisation" as "*any* organisation of workers or of employers for furthering and defending the interests of workers or of employers" (emphasis added). Canada ratified Convention No. 87 in 1972. The Convention's broadly worded provisions confirm precisely what I have discussed above, which is that discriminatory treatment implicates not only an excluded group's dignity interest, but also its basic freedom of association. This is further confirmed by the fact that Article 2 operates not only on the basis of sex, race, nationality and other traditional grounds of discrimination, but on the basis of *any* distinction, including occupational status (see L. Swepston, "Human rights law and freedom of association: Development through ILO supervision" (1998), 137 *Int"l Lab. Rev.* 169, at pp. 179-180). Nowhere is this clearer than in Article 1 of *Convention (No. 11) concerning the Rights of Association and Combination of Agricultural Workers*, 38 UNTS 153, which obliges ratifying member states to secure to "all those engaged in agriculture" the same rights of association as to industrial workers; the convention makes no distinction as to the type of agricultural work performed. Although provincial jurisdiction has prevented Canada from ratifying Convention No. 11, together these conventions provide a normative foundation for prohibiting *any* form of discrimination in the protection of trade union freedoms (see J. Hodges-Aeberhard, "The right to organise in Article 2 of Convention No. 87: What is meant by workers 'without distinction whatsoever'?" (1989), 128 *Int"l Lab. Rev.* 177). This foundation is fortified by *Convention (No. 141) concerning Organisations of Rural Workers and Their Role in Economic and Social Development (ILO Official Bulletin*, vol. LVIII, 1975, Series A, No. 1, p. 28) which extends, under Article 2, the freedom to organize to "any person engaged in agriculture, handicrafts or a related occupation in a rural area, whether as a wage earner or, ... as a tenant, sharecropper or small owner-occupier".[377]

The majority also referred to the work of the International Labour Organization when discussing the collective dimension of section 2(d) of the *Charter*,[378] that is, the interpretation of the right to organize in labour associations recognized by the ILO Committee of Experts on the Application of Conventions and Recommendations and the ILO Committee on Freedom

---

377 *Dunmore* v. *Ontario (Attorney General)*, *supra* note 375, at para. 27 (emphasis in the original).
378 *Ibid.*, at para. 16.

of Association.[379] Finally, a reference was made to a complaint made to the International Labour Organization in the present case.[380] In the end, the majority held that freedom of association was unjustifiably breached because agricultural workers are substantially incapable of exercising their right to organise without the benefit of the legislative scheme under scrutiny. Justice Major, dissenting, failed to see how the present situation was in any way different from that in *Delisle v. Canada (Deputy Attorney General)*.[381]

Opponents of the trade union movement have also invoked international law and the *Charter* in order to attack the "closed shop". The conformity of the closed shop with freedom of association has already been debated before the European Court of Human Rights. In *Young, James and Webster*,[382] the Court ruled that legislation requiring British rail workers to belong to a specific union breached their rights under article 11(1) of the *European Convention on Human Rights* and was not an acceptable limitation contemplated by article 11(2). In *Bhindi* v. *B.C. Projectionists*, the British Columbia Supreme Court indicated that the European case might have had a bearing if the provisions of the province's *Labour Code* were being attacked. But as the matter was purely contractual, the *Charter* could not apply.[383]

In *Lavigne* v. *Ontario Public Service Employees Union*, compulsory dues contributions to trade unions was contested pursuant to section 2(d) of the *Charter*. The petitioner invoked the report of the European Commission on Human Rights in the British Rail closed shop case.[384] Justice Wilson wrote:

> It is my opinion, however, that *Young, James and Webster* actually provides scanty support for the appellant's position. As was the case in *Oil, Chemical* [*Oil, Chemical & Atomic Workers' Int'l Union* v. *Imperial Oil Ltd.*, [1963]

---

379 International Labour Office. Freedom of Association Committee, *Freedom of Association: Digest of decisions and principles of the Freedom of Association Committee of the Governing Body of the ILO*, 4th ed., Geneva: International Labour Office, 1996; and International Labour Office, Voices for Freedom of Association, Labour Education, 1998/3, No. 112, Geneva: International Labour Office, 1998.

380 *Canadian Labour Congress* v. *Canada (Ontario)*, Case No. 1900, Report No. 308, *ILO Official Bulletin*, vol. LXXX, 1997, Series B, No. 3, at para. 145-146 & 187.

381 *Delisle* v. *Canada*, *supra* note 364.

382 *Young, James and Webster* v. *United Kingdom* (App. Nos. 7601/76 and 7806/77), (1980) 9 DR 126, 3 EHRR 20. See: A. Drzemczewski & F. Wooldridge, "The Closed Shop Case in Strasbourg", (1982) 31 *International and Comparative Law Quarterly* 396.

383 *Bhindi* v. *BC Projectionists, Loc. 348 of Int. Alliance of Picture Machine Operators of U.S. and Canada*, (1985) 20 DLR (4th) 386, 63 BCLR 352, 86 CLLC 14,001 (SC), affirmed, (1986) 4 BCLR (2d) 145 (CA), leave to appeal refused, (1986) 73 N.R. 399n (SCC). See also *Canadian Imperial Bank of Commerce* v. *Rifou*, (1986) 13 CCEL 293, 72 NR 12 (FCA).

384 *Young, James and Webster* v. *United Kingdom*, *supra* note 382.

S.C.R. 584, 13 D.L.R. (4th) 584] and unlike the present case, the impugned article of the collective agreement provided for a "closed shop". More crucial is the fact that the commission expressly refused to base it decision on a right not to associate, a point which is made clear by the commission's statement at pp. 26-27 that it did "not have to discuss the more general question whether or not the positive freedom guaranteed by Article 11(1) implies also a negative freedom". Indeed, the gist of the decision is that the complainants" positive associational rights were violated because they were prohibited from joining a union of their choosing. That the heart of the decision rested on this footing is made abundantly clear by the following remarks of the commission at p. 26:

> As regards the individual to whom the rights mentioned in Article 11 are guaranteed, these words imply that a worker must be able to choose the union which in his opinion best protects his interests, *and if he considers that none of the existing trade unions does so effectively, to form together with others a new one.* This is particularly important since unions, as these cases show, may have political affiliations.[385]

Curiously, the judgment of the European Court that followed the Commission's report was not mentioned by Justice Wilson.[386]

In *Beck* v. *Edmonton (City)*,[387] Miller J of the Alberta Court of Queen's Bench cited a more recent decision of the European Court of Human Rights, *Sigurjonsson* v. *Iceland*,[388] which considered legislation requiring a taxi driver to join a particular trade union as a condition for obtaining a licence. The European Court found that such a provision violated the right to "freedom of association with others", guaranteed by article 11 of the *European Convention on Human Rights*.

In *R. v. Advance Cutting & Coring Ltd.*,[389] Trudel J of the Quebec Superior Court referred to both the decisions of the European Court of

---

385 *Lavigne* v. *Ontario Public Service Employees Union*, [1991] 2 SCR 211, 81 DLR (4th) 545, 4 CRR 193, 91 CLLC 14,029, 3 OR (3d) 511, 126 NR 161, 48 OAC 241, reconsideration refused, (1991) 4 OR (3d) xii (SCC), at 255-256 (SCR) (emphasis in the original). See also, on this issue: *Lapalme* v. *Union des producteurs agricoles*, [2000] RJQ 1115 (SC).

386 *Young, James and Webster* v. *United Kingdom, supra* note 382.

387 *Beck* v. *Edmonton (City)*, [1994] 1 WWR 248 (Alta QB).

388 *Sigurjonsson* v. *Iceland*, 30 June 1993, Series A, No. 264. See also on this point: *Wilson, National Union of Journalists* et al. v. *United Kingdom* (App. No. 30668/96), 2 July 2002; *Chassagnou* et al. v. *France* (App. No. 25088/94), 29 April 1999; and *Sibson* v. *United Kingdom*, 20 April 1993, Series A, No. 258-A.

389 *R. v. Advance Cutting & Coring Ltd.*, (1998) 1998 CarswellQue 302, (sub nom. *Thériault c. R.*) [1998] RJQ 911 (CS), affirmed, [2001] 3 SCR 209, 205 DLR (4th) 385, 87 CRR (2d) 189. See also: Jamie Cameron, "The 'Second Labour Trilogy': A Comment on *R. v. Advance Cutting, Dunmore* v. *Ontario*, and *RWDSU* v. *Pepsi-Cola*", (2002) 16 *Supreme Court Law Review* (2d) 67.

Human Rights in *Young, James et Webster*[390] and *Sigurjonsson* v. *Iceland*,[391] which she distinguished from the facts of the case at hand, as well at to the universal human rights regime found in the *International Covenant on Civil and Political Rights* [392] and the *International Covenant on Economic, Social and Cultural Rights*,[393] the applicable norm she observed not being implemented domestically.[394] Noting that the Supreme Court, in *Lavigne* v. *Ontario Public Service Employees Union*,[395] did not seem to have settled whether freedom of association includes the right not to associate, Justice Trudel concluded that the statutory regime at issue,[396] which forced construction workers to belong to a union but gave them a choice between several representative organisations, was not in violation of section 2(d) of the *Charter*.

At the Supreme Court of Canada, the decision was split five to four in favour of upholding the constitutionality of the legislation.[397] Except for Justice L'Heureux-Dubé, all of the justices participating in the judgment interpreted *Lavigne* v. *Ontario Public Service Employees Union*[398] as holding that the right not to associate was guaranteed in section 2(d) of the *Charter*; they disagreed however on the extent of that negative right. Writing the main set of reasons for the majority, Justice LeBel expressed the view that not all forms of compelled labour association are incompatible with *Charter* values and the freedom of association guarantee. In fact, to trigger the application of section 2(d), the impugned legislation compelling membership in a union must impose a form of ideological conformity, which had not been established in this case. Under a separate heading,[399] Justice Lebel considered the *European Convention on Human Rights*[400] and the caselaw of the European Court of Human Rights, including *Young, James et Webster* and *Sigurjonsson* v. *Iceland,* already mentioned, but also *Le Compte, Van Leuven and De Meyere*[401] and *Gustafsson* v. *Sweden*,[402] also

---

390 *Young, James and Webster* v. *United Kingdom, supra* note 382.

391 *Sigurjonsson* v. *Iceland, supra* note 388.

392 *Supra* note 369, art. 22.

393 (1976) 993 UNTS 3, [1976] CTS 46, art. 8.

394 *R.* v. *Advance Cutting & Coring Ltd., supra* note 389, at 929-929.

395 *Lavigne* v. *Ontario Public Service Employees Union, supra* note 385.

396 *Act Respecting Labour Relations, Vocational Training and Manpower Management in the Construction Industry*, RSQ, c. R-20, ss. 28-40, 85.5, 85.6, 119.1, 120.

397 *R.* v. *Advance Cutting & Coring Ltd.*, [2001] 3 SCR 209, 205 DLR (4th) 385, 87 CRR (2d) 189.

398 *Lavigne* v. *Ontario Public Service Employees Union, supra* note 385.

399 *R.* v. *Advance Cutting & Coring Ltd., supra* note 397, at para. 249-251.

400 (1955) 213 UNTS 221, ETS 5, art. 11.

401 *Le Compte, van Leuven and de Meyere* v. *Belgium*, 23 June 1981, Series A, No. 43, 4 EHRR 1.

402 *Gustafsson* v. *Sweden* (App. No. 15573/89), 25 April 1996, Reports 1996-II.

supporting a qualified right not to associate, as well as another judgment outside labour relations, which dealt with hunter associations, *Chassagnou et al.* v. *France.*[403]

Justice L'Heureux-Dubé opined that "*Lavigne* is neither authoritative nor persuasive on the issue of the protection under s. 2(d) of a 'right not to associate'".[404] She felt there was no need to develop a new constitutional doctrine. She also commented on the caselaw of the European Court of Human Rights – *Sigurjonsson* v. *Iceland* and *Chassagnou* et al. v. *France* – emphasising the different methodology adopted in this regional human rights legal regime with respect to the present issue. "In any event", concluded Justice L'Heureux-Dubé on this point, "the *European Convention* cannot dictate the way the *Canadian Charter* does protect fundamental rights."[405] Dissenting on the conclusion that there was no infringement of section 2(d), Justice Bastarache (with McLachlin CJ, Major and Binnie JJ) invoked the *Universal Declaration of Human Rights*[406] and the *International Covenant on Economic, Social and Cultural Rights.*[407] These instruments were interpreted as supporting the view that there is a right not to associate guaranteed in section 2(d).[408] The dissent would have allowed less qualification of that negative right however.

In *Pruden Building Ltd.* v. *Construction & General Workers Union, Local 92*, Justice Sinclair of the Alberta Court of Queen's Bench also considered article 11(1) of the *European Convention*. He referred to three European cases indicating that freedom of association did not include a guaranteed right to a negotiated collective agreement.[409] The Federal Court of Appeal has considered article 11 of the *European Convention*[410] in assessing the validity of section 61.5(9)(b) of the *Canada Labour Code,*[411] which deals with wrongful dismissal of unorganized employees. Definitions from international law were helpful to Justice Beetz, who rendered judgment

---

403 *Chassagnou and others* v. *France, supra* note 388.
404 *R.* v. *Advance Cutting & Coring Ltd., supra* note 397, at para. 57.
405 *Ibid.*, para. 78.
406 GA Res. 217 A (III), UN Doc. A/810, article 20.
407 *Supra* note 393, art. 6 and 8. See also, using this international convention: *Canadian Egg Marketing Agency* v. *Richardson*, [1998] 3 SCR 157, at para. 60.
408 *R.* v. *Advance Cutting & Coring Ltd., supra* note 397, at paras. 10-15 & 30.
409 (1984) [1985] 1 WWR 42, 33 Alta LR (2d) 295, 85 CLLC 14,004, 13 DLR (4th) 584, 55 AR 371, 14 CRR 117 (Alta QB). The three cases were *Young, James and Webster* v. *United Kingdom, supra* note 382; *Swedish Engine Drivers Union* v. *Sweden*, 6 February 1976, Series A, No. 20, 1 EHRR 617, 58 ILR 19; *National Union of Belgian Police* v. *Belgium*, 27 October 1975, Series A, No. 19, 1 EHRR 578, 57 ILR 262. See: R. Pelloux, "Trois affaires syndicales devant la Cour européenne des droits de l'homme", [1976] *Annuaire français de droit international* 121.
410 *Canadian Imperial Bank of Commerce* v. *Rifou, supra* note 383.
411 RSC 1985, c. L-2.

for the court in *Bell Canada* v. *Quebec (CSST)*. He relied on the preamble to the *Constitution of the International Labour Organization*[412] and on article 7 of the *International Covenant on Economic, Social and Cultural Rights* in concluding that the term "working conditions" encompasses the health and safety of workers.[413] In *Slaight Communications* v. *Davidson*, Chief Justice Dickson referred to article 6 of the *International Covenant on Economic, Social and Cultural Rights* in declaring that the right to work is a fundamental value in a free and democratic society.[414] In *Lakeland College Faculty Association* v. *Lakeland College*, Lefsrud J opined that his interpretation of section 2(d) of the *Charter* did not "present a conflict with the international covenants".[415]

4.3   Political Rights

Sections 3, 4 and 5 of the *Canadian Charter* address political rights:

3.   Every citizen of Canada has the right to vote in an election of members of the House of Commons or of a legislative assembly and to be qualified for membership therein.

4. (1)   No House of Commons and no legislative assembly shall continue for longer than five years from the date fixed for the return of the writs of a general election of its members.

(2)   In time of real or apprehended war, invasion or insurrection, a House of Commons may be continued by Parliament and a legislative assembly may be continued by the legislature beyond five years if such continuation is not opposed by the votes of more than one-third of the members of the House of Commons or the legislative assembly, as the case may be.

5.   There shall be a sitting of Parliament and of each legislature at least once every twelve months.

These three provisions are obviously very specific to Canada. Nevertheless, they have significant parallels in the international instruments. For example, article 21 of the *Universal Declaration of Human Rights* recognizes the right of everyone to take part in the government of his or her country, directly or through freely chosen representatives, and the right of equal

---

412   *Instrument for the Amendment of the Constitution of the International Labour Organization, with Annexed Constitution*, (1946) 15 UNTS 15, [1946] CTS 48.

413   *Bell Canada* v. *Québec*, [1988] 1 SCR 749, 51 DLR (4th) 161, 85 NR 295, 21 CCEL 1, 15 QAC 217, at 806 (SCR).

414   *Slaight Communications Inc.* v. *Davidson*, [1989] 1 SCR 1038, 59 DLR (4th) 416, 93 NR 183, 89 CLLC 14,031, 26 CCEL 85, 40 CRR 100, at 1056 (SCR).

415   *Lakeland College Faculty Association* v. *Lakeland College*, (1995) 35 Alta LR (3d) 95, 176 AR 303 (QB), reversed, (1998) 62 Alta LR (3d) 52, 223 AR 1, 162 DLR (4th) 338 (CA).

access to public service in his country. Furthermore, it affirms that "[t]he will of the people shall be the basis of the authority of government; this will shall be expressed in periodic and genuine elections which shall be by universal and equal suffrage and shall be held by secret vote or by equivalent free voting procedures". The *International Covenant on Civil and Political Rights*, at article 25, contains similar provisions, as do the different regional instruments.[416] Sections 4 and 5 of the *Charter*, for what may be obvious reasons, do not appear to have generated any caselaw; the same cannot be said for section 3.

In *Thomson Newspapers Co.* v. *Canada (Attorney General)*, Justice Somers of the Ontario Court (General Division) referred to some of these international provisions concerning elections, noting that "[t]he philosophy underlying the *Charter* can be derived from the international human rights documents reflective of Canada's commitments and from which the *Charter*'s drafters drew inspiration", concluding that the right to vote ". . .must be read broadly to encompass the right to vote in free genuine multi-candidate elections. Section 3 must protect more than the bare right to mark a ballot, otherwise it would be a purely formalistic guarantee."[417] This case challenged the provision of the *Canada Elections Act*[418] prohibiting the publication of opinion surveys during the last three days of the campaign in federal elections based on freedom of expression and on the right to vote. At the Supreme Court of Canada, the majority's decision was based on section 2(b) of the *Charter* only, leaving to another day the determination of the scope of section 3 in terms of access to information during an election.[419] Nevertheless, in his reasons for the majority, Bastarache J made

---

416   *Protocol* [No. 1] *to the Convention for the Protection of Human Rights and Fundamental Freedoms*, (1955) 213 UNTS 262, ETS 9, art. 3; *American Declaration of the Rights and Duties of Man*, OAS Doc. OEA/Ser. L./V/II.23, doc. 21, rev. 6, arts. XX, XIV; *American Convention on Human Rights*, (1979) 1144 UNTS 123, OASTS 36, art. 23; *African Charter on Human and People's Rights*, OAU Doc. CAB/LEG/67/3 rev. 5, 4 EHRR 417, 21 *ILM* 58, art. 13; *International Convention on the Elimination of All Forms of Racial Discrimination*, (1969) 660 UNTS 195, [1976] CTS 47, art. 5(c); *Convention on the Elimination of Discrimination Against Women*, (1981) 1249 UNTS 13, [1982] CTS 31, art. 7. Also: "Document of the Copenhagen Meeting of the Conference on the Human Dimension of the CSCE", 1989, paras. 5.1, 6, 7. See also: Gérald-A. Beaudoin, "Les droits démocratiques (articles 3, 4 et 5)", in Gérald-A. Beaudoin & Errol P. Mendes, eds., *Canadian Charter of Rights and Freedoms*, 4th ed., Markham, Ont., LexisNexis Butterworths, 2005, pp. 359-409, at 363-364.

417   *Thomson Newspapers Co.* v. *Canada (Attorney General)*, (1995) 24 OR (3d) 109 (Gen Div), affirmed, (1996) 1996 CarswellOnt 2942 (CA), leave to appeal allowed, (1997) 41 CRR (2d) 375n (SCC), reversed, (1998) 1998 CarswellOnt 1981 (SCC), at 136 (OR).

418   *Canada Elections Act*, RSC, 1985, c. E-2, s. 322.1.

419   *Thomson Newspapers Co.* v. *Canada (Attorney General)*, [1998] 1 SCR 877, at para. 82-84. See also: *Somerville* v. *Canada (Attorney General)*, (1996) 136 DLR (4th) 205 (Alta CA); and *Canada (Procureur général)* c. *Barrette*, [1994] RJQ 671 (CA).

comments about section 3 which are of some interest. He recalled that McLachlin J, as she then was, in *Reference re Provincial Electoral Boundaries (Sask.)*[420] identified the purpose of this *Charter* guarantee as being the protection of the right to effective representation, and then wrote:

> This position accords with the jurisprudence of the European Court of Human Rights and the European Commission of Human Rights. Article 3 of the First Protocol to the European *Convention for the Protection of Human Rights and Fundamental Freedoms*, March 20, 1952, Europ. T.S. No. 9, provides that parties to the Convention "undertake to hold free elections at reasonable intervals by secret ballot, under conditions which will ensure the free expression of the opinion of the people in the choice of the legislature". The European Court has held that this provision guarantees the right to vote; see Eur. Court H.R., *Mathieu-Mohin and Clerfayt* case, judgment of 2 March 1987, Series A No. 113 However, neither the European Court nor the European Commission has equated the right to vote with a right to information *per se*. Rather, in *Mathieu-Mohin and Clerfayt, supra*, the European Court equated the right to vote with the right to participate in the electoral process. This same principle was applied by the European Commission in *Bowman v. United Kingdom* (1996), 22 E.H.R.R. C.D. 13. In that case, the Commission considered legislation that restricted "single-issue" campaigning by individuals other than the electoral candidates. The applicant, who had been charged for distributing leaflets outlining the views of three electoral candidates on abortion, complained that her right to free expression had been violated. The Commission agreed and held that there was an unjustified violation of freedom of expression. With regard to the applicant's right to vote, the Commission wrote, at p. CD18:

> > The Commission has had regard to whether the expression of opinion or information on "single issues" addressed by individuals or groups with strongly-held views may operate in particular constituencies so as to "distort" election results. It has previously considered in the context of Article 3 of the First Protocol . . . that one of the legitimate objectives of national electoral systems is to channel currents of thought so as to promote the emergence of a sufficiently clear and coherent political will. . . . *The Government has not, however, produced any argument to the effect that "single issue" campaigning of the kind illustrated in the applicant's case would distract voters from the political platforms which are the basis of national party campaigns to such a degree as would hinder the electoral process.*[421]

---

420   *Reference re Provincial Electoral Boundaries (Sask)*, [1991] 2 SCR 158, at 183. See also: *Harper* v. *Canada (Attorney General)*, [2004] 1 SCR 827; *Figueroa* v. *Canada (Attorney General)*, [2003] 1 SCR 912, 227 DLR (4th) 1, 108 CRR (2d) 66, 176 OAC 89; *Harvey* v. *New Brunswick (Attorney General)*, [1996] 2 SCR 876; and *Haig* v. *Canada*, [1993] 2 SCR 995.

421   *Thomson Newspapers Co.* v. *Canada (Attorney General)*, *supra* note 419, at para. 83 (emphasis in the original).

Although it was not decided on the basis of section 3 of the *Charter*, ironically, it is with respect to the right to vote that references to international human rights law thus abound in this case.

Restrictions on the right to vote by certain groups have been challenged based on section 3 of the *Charter*. The question of the right to vote and to participate in political activity of specific groups such as the mentally handicapped, penitentiary inmates, Aboriginal peoples,[422] judges and Crown attorneys is very much alive in Canadian law, and international jurisprudence may be of some help to the courts in determining the scope of such political rights and what, if any, reasonable limits may be imposed.[423] Even prior to the coming into force of the *Charter*, it would seem that political rights were broadened in order to give effect to the *International Covenant on Civil and Political Rights*. That, at any rate, is what one can read in *C.F. et al.* v. *Canada*, a decision of the Human Rights Committee:

> On 19 August 1976, the International Covenant on Civil and Political Rights and the Optional Protocol thereto entered into force for Canada. In order to bring the Quebec Election Act into conformity with the provisions of article 25 of the Covenant, several amendments to the Act were adopted by the National Assembly of Quebec on 13 December 1979, establishing, *inter alia*, the right of every inmate to vote in general elections in Quebec.[424]

Penitentiary inmates in Quebec, relying on article 25 of the *International Covenant on Civil and Political Rights*, had challenged legislation that denied them the right to vote in federal elections. Their petition was declared inadmissible because the Committee considered that an application for declaratory judgment in the Federal Court, Trial Division, constituted an effective domestic remedy.

Subsequently, in *Lévesque* v. *Canada*, the legislation was attacked successfully, by means of just such a motion for declaratory judgment before the Federal Court, although the court did no more than take note of the

---

422   A provision of the *Indian Act*, RSC 1985, c. I-5, denying band members who are not resident on a reserve the right to vote was successfully challenged in *Batchewana Indian Band* v. *Batchewana Indian Band*) [1994] 1 FC 394 (TD), varied, [1997] 1 FC 689 (CA), leave to appeal allowed, (1997) 215 NR 239n, [1999] 2 SCR 203, reconsideration refused, (2000) 2000 CarswellNat 2393 (SCC). International human rights law is cited in the judgment, which is based on section 15, and not section 3, of the *Canadian Charter*.

423   See, for example: *E.* v. *Switzerland* (App. No. 10279/83), (1984) 27 European Convention on Human Rights Yearbook 149, 38 DR 124, a case of the European Commission of Human Rights dealing with the right of a judge to participate in public political debate.

424   *C.F.* v. *Canada* (No. 113/1981), UN Doc. CCPR/C/24/D/113/1981, UN Doc. CCPR/C/OP/1, p. 13, 7 *Human Rights Law Journal* 300, [1986] *Canadian Human Rights Yearbook* 185, para. 3.1.

international law arguments.[425] In its published decision in *C.F.* v. *Canada*, the Human Rights Committee included a "Follow Up" annotation, which reads as follows:

> The Canadian Government has informed the Committee that pursuant to a decision dated 2 December 1985 in the case *Lévesque* v. *Attorney-General of Canada*, the Federal Court of Canada upheld the right of penitentiary prisoners in Quebec to vote in provincial elections and ordered the Federal Minister of Justice and the Solicitor General to make the necessary arrangements to put this into effect.[426]

In *Sauvé* v. *Canada (Chief Electoral Officer)*,[427] the provision of the *Canada Elections Act*[428] disqualifying prisoners serving sentences of two years or more in a correctional institution from voting in federal elections was challenged under section 3 of the *Canadian Charter*. The case was decided on the basis of whether or not such a restriction was justified in a free and democratic society pursuant to section 1, the respondents having conceded that there was a violation of the constitutional right to vote. The Supreme Court was divided, five to four, on whether the measure satisfied the *Oakes* test, a disagreement that was rooted in the very approach to the limitation clause in the context that "involves evaluating choices regarding social or political philosophies and relates to shaping, giving expression, and giving practical application to communal values".[429] It was, therefore, in an attempt to show the existing range of reasonable and rational balances that have been struck between the different societal and individual interests at stake that the dissent *per* Gonthier J examined the situations in the Canadian provinces and within the international community.[430] The latter included references to the situation in the European human rights regime,

---

425 *Lévesque* v. *Canada (AG)*, [1986] 2 FC 287, 25 DLR (4th) 184, 7 CHRR D/3617, 20 CRR 15 (TD).

426 *C.F.* v. *Canada, supra* note 424.

427 *Sauvé* v. *Canada (Chief Electoral Officer)*, [2002] 3 SCR 519, 218 DLR (4th) 577, 168 CCC (3d) 449, 5 CR (6th) 203, 98 CRR (2d) 1. See also: *Driskell* v. *Manitoba (Attorney General)*, (1999) 67 CRR (2d) 147 (Man QB); and Chantal Sauriol, "Droit de vote des détenus: le Parlement est-il encore souverain?", in *Développements récents en droit administratif et constitutionnel (2003)*, Cowansville: Éditions Yvon Blais, 2003, pp. 119-141.

428 *Canada Elections Act*, RSC 1985, c. E-2, s. 51(e).

429 *Sauvé* v. *Canada (Chief Electoral Officer), supra* note 427, at para. 83.

430 *Ibid.*, at para. 122-134. The examination included international law but also foreign law, such as that in the United States of America, European countries (Armenia, Austria, Bosnia and Herzegovina, Bulgaria, Croatia, Cyprus, the Czech Republic, Denmark, Estonia, Finland, France, Germany, Greece, Hungary, Iceland, Ireland, Latvia, Lithuania, Luxembourg, Macedonia, Malta, Netherlands, Norway, Poland, Romania, Russia, San Marino, Slovenia, Spain, Sweden, Switzerland, Ukraine and the United Kingdom), Australia, and New Zealand.

including the *European Convention on Human Rights* and its *Protocol No. 1*,[431] and relevant cases decided by the European Commission of Human Rights[432] and the European Court of Human Rights.[433] He also referred to the *International Covenant on Civil and Political Rights* [434] and a General Comment of the United Nations Human Rights Committee to the effect that restrictions on the right to vote should be "objective and reasonable" and that "[i]f conviction for an offence is a basis for suspending the right to vote, the period of such suspension should be proportionate to the offence and the sentence".[435] Even a publication by an international non-governmental organization was mentioned.[436]

Section 3 of the *Charter* has also been invoked in cases dealing with electoral boundaries, the main one being *Reference re Electoral Boundaries Commission Act (Sask.)*. At the Saskatchewan Court of Appeal, reference was made to article 25 of the *International Covenant on Civil and Political Rights*, noting that "our nation supports this fundamental notion",[437] namely the right to vote. This provision of the *Covenant* was one of a series of arguments used by the Court in ruling that the right to participate in free and fair elections must be real and not illusory, and that electoral boundaries that result in urban constituencies with more voters than rural constituencies frustrate the right to genuine democratic participation. The case went to the Supreme Court of Canada, where the appeal was allowed in a majority judgment which, without recourse to international human rights law, held that section 3 of the *Canadian Charter* was not breached because it does not guarantee absolute equality of voting power.[438]

431 *Protocol* [No. 1] *to the Convention for the Protection of Human Rights and Fundamental Freedoms, supra* note 416, article 3.
432 *X.* v. *Netherlands* (App. No. 6573/74), (1974) 1 DR 87; *H.* v. *Netherlands* (App. No. 9914/82), (1983) 33 DR 242; *Holland* v. *Ireland* (App. No. 24827/94), (1998) 93-A DR 15.
433 *Mathieu-Mohin and Clerfayt* v. *Belgium*, 2 March 1987, Series A, No. 113.
434 (1976) 999 UNTS 171, [1976] CTS 47, art. 25.
435 "General Comment No. 25 (57), The right to participate in public affairs, voting rights and the right of equal access to public service", UN Doc. CCPR/C/21/Rev.1/Add.7.
436 Penal Reform International, *Making Standards Work – An International Handbook on Good Prison Practice*, The Hague: Penal Reform International, 1995.
437 *Reference re Provincial Electoral Boundaries (Sask.)*, [1991] 3 WWR 593, 78 DLR (4th) 449, 90 Sask R 174 (CA), reversed, (1991) 1991 CarswellSask 188 (SCC), at 457 (DLR).
438 *Reference re Electoral Boundaries Commission Act (Sask), supra* note 420. It appears that this conclusion is in line with the view of the United Nations Human Rights Committee expressed in "General Comment No. 25 (57), The right to participate in public affairs, voting rights and the right of equal access to public service", UN Doc. CCPR/C/21/Rev.1/Add.7, at para. 21, to the effect that electoral boundaries "should not distort the distribution of voters or discrimination against any group and should not exclude or restrict unreasonably the right of citizens to choose their representatives

The right to democratic elections is sometimes linked, in international human rights law, to the right of peoples to self-determination. This is the concept of "internal self-determination", as distinct from "external self-determination", which is often associated with secession.[439] Yukon Territory politician Tony Penikett invoked article 1 of the *International Covenants* (the provision is identical in both *Covenants*), which provides for the right of peoples to self-determination, in an unsuccessful challenge to the Meech

---

freely." See also: Mark Carter, "Reconsidering the Charter and Electoral Boundaries", (1999) 22 *Dalhousie Law Journal* 53; Ronald E. Fritz, "Challenging Electoral Boundaries under the Charter: Judicial Deference and Burden of Proof", (1999) 5 *Revue d'études constitutionnelles*. 1.

439 On self-determination in international law, see: Robert McCorquodale, ed., *Self-Determination in International Law*, Aldershot, United Kingdom: Ashgate/Dartmouth, 2000; Edward McWhinney, *The United Nations and a New World Order for a New Millenium: Self-Determination, State Succession and Humanitarian Intervention*, Boston: Kluwer Law International, 2000; Thomas D. Musgrave, *Self-Determination and National Minorities*, New York: Oxford University Press, 2000; Joshua Castellino, *International Law of Self-Determination: The Interplay of the Politics of Territorial Possession with Formulations of Post-Colonial "National" Identity*, London: Kluwer Law International, 2000; Michael J. Kelly, "Political Downsizing: The Re-Emergence of Self-Determination, and the Movement toward Smaller, Ethnically Homogenous States", (1999) 47 *Drake Law Review* 209; Théodore Christakis, *Le droit à l'autodétermination en dehors des situations de décolonisation*, Paris: La documentation française, 1999; Hurst Hannum, "The Right of Self-Determination in the Twenty-First Century", (1998) 55 *Washington & Lee Law Review* 773; Helen Quane, "The United Nations and the Evolving Right to Self-Determination" (1998), 47 *International and Comparative Law Quarterly* 537; Manuel Rodriguez-Orellana, "Human Rights Talk . . . and Self-Determination, Too!", (1998) 73 *Notre Dame Law Review* 1391; W. Danspeckgruber & Arthur Watts, eds., *Self-Determination and Self-Administration: A Sourcebook*, Boulder, Colorado: Lynne Rienner Publishers, 1997; Jerome Wilson, "Ethnic Groups and the Right to Self-Determination", (1996) *Connecticut Journal of International Law* 433; Gregory H. Fox, "Self-Determination in the Post-Cold War Era: A New Internal Focus?", (1995) 16 *Michigan Journal of International Law* 733; Antonio Cassese, *Self Determination of Peoples: A Legal Reappraisal*, Cambridge: Cambridge University Press, 1995; Martti Koskenniemi, "National Self-determination Today: Problems of Legal Theory and Practice", (1994) 43 *International and Comparative Law Quarterly* 241; Christian Tomuschat, ed., *Modern Law of Self-Determination*, Dordrecht: Martinus Nijhoff, 1993; Thomas M. Franck, "Postmodern Tribalism and the Right to Secession", in Catherine M. Brölmann, Rene Lefeber & Marjoleine Y.A. Zieck, eds., *Peoples and Minorities in International Law*, Dordrecht, Martinus Nijhoff Publishers, 1993, pp. 3-27; Thomas M. Franck. "The Emerging Right to Democratic Governance", (1992) 86 *American Journal of International Law* 46; Hurst Hannum, *Autonomy, Sovereignty and Self-Determination: The Accommodation of Conflicting Rights*, Philadelphia: University of Pennsylvania Press, 1990.

Lake accord of 1987.[440] Confronted with the failure of the *Canadian Charter* to recognize explicitly the right to self-determination, despite the fact that it forms part of Canada's international obligations under the *Covenant*, Penikett argued:

> Although many of the guarantees in the international documents are covered by the Charter of Rights it is submitted that there is an independent requirement of the government to observe its international treaties and that those rights in the international documents which are broader than rights set out in the Charter of Rights are equally binding on Canada. For the purposes of the declaration sought, the Petitioners do not ask the court to find that the international obligations by which Canada is bound prevail over domestic legislation. Rather, the Petitioners seek a declaration that the proposed Constitutional Amendment, 1987, is inconsistent with Canada's international obligations.
>
> The right of self-determination has been defined as the right of a people to shape its own political, economic and cultural destiny. The principle is most frequently applied in the international scene as a legal justification for revolution or the proclaiming of a national sovereign identity. It is submitted that the principle is nevertheless applicable to a group such as those within the Yukon Territory who share a common appreciation of cultural background, history and geographic area.[441]

Justice David C. McDonald, sitting as a judge of the Yukon Territory Supreme Court, dismissed the claim because "[t]he provisions of the International Covenant on Civil and Political Rights are not part of the domestic law of Canada and do not create rights enforceable by a remedy in a Canadian court".[442] The judgment was upheld on appeal.[443]

---

440 The Final Report of the Special Joint Committee of the Senate and the House of Commons on the Constitution of Canada, tabled in the House of Commons on 16 March 1972, considered explicit recognition of the right to self-determination in the *Constitution*, noting that it was contemplated by article 1 of the *International Covenant on Civil and Political Rights* as well as in the *Charter of the United Nations*. The Report observed that "[t]he principle of self-determination, while not entirely new in Canadian history, has had a new currency in Quebec since 1960". It went on to note that "[t]he right to secede as an expression of self-determination is not generally recognized in federal constitutions". It proposed a muted recognition of the principle that nevertheless avoided explicit use of the term "self-determination". "Final Report, 16 March 1972", in Anne F. Bayefsky, *Canada's Constitution Act 1982 & Amendments, A Documentary History*, Toronto: McGraw-Hill Ryerson, 1989, pp. 224-308, at 235.

441 *Penikett* v. *R*, [1987] 5 WWR 691, 20 CRR 107, 2 YR 262 (SC), reversed, [1988] 2 WWR 481, 45 DLR (4th) 108, 21 BCLR (2d) 1 (YT CA), leave to appeal refused, (1988) 88 N.R. 320n (SCC), at 733 (WWR).

442 *Ibid.*, at 734.

443 *Penikett* v. *R.*, [1988] 2 WWR 481 (YT CA), leave to appeal refused, (1988) 88 N.R. 320n (SCC).

The 1998 *Reference re Secession of Quebec*[444] provided an opportunity for the Supreme Court of Canada to address issues of self-determination, including the role of international law, when it was asked to give an advisory opinion on the legality and consequences of a unilateral secession by the province of Quebec. The three questions submitted by the Governor in Council of Canada read as follows:

1. Under the Constitution of Canada, can the National Assembly, legislature or government of Quebec effect the secession of Quebec from Canada unilaterally?

2. Does international law give the National Assembly, legislature or government of Quebec the right to effect the secession of Quebec from Canada unilaterally? In this regard, is there a right to self-determination under international law that would give the National Assembly, legislature or government of Quebec the Right to effect the secession of Quebec from Canada unilaterally?

3. In the event of a conflict between domestic and international law on the right of the National Assembly, legislature or government of Quebec to effect the secession of Quebec from Canada unilaterally, which would take precedence in Canada.[445]

As suggested by the formulation of the questions, the two aspects of the issue were treated separately, which means that the numerous references to international law were not made in order to assist in the interpretation of the Constitution of Canada for the purpose of question 1.

---

444 *Reference re Secession of Quebec*, [1998] 2 SCR 217, 161 DLR (4th) 385, 55 CRR (2d) 1. For all the judicial materials pertaining to this case, including expert opinions by James Crawford, Luzius Wildhaber, Thomas Franck, Alain Pellet, Malcolm Shaw and George Abi-Saab, see Anne F. Bayefsky, ed., *Self-Determination in International Law – Quebec and Lessons Learned*, The Hague: Kluwer Law International, 2000. See also: Daniel Turp, *Le droit de choisir: Essais sur le droit du Québec à disposer de lui-même*, Montreal: Éditions Thémis, 2001; Sujit Choudhry & Robert Howse, "Constitutional Theory and the Quebec Secession Reference", (2000) 13 *Canadian Journal of Law & Jurisprudence* 143; Nathalie Des Rosiers, "From Québec Veto to Québec Secession: The Evolution of the Supreme Court of Canada on Québec-Canada Disputes",(2000) 13 *Canadian Journal of Law & Jurisprudence* 171; David Schneiderman, ed., *The Quebec Decision: Perspectives on the Supreme Court Ruling on Secession*, Toronto: Lorimer, 1999; Stephen J. Toope, "Case Comment on the Reference Re Secession of Quebec", (1999) 93 *American Journal of International Law* 519; Patrick J. Monahan, "The Public Policy Role of the Supreme Court of Canada in the *Secession Reference*", (1999) 11 *National Journal of Constitutional Law* 65; Mark D. Walters, "Nationalism and the Pathology of Legal Systems: Considering the *Quebec Secession Reference* and the Lessons for the United Kingdom", (1999) 62 *Modern Law Review* 371; David J. Mullan, "Quebec Unilateral Secession Reference: 'A Ruling that Will Stand the Test of Time'", (1998) 9 *Public Law Review* 231.
445 *Reference re Secession of Quebec*, [1998] 2 SCR 217, 161 DLR (4th) 385, 55 CRR (2d) 1, para. 2.

In fact, in answering question 2, the Court did little more than cut and paste uncontroversial passages in international instruments on self-determination,[446] including article 1(2) and 55 of the *Charter of the United Nations*[447] and article 1 of both the *International Covenant on Civil and Political Rights* and the *International Covenant on Economic, Social and Cultural Rights*, as well as the 1970 United Nations General Assembly's *Declaration on Principles of International Law concerning Friendly Relations*,[448] the *Helsinki Final Act*,[449] *Vienna Declaration and Programme of Action* of the the 1993 United Nations World Conference on Human Rights[450] and the 1995 United Nations General Assembly's *Declaration on the Occasion of the Fiftieth Anniversary of the United Nations*.[451] Other international documents also referred to included the concluding document of the 1986 Conference on Security and Co-operation in Europe's *Concluding Document of the Vienna Meeting*[452] and the 1991 European Community's *Guidelines on the Recognition of New States in Eastern Europe and in the Soviet Union*.[453] In the end, the Court opined that the province of Quebec, even if one characterizes it as a "people" (a concept whose precise definition was left undetermined), is not entitled to a right to external self-determination under the existing circumstances – which involve no colonization, oppression or denial of government access – and thus does not hold a right to secede unilaterally from Canada under international law.[454]

Of interest with respect to clarifying the role of international human rights in Canadian constitutional law, in the *Secession Reference* two objections were raised by the *amicus curiae* challenging the jurisdiction of the Supreme Court.[455] First, it was argued that question 2 was one of "pure" international law, which means that a domestic court inappropriately acts

---

446   *Ibid.*, at para. 115-121. See also: William A. Schabas, "Twenty-Five Years of Public International Law at the Supreme Court of Canada", (2000) 79 *Canadian Bar Review* 174, at 191-193.
447   *Charter of the United Nations*, [1945] CTS 1945 7.
448   "Declaration on Principles of International Law Concerning Friendly Relations and Co-operation Among States in Accordance with the Charter of the United Nations", GA Res. 2625 (XXV).
449   "Conference on Security and Cooperation in Europe, Final Act", 1 August 1975.
450   *Vienna Declaration and Programme of Action*, UN Doc. A/CONF.157/24, (1993) 14 *Human Rights Law Journal* 352.
451   "Declaration on the Occasion of the Fiftieth Anniversary of the United Nations", GA Res. 50/6.
452   "Concluding Document of the Vienna Meeting of the Conference on Security and Cooperation in Europe", 19 January 1989.
453   "Guidelines on the Recognition of New States in Eastern Europe and in the Soviet Union", 16 December 1991, (1992) 31 *ILM* 1486.
454   *Reference re Secession of Quebec*, *supra* note 445, at para. 138.
455   *Ibid.*, at paras. 20-23.

as an international tribunal in answering it; and, second, it was suggested that question 2 was beyond the competence of the Court because it required the application of international law rather than domestic law. Both objections were rejected. On the one hand, there was no contention to "act as" or be a substitute for an international tribunal, nor would an answer to question 2 "purport to bind any other state or international tribunal that might subsequently consider a similar question".[456] On the other hand, the Supreme Court has used international law on numerous occasions in order to decide legal issues within the Canadian legal system, including in reference cases.[457] The truth of the matter here is that, "a consideration of international law in the context of this Reference about the legal aspects of the unilateral secession of Quebec is not only permissible but unavoidable".[458] These statements are helpful in confirming that, although the international and domestic spheres (including their judicial instances) are separate and distinct pursuant to the Westphalian model of international relations,[459] international law may have an impact on the interpretation and application of Canadian law, including constitutional law such as *Charter* rights and freedoms.[460]

4.4   Mobility Rights

The *Canadian Charter* sets out mobility rights in section 6.

6. (1) Every citizen of Canada has the right to enter, remain in and leave Canada.
   (2) Every citizen of Canada and every person who has the status of a permanent resident of Canada has the right
     a) to move to and take up residence in any province; and
     b) to pursue the gaining of a livelihood in any province.
   (3) The rights specified in subsection (2) are subject to

---

456   *Ibid.*, at para. 20.
457   *Ibid.*, at para. 22. The Court referred to: *Reference Powers to Levy Rates on Foreign Legations and High Commissioners' Residence*, [1943] SCR 208; *Reference re Ownership of Offshore Mineral Rights of British Columbia*, [1967] SCR 792; and *Reference re Newfoundland Continental Shelf*, [1984] 1 SCR 86.
458   *Ibid.*, para. 23.
459   See: Stéphane Beaulac, *The Power of Language in the Making of International Law – The Word Sovereignty in Bodin and Vattel and the Myth of Westphalia*, Leiden & Boston: Martinus Nijhoff Publishers, 2004, at 67-70.
460   See: Stéphane Beaulac, "L'interprétation de la Charte: reconsidération de l'approche téléologique et réévaluation du rôle du droit international", in Gérald-A. Beaudoin & Errol P. Mendes, eds., *Canadian Charter of Rights and Freedoms*, 4th ed., Markham, Ont., LexisNexis Butterworths, 2005, pp. 25-69; reprinted in (2005) 27 *Supreme Court Law Review* (2d) 1.

a) any laws or practices of general application in force in a province other than those that discriminate among persons primarily on the basis of province of present or previous residence; and

b) any laws providing for reasonable residency requirements as a qualification for the receipt of publicly provided social services.

(4) Subsections (2) and (3) do not preclude any law, program or activity that has as its object the amelioration in a province of conditions of individuals in that province who are socially or economically disadvantaged if the rate of employment in that province is below the rate of employment in Canada.

According to article 13 of the *Universal Declaration of Human Rights*, "[e]veryone has the right to freedom of movement and residence within the borders of each state" and "[e]veryone has the right to leave any country, including his own, and to return to his country". Corresponding provisions, with minor differences, appear in article 12 of the *International Covenant on Civil and Political Rights* and in the regional instruments.[461] The international instruments provide relatively elaborate limitations clauses in order to define the scope of mobility rights,[462] a function that is fulfilled, in the case of the *Canadian Charter*, by section 1.

The *International Covenant on Civil and Political Rights* provides for a right of "everyone. . .to leave any country, including his own",[463] adding that "[n]o one shall be arbitrarily deprived of the right to enter his own country".[464] The *Covenant* provides no protection against expulsion of cit-

---

461 *Protocol No. 4 to the European Convention on Human Rights*, ETS 46, arts. 2, 3, 4; *American Declaration of the Right and Duties of Man*, OAS Doc. OEA/Ser. L./V/II.23, doc. 21, rev. 6, art. 8; *American Convention on Human Rights*, (1979) 1144 UNTS 123, OASTS 36, art. 22; *African Charter of Human and Peoples' Rights*, OAU Doc. CAB/LEG/67/3 rev. 5, 4 EHRR 417, 21 *ILM* 58, art. 12; *Convention on the Rights of the Child*, GA Res. 44/25, art. 10; *Convention on the Elimination of Discrimination Against Women*, (1981) 1249 UNTS 13, [1982] CTS 31, art. 15(4); *International Convention on the Elimination of All Forms of Racial Discrimination* (1969) 660 UNTS 195, [1976] CTS 47, art. 5(d)i, ii)). Also: "Conference on Security and Cooperation in Europe, Final Act" ("Helsinki Final Act"), 1 August 1975, preamble on human contacts; "Document of the Copenhagen Meeting of the Conference on the Human Dimension of the CSCE", 1989, paras. 9.5, 19; "Document of the Moscow Meeting of the Conference on the Human Dimension of the CSCE", 1991, para. 33.

462 *International Covenant on Civil and Political Rights, supra* note 434, art. 12(3); *Protocol No. 4 to the European Convention on Human Rights, ibid.,* art. 2(3), (4); *American Convention on Human Rights, ibid.,* art. 22 (3), (4).

463 *International Covenant on Civil and Political Rights, supra* note 434, art. 12(2). See also: *Protocol no. 4 to the European Convention on Human Rights, supra* note 461, art. 2(2); *American Convention on Human Rights, supra* note 461, art. 22(2).

464 *International Covenant on Civil and Political Rights, supra* note 434, art. 12(4). See also: *Protocol No. 4 to the European Convention on Human Rights, supra* note 461, art. 3(2); *American Convention on Human Rights, supra* note 461, art. 22(5).

izens. Nevertheless, this right can be found in other instruments, namely *Protocol No. 4 to the European Convention on Human Rights*[465] and the *American Convention on Human Rights*.[466]

All citizens and all permanent residents are entitled, according to paragraph 6(2) of the *Charter*, to live and earn their living in any province. These rights are subject to specific limitations, set out in paragraphs (3) and (4). A right similar to that in paragraph 6(2) of the *Charter* appears in article 12(1) of the *International Covenant on Civil and Political Rights*, except that the latter applies to "[e]veryone lawfully within the territory".[467] In *Black* v. *Law Society of Alberta*, the Alberta Court of Appeal extensively reviewed European jurisprudence under both the *European Convention on Human Rights* and the *Treaty of Rome* in determining that restrictions on lawyers practising in other jurisdictions, enacted by the Benchers of the Alberta Bar, were *ultra vires*.[468] The Supreme Court of Canada referred to a tendency to eliminate residency requirements for the practice of law within the European Economic Community (now the European Union), and cited a judgment rendered by the European Court of Justice holding that the Paris Bar Council could not refuse membership to a German national seeking to set up a branch office.[469]

Without specific references to provisions of international law instruments, Justices Iacobucci and Bastarache, for the majority in *Canadian Egg Marketing Agency* v. *Richardson*, noted that section 6 of the *Charter* was "closely mirroring the language of international human rights treaties", and thus clearly "responds to a concern to ensure one of the conditions for the preservation of the basic dignity of the person".[470] They also referred to the words of Justice La Forest in *Black* v. *Law Society of Alberta* in explaining that the actual mobility guarantee is limited to the right to pursue a livelihood subject to the same laws as residents, which means that section 6 "is not violated by legislation regulating any particular *type* of economic activity, but rather by the *effect* of such legislation on the fundamental right to pursue a livelihood on an equal basis with others".[471] Such a general reference to

---

465 *Protocol no. 4 to the European Convention on Human Rights, supra* note 461, art. 3(1).

466 *American Convention on Human Rights, supra* note 461, art. 22(5).

467 See also: *Protocol No. 4 to the European Convention on Human Rights, supra* note 461, art. 2(1); *American Convention on Human Rights, ibid.*, art. 22(1).

468 *Black* v. *Law Society of Alberta*, [1986] 3 WWR 591, 27 DLR (4th) 527, Alta LR (2d) 1, 68 AR 259, 20 Admin LR 140, 20 CRR 177 (CA), affirmed, [1989] 1 SCR 591.

469 *Ibid.*, p. 623. See also: Pierre Blache, "Les libertés de circulation et d'établissement", in Gérald-A. Beaudoin & Errol P. Mendes, eds., *Canadian Charter of Rights and Freedoms*, 3rd ed., Toronto: Carswell, 1996, pp. 387-413.

470 *Canadian Egg Marketing Agency* v. *Richardson*, [1998] 3 SCR 157, at para. 60. See also: Armand de Mestral & Jan Winter, "Mobility Rights in the European Union and Canada", (2001) 46 *McGill Law Journal* 979.

471 *Canadian Egg Marketing Agency* v. *Richardson, ibid.*, at para. 61 (emphasis in original).

the language of international human rights law in the context of section 6 of the *Canadian Charter*, as *per* Iacobucci and Bastarache JJ in *Canadian Egg Marketing Agency* v. *Richardson*,[472] was endorsed by the New Brunswick Court of Appeal in *Rombaut* v. *New Brunswick (Minister of Health and Community Services)*, a case dealing with the ability of a physician to practice medicine in a province.[473]

In *Re Federal Republic of Germany and Rauca*, the Ontario Court of Appeal concluded that extradition of Canadian citizens, although at first glance expressly prohibited by section 6, was in fact a reasonable limit within the meaning of section 1. The Court noted that nowhere in the *International Covenant on Civil and Political Rights* or in the *European Convention on Human Rights* is there a right not to be extradited, and that extradition of nationals was actually contemplated by the members of the Council of Europe when the right to remain in one's own country was detailed in *Protocol No. 4 to the European Convention on Human Rights*.[474]

The Supreme Court of Canada examined this issue in *United States* v. *Cotroni*, which involved extradition of a Canadian national.[475] In *Cotroni*, Justice La Forest concluded that had section 6(1) of the *Charter* been intended to protect solely against expulsion, banishment or exile, this would have been expressed clearly, adding that his approach was "fortified by the fact that in enacting this clause several familiar models appear to have been ignored".[476] The familiar models included article 3(1) of *Protocol No. 4 to the European Convention on Human Rights*, whose explanatory reports[477] suggest that extradition is "outside the scope" of the provisions. European jurisprudence also suggests a degree of tolerance for the extradition of nationals, he wrote. As for the *International Covenant on Civil and Political*

---

472   *Ibid.*
473   *Rombaut* v. *New Brunswick (Minister of Health and Community Services)*, (2001) 240 NBR (2d) 258 (CA). See also: *British Columbia Native Women's Society* v. *R.*, [2001] 4 FC 191 (TD), at para. 63.
474   *Re Federal Republic of Germany and Rauca*, (1983) 145 DLR (3d) 638, 4 CCC (3d) 385, 41 OR (2d) 223, 4 CRR 42, 34 CR (3d) 97 (CA), at 655 (DLR).
475   See also: *Cook* v. *Canada (Minister of Justice)*, (2003) 168 CCC (3d) 184 (BC CA), which recently reaffirmed that the extradition process must live up to Canada's international obligations.
476   *United States of America* v. *Cotroni; United States of America* v. *El Zein*, [1989] 1 SCR 1469, (sub nom. *United States v. Cotroni*) 48 CCC (3d) 193, (sub nom. *United States v. El Zein*) 96 NR 321, (sub nom. *El Zein c. Centre de Prévention de Montréal*) 42 CRR 101, (sub nom. *El Zein c. Centre de Prévention de Montréal*) 23 QAC 182, at 1481 (SCR).
477   The Council of Europe has a practice of publishing "explanatory reports" to accompany its human rights treaties. These constitute a form of official commentary on the instrument, and compensate for the fact that most of the *travaux préparatoires* of the *Convention*'s protocols remain confidential.

Rights, Justice La Forest noted that article 12 did not contain a right to remain in one's country, although it encompassed all of the other rights found in paragraphs 6(1) and 6(2)(a) of the *Charter*. Justice La Forest concluded that despite the fact that extradition of a Canadian national was a *prima facie* violation of section 6(1), it stood on the outer edges of the core values protected by the *Charter*, and was a reasonable limit within the meaning of section 1.[478] Justice Wilson, who also relied on international law in her reasoning, reached the opposite conclusion. Section 6(1) is clear and unambiguous, she stated and, referring to *Protocol No. 4 to the European Convention on Human Rights*, she noted that were extradition to be excluded from the scope of the *Charter* this would have been stated in specific terms.[479]

In contrast with the international instruments,[480] the *Canadian Charter* provides no formal recognition of the rights of aliens or of a right of asylum.[481] The *European Convention on Human Rights* also envisages pro-

---

478 *United States of America* v. *Cotroni, United States of America* v. *El Zein, supra*, note 476, at 1480-1481 (SCR). See also *United States of America* v. *Kwok*, [2001] 1 SCR 532, at para. 60; and *United States* v. *Burns and Rafay*, [2001] 1 SCR 283, 195 DLR (4th) 1, [2001] 3 WWR 193, 151 CCC (3d) 97, 39 CR (5th) 205, 81 CRR (2d) 1, 85 BCLR (3d) 1, at para. 41. For recent cases of application of *Cotroni*, where the international law argument with respect to section 6 of the *Charter* was made as well, see: *Van Vlymen* v. *Canada (Solicitor General)*, (2004) 258 FTR 1 (Eng.), 189 CCC (3d) 538, 123 CRR (2d) 101 (FC); *United States of America* v. *Latty*, (2004) 237 DLR (4th) 652, 183 CCC (3d) 126 (Ont. CA), leave to appeal allowed, (2004) 2004 CarswellOnt 4090 (SCC), affirmed, (2006) 2006 CarswellOnt 4450 (SCC); *United States of America* v. *Turenne*, (2004) 187 Man R (2d) 45, 187 CCC (3d) 375 (CA), leave to appeal refused, (2004) 2004 CarswellMan 510 (SCC); *United States of America* v. *Wacjman*, (2002) [2003] RJQ 71, 171 CCC (3d) 134 (CA), leave to appeal refused, (2003) 2003 CarswellQue 697 (SCC); and *Solis* v. *Canada (Minister of Citizenship and Immigration)*, (1998) 147 FTR 272, 53 CRR (2d) 170, 47 Imm LR (2d) 89 (TD), affirmed, (2000) 2000 CarswellNat 539 (Fed CA), leave to appeal refused, (2000) 2000 CarswellNat 2719 (SCC).

479 *United States of America* v. *Cotroni, United States of America* v. *El Zein, supra* note 476, *at* 1505 (SCR).

480 *Universal Declaration on Human Rights*, GA Res. 217 A (III), UN Doc. A/810, art. 14; *International Covenant on Civil and Political Rights*, (1976) 999 UNTS 171, [1976] CTS 47, arts. 12, 13; *Protocol No. 4 to the European Convention on Human Rights*, *supra* note 461, arts. 2, 4. See also: *Hammel* v. *Madagascar* (No. 155/1983), UN Doc. CCPR/C/OP/1, p. 179, 6 *DJI* 500.

481 *Chieu* v. *Canada (Minister of Citizenship and Immigration)*, [2002] 1 SCR 84; *Huynh* v. *R.*, [1995] 1 FC 633 (TD), affirmed, (1996) 34 Imm LR (2d) 199 (CA), leave to appeal refused, (1996) 206 NR 238n (SCC); *Chiarelli* v. *Canada (Minister of Employment and Immigration)*, [1992] 1 SCR 711; and *Vincent* v. *Canada (Minister of Employment and Immigration)*, [1983] 1 FC 1057, 148 DLR (3d) 385, 48 NR 214 (CA), leave to appeal allowed, (1983) 53 NR 315 (SCC), affirmed, [1985] 2 SCR xiii (SCC). Aliens do of course enjoy the protection of the *Charter: Singh* v. *Canada (Minister of*

tection against collective expulsions,[482] including collective expulsion of aliens.[483] The *American Convention on Human Rights* goes even further, recognizing that "[i]n no case may an alien be deported or returned to a country, regardless of whether or not it is his country of origin, if in that country his right to life or personal freedom is in danger of being violated because of his race, nationality, religion, social status, or political opinions".[484] This protection is essentially comparable to that provided by the *Convention Relating to the Status of Refugees*, to which Canada is a party.[485]

In *Mobarakizadeh* v. *Canada*, Justice Nadon of the Federal Court of Canada (Trial Division) observed that "[t]he right to travel or move freely has been recognized. . .as a universal human right in Article 2 of the [European] Convention for the Protection of Human Rights and Fundamental Freedoms [*sic*] and Article 12 of the International Covenant on Civil and Political Rights". Because he considered that a passport was essential to the meaningful exercise of the right to travel, Justice Nadon concluded "the Charter may have the effect of imposing restrictions on the exercise of what has heretofore been regarded as an absolute discretionary power".[486] The confiscation of one's passport has once been recognised as a violation of mobility rights in section 6 of the *Charter*,[487] although the actual issue of whether or not there is a general constitutional right to a passport has yet to receive a definite answer.[488]

Exploiting a possible inconsistency between the applicable provisions of the *Canadian Charter* and those of the *International Covenant on Civil and Political Rights*, non-citizens have invoked an alleged right to remain in Canada in accordance with article 12(4) of the *Covenant*: "No one shall be arbitrarily deprived of the right to enter his own country." One case involved a man born in Scotland who had lived in Canada from the age of seven. As a result of a series of convictions for petty crime, proceedings were taken to strip him of his permanent residence status and to expel him from Canada. He argued that

Employment and Immigration), [1985] 1 SCR 177, 17 DLR (4th) 422, 58 NR 1, 14 CRR 13, 12 Admin LR 137.

482 *Protocol No. 4 to the European Convention on Human Rights, supra* note 461, art. 3(1).
483 *Ibid.*, art. 4. Also: *American Convention on Human Rights, supra* note 461, art. 22(9).
484 *American Convention on Human Rights, supra* note 461, art. 22(8).
485 (1954) 189 UNTS 137, [1969] CTS 7.
486 *Mobarakizadeh* v. *Canada*, (1993) 72 FTR 30, 23 Imm LR (2d) 93, at para. 22. See also, on this issue, the recent case at the United Nations Human Rights Committee, *Loubna El Ghar* v. *Libyan Arab Jamahiriya* (No. 1107/2202), UN Doc. CCPR/C/82/D/1107/2002.
487 *Droit de la famille – 2565*, [1997] RDF 93 (SC).
488 However, see the *obiter dictum* of Cory J. in *R.* v. *Nikal*, [1996] 1 SCR 1013, at para. 96. See also: *Black* v. *Canada (Prime Minister)*, (2001) 199 DLR (4th) 228, 54 OR (3d) 215 (CA); and *Mahmood* v. *Canada*, (2000) 189 FTR 140, 5 Imm LR (3d) 306.

for all practical purposes, Canada is his own country. His deportation from Canada would result in an absolute statutory bar from reentering Canada. It is noted in this context that article 12(4) does not indicate that everyone has the right to enter his country of nationality or of birth but only "his own country". Counsel argues that the U.K. is no longer the author's "own country", since he left it at the age of seven and his entire life is now centred upon his family in Canada – thus, although not Canadian in a formal sense, he must be considered *de facto* a Canadian citizen.[489]

The Canadian government answered that the decision to deport was

> justified by the facts of the case and by Canada's duty to enforce public interest statutes and protect society. Canadian courts have held that the most important objective for a government is to protect the security of its nationals. This is consistent with the view expressed by the Supreme Court of Canada that the executive arm of government is pre-eminent in matters concerning the security of its citizens . . . and that the most fundamental principle of immigration law is that non-citizens do not have an unqualified right to enter or remain in the country.[490]

The Human Rights Committee dismissed the petition, noting that the phrase "his own country" as a concept "applies to individuals who are nationals and to certain categories of individuals who, while not nationals in a formal sense, are also not 'aliens' within the meaning of article 13, although they may be considered as aliens for other purposes".[491] Some dissenting members of the Committee argued that the decision failed to consider the raison d'être of article 12 of the *Covenant*, which protects the right to enter one's "own country" because "it is deemed unacceptable to deprive any person of close contact with his family, or his friends or, put in general terms, with the web of relationships that form his or her social environment". They continued: "For the rights set forth in article 12, the existence of a formal link to the State is irrelevant; the Covenant is here concerned with the strong personal and emotional links an individual may have with the territory where he lives and with the social circumstances obtaining in it. This is what article 12, paragraph 4, protects."[492]

The Committee's approach in this case was largely confirmed in its General Comment on article 12, issued in 1999.[493] Nevertheless, the prin-

---

489 *Stewart* v. *Canada* (No. 538/1993), UN Doc. CCPR/C/58/D/538/1993; para. 3.4. Followed in *Canepa* v. *Canada* (No. 558/1993), UN Doc. CCPR/C/59/D/558/1993.
490 *Ibid.*, para. 5.3
491 *Ibid.*, para. 12.3.
492 *Ibid.*, Individual opinion by Elizabeth Evatt and Cecilia Medina Quiroga, co-signed by Francisco José Aguilar Urbina, dissenting.
493 "General Comment No. 27 (67), Freedom of movement (Article 12)", UN Doc. CCPR/C/21/Rev.1/Add.9.

cipal commentator on the *Covenant*, Manfred Nowak, prefers the view of the dissenters.[494]

4.5   Legal Rights

Sections 7 to 14 form the "legal rights" provisions of the *Charter*. Professor Maxwell Cohen has suggested that these texts are ". . .redolent with the classic rules. These sections owe less, perhaps, to the international law than to the great Anglo-Canadian/Anglo-American traditions and to the French Declaration on the Rights of Man of 1789."[495] Yet there are broad parallels with the international instruments of which the courts have made ample use. They have also commented on the differences between the *Canadian Charter* and the international documents in ruling on what the Canadian drafters had chosen to leave out. Finally, the appreciation made by international tribunals of such highly factual issues as unreasonable delay, wrongful detention and cruel and unusual treatment or punishment has assisted Canadian jurists in applying the *Charter*.

4.5.1   Life, Liberty and Security of the Person

Section 7 of the *Canadian Charter* enshrines the right to "life, liberty and security of the person", adding that it may not be deprived except in accordance with "principles of fundamental justice": "Everyone has the right to life, liberty and security of the person and the right not to be deprived thereof except in accordance with the principles of fundamental justice." Although international law is of considerable relevance to construction of this provision, the match is far from obvious. At the outset, it must be noted that "fundamental justice" is a Canadian creation; no such term appears in any of the international instruments.

The *Universal Declaration of Human Rights* affirms that "[e]veryone has the right to life, liberty and security of person". The drafters of the *Universal Declaration*, among them the Canadian law professor John P. Humphrey, devised this text after examining various domestic models, including the Fifth Amendment to the United States *Constitution*, which affirms the right not to be deprived of life, liberty, or property "without due process of law". However, the *Universal Declaration*, like the *Canadian Charter*, views the right to life, liberty and security in a manner going well beyond the procedural fairness approach of the American instruments.

---

494   Manfred Nowak, *Covenant on Civil and Political Rights, CCPR Commentary*, 2nd ed., Kehl, Strasbourg, Arlington: N.P. Engel, 2005.

495   Maxwell Cohen, "Towards a Paradigm of Theory and Practice: The Canadian Charter of Rights and Freedoms – International Law Influences and Interactions", [1986] *Canadian Human Rights Yearbook* 47.

The subsequent human rights treaties have not treated "life, liberty and security of person" in a single, coherent provision. The right to life has been singled out in a specific text that affirms a principle, and then describes its permissible exceptions, notably the death penalty[496] and, in the case of the *European Convention on Human Rights*, self defence and the use of lethal force against fleeing felons.[497] Liberty and security of the person are dealt with in a distinct article, concerned essentially with those who are detained by state authorities. According to article 9(1) of the *International Covenant on Civil and Political Rights*,

> [e]veryone has the right to liberty and security of person. No one shall be subjected to arbitrary arrest or detention. No one shall be deprived of his liberty except on such grounds and in accordance with such procedure as are established by law.[498]

Thus, the *Covenant* and similar provisions in the regional instruments might imply that "liberty and security of the person" should be seen in the relatively narrow context of arrest or detention.

The international authorities were invoked in this sense by Federal Court of Appeal Justice Pratte in an early *Charter* judgment, *Operation Dismantle Inc. v. Canada*, that imposed a very narrow construction on section 7:

> According to the established jurisprudence of the European Court of Human Rights, the phrase "liberty and security of the person" must be read as a whole in referring to freedom from arrest and detention and the protection against arbitrary interference with that liberty. . .In my opinion, that expression is used in the same meaning in section 7 of the Charter. The only security that is protected by that provision is, in my opinion, the security against arbitrary arrest or detention.[499]

---

496 *International Covenant on Civil and Political Rights, supra* note 480, art. 6(2); *American Declaration of the Right and Duties of Man*, OAS Doc. OEA/Ser. L./V/II.23, doc. 21, rev. 6, art. I; *American Convention on Human Rights*, (1979) 1144 UNTS 123, OASTS 36, art. 4(2); *Convention on the Rights of the Child*, GA Res. 44/25, art. 6. Also: "Document of the Copenhagen Meeting of the Conference on the Human Dimension of the CSCE", 1989, para. 17; "Document of the Moscow Meeting of the Conference on the Human Dimension of the CSCE", 1991, para. 36.

497 *European Convention on Human Rights*, (1955) 213 UNTS 221, ETS 5, art. 2.

498 See also articles 10 and 11 of the *International Covenant on Civil and Political Rights, supra* note 480. Also: *American Convention on Human Rights, supra* note 496, art. 7; *European Convention on Human Rights, ibid.* art. 5(1); *African Charter of Human and Peoples' Rights*, OAU Doc. CAB/LEG/67/3 rev. 5, 4 EHRR 417, 21 *ILM* 58, art. 6.

499 *Operation Dismantle Inc. v. Canada*, [1983] 1 FC 745, 3 DLR (4th) 193, 49 NR 363, 39 CPC 120 (CA), affirmed, [1985] 1 SCR 441, at 200 (DLR). See also: *de Mercado v. Canada*, (March 19, 1984) Doc T-2588-83, [1984] FCJ No 236 (TD); *Piche v. Canada (Solicitor General)*, (1984) 1984 CarswellNat 830, [1984] FCJ No 1008 (TD); *R. v. Cassidy*, (May 15, 1987) Doc 179/87, [1987] OJ No 1497 (Dist Ct).

In a case dealing with legislation enabling police officers to suspend drivers' licences on the spot where intoxication is suspected, the Alberta Court of Appeal referred to article 9 of *International Covenant on Civil and Political Rights*: "There, also, the term liberty does not appear to extend beyond the concept of physical liberty."[500] But, according to Justice O'Leary of the Alberta Court of Queen's Bench:

> I am not persuaded that the right to liberty guaranteed by s. 7 should be limited to matters of physical restraint of the person. In both the International Covenant on Civil and Political Rights and the European Convention on Human Rights, the right to "liberty and security of the person" is stated in a context which clearly restricts the meaning of these words to the area of arrest and detention. In contrast, s. 7 stands alone. . .[501]

Indeed, as a general rule, the Canadian courts have been cautious in applying article 9 of the *Covenant*, and its equivalent in the regional treaties, so as to limit the scope of section 7 of the *Charter*.[502] Distinguishing Justice Pratte's remarks in *Operation Dismantle*, Justice Parker of the Ontario High Court of Justice remarked:

> Given the differences in the structure between section 7 of the Charter and article 5 of the [European] Convention, and that the Convention was drafted as a process of negotiation among sovereign states, many having legal systems significantly different than ours, I do not find that the interpretation of the phrase "liberty and security of the person" in the European context offers much persuasive guidance in resolving the issues before this court.[503]

His views were endorsed by the Court of Appeal, which considered European jurisprudence and article 9 of the *International Covenant on Civil and Political Rights* to be of "little significance" in interpreting section 7.[504]

---

500 *R. v. Neale*, [1986] 5 WWR 577, 28 CCC (3d) 345, 52 CR (3d) 376, 43 MVR 194, 26 CRR 1, 46 Alta LR (2d) 225, 71 AR 337 (CA), leave to appeal refused, [1987] 1 S.C.R. xi (note).

501 *Re Rowland and R.*, (1984) 10 DLR (4th) 724, 13 CCC (3d) 367, 33 Alta LR (2d) 252, 56 AR 10, 28 MVR 239 (QB), at 733 (DLR). A similar view was taken by Justice Kroft of the Manitoba Court of Queen's Bench in *Gershman Produce Co. Ltd.* v. *Motor Transport Board*, [1985] 2 WWR 63, 14 DLR (4th) 722, 32 Man R (2d) 308, 31 MVR 67, 15 CRR 68, 10 Admin LR 253 (QB), reversed, (1985) 1985 CarswellMan 212 (CA).

502 Justice Smith of the Ontario High Court seemed unimpressed with the argument that section 7 should be interpreted "with an eye to the Covenant": *Re Evans and R.*, (1987) 30 CCC (3d) 1, 55 CR (3d) 276 (Ont HC).

503 *R. v. Morgentaler*, (1984) 12 DLR (4th) 502, 14 CCC (3d) 258, 41 CR (3d) 193, 47 OR (2d) 353, 11 CRR 116 (HC), affirmed, (1984) 14 C.R.R. 107 (CA), at 403 (OR).

504 *R. v. Morgentaler*, (1986) 22 DLR (4th) 641, 22 CCC (3d) 353, 48 CR (3d) 1, 52 OR (2d) 353, 11 OAC 81, 17 CRR 223 (CA), at 663 (DLR), reversed, [1988] 1 SCR 30, (1988) 31 CRR 1, 37 CCC (3d) 449, 44 DLR (4th) 365, 62 CR (3d) 1, 82 NR 1.

But in *B.(R.)* v. *Children's Aid Society of Metropolitan Toronto*, Chief Justice Lamer of the Supreme Court of Canada revived the rather conservative view of section 7 originally advanced by Justice Pratte of the Federal Court of Appeal. In a case dealing with the refusal of parents to authorize a blood transfusion for their child, Chief Justice Lamer noted the similarity between article 9(1) of the *International Covenant on Civil and Political Rights* and section 7 of the *Canadian Charter*. He observed that selected decisions of the Human Rights Committee showed the provision had been "invoked in cases of allegedly unlawful arrest, detention, imprisonment, mistreatment and torture". But he added that he had not "found any decision that raised any question other than a violation of the physical dimension of the person". The Chief Justice also referred to article 5(1) of the *European Convention on Human Rights*, decisions of the European Court of Human Rights, article 7 of the *American Convention on Human Rights*, article 6 of the *African Charter of Human and Peoples' Rights*, article 3 of the *Universal Declaration of Human Rights* and articles I and XXV of the *American Declaration of the Rights and Duties of Man*, noting that they too contemplated the question of liberty and security from the standpoint of physical liberty alone. "I am fully aware that the weight to be given to the foregoing may be uncertain," he concluded, "but nevertheless I believe that it provides an additional indication, at least, of the scope that the framers of the *Charter* may have intended to give to the expression 'right to liberty' in the context of s. 7."[505]

A recent example where the right to "liberty" in section 7 of the *Charter* was given a large scope with the help of international human rights law is found in the minority set of reasons *per* Justice La Forest in *Godbout* v. *Longueuil (City)*,[506] a case concerning the residence requirement imposed by a municipality for all new permanent employees. The majority of the Supreme Court of Canada decided the issue on the basis of the right to privacy as set out in section 5 of Quebec's *Charter of Human Rights and Freedoms*,[507] refusing to express any opinion on section 7 and its scope because submissions from interested parties were not made. The minority did address this argument and held that the ambit of section 7's protection included the right to make fundamentally personal choices without the interference of the state, such as choosing where to establish one's home. In giving such a broad reading of the constitutional right to "liberty", Justice

---

505   *B. (R.)* v. *Children's Aid Society of Metropolitan Toronto*, [1995] 1 SCR 315, 122 DLR (4th) 1, 176 NR 161, at 349-350 (SCR). Cited in: *Heuman (Next Friend of)* v. *Andrews*, (2005) 2005 CarswellAlta 1603, [2005] AJ No 1509 (QB).

506   *Godbout* v. *Longueuil (City)*, [1997] 3 SCR 844, 152 DLR (4th) 577, 47 CRR (2d) 1.

507   *Charter of Human Rights and Freedoms*, RSQ, c. C-12, s. 5, which reads: "Every person has a right to respect to his private life."

La Forest relied on article 12 of the *International Covenant on Civil and Political Rights*[508] and noted that "the right to choose where to reside is itself enshrined as one of the Covenant's fundamental guarantees".[509]

Although most litigation concerning section 7 and international law has focussed on the "liberty and security" component, there have been a few decisions considering the right to life. In *Rodriguez v. British Columbia (Attorney General)*, which concerned voluntary euthanasia, Justice Sopinka of the Supreme Court of Canada referred to legislation in the United Kingdom that was similar to the impugned *Criminal Code* provision.

> In the Application No. 10083/82, *R. v. United Kingdom* (1983), 33 D.R. 270, the European Commission of Human Rights considered whether s. 2 of the *Suicide Act, 1961* violated either the right to privacy in Article 8 or freedom of expression in Article 10 of the *Convention for the Protection of Human Rights and Fundamental Freedoms*. The applicant, who was a member of a voluntary euthanasia association, had been convicted of several counts of conspiracy to aid and abet a suicide for his actions in placing persons with a desire to kill themselves in touch with his co-accused who then assisted them in committing suicide. The European Commission held (at pp. 271-272) that the acts of aiding, abetting, counselling or procuring suicide were "excluded from the concept of privacy by virtue of their trespass on the public interest of protecting life, as reflected in the criminal provisions of the 1961 Act," and upheld the applicant's conviction for the offence. Further, the Commission upheld the restriction on the applicant's freedom of expression, recognizing (at p. 272):
> > . . .the State's legitimate interest in this area in taking measures to protect, against criminal behaviour, the life of its citizens particularly those who belong to especially vulnerable categories by reason of their age or infirmity. It recognizes the right of the State under the Convention to guard against the inevitable criminal abuses that would occur, in the absence of legislation, against the aiding and abetting of suicide.
> Although the factual scenario in that decision was somewhat different from the one at bar, it is significant that neither the European Commission of Human Rights nor any other judicial tribunal has ever held that a state is prohibited on constitutional or human rights grounds from criminalizing assisted suicide.[510]

Canadian courts have been cautious in giving section 7 of the *Charter* a scope that goes beyond the core civil and political rights, although they are clearly aware that international law may well suggest such an approach. According to the Supreme Court of Canada, in *Irwin Toy*:

508 *Supra*, note 480, article 12(1), which reads: "Everyone lawfully within the territory of a State shall, within that territory, have the right to liberty of movement and freedom to choose his residence."
509 *Godbout* v. *Longueuil (City)*, *supra* note 506, at para. 69.
510 *Rodriguez* v. *British Columbia (Attorney General)*, [1993] 3 SCR 519, 79 CCC (3d) 1, [1993] 3 WWR 553, 76 BCLR (2d) 145, 24 CR (4th) 281, 17 CRR (2d) 193, 56 WAC 1, 158 NR 1, at 602-603 (SCR) (*per* Sopinka J.).

The intentional exclusion of property from s. 7, and the substitution therefore of "security of the person" has, in our estimation, a dual effect. First, it leads to a general inference that economic rights as generally encompassed by the term "property" are not within the perimeters of the s. 7 guarantee. This is not to declare, however, that no right with an economic component can fall within "security of the person". Lower courts have found that the rubric of "economic rights" embraces a broad spectrum of interests, ranging from such rights, included in various international covenants, as rights to social security, equal pay for equal work, adequate food, clothing and shelter, to traditional property – contract rights. To exclude all of these at this early moment in the history of Charter interpretation seems to us to be precipitous. We do not, at this moment, choose to pronounce upon whether those economic rights fundamental to human life or survival are to be treated as though they are of the same ilk as corporate-commercial economic rights.[511]

Contemplating the possibility of giving section 7 a larger scope, in *Service Employees' International Union Local 204* v. *Broadway Manor Nursing Home*,[512] Justice O'Leary of the Ontario Divisional Court referred to publications of the Law Reform Commission of Canada, where "security of the person" is defined as "not only protection of one's physical integrity, but the provision of necessaries for its support".[513]

In *Singh* v. *Minister of Manpower and Immigration*, Justice Wilson of the Supreme Court of Canada referred to article 25(1) of the *Universal Declaration* and its relevance in construing section 7 of the *Charter*. She noted that the Law Reform Commission of Canada has already made the connection, and that:

> Commentators have advocated the adoption of a similarly broad conception of "security of the person" in the interpretation of s. 7 of the Charter. . .For

---

511 *Irwin Toy* v. *Quebec (AG)*, [1989] 1 SCR 927, 39 CRR 193, 25 CPR (3d) 417, 58 DLR (4th) 577, 94 NR 167, 24 QAC 2, at 1003-1004 (SCR). Cited in: *R.* v. *Rehberg*, (1993) 127 NSR (2d) 331, 355 APR 331 (NS SC), at 354; *Chippewa of the Thames Indian Band Number 42* v. *Ontario Hydro*, (1995) 1995 CarswellOnt 2483, [1995] OJ No 487 (Gen Div); *Haddock* v. *Ontario (Attorney General)*, (1990) 73 OR (2d) 545 (HC), at 560; *Howard* v. *Architectural Inst. of BC*, (1990) 40 BCLR (2d) 315 (SC), at 319; *Hernandez* v. *Palmer*, (1992) 46 MVR (2d) 26 (Ont Gen Div); *Conrad v. Halifax (County)*, (1993) 1993 CarswellNS 208, [1993] NSJ No 342 (SC), affirmed, (1994) 1994 CarswellNS 352 (CA), leave to appeal refused, (1994) 178 NR 396n (SCC); *Clark* v. *Peterborough Utilities Commission*, (1995) 24 OR (3d) 7 (Gen Div), affirmed, (1998) 40 OR (3d) 409 (CA); *A & L Investments* v. *Ontario*, (1998) 152 DLR (4th) 692, 36 OR (3d) 127 (CA), leave to appeal refused, (1998) 111 OAC 399n (SCC), leave to appeal refused, (1998) 111 OAC 396n (SCC); and *Criminal Trial Lawyers' Assn.* v. *Alberta (Solicitor General)*, (2004) 188 CCC (3d) 538, 122 CRR (2d) 49 (Alta QB).

512 (1983) 44 OR (2d) 392 (Div. Ct.), reversed, (1984) 1984 CarswellOnt 829 (CA), leave to appeal refused, (1985), 8 OAC 320n (SCC), at 448-449 (OR).

513 Law Reform Commission of Canada, *Medical Treatment and Criminal Law, Working Paper No. 26*, Ottawa: Supply and Service Canada, 1980, at 6.

purposes of the present appeal it is not necessary, in my opinion, to consider whether such an expansive approach to security of the person in s. 7 of the Charter should be taken.[514]

Justice Wilson returned to section 7 in her dissenting opinion in *R. v. Jones*.[515] Again relying on international law, she held that the right to parental choice in the education of children is a part of section 7 of the *Charter*. She noted that this right is "widely recognized", and in support of her reasoning she referred to article 8(1) of the *European Convention* and article 2 of the *First Protocol* to the *European Convention*.

Subsequently, the Ontario Court of Appeal gave section 7 an extensive scope, and found within it a constitutional right to legal aid, despite the rather glaring absence of an express provision to that effect in sections 10 or 11 of the *Charter*: ". . .the concept of the right to counsel had evolved into a social right or a human right implying an obligation on the state to provide counsel for an accused who lacks sufficient means to pay a lawyer. . . This evolution is reflected in the provisions of the International Covenant on Civil and Political Rights and the European Convention on Human Rights."[516] The Court of Appeal could also have cited relevant European caselaw in defense of its position.[517]

The Supreme Court of Canada addressed directly the issue of whether or not section 7 of the *Charter* should be interpreted broadly enough to include economic rights in *Gosselin* v. *Quebec (Procureur general)*,[518] concerning the validity of a differential welfare scheme providing for reduced benefits for young people not participating in training programmes. For the majority, Chief Justice McLachlin noted, without references to international human rights law, that the dominant position in Canadian caselaw dictates a narrow interpretation to the expression "life, liberty and security of the person", one limited to the protection against state measures concerning the administration of justice (although not one constrained to

---

514   *Singh* v. *Minister of Employment and Immigration, supra* note 481, at 207. Cited without approval in: *Chaoulli* v. *Québec (Procureur général)*, [2000] RJQ 786 (SC), affirmed, [2002] RJQ 1205 (CA), reversed, [2005] 1 SCR 791.

515   *R.* v. *Jones*, [1986] 2 SCR 284, 31 DLR (4th) 569, 28 CCC (3d) 513, 69 NR 241, [1986] 6 WWR 577, 47 Alta LR (2d) 97, 73 AR 133, at 319.

516   *R.* v. *Rowbotham*, (1988) 41 CCC (3d) 1, 35 CRR 207, 25 OAC 321, 63 CR (3d) 113 (CA), at 62 (CCC).

517   See, for example: *Airey* v. *Ireland*, 2 February 1981, Series A, No. 41, 3 EHRR 592, 67 ILR 388, which deals with a right to legal aid in matrimonial matters.

518   *Gosselin* v. *Quebec (Procureur general)*, [2002] 4 SCR 429, 221 DLR (4th) 257, 100 CRR (2d) 1, 44 CHRR D/363. See also: *Siemens* v. *Manitoba (Attorney General)*, (2002) [2003] 1 SCR 6, at para. 45. For a recent consideration by the Supreme Court of Canada of this issue, but under the *Canadian Bill of Rights*, SC 1960, c. 44, see: *Authorson* v. *Canada (Attorney General)*, [2003] 2 SCR 40, 66 OR (3d) 734, 227 DLR (4th) 385, 109 CRR (2d) 220, 4 AdminLR (4th) 167, 175 OAC 363.

criminal law).[519] The question whether section 7 of the *Charter* could encompass rights or interests unconnected to the administration of justice remains open, however, because of some judicial pronouncements by the Court that were neither endorsed nor rejected by Chief Justice McLachlin. She wrote:

> One day s. 7 may be interpreted to include positive obligations. To evoke Lord Sankey's celebrated phrase in *Edwards v. Attorney-General for Canada*, [1930] A.C. 124 (P.C.), at p. 136, the *Canadian Charter* must be viewed as "a living tree capable of growth and expansion within its natural limits": see *Reference re Provincial Electoral Boundaries (Sask)*, [1991] 2 SCR 158, at p. 180, *per* McLachlin J. It would be a mistake to regard s. 7 as frozen, or its content as having been exhaustively defined in previous cases.[520]

The majority did not determine whether or not section 7 of the *Charter* could be a source of positive rights, but whether in the present case the right to a level of social assistance sufficient to meet basic needs falls within the ambit of the constitutional guarantee. The majority concluded in the negative; two dissenting judges were of the contrary view.[521] After citing the Chief Justice Dickson's dictum in *Irwin Toy*, Justice Arbour wrote:

> [T]he rights at issue in this case are so connected to the sorts of interests that fall under s. 7 that it is a gross mischaracterization to attach to them the label of "economic rights". Their only kinship to the economic "property" rights that are *ipso facto* excluded from s. 7 is that they involve some economic value. But if this is sufficient to attract the label "economic right", there are few rights that would not be economic rights. It is in the very nature of rights that they crystallize certain benefits, which can often be quantified in economic terms. What is truly significant, from the standpoint of inclusion under the rubric of s. 7 rights, is not therefore whether a right can be expressed in terms of its economic value, but as Dickson C.J. suggests, whether it "fall[s] within 'security of the person'" or one of the other enumerated rights in that section. It is principally because corporate-commercial "property" rights fail to do so, and not because they contain an economic component *per se*, that they are excluded

---

519 See: *New Brunswick (Minister of Health and Community Services)* v. *G. (J.)*, [1999] 3 SCR 46; and, *Blencoe* v. *British Columbia (Human Rights Commission)*, [2000] 2 SCR 307, 190 DLR (4th) 513, [2000] 10 WWR 567, 23 Admin LR (3d) 175, 38 CHRR D/153, 2 CCEL (3d) 165, 77 CRR (2d) 189, 81 BCLR (3d) 1. See also: Philip Bryden, "*Blencoe* v. *British Columbia Human Rights Commission*", (1999) 33 *University of British Columbia Law Review* 153.

520 *Gosselin* v. *Quebec*, *supra* note 518, at para. 82. On section 7 of the *Charter* and positive obligations, see: David Wiseman, "The Charter and Poverty: Beyond Injusticiability", (2001) *University of Toronto Law Journal* 425.

521 The Chief Justice, with Gonthier, Iacobucci, Major and Binnie JJ, formed the majority; the dissenting judges, all of whom eparate opinions, were L'Heureux-Dubé, Bastarache, Arbour and LeBel JJ. Justices L'Heureux-Dubé and Arbour concluded that there was an unjustifiable section 7 *Charter* infringement.

from s. 7. Conversely, it is because the right to a minimum level of social assistance is clearly connected to "security of the person" and "life" that it distinguishes itself from corporate-commercial rights in being a candidate for s. 7 inclusion.[522]

Interestingly, in the international arena, the Canadian government has given a very broad interpretation to the scope of the terms "life, liberty and security of the person", one that includes not only civil and political rights but also economic, social and cultural rights. In its initial report to the Human Rights Committee pursuant to article 40 of the *International Covenant on Civil and Political Rights*, Canada explained its compliance with article 6 of the *Covenant* ("the right to life") with reference to occupational health and safety legislation,[523] family allowances[524] and old age pensions.[525] In its supplementary report, Canada stated that "[a]rticle 6 of the Covenant requires Canada to take the necessary legislative measures to protect the right to life. These measures, as indicated by Canada in its report, may relate to the protection of the health or social well-being of individuals."[526] In its third periodic report, Canada claimed that pursuant to article 6 of the *Covenant*, it had established a range of social and economic assistance programmes.[527] In the fifth periodic report, under the heading of article 6, Canada spoke principally of the issue of homelessness.[528] Such a large interpretation of the right to life is consistent with that proposed by the Human Rights Committee in its first general comment on article 6,[529] and has been supported by some academic writers.[530]

International law has also proved to be highly relevant as a source of "principles of fundamental justice". In discussing the meaning of the expression as it is contemplated by section 7, Lamer J (as he then was) in

---

522 *Gosselin* v. *Quebec, supra* note 518, para. 310.
523 UN Doc. CCPR/C/1/Add.43, pp. 20-21.
524 SC 1973-74, c. 44
525 SRC 1970, c. O-6.
526 UN Doc. CCPR/C/1/Add.62, p. 25.
527 UN Doc. CCPR/C/51/Add.1, p. 5.
528 UN Doc. CCPR/C/CAN/2004/5, paras. 36-40.
529 "General Comment No. 6 (16), The Right to Life (Article 6)", UN Doc CCPR/C/21/Add.1, UN Doc A/37/40, Annex V, pp. 382-383, para. 5.
530 Bertrand G. Ramcharan, "The Right to Life", (1983) 30 *Netherlands International Law Review* 297; Bertrand G. Ramcharan, "The Concept and Dimensions of the Right to Life", in Bertrand G. Ramcharan, ed., *The Right to Life in International Law*, Dordrecht/Boston/Lancaster: Martinus Nijhoff Publishers, 1985, pp. 1-32; Daniel Prémont, ed., *Essais sur le concept de "droit de vivre" en mémoire de Yougindra Khushalani*, Brussels: Bruylant, 1988; Thomas Desch, "The Concept and Dimensions of the Right to Life – As Defined in International Standards and in International and Comparative Jurisprudence", (1985-86) 36 *Osterreichische Zeitschrift für Offentliches Recht und Volkerrecht* 77.

Reference Re B.C. Motor Vehicle Act was the first to note that one of the sources of these principles is international human rights law:

> Thus, ss. 8 to 14 provide an invaluable key to the meaning of "principles of fundamental justice". Many have been developed over time as presumptions of the common law, others have found expression in the international conventions on human rights. All have been recognized as essential elements of a system for the administration of justice which is founded upon a belief in "the dignity and worth of the human person" (preamble to the *Canadian Bill of Rights*, RSC. 1970, App. III) and on the "rule of law" (preamble to the *Canadian Charter of Rights and Freedoms*).[531]

An example is found in *Reference re ss. 193 & 195.1(1)(c) of the Criminal Code (Canada)*, where Justice Lamer referred to article 7 of the *European Convention* in support of the notion that section 7 of the *Charter* encompasses a "void for vagueness" doctrine.[532]

In *R. v. Finta*, Justice Tarnopolsky of the Ontario Court of Appeal disposed of an argument that alleged certain sections of the *Criminal Code* to be contrary to principles of fundamental justice, and thus in breach of section 7 of the *Charter*, because they might have created retroactive infractions by making reference to article 15 of the *International Covenant on Civil and Political Rights*, noting that it "binds Canada in international law".[533] After recongizing that principles of fundamental justice could be derived from international human rights law, Justice Rosenberg of the Ontario Court of Justice stated that section 7 of the *Charter* included a right to a safe work environment.[534] He referred specifically to the preamble of the *Constitution of the International Labour Organization*,[535] article 16 of *ILO Convention No. 155*,[536] and article 7 of the *International Covenant on Civil and Political Rights*. Some years later, Justice Rosenberg (by then at the Ontario Court of Appeal) invoked article 12 of the *International Covenant on Economic, Social and Cultural Rights*, which affirms "the right of eve-

---

531 *Reference re British Columbia Motor Vehicle Act*, (1985) [1985] 2 SCR 486, 23 CCC (3d) 289, 63 NR 266, 24 DLR (4th) 536, 48 CR (3d) 289, [1986] 1 WWR 481, 69 BCLR 145, 36 MVR 240, 18 CRR 30, at 503 (SCR). These comments are cited by Wilson J in *Thomson Newspapers* v. *Canada (Director of Investigation and Research, Restrictive Practices Commission)*, [1990] 1 SCR 425, 67 DLR (4th) 161, 54 CCC (3d) 417, at 462 (SCR). Generally, see also: Alan Young, "Fundamental Justice and Political Power: A Personal Reflection on Twenty Years in the Trenches", (2002) 16 *Supreme Court Law Review* (2d) 121.

532 [1990] 1 SCR 1123, [1990] 4 WWR 481, 77 CR (3d) 1, 56 CCC (3d) 65.

533 *R. v. Finta,* (1992) 92 DLR (4th) 1 (Ont CA), affirmed, [1994] 1 SCR 701, 88 CCC (3d) 417, 112 DLR (4th) 513, 150 NR 370, at 63-64 (DLR).

534 *Everingham* v. *Ontario*, (1993) 1993 CarswellOnt 719, [1993] OJ No 55 (Ont Gen Div)

535 (1946) 15 UNTS 15, [1946] CTS 48.

536 *ILO Convention (No. 155) concerning Occupational Safety and Health and the Working Environment*, (1983) 1331 UNTS 279. Canada has not ratified this treaty.

ryone to the enjoyment of the highest attainable standard of physical and mental health", in holding that the absolute prohibition on the possession and cultivation of marijuana for personal medical use violates section 7.[537]

In *Canada* v. *Schmidt*, Justice La Forest relied on a decision of the European Commission[538] in declaring that surrender of a fugitive in certain circumstances could constitute a violation of principles of fundamental justice, for example where torture might be involved upon extradition.[539] His remarks were cited approvingly by Justice Hugessen, in the case of *Kindler v. Canada (Minister of Justice)*, who wrote: "La Forest J.'s reference to the *Altun* case makes this abundantly clear: it is quite simply unthinkable that any Canadian court or government could countenance the extradition of any criminal, no matter how heinous his crime, to suffer torture at the hands of a foreign state."[540] The decision of the Supreme Court of Canada in *Kindler*,[541] as well as more recent judgments on the issue of extradition and death penalty (or other forms of torture) are examined below, under the heading "Cruel and Unusual Treatment or Punishment", because they have traditionally involved both section 7 and section 12 of the *Charter*.

Similarly, in cases of expulsions or deportations to a country where there are serious risks of torture, international human rights law has become a very important factor in the interpretation of the "principles of fundamental

---

537 *R.* v. *Parker*, (2000) 188 DLR (4th) 385, 146 CCC (3d) 193, 49 OR (3d) 481 (CA). See also: *R.* v. *Krieger*, (2003) 225 DLR (4th) 183 (Alta CA), leave to appeal refused, (2003) 327 NR 390n (SCC).

538 *Altun* v. *Federal Republic of Germany* (App. No. 10308/82), (1983) 36 DR 209, 5 EHRR 651.

539 *Canada* v. *Schmidt*, [1987] 1 SCR 500, 33 CCC (3d) 193, 39 DLR (4th) 18, 58 CR (3d) 1, 28 CRR 280, 76 NR 12, 61 OR (2d) 530. Cited in: *United States of America* v. *Doyer*, (1992) (sub nom. *United States of America* v. *Doyer*) 77 CCC (3d) 203 (Que. CA), reversed, (1993) 1993 CarswellQue 169 (SCC); *Hong Kong* v. *Chan*, (1996) 113 CCC (3d) 270 (Que. CA), leave to appeal refused, (22 mai 1997), no 25761 (SCC); *Gwynne* v. *Canada (Minister of Justice)*, (1998) 50 CRR (2d) 250 (BCCA), leave to appeal refused, [1998] 1 SCR ix; *United Mexican States* v. *Ortega*, (2004) 237 DLR (4th) 281, 183 CCC (3d) 75, 117 CRR (2d) 191 (BC SC), reversed, (2005) 2005 CarswellBC 1142 (CA), leave to appeal allowed, (2005) 2005 CarswellBC 2473 (SCC), reversed, (2006) 2006 CarswellBC 1789 (SCC); *United States of America* v. *Cobb*, [2001] 1 SCR 587, reconsideration refused, (2001) 2001 CarswellOnt 2045 (SCC). See also: *United States of America* v. *Redha*, [2003] 11 WWR 707, 176 Man R (2d) 21, 28 Imm LR (3d) 135 (QB); Dianne L. Martin, "Extradition, the Charter, and Due Process: Is Procedural Fairness Enough?", (2002) 16 *Supreme Court Law Review* (2d) 161.

540 *Kindler* v. *Canada (Minister of Justice)*, [1989] 2 FC 492, 46 CCC (3d) 257, 91 NR 359, 42 CRR 262, 69 CR (3d) 38, 25 FTR 240n (CA), leave to appeal allowed, (1989) 102 NR 158n (S.C.C.), affirmed, [1991] 2 SCR 779, 67 CCC (3d) 1, 84 DLR (4th) 438, 6 CRR (2d) 193, 129 NR 81, at 508 (FC).

541 *Kindler* v. *Canada (Minister of Justice)*, [1991] 2 SCR 779, 67 CCC (3d) 1, 84 DLR (4th) 438, 6 CRR (2d) 193, 129 NR 81.

justice" in section 7 of the *Charter*.[542] The 2001 decision of the Supreme Court of Canada in *Suresh v. Canada (Minister of Citizenship and Immigration)*[543] is the most significant development in that regard, where it was held that, save in the most extraordinary circumstances, the *refoulement* of an asylum seeker in such a situation is an unjustifiable violation of the constitutional requirements of fundamental justice. In reviewing how the administrative power under section 53(1) of the *Immigration Act*[544] was exercised by the Minister, the Court considered in detail not only the Canadian perspective on the issue but also the international one. It first addressed the argument that the absolute prohibition on torture was a norm of *jus cogens*, a notion codified in sections 53 and 64 of the *Vienna Convention on the Law of Treaties*.[545] As a national court responsible for the interpretation and application of national law, the Supreme Court of Canada was wise in handling this tricky question:

> Although this Court is not being asked to pronounce on the status of the prohibition on torture in international law, the fact that such a principle is included in numerous multilateral instruments, that it does not form part of any known domestic administrative practice, and that it is considered by many academics to be an emerging, if not established peremptory norms, suggests that it cannot be easily derogated from.[546]

---

542 See: *Bhatti v. Canada (Minister of Citizenship and Immigration)*, (1996) 120 FTR 123, 35 Imm LR (2d) 192; *Sivakumar v. Canada (Minister of Citizenship and Imigration)*, [1996] 2 FC 872.

543 *Suresh v. Canada (Minister of Citizenship and Immigration)*, [2002] 1 SCR 3, 208 DLR (4th) 1, 37 Admin LR (3d) 159, 90 CRR (2d) 1. Cited in: *Almrei v. Canada (Minister of Citizenship and Immigration)*, [2005] 3 FCR 142 (CA); *Jaballah (Re)*, (2005) 261 FTR 35, 44 Imm LR (3d) 181 (TD); *Thanabalasingham v. Canada (Minister of Citizenship and Immigration)*, (2005) 250 DLR (4th) 33, 46 Imm LR (3d) 131 (FC TD), reversed, (2006) 2006 CarswellNat 25 (FCA); and *John v. Canada (Minister of Citizenship and Immigration)*, (2003) 231 FTR 248 (TD). For a case comment, see: Stéphane Beaulac, "The *Suresh* Case and Unimplemented Treaty Norms", (2002) 15 *Revue québecoise de droit international* 221.

544 *Immigration Act*, RSC 1985, c. I-2.

545 (1969) 1155 UNTS 331, [1980] CTS 37, 8 ILM 679. Article 53 of the *Vienna Convention offers* the following definition of *jus cogens* or "peremptory norms": "For the purposes of the present Convention, a peremptory norm of general international law is a norm accepted and recognized by the international community of States as a whole as a norm from which no derogation is permitted and which can be modified only by a subsequent norm of general international law having the same character."

546 *Suresh v. Canada (Minister of Citizenship and Immigration)*, *supra* note 543, at para. 65.

The international legal instruments include common article 3 to the 1949 *Geneva Conventions*,[547] the *Universal Declaration of Human Rights*;[548] the *Declaration on the Protection of All Persons from Being Subjected to Torture and Other Cruel, Inhuman or Degrading Treatment or Punishment*;[549] the *International Covenant on Civil and Political Rights*;[550] the *European Convention on Human Rights*;[551] the *American Convention on Human Rights*;[552] *the African Charter on Human and People' Rights*;[553] and the *Universal Islamic Declaration of Human Rights*.[554] The Court also referred to a judgment of the International Criminal Tribunal for the former Yugoslavia, *Prosecutor* v. *Furundžija*,[555] and the celebrated *Pinochet* case of the British courts: *R. v. Bow Street Metropolotan Stipendiary Magistrate, Ex parte Pinochet Ugarte (No. 3)*.[556]

Then the Court considered, specifically, three treaties to help identify the situation at international law concerning deportation where there was a risk of torture. The first two, the *International Covenant on Civil and Political Rights*[557] and the *Convention Against Torture and Other Cruel, Inhuman and Degrading Treatment or Punishment*,[558] prescribe an absolute prohibition to deport to torture, while the third one, the *Convention Relating to the Status of Refugees*[559] (unlike the first two, a treaty that is partially

---

547 *Geneva Convention for the Amelioration of the Condition of the Wounded and Sick in Armed Forces in the Field*, (1950) 75 UNTS 31, [1965] CTS 20; *Geneva Convention for the Amelioration of the Condition of the Wounded, Sick and Shipwrecked Members of the Armed Forces at Sea*, (1950) 75 UNTS 85, [1965] CTS 20; *Geneva Convention Relative to the Treatment of Prisoners of War*, (1950) 75 UNTS 135, [1965] CTS 20; *Geneva Convention Relative to the Protection of Civilian Persons in Time of War*, (1950) 75 UNTS 287, [1965] CTS 20.

548 GA Res. 217 A (III), UN Doc. A/810, art. 5.

549 GA Res. 3452 (XXX), UN Doc. A/10034 (1975).

550 (1976) 999 UNTS 171, [1976] CTS 47, art. 7.

551 (1955) 213 UNTS 221, ETS 5, art. 3.

552 (1979) 1144 UNTS 123, OASTS 36, art. 5.

553 OAU Doc. CAB/LEG/67/3 rev. 5, 4 EHRR 417, 21 *ILM* 58, art. 5.

554 (1982) 4 EHRR 433, art. VII.

555 *Prosecutor* v. *Furundžija* (Case No. IT-95-17/1-T), Judgment, 10 December 1998.

556 [1999] 2 WLR 827 (HL).

557 *Supra* note 550, arts. 4 and 7, as interpreted by the United Nations Human Rights Committee in "General Comment No. 20 (44), Replaces general comment 7 concerning prohibition of torture and cruel treatment or punishment (Article 7)", UN Doc. HRI/GEN/1/Rev. 1.

558 *Convention Against Torture and Cruel, Inhuman or Degrading Treatment or Punishment*, UN Doc. A/39/51, annex, [1987] CTS 36, arts. 1, 2, 3 and 16. The Court noted that these provisions enjoy a dominant status in international law. See: "Conclusions and Recommendations of the Committee against Torture: Canada", UN Doc. CAT/C/XXV/Concl.4 (2000).

559 *Convention Relating to the Status of Refugees*, (1954) 189 UNTS 137, [1969] CTS 29, art. 33.

incorporated into Canadian law), provides for a prohibition that is quasi-total, because there is an exception when national security interests are at stake. But the Court disregarded the lack of legislative transformation of the former two instruments, which contrast with the latter treaty, and held that the absolute prohibition "on returning a refugee to face a risk of torture reflects the prevailing international norm".[560] In interpreting Canadian law, "[t]his is the norm which best informs the content of the principles of fundamental justice".[561] However, inconsistently with this international perspective, which would even have a flavour of *jus cogens*, the Supreme Court of Canada in the end left the door open under section 7 of the *Charter* to an exception based upon national security reasons to the prohibition to deport where there is a risk of torture.[562]

The companion case to *Suresh* at the Supreme Court of Canada, *Ahani v. Canada (Minister of Citizenship and Immigration)*,[563] was decided differently. The Court refused to order a new hearing and confirmed the deportation order. Having exhausted all domestic remedies, Ahani submitted a petition to the United Nations Human Rights Committee under the *Optional Protocol to the International Covenant of Civil and Political Rights*.[564] The international instance made a request for interim measures of

---

560   *Suresh* v. *Canada (Minister of Citizenship and Immigration)*, *supra*, note 543, at para. 72. To the same effect, see also: *Philippines (Republic)* v. *Pacificador*, (1999) (sub nom. *Philippines (Republic)* v. *Pacificador*) 60 CRR (2d) 126 (Ont Gen Div), at para. 61; and *Farhadi* v. *Canada (Minister of Citizenship and Immigration)*, [1998] 3 FC 315 (TD), reversed, (2000) 257 NR 158 (CA), referred for consideration, (2002) 2002 CarswellNat 69 (SCC), at para. 45.

561   *Suresh* v. *Canada (Minister of Citizenship and Immigration)*, *supra* note 543, at para. 75.

562   *Ibid.*, at para. 129.

563   *Ahani* v. *Canada (Minister of Citizenship and Immigration)*, [2002] 1 SCR 72, 208 DLR (4th) 57, 90 CRR (2d) 47. On those issues, see also: *Thamotharampillai* v. *Canada (Minister of Citizenship and Immigration)*, (2001) 84 CRR (2d) 346, 14 Imm LR (3d) 201 (FCA); *Ithibu* v. *Canada (Minister of Citizenship and Immigration)*, (2001) 202 FTR 233, 13 Imm LR (3d) 251 (TD); *Rasa* v. *Canada (Minister of Citizenship and Immigration)*, (2000), 191 FTR 129, 75 CRR (2d) 105, 6 Imm LR (3d) 52 (TD); *Said* v. *Canada (Minister of Citizenship and Immigration)*, [1999] 2 FC 592 (TD), reversed, (2000) 2000 CarswellNat 2350 (CA); *Williams* v. *Canada (Minister of Citizenship and Immigration)*, [1997] 2 FC 646 (CA), leave to appeal refused, (1997) 150 D.L.R. (4th) viii (note) (SCC); *Sinnappu* v. *Canada (Minister of Citizenship and Immigration)*, [1997] 2 FC 791 (TD), affirmed, (1999) 1999 CarswellNat 2891 (Fed CA); *Ghorvei* v. *Canada (Minister of Citizenship and Immigration)*, (1997) 138 FTR 149 (TD); *Singh* v. *Canada (Minister of Citizenship and Immigration)*, (1997) 50 CRR (2d) 176 (FC TD); *Bavi* v. *Canada (Minister of Citizenship and Immigration)*, (1996) 106 FTR 153 (TD).

564   *Ahani* v. *Canada* (No. 1051/2002), UN Doc. CCPR/C/80/D/1051/2002, cited in *Charkaoui (Re)*, [2005] 2 FCR 299 (CA), leave to appeal allowed, (2005) 346 NR 393n (S.C.C.), at para. 140.

protection (the equivalent of a domestic interlocutory injunction, to avoid irreparable harm while the case is pending) to Canada, asking to delay deportation until the full consideration by it of Ahani's case, which was declined by the federal government.[565] Ahani then applied to the Canadian courts, invoking the interim measures request of the Human Rights Committee in support of a motion for a provisional injunction, again relying on section 7 of the *Charter*.[566] The majority of the Ontario Court of Appeal, *per* Laskin JA, decided against reviewing the government's decision and Ahani was indeed sent back to Iran. All members of the bench agreed that the international norms had no direct legal effect domestically, because "Canada has never incorporated either the Covenant or the Protocol into Canadian law by implementing legislation".[567] Justice Laskin further wrote that it would be untenable to "convert a non-binding request, in a Protocol which has never been part of Canadian law, into a binding obligation enforceable in Canada by a Canadian court".[568]

On the merits, the Human Rights Committee concluded that Canada had violated the *International Covenant on Civil and Political Rights* by sending Ahani to Iran. The Committee said there was a breach of article 9 with respect to arbitrary detention and lack of access to court. It noted that

> detention on the basis of a security certification by two Ministers on national security grounds does not result ipso facto in arbitrary detention, contrary to article 9, paragraph 1. However, given that an individual detained under a security certificate has neither been convicted of any crime nor sentenced to a term of imprisonment, an individual must have appropriate access, in terms of article 9, paragraph 4, to judicial review of the detention, that is to say, review of the substantive justification of detention, as well as sufficiently frequent review.

Because of lengthy delay in the Federal Court proceedings, the Committee concluded that article 9(4) had indeed been breached.[569] According to the Committee:

565 The interim measures issue before the Human Rights Committee is discussed in Chapter 3, *supra*, at 164-167.

566 *Ahani* v. *Canada (Attorney General)*, (2002) 58 OR (3d) 107, 91 CRR (2d) 145, 19 Imm LR (3d) 231 (CA), leave to appeal refused, (2002) [2002] SCCA 62, 2002 CarswellOnt 1651 (SCC). See also: Jo M. Pasqualucci, "Interim Measures in International Human Rights: Evolution and Harmonization", (2005) 38 *Vanderbilt Journal of Transnational Law* 1; and Joanna Harrington, "Punting Terrorists, Assassins and Other Undesirables: Canada, the Human Rights Committee and Requests for Interim Measures of Protection", (2003) 48 *McGill Law Journal* 55.

567 *Ahani* v. *Canada (Attorney General)*, *ibid.*, at para. 31.

568 *Ibid.*, at para. 33. Followed in *Dadar* v. *Minister of Citizenship and Immigration*, 2006 FC 382, para. 17.

569 *Ahani* v. *Canada*, *supra* note 564 at paras. 10.3-10.4.

[T]he failure of the State party to provide him, in these circumstances, with the procedural protections deemed necessary in the case of *Suresh*, on the basis that the present author had not made out a prima facie risk of harm fails to meet the requisite standard of fairness. The Committee observes in this regard that such a denial of these protections on the basis claimed is circuitous in that the author may have been able to make out the necessary level of risk if in fact he had been allowed to submit reasons on the risk of torture faced by him in the event of removal, being able to base himself on the material of the case presented by the administrative authorities against him in order to contest a decision that included the reasons for the Minister's decision that he could be removed. The Committee emphasizes that, as with the right to life, the right to be free from torture requires not only that the State party not only refrain from torture but take steps of due diligence to avoid a threat to individual of torture from third parties.[570]

The Committee concluded with a reference to the Supreme Court's holding in *Suresh* that deportation of an individual where a substantial risk of torture had been found to exist was not necessarily precluded in all circumstances. The Committee reminded the Supreme Court of Canada that "the prohibition on torture, including as expressed in article 7 of the Covenant, is an absolute one that is not subject to countervailing considerations".[571]

The same year that it issued *Suresh* and *Ahani*, in *Burns and Rafay* the Supreme Court of Canada also made numerous international references in a section 7 analysis concerning extradition to a State where capital punishment might be imposed. Noting that "principles of fundamental justice" were drawn from "basic tenets of our legal system", the Court concluded in this context that the abolition of the death penalty had emerged as a major Canadian initiative at the international level, and that it reflected a concern increasingly shared by most of the world's democracies. The Court referred to resolutions adopted by the United Nations Commission on Human Rights calling not only for the abolition of the death penalty but also "request[ing] States that have received a request for extradition on a capital charge to reserve explicitly the right to refuse extradition in the absence of effective assurances from relevant authorities of the requesting State that capital punishment will not be carried out".[572] According to the Supreme Court, "Canada supported these initiatives. When they are combined with other examples of Canada's international advocacy of the abolition of the death penalty itself, as described below, it is difficult to avoid the conclusion that in the Canadian view of fundamental justice, capital punishment is unjust

---

570   *Ibid.*, para. 10.7.
571   *Ibid.*, para. 10.10.
572   Citing CHR Resolutions 1999/61 (adopted 28 April 1999) and 2000/65 (adopted 27 April 2000).

and it should be stopped."[573] The Court cited remarks by a Canadian representative to the Commission on Human Rights, made in the context of adoption of one of the death penalty resolutions: "Suggestions that national legal systems needed merely to take into account international laws [were] inconsistent with international legal principles. National legal systems should make sure they were in compliance with international laws and rights, in particular when it came to the right to life."[574]

Regrettably, the Court's glowing assessment of Canadian human rights diplomacy may have been a bit overstated. In 1999, Canada nearly sabotaged the resolution in the Commission on Human Rights when its European promoters attempted to add the famous paragraph dealing with extradition, which the Supreme Court found to be so significant.[575] Far from being buried in obscure United Nations documents, Canada's discomfort with the resolution was reported in *The Globe and Mail* a few weeks after the first hearing in *Burns and Rafay* before the Supreme Court of Canada.[576]

The principles of fundamental justice in section 7 of the *Charter* were also interpreted in view of Canada's international human rights obligations under the *Convention on the Rights of the Child* in the case of *Francis (Litigation Guardian of)* v. *Canada (Minister of Citizenship and Immigration)*.[577] The issue was whether or not there was a constitutional duty to give consideration to Canadian-born children and to make sure their rights and interests were considered in a deportation proceeding taken against their mother under the *Immigration Act*. This case was thus similar to *Baker v. Canada (Minister of Citizenship and Immigration)*,[578] except for the *Charter*

---

573   *United States* v. *Burns and Rafay*, [2001] 1 SCR 283, 195 DLR (4th) 1, [2001] 3 WWR 193, 151 CCC (3d) 97, 39 CR (5th) 205, 81 CRR (2d) 1, 85 BCLR (3d) 1, para. 84.

574   *Ibid.*, para. 85, citing Press Release HR/CN/788 (7 April 1997).

575   See: Ilias Bantekas & Peter Hodgkinson, "Capital Punishment at the United Nations: Recent Developments", (2000) 11 *Criminal Law Forum* 23, at 31.

576   Daniel LeBlanc, "Canada wants UN to soften extradition proposal", *The Globe and Mail*, 19 April 1999, p. A3; Daniel LeBlanc, "EU firm on extradition proposal", *The Globe and Mail*, 20 April 1999, p. A2.

577   *Francis (Litigation Guardian of)* v. *Canada (Minister of Citizenship and Immigration)*, (1998) 40 OR (3d) 74, 160 DLR (4th) 557, 52 CRR (2d) 329 (Ont Gen Div), reversed, 49 OR (3d) 136 (Ont CA), leave to appeal allowed, (2000) 257 NR 200n (SCC), but motion to quash on grounds that the case was moot granted on 6 November 2000, SCC no. 27615.

578   *Baker* v. *Canada (Minister of Citizenship and Immigration)*, (1995) 101 FTR 110, 31 Imm LR (2d) 150, affirmed, [1997] 2 FC 127, reversed, [1999] 2 SCR 817, 174 DLR (4th) 193, 14 Admin LR (3d) 173, 1 Imm LR (3d) 1, 243 NR 22. For similar pronouncements, see also: *De Guzman* v. *Canada (Minister of Citizenship and Immigration)*, [2005] FCJ No 2119, 2005 CarswellNat 4381 (CA), leave to appeal refused, (2006) 2006 CarswellNat 1694 (SCC); *Varga* v. *Canada (Minister of Citizenship and Immigration)*, (2005) [2005] FCJ No 1570, 2005 CarswellNat 2963 (FC); *Fraser* v. *Canada (Attorney General)*, (2005) 2005 CarswellOnt 7457, [2005] OJ No 5580 (SCJ); *Vallée*

argument, in which the majority of the Supreme Court of Canada *per* L'Heureux-Dubé J made the groundbreaking statement that unimplemented treaty norms can play a role in the interpretation and application of domestic law.[579] In the *Francis* case, Justice McNeely of the Ontario Court (General Division) also ignored the fact that the *Convention on the Rights of the Child* has not been incorporated in Canada and referred to several of its provisions to help give a constitutional protection of children's interests in the deportation hearing of their mother.[580] Similarly, the dissenting judges at the Supreme Court of Canada in *Winnipeg Child and Family Services v. K.L.W.*,[581] a case concerning the statutory power to remove a child from a parent's custody without prior judicial authorization in non-emergency sit-

---

v. *Commission des droits de la personne et des droits de la jeunesse*, [2005] RJQ 961 (CA); *Bouzari* v. *Iran (Islamic Republic)*, (2004) 71 OR (3d) 675, 243 DLR (4th) 406, 122 CRR (2d) 26 (CA), leave to appeal refused, (2005) 2005 CarswellOnt 292 (SCC); *De Guzman* v. *Canada (Minister of Citizenship and Immigration)*, (2004) 257 FTR 290, 245 DLR (4th) 341, 40 Imm LR (3d) 256 (TD), affirmed, (2005) 51 Imm LR (3d) 17 (CA), leave to appeal refused, (2006) 2006 CarswellNat 1694 (SCC); *Schreiber* v. *Canada (Attorney General)*, [2002] 3 SCR 269, (sub nom. *Schreiber* v. *Federal Republic of Germany*) 216 DLR (4th) 513, 167 CCC (3d) 51, 164 OAC 354; *Lalonde* v. *Ontario (Commission de restructuration des services de santé)*, (2001) 208 DLR (4th) 577, 38 Admin LR (3d) 1, 89 CRR (2d) 1 (CA), additional reasons at, (2002) 2002 CarswellOnt 336 (CA); *114957 Canada Ltée (Spraytech, Société d'arrosage) v. Hudson (Town)*, [2001] 2 SCR 241; and *R.* v. *Demers*, (1999) 176 DLR (4th) 741, 137 CCC (3d) 297 (BC SC), affirmed, (2003) 102 CRR (2d) 367 (BC CA), leave to appeal refused, (2003) 321 NR 399n (SCC).

579   Among the numerous commentators on this seminal decision, see: René Provost, "Le juge mondialisé: légitimité judiciaire et droit international au Canada", in Marie-Claude Belleau & François Lacasse, eds., *Claire L'Heureux-Dubé à la Cour suprême du Canada, 1987-2002*, Montreal: Wilson & Lafleur, 2004, pp. 569-603; Stéphane Beaulac, "National Application of International Law: The Statutory Interpretation Perspective", (2003) 41 *Canadian Yearbook of International Law* 225; Hugh Kindred, "Canadians as Citizens of the International Community: Asserting Unimplemented Treaty Rights in the Courts", in Stephen G. Coughlan & Dawn Russell, eds., *Citizenship and Citizen Participation in the Administration of Justice*, Montreal: Thémis, 2002, pp. 263-287; Jutta Brunée & Stephen J. Toope, "A Hesitant Embrace: The Application of International Law by Canadian Courts", (2002) 40 *Canadian Yearbook of International Law* 3; and Karen Knop, "Here and There: International Law in Domestic Courts", (2000) 32 *New York University Journal of International Law & Policy* 501.

580   *Francis (Litigation Guardian of)* v. *Canada (Minister of Citizenship and Immigration)*, *supra* note 577, at 563-564. See also: *Jones (Litigation guardian of)* v. *Canada (Minister of Citizenship and Immigration)*, (1999) 93 OTC 331, 1999 CarswellOnt 1161 (SCJ).

581   *Winnipeg Child and Family Services* v. *KLW*, [2000] 2 SCR 519; McLachlin CJ and Arbour J were in dissent. As for the majority, *per* L'Heureux-Dubé J, the references to the *Convention on the Rights of the Child*, GA Res. 44/25, were merely to assist in ascertaining the social context and legislative framework within which the section 7 analysis was undertaken; *ibid.*, at paras. 73 and 81.

uations,[582] made references to the *Convention on the Rights of the Child* in identifying the substantive content of fundamental justice. The dissent concluded that there was an unjustifiable violation of section 7 of the *Charter*.[583]

In *Canadian Foundation for Children, Youth and the Law v. Canada (Attorney General)*, dealing with the exemption for parents and teachers from criminal sanctions for using reasonable corrective force on children or pupils, pursuant to section 43 of the *Criminal Code*, the Supreme Court of Canada referred to international human rights law for the interpretation of section 7 of the *Charter*. The argument that the "best interest of the child" was a principle of fundamental justice was rejected by Chief Justice McLachlin, for the majority, because it failed the second and third criteria of the three-pronged test developed in caselaw.[584] The requirement of being a legal principle was met, as evidenced by both international law and domestic law. As regards the former, the Chief Justice wrote: "Canada is a party to international conventions that treat 'the best interests of the child' as a legal principle: see the *Convention on the Rights of the Child*, Can. T.S. 1992 No. 3, Art. 3(1), and the *Convention on the Elimination of Discrimination Against Women*, Can. T.S. 1982 No. 31, Arts. 5(b) and 16(1)(d)."[585] Then followed references to statutory provisions in federal and provincial legislation. Albeit a legal principle, the majority opined that the "best interest of the child" is not a foundational requirement for Canada's societal notion of justice, nor does it provide a justiciable legal standard that courts can identify with some precision, thus failing the last two criteria of the test.[586] The Chief Justice invoked international law in support of her argument that the "best interest of the child" principle did not meet the second of the three criteria, requiring a legal principal to be "a foundational requirement for the dispensation of justice". She noted that article 3(1) of the *Convention on the Rights*

---

582 On this issue, see also: *New Brunswick (Minister of Health and Community Services) v. G. (J.)*, [1999] 3 SCR 46.

583 *Winnipeg Child and Family Services* v. *KLW, supra* note 581, at paras. 7-8.

584 The test was developed in the following cases: *Reference re British Columbia Motor Vehicle Act*, (1985) [1985] 2 SCR 486, 23 CCC (3d) 289, 63 NR 266, 24 DLR (4th) 536, 48 CR (3d) 289, [1986] 1 WWR 481, 69 BCLR 145, 36 MVR 240, 18 CRR 30, at 503; *Rodriguez* v. *British Columbia (Attorney General)*, [1993] 3 SCR 519, 79 CCC (3d) 1, [1993] 3 WWR 553, 76 BCLR (2d) 145, 24 CR (4th) 281, 17 CRR (2d) 193, 56 WAC 1, 158 NR 1, at 590 (SCR); and *R.* v. *Malmo-Levine*, [2003] 3 SCR 571, 233 DLR (4th) 415, [2004] 4 W.W.R. 407, 179 CCC (3d) 417, 114 CRR (2d) 189, 16 CR (6th) 1, 23 BCLR (4th) 1, at para. 113.

585 *Canadian Foundation for Children, Youth and the Law* v. *Canada (Attorney General)*, [2004] 1 SCR 76, 70 OR (3d) 95, 234 DLR (4th) 257, 180 CCC (3d) 353, 115 CRR (2d) 88, 16 CR (6th) 203, 46 RFL (5th) 1, 183 OAC 1, at para. 9. Cited in: *Hiemstra* v. *Hiemstra*, (2005) 44 Alta LR (4th) 315 (QB).

586 *Ibid.*, at paras. 10-11.

of the Child describes the "best interests of the child" as "*a* primary consideration" rather than "*the* primary consideration".[587]

4.5.2   Unreasonable Search and Seizure

There is no provision in any of the international instruments that is comparable to section 8 of the *Canadian Charter*, whose wording is undoubtedly derived from article IV of the United States *Bill of Rights*: "Everyone has the right to be secure against unreasonable search or seizure."[588] However, in its interpretation of section 8, the Supreme Court of Canada has held that the "interest" protected by the provision is privacy.[589] The right to privacy is explicitly protected by the international instruments. For example, article 12 of the *Universal Declaration of Human Rights* states that "[n]o one shall be subjected to arbitrary interference with his privacy, family, home or correspondence, nor to attacks upon his honour and reputation".[590]

Canadian courts have referred occasionally to the international law provisions concerning privacy, in refugee claimant cases raising such issues as sexual orientation.[591] The European Court of Human Rights has estab-

---

587   *Ibid.*, para. 10 (emphasis in original). Chief Justice McLachlin expressly referred to the wording of L'Heureux-Dubé J's reasons in *Baker* v. *Canada (Minister of Citizenship and Immigration)*, *supra* note 578, at para. 75.

588   See: François Chevrette, Hugo Cyr & François Tanguay-Renaud, "La protection lors de l'arrestation, la détention et la protection contre l'incrimination rétroactive", in Gérald-A. Beaudoin & Errol P. Mendes, eds., *Canadian Charter of Rights and Freedoms*, 4th ed., Markham, Ont., LexisNexis Butterworths, 2005, pp. 595-789, at 597-598.

589   *Hunter* v. *Southam Inc.*, [1984] 6 WWR 577, 41 CR (3d) 97, 33 Alta LR (2d) 193, 27 BLR 297, 84 DTC 6467, [1984] 2 SCR 145, (sub nom. *Hunter v. Southam Inc.*) (1984) 11 DLR (4th) 641, 14 CCC (3d) 97, 2 CPR (3d) 1, (sub nom. *Hunter v. Southam Inc.*) 55 AR 291, 9 CRR 355, (sub nom. *Hunter v. Southam Inc.*) 55 NR 241. The right to privacy may also appear in the *Charter* as a reasonable limit on freedom of expression, according to Justice La Forest, who relied on the *International Covenant on Civil and Political Rights* and the *European Convention on Human Rights*: *Edmonton Journal* v. *Alta (AG)*, [1989] 2 SCR 1326, 64 DLR (4th) 577, [1990] 1 WWR 557, 41 CPC (2) 109, 45 CRR 1, 103 AR 321, 71 Alta LR (2d) 273, 102 NR 321. Justice Wilson also found that a concern for privacy underlies sections 11(c) and 13 of the *Charter*: *Thomson Newspapers* v. *Canada (Director of Investigation and Research, Restrictive Practices Commission)*, [1990] 1 SCR 425, 67 DLR (4th) 161, 54 CCC (3d) 417, at 480 (SCR).

590   See also: *International Covenant on Civil and Political Rights*, *supra* note 550, art. 17; *American Convention on Human Rights*, *supra* note 532, art. 11para. 2; *European Convention on Human Rights*, *supra* note 551, art. 8. These provisions were cited by Justice L'Heureux-Dubé in *R.* v. *O'Connor*, [1995] 4 SCR 411, at 484.

591   *R. (U.W.) (Re)*, [1991] CRDD 501; *V. (O.Z.) (Re)*, [1993] CRDD 164. See also: Philip Girard, "The Protection of the Rights of Homosexuals under the International Law of Human Rights: European Perspectives", [1986] *Canadian Human Rights Yearbook* 3.

lished guidelines for civil search procedures, conducted pursuant to Anton Piller orders issued by common law courts, if such searches and seizures are not to violate the right to privacy.[592] A Nova Scotia Court has referred to article 8 of the *European Convention on Human Rights* in ruling that a search of a domicile was illegal.[593]

Recently, the Ontario Court of Appeal made reference to the protection of private life under the European human rights regime in a case challenging the constitutionality of the retention of fingerprints following the withdrawal of criminal charges.[594] To help determine whether, under section 8 of the *Charter*, there remains a reasonable expectation of privacy in such situations, Justice Feldman examined the law in other common law countries – Scotland, New Zealand, Tasmania in Australia, and several states in the United States – which provide for the destruction or return of fingerprints upon acquittal or withdrawal of charges. Then he noted a 1984 change in English criminal procedure, which allowed authorities to keep fingerprints and DNA upon acquittal or withdrawal of charges, was unsuccessfully challenged under article 8 of the *European Convention on Human Rights*.[595] The issue of whether there is still an expectation of privacy with regard to such samples was left unanswered, because the British case turned on the weighing of individual versus state interests.[596] In the end, the Ontario Court of Appeal opined that there is some privacy interest in retained fingerprints. However, the constitutional argument was dismissed because the balance of interests that had been struck was deemed appropriate.

4.5.3   Rights Upon Arrest and Detention

Sections 9 and 10 of the *Canadian Charter* deal with the rights of those subject to detention, imprisonment and arrest.

9. Everyone has the right not to be arbitrarily detained or imprisoned.
10. Everyone has the right on arrest or detention
   a) to be informed promptly of the reasons therefor;
   b) to retain and instruct counsel without delay and to be informed of that right; and
   c) to have the validity of the detention determined by way of *habeas corpus* and to be released if the detention is not lawful.

592 *Chappell* v. *United Kingdom*, 30 March 1989, Series A, No. 152, 12 EHRR 1.
593 *R.* v. *Comeau*, (1991) 101 NSR. (2d) 425, 275 APR 425 (NS Co Ct), at 428.
594 *R.* v. *Dore*, (2002) 166 CCC (3d) 225, 4 CR (6th) 81, 96 CRR (2d) 49 (Ont CA).
595 *R. (on the application of S.)* v. *The Chief Constable of South Yorkshire; R. (on the application of Marper)* v. *Chief Constable of South Yorkshire*, [2002] EWHC 478 (Admin.).
596 On this point, see: Gérald-A. Beaudoin, "L'équilibre délicat entre la sécurité publique et les droits individuels: le point de vue d'un législateur", [2003] *Revue du Barreau* (numéro spécial) 75.

There are some rather elaborate corresponding provisions on this subject in the international instruments. The *Universal Declaration of Human Rights*, in article 9, provides succinctly that "[n]o one shall be subjected to arbitrary arrest, detention or exile". The provisions of the *International Covenant on Civil and Political Rights* are considerably more detailed. They prohibit arbitrary arrest or detention, accord a right to be informed, at the time of arrest, of the reasons for arrest and of any charges, and specify that an individual arrested or detained on a criminal charge shall be brought promptly before a judge or other officer authorized by law to exercise judicial power.[597] According to the Human Rights Committee, the term "deprivation of liberty", as found in article 9(1) of the *International Covenant on Civil and Political Rights*, "is applicable to all deprivations of liberty, whether in criminal cases or in other cases such as, for example, mental illness, vagrancy, drug addiction, educational purposes, immigration control, etc."[598] Several specialized declarations assist in completing the rights international law recognizes in the case of arrest or detention, although as these are not international treaties they do not carry the same legal force.[599]

The international instruments also include specific provisions that deal with the rights of those detained. These might well be applicable in developing the scope of section 9, although it would appear that most *Charter* litigation dealing with prison conditions has focussed instead on section 12. Article 10 of the *International Covenant on Civil and Political Rights* declares that "[a]ll persons deprived of their liberty shall be treated with humanity and with respect for the inherent dignity of the human person". They are to be segregated from convicted persons, and treated separately under conditions appropriate to their status as unconvicted persons. Juveniles are to be segregated from adults.[600] Furthermore, "[t]he penitentiary system shall comprise treatment of prisoners the essential aim of which shall be their reformation and social rehabilitation".

---

597 *International Covenant on Civil and Political Rights*, (1976) 999 UNTS 171, [1976] CTS 47, art. 9. See also: *American Convention on Human Rights*, (1979) 1144 UNTS 123, OASTS 36, art. 7; *European Convention on Human Rights*, (1955) 213 UNTS 221, ETS 5, art. 5; *African Charter of Human and Peoples' Rights*, OAU Doc. CAB/LEG/ 67/3 rev. 5, 4 EHRR 417, 21 *ILM* 58, art. 6. Also: "Document of the Moscow Meeting of the Conference on the Human Dimension of the CSCE", 1991, para. 23.

598 "General Comment 8 (16), Right to liberty and security of persons (Article 9)", UN Doc. CCPR/C/21/Add.1, UN Doc. CCPR/C/Add.1, Vol. II, p. 383, 9 EHRR 176.

599 Jiri Toman, "The Treatment of Prisoners: Development of Legal Instruments and Quasi-Legal Standards", in Gudmundur Alfredsson & Peter Macalister-Smith, *The Living Law of Nations*, Kehl: Engel, 1996, pp. 421-439.

600 Canada formulated a reservation to a similar provision in the *Convention on the Rights of the Child, supra* note 581, art. 37(c). Canada said it reserved the right not to separate adults and children in cases where it was not possible or appropriate.

International authorities have provided assistance to Canadian courts in defining the word "detention" as it appears in sections 9 and 10 of the *Charter*.[601] In one early *Charter* case, the Alberta Court of Queen's Bench considered article 5 of the *European Convention on Human Rights* and the interpretation given the word "detention" by the European Commission of Human Rights[602] to be "helpful" in the construction of section 9 of the *Charter*.[603] Justice Veit noted that the European Commission had considered the length of time of the restraint, and the purpose and circumstances surrounding the detention in determining whether there had been a violation of the individual's civil rights. In *R. v. Konechny*, Justice Lambert of the British Columbia Court of Appeal observed that article 9 of the *International Covenant on Civil and Political Rights* "must have been in the contemplation of the framers of the charter". Subscribing to the view that in resolving a difficulty in interpreting the *Charter* it is proper to look at the *International Covenant on Civil and Political Rights*, he extended the protection of the *Charter* to confinement going beyond confinement based on grounds and procedures established by law.[604] Referring to cases decided by the European Court of Human Rights,[605] Justice Then, of the Ontario Court of Justice, observed that the *European Convention on Human Rights* allows for detention "when it is reasonably considered necessary to prevent [a person from] committing an offence, though the European Human Rights Court has taken a relatively restrictive view of this provision".[606] The *European Convention* provision on detention is actually rather archaic, authorizing, for example, "the lawful detention of persons for the prevention of the spreading of infectious diseases, of persons of unsound mind, alcoholics or drug addicts or vagrants".[607]

The right to retain and instruct counsel is set out in section 10(b) of the *Charter*, and is clearly a right that obtains at the stage of arrest and detention.

---

601 See generally: Simon Roy, "Le rôle de l'accusé dans la poursuite criminelle", in Gérald-A. Beaudoin & Errol P. Mendes, eds., *Canadian Charter of Rights and Freedoms*, 4th ed., Markham, Ont., LexisNexis Butterworths, 2005, pp. 791-874, at 799-803.

602 *X. v. Austria* (App. No. 8278/78), (1980) 18 DR 154; *X. v. Federal Republic of Germany* (App. No. 8819/79), (1981) 24 DR 158; *X and Y v. Sweden* (App. No. 7376/76), (1977) 7 DR 123; *Ireland v. United Kingdom*, (1976) 19 European Convention on Human Rights Yearbook 512.

603 *R. v. King*, [1984] 4 WWR 531, 31 Alta LR 253, 27 MVR 212 (QB).

604 *R. v. Konechny*, (1983) [1984] 2 WWR 481, 6 DLR (4th) 350, 10 CCC (3d) 233, 38 CR (3d) 69, 25 MVR 132 (BC CA), leave to appeal refused, (1984) 55 NR 156A (SCC), at 490 (WWR).

605 *Matznetter v. Austria*, 10 November 1969, Series A, No. 10, 1 EHRR 199; *Guzzardi v. Italy*, 6 November 1980, Series A, No. 39, 3 EHRR 333.

606 *R. v. Budreo*, (1996) 104 CCC (3d) 245 (Ont Gen Div), affirmed, (2000) 70 CRR (2d) 203 (Ont CA), leave to appeal refused, [2001] 1 SCR vii, at 270 (CCC).

607 *European Convention on Human Rights*, *supra* note 597, art. 5(1)(e).

The international instruments formally contemplate the right to counsel only at the trial stage. According to the *International Covenant on Civil and Political Rights*, there is a right to "communicate with counsel" in preparation of trial[608] as well as to be defended by counsel of the defendant's choice. An exception is the *Rome Statute of the International Criminal Court*, which recognizes a right to counsel even for a suspect who is being questioned.[609] The international human rights instruments are clearly more explicit on the subject of state funding for counsel. Under the *International Covenant*, a defendant is entitled "to have legal assistance assigned to him, in any case where the interests of justice so require, and without payment by him in any such case if he does not have sufficient means to pay for it".[610] The *European Convention* also provides that legal assistance be provided free of charge "when the interest of justice so require".[611] The *American Convention on Human Rights* is similarly somewhat equivocal on the subject of free legal assistance, providing for "[t]he inalienable right to be assisted by counsel provided by the State, paid or not as the domestic law provides, if the accused does not defend himself personally or engage his own counsel within the time period established by law".[612] Thus, the international instruments envisage a right to state-funded counsel in certain circumstances, although the right is clearly far from absolute.

In *Deutsch v. Law Society Legal Aid Fund*, the Ontario Divisional Court compared the European and Canadian provisions and concluded that a right to state-funded counsel could not be read into the *Charter*. Reference was made to the minutes of the Hays-Joyal Committee, where this discrepancy between the draft provisions of the *Canadian Charter* and the relevant articles of the *International Covenant on Civil and Political Rights* and the *European Convention on Human Rights* had been raised and where, upon the representations of Justice Minister Jean Chrétien who argued that free legal assistance was adequately covered by provincial legal aid plans, it was agreed not to entrench such a right. However, Justice Craig noted that in "rare cases", by application of sections 7 and 11(d) of the *Charter*, "it seems to follow that there is an entrenched right to funded counsel".[613] In *R. v. Rowbotham*, Justices Martin, Grange and Cory (as he then was) of the Ontario Court of Appeal approved of the comments in *Deutsch*, after referring to relevant provisions in the *International Covenant on Civil and*

---

608 *International Covenant on Civil and Political Rights, supra* note 597, art. 14(3)(b).
609 *Rome Statute of the International Criminal Court*, UN Doc. A/CONF.183/9, art. 55(2)(e).
610 *International Covenant on Civil and Political Rights, supra* note 597, art. 14(3)(d).
611 *European Convention on Human Rights, supra* note 597, art. 6(3).
612 *American Convention on Human Rights, supra* note 597, art. 8(2)(e).
613 *Deutsch v. Law Society Legal Aid Fund*, (1985) 11 OAC 30, 48 CR (3d) 166, 16 CRR 349 (Div Ct), at 173-4 (CR).

Political Rights and the *European Convention on Human Rights*, and declared that a stay of proceedings was the appropriate remedy under section 24(1) where the right to funded counsel had been violated.[614]

The Alberta Court of Queen's Bench also referred to the international provisions where a motion for postponement, based on a refusal of legal aid by the relevant authorities, had been dismissed. The accused had argued that his *Charter* rights had been denied, in that he did not have adequate additional time to prepare his defence.[615] In *R.* v. *Robinson*, the Alberta Court of Appeal noted that the right to counsel was "less than absolute" in the provisions of both the *European Convention on Human Rights* and the *International Covenant on Civil and Political Rights*. According to Justice McClung:

> Despite the fact that the proposed clause mirrors the powers furnished the Court of Appeal by s. 684, it was rejected. It was rejected after the joint committees heard evidence and weighed the competing articles found in the International Covenant on Civil and Political Rights, the European Convention on Human Rights and Fundamental Freedoms and the Sixth Amendment to the United States Constitution. It cannot be assumed that the committee was unmindful of the extended right-to-counsel jurisprudence of the U.S. federal courts that is relied upon by the applicants in this case, but which, as a Constitutional safeguard, has been consistently refused in Canada.[616]

But rather than view the international instruments as limiting the right to counsel, Justice Lamer of the Supreme Court of Canada, in *R.* v. *Brydges*, found that article 14(3)(d) of the *International Covenant on Civil and Political Rights* stressed the importance of the right to counsel. He wrote: "[T]he right to retain and instruct counsel [. . .] also means the right to have access to counsel free of charge where the accused meets certain financial criteria set up by the provincial Legal Aid plan, and the right to have access to immediate, although temporary, advice from duty counsel irrespective of financial status."[617] The Supreme Court returned to the right to counsel issue in *R.* v. *Prosper*. Chief Justice Lamer stressed that the issue arising under section 10(b) of the *Charter* is not a general right to state-funded legal assistance, but rather the more limited issue of a right to free and immediate legal advice upon detention. The Chief Justice noted that no such right can be found expressly in section 10(b), and moreover that the preparatory work

---

614 *R.* v. *Rowbotham*, (1988) 41 CCC (3d) 1, 35 CRR 207, 25 OAC 321, 63 CR (3d) 113 (CA), at 69-70 (CCC).

615 *R.* v. *Stiopu; Mackay* v. *R.*, (1984) 8 CRR 216 (Alta QB), affirmed, (1984) 8 CRR 216 at 217n (CA).

616 *R.* v. *Robinson*, (1990) 51 CCC (3d) 452, 70 Alta LR (2d) 31, 63 DLR (4th) 289, 100 AR 26, 73 CR (3d) 81 (CA), at 114 (CR).

617 *R.* v. *Brydges*, [1990] SCR 190, [1990] 2 WWR 220, 71 Alta LR (2d) 145, 103 NR 282, 74 CR (3d) 129, 53 CCC (3d) 330, 104 AR 124, 46 CRR 236, at 349-350 (CCC).

of the *Canadian Charter* indicates that such a provision was expressly rejected.[618] The Chief Justice did not refer to international law in his reasons. His conclusion that section 10(b) imposes no substantive constitutional obligation upon governments to ensure the availability of duty counsel upon arrest or detention was endorsed by Justice L'Heureux-Dubé, who wrote for the minority. She referred approvingly to the reasons of the Alberta Court of Appeal in *R. v. Robinson*,[619] which cite the relevant texts in the *International Covenant on Civil and Political Rights* and the *European Convention on Human Rights*.[620]

A similar utilisation of international human rights law, to help give a generous scope to section 10(b) of the *Canadian Charter*, occurred in *R. v. Cornelio*.[621] Referring to the presumption that Canada's constitutional protection is at least as great as that under international law, Justice Molloy resorted to the *International Covenant on Civil and Political Rights*, at article 14(3), providing for the right to have a lawyer of one's choice. In *R. v. M. (B.)*,[622] it was the *Convention on the Rights of the Child*[623] that was used to reinforce the interpretation of the right to counsel, again in the context of legal aid, this time under the *Young Offenders Act*.[624] The Quebec Court of Appeal once cited a statement of principle adopted at the Third United Nations Congress on the Prevention of Crime and Treatment of Offenders that stressed "that adequate and timely legal assistance must be available as of right to all arrested and accused persons at a sufficiently early stage in the criminal process adequately to protect their human rights and to ensure the fair and non-discriminatory application of the criminal law to all citizens".[625]

Section 10(c) entrenches the historic writ of *habeas corpus*, which is the classic remedy against unlawful detention. Although the international instruments do not use the common law term of *habeas corpus*, they also provide that "[a]nyone who is deprived of his liberty by arrest or detention shall be entitled to take proceedings before a court, in order that that court may decide without delay on the lawfulness of his detention and order his release if the detention is not lawful".[626] Although international human rights

---

618 *R. v. Prosper*, [1994] 3 SCR 236, at 266-267.

619 *Supra* note 616.

620 *R. v. Prosper*, *supra* note 618, at 286-287.

621 *R. v. Cornelio*, (1998) 58 CRR (2d) 43 (Ont Gen Div).

622 *R. v. M. (B.)*, (1998) 128 CCC (3d) 149, 54 CRR (2d) 241 (Ont Prov Div).

623 *Convention on the Rights of the Child*, GA Res. 44/25, art. 40(4).

624 *Young Offenders Act*, RSC 1985, c. Y-1, s. 11(4).

625 *Dubois v. R.*, [1990] RJQ 681, 27 QAC 241 (CA), at 688 (RJQ).

626 *International Covenant on Civil and Political Rights*, *supra* note 597, art. 9(4); *European Convention on Human Rights*, *supra* note 597, art. 5(4); *American Convention on Human Rights*, *supra* note 597, art. 7(6).

law provides abundant and intriguing authorities on the subject of *habeas corpus*, it has yet to be cited by Canadian courts in the construction and application of section 10(c) of the *Charter*.

4.5.4   Rights in Criminal and Penal Proceedings

Rights in "criminal and penal matters" are set out in section 11 of the *Canadian Charter*:

11. Any person charged with an offence has the right
  a) to be informed without unreasonable delay of the specific offence;
  b) to be tried within a reasonable time;
  c) not to be compelled to be a witness in proceedings against that person in respect of the offence;
  d) to be presumed innocent until proven guilty according to law in a fair and public hearing by an independent and impartial tribunal;
  e) not to be denied reasonable bail without just cause;
  f) except in the case of an offence under military law tried before a military tribunal, to the benefit of trial by jury where the maximum punishment for the offence is imprisonment for five years or a more severe punishment;
  g) not to be found guilty on account of any act or omission unless, at the time of the act or omission, it constituted an offence under Canadian or international law or was criminal according to the general principles of law recognized by the community of nations;
  h) if finally acquitted of the offence, not to be tried for it again and, if finally found guilty and punished for the offence, not to be tried or punished for it again; and
  i) if found guilty of the offence and if the punishment for the offence has been varied between the time of commission and the time of sentencing, to the benefit of the lesser punishment.

The rights set out in section 11 of the *Canadian Charter* are quite specifically confined to individuals already "charged with an offence" in criminal and penal matters. They do not, then, apply to civil or administrative proceedings, as the Alberta Court of Queen's Bench recently reaffirmed in the 2005 case of *Alberta* v. *Kingsway General Insurance Co.*[627] This is in clear distinction with the international provisions, which contemplate the right to a fair trial in a broader context. For example, article 14 of the *International Covenant on Civil and Political Rights* declares that "[a]ll persons shall be equal before the courts and tribunals", and that "[i]n the determination of any criminal charge against him, or of his rights and obligations in a suit at law, everyone shall be entitled to a fair and public hearing by a competent,

---

627 *Alberta* v. *Kingsway General Insurance Co.*, (2005) 258 DLR (4th) 507, 53 Alta LR (4th) 147 (QB), at paras. 90-91.

independent and impartial tribunal established by law".[628] The international models then go on to set out a much more detailed catalogue of procedural rights applicable specifically to those charged with criminal offences. In other words, they protect a more limited range of judicial guarantees in the case of non-criminal matters. The issue of whether to recognize a broad right to a fair trial was debated by the Hays-Joyal Committee when a draft of the *Canadian Charter* was being considered by Parliament, but it decided that non-criminal and non-penal proceedings should not fall within the ambit of section 11.[629]

In *Re Lazarenko and Law Society of Alberta*, an attorney threatened with disbarment argued that section 11(c) of the *Charter* (the right not to be compelled to be a witness in proceedings against one's self) could apply, because an "offence" had been charged. Comparisons were made between the *European Convention on Human Rights* and the *Charter*, which speaks only of an offence, in order to broaden section 11 to the disciplinary proceedings under the *Bar Act*. The court accepted this reasoning, only to conclude that the offending provision met the *Charter*'s section 1 test.[630]

In *Re Trumbley and Fleming*, the Ontario Court of Appeal was asked to apply section 11 in the context of disciplinary proceedings under the *Police Act*. The Court referred to articles 6(2) and 6(3) of the *European Convention* and article 14(2) of the *International Covenant on Civil and Political Rights*, where the expression "everyone charged with a criminal offence" is employed. According to the Court:

> I think the European Convention may have influenced the drafting of the same term in the Canadian Bill of Rights in 1960 but in the light of the Canadian history of what is the text of s. 2(f) in this document, discussed above, I would not infer from a comparison between these international documents and s. 11 of the Charter an intention to extend its coverage beyond federal and provincial prosecutions.[631]

---

628 *International Covenant on Civil and Political Rights*, *supra* note 597, art. 14(1). See also: *European Convention on Human Rights*, *supra* note 597, art. 6(1); *American Convention on Human Rights*, *supra* note 597, art. 8(1). Also: "Document of the Copenhagen Meeting of the Conference on the Human Dimension of the CSCE", 1989, paras. 5.16-5.19; "Document of the Moscow Meeting of the Conference on the Human Dimension of the CSCE", 1991, para. 23.1(v).

629 See Michael Bothe, "La protection des droits fondementaux au Canada", *Jahrbuch des öffentlichen Rechts der Gegenwart*, 1986, at 304.

630 *Re Lazarenko and Law Society of Alberta*, (1983) [1984] 2 WWR 24, (sub nom. *Lazarenko v. Law Society (Alberta)*) 4 DLR (4th) 389, 29 Alta LR (2d) 28, 50 AR 337 (QB).

631 *Re Trumbley and Fleming*, (1986) (sub nom. *Trumbley v. Fleming*) 29 DLR (4th) 557, 55 OR (2d) 570, 15 OAC 279, 24 CRR 333, 21 Admin LR 232 (CA), affirmed, (1987) 1987 CarswellOnt 948 (SCC), affirmed, (1987) 1987 CarswellOnt 947 (SCC), affirmed, (1987) 1987 CarswellOnt 949 (SCC).

4.5.4.1   The Right to be Informed of the Specific Offence

Section 11(a) of the *Canadian Charter* (the right to be informed without unreasonable delay of the specific offence) has provided one of the clearest examples of international law being applied and explicitly used to resolve uncertainty about the meaning of the *Charter*. According to Justice Linden of the Ontario High Court of Justice (as he then was):

> Although legislation has not been enacted to incorporate the United Nations International Covenant on Civil and Political Rights into the domestic law of Canada, the Covenant can be used to help construe ambiguous provisions of a domestic statute, if there are no provisions of the domestic statute contrary to the portions of the Covenant being relied upon. Since the meaning of s. 11(a) is not completely clear on its face, resort should be had to the Covenant as a tool of statutory interpretation.[632]

Justice Linden noted that the *International Covenant on Civil and Political Rights* is more expansive in its wording than the *Canadian Charter*, and that it refers not only to a right "to be informed. . .of the specific offence" but also of the right to be informed of the "nature and cause of the charge".

> Surely the words "nature and cause of the charge" do not include the mode of procedure to be employed in prosecuting the offence. Since the Parliament of Canada is presumed not to act in violation of its international obligations, s. 11(a) of the Charter should be construed in a manner consistent with art. 14 of the Covenant. As a result, I must conclude that the right to be informed of the "specific offence" means the right to be informed of the substantive offence and the acts or conduct which allegedly form the basis of that charge.[633]

4.5.4.2   Trial Within a Reasonable Time

The explanatory notes accompanying the 5 October 1980 draft of the *Canadian Charter* indicate that section 11(b), which provides for the right to be tried without unreasonable delay, was drawn from the *International Covenant on Civil and Political Rights*[634] and the *European Convention on Human Rights*.[635] In *R.* v. *Beason*, it was held that the right to a trial within a reasonable period of time existed prior to the *Charter*, because it had been incorporated in the *European Convention on Human Rights* and the *Inter-*

---

632   *Re R. and Warren*, (1983) 35 CR (3d) 173, 6 CRR 82 (Ont. HC), at 86 (CRR).

633   *Ibid.*; followed in *R.* v. *Harmouche*, [1984] CSP 1069 (Que CSP) and in *R.* v. *Cancor Software Corp*, (1990) 58 CCC (3d) 53, 40 OAC 122 (CA), leave to appeal refused, (1991) 130 NR 394n (SCC).

634   (1976) 999 UNTS 171, [1976] CTS 47, art. 9(3).

635   (1955) 213 UNTS 221, ETS 5, art. 5(3). Noted by Justice McKay in *Re R. and Carter*, (1984) 4 DLR (4th) 746, 9 CCC (3d) 173, 36 CR (3d) 346 (BCSC), affirmed, (1984) 1984 CarswellBC 532 (CA), affirmed, (sub nom. *Carter* v. *R.*) [1986] 1 SCR 981. See also: Michael Bothe, *supra* note 629, at 302.

national Covenant on Civil and Political Rights, as well as in the *Magna Carta*, the Sixth Amendment to the United States *Constitution*, and other documents of general significance. According to Justice Fitzpatrick of the Ontario High Court, section 11(b) "has only reaffirmed a right which existed in Canada from long before the *Canadian Charter* came into force".[636] A totally opposite result was reached by Justice de Weerdt of the Northwest Territories Supreme Court. Noting that the right to a speedy trial does not appear in the *Universal Declaration of Human Rights*, the learned judge concluded "that this is to be regarded as a new right under the *Canadian Charter of Rights and Freedoms*".[637]

The courts have frequently referred to international law and jurisprudence in interpreting the meaning of section 11(b) and in determining what is in fact "a reasonable time". Just as "reasonable" in section 1 may invite reference to international sources, so also it does in section 11(b). Canadian courts have looked at the facts in both international and United States cases in order to decide how long is "reasonable".[638]

Rather early on in *Charter* interpretation, the issue of whether or not the right accorded by section 11(b) applied to "pre-charge" as well as "post-charge" was a frequent subject of contention before the Canadian courts. In the first of many decisions on the subject,[639] Justice McDonald referred to the *International Covenant on Civil and Political Rights* and the *European Convention on Human Rights*, as well as to *König v. Federal Republic of Germany*,[640] an early case of the European Court of Human Rights. His reasons were frequently cited by other courts.[641] The matter was subsequently settled by the Supreme Court of Canada in *R. v. Carter*, which excluded "pre-charge delay" from the section 11 computation, although without resorting to international law in its reasoning.[642] In a subsequent decision, Justice Lamer referred to three European cases in order to demonstrate that "pre-charge delay" comes to an end and section 11 delay begins

---

636 *R. v. Beason*, (1984) 5 CRR 29 (Ont. HC) at 32, reversed, (1983) 7 CRR 65 (CA).
637 *Re Panarctic Oils Limited and R.*, (1982) 141 DLR (3d) 138, 69 CCC (2d) 393, 38 AR 447, 2 CRR 358 (NWT SC), at 145 (DLR); followed in *R. v. Whissel Industries*, (1983) 2 CRD. 725.310-30 (Alta PC).
638 See *R. v. Mills*, [1986] 1 SCR 863, 58 OR (2d) 544n, 16 OAC 81, 29 DLR (4th) 161, 26 CCC (3d) 481, 52 CR (3d) 1, 67 NR 241, at 931 (SCR).
639 *R. v. Cameron*, [1982] 6 WWR 270, 70 CCC (2d) 532, 29 CR (3d) 73, 39 AR 194, 22 Alta LR (2d) 1, 1 CRR 289 (QB), affirmed, [1983] 2 WWR 671 (CA).
640 *König v. Federal Republic of Germany*, 10 March 1980, Series A, No. 36, 2 EHRR 170, 59 ILR 370, 17 *ILM* 1151.
641 *Re Regina and Carter, supra* note 635; *R. v. Dahlem*, (1983) 25 Sask R 10 (QB); *R. v. Chartrand*, (1983) 19 Man R (2d) 344 (Co Ct).
642 *Carter v. R.*, (1984) 4 DLR (4th) 746, 9 CCC (3d) 173, 36 CR (3d) 346 (BCSC), affirmed, (1984) 1984 CarswellBC 532 (CA), affirmed, (sub nom. *Carter v. R.*) [1986] 1 SCR 981; and see also *R. v. Morin*, [1992] 1 SCR 771.

when the individual is first exposed to the charge, by summons or arrest, and not, as had been argued by the Crown, when the trial court is formally seized with the case.[643]

In *R.* v. *Rahey*,[644] Justice La Forest referred to the *European Convention on Human Rights* and its jurisprudence in explicitly resolving the ambiguity surrounding the term "to be tried"/"d'être jugée". He noted that the French version of article 7 of the *European Convention on Human Rights* also uses the term "jugée", and that this implies the right not only to begin the trial but also to be judged and sentenced with dispatch.[645] Article 7 of the *European Convention* had been interpreted by the European Court of Human Rights in this manner, and Justice La Forest relied on its decision in reaching a similar conclusion.[646]

In a subsequent decision, *R.* v. *Conway*,[647] Justice La Forest did not seem concerned by another important conclusion of the European Court of Human Rights in *Wemhoff*, namely that the right to be tried within a reasonable delay includes the appeal of the case subsequent to a conviction. Justice Sopinka, in dissent, quoted *Wemhoff* in support of his reasons in *Conway*, noting that although article 5(3) of the *European Covenant* did not cover the appeal procedure, there was no doubt that such protection was accorded by article 6(1). The Human Rights Committee reached a similar conclusion in *Pinkney* v. *Canada*.[648]

---

643 *R.* v. *Kalanj*, [1989] 1 SCR 1594, 48 CCC (3d) 459, 96 NR 191, [1989] 6 WWR 577, 70 CR (3d) 260.

644 *R.* v. *Rahey*, [1987] 1 SCR 588, 33 CCC (3d) 289, 75 NR 81, 33 CRR 279, 57 CR (3d) 289, 78 NSR (2d) 183, 193 APR 183, 39 DLR (4th) 481. See also: *R.* v. *Potvin*, [1993] 2 SCR 880, 105 DLR (4th) 214, 155 NR 241, 23 CR (4th) 10, 83 CCC (3d) 97, at 899 (SCR) (*per* La Forest) and 912 (*per* Sopinka); *R.* v. *Sapara*, [2002] 10 WWR 350, 5 Alta LR (4th) 284 (QB); and *R.* v. *Peters*, (2002) 2002 CarswellQue 1344, [2002] JQ no 701 (PC), affirmed, (2004) 2004 CarswellQue 829 (CA).

645 On interpretation of bilingual treaties, see also the comments of Justice Vancise of the Saskatchewan Court of Appeal in *Saskatchewan Human Rights Commission* v. *Kodellas*, (1989) 60 DLR (4th) 143 (Sask CA), at 184-185, and *R.* v. *Racette*, [1988] 2 WWR 318, 39 CCC (3d) 289, 6 MVR (2d) 55 (Sask CA), at 309-310 (CCC).

646 *Wemhoff* v. *Federal Republic of Germany*, 27 June 1968, Series A, No. 7, 1 EHRR 55, 41 ILR 281. *Wemhoff* was also cited by Justice Lamer in *R.* v. *Mills*, supra note 638, at 227 (DLR), in support of the point that difficulties in investigating a case would be a factor in appreciating the time requirements inherent in a case.

647 *R.* v. *Conway*, [1989] 1 SCR 1659, 49 CCC (3d) 289, 70 CR (3d) 209, 40 CRR 1, 96 NR 241, 34 OAC 165.

648 *Pinkney* v. *Canada* (No. 27/1978), UN Doc. CCPR/C/14/D/27/1977, UN Doc. CCPR/ 3/Add.1, Vol. II, p. 385, UN Doc. CCPR/C/OP/1, p. 95, 2 *Human Rights Law Journal* 344, [1983] *Canadian Human Rights Yearbook* 315. In applying the international authorities to the *Canadian Charter*, it is important to note that the former provide formally for a right of appeal from a criminal conviction, something that does not appear in the *Charter*.

Judge Payne of the Ontario Provincial Court – Criminal Division, also cited the *Wemhoff* case with respect to the various criteria applicable in assessing delay, and specifically "difficulties in the investigation of the case (its complexity in respect of facts or number of witnesses or co-accused, need to obtain evidence abroad, etc.)".[649] In *R. v. Porter, R. v. Hurlburt*, an individual acquitted at trial argued that the Crown's application for leave to appeal would result in a lengthy and costly hearing, and that this violated his rights under section 11(b). Justice Macdonald of the Nova Scotia Court of Appeal referred to article 5(3) of the *European Convention on Human Rights*, and to scholarly commentary on the provision, in dismissing the respondent's argument. Although the international instruments echo the right to trial without unreasonable delay, they do not necessarily forbid lengthy pre-trial detention.[650]

4.5.4.3   The Right Not to be Compelled to be a Witness

Section 11(c) of the *Canadian Charter* was drawn from article 14(3)(g) of the *International Covenant on Civil and Political Rights*, as well as from section 2 of the *Canadian Bill of Rights*.[651] The *Covenant* declares that no accused shall be "compelled to testify against himself or to confess guilt".[652] In *R. v. Dubois*, the Alberta Court of Appeal found it significant that neither the *European Convention on Human Rights* nor the *Universal Declaration of Human Rights* provide any explicit right against self-incrimination.[653]

4.5.4.4   The Presumption of Innocence

The presumption of innocence is recognized in all of the international instruments,[654] although its scope remains enigmatic. In *R. v. Oakes*, Chief

---

649 *R. v. Hickey*, (24 February 1987) Payne Prov. Ct. J., [1987] OJ No 1924 (Prov Ct).

650 *R. v. Porter; R. v. Hurlburt*, (1988) 213 APR 91, 84 NSR (2d) 91 (CA), at 96 (APR).

651 Michael Bothe, *supra* note 629.

652 *International Covenant on Civil and Political Rights, supra* note 634, art. 14(3)(g). See also: *American Convention on Human Rights*, (1979) 1144 UNTS 123, OASTS 36, art. 8(2)(g); *Convention on the Rights of the Child, supra* note 623, art. 40(2)(b)(iv).

653 *R. v. Dubois*, [1984] 3 WWR 594, 8 DLR (4th) 589, 11 CCC (3d) 453, 39 CR (3d) 281, 31 Alta LR (2d) 16, 51 AR 210, 9 CRR 61 (CA), reversed, [1985] 2 SCR 350. In *Thomson Newspapers* v. *Canada (Director of Investigation and Research, Restrictive Practices Commission)*, [1990] 1 SCR 425, 67 DLR (4th) 161, 54 CCC (3d) 417, Justice Wilson looked to English, American and Australian authorities in reasoning that "the right of compellability and the right against self-incrimination are thus fundamental precepts of democratic societies which respect individual rights and freedoms", and did not even mention international human rights sources.

654 *Universal Declaration of Human Rights*, GA Res. 217 A (III), UN Doc. A/810, art. 11; *American Declaration of the Rights and Duties of Man*, OAS Doc. OEA/Ser. L./V/II.23, doc. 21, rev. 6, art. XXVI; *International Covenant on Civil and Political Rights, supra*

Justice Dickson of the Supreme Court of Canada referred extensively to the international instruments and jurisprudence concerning the presumption of innocence. They provide "further evidence of the widespread acceptance of the principle of the presumption of innocence", he said.[655] In *Oakes* in the Ontario Court of Appeal,[656] Justice Martin had noted the similarity between article 6(2) of the *European Convention* and section 11(d) of the *Charter*. He examined the existence of reverse onus clauses in Europe, and specifically in section 30(2) of the United Kingdom's *Sexual Offences Act*, whose legality had been upheld by the European Commission on Human Rights in *X. v. United Kingdom*. The test was one of a rational connection between the proven fact (living with a prostitute) and the presumed fact (living off the avails of prostitution).[657]

Justice Michel Proulx of the Quebec Court of Appeal insisted upon the importance of giving a broad application to the presumption of innocence. Referring to decisions of the European Commission on Human Rights, he wrote that the presumption must extend to the pre-trial phases of the criminal process.[658]

4.5.4.5   The Right to a Fair and Public Hearing

With respect to the right to a fair and public hearing, the international provisions appear to go considerably further that the *Charter* in allowing *in camera* proceedings. Pursuant to section 11(d) of the *Charter*, criminal and

---

note 634, art. 14(2); *American Convention on Human Rights, supra* note 652, art. 8(2); *European Convention on Human Rights, supra* note 635, art. 6(2); *African Charter of Human and Peoples' Rights*, OAU Doc. CAB/LEG/67/3 rev. 5, 4 EHRR 417, 21 *ILM* 58, art. 7(1)(b); *Convention on the Rights of the Child, supra* note 623, art. 40(2)(b)(i).

655 *R. v. Oakes*, [1986] 1 SCR 103, 24 CCC (3d) 321, 50 CR (3d) 1, 26 DLR (4th) 200, 53 OR (2d) 719n, 65 NR 87, 19 CRR 308, 14 OAC 335, at 120 (SCR). Also: *R. v. Atherton*, (June 23, 1987) Babe Prov. Ct. J., [1987] OJ No 1940 (Ont Prov Ct); *R. v. Coles*, (1994) 121 Nfld & PEIR 155, 377 APR 155 (Nfld TD), at 157; *R. v. D.O.L.*, (1991) 73 Man R (2d) 238, 6 CR (4th) 277, 65 CCC (3d) 465 (CA), reversed, [1993] 4 SCR 419, at 493-494 (CCC); *Fédération des infirmières et infirmiers du Québec* v. *Québec (Procureur général)*, [1991] RJQ 2607 (CS), reversed, (sub nom. *Centrale de l'enseignement du Québec c. Québec (procureur général)*) [1998] RJQ 2897 (CA), leave to appeal refused, (1998) 245 NR 199n (SCC), at 2632-2633 (RJQ).

656 *R. v. Oakes*, (1983) 145 DLR (3d) 123, 40 OR (2d) 660, 2 CCC (3d) 339, 32 CR (3d) 193, 3 CRR 289 (CA), affirmed, [1986] 1 SCR 103, 24 CCC (3d) 321, 50 CR (3d) 1, 26 DLR (4th) 200, 53 OR (2d) 719n, 65 NR 87, 19 CRR 308, 14 OAC 335; see also *R. v. Leclerc*, [1982] CS 1001, 1 CCC (3d) 422 (Que SC).

657 *X. v. United Kingdom* (App. No. 5124/71), *X. v. United Kingdom* (App. No. 5124/71), (1973) 42 Coll. 135.

658 *R. v. Pearson*, [1990] RJQ 2438, 59 CCC (3d) 406, 79 CR (3d) 90, 5 CRR (2d) 164 (CA), reversed [1992] 3 SCR 665, at 423 (CCC), citing *Krause* v. *Switzerland* (App. No. 7986/77), (1980) 13 DR 73 and *R.F. and S.F.* v. *Austria* (App. No. 10847/84), (1985) 44 DR 238.

penal proceedings must be held in public, subject only to the limitations of section 1 of the *Charter*, to which the courts have given a very strict construction.[659] If applicable, the international instruments would presumably be used to defend limits on the open court principle. The European Court's celebrated *Sunday Times Case*[660] also deals with the right to comment on judicial proceedings. In the "collision" between sections 11(d) and 2(b) of the *Canadian Charter, Sunday Times* may be used, as it was in *R. v. Sophonow*, to tip the balance in favour of the press.[661]

In *Re Walton and Attorney-General of Canada*,[662] the Northwest Territories Superior Court observed that the right to a public hearing is formally recognized by article 10 of the *European Convention of Human Rights*. And in *Valente* v. *R.*, Justice Le Dain of the Supreme Court of Canada referred to article 6 of the *European Convention* in this context, but without any specific conclusion.[663]

4.5.4.6   An Independent and Impartial Tribunal

Justice is to be rendered, according to section 11(d) of the *Charter*, by an "independent and impartial tribunal". Identical wording appears in the international models.[664] A non-binding instrument adopted in 1983 at the World Conference on the Independence of Justice, held in Montreal, the *Universal Declaration of the Independence of Justice*[665] has been frequently

---

659 *Re Southam Inc. and R. (No. 1)*, (1983) 146 DLR (3d) 408, 3 CCC (3d) 515, 41 OR (2d) 113, (sub nom. *R.* v. *Southam Inc.*) 33 RFL (2d) 279, 34 CR (3d) 27 (CA).
660 *Sunday Times* v. *United Kingdom*, 26 April 1979, Series A, No. 30, 2 EHRR 245, 58 ILR 491.
661 *R.* v. *Sophonow (No. 2)*, (1983) 150 DLR (3d) 590, 6 CCC (3d) 396, 34 CR (3d) 287, 21 Man R (2d) 110, 5 CRR 331 (CA), affirmed, (1984) 31 Man R (2d) 8 (SCC).
662 *Re Walton and Attorney-General of Canada*, (1984) [1985] 1 WWR 122, 13 DLR (4th) 379, (sub nom. *Walton* v. *Canada (Attorney General)*) 15 CCC (3d) 65, [1984] NWTR 353 (SC).
663 [1985] 2 SCR 673, 24 DLR (4th) 161, 23 CCC (3d) 193, 49 CR (3d) 97, 52 OR (2d) 779, 37 MVR 9, 64 NR 1, 19 CRR 354, 14 OAC 79.
664 *Universal Declaration of Human Rights, supra* note 654, art. 10; *International Covenant on Civil and Political Rights, supra* note 634, art. 14(1); *American Convention on Human Rights, supra* note 652, art. 8(1); *European Convention on Human Rights, supra* note 635, art. 6(1). The *African Charter of Human and Peoples' Rights, supra* note 654, art. 7(1)(b) refers to a "competent" tribunal, while art. 7(1)(d) refers to an "impartial" tribunal. The *Convention on the Rights of the Child*, GA Res. 44/25, art. 40(2)(b)(iv) speaks of tribunals which are "competent, independent and impartial".
665 *Universal Declaration of the Independance of Justice*, in Shimon Shetreet & Jules Deschênes, *Judicial Independence*, Dordrecht/Boston/Lancaster: Nijhoff, 1985. Cited in: *R.* v. *Beauregard*, [1986] 2 SCR 56, at 74; *Valente* v. *R., supra* note 663; *Québec (PG)* v. *Lippé*, [1990] RJQ 2200, 60 CCC (3d) 34, 80 CR (3d) 1 (CA), reversed, (sub nom. *R. c. Lippé*) [1991] 2 SCR 114, (sub nom. *R. v. Lippé*) 64 CCC (3d) 513, (sub nom. *Lippé* v. *Québec (Procureur général)*) 128 NR 1, 5 CRR (2d) 31, 39 QAC 241, at

referred to by Canadian courts in order to assess the scope of the term "independent and impartial tribunal" found in section 11(d). As McDonald J stated, in *R. v. Campbell*, "the provisions of the Montreal Declaration are consistent with a purposive and liberal analysis of s. 11(d)". He continued: "Of course the provisions of these instruments are not binding in Canadian constitutional law, but they are important indications of what the acceptable minimal standards are internationally."[666]

In *R. v. Lippé*, Justice Gonthier of the Supreme Court of Canada noted, in his concurring judgment, with reference to article 2.02 of the *Universal Declaration on the Independence of Justice*, that independence from government is an important aspect of "judicial independence". However, relying principally on caselaw of the European Court of Human Rights in the application of article 6(1) of the *European Convention on Human Rights*,[667] he said that an independent tribunal is also one which is independent of the parties to the litigation.[668]

In *Lippé*, Justice Tourigny of the Quebec Court of Appeal invoked European caselaw so as to stress the relationship between independence and impartiality, noting that "the former [is] essentially designed to ensure the latter".[669] In *Lowther*, Justice MacDonald of the Prince Edward Island Supreme Court – Trial Division referred to European caselaw.[670] Justice Glube of the Nova Scotia Supreme Court, Trial Division, also referred to a resolution dealing with the independence of the judiciary, in which it is stated that judges are not to be compelled to testify on confidential or secret

---

541 (CCC); *Lowther v. Prince Edward Island*, 122 Nfld & PEIR 221, 379 APR 221 (PEI TD), reversed, (1995), 129 Nfld & PEIR 267 (CA), leave to appeal allowed, (1996) 45 APR 90n (SCC), at 229 (Nfld & PEIR); *Southam Inc. v. Québec (Procureur général)*, [1993] RJQ 2374 (SC), at 2386; *MacKeigan and other Justices v. Hickman and other Justices*, (1988) 85 NSR (2d) 219, 216 APR 219 (TD), affirmed, (1988) (sub nom. *MacKeigan, J.A. v. Royal Comm. (Marshall Inquiry)*) 87 NSR (2d) 443 (CA), affirmed, [1989] 2 SCR 796, at 232 [NSR]; *Gratton v. Canada (Canadian Judicial Council)*, (1994) 78 FTR 214, at 234 [FTR]; *Ruffo v. Conseil de la magistrature*, [1992] RJQ 1796 (CA), affirmed, (1995) 1995 CarswellQue 183 (SCC), at 1810 [1796]; *R. v. Temela*, (1992) 71 CCC (3d) 276, 9 CRR (2d) 302 (NWT CA), at 289 (CCC).

666 *R. v. Campbell*, [1995] 2 WWR 469, 160 AR 81, 25 Alta LR (3d) 158 (QB), affirmed, [1995] 8 WWR 747 (CA), reversed (sub nom. *Reference re Remuneration of Judges of the Provincial Court of Prince Edward Island*) [1997] 3 SCR 3, at 124 (AR).

667 *Ringeisen v. Austria*, 16 July 1971, Series A, No. 13, 1 EHRR 455, 56 ILR 442; *Le Compte, van Leuven and de Meyere v. Belgium*, 23 June 1981, Series A, No. 43, 4 EHRR 1; *Piersack v. Belgium*, 1 October 1982, Series A, No. 53; *Campbell and Fell v. United Kingdom*, 28 June 1984, Series A, No. 80.

668 *R. v. Lippé*, *supra* note 665, at 154 (SCR). See also: *R. v. Musselman*, (2004) 25 CR (6th) 295 (Ont SCJ).

669 *Québec (PG) v. Lippé*, *supra* note 665, at 43 (CCC), citing *Bramelid v. Sweden* (App. No. 8588/79), (1983) 29 DR 64, 5 EHRR 249.

670 *Lowther v. Prince Edward Island*, *supra* note 665.

matters, adopted by the Seventh United Nations Congress on the Prevention of Crime and the Treatment of Offenders, in which Canada participated actively.[671]

Judicial salaries and working conditions have given rise to considerable litigation, and the courts have referred to the *Declaration*'s relatively detailed provisions in this connection. Specifically, the *Universal Declaration on the Independence of Justice* states that:

> 2.21 a) During their terms of office, judges shall receive salaries, and after retirement, they shall receive pensions.
>
> b) The salaries and pensions of judges shall be adequate, commensurate with the status, dignity and responsibility of their office, and be regularly adjusted to account fully for price increases.
>
> c) Judicial salaries shall not be decreased during the judges' term of office, except as a coherent part of an overall public economic measure.

Chief Justice Dickson of the Supreme Court of Canada, in *R.* v. *Beauregard*, invoked article 2.21(a) of the *Declaration* in order to construe section 11(d) of the *Charter*.[672] In *R.* v. *Doyle*, the Northwest Territories Court of Appeal cited these provisions and observed that "financial security has been recognized as a central component of the international concept of judicial independence".[673]

In *Manitoba Provincial Judges Assn.* v. *Manitoba (Minister of Justice)*[674] the Supreme Court of Canada referred to the *Universal Declaration* and other international material to help decide the constitutional issue of judicial independence through institutional financial security, both under section 11(d) of the *Charter* and section 100 of the *Constitution Act, 1867*. In considering the requirement that judicial salaries may not fall below a minimum level, Chief Justice Lamer, for the majority, wrote:

> The idea of a miminum salary has been recognized in a number of international instruments. Article 11 of the *Basic Principles on the Independence of the*

---

671 *MacKeigan and other Justices* v. *Hickman and other Commissioners, supra* note 665, at 232.

672 *R.* v. *Beauregard, supra* note 665, at 75.

673 *R.* v. *Temela, supra* note 665. Also cited in: *Lowther* v. *Prince Edward Island, supra* note 665; *R.* v. *Campbell, supra* note 666, at 124 (AR); *R.* v. *Avery,* (1995) 1995 CarswellPEI 124, [1995] PEIJ No 118 (TD); *Judges of the Provincial Court (Manitoba)* v. *Manitoba,* (1995) 102 Man R (2d) 51 (CA), leave to appeal allowed, (1996) 131 WAC 238n (SCC), reversed, (sub nom. *Reference re Remuneration of Judges of the Provincial Court of Prince Edward Island*) [1997] 3 SCR 3.

674 *Judges of the Provincial Court (Manitoba)* v. *Manitoba* (a.k.a. *Reference re Remuneration of Judges of the Provincial Court of Prince Edward Island; Provincial Court Judges Assn. (Manitoba)* v. *Manitoba (Minister of Justice),* (sub nom. *Reference re Remuneration of Judges of the Provincial Court of Prince Edward Island*) [1997] 3 SCR 3.

Judiciary, which was adopted by the Seventh United Nations Congress on the Prevention of Crime and the Treatment of Offenders, states that:

> 11. The term of office of judges, their independence, security, *adequate remuneration*, conditions of service, pensions and the age of retirement *shall be adequately secured by* law. [Emphasis added.]

The U.N. Basic Principles were endorsed by the United Nations General Assembly on November 29, 1985 (A/RES/40/32), which later invited government "to respect them and to take them into account within the framework of their national legislation and practice" (A/RES/40/146) on December 12, 1985. A more recent document is the *Draft Universal Declaration on the Independence of* Justice, which the United Nations Commission on Human Rights invited government to take into account when implementing the U.N. Basic Principles (resolution 1989/32). Article 18(b) provides that:

> The salaries and pensions of judges shall be adequate, commensurate with the status, dignity and responsibility of their office, and shall be periodically reviewed to overcome or minimize the effect of inflation.[675]

This question had been left unanswered in the *Beauregard* case.[676] Here, a majority of six, with a lone dissenter, expressed the opinion that there are indeed minimum levels of judicial remuneration to ensure institutional judicial independence.

The provisions of the *Universal Declaration on the Independence of Justice* dealing with discipline of judges have also been invoked on several occasions. The *Universal Declaration* affirms that discipline of judges must be independent of the executive,[677] and that the power to remove a judge "should preferably be vested in a judicial tribunal,"[678] and that proceedings for removal held before a court or a board predominantly composed of members of the judiciary and selected by the judiciary.[679]

4.5.4.7   Reasonable Bail

Section 11(e) of the *Charter* establishes a right not to be denied reasonable bail without just cause. There is no "reasonable bail" provision as such in the *International Covenant on Civil and Political Rights*, although it states that detention in custody while awaiting trial "shall not be the general rule".[680] The *Covenant* provides that interim release may be conditional on

675 *Ibid.*, at para. 194 (emphasis in the original).
676 *R.* v. *Beauregard, supra* note 665.
677 *Universal Declaration on the Independence of Justice, supra* note 665, art. 4(a).
678 *Ibid.*, art. 4(b).
679 Cited in: *Gratton* v. *Canada (Canadian Judicial Council)*, (1994) 78 FTR 214; *R.* v. *Campbell, supra* note 666, at 124 (AR).
680 *International Covenant on Civil and Political Rights*, (1976) 999 UNTS 171, [1976] CTS 47, art. 9(3). See also: *American Convention on Human Rights, supra* note 652, art. 7(5); *European Convention on Human Rights*, (1955) 213 UNTS 221, ETS 5, art. 5(3).

guarantees, but nowhere is it stated that these guarantees be "reasonable". The *European Convention* provides that trial must take place "within a reasonable time" or else the accused released pending trial. Such release "may be conditioned by guarantees to appear for trial". The *American Convention* provisions are comparable to those of the *European Convention*. Absence of an express requirement that such bail be "reasonable" has not stopped the European Court of Human Rights from reading this into the provision, holding that bail "must therefore be assessed principally by reference to [the accused], his assets and his relationship to the persons who are to provide the security".[681] In requiring that bail be "reasonable", the *Canadian Charter* goes further than the international instruments. Perhaps it is no surprise, then, that no reported cases deal with the application of international law to section 11(e) of the *Canadian Charter*.

4.5.4.8   *Trial by Jury*

Section 11(f) of the *Charter* enshrines the right to trial by jury under certain circumstances. International law recognizes no right to trial by jury and in many domestic legal systems such forms of lay or popular participation in criminal justice are unknown.

4.5.4.9   Nullum Crimen Sine Lege

Section 11(g) of the *Canadian Charter* has the distinction of making express reference to international law. It protects individuals against retroactive or retrospective operation of criminal and penal law, unless the charge constituted "an offence under Canadian or international law or was criminal according to the general principles of law recognized by the community of nations". This reference was added during the Hays-Joyal Committee discussion of the *Charter* so that section 11(g) would not be a bar to prosecution for war crimes. Its addition was justified by reference to article 15 of the *International Covenant on Civil and Political Rights*. Article 15(1) of the *Covenant* states: "No one shall be held guilty of any criminal offence on account of any act or omission which did not constitute a criminal offence, under national or international law, at the time when it was committed."[682]

The *Canadian Charter* completes the reference to "national or international law", which appears in the various international instruments, with

---

681   *Neumeister* v. *Austria*, 27 June 1968, Series A, No. 7, 1 EHRR 91, 41 ILR 316, at 129 (EHRR).

682   See also: *Universal Declaration of Human Rights*, *supra* note 654, art. 11(2); *American Declaration of the Rights and Duties of Man*, *supra* note 654, art. XXVI; *American Convention on Human Rights*, *supra* note 652, art. 9; *European Convention on Human Rights*, *supra* note 680, art. 7(1); *African Charter of Human and Peoples' Rights*, *supra* note 654, art. 7(2).

an innovation: "or as criminal according to the general principles of law recognized by the community of nations". The text resembles, although it is not identical to, a provision in article 38 of the *Statute of the International Court of Justice.* The reference is probably superfluous, because "general principles" are encompassed within "international law".

The international models generally associate the rule against retroactive criminal offences with a guarantee of the right to the lighter penalty, where it has been changed since the time the crime was committed. The *Charter* separates the two, placing the right to the lighter penalty in section 11(i). The international models accord pre-eminence to the right against retroactive infractions, placing it in the category of non-derogable norms.[683] It is often said that this right is one of the core norms of international human rights, together with the right to life, and the prohibition of slavery and torture. Nevertheless, international courts have tended to give the prohibition on retroactive prosecution a rather liberal construction.[684]

Canada amended the *Criminal Code* in the mid-1980s in order to permit prosecution for war crimes and crimes against humanity where, under the ordinary rules of the *Code,* Canadian courts would be without jurisdiction. The amendments followed recommendations of the Deschênes Commission and were aimed at prosecutions relating to the Second World War, although they are applicable in the case of such crimes wherever and whenever they were committed. In the *Finta* case, the Supreme Court of Canada endorsed the opinion of the Deschênes Commission that section 11(g) of the *Charter* adopted customary international law into Canadian law.[685] According to Justice Cory, writing for a majority of the Supreme Court of Canada, "[s]ection 11(g) of the *Charter* allows customary international law to form a basis for the prosecution of war criminals who have violated general principles of law recognized by the community of nations regardless of

---

683   *International Covenant on Civil and Political Rights, supra* note 680, art. 4(2); *American Convention on Human Rights, supra* note 652, art. 27(20; *European Convention on Human Rights, supra* note 680, art. 15(2).

684   *S.W.* v. *United Kingdom,* 22 November 1995, Series A, No. 335-B, paras. 35-36; *C.R.* v. *United Kingdom,* 22 November 1995, Series A, No. 335-B, paras. 33-34; *Streletz, Kessler and Krenz* v. *Germany* (App. Nos. 34044/96, 35532/97 and 44801/98), 22 March 2001, para. 49; *Prosecutor* v. *Tadić* (Case No. IT-94-1-AR72), Separate Opinion of Judge Sidhwa on the Defence Motion for Interlocutory Appeal on Jurisdiction, 2 October 1995, para. 72; *Prosecutor* v. *Hadžihasanović* et al. (Case No. IT-01-47-AR72), Decision on Interlocutory Appeal Challenging Jurisdiction with respect to Command Responsibility, 16 July 2003, para. 34; *Prosecutor* v. *Norman* (Case No. SCSL-04-14-AR72(E)), Decision on Preliminary Motion Based on Lack of Jurisdiction (Child Recruitment), 31 May 2004.

685   *R.* v. *Finta,* (1992) 92 DLR (4th) 1 (Ont CA), affirmed, [1994] 1 SCR 701, 88 CCC (3d) 417, 112 DLR (4th) 513, 150 NR 370, at 734 (SCR).

when or where the criminal act or omission took place".[686] The new *Code* provisions were attacked as being contrary to the prohibition of retroactive or retrospective offences, in that they sought to punish individuals for offences that were not recognized as crimes at the time of their commission.

The argument is not a new one, and it had been invoked by several of the defendants at the trial of the major war criminals in Nuremberg. The defence was rejected by the trial judges,[687] as well as in subsequent war crimes prosecutions.[688] According to one of the Nuremberg prosecutors:

> With regard to "crimes against humanity", this at any rate is clear: the Nazis, when they persecuted and murdered countless Jews and political opponents in Germany, knew that what they were doing was wrong and that their actions were crimes which had been condemned by the criminal law of every civilized State. When these crimes were mixed with the preparation for aggressive war and later with the commission of war crimes in occupied territories, it cannot be a matter of complaint that a procedure is established for their punishment.[689]

Justice Callaghan of the Ontario High Court, who presided over the trial of Imre Finta, dismissed the challenge, drawing on the Deschênes Commission and making extensive reference to international humanitarian and human rights law. He wrote:

> In addition to the legislative history of s. 11 (g), the Deschênes Commission indicates, in considerable detail, that foreign legislation, international jurisprudence, international instruments and opinions of jurists here and abroad, carries a "fateful meaning for war criminals" and that the section has removed the traditional barrier of non-retrospectivity: Deschênes Commission, pp. 143-8.
>
> It is incumbent upon us to answer the threshold question, therefore, as to whether war crimes and crimes against humanity were, during World War II, offences at international law or criminal according to the general principles of law recognized by the community of nations.
>
> A brief review of international conventions, agreements and treaties, clearly demonstrate that, by World War II, war crimes or crimes against humanity were recognized as an offence at international law, or criminal according to the general principles of law recognized by the community of nations.[690]

Justice Callaghan reviewed such international instruments as the *Hague Convention* of 1907, the *Treaty of Versailles*, and the *Charter* of the Nurem-

---

686 *Ibid.*, at 807 (SCR).
687 *France* et al. v. *Goering* et al., (1946) 23 *Trial of the Major War Criminals before the International Military Tribunal*, 13 ILR 203, at 461-465.
688 *United States of America* v. *Alstötter et al.* ("Justice trial"), (1948) 3 TWC 1, 6 LRTWC 1, 14 ILR 274, at 41-49 (TWC).
689 Quoted in *R.* v. *Finta*, *supra* note 685, at 736 (SCR).
690 *R.* v. *Finta*, (1989) 50 CCC (3d) 236, 64 CR (3d) 223, 44 CRR 23 (Ont HC), additional reasons at, (1987) 50 CCC 236 (Ont HC), at 247 (CCC).

berg tribunal.[691] He concluded that the treaties, agreements and conventions dealing with war crimes were "ample evidence" that they had either been recognized at international law or that they formed part of the general principles of law recognized by the community of nations.[692]

In the Ontario Court of Appeal, Justice Tarnopolsky disposed of the argument based on the alleged retroactivity of the crimes against humanity provisions by simply citing article 15 of the *International Covenant on Civil and Political Rights*, noting it "binds Canada in international law" and that section 11(g) of the *Charter* accords with it.[693] This is of course no real answer to the challenge based on the retroactivity of the legislation.

On appeal to the Supreme Court of Canada, Justice La Forest, dissenting, distinguished between war crimes and crimes against humanity. In his view, the prohibition against war crimes had been derived from Christian codes of conduct, the rules of chivalry and the writing of commentators such as Hugo Grotius. This "customary European law" was confirmed and developed in important treaties, of which the *Hague Conventions* of 1899 and 1907 were the most important, he wrote.[694] Turning to "the somewhat uncertain status of crimes against humanity", Justice La Forest said he favoured an approach by which "the strongest source in international law

---

691   *Agreement for the Prosecution of the Major War Criminals of the European Axis, and Charter of the International Military Tribunal*, (1946) 82 UNTS 279. The *Charter of the International Military Tribunal* has been cited in many Canadian judicial decisions: *R. v. Finta, ibid.*; *Gould v. Yukon Order of Pioneers*, (1991) 87 DLR (4th) 618, 14 CHRR D/176 (YTSC), affirmed, (1993) 100 DLR (4th) 596 (YTCA), affirmed, [1996] 1 SCR 571; *Canada v. Mehmet*, [1992] 2 FC 598 (CA); *Rudolph v. Canada (Minister of Employment and Immigration)*, (1992) 91 DLR (4th) 686 (Fed CA), leave to appeal refused, (1992) 93 DLR (4th) vii (note) (SCC); *Sivakumar v. Canada*, (1993) [1994] 1 FC 433 (CA), leave to appeal refused, (1994) 175 NR 324n (SCC); *Ramirez v. Canada*, [1992] 2 FC 306, 89 DLR (4th) 173, 135 NR 390 (CA); *Aden v. Canada*, [1994] 1 FC 625, 23 Imm LR (2d) 50 (TD); *R. v. Finta*, *supra* note 685; *Maslova v. Canada (Minister of Citizenship and Immigration)*, (1994) 86 FTR 34 (TD); *Gonzalez v. Canada (Minister of Employment and Immigration)*, [1994] 3 FC 646 (CA); *Sumaida v. Canada (Minister of Citizenship and Immigration)*, [2000] 3 FC 66 (CA *Pushpanathan v. Canada (Minister of Employment and Immigration)*, [1998] 1 SCR 982, amended, [1998] 1 SCR 1222; *Zrig v. Canada (Minister of Citizenship and Immigration)*, [2003] 3 FC 761 (CA); *Oberlander v. Canada (Attorney General)*, [2005] 1 FCR 3 (CA).

692   In its periodic reports pursuant to the *International Convention on the Elimination of All Forms of Racial Discrimination*, (1969) 660 UNTS 195, [1976] CTS 47, under the heading "Article 4. Measures Relating to War Criminals/Prosecution of alleged war crime perpetrators", Canada provided "progress reports" on the prosecution of Finta: see the ninth report, UN Doc. CERD/C/159/Add.3, para. 47, and the tenth report, UN Doc. CERD/C/185/Add. 3, para. 26. In its "Seventeenth and eighteenth report", UN Doc. CERD/C/CAN/18, pp. 74-75, Canada reported on other prosecutions involving hate crimes.

693   *R. v. Finta*, *supra* note 685, at 763-764.

694   *Ibid.*, at 782 (SCR).

for crimes against humanity was the common domestic prohibitions of civilized nations".[695]

Justice Cory, writing for the majority of the Supreme Court of Canada in *Finta*, reviewed two different theories on the alleged retroactivity of crimes against humanity. The first refers essentially to treaty provisions, and specifically the so-called "Martens clause" found in the preamble to the two *Hague Conventions*:

> Until a more complete code of the laws of war has been issued, the High Contracting Parties deem it expedient to declare that, in cases not included in the Regulations adopted by them, the inhabitants and the belligerents remain under the protection and the rule of the principles of the law of nations, as they result from the usages established among civilized peoples, from the laws of humanity, and the dictates of the public conscience.[696]

The second approach, espoused by professors Hans Kelsen and Georg Schwarzenberger, considers that punishment for crimes against humanity at the end of the Second World War was indeed a case of *ex post facto* legislation. Nevertheless, this was justifiable because it was necessary because the deeds of the Nazi and Japanese regimes "could not go unpunished".[697] Justice Cory said he preferred the second approach, and cited Hans Kelsen's solution to the dilemma of retroactivity:

> A retroactive law providing individual punishment for acts which were illegal though not criminal at the time they were committed, seems also to be an exception to the rule against *ex post facto* laws. The London Agreement is such a law. It is retroactive only in so far as it established individual criminal responsibility for acts which at they time they were committed constituted violations of existing international law, but for which this law has provided only collective responsibility. The rule against retroactive legislation is a principle of justice. Individual criminal responsibility represents certainly a higher degree of justice than collective responsibility, the typical technique of primitive law. Since the internationally illegal acts for which the London Agreement established individual criminal responsibility were certainly also morally most objectionable, and the persons who committed these acts were certainly aware of their immoral character, the retroactivity of the law applied to them can hardly be considered as absolutely incompatible with justice. Justice required the punishment of these men, in spite of the fact that under positive law they were not punishable at the time they performed the acts made punishable with retroactive force. In case two postulates of justice are in conflict with each

---

695 *Ibid.*, at 783.
696 *International Convention with Respect to the Laws and Customs of War by Land* (Convention no 2), [1942] CTS 6, preamble. Cited in *R.* v. *Finta, supra* note 685, at 871; *Rudolph* v. *Canada (Minister of Employment and Immigration), supra* note 691, at 690.
697 *R.* v. *Finta, supra* note 685, at 872.

other, the higher one prevails; and to punish those who were morally responsible for the international crime of the second World War may certainly be considered as more important than to comply with the rather relative rule against *ex post facto* laws open to so many exceptions.[698]

Justice Cory concluded that Kelsen's approach is "eminently sound and reasonable. I would adopt it as correct and apply it in reaching the conclusion that the provisions in question do not violate the principles of fundamental justice."[699]

Kelsen's theory, adopted by the majority, is indeed entirely satisfactory as an answer to a challenge based on section 7 of the *Charter*. However, the majority in *Finta* gave no clear answer to the challenge based on section 11(g). Indeed, Kelsen's approach amounts to an admission of a violation of section 11(g) because he conceded that prosecution for crimes against humanity committed prior to 1945 violated the rule against retroactive infractions, which he called "rather relative". His arguments might be valid in an analysis under section 1, once the violation of section 11(g) is established. However, as we have mentioned above, international human rights now considers the prohibition of retroactive offences to be one of its most fundamental rules, and it is hard to see how its significance can be reduced in keeping with Kelsen's suggestion.

The latest decision of the Supreme Court of Canada dealing with international criminal law, *Mugesera v. Canada (Minister of Citizenship and Immigration)*,[700] did not raise issues of retroactivity of the law.

4.5.4.10   Double Jeopardy

Section 11(h) of the *Charter* sets out the rule against double jeopardy,[701] which is known in international human rights law as the principle of *non bis in idem* or *ne bis in idem*.[702] According to article 14(7) of the *International Covenant on Civil and Political Rights*, "[n]o one shall be liable to be tried or punished again for an offence for which he has already been finally convicted or acquitted in accordance with the law and penal procedure of

---

698   Hans Kelsen, "Will the Judgment in the Nuremberg Trial Constitute a Precedent in International Law?", (1947) 1 *International Law Quarterly* 153, at 165. Cited in: *R. v. Finta*, *supra* note 685, at 873-874 (SCR).

699   *R. v. Finta*, *supra* note 685, at 874 (SCR)

700   *Mugesera* v. *Canada (Minister of Citizenship and Immigration)*, [2005] 2 SCR 100.

701   See also: *Criminal Code*, RSC 1985, c. C-46, s. 607.

702   See: Yannick Landry & Virginie Désilets, "Les garanties juridiques", in Gérald-A. Beaudoin & Errol P. Mendes, eds., *Canadian Charter of Rights and Freedoms*, 4th ed., Markham, Ont., LexisNexis Butterworths, 2005, pp. 875-921, at 896.

each country".[703] Perhaps a suggestion that it is of only secondary importance in the hierarchy of human rights, the protection against double jeopardy does not appear in the *Universal Declaration of Human Rights* or in
the *European Convention on Human Rights*. On the other hand, the *European Convention* has been completed with a number of protocols. *Protocol
No. 7 to the European Convention on Human Rights* not only adds the right
of *non bis in idem*, it elevates it to the category of non-derogable rights.
Interestingly, the right is also subject to an exception: "2.The provisions of
the preceding paragraph shall not prevent the re-opening of the case in
accordance with the law and penal procedure of the State concerned, if there
is evidence of new or newly discovered facts, or if there has been a fundamental defect in the previous proceedings, which could affect the outcome
of the case."[704]

Justice McDonald of the Alberta Court of Queen's Bench referred to
the *International Covenant on Civil and Political Rights* to assist in resolving ambiguity in section 11(h) of the *Canadian Charter*, because he found
it to be unclear whether "finally/définitivement" qualified the words "found
guilty and punished for/. . .dont il a été définitivement déclaré coupable et
puni". His judgment, in *R. v. T.R.*, reads:

> It is evident that the words "and punished for" were added to what was otherwise
> a simple adoption of article 14(7) of the International Covenant on Civil and
> Political Rights, to which Canada has been a party since 1976. . .It is unlikely
> that in adding the words "and punished for" the Canadian draftsman intended
> that the word "finally" would apply to that phrase. If he had so intended, he
> would have repeated the word "finally" as part of that phrase.[705]

4.5.4.11   *Lesser Punishment*

Section 11(i) of the *Charter* provides a right "if found guilty of the
offence and if the punishment for the offence has been varied between the
time of commission and the time of sentencing, to the benefit of the lesser
punishment". The international models go somewhat further, providing:
"Nor shall a heavier penalty be imposed than the one that was applicable at
the time when the criminal offence was committed. If, subsequent to the
commission of the offence, provision is made by law for the imposition of

703 See also: *American Convention on Human Rights*, (1979) 1144 UNTS 123, OASTS 36,
     art. 8(4); *Convention on the Rights of the Child*, GA Res. 44/25, Annex, [1992] CTS 3,
     art. 40(2)(iv).
704 *Protocol No. 7 to the European Convention on Human Rights*, ETS 117, art. 4.
705 *R. v. T.R.*, (1984) 28 Alta LR (2d) 383, 50 AR 56 (QB), at 63 (AR).

the lighter penalty, the offender shall benefit thereby."[706] Justice Smith of
the Ontario High Court of Justice, in *Re Evans and the Queen*, identified a
difference between the provisions of section 11(i) of the *Canadian Charter*
and those of article 15 of the *International Covenant on Civil and Political
Rights*. Section 11(i) "falls short" of the "broad wording" used in the *International Covenant on Civil and Political Rights*, said the learned judge.

> Section 11 is limited to the prohibition of a variation of the punishment between
> the time of commission of the offence and the time of sentencing. It was open
> to the framers of the Charter to widen the scope of a permissible change in
> penalty after the commission of the offence so as to encompass all charges.[707]

Justice Smith added that the kind of penalty contemplated (release under
parole) is not included in article 15 of the *Covenant*, and that "[a]t any rate,
article 15 of the *Covenant*, as already stated, has not been made a part of
the domestic law of Canada".[708] In *Re Mitchell and the Queen*, Justice
Linden of the Ontario High Court (as he then was) reached a similar conclusion.[709] He reasoned that article 15 of the *International Covenant on Civil
and Political Rights* and section 11(i) of the *Canadian Charter* were in
"conflict", and that consequently article 15 could not be used as an aid to
interpretation of other sections of the *Charter*, namely sections 9 and 12.
The reasons of Justice Linden were fully endorsed by Justice La Forest of
the Supreme Court of Canada in *R. v. Milne*.[710]

Some of the procedural guarantees recognized in the international instruments, including article 14 of the *International Covenant on Civil and
Political Rights* to which Canada is bound, were not included in section 11
of the *Charter*. Unlike the *Covenant*, the *Charter* makes no special mention
of a right to counsel, at the trial stage, or for the examination of witnesses,
although this is most certainly subsumed within the guarantee to a fair trial
provided by section 11(d). The *Covenant* sets out an express right to review

706 *International Covenant on Civil and Political Rights*, *supra* note 680, art. 15(1). See
     also: *Universal Declaration of Human Rights*, GA Res. 217 A (III), UN Doc. A/810,
     art. 11(2); *American Convention on Human Rights*, *supra* note 703, art. 9; *European
     Convention on Human Rights*, *supra* note 680, art. 7(1).
707 *Re Evans and R.*, (1987) 30 CCC (3d) 1, 55 CR (3d) 276 (Ont HC), at 5 (CCC).
708 *Ibid.*, at 6.
709 *Re Mitchell and R.*, (1983) 150 DLR (3d) 449, 6 CCC (3d) 193, 35 CR (3d) 225,42 OR
     (2d) 481 (HC). See, however, *R. v. Konechny*, (1983) [1984] 2 WWR 481, 6 DLR (4th)
     350, 10 CCC (3d) 233, 38 CR (3d) 69, 25 MVR 132 (BC CA), leave to appeal refused,
     (1984) 55 NR 156A (SCC), at 240-241 (CCC), (*per* Lambert J., dissenting).
710 *R. v. Milne*, [1987] 2 SCR 512, 46 DLR (4th) 487, 81 NR 36, 32 CRR 97, 61 CR (3d)
     55, 25 OAC 100, 38 CCC (3d) 502. See also: *R. v. Dussault*, [1993] RJQ 2087 (CA),
     at 2091.

of a conviction by a higher tribunal.[711] It also provides for a right of compensation to a person who has been wrongfully convicted as a result of a miscarriage of justice.[712] Arguably, these rights may be read into the *Charter* via sections 11(d), 7 and 24(1), although there are as yet no Canadian authorities on the point.

4.6   Cruel and Unusual Treatment or Punishment

The prohibition of cruel and unusual treatment or punishment can be found in all of the general human rights treaties, although its wording varies somewhat from instrument to instrument.[713] The Canadian formulation is derived from the English *Bill of Rights* of 1689[714] and the Eighth Amendment to the United States *Constitution*. The *Universal Declaration of Human Rights*, the *International Covenant on Civil and Political Rights*, the *Convention on the Rights of the Child* and the *American Convention on Human Rights* refer to "cruel, inhuman or degrading treatment or punishment". The *American Declaration of the Rights and Duties of Man* speaks of "cruel, infamous or unusual punishment", while the *European Convention on Human Rights* uses the expression "inhuman or degrading treatment or punishment". Common article 3 to the *Geneva Conventions*, which is often described as a codification of a customary norm, prohibits "cruel treatment". The Human Rights Committee has said that "[i]t may not be necessary to draw sharp distinctions between the various prohibited forms of treatment or punishment. These distinctions depend on the kind, purpose and severity of the particular treatment." [715]

All of the international models associate "cruel treatment" and its synonyms with "torture", with the exception of the *American Declaration*.

---

711 *International Covenant on Civil and Political Rights*, (1976) 999 UNTS 171, [1976] CTS 47, art. 14(5).

712 *Ibid.*, art. 14(6).

713 *Universal Declaration of Human Rights, supra* note 706, art. 5; *International Covenant on Civil and Political Rights, supra* note 711, art. 7; *American Declaration of the Rights and Duties of Man*, OAS Doc. OEA/Ser. L./V/II.23, doc. 21, rev. 6, art. XXVI; *American Convention on Human Rights, supra* note 703, art. 5(2); *African Charter of Human and Peoples' Rights*, OAU Doc. CAB/LEG/67/3 rev. 5, 4 EHRR 417, 21 *ILM* 58, art. 5; *Convention on the Rights of the Child, supra* note 703, art. 37(a). Also: "Document of the Copenhagen Meeting of the Conference on the Human Dimension of the CSCE", 1989, para. 16.

714 1 Will & Mary, 2nd Sess., c. 2.

715 "General Comment No. 7 (16), Torture or cruel, inhuman or degrading treatment or punishment (Article 7)", UN Doc. CCPR/3/Add.1, p. 383, para. 2; General Comment No. 7 was replaced by "General Comment No. 20 (44), Replaces general comment 7 concerning prohibition of torture and cruel treatment or punishment (Article 7)", UN Doc. HRI/GEN/1/Rev. 1.

Several specialized treaties also deal with the norm, of which the most important is the *Convention Against Torture and Other Cruel, Inhuman and Degrading Treatment or Punishment*.[716] Canada ratified the *Convention* in 1987; Parliament amended the *Criminal Code* in order to incorporate a specific offence of "torture"[717] so as to comply with the *Convention*, which requires all States parties to "ensure that all acts of torture are offences under its criminal law" and to make them punishable with "appropriate penalties".[718]

Canadian courts have made relatively rare use of international law in their interpretation of section 12 of the *Charter*. This may be because the international authorities are usually concerned with forms of extreme ill-treatment that are widespread in certain parts of the world but, fortunately, virtually unknown in Canada. Interestingly, the caselaw of the European Commission and the European Court of Human Rights on the subject of cruel punishment is also rather slender, although there have been isolated attempts to enlarge the scope of article 3 of the *European Convention* to cover such forms of inhuman treatment as discrimination based on race or gender.[719] The international authorities have also distinguished between "torture" and "other acts of cruel, inhuman or degrading treatment or punishment which do not amount to torture".[720]

Torture is defined in the United Nations *Convention Against Torture* as

> ... act by which severe pain or suffering, whether physical or mental, is intentionally inflicted on a person for such purposes as obtaining from him or a third person information or a confession, punishing him for an act he or a third person has committed or is suspected of having committed, or intimidating

---

716   UN Doc. A/39/51, annex, [1987] CTS 36. Also: *European Convention for the Prevention of Torture and Inhuman or Degrading Treatment or Punishment*, (1987) ETS 126, 27 ILM 1152; *Inter-American Convention to Prevent and Punish Torture*, (1985) OASTS 67. On the *European Convention*, see: Malcolm Evans & Rod Morgan, *Preventing Torture:A Study of the European Convention for the Prevention of Torture and Inhuman or Degrading Treatment or Punishment*, Oxford: Clarendon Press, 1998.

717   SC 1987, c. 13. The amended *Code* provisions are currently section 269.1, which creates the offence of torture, and section 7(3.7), which gives Canadian courts jurisdiction over the offence of torture where the offender is present in Canada even if the crime was committed elsewhere, where the crime was committed on a Canadian ship, and where either the offender or the victim are Canadian citizens.

718   *Convention Against Torture and Other Cruel, Inhuman and Degrading Treatment or Punishment, supra* note 716, art. 4.

719   *East African Asians* v. *United Kingdom* (App. Nos. 4403/70-4419/70, 4423/70, 4434/70, 4443/70, 4476/70-4478/70, 4486/70, 4501/70, 4526/70-4530/70), (1994) 15 *Human Rights Law Journal* 215.

720   *Convention Against Torture and Other Cruel, Inhuman and Degrading Treatment or Punishment, supra* note 716, art. 16.

or coercing him or a third person, or for any reason based on discrimination of any kind, when such pain or suffering is inflicted by or at the instigation of or with the consent or acquiescence of a public official or other person acting in an official capacity.

But, adds the *Convention*, "[i]t does not include pain or suffering arising only from, inherent in or incidental to lawful sanctions".[721] "Cruel, inhuman and degrading treatment or punishment" is not defined in the *Convention Against Torture*, which treats it as a residual category for acts that do not rise to the level of torture.[722]

In an early case filed by Ireland against the United Kingdom, the European Court of Human Rights concluded that certain acts of harsh treatment involving the abuse of detainees in Northern Ireland, which included sleep deprivation and placing inmates in soundproof rooms, did not reach the threshold of "torture", preferring to describe them as acts of "inhuman and degrading treatment".[723] Article 3 of the *European Convention on Human Rights* prohibits both "torture" and "inhuman and degrading treatment", so the distinction is only one of degree. Perhaps the absence of any reference to "torture" in the *Canadian Charter* should be taken to suggest that there is no meaningful distinction in Canadian law between the two categories. Justice McDonald of the Alberta Court of Queen's Bench referred to *Ireland* v. *United Kingdom* in interpreting section 12 of the *Canadian Charter*. Basing himself on the European jurisprudence, he concluded that "treatment" encompasses more than simply penal treatment.[724]

Many of the cases concern hypothetical torture or inhuman or degrading treatment, because they involve the extradition, expulsion or transfer of individuals to other countries. Canadian courts have looked to international authorities for guidance in this area. As the Federal Court of Appeal explained, in *Suresh*: "It is generally acknowledged that the risk of torture must be assessed on the grounds that go beyond 'mere theory' or 'suspicion' but something less than 'highly probable'. The risk or danger of torture

---

721 *Ibid.*, art. 1.

722 GA Res. 39/46, annex, article 16(1).

723 *Ireland* v. *United Kingdom*, 18 January 1978, Series A, No. 25, 2 EHRR 25, 59 ILR 188. See: David Bonner, "Ireland v. United Kingdom", (1978) 27 *International and Comparative Law Quarterly* 897; Louise Doswald-Beck, "What does the Prohibition of 'Torture or Inhuman or Degrading Treatment or Punishment' Mean? The Interpretation of the European Commission and Court of Human Rights", (1978) 25 *Netherlands International Law Review* 24; Peter J. Duffy, "Article 3 of the European Convention on Human Rights", (1983) 32 *International and Comparative Law Quarterly* 316.

724 *Soenen* v. *Director of Edmonton Remand Centre*, (1983) [1984] 1 WWR 71, 3 DLR (4th) 658, 8 CCC (3d) 224, 35 CR (3d) 206, (1984) 48 AR 31, 28 Alta LR (2d) 31, 6 CRR 368 (QB).

must be 'personal and present'."[725] Justice McKeown of the Trial Division of the Federal Court had said this was the approach adopted by the European Court of Human Rights, referring to *Chahal* v. *United Kingdom*.[726] He also referred to the first General Comment of the Committee Against Torture:

> Bearing in mind that the State party and the Committee are obliged to assess whether there are substantial grounds for believing that the author would be in danger of being subjected to torture were he/she to be expelled, returned or extradited, *the risk of torture must be assessed on grounds that go beyond mere theory or suspicion. However, the risk does not have to meet the test of being highly probable.*[727]

In a subsequent ruling, Justice Gauthier of the Federal Court, Trial Division, noted that the Committee Against Torture and international tribunals have not tended to distinguish between a possibility of torture versus a probability. He cited a ruling of the Committee of Torture in this respect:

> The Committee *considers that in the present case substantial grounds exist for believing that the author would be in a danger of being subjected to torture.* The Committee has noted the author's ethnic background, alleged political affiliation and detention history as well as the fact, which has not been disputed by the State party, that he appears to have deserted from the army and to have left Zaire in a clandestine manner and, when formulating an application for asylum, to have adduced arguments which may be considered defamatory towards Zaire. The Committee *considers that*, in the present circumstances, *his return* to Zaire *would* have the *foreseeable and necessary consequence* of exposing him to a *real risk* of being detained and tortured. Moreover, the belief that "substantial grounds" exist within the meaning of article 3, paragraph 1, is strengthened by "the existence in the State concerned of a consistent pattern

---

725 *Suresh* v. *Canada (Minister of Citizenship and Immigration)*, [2000] 2 FC 592, 183 DLR (4th) 629, 252 NR 1, 18 Admin L.R. (3d) 159, 5 Imm LR (3d) 1 (CA), leave to appeal allowed, (2000) 2000 CarswellNat 879 (SCC), reversed, (2002) 2002 CarswellNat 7 (SCC).

726 *Suresh* v. *Canada (Minister of Citizenship and Immigration)*, (1999) 173 FTR 1, 50 Imm LR (2d) 183, 65 CRR (3d) 344 (TD), affirmed, (2000) 2000 CarswellNat 25 (CA), leave to appeal allowed, (2000) 2000 CarswellNat 879 (SCC), reversed, (2002) 2002 CarswellNat 7 (SCC), citing *Chahal* v. *United Kingdom*, 15 November 1997, (1997) 23 EHRR 413.

727 "General Comment No. 1, Implementation of article 3 of the Convention in the context of article 22", UN Doc. A/53/44, annex IX. Cited *ibid.*, at para. 47 (emphasis in the original). The General Comment was also cited at: *Yi Mei Lei* v. *Minister of Citizenship and Immigration*, 2003 FC 1514, affirmed, (2005) 2005 CarswellNat 30 (FCA), leave to appeal refused, (2005) 2005 CarswellNat 1112 (SCC), para. 34.

of gross, flagrant or mass violations of human rights", within the meaning of article 3, paragraph 2.[728]

In the first important consideration of section 12 by the Supreme Court of Canada, *R. v. Smith*,[729] Justice Lamer referred to article 7 of the *International Covenant on Civil and Political Rights*, which prohibits torture or cruel, inhuman or degrading treatment or punishment. In *Smith*, the issue was the minimum seven-year sentence for importing narcotics, provided for by the *Narcotic Control Act*.[730] The Supreme Court declared the impugned provision to be unconstitutional. Justice Lamer found that there was no relevant jurisprudence on article 7 of any assistance, "as most of the cases that have addressed the provision have dealt with the conditions of imprisonment or the type of treatment". Justice Lamer also cited article 3 of the *European Convention on Human Rights* and article 5 of the *Universal Declaration of Human Rights*, but considered that they were of little help. There is, nevertheless, useful authority from the European Court of Human Rights that has addressed the nature of criminal penalties, in particular in the area of corporal punishment and capital punishment.

In *Ocalan*, a Chamber of the European Court said

> . . . that in assessing whether a given treatment or punishment is to be regarded as inhuman or degrading for the purposes of Article 3 it cannot but be influenced by the developments and commonly accepted standards in the penal policy of the member States of the Council of Europe in this field. Moreover, the concepts of inhuman and degrading treatment and punishment have evolved considerably since the Convention came into force in 1950. . .[731]

In *Hussain v. United Kingdom*, a case that concerned sentencing of juvenile offenders to indefinite terms of imprisonment, the European Court of Human Rights looked at the absence of a right of judicial review in the United Kingdom for detained former juvenile criminals, and stated: "A failure to have regard to the changes that inevitably occur with maturation would mean that young persons detained under section 53 would be treated as having forfeited their liberty for the rest of their lives, a situation which, as the applicant and the Delegate of the Commission pointed out, might give rise to questions under Article 3 (Article 3) of the [*European Convention*

---

728 *Mutombo v. Switzerland* (No. 13/1993), UN Doc. A/49/44, p. 45, cited in *Yi Mei Lei v. Minister of Citizenship and Immigration*, 2003 FC 1514, affirmed, (2005) 2005 FCA 1, leave to appeal refused, (2005) 343 NR 197n (SCC), para. 39 (emphasis added by the Federal Court).

729 *R. v. Smith*, [1987] 1 SCR 1045, [1987] 5 WWR 1, 31 CRR 193, 75 NR 321, 15 BCLR (2d) 273, 58 CR (3d) 193, 34 CCC (3d) 97, 40 DLR (4th) 435.

730 RSC 1985, c. N-1.

731 *Öcalan v. Turkey* (App. No. 46221/99), 12 May 2005, para. 163.

of Human Rights]."[732] It may well be that at some future date, the European Court declares certain penalties that are today commonly used in Western democracies, including Canada, to be contrary to article 3 of the *European Convention*,[733] just as it has noted the evolving incompatibility of capital punishment with European human rights law since 1950, when the death penalty was still well accepted among European States.

In *Canadian Foundation for Children, Youth and the Law v. Canada (Attorney General)*, the Supreme Court of Canada rejected a challenge to section 43 of the *Criminal Code* that allows corporal punishment of children as an exception to the prohibition on assault. Article 19(1) of the *Convention on the Rights of the Child* prohibits physical violence directed towards children, and requires State Parties to "protect the child from all forms of physical or mental violence, injury or abuse, neglect or negligent treatment, maltreatment or exploitation",[734] as Chief Justice McLachlin, who wrote for the majority, observed.[735] However, she noted that there was no explicit prohibition of all corporal punishment of children in either the *Convention on the Rights of the Child* or the *International Covenant on Civil and Political Rights*. Chief Justice McLachlin looked to European Court of Human Rights caselaw so as to determine whether corporal punishment was severe enough to fall within the ambit of the international prohibition of inhuman or degrading treatment. She cited a holding of the European Court by which the assessment must take account of "all the circumstances of the case, such as the nature and context of the treatment, its duration, its physical and mental effects and, in some instances, the sex, age and state of health of the victim".[736] According to the Chief Justice, "[t]hese factors properly focus on the prospective effect of the corrective force upon the child, as required by s. 43"[737] of the *Criminal Code*. Moreover, she noted that in its monitoring of compliance with the *International Covenant on Civil and Political Rights*, the United Nations Human Rights Committee had ex-

---

732 *Hussain* v. *United Kingdom* (App. No. 21928/93), 21 February 1996, Reports 1996-I, para. 53.

733 The German Constitutional Court has suggested that life imprisonment without possibility of parole constitutes cruel, inhuman and degrading punishment: [1977] 45 BVerfGE 187, 228. See generally: Dirk van Zyl Smit, "Is Life Imprisonment Constitutional? – The German Experience", [1992] *Public Law* 263; Dirk van Zyl Smit, "Life Imprisonment as an Ultimate Penalty in International Law: A Human Rights Perspective", (1999) 9 *Criminal Law Forum* 5.

734 *Convention on the Rights of the Child*, *supra* note 703, art. 19(1).

735 *Canadian Foundation for Children, Youth & the Law* v. *Canada (Attorney General)*, [2004] 1 SCR 76, 70 OR (3d) 95, 234 DLR (4th) 257, 180 CCC (3d) 353, 115 CRR (2d) 88, 16 CR (6th) 203, 46 RFL (5th) 1, 183 OAC 1, at para. 33.

736 *A.* v. *United Kingdom*, 25 September 1998, 1998-VI, 2692, pp. 2699-2700.

737 *Canadian Foundation for Children, Youth and the Law* v. *Canada (Attorney General)*, *supra* note 735, at para. 34.

pressed the view that corporal punishment of children in schools engages the prohibition of degrading treatment or punishment in article 7 of the *Covenant*, but that the "Committee has not expressed a similar opinion regarding parental use of mild corporal punishment".[738]

Invoking international law in support of her arguments, Justice Arbour dissented from the majority on the permissibility of the defence of reasonable chastisement of children and pupils that is found in section 43 of the *Criminal Code*. Justice Arbour referred to the Concluding Observations of the Committee on the Rights of the Child, with respect to the periodic report of the United Kingdom, a State with a provision in its criminal law that is similar to section 43. The Committee had observed: *"The imprecise nature of the expression of reasonable chastisement as contained in these legal provisions may pave the way for it to be interpreted in a subjective and arbitrary manner.* Thus, the. . .legislative and other measures relating to the physical integrity of children do not appear to be compatible with the provisions and principles of the Convention."[739] Justice Arbour remarked that "the Committee has not recommended clarifying these laws so much as abolishing them entirely".[740] She also cited the Committee's Concluding Observations on Canada's First Report:

> Penal legislation allowing corporal punishment of children by parents, in schools and in institutions where children may be placed [, should be considered for review]. *In this regard. . .physical punishment of children in families [should] be prohibited.* In connection with the child's right to physical integrity. . .and in the light of the best interests of the child,. . .the possibility of introducing new legislation and follow-up mechanisms to prevent violence within the family [should be considered], and. . .educational campaigns [should] be launched with a view to changing attitudes in society on the use of physical punishment in the family *and fostering the acceptance of its legal prohibition.*[741]

In its most recent Concluding Observations concerning Canada, as Justice Arbour noted, the Committee on the Rights of the Child

> . . .expressed "deep concern" that Canada had taken "no action to remove section 43 of the Criminal Code" and recommended the adoption of legislation to remove the existing authorization of the use of "reasonable force" in disciplining children and explicitly prohibit all forms of violence against children,

---

738 *Ibid.*, para. 33, citing UN Doc. A/50/40, at paras. 426 and 434; UN Doc. A/54/40) (1999), para. 358; UN Doc. A/55/40, paras. 306 and 429.
739 *Ibid.*, para. 186 (emphasis added by Arbour J.), citing UN Doc. CRC/C/38, para. 218.
740 *Ibid.*, para. 187.
741 *Ibid.*, para. 187 (emphasis added by Arbour J.), citing UN Doc. CRC/C/43, at para. 93.

however light, within the family, in schools and in other institutions where children may be placed.[742]

Section 12 is most certainly applicable to prison conditions, a subject on which there is considerable international material. The *International Covenant on Civil and Political Rights* also contains a provision specifically addressed to "persons deprived of their liberty", requiring that they "be treated with humanity and with respect for the inherent dignity of the human person".[743] The preamble of the *International Covenant on Civil and Political Rights*, which refers to the "inherent dignity of the human person", has also been cited in the context of treatment of prisoners.[744] Prison conditions are also dealt with in specific instruments, notably the *Standard Minimum Rules for the Treatment of Prisoners.*[745] Canadian courts might well refer to such documents as the reports of the European Committee for the Prevention of Torture, which contain detailed assessments of prison conditions in the United Kingdom, Ireland and continental Europe, as well as the summary records of the United Nations Committee Against Torture in the examination of periodic reports by States parties. To date, these sources have not been cited in reported cases, however.

Because cruel and unusual punishment continues to be practiced on a fairly general scale in many States, issues arise regularly before Canadian courts where expulsion or extradition is involved. In *Kindler* v. *Canada*, the Supreme Court made frequent use of international law in assessing whether section 12 could apply extraterritorially. Justice Cory referred to the "European position", noting that the European cases decided under the *European Convention on Human Rights* "are useful in their indication of a judicial trend in the consideration of extradition cases where a fugitive may be subjected to cruel and unusual punishment or treatment".[746] The Strasbourg organs had, in effect, taken a different view of the subject than the majority of the Supreme Court of Canada, giving the *Convention* an extraterritorial effect in cases where there exists the possibility of a breach of

---

742 *Ibid.*, para. 188, UN Doc. CRC/C/15/Add. 215, paras. 32-33.
743 *International Covenant on Civil and Political Rights*, (1976) 999 UNTS 171, [1976] CTS 47, art. 10.
744 *Stanley* v. *Royal Canadian Mounted Police*, (1987) 8 CHRR D/3799 (Can Human Rights Trib).
745 ESC Res. 663C(XXIV); as amended, ESC Res. 2076(LXII). On the *Standard Minimum Rules*, see: Roger S. Clark, *The United Nations Crime Prevention and Criminal Justice Program, Formulation of Standards and Efforts at Their Implementation*, Philadelphia: Pennsylvania University Press, 1994, at 145-179.
746 *Kindler* v. *Canada (Minister of Justice)*, [1991] 2 SCR 779, 67 CCC (3d) 1, 84 DLR (4th) 438, 6 CRR (2d) 193, 129 NR 81, at 820 (SCR). Cited in: *R.* v. *Vaughan*, [2004] OTC 79, 2004 CarswellOnt 293 (SCJ), at para. 43-46.

article 3, which corresponds to section 12 of the *Charter*.[747] He noted particularly one of the European Court's more important and significant judgments:

> [T]he decision by a Contracting State to extradite a fugitive may give rise to an issue under Article 3, and hence engage the responsibility of that State under the Convention, where substantial grounds have been shown for believing that the person concerned, if extradited, faces a real risk of being subjected to torture or to inhuman or degrading treatment or punishment in the requesting country. The establishment of such responsibility inevitably involves an assessment of conditions in the requesting country against the standards of Article 3 of the Convention. Nonetheless, there is no question of adjudicating on or establishing the responsibility of the receiving country, whether under general international law, under the Convention or otherwise. In so far as any liability under the Convention may be incurred, it is liability incurred by the extraditing Contracting State by reason of its having taken action which has as a direct consequence the exposure of an individual to proscribed ill-treatment.[748]

In the same context, Justice McLachlin, writing for the majority, referred to *Soering* and an earlier case that had been heard by the European Commission, *Kirkwood* v. *United Kingdom*,[749] in which an argument based on the death row phenomenon in California was dismissed. She concluded that "the fact that two tribunals reached different views on not dissimilar cases illustrates the complexity of the issue and supports the view that courts should not lightly interfere with executive decisions on extradition matters".[750] This reveals a misunderstanding of the hierarchical relationship between the European Commission and the European Court of Human Rights. Moreover, Justice McLachlin distorted the Commission's decision in *Kirkwood*. In fact, although it found the factual basis of the case to be insufficient for a violation of the *Convention*, the Commission said it considered "that notwithstanding the terms of article 2(1), it cannot be excluded that the circumstances surrounding the protection of one of the other rights contained in the Convention might give rise to an issue under article 3".[751]

The majority of the Supreme Court of Canada, however, refused to follow the approach of the European Commission and the European Court,

---

747 Justice Cory cited three European Commission on Human Rights cases: *X.* v. *Federal Republic of Germany* (App. No. 6315/73), (1974) 1 DR 73; *Kirkwood* v. *United Kingdom* (App. No. 10479/83), (1984) 27 European Convention on Human Rights Yearbook 170, 37 DR 158; *Altun* v. *Federal Republic of Germany* (App. No. 10308/82), (1983) 36 DR 209, 5 EHRR 651.

748 *Soering* v. *United Kingdom*, 7 July 1989, Series A, No. 161, 11 EHRR 439, at 36 (cited by Cory J in *Kindler* v. *Canada*, *supra* note 746, at 823).

749 *Kirkwood* v. *United Kingdom*, *supra* note 747.

750 *Kindler* v. *Canada*, *supra* note 746, at 856.

751 *Kirkwood* v. *United Kingdom*, *supra* note 747, at 184 [D.R.].

at least with respect to section 12. Nevertheless, it did not depart from comments made by Justice La Forest in an earlier judgment and inspired by the European precedents holding section 7 of the *Charter* to have an extraterritorial effect in extradition cases. Moreover, in *Kindler* the majority took the view that section 12 was of relevance in determining the content of section 7, a reasoning that borders on tautology.[752]

Even though the majority of the court refused to give extraterritorial effect to section 12, some of the extraterritorial cases shed light indirectly on section 12 of the *Charter*, in that they suggest the interpretation that the Supreme Court would give were the form of ill treatment that is practised abroad to be allowed in Canada. On more than one occasion, Canadian courts have suggested that sentences imposed in other countries, while not sufficiently shocking as to block extradition, would probably be deemed cruel and unusual punishment in Canada.[753] This subject is of particular interest with respect to the death penalty which, although removed from the *Criminal Code* in 1976[754] and from the *Code of Military Justice* in 1998,[755] continues on occasion to be promoted by some reactionary politicians. On 25 November 2005, Canada acceded to the *Second Optional Protocol to the International Covenant on Civil and Political Rights* and thereby accepted as an international obligation the irrevocable abolition of the death penalty. In a press release issued at that time, the Minister of Justice, Irwin Cotler, said: "Canada has been abolitionist in practice for decades – no one has been executed in Canada since 1962. By acceding to the UN treaty, we not only formalize our long-standing support for the abolition of the death penalty, but take our place at the forefront of the international struggle toward abolition."[756]

In *Kindler* v. *Canada*, Justice Peter Cory presented a detailed review of what he entitled "Twentieth Century Developments: The International Protection of Human Dignity". Justice Cory, whose dissenting views were endorsed by the Chief Justice and Justice Sopinka, took the position that extradition to a State where the death penalty would be imposed would constitute a breach of section 12. Justice Cory referred to the preamble of

---

752 *Canada* v. *Schmidt*, [1987] 1 SCR 500, 33 CCC (3d) 193, 39 DLR (4th) 18, 58 CR (3d) 1, 28 CRR 280, 76 NR 12, 61 OR (2d) 530.

753 For a recent example, *R.* v. *Jamieson*, [1994] RJQ 2144 (CA), leave to appeal allowed, (1995) 94 CCC (3d) vi (SCC), reversed, (sub nom. *United States v. Jamieson*) [1996] 1 SCR 465 (*per* Baudouin JA). The judgment of the Quebec Court of Appeal was reversed by the Supreme Court of Canada, which endorsed the views of dissenting Justice Jean-Louis Baudouin.

754 *Criminal Law Amendment Act (No. 2), 1976*, SC 1974-75-76, c. 105.

755 SC 1998, c. 35, ss. 24-27.

756 "Canada Supports International Efforts Toward Abolition of the Death Penalty", Department of Justice Press Release No. 238, 25 November 2005.

the *Charter of the United Nations*, the *Universal Declaration of Human Rights*, the *International Covenant on Civil and Political Rights* and the *American Convention on Human Rights* as evidence of "[t]he commitment of the international community to human dignity and the trend of western nations to abolish the death penalty [which] parallels Canada's own stance".[757] Interestingly, although he based his conclusions on section 12 of the *Charter*, Justice Cory cited the right to life provisions of the international instruments, which are more closely analogous to section 7 of the *Charter* than they are to section 12.

Justice Cory went on to refer to recent developments on the death penalty in international law, notably the adoption of the *Second Optional Protocol to the International Covenant on Civil and Political Rights* by the United Nations General Assembly in 1989.[758] Justice Cory noted that Canada voted in favour of the *Protocol*, and cited Canadian statements in the Commission on Human Rights during the drafting of the instrument. Canada had declared that "there was merit in the elaboration of a second optional protocol" and that "[t]here was no doubt that the United Nations would be honouring human dignity by enshrining the principle of the abolition of the death penalty in an international instrument".[759]

Justice La Forest, writing for the majority, did not view the international trend towards abolition of capital punishment as enthusiastically as his colleague. Justice La Forest said that the failure of the major international treaties to condemn the death penalty outright contrasted with "the overwhelming universal condemnation that has been directed at practices such as genocide, slavery and torture".[760] Noting that despite certain trends, "[t]here is. . .no international norm" providing for abolition of the death penalty, he said that only one international instrument, *Protocol No. 6 to the European Convention*, prohibited the use of the death penalty.[761] This was quite simply an error. Not only did there also exist two other protocols to the *International Covenant on Civil and Political Rights* and the *American Convention on Human Rights* that are to the same effect as the European instrument,[762] the *American Convention on Human Rights* also provides that

---

757   *Kindler* v. *Canada*, *supra* note 746, at 804-807 (SCR).
758   *Second Optional Protocol to the International Covenant on Civil and Political Rights Aimed at Abolition of the Death Penalty*, UN Doc. A/RES/44/128, annex.
759   *Kindler* v. *Canada*, *supra* note 746, at 809 (SCR).
760   *Ibid.*, at 833.
761   *Ibid.*, at 833-834.
762   Since the decision, a second protocol to the *European Convention* concerning capital punishment has been adopted and entered into force: *Protocol No. 13 to the Convention for the Protection of Human Rights and Fundamental Freedoms, concerning the abolition of the death penalty in all circumstances*, ETS No. 187. *Protocol No. 6* concerned the death penalty in peacetime. *Protocol No. 13* prohibits the death penalty at all times.

States that have already abolished the death penalty may not reintroduce it. A significant number of States in the Organization of American States are bound as a question of international law not to impose the death penalty. When the number of States parties to these four instruments is totalled, approximately seventy-five States are now abolitionist as a question of international law, including Canada, although to be fair to Justice La Forest when he wrote his reasons in *Kindler*, the number was much smaller then. Thus, an international norm does indeed exist, although it is not yet unanimous.

In *Soering*, the European Court of Human rights had not ruled directly on the death penalty, considering itself to be bound by article 2 of the *European Convention on Human Rights* which recognized capital punishment as an exception to the right to life. The European Court focussed on what is known as the "death row phenomenon", a term used to describe the years of agony suffered by the condemned.[763] In Soering's case, this wait for execution in Virginia was likely to take six to eight years. The Court held such treatment to be inhuman and degrading, and therefore contrary to article 3 of the *European Convention on Human Rights*. Justice Cory did not, however, reach any conclusions on the "death row phenomenon", although it was indeed relevant to the case of Kindler and a companion case, that of Charles Ng. He addressed his analysis to the death penalty as such. Unlike the *European Convention*, there is nothing in the right to life provision of the *Canadian Charter* explicitly recognizing the death penalty. Justice Cory developed his argument around the notion of dignity, which he said was central to international human rights law, and which necessarily proscribed capital punishment.

Justice Cory was not the only member of the Court to refer to the *Soering case* in his reasons. In fact, there was something of a debate among the judges concerning the interpretation and the scope to be given to the European Court's judgment. Justice La Forest dismissed the significance of *Soering*, which involved extradition to the United States from the United Kingdom for a capital crime, because the European Court had referred to a number of extenuating circumstances, such as Soering's young age.[764] However, Justice Cory said that "on my reading of the decision neither his youth nor his country of origin were either crucial to or determinative of the result".[765] Since the *Kindler* judgment, Justice La Forest's views have been

763 *Soering* v. *United Kingdom, supra* note 748.
764 *Kindler* v. *Canada, supra* note 746, at 835.
765 *Ibid.*, at 823.

criticized by courts elsewhere in the world,[766] and the broad interpretation of the *Soering* case advanced by Justice Cory has been endorsed by no less than the Judicial Committee of the Privy Council.[767]

There is probably no more dramatic example in Canadian caselaw of how the courts have been influenced to change their views by the evolving landscape of international law than the sequel to *Kindler* and *Ng*, which came before the Supreme Court of Canada a decade later. In *Burns and Rafay*,[768] a unanimous Court essentially reversed its earlier opinion, holding that extradition to a State where the death penalty might be imposed would only be constitutionally admissible in "exceptional circumstances". The ruling was somewhat a compromise, probably the result of the changing composition of the bench. Three of the members of the majority in *Kindler* and *Ng*, were still on the Court, and they were understandably reluctant to overtly overturn their earlier decision. Ruling that extradition might still be allowed in "exceptional circumstances" provided them with a graceful distinction. None of the dissenters in the earlier decisions remained on the bench, and so there was no issue of any dilution of their earlier views, which were quite absolute on the subject, in the interests of compromise. Ironically, then, it seems it was the departure of the three dissenters in *Kindler* and *Ng*, Justices Sopinka, Cory and Lamer, that set the stage for revision of those judgments by the majority. But the catalyst in the entire process was the dramatic evolution in international law and practice with respect to capital punishment, to which the Court made abundant reference.

In *Burns and Rafay*, the Court pointed to a range of international initiatives aimed at abolition of capital punishment, "with the government of

---

766 *Catholic Commission for Justice and Peace in Zimbabwe* v. *Attorney-General et al.*, (1993) 1 ZLR 242 (S), 4 SA 239), 14 *Human Rights Law Journal* 323 (ZSC). See also the discussion of the *Kindler* case in *S.* v. *Makwanyane*, 1995 (3) SA 391, (1995) 16 *Human Rights Law Journal* 154.

767 *Pratt* et al. v. *Attorney General for Jamaica* et al., [1993] 4 All ER 769, [1993] 2 LRC 349, [1994] 2 AC 1, [1993] 3 WLR 995, 43 WIR 340, 14 *Human Rights Law Journal* 338, 33 ILM 364 (JCPC). Kindler's petition to the Human Rights Committee was unsuccessful: *Kindler* v. *Canada* (No. 470/1991), UN Doc. CCPR/C/48/D/470/1991, UN Doc. A/48/40, Vol. II, 138, 14 *Human Rights Law Journal* 307. However, Charles Ng won a victory before the Committee, which ruled that his extradition to a State where the death penalty would be imposed in an inhuman manner, namely the gas chamber, breached article 7 of the *Covenant*: *Ng* v. *Canada* (No. 469/1991), UN Doc. CCPR/C/49/D/469/1991, UN Doc. A/49/40, Vol. II, p. 189, 15 *Human Rights Law Journal* 149.

768 *United States* v. *Burns and Rafay*, [2001] 1 SCR 283, 195 DLR (4th) 1, [2001] 3 WWR 193, 151 CCC (3d) 97, 39 CR (5th) 205, 81 CRR (2d) 1, 85 BCLR (3d) 1. See: William A. Schabas, "Case Comment: *United States* v. *Burns*", (2001) 95 *American Journal of International Law* 666; William A. Schabas, "From *Kindler* to *Burns*: International Law is Nourishing the Constitutional Living Tree", in Gérard Cohen-Jonathan & William Schabas, eds., *La peine capitale et le droit international des droits de l'homme*, Paris: L.G.D.J. Diffuseur, 2003, pp. 143-156.

Canada often in the forefront".[769] The Court took note of a number of important instruments and sources, including a report of the United Nations Special Rapporteur on Extrajudicial, summary or arbitrary executions, resolutions of the United Nations Commission on Human Rights, resolutions of the Parliamentary Assembly of the Council of Europe and the European Parliament, and the European Union General Affairs Council's 1998 declaration stating: "The [European Union] will work towards the universal abolition of the death penalty as a strongly held policy now agreed by all [European Union] Member States." The Supreme Court of Canada pointed to the various protocols aimed at abolition adopted within the universal and regional human rights systems, noting that Canada had told the Human Rights Committee that its position on accession to the *Second Optional Protocol to the International Covenant on Civil and Political Rights* was being given "careful consideration". Finally, the Court pointed to the exclusion of capital punishment in the Statutes of the two ad hoc international criminal tribunals established by the United Nations Security Council for the former Yugoslavia and Rwanda, "despite the heinous nature of the crimes alleged against the accused individuals. This exclusion was affirmed in the Rome Statute of the International Criminal Court, signed on December 18, 1998 and ratified on July 7, 2000 by Canada." The Court repeated an affirmation it had made in *Kindler* and *Ng* to the effect that there was no "international law norm against the death penalty, or against extradition to face the death penalty". Nevertheless, and here it was departing from the conservative approach of the majority in the earlier judgments, in *Burns and Rafay* the Court said international developments showed "significant movement towards acceptance internationally of a principle of fundamental justice that Canada has already adopted internally, namely the abolition of capital punishment".[770] According to the Court:

> The existence of an international trend against the death penalty is useful in testing our values against those of comparable jurisdictions. This trend against the death penalty supports some relevant conclusions. First, criminal justice, according to international standards, is moving in the direction of abolition of the death penalty. Second, the trend is more pronounced among democratic states with systems of criminal justice comparable to our own. The United States (or those parts of it that have retained the death penalty) is the exception, although of course it is an important exception. Third, the trend to abolition in the democracies, particularly the Western democracies, mirrors and perhaps corroborates the principles of fundamental justice that led to the rejection of the death penalty in Canada.[771]

---

769   *Ibid.*, para. 85.
770   *Ibid.*, paras. 85-88.
771   *Ibid.*, para. 92.

It now seems fairly clear, in light of recent caselaw of the Human Rights Committee,[772] together with Canada's accession to the *Second Optional Protocol*, that even were the government to invoke "exceptional circumstances" as a justification for rendition without assurances not to impose the death penalty, this would run afoul of Canada's international obligations, even if it might still be constitutionally acceptable.

4.7   Protection Against Self-Incrimination

Section 13 of the *Canadian Charter* states: "A witness who testifies in any proceedings has the right not to have any incriminating evidence so given used to incriminate that witness in any other proceedings, except in a prosecution for perjury or for the giving of contradictory evidence." This provision was not drawn from international law; it derives from the *Canadian Bill of Rights* and the United States *Bill of Rights*.[773] Justice Kerens of the Alberta Court of Appeal, noted that the international instruments offer no explicit rule against self-incrimination, but added that article 11 of the *Universal Declaration of Human Rights* and article 8 of the *European Convention on Human Rights* "command respect for privacy, family home and correspondence", and found there a similar form of protection.[774]

4.8   Right to an Interpreter

"The priority given to the right to interpreter assistance of criminally accused persons. . .is echoed in international human rights instruments," wrote Chief Justice Lamer in *R*. v. *Tran*,[775] referring to the *International Covenant on Civil and Political Rights*[776] and the *European Convention on*

---

772 *Judge* v. *Canada* (No. 829/1998), UN Doc. CCPR/C/78/D/829/1998.

773 Michael Bothe, "La protection des droits fondementaux au Canada", *Jahrbuch des öffentlichen Rechts der Gegenwart*, 1986, at 304; Morris Manning, *Rights, Freedoms and the Courts: A Practical Analysis of the* Constitution Act, 1982, Toronto: Emond-Montgomery, 1983, at 451.

774 *R*. v. *Dubois*, [1984] 3 WWR 594, 8 DLR (4th) 589, 11 CCC (3d) 453, 39 CR (3d) 281, 31 Alta LR (2d) 16, 51 AR 210, 9 CRR 61 (CA), reversed, [1985] 2 SCR 350, at 594-595 (WWR). The notion that "privacy" is the underlying rationale for the protection against self-incrimination is supported by comments of Justices Wilson and Sopinka in *Thomson Newspapers* v. *Canada (Director of Investigation and Research, Restrictive Practices Commission)*, [1990] 1 SCR 425, 67 DLR (4th) 161, 54 CCC (3d) 417.

775 *R*. v. *Tran*, [1994] 2 SCR 951, at 969.

776 *International Covenant on Civil and Political Rights*, (1976) 999 UNTS 171, [1976] CTS 47, art. 14(3)(f). See also: *American Convention on Human Rights*, (1979) 1144 UNTS 123, OASTS 36, art. 8(2)(a); *Convention on the Rights of the Child*, GA Res. 44/25, art. 40(2)(b)(vi).

Human Rights.[777] The *Covenant* includes the right "[t]o have the free assistance of an interpreter if he cannot understand or speak the language used in court" in its list of minimum guarantees for the determination of a criminal charge. It also specifies that an accused is "[t]o be informed promptly and in detail in a language which he understands of the nature and cause of the charge against him."[778]

The issue of interpretation is hardly controversial in criminal matters, but issues have arisen when counsel have attempted to extend the guarantee to civil and administrative proceedings.[779] On this subject, the international instruments give little guidance, because they apply only to criminal matters.[780] Justice Skipp of the British Columbia Supreme Court referred to article 14(3)(f) of the *International Covenant on Civil and Political Rights* in ruling on an application to appoint an interpreter in a civil case. The interpreter is without doubt provided free, he noted, but nowhere does the *Covenant* say that the court should pay when the matter is not criminal.[781] The application was dismissed, although the judge noted that appointment of a court-remunerated interpreter, pursuant to section 14 of the *Charter*, could not be ruled out in a particularly needy case. The European Court of Human Rights has held that there is a right not only to an interpreter, but to one provided free by the court, even in an administrative-type hearing for violation of a regulatory matter.[782] Justice Lacourcière of the Ontario Court of Appeal referred to the *European Convention* in support of the importance of the right to an interpreter, even in an administrative matter.[783]

777 *European Convention on Human Rights*, (1955) 213 UNTS 221, ETS 5, art. 6(3)(e).
778 *International Covenant on Civil and Political Rights*, *supra* note 776, art. 14(3)(a). See also: *American Convention on Human Rights*, *supra* note 776, art. 8(2)(a); *European Convention on Human Rights*, *ibid.*, art. 6(3)(a)
779 In immigration and refugee law, for instance, see: *Mohammadian* v. *Canada (Minister of Citizenship and Immigration)*, [2001] 4 FC 85 (FCA), leave to appeal refused, (2002) 292 NR 195n (SCC).
780 Yannick Landry & Virginie Désilets, "Les garanties juridiques", in Gérald-A. Beaudoin & Errol P. Mendes, eds., *Canadian Charter of Rights and Freedoms*, 4th ed., Markham, Ont., LexisNexis Butterworths, 2005, at 911.
781 *Wyllie* v. *Wyllie*, (1987) 37 DLR (4th) 376 (BC SC).
782 *Öztürk* v. *Germany*, 21 February 1984, Series A, No. 73; see also *Luedicke, Belkacem and Koç* v. *Germany*, 10 March 1980, Series A, No. 36, 2 EHRR 433, 59 ILR 463. See: P. Stanfield, "Right to Free Assistance of an Interpreter in Judicial Proceedings Concerning a 'Regulatory Offence'/Öztürk Case", (1984) 4 *Human Rights Law Journal* 293.
783 *Roy* v. *Hackett*, (1987) 62 OR (2d) 351 (CA). The reference is in error, however, in citing article 14(3)(a) of the *European Convention of Human Rights*, *supra* note 777, when he meant article 6(3)(a). Article 14(3)(a) of the *International Covenant on Civil and Political Rights* supra note 776, would have been a better reference.

4.9   Equality Rights

"All human beings are born free and equal in dignity and rights", states the first sentence of article 1 of the *Universal Declaration of Human Rights*. Professor Maxwell Cohen has described equality rights as ". . .the central altar in the modern cathedral of international human rights. Non-discrimination and equality are at the very heart of the assertion of dignity and opportunity, of recognition and respect."[784] In Canadian law, the right to equality has been of particular importance because, in addition to its recognition in section 15 of the *Canadian Charter*,[785] it has occupied the attention of federal and provincial legislators in the various anti-discrimination statutes and codes.

The influence of international norms in this branch of Canadian law is unquestionable. Two of the provincial codes, those of Ontario[786] and the Yukon Territory,[787] actually make specific reference to the *Universal Declaration of Human Rights* in their texts. Although the *Canadian Charter* affirms a general right to equality, it is only applicable, pursuant to section 32, to legislation and to state action.[788] The provincial and federal anti-discrimination statutes are also applicable in the private sector, and normally confine their scope to discrimination in employment, housing, education, transport and other goods and services normally offered to the public. Quebec's *Charter of Human Rights and Freedoms* is an exception, in that it comprises not only the classic anti-discrimination provisions of the provincial codes, but also an extensive list of political, legal, economic, social and cultural rights.[789] Furthermore, by virtue of section 52, the Quebec

---

784   Maxwell Cohen, "Towards a Paradigm of Theory and Practice: The Canadian Charter of Rights and Freedoms – International Law Influences and Interactions", [1986] *Canadian Human Rights Yearbook* 47, at 67.

785   See: William Black & Lynn Smith, "The Equality Rights", in Gérald-A. Beaudoin & Errol P. Mendes, eds., *Canadian Charter of Rights and Freedoms*, 4th ed., Markham, Ont., LexisNexis Butterworths, 2005, pp. 925-1024.

786   *Ontario Human Rights Code*, RSO 1990, c. H.19, preamble.

787   *Human Rights Act*, SY 1987, c. 3, s. 1.

788   *Retail, Wholesale & Department Store Union, Local 580* v. *Dolphin Delivery Ltd.*, [1984] 3 WWR 481, 52 BCLR 1, 84 CLLC 14,036, 10 DLR (4th) 198 (CA), affirmed, [1986] 2 SCR 573.

789   *Charter of Human Rights and Freedoms*, RSQ, c. C-12. In *Devine* c. *Québec (Procureur général)*, [1982] CS 355, Justice Dugas of the Quebec Superior Court stated that the *Universal Declaration of Human Rights*, the *International Covenant on Civil and Political Rights*, and the *European Convention on Human Rights*, were all models for the Quebec *Charter of Human Rights and Freedoms*, RSQ, c. C-12 (at pp. 375-376). The explanatory notes accompanying the original draft articles of the Quebec *Charter*, proposed by F.R. Scott, Jean Beetz, G. LeDain and Jacques-Yvan Morin as amendments to the *Civil Code*, refer in a general way to the *Convention for the Prevention and Punishment of the Crime of Genocide*, the *Universal Declaration of Human Rights*, and

Charter is paramount with respect to other provincial legislation and, in case of conflict, the impugned text may be declared inoperative.

The *International Covenant on Civil and Political Rights* considers equality rights in two important provisions, articles 2(1) and 26. These declare:

> 2 (1). Each State Party to the present Covenant undertakes to respect and to ensure to all individuals within its territory and subject to its jurisdiction the rights recognized in the present Covenant, without distinction of any kind, such as race, colour sex, language, religion, political or other opinion, national or social origin, property, birth or other status.
>
> 26. All persons are equal before the law and are entitled without any discrimination to the equal protection of the law. In this respect, the law shall prohibit any discrimination and guarantee to all persons equal and effective protection against discrimination on any ground such as race, colour, sex, language, religion, political or other opinion, national or social origin, property, birth or other status.

The *International Covenant on Civil and Political Rights* offers additional guarantees of equality in articles 3 (men and women), 14(1) (before the courts), 23(4) (spouses), 24 (children) and 25 (public affairs). Article 2(1) of the *Covenant* applies only to "the rights recognized in the present Covenant", whereas article 26 is much broader. Article 26 more closely resembles section 15 of the *Canadian Charter*, in that it suggests a degree of substantive protection and an independent, autonomous right to equality, even in the case of rights that are not formally set out within the *Covenant*. Moreover, by use of the term "such as", it indicates an open enumeration and invites the courts to read in analogous grounds of discrimination that are not specifically set out in the text. A right to equality before and equal protection of the law that is broadly similar in scope to that of article 26 of the *International Covenant on Civil and Political Rights* appears in article 7 of the *Universal Declaration of Human Rights*, article 24 of the *American Convention on Human Rights* and article 3 of the *African Charter of Human and Peoples' Rights*.

Some of the international instruments differ from section 15 of the *Charter* in that they only secure individuals from discrimination with respect to rights and freedoms set out therein. Accordingly, they contain clauses

---

the *Charter of the United Nations*, and indicate that section 5 of the *Quebec Charter* (the right to privacy) was directly inspired by article 12 of the *Universal Declaration of Human Rights*: Civil Code Revisions Office, *Report of the Civil Rights Committee*, Quebec City, 1966. In *Wong* v. *Hughes Petroleum Ltd.*, (1983), 28 Alta LR (2d) 155, 46 AR 276, 4 CHRR D/1488 (Q.B.), the Court noted similarities between section 10 of the *Quebec Charter* and article 1 of the *International Convention on the Elimination of All Forms of Racial Discrimination*.

similar to article 2(1) of the *International Covenant on Civil and Political Rights*, but not equivalent to article 26 of that instrument. This is notably the case with the *European Convention on Human Rights*. The *European Convention on Human Rights* states, at article 14: "The enjoyment of the rights and freedoms set forth in this Convention shall be secured without discrimination on any ground such as sex, race, colour, language, religion, political or other opinion, national or social origin, association with a national minority, property, birth or other status."[790] In 2000, the Council of Europe adopted *Protocol No. 12*, which amends the *European Convention on Human Rights* in order to add a guarantee of substantive equality: "The enjoyment of any right set forth by law shall be secured without discrimination on any ground such as sex, race, colour, language, religion, political or other opinion, national or social origin, association with a national minority, property, birth or other status."[791] The *Convention on the Rights of the Child* declares: "States Parties shall respect and ensure the rights set forth in the present Convention to each child within their jurisdiction without discrimination of any kind, irrespective of the child's or his or her parent's or legal guardian's race, colour, sex, language, religion, political or other opinion, national, ethnic or social origin, property, disability, birth or other status."[792] The approach of these treaties is comparable to that taken by the Quebec legislature in section 10 of the *Charter of Human Rights and Freedoms*, as the Quebec Human Rights Tribunal has often pointed out.[793] Al-

---

790 *Supra* note 777, art. 14. See: Graham Zellick, "The European Convention on Human Rights: Its Significance for Charter Litigation", in R.J. Sharpe, ed., *Charter Litigation*, Toronto: Butterworths, 1987, p. 119.

791 *Protocol No. 12 to the Convention for the Protection of Human Rights and Fundamental Freedoms*, ETS 177.

792 *Convention on the Rights of the Child, supra* note 776, art. 2(1).

793 *Commission des droits de la personne du Québec* v. *Commission scolaire Saint-Jean-sur-Richelieu*, [1991] RJQ 3003 (TDPQ), varied, [1994] RJQ 227 (CA); *Commission des droits de la personne du Québec* v. *Immeubles Ni/Dia Inc.*, [1992] RJQ 2977 (TDPQ); *Commission des droits de la personne du Québec* v. *Commission scolaire régionale Chauveau*, (1993) 18 CHRR D/433 (TDPQ), reversed, (1994) 1994 CarswellQue 265 (CA), leave to appeal refused, (1995) 186 NR 79n (SCC), reconsideration refused, (21 novembre 1996) no 24291 (SCC); *M.L. and Commission des droits de la personne et des droits de la jeunesse du Québec* v. *Maison des jeunes*, (1998) 1998 CarswellQue 2602, [1998] JTDPQ no 31 (TDPQ); *Forget et Québec (Commission des droits de la personne et des droits de la jeunesse)* v. *Bertrand*, [2001] RJQ 1684 (TDPQ); *Commission des droits de la personne et des droits de la jeunesse* v. *Commission scolaire des Phares*, [2005] RJQ 309 (TDPQ), leave to appeal allowed, (2005) 2005 CarswellQue 968 (CA), varied, (2006) 2006 CarswellQue 303 (CA). See also the comments of the Quebec Court of Appeal in *Ville de Québec* v. *Commission des droits de la personne*, [1989] RJQ 831, 11 CHRR D/500 (CA), leave to appeal refused, (1989) 103 NR 160 (note) (SCC), at D/508 [CHRR]; and in *Québec (Commission des droits de la personne et des droits de la jeunesse)* v. *Montréal (Ville)*, [1998] RJQ 688 (CA), affirmed, [2000] 1 SCR 665, at para. 65.

though the scope of the regional treaties is less broad than that of the *Covenant*, their caselaw may allow for a larger view of equality rights precisely because of the specificity of each region. This is certainly the situation in Europe, and the Strasbourg organs have given a larger reading to equality rights in the case of unmarried families than the Human Rights Committee, as our courts have been quick to observe.[794]

One of the principal article 26 cases before the Human Rights Committee concerns a violation by Canada of the right to equality in access to state-funded parochial schools.[795] The Human Rights Committee has also examined the right to equality in cases dealing with discrimination on grounds of political opinion,[796] race,[797] citizenship or residence,[798] religion or belief[799] and language.[800] It was initially somewhat timid in applying article 26 to rights not set out in the *Covenant*, but in a series of decisions it extended its scope to economic and social rights found in the *International Covenant on Economic, Social and Cultural Rights*.[801]

There are also several important specialized conventions dealing with discrimination, notably the *International Convention on the Elimination of All Forms of Racial Discrimination*, the *Convention on the Elimination of Discrimination Against Women, I.L.O Convention (No. 111) Concerning*

---

794 *Commission des droits de la personne du Québec* v. *Immeubles Ni/Dia Inc.*, *ibid.*, at 2982.

795 *Waldman* v. *Canada* (No. 694/1996), UN Doc. CCPR/C/67/D/694/1996. *Waldman* is discussed in some detail in Chapter 3, at 163-164.

796 *Orihuela* v. *Peru* (No. 309/1988), UN Doc. CCPR/C/48/D/309/1988; *Bwalya* v. *Zambia* (No. 314/1988), UN Doc. CCPR/C/48/D/314/1988, *Bahamonde* v. *Equatorial Guinea* (No. 468/1991), UN Doc. CCPR/C/49/D/468/1991; *Gedumbe* v. *Democratic Republic of Congo* (No. 641/1995), UN Doc. CCPR/C/75/D/641/1995.

797 *Drobek* v. *Slovakia* (No. 643/1995), UN Doc. CCPR/C/60/D/643/1995; *Singh* v. *Canada* (No. 761/1997), UN Doc. CCPR/C/60/D/761/1997; *Jonassen et al.* v. *Norway* (No. 942/2000), UN Doc. CCPR/C/76/D/942/2000.

798 *Simunek et al.* v. *Czech Republic* (No. 516/1992), UN Doc. CCPR/C/54/D/516/1992; *Adam.* v. *Czech Republic* (No. 586/1994), UN Doc. CCPR/C/57/D/586/1994; *Brok et al.* v. *Czech Republic* (No. 774/1997), UN Doc. CCPR/C/73/D/774/1997.

799 *Foin* v. *France* (No. 666/1995), UN Doc. CCPR/C/67/D/666/1995.

800 *Ignatane* v. *Latvia* (No. 884/1999), UN Doc. CCPR/C/72/D/884/1999; *Diergaardt et al.* v. *Namibia* (No. 760/1997), UN Doc. CCPR/C/69/D/760/1997.

801 *Zwaan-de Vries* v. *The Netherlands* (No. 182/1984), UN Doc. CCPR/C/OP/2, p. 209, 9 *Human Rights Law Journal* 256, 7 ILLR 25; *Danning* v. *Netherlands* (No. 180/1984), UN Doc. CCPR/C/OP/2, p. 205, 9 *Human Rights Law Journal* 259; *Pauger* v. *Austria* (No. 716/1996), UN Doc. CCPR/C/65/D/716/1996; *Vos* v. *Netherlands* (No. 786/1997), UN Doc. CCPR/C/66/D/786/1997; *Müller* et al. v. *Namibia* (No. 919/2000), UN Doc. CCPR/C/74/D/919/2000. Note that the non-discrimination portion of article 2(1) of the *International Covenant on Economic, Social and Cultural Rights* (1976) 993 UNTS 3, [1976] CTS 46 is identical to article 2(1) of the *International Covenant on Civil and Political Rights*, *supra* note 776. Article 10(3) of the *International Covenant on Economic, Social and Cultural Rights* prohibits discrimination against children.

Discrimination in Employment[802] and the *UNESCO Convention on Discrimination in Education.*[803] (which Canada has never ratified). As yet, there are no specialized conventions dealing with discrimination based on religion, although the General Assembly has adopted a declaration on the subject.[804] These instruments provide detailed definitions of discrimination, and they review the types of measures that States should undertake to combat it in their respective spheres.[805] For example, article 1(1) of the *International Convention on the Elimination of All Forms of Racial Discrimination* states:

> In this Convention, the term "racial discrimination" shall mean any distinction, exclusion, restriction or preference based on race, colour, descent, or national or ethnic origin which has the purpose or effect of nullifying or impairing the recognition, enjoyment or exercise, on an equal footing, of human rights and fundamental freedoms in the political, economic, social, cultural or any other field of public life.

Article 1 of the *Convention on the Elimination of Discrimination Against Women* declares:

> For the purposes of the present Convention, the term "discrimination against women" shall mean any distinction, exclusion or restriction made on the basis of sex which has the effect or propose of impairing or nullifying the recognition, enjoyment or exercise by women, irrespective of their marital status, on a basis

---

802 (1960) 361 UNTS 31.

803 (1960) 429 UNTS 93. See: P. Mertens, "L'application de la Convention et de la Recommandation de l'UNESCO concernant la lutte contre la discrimination dans le domaine de l'enseignement, Un bilan provisoire", (1974) 1 *Revue des droits de l'homme* 91. Other relevant instruments adopted by UNESCO dealing with discrimination include: *UNESCO Declaration on Race and Racial Prejudice*, UNESCO Doc. 14 C/3/1.2, 1978, and *Declaration of the Principles of International Cultural Co-operation*, UNESCO Doc. 14 C/8/1.1/2, 1966.

804 *Declaration on the Elimination of All Forms of Intolerance and Discrimination based on Religion and Belief*, GA Res. 35/55; cited in *Québec (Commission des droits de la personne) c. Autobus Legault inc.*, (sub nom. *Bédard et Commission des droits de la personne du Québec* v. *Autobus Legault Inc.*) [1994] RJQ 3027 (CS), reversed, (sub nom. *Autobus Legault Inc.* c. *Commission de droits de la personne & des droits de la jeunesse*) [1998] RJQ 3022 (CA), leave to appeal refused, (sub nom. *Commission des droits de la personne & des droits de la jeunesse (Qué.)* v. *Autobus Legault Inc.*) 250 N.R. 198n (SCC). See also the *Vienna Declaration and Programme of Action*, (1976) 993 UNTS 3, [1976] CTS 46, para. 22.

805 As was done by the Federal Court in *Schachter* v. *Canada*, [1988] 3 FC 515, 52 DLR (4th) 525, 18 FTR 199, 88 CLLC 14,021, 20 CCEL 301, 9 CHRR D/5320 (TD), affirmed, (1990) 1990 CarswellNat 677 (Fed CA), reversed, (1992) 1992 CarswellNat 658 (SCC). Also: *Andrews* v. *Law Society of BC*, [1986] 4 WWR 242, 27 DLR (4th) 600, 91 NR 255 (BC CA) at 251 (WWR), affirmed, [1989] 1 SCR 143, 56 DLR (4th) 1, [1989] 2 WWR 289, 36 CRR 193, 25 CCEL 255, 10 CHRR D/5719, 34 BCLR (2d) 273, 91 NR 255, (*per* McLachlin JA).

of equality of men and women, of human rights and fundamental freedoms in the political, economic, social, cultural, civil and any other field.

After noting the differences between the *Charter*, which relies on section 1, and the international models, the Saskatchewan Court of Appeal held that the the term "discrimination" in section 15 of the *Canadian Charter* has "essentially the same general meaning" as that found in the specialized human rights treaties mentioned above. The Court continued: "Picking up on the definition common to these treaties, and assuming the whole of the section is modified by the phrase 'without discrimination', we construe the term to mean any distinction, exclusion, restriction, or preference whose purpose or effect is to nullify or impair the enjoyment of the forms of equality enshrined in the section."[806] The Quebec Human Rights Tribunal has relied on the *International Convention on the Elimination of All Forms of Racial Discrimination* in addressing the issue of racial discrimination under the Quebec *Charter*.[807]

But in *Gould* v. *Yukon Order of Pioneers*, Justice Wachowich of the Yukon Territory Supreme Court said he had "a number of concerns" with applying the definition of "discrimination" in the *Convention on the Elimination of Discrimination Against Women* to the Yukon *Human Rights Act*. He noted that it was a specific convention that needed to be considered within the context of international human rights law overall, and concluded that it was "inappropriate to insist on an equivalent meaning for domestic legislation. . .[A]s an aid to interpretation I find [the *Convention on the Elimination of Discrimination Against Women*] to be of little assistance."[808]

806 *Reference re Use of French in Criminal Proceedings in Saskatchewan*, [1987] 5 WWR 577, 44 DLR (4th) 16, 43 CRR 189, 36 CCC (3d) 353 (Sask CA). See also: *W. (D.S.)* v. *H. (R.)*, (1988) 1988 CarswellSask 341, [1988] S.J. No. 732 (CA), leave to appeal refused, (1989) 62 D.L.R. (4th) viii (SCC).

807 *Commission des droits de la personne du Québec v. Commission scolaire Deux-Montagnes*, [1993] RJQ 1297 (TDPQ); *Gagnon et Commission des droits de la personne et des droits de la jeunesse du Québec* v. *Quévillon*, (1999) 1999 CarswellQue 1138, [1999] JTDPQ no 6 (TDPQ); *Bia-Domingo et Québec (Commission des droits de la personne et des droits de la jeunesse)* v. *Sinatra*, (1999) 1999 CarswellQue 3292, [1999] JTDPQ no 19 (TDPQ); *Délicieux et Québec (Commission des droits de la personne et des droits de la jeunesse)* v. *Yazbeck*, (2001) 2001 CarswellQue 2220, [2001] TDPQ 12 (TDPQ); *Commission des droits de la personne et des droits de la jeunesse* v. *Collège Montmorency*, [2004] RJQ 1381 (TDPQ); *Commission des droits de la personne et des droits de la jeunesse* v. *Pettas*, (2005) 2005 CarswellQue 3317, [2005] JTDPQ no 7 (TDPQ).

808 *Gould* v. *Yukon Order of Pioneers*, (1991) 87 DLR (4th) 618, 14 CHRR D/176 (YTSC), affirmed, (1993) 100 DLR (4th) 596 (YTCA), affirmed, [1996] 1 SCR 571, at D/188. See also: *AG Canada* v. *Stuart*, (1982) [1983] 1 FC 651, 137 DLR (3d) 740, 44 NR 320 (CA), leave to appeal refused, (1982) 1982 CarswellNat 600 (SCC); and *Leroux* v. *Co-operators General Insurance Co.*, (1990) 65 DLR (4th) 702 (Ont HC), reversed, (1991) 83 DLR (4th) 694 (Ont CA).

In *Schacter* v. *Canada*, Justice Strayer of the Federal Court, Trial Division, referred to the *Convention on the Elimination of Discrimination Against Women* and the *Declaration on the Elimination of Discrimination Against Women*[809] in ruling that section 32 of the *Unemployment Insurance Act* constituted an infringement of section 15 of the *Charter*.[810] According to the *Unemployment Insurance Act*, adoptive parents, either male or female, may obtain benefit during "maternity leave" at the time of adoption, whereas in the case of natural parents, benefit is only available to the mother.[811] Justice Strayer wrote:

> These internationally adopted objectives, and in the latter case obligations [*i.e.*, the *Convention on the Elimination of Discrimination Against Women*], reinforce the view that Canadian society is committed to equalizing the role of parents in the care of children as much as possible, for the benefit of the family in general and in particular for the achievement of greater equality in the workplace for women.[812]

In *R. v. Ewanchuk*,[813] Justices L'Heureux-Dubé and Gonthier, in concurring reasons, made reference to the *Convention on the Elimination of Discrimination Against Women*, as well as to the work of the *Committee on the Elimination of Discrimination against Women*[814] and to the *Declaration on the Elimination of Violence against Women*,[815] in a *Charter*-informed contextual interpretation of relevant criminal law provisions. At issue was whether, in a sexual assault case, the trial judge had erred in applying a defence of "implied consent" pursuant to sections 265(3), 273.1 and 273.2 of the *Criminal Code*, a question that the majority of the Alberta Court of Appeal *per* McClung JA answered in the negative. The case became famous because of the stern rebuke Justice L'Heureux-Dubé gave to the latter for his "plainly inappropriate"[816] remarks and for the use of "myths and stereotypes in dealing with sexual assault complaints".[817] The day after the judgment was released, Justice McClung published a letter in the *National*

---

809 GA Res. 2263 (XXII).
810 Provisions of the unemployment insurance legislation of the Netherlands providing that married women who were neither breadwinners nor permanently separated were ineligible for benefit have been challenged before the Human Rights Committee as contrary to article 26 of the *International Covenant on Civil and Political Rights*: *Zwaan-de Vries* v. *Netherlands* (No. 182/1984), *supra* note 801. The Committee held that "such a differentiation is not reasonable" and in breach of the *Covenant*.
811 *Unemployment Insurance Act*, RSC 1985, c. U-1.
812 *Schachter* v. *Canada*, *supra* note 805, at 210 (FTR).
813 *R. v. Ewanchuk*, [1999] 1 SCR 330.
814 "General Recommendation No. 19, Violence against women", UN Doc. A/47/38.
815 "Declaration on the Elimination of Violence against Women", GA Res. 48/104.
816 *R. v. Ewanchuk*, *supra* note 813, at para. 91.
817 *Ibid.*, at para. 95.

Post attacking Justice L'Heureux-Dubé's integrity, tarnishing his office and writing one of the darker chapters in the history of the Canadian judiciary.[818]

On the important issue of pay equity between men and women, Justice Julien of the Quebec Superior Court, in *Syndicat de la fonction publique v. Procureur general du Québec*, rendered a highly significant judgment challenging Quebec's *Pay Equity Act*,[819] in which international legal instruments on discrimination against women played a central role:

> Lorsque le législateur québécois adopte la Loi, il ne peut ignorer l'environnement juridique relié au droit international. Le Québec connaît le contenu des engagements pris par le Canada. Son gouvernement adhère aux principes d'égalité et de droits fondamentaux auxquels le Canada et les États membres de l'ONU souscrivent. Il n' a pas de doute que le Québec se veut au diapason des valeurs modernes reliées au respect des droits de la personne. Le droit à l'égalité prévu à la Charte canadienne et à la Charte québécoise doit être interprété dans le sens des engagements internationaux du Canada.[820]

In addition to the *Universal Declaration of Human Rights*, the *International Covenant on Economic, Social and Cultural Rights* and the *Convention on the Elimination of Discrimination Against Women*, Justice Julien also referred to *ILO Convention (No. 100) Concerning Equal Remuneration for Men and Women Workers for Work of Equal Value*,[821] the *Implementation of the Nairobi Forward-looking Strategies for the Advancement of Women*,[822] the *Beijing Declaration and Platform for Action*[823] and the *Copenhagen Declaration on Social Development and the Programme of Action of the World Summit for Social Development*.[824]

The international models do not include a limitation clause specifically addressed to equality rights, unlike the *Canadian Charter*, where section 1 applies in any section 15 litigation. As a result, international tribunals have developed an internal definitional limitation on the right to equality. In applying the norm of non-discrimination, the Committee takes the view that not all distinction is prohibited, but that any discriminatory treatment must be justifiable using "reasonable and objective criteria".[825] Similarly, the European Court of Human Rights has held that the norm is violated if a

818 On this episode, see: Hester Lessard, "Farce or Tragedy?: Judicial Backlash and Justice McClung", (1999) 10 *Constitutional Forum* 65.
819 RSQ, c. E-12.001.
820 *Syndicat de la fonction publique* v. *Procureur général du Québec*, [2004] RJQ 524 (SC), at para. 881-882.
821 (1953) 165 UNTS 303, [1973] CTS 37.
822 GA Res. 40/108, UN Doc. A/CONF.116/28/Rev.1 (1986).
823 UN Doc. A/CONF.177/20, UN Doc. A/CONF.177/20/Add.1.
824 UN Doc. A/CONF.166/9.
825 *Kavanagh* v. *Ireland* (No. 819/1998), UN Doc. CCPR/C/71/D/819/1998, para. 12.

distinction has no "objective and reasonable justification".[826] The justification is evaluated with respect to the aim and effects of the measure being analysed. Differential treatment must pursue a legitimate aim. Furthermore, article 14 is breached where there is an absence of proportionality between the aim and the means to achieve it.[827]

In the early decisions under section 15, which came into force on 17 April 1985 three years after the *Charter* as a whole,[828] Canadian courts found article 14 of the *European Convention*, with its already abundant jurisprudence and learned commentary, to be of assistance in construction of the *Charter* provision. According to the Saskatchewan Court of Appeal, article 14 of the *European Convention* provides an equivalent to the section 1 test, that is, a mechanism for distinguishing between justified and unjustified forms of discrimination.[829] Justice Cameron referred to the European Court's application of article 14 of the *Convention* in the *Belgian Linguistic Case (No. 2)*,[830] and noted that its approach, like that of Justice McIntyre of the Supreme Court of Canada to the *Canadian Bill of Rights* in *R. v. MacKay*,[831] could be considered "relevant" to the construction of section 15.[832]

Article 14 of the *European Convention* and the *Belgian Linguistic* case were examined by Justice McIntyre in the Supreme Court of Canada's first judgment dealing with section 15 of the *Charter*.[833] He noted that there is no specific "reasonable limits" test set out in article 14 or elsewhere in the *European Convention* with respect to the equality provisions, but that nev-

---

826 *Barthold* v. *Federal Republic of Germany*, 25 March 1985, Series A. No. 90, 7 EHRR 383. See: R. Pelloux, "L'arrêt de la Cour européenne des droits de l'homme dans l'affaire linguistique belge (fond)", [1968] *Annuaire français de droit international* 201.

827 See: *British Columbia and Yukon Territory Building and Construction Trades Council* v. *Attorney General of British Columbia*, [1985] 6 WWR 726 (BC SC), at 734.

828 Something Judge Charles found difficult to explain, in light of Canada's international commitments: *R.* v. *MacDonald*, (1982) 16 MVR 101 (Ont Prov Ct), reversed, (1982) 17 MVR 185 (Ont Co Ct).

829 *Reference Re Use of French in Criminal Proceedings in Saskatchewan*, *supra* note 806; see also *Quebec Protestant School Boards* v. *A-G Quebec (No. 2)*, [1982] CS 273, 140 DLR (3d) 33, 3 CRR 114, affirmed, (1983) 1 DLR (4th) 573 (CA), affirmed, [1984] 2 SCR 66; *Williams* v. *Haugen*, *supra* note 806.

830 *Belgian Linguistic Case (No. 2)*, 23 July 1968, Series A, No. 6, 1 EHRR 252, 45 ILR 114.

831 [1980] 2 SCR 370; decided under the *Canadian Bill of Rights*.

832 *Reference Re Use of French in Criminal Proceedings in Saskatchewan*, *supra* note 806, at page 605 (WWR).

833 *Andrews* v. *Law Society of British Columbia*, [1989] 1 SCR 143. For an analysis of the *Belgian Linguistic Case*, and more generally the treatment of "discrimination" by international human rights instruments and tribunals, see: Marc Bossuyt, *L'interdiction de la discrimination dans le droit international des droits de l'homme*, Brussels: Etablissements Emile Bruylant, 1976.

ertheless such a test has been imposed by the caselaw of the European Court.[834] He drew the analogy with the test that he had proposed in *MacKay*, where the equality provisions of the *Canadian Bill of Rights* had no express limitation test, and where one had to be devised by the court. The situation is not the same under the *Canadian Charter*, because such a test is provided by section 1, Justice McIntyre explained. As a result, in analysing an alleged violation of section 15(1) of the *Charter*, the courts must pass immediately to section 1 once there has been a finding of discrimination; there is no additional "test" implied in section 15(1). As Justice McIntyre explained, "[t]he distinguishing feature of the *Charter*, unlike the other enactments, is that the consideration of such limiting factors is made under s. 1."[835] In *Andrews*, the Supreme Court concluded that the first question to be addressed under section 15 is whether or not there has been discrimination. Once this is determined, it is for the state to attempt to justify it under section 1.

The Ontario Court of Appeal, in *R. v. Century 21 Ramos Realty Inc. and Ramos*, compared the English and French versions of article 14 of the *European Convention on Human Rights*. It held that the English formulation "without discrimination" was more appropriate than the French "sans distinction aucune", as this conveyed the sense that prohibited discrimination must be pejorative and must go beyond a merely "neutral" differentiation.[836]

Canada was charged before the Human Rights Committee with violating article 26 of the *International Covenant on Civil and Political Rights* by discriminatory practices at C.N. Rail preventing Sikhs from wearing turbans and requiring them to wear safety helmets, contrary to their religious obligations. This celebrated case had already been addressed by the Supreme Court of Canada, which found that Bhinder was not the victim of discrimination.[837] Having exhausted his local remedies, Bhinder petitioned the Human Rights Committee, which concluded:

> The Committee notes that in the case under consideration legislation which, on the face of it, is neutral in that it applies to all persons without distinction, is said to operate in fact in a way which discriminates against persons of the

---

834 The Inter-American Court of Human Rights has adopted the same interpretation as the European Court, referring expressly to the *Belgian Linguistic Case: Proposed Amendments to the Naturalization Provisions of the Political Constitution of Costa Rica*, Advisory Opinion OC-4/84, Series A No. 4, (1984) 5 *Human Rights Law Journal* 161, 79 ILR 282.

835 *Andrews* v. *Law Society of British Columbia*, supra note 833, at 178 (SCR).

836 *R. v. Century 21 Ramos Realty Inc. and Ramos*, (1987) 32 CCC (3d) 353, 87 DTC 5158, 29 CRR 320, 58 OR (2d) 737, 56 CR (3d) 150, [1987] 1 CTC 340 (CA), at 334 (CRR), leave to appeal refused, (1987) 56 C.R. (3d) xxviii (SCC).

837 *Bhinder* v. *Canadian National*, [1985] 2 SCR 561, 23 DLR (4th) 481, 17 Admin LR 111, 9 CCEL 135, 86 CLLC 17,003, 63 NR 185.

Sikh religion. . .If the requirement that a hard hat be worn is regarded as raising issues under article 18 [freedom of religion] then it is a limitation that is justified by reference to the grounds laid down in article 18, paragraph 3. If the requirement that a hard hat be worn is seen as a discrimination *de facto* against persons of the Sikh religion under article 26, then, applying criteria now well established in the jurisprudence of the Committee, the legislation requiring the workers in federal employment be protected from injury and electric shock by the wearing of hard hats is to be regarded as reasonable and directed towards objective purposes that are compatible with the Covenant.[838]

Interestingly, at about the same time as the Human Rights Committee released its views in *Bhinder*, the Supreme Court of Canada reversed itself, declaring its judgment in *Bhinder* to have been erroneous.[839]

On the other hand, the Human Rights Committee found that Canada had violated article 26 of the *Covenant* by denying a general right to State funded parochial schools, given the existence of a publicly-financed system for the Catholic religion. According to the Human Rights Committee,

The Committee has noted the State party's argument that the aims of the State party's secular public education system are compatible with the principle of nondiscrimination laid down in the Covenant. The Committee does not take issue with this argument but notes, however, that the proclaimed aims of the system do not justify the exclusive funding of Roman Catholic religious schools. It has also noted the author's submission that the public school system in Ontario would have greater resources if the Government would cease funding any religious schools. In this context, the Committee observes that the Covenant does not oblige States parties to fund schools which are established on a religious basis. However, if a State party chooses to provide public funding to religious schools, it should make this funding available without discrimination. This means that providing funding for the schools of one religious group and not for another must be based on reasonable and objective criteria. In the instant case, the Committee concludes that the material before it does not show that the differential treatment between the Roman Catholic faith and the author's religious denomination is based on such criteria. Consequently, there has been a violation of the author's rights under article 26 of the Covenant to equal and effective protection against discrimination.[840]

Waldman had, of course, exhausted his domestic remedies in a case that went to the Supreme Court of Canada, where it was known as *Adler*.[841]

---

838 *Bhinder* v. *Canada* (No. 208/1986), UN Doc. CCPR/C/37/D/208/1986, UN Doc. A/45/40, Vol. II, p. 50, [1989-90] *Canadian Human Rights Yearbook* 306.

839 *Central Alberta Dairy Pool* v. *Alberta (Human Rights Commission)*, [1990] 2 SCR 489.

840 *Waldman* v. *Canada* (No. 694/1996), UN Doc. CCPR/C/67/D/694/1996, para. 10.6.

841 *Adler* v. *Ontario*, [1996] 3 SCR 609, 30 OR (3d) 642n, 140 DLR (4th) 385, 40 CRR (2d) 1, 95 OAC 1, affirmed, [1987] 4 WWR 385, 33 CCC (3d) 402, 29 CRR 244, 56 Sask R 129, 59 CR (3d) 223, 39 DLR (4th) 731 (Sask CA), affirmed, [1989] 1 SCR 342.

There were no international references when the issue was argued at the Supreme Court. The views of Justice L'Heureux-Dubé, who dissented from the majority, were largely confirmed in the views of the Human Rights Committee.

Both the *International Covenant* and the *European Convention* contain "open" rather than "closed" enumerations, and this inspired the *Charter* drafters who in the same fashion left it to the courts to apply section 15 to unspecified forms of discrimination.[842] In *Re MacVicar and Superintendent of Family and Child Services et al.*, Justice Huddart of the British Columbia Supreme Court referred to article 14 of the *European Convention on Human Rights* in determining that the enumeration in section 15 of the *Charter* was not exhaustive. In *Condon v. Prince Edward Island*, the Prince Edward Island Supreme Court (Trial Division) relied on, *inter alia*, the *Universal Declaration of Human Rights* in holding that political belief was an analogous ground of discrimination under section 15 of the *Charter*.[843] Canadian courts may well look to international authorities dealing with vulnerable groups, such as the disabled,[844] in order to add categories to section 15's enumeration. International law continues to evolve and categories that were once excluded or marginalized are now being recognized, which ought to have an effect domestically.[845] However, such recourse to international law to interpret section 15 of the *Charter* has been somewhat limited.[846]

---

842   See: Anne F. Bayefsky, "The Principle of Equality or Non-Discrimination in International Law", (1990) 11 *Human Rights Law Journal* 1, at 5.

843   *Condon* v. *Prince Edward Island*, (2002) 214 Nfld & PEIR 244 (PEI TD), affirmed, (2006) 253 Nfld & PEIR 265 (CA), additional reasons, (2006) 2006 CarswellPEI 39 (CA), at paras. 56 and 60.

844   *Mahon* v. *Canadian Pacific Ltd.*, (1986), 7 CHRR D/3278 (CHRT), reversed, (1987) 40 DLR (4th) 586 (Fed CA), leave to appeal refused, (1987) 86 NR 263n (SCC), at D/3284-D/3285 [CHRR]; *Lisenko* v. *Commission scolaire Saint-Hyacinthe Val Monts*, JE 96-787 (TDPQ); *Bales* v. *School District No. 23*, (1984) 54 BCLR 203 (SC), at 220; *Commission des droits de la personne du Québec* v. *Commission scolaire régionale Chauveau*, [1993] RJQ 929, 18 CHRR D/433 (TDPQ); *Gaumond et Commission des droits de la personne du Québec* v. *Société de transport de la communauté urbaine de Montréal*, [1996] RJQ 2063 (TDPQ).

845   For instance, see: *Québec (Commission des droits de la personne et des droits de la jeunesse)* v. *Montréal (City)*, [2000] 1 SCR 665, at paras. 73-75, and *Granovsky* v. *Canada (Minister of Employment and Immigration)*, [2000] 1 SCR 703, 186 DLR (4th) 1, 50 CCEL (2d) 177, 253 NR 329, at paras. 34-35, where the Supreme Court of Canada noted that the word "handicap" was not found in the leading international instruments such as the *Universal Declaration of Human Rights* and the two *International Covenants*, but went further in its quest and, although acknowledging that there is no consistent definition at international law, made use of two international documents to help shed light on the term: "World Programme of Action concerning Disabled Persons", UN Doc. A/RES/37/52, and *International Classification of Impairments, Disabilities,*

Perhaps more intriguing for the Canadian courts is the absence of categories, such as age, from the international enumerations. "Age had not

and *Handicaps: A Manual of Classification Relating to the Consequences of Disease.* Geneva: World Health Organization, 1980.

846 This situation contrasts with the frequent use of international human rights law in interpreting the equality provisions of the Quebec *Charter of Human Rights and Freedoms*, RSQ, c. C-12, especially section 10, at both stages of the analysis. Under the leadership of Justice Rivet, the Quebec Human Rights Tribunal has been particularly receptive to international instruments; see: *Commission des droits de la personne du Québec* v. *Brzozowski*, [1994] RJQ 1447 (TDPQ); *Commission des droits de la personne du Québec* v. *Autobus Legault inc.*, (sub nom. *Bédard et Commission des droits de la personne du Québec* v. *Autobus Legault Inc.*) [1994] RJQ 3027 (CS), reversed, (sub nom. *Autobus Legault Inc.* c. *Commission de droits de la personne & des droits de la jeunesse*) [1998] RJQ 3022 (CA), leave to appeal refused, (sub nom. *Commission des droits de la personne & des droits de la jeunesse (Qué.)* v. *Autobus Legault Inc.*) 250 N.R. 198n (SCC); *Commission des droits de la personne du Québec* v. *J.M. Brouillette Inc.*, (1994) 23 CHRR D/495 (TDPQ); *Chiasson et Commission des droits de la personne du Québec* v. *Centre d'accueil Villa Plaisance*, [1995] RJQ 511 (TDPQ); *Bénéficiaires du Centre d'accueil Pavillon Saint-Théophile et Commission des droits de la personne du Québec* v. *Coutu*, [1995] RJQ 1628 (TDPQ), reversed, (1998) 1998 CarswellQue 907 (CA); *Gaumond et Commission des droits de la personne du Québec* v. *Société de transport de la communauté urbaine de Montréal, supra* note 844; *Roy et Commission des droits de la personne et des droits de la jeunesse du Québec* v. *Maksteel Québec Inc.*, [1997] RJQ 2891 (TDPQ), reversed, (2000) 2000 CarswellQue 2765 (CA), leave to appeal allowed, (2001) 2001 CarswellQue 1914 (SCC), affirmed, (2003) 2003 CarswellQue 2475 (SCC); *Dubé et Commission des droits de la personne et des droits de la jeunesse du Québec* v. *Martin*, (1997) 1997 CarswellQue 799, [1997] TDPQ 21 (TDPQ); *M.L. and Commission des droits de la personne et des droits de la jeunesse du Québec* v. *Maison des jeunes, supra* note 793; *Landriau et Commission des droits de la personne et des droits de la jeunesse du Québec* v. *Beaublanc inc.*, [1999] RJQ 1875 (TDPQ); *Bia-Domingo et Québec (Commission des droits de la personne et des droits de la jeunesse)* v. *Sinatra, supra* note 807; *Gagnon et Commission des droits de la personne et des droits de la jeunesse du Québec* v. *Quévillon, supra* note 807; *Rhéaume et Québec (Commission des droits de la personne et des droits de la jeunesse)* v. *Université Laval*, [2000] RJQ 2156 (TDPQ), reversed, (2005) 2005 CarswellQue 127 (CA); *Boisvert et Québec (Commission des droits de la personne et des droits de la jeunesse)* v. *Nicolet (Ville)*, [2001] RJQ 2735 (TDPQ); *Délicieux et Québec (Commission des droits de la personne et des droits de la jeunesse)* v. *Yazbeck, supra* note 807; *Forget et Québec (Commission des droits de la personne et des droits de la jeunesse)* v. *Bertrand*, [2001] RJQ 1684 (TDPQ); *O'Connor et Québec (Commission des droits de la personne et des droits de la jeunesse)* v. *Sfiridis*, (2002) 2002 CarswellQue 768, [2002] JTDPQ no 3 (TDPQ); *Commission des droits de la personne et des droits de la jeunesse du Québec* v. *Gagné*, (2003), 2003 CarswellQue 445, [2002] JTDPQ no 23 (TDPQ); *Commission des droits de la personne et des droits de la jeunesse du Québec* v. *Société de l'assurance automobile du Québec*, [2003] RJQ 1737 (TDPQ); *Commission des droits de la personne et des droits de la jeunesse* v. *Vallée*, [2003] RJQ 2009, 18 CCLT (3d) 27 (TDPQ), varied, [2005] RJQ 961 (CA); *Commission des droits de la personne et des droits de la jeunesse agissant en faveur de F.R.* v. *Caisse populaire Desjardins d'Amqui*, [2004] RJQ 355 (TDPQ); *Commission des droits de la personne*

fully emerged as an unacceptable ground of discrimination when the early international human rights documents were adopted", commented Justice La Forest in *McKinney* v. *University of Guelph*.[847] He referred to a General Assembly Resolution adopted in 1973[848] as evidence that "[t]he evolving right against discrimination on the ground of age is gaining ground".[849] Justice La Forest noted that the General Assembly's text was carefully worded, and discouraged discriminatory practices in employment based exclusively on age "wherever and whenever the overall situation allows".[850] The Ontario Court of Appeal seemed troubled by the fact that "age" was not enumerated as a prohibited form of discrimination in the *Universal Declaration of Human Rights* when it referred to that instrument's equality provisions.[851] In another Ontario case,[852] raising the issue of whether children under the age of sixteen are entitled in their own right to welfare assistance, a reference was made to the *Convention on the Rights of the Child*, particularly the definition of "child" in article 1 as a "human being below the age of 18 years unless, under the law applicable to the child, majority is attained earlier".[853]

International authorities may be quite helpful in addressing specific cases of unequal treatment, to determine whether these are in fact discrim-

---

et des droits de la jeunesse v. *Commission scolaire Des Phares*, [2005] RJQ 309 (TDPQ), leave to appeal allowed, (2005) 2005 CarswellQue 968 (CA), varied, (2006) 2006 CarswellQue 303 (CA); *Commission des droits de la personne et des droits de la jeunesse* v. *Poirier*, (2004) 2004 CarswellQue 907, [2004] JTDPQ no 5 (TDPQ); *Commission des droits de la personne et des droits de la jeunesse* v. *Collège Montmorency*, *supra* note 807; *Commission des droits de la personne et des droits de la jeunesse* v. *Pettas*, *supra* note 807.

847   *McKinney* v. *University of Guelph*, (1988) 46 DLR (4th) 193, 29 Admin LR 227, 24 OAC 241, affirmed, [1990] 3 SCR 229, 76 DLR (4th) 545, 91 CLLC 17,004, 13 CHRR D/171, 45 OAC 1, 118 NR 1, 2 OR (3d) 319n, at 295 (SCR).

848   "Questions of the Elderly and the Aged", GA Res. 3137 (XXVIII).

849   *McKinney* v. *University of Guelph*, *supra* note 847, at 296 (SCR).

850   *Ibid.*, at 297-298, 303.

851   *McKinney* v. *University of Guelph*, (1987) 46 DLR (4th) 193, 29 Admin LR 227, 24 OAC 241 (CA), affirmed, (1990) 1990 CarswellOnt 1019 (SCC). See K.J. Partsch, "The Contribution of Universal International Instruments on Human Rights", in Armand De Mestral et al., eds., *The Limitation of Human Rights in Comparative Constitutional Law*, Cowansville: Editions Yvon Blais, 1986, pp. 63-74, at 72: "The list of prohibited criteria in article 26, International Covenant on Civil and Political Rights differs from that in subsection 15(1) of the *Canadian Charter*. Age, mental or physical disability do not appear in the *Covenant*, and for good reasons. Property, language, political or other opinions, birth or other status appear only in the *Covenant* but not in subsection 15(1)."

852   *Mohamed* v. *Metropolitan Toronto (Department of Social Services, General Manager)*, (1996) 133 DLR (4th) 108 (Ont Div Ct), leave to appeal allowed, (1996) 1996 CarswellOnt 2271 (CA), at para. 37.

853   See also *Ontario (Attorney General)* v. *Pyke*, (1998) 167 DLR (4th) 170 (Ont Div Ct), at para. 29.

inatory within the meaning of section 15. For example, the Inter-American Court has held that differential residence requirements for citizenship applications, depending on national origin, are not "inconsistent with the nature and purpose of the grant of nationality to expedite the naturalization procedures for those who objectively shared much closer historical, cultural and spiritual bonds with the people of Costa Rica". The Court added: "No discrimination exists if the difference in treatment has a legitimate purpose and if it does not lead to situations which are contrary to justice, to reason or to the nature of things." An attempt by the government to justify differential treatment of immigration or citizenship applications based on national or linguistic origin would find some support in this decision. In the same Inter-American Court case, a violation of the equality provisions of the *American Convention on Human Rights* by Costa Rica's naturalization legislation was found because the provisions treated foreign women who married Costa Rican men differently than foreign men who married Costa Rican women.[854]

The Human Rights Committee has considered whether differences in social benefits, based on whether or not the beneficiaries are legally married or merely cohabiting, constitute discrimination:

> The right to equality before the law and to equal protection of the law without any discrimination does not make all differences of treatment discriminatory. A differentiation based on reasonable and objective criteria does not amount to prohibited discrimination within the meaning of article 26 [of the *International Covenant on Civil and Political Rights*]. . .the decision to enter into a legal status by marriage, which provides, in Netherlands law, both for certain benefits and for certain duties and responsibilities, lies entirely with the cohabiting persons. By choosing not to enter into marriage, Mr Danning and cohabitant have not, in law, assumed the full extent of the duties and responsibilities incumbent on married couples. Consequently, Mr Danning does not receive the full benefits provided for in Netherlands law for married couples. The Committee concludes that the differentiation complained of by Mr Danning does not constitute discrimination, in the sense of article 26 of the Covenant.[855]

In *Schafer v. Canada (Attorney General)*,[856] the issue was whether section 15 of the *Charter* was infringed by a statutory scheme in Ontario that provided better maternity and parental benefits to biological parents than to adoptive parents. International human rights law instruments were

---

854 *Proposed Amendments to the Naturalization Provisions of the Political Constitution of Costa Rica,* Advisory Opinion OC-4/84, *supra* note 834, at 301.

855 *Danning v. Netherlands* (No. 180/1984), UN Doc. CCPR/C/OP/2, p. 205, 9 *Human Rights Law Journal* 259, paras. 13-14.

856 *Schafer v. Canada (Attorney General),* (1996) 135 DLR (4th) 707 (Ont Gen Div), reversed, (1997) 149 DLR (4th) 705 (Ont CA), leave to appeal refused, (1998) 49 CRR (2d) 186 (SCC).

invoked – such as the *Universal Declaration of Human Rights*,[857] the *Convention on the Rights of the Child*[858] and an International Labour Organization instrument[859] – but they were not used in holding that there was an unjustifiable *Charter* violation in this case. This conclusion was overturned in part by the Ontario Court of Appeal, which did not refer to the international law sources.[860]

Provisions of the *Indian Act*[861] denying band members who are not resident on reservations the right to vote in band elections was challenged under section 15 of the *Charter* in *Batchewana Indian Band* v. *Batchewana Indian Band*.[862] Justice Strayer of the Federal Court referred to the views of the Human Rights Committee in *Lovelace* v. *Canada*, which held another provision of the *Indian Act* to be contrary to the *International Covenant on Civil and Political Rights*.[863] Justice Strayer noted that "[w]hile the U.N. Human Rights Committee found that paragraph 12(1)(b) discriminated on the grounds of sex in depriving Mrs. Lovelace of Indian status, the Covenant had not been in force when that happened."[864] But although it is true that the repeal of section 12(1)(b) was associated with the entry into force of section 15 of the *Charter*, the real basis of the Human Rights Committee's views in *Lovelace* that there had been a breach of the *Covenant* was article 27, which protects the right of individuals belonging to ethnic, religious or linguistic minorities, in community with the other members of their group, to enjoy their own culture, to profess and practise their own religion, or to use their own language. Only one member of the eighteen-person Commit-

---

857   GA Res. 217 A (III), UN Doc. A/810, art. 10.
858   GA Res. 44/25, preamble and arts. 23, 24 & 26.
859   *ILO Maternity Protection Convention 1919, (No. 3)*, revised by *ILO Maternity Protection Convention, 1952 (No. 103)* and, since *Schafer*, by *ILO Maternity Protection Convention, 2000 (No. 183)*.
860   *Schafer* v. *Canada (Attorney General)*, *supra* note 856.
861   *Indian Act*, SRC 1985, c. I-5, preamble and arts. 23, 24 and 26.
862   [1994] 1 FC 394 (TD), varied, [1997] 1 FC 689 (CA), leave to appeal allowed, (1997) 215 NR 239n, [1999] 2 SCR 203, reconsideration refused, (2000) 2000 CarswellNat 2393 (SCC).
863   *Lovelace* v. *Canada* (No. 24/1977), UN Doc. CCPR/C/13/D/24/1977, UN Doc. CCPR/3/Add.1, Vol. II, p. 320, UN Doc. CCPR/C/OP/1, p. 83, [1983] *Canadian Human Rights Yearbook* 306, 68 ILR 17. For some of the judicial aftermath of *Lovelace*, see: *Raphaël* v. *Montagnais du Lac St-Jean Band*, (1995) 23 CHRR D/259 (Can. Human Rights Trib.).
864   *Batchewana Indian Band* v. *Batchewana Indian Band* [1994] 1 FC 394 (TD), varied, [1997] 1 FC 689 (CA), leave to appeal allowed, (1997) 215 NR 239n, [1999] 2 SCR 203, reconsideration refused, (2000) 2000 CarswellNat 2393 (SCC), at 414, note 18.

tee actually concluded that there had also been a breach of the non-discrimination provision, article 26.[865]

Several of the international instruments recognize a right to marry.[866] Although the right is quite distinct from the non-discrimination provisions considered in *Miron* v. *Trudel*, it was invoked by Justice Gonthier of the Supreme Court of Canada in order to confirm "what in my view requires little if any confirmation, namely that marriage is both a basic social institution and a fundamental right which states can legitimately legislative to foster".[867] Justice Gonthier, who drafted the reasons for the minority in *Miron*, used the argument in the context of section 15 in order to justify legislation that distinguished between married and unmarried or "common law" couples. The Supreme Court did not resort to international law in another of its 1995 equality trilogy cases, dealing with the rights of homosexual couples, and there is in fact little in the instruments upon which to build much of a case.[868] This was confirmed in the advisory opinion sought by the Federal Government in *Reference re Same-Sex Marriage*,[869] where the Supreme Court of Canada made no international references in holding that the proposed legislation extending the capacity to marry persons of the same sex was consistent with the *Charter*.

The international law provisions on the right to marry generally grant this to "men and women". The wording is ambiguous, and seems capable of supporting a variety of interpretations. It is doubtful that at the time these provisions were adopted, their drafters even contemplated the possibility of same-sex marriage. Caselaw of the European Court of Human Rights supports the view that a right to marry is confined to heterosexual couples.[870] Similarly, the Human Rights Committee has held: "Use of the term 'men and women', rather than the general terms used elsewhere in Part III of the Covenant, has been consistently and uniformly understood as indicating that the treaty obligations of States parties stemming from article 23, para-

---

865 *Lovelace* v. *Canada, supra* note 863, Individual opinion appended to the Committee's views at the request of Mr. Nejib Bouziri.

866 *Universal Declaration of Human Rights, supra* note 857, art. 16(1); *International Covenant on Civil and Political Rights*, (1976) 999 UNTS 171, [1976] CTS 47, art. 23(2); *American Convention on Human Rights*, (1979) 1144 UNTS 123, OASTS 36, art. 17(2); *European Convention on Human Rights*, (1955) 213 UNTS 221, ETS 5, art. 12.

867 *Miron* v. *Trudel*, [1995] 2 SCR 418, 181 NR 253, 81 OAC 253, at 450 (SCR).

868 *Egan* v. *Canada*, [1995] 2 SCR 513, 182 NR 161.

869 *Reference re Same-Sex Marriage*, [2004] 3 SCR 698.

870 *Rees* v. *United Kingdom*, 17 October 1986, Series A, No. 106. According to paragraph 19, "the right to marry guaranteed by Article 12 refers to the traditional marriage between persons of the opposite biological sex". In *Cossey* v. *United Kingdom*, 27 September 1990, Series A, No. 184, at para. 18, the European Court of Human Rights said recent developments "cannot be said to evidence any general abandonment of the traditional concept of marriage".

graph 2, of the Covenant is to recognize as marriage only the union between a man and a woman wishing to marry each other."[871] Two Committee members wrote that while they agreed with the conclusion, it

> . . .should not be read as a general statement that differential treatment between married couples and same-sex couples not allowed under the law to marry would never amount to a violation of article 26. . . .Therefore, a denial of certain rights or benefits to same-sex couples that are available to married couples may amount to discrimination prohibited under article 26, unless otherwise justified on reasonable and objective criteria.[872]

4.10   Minority Rights

Maxwell Cohen and Anne F. Bayefsky considered that the official language provisions and minority language educational rights provisions of the *Canadian Charter* contained in sections 16 to 23 were "uniquely Canadian" and unlikely to provoke any application of international law.[873] But the Supreme Court of Canada has sent out a slightly different message. "Language rights are a well known species of human rights and should be approached accordingly", wrote Justice La Forest in *R. v. Mercure*.[874] Justice La Forest referred explicitly to article 27 of the *International Covenant on Civil and Political Rights*, which recognizes the right of linguistic minorities to use their own language. After attempts to invoke caselaw under the *European Convention* were first summarily dismissed by the Quebec Court of Appeal in one of the *Charter of the French Language* cases, the Supreme Court of Canada indicated that it was more receptive to international precedents, which prompted the Quebec Court of Appeal to revise its position.[875]

Article 27 of the *International Covenant on Civil and Political Rights* recognizes the rights of linguistic minorities "to use their own language".[876] The Human Rights Committee has found that language is also protected by

---

871   *Joslin et al. v. New* Zealand (No. 902/1999), UN Doc. CCPR/C/75/D/902/1999, paras. 8.2. and 8.3.

872   *Ibid.*, Individual opinion of Committee members Mr. Rajsoomer Lallah and Mr. Martin Scheinin (concurring).

873   Maxwell Cohen & Anne F. Bayefsky, "The Canadian Charter of Rights and Freedoms and International Law", (1983) 61 *Canadian Bar Review* 265, at 268.

874   *R. v. Mercure*, [1988] 1 SCR 234, 48 DLR (4th) 1, 39 CCC (3d) 385, [1988] 2 WWR 577, 65 Sask R 1, 83 NR 81, at 268 (SCR).

875   This is discussed *supra* at 300-302.

876   Considered by the Human Rights Committee in *J.H.* v. *Canada* (No. 187/1985), UN Doc. CCPR/C/OP/2, p. 63, 6 *Human Rights Law Journal* 240, [1986] *Canadian Human Rights Yearbook* 195; *S.R.* v. *France* (No. 243/1987), UN Doc. CCPR/C/31/D/243/1987, UN Doc. CCPR/C/OP/2, p. 72.

article 19, which governs freedom of expression.[877] The Human Rights Committee has declared that "positive measures by States may also be necessary to protect the identity of a minority and the rights of its members to enjoy and develop their. . .language".[878] The *Vienna Declaration and Programme of Action*, adopted at the Vienna Conference on Human Rights in 1993, affirms that "persons belonging to minorities have the right. . .to use their own language in private and in public, freely and without interference or any form of discrimination".[879] The *Convention on the Rights of the Child* has a similar provision, adding the dimension of indigenous peoples: "In those States in which ethnic, religious or linguistic minorities or persons of indigenous origin exist, a child belonging to such a minority or who is indigenous shall not be denied the right, in community with other members of his or her group, to enjoy his or her own culture, to profess and practise his or her own religion, or to use his or her own language."[880] The regional instruments are more cautious, and lack a comparable minority rights provision, although the *European Convention on Human Rights* does prohibit discrimination based on "association with a national minority".[881]

The *Canadian Charter* is quite limited in the scope it allows to minority rights.[882] There is no evidence in the preparatory work of the *Charter* of any attempt to integrate the rather timid provisions of article 27 of the *International Covenant on Civil and Political Rights* into the *Charter*. Recently, there has been renewed interest in international human rights law concerning minority rights, and this has led to a *Declaration* adopted by the United Nations General Assembly,[883] as well as a *Framework Convention* adopted by the Council of Europe. The Council of Europe's *Framework Convention* is largely inspired by the *Copenhagen Document* of the Conference on Security and Cooperation in Europe (now the Organization for Security and Cooperation in Europe); Canada, which is a member of the OSCE, played

877 *Ballantyne and Davidson, and McIntyre* v. *Canada* (Nos. 359/1989 and 385/1989), UN Doc. CCPR/C/47/D/385/1989, UN Doc. A/48/40, Vol. II, p. 91, 14 *Human Rights Law Journal* 171, 11 *Netherlands Quarterly of Human Rights* 469.

878 "General Comment No. 24 (52), Issues relating to reservations made upon ratification or accession to the Covenant or the Optional Protocols thereto, or in relation to declarations under article 41 of the Covenant", UN Doc. CCPR/C/21/Rev.1/Add.6, para. 6.2.

879 *Vienna Declaration and Programme of Action*, UN Doc. A/CONF.157/24, (1993) 14 *Human Rights Law Journal* 352, para. 5, at 353 (*HRLJ*).

880 *Convention on the Rights of the Child*, *supra* note 858, art. 30.

881 *European Convention on Human Rights*, *supra* note 866, art. 14.

882 See: Mark Power & Pierre Foucher, "Language Rights and Education", in Gérald-A. Beaudoin & Errol P. Mendes, eds., *Canadian Charter of Rights and Freedoms*, 4th ed., Markham, Ont., LexisNexis Butterworths, 2005, pp. 1093-1167.

883 "Declaration on the Rights of Persons Belonging to National or Ethnic Religious and Linguistic Minorities", UN Doc. A/RES/48/138, 14 *Human Rights Law Journal* 54.

an important role in drafting the minority rights provisions of the *Copenhagen Document*.[884]

Only two linguistic minorities are recognized by the *Canadian Charter*, and they are granted the detailed rights set out in section 23 of the *Charter*. However, the right of individuals belonging to linguistic minorities to use their own language receives a limited degree of protection from section 2(b) of the *Charter*.[885] Minorities may also invoke the provisions of section 27 of the *Canadian Charter*, which is a purely interpretative provision: "This Charter shall be interpreted in a manner consistent with the preservation and enhancement of the multicultural heritage of Canadians." According to Justices Cory and Iacobucci in *R. v. Zundel*, the model for section 27 of the *Charter*, which recognizes the multicultural heritage of Canadians, is article 27 of the *International Covenant on Civil and Political Rights*.[886] Canada has explained to the Human Rights Committee that it does not adopt a "melting pot" approach to minorities, and that this is dictated by section 27 of the *Charter*.[887]

In *Big M Drug Mart*, Justice Belzil of the Alberta Court of Appeal considered the minority language education provisions found in section 29 of the *Charter* in an effort to demonstrate that Canada has not taken a position against an established religion. He observed that the *International Covenant on Civil and Political Rights* does not proscribe established state religions, and that anti-establishmentarianism is "noticeably absent" from the *American Declaration of the Rights and Duties of Man*. In light of the international authorities, Justice Belzil concluded that the omission of an anti-establishment declaration in section 29 was "obviously intentional".[888]

Aboriginal groups have frequently attempted to invoke international human rights law before Canadian, and international, tribunals. As early as the 1920s, they were present at the League of Nations in efforts to enforce fundamental rights. Their efforts have been hampered by the relatively underdeveloped state of the protection of aboriginal rights. The only applicable normative instrument, *ILO Convention No. 169 Concerning Indige-*

---

884 "Document of the Copenhagen Meeting of the Conference on the Human Dimension of the CSCE", 1989, paras. 31-36.

885 *Ford* v. *Québec (AG)*, [1988] 2 SCR 712, 54 DLR (4th) 577, 19 QAC 69, 36 CRR 1, 90 NR 84, 10 CHRR D/5559. The same view of the role of "freedom of expression" in the protection of the right to use minority languages is taken by the Human Rights Committee: *Ballantyne and Davidson, and McIntyre* v. *Canada* (Nos. 359/1989 and 385/1989), UN Doc. CCPR/C/47/D/385/1989, UN Doc. A/48/40, Vol. II, p. 91, 14 *Human Rights Law Journal* 171, 11 *Netherlands Quarterly of Human Rights* 469.

886 *R.* v. *Zundel*, [1992] 2 SCR 731, 95 DLR (4th) 202, 16 CR (4th) 1, 75 CCC (3d) 449, at 815 (SCR).

887 UN Doc. CCPR/C/SR.1013, (3). See also: UN Doc. CCPR/C/SR.211, para. 26.

888 *R.* v. *Big M Drug Mart Ltd.*, [1984] 1 WWR 625, 5 DLR (4th) 121, 9 CCC (3d) 310, 28 Alta LR (2d) 289, 49 AR 194, 7 CRR 92 (CA), affirmed, [1985] 1 SCR 295.

nous and Tribal Peoples in Independent Countries, has not been ratified by Canada.[889] A draft declaration on the rights of indigenous peoples,[890] which was developed by the United Nations Working Group on Indigenous Populations, was presented in 1994.[891] The project has since been taken up by an intersessional working group set up by the Commission on Human Rights in 1995,[892] in which Canada is an active participant.[893] Although it was hoped that the draft declaration would be adopted by the General Assembly in 2004, material disagreements particularly in regard to indigenous peoples' right of self-determination have blocked a possible agreement.[894] In 1997, the Inter-American Commission on Human Rights approved a draft declaration on the rights of indigenous peoples[895] which is scheduled to be adopted by the Organization of American States General Assembly.[896]

In attempts to make use of the petition mechanism created by the *Optional Protocol to the International Covenant*, Canadian Aboriginal groups have invoked the provisions of both article 27 of the *International Covenant on Civil and Political Rights*, which protects individuals belonging to ethnic, linguistic and religious minorities, and article 1, which enshrines the right of peoples to self-determination. Like article 27, article 1 has no direct counterpart in the *Canadian Charter*. The Human Rights Committee has held that individual petitions invoking article 1 are inadmissible, because the right to self-determination belongs to peoples and not

---

889   ILO, *Official Bulletin*, vol. LXXII, 1989, Ser. A., no. 2, p. 63; entered into force September 5, 1991. Ratifications have been filed by Bolivia, Colombia, Costa Rica, Mexico, Norway, Paraguay and Peru.

890   On the draft declaration generally, see: Caroline E. Foster, "Articulating Self-Determination in the Draft Declaration on the Rights of Indigenous Peoples", (2001) 12 *European Journal of International Law* 141.

891   UN Doc. E/CN.4/Sub.2/1994/2/Add.1.

892   CHR Res. 1995/32, 3 March 1995.

893   See: Canada, Minister of Indian and Northern Development, *Aboriginal Self Government: The Government of Canada's Approach to Implementation of the Inherent Right and the Negotiation of Aboriginal Self-Government*, Ottawa: Public Works and Government Services Canada, 1995, presented to the Commission of Human Rights intersessional working group on 31 October 1996.

894   See: Patrick Thornberry, *Indigenous Peoples and Human Rights*, Manchester: Manchester University Press, 2002.

895   *American Declaration on the Rights of Indigenous Peoples*, OEA/Ser/L/V/.II.95 Doc.6, 26 February 1997.

896   The Organization of American States affirmed its intention to adopt the draft declaration in a resolution: Organization of American States General Assembly, Res. 1851 (XXXXII-0/02), 4 June 2002.

individuals.[897] However, the Committee has, on two occasions, found Canada to be in violation of article 27 in cases involving aboriginal rights.[898] Recently, the Committee rendered its opinion on the communication of *Apirana Mahuika et al.* v. *New Zealand*,[899] where it reiterated its view that while article 1 is not enough in itself to support a complaint, it may nevertheless be relevant to the interpretation and application of other rights guaranteed in the *International Covenant on Civil and Political Rights*.

In *Montana Band of Indians* v. *Canada*, four Bands sought a declaration from the Federal Court (Trial Division) that articles 1 and 27 of the *International Covenant* are binding on Canada. They also invoked customary international law in support of their application. The Bands submitted that ". . .although, by reason of their being aboriginal people they are not a minority in the usual sense, nevertheless they are entitled to the benefit of Article 27, being a minority for the purposes of the said Article". Justice Jerome concluded that the failure of the Band to identify a specific grievance meant that such a claim must be struck.[900]

4.11   Right to a Remedy

Rights are illusory if they have no remedies.[901] Section 24 of the *Charter* entitles anyone whose rights have been violated to seek redress before an appropriate tribunal.[902] As the Supreme Court of Canada has stated, however, this does not involve "the wholesale invention of a parallel system for the administration of *Charter* rights over and above the machinery already

---

897 *Marshall* et al. (*Micmaq Tribal Society*) v. *Canada* (No. 205/1986), UN Doc. CCPR/C/43/D/205/1986, UN Doc. A/47/40, p. 213; *Lubicon Lake Band (Bernard Ominayak)* v. *Canada* (No. 167/1984) UN Doc. CCPR/C/38/D/167/1984, UN Doc. A/45/40, Vol. II, p. 1, 11 *Human Rights Law Journal* 305, [1991-92] *Canadian Human Rights Yearbook* 221.

898 *Lovelace* v. *Canada* (No. 24/1977), UN Doc. CCPR/C/13/D/24/1977, UN Doc. CCPR/3/Add.1, Vol. II, p. 320, UN Doc. CCPR/C/OP/1, p. 83, [1983] *Canadian Human Rights Yearbook* 306, 68 ILR 17; *Lubicon Lake Band (Bernard Ominayak)* v. *Canada* (No. 167/1984), *ibid.*

899 *Mahuika et al.* v. *New Zealand* (No. 547/1993), UN Doc. CCPR/C/70/D/547/1993.

900 *Montana Band of Indians* v. *Canada*, [1990] 2 FC 198 (TD), reversed, (1991) 120 NR 200 (CA), leave to appeal refused, (1991) 136 NR 421n (SCC), at 203 (FC).

901 This typically common law idea originally comes from a three centuries-old English case, *Ashby* v. *White*, (1703) 2 Ld. Raym. 938, at 953, in which Chief Justice Holt said that "it is a vain thing to imagine a right without a remedy".

902 See: Dale Gibson, "Enforcement of the Canadian Charter of Rights and Freedoms", in Gérald-A. Beaudoin & Errol P. Mendes, eds., *Canadian Charter of Rights and Freedoms*, 4th ed., Markham, Ont., LexisNexis Butterworths, 2005, pp. 1321-1398; and Kent Roach, *Constitutional Remedies in Canada* (looseleaf), Toronto: Canada Law Book, 1994.

available for the administration of justice".[903] Section 24 is directly inspired by international human rights law. It was proposed to the Hays-Joyal Committee following representations by the Canadian Bar Association to the effect that its omission would violate the *International Covenant on Civil and Political Rights*.[904] According to article 2(3) of the *Covenant*:

Each State Party to the present Covenant undertakes:

(a) To ensure that any person whose rights or freedoms as herein recognized are violated shall have an effective remedy, notwithstanding that the violation has been committed by persons acting in an official capacity;

(b) To ensure that any person claiming such a remedy shall have his right thereto determined by competent judicial, administrative or legislative authorities, or by any other competent authority provided for by the legal system of the State, and to develop the possibilities of judicial remedy;

(c) To ensure that the competent authorities shall enforce such remedies when granted.

The right to *habeas corpus* is, of course, also found in section 10(c) of the *Canadian Charter*. Unlike the international instruments, including the *Covenant*, the *Canadian Charter* does not recognize a right to compensation where an individual has been wrongly convicted and punished for a criminal offence.[905]

The right to an appropriate remedy was discussed by Justice Lamer, as he then was, in *R. v. Mills*,[906] who noted that section 24 of the *Charter* is consistent with article 8 of the *Universal Declaration* and article 2 of the *International Covenant on Civil and Political Rights*. Similar provisions can be found in the other international instruments.[907] The international

---

903 *R. v. Mills*, [1986] 1 SCR 863, 58 OR (2d) 544n, 16 OAC 81, 29 DLR (4th) 161, 26 CCC (3d) 481, 52 CR (3d) 1, 67 NR 241.

904 Maxwell Cohen & Anne F. Bayefsky, "The Canadian Charter of Rights and Freedoms and International Law", (1983), 61 *Canadian Bar Review* 265, at 304.

905 *International Covenant on Civil and Political Rights*, (1976) 999 UNTS 171, [1976] CTS 47, art. 14(6); *American Convention on Human Rights*, (1979) 1144 UNTS 123, OASTS 36, art. 10. Both the *Covenant* (art. 6(4)) and the *American Convention* (art. 4(4)) provide for a right to seek amnesty, pardon or commutation in the case of a death sentence. The *American Convention* also recognizes a "right of reply" in the case of defamation (art. 14).

906 *Supra* note 903, at 881 (SCR). His remarks are cited in: *Mooring v. Canada (National Parole Board)*, [1996] 1 SCR 75, 104 CCC (3d) 97. See also: *R. v. Ward*, (1989) 43 CRR 174 (Man Prov Ct).

907 *American Declaration of the Rights and Duties of Man*, OAS Doc. OEA/Ser. L./V/II.23, doc. 21, rev. 6, art. XVIII; *American Convention on Human Rights, supra* note 905, art. 25; *European Convention on Human Rights*, (1955) 213 UNTS 221, ETS 5, art. 13; *Helsinki Final Act*, Principle VII; "Document of the Copenhagen Meeting of the Conference on the Human Dimension of the CSCE", 1989, para. 40.5; "Document of the

human rights instruments also recognize a specific remedy be available to "[a]nyone who is deprived of his liberty by arrest or detention. . .to take proceedings before a court, in order that that court may decide without delay on the lawfulness of his detention and order his release if the detention is not lawful."[908] Recently, in an action against the Canadian government for damages and other remedies arising out of a head tax imposed on Chinese immigrants between 1885 and 1923, the plaintiffs grounded their claim in domestic constitutional law, but also in international law, invoking as an aid to interpretation the *Charter of the United Nations*, the *Universal Declaration of Human Rights*, the *International Covenant on Economic, Social and Cultural Rights*, the *International Covenant on Civil and Political Rights*, the United Nations *Declaration on the Elimination of All Forms of Racial Discrimination* and the *International Convention on the Elimination of All Forms of Racial Discrimination*. In the end, however, the argument was rejected by Justice Cumming of the Ontario Superior Court of Justice because it "would necessarily involve the application of norms and principles that did not exist at the material times".[909]

In *BCGEU* v. *Attorney-General of British Columbia*, Chief Justice Dickson discussed the question of remedy with reference to a judgment of the European Court of Human Rights:

> To paraphrase the European Court of Human Rights in *Golder* v. *U.K.*, (1975) 1 E.H.R.R. 524 at 537, it would be inconceivable that Parliament and the provinces would describe in such detail the rights and freedoms guaranteed by the Charter and should not first protect that which alone makes it in fact possible to benefit from such guarantees, that is access to a court. As the Court of Human Rights truly stated: "The fair, public and expeditious characteristics of judicial proceedings are of no value at all if there are no judicial proceedings.[910]

Moscow Meeting of the Conference on the Human Dimension of the CSCE", 1991, paras. 18.2-18.4.

908   *International Covenant on Civil and Political Rights, supra* note 905, art. 9(4); *European Convention on Human Rights, ibid.*, art. 5(4); *American Convention on Human Rights, supra* note 905, art. 7(6); *Convention on the Rights of the Child*, GA Res. 44/25, art. 37(d).

909   *Mack* v. *Canada (Attorney General)*, (2001) 55 OR (3d) 113 (SC), affirmed, (2002) 60 OR (3d) 737, 217 DLR (4th) 583, 96 CRR (2d) 254, 165 OAC 17 (CA), leave to appeal refused, (2003) 319 NR 196n (SCC), at para. 40.

910   *BCGEU* v. *Attorney-General of British Columbia*, [1988] 2 SCR 214, 53 DLR (4th) 1, 44 CCC (3d) 289, [1988] 6 WWR 577, 71 Nfld. & PEIR. 93, 22 APR 93, 30 CPC (2d) 221, 88 CLLC 14,047, 87 NR 241, 31 BCLR (2d) 273. See also: *Re BC Govt. Employees Union*, [1985] 5 WWR 421 (BC CA), leave to appeal allowed, [1985] 2 SCR vi (SCC), affirmed, (1988) 1988 CarswellBC 762 (SCC), at p 427 (SCR). For a discussion of the situation in European law, see: Jean-François Flauss, "Le droit à un recours effectif: l'art. 13 de la Convention européenne des droits de l'Homme dans la jurisprudence de la Commission et de la Cour", in Gérald-A. Beaudoin, *Vues canadiennes et européennes*

International courts frequently order that a remedy be provided where the State Party is in violation of the petitioner's human rights. In the case of the European Court of Human Rights, this can also involve an award of damages and recovery of judicial costs.[911]

4.12   Derogation and Section 33 Procedure

Although it has rarely been used, one of the most controversial sections of the *Canadian Charter* at the time it was adopted is what is known as the derogation, "override" or "notwithstanding" clause:[912]

33. (1) [Exception where express declaration] Parliament or the legislature of a province may expressly declare in an Act of Parliament or of the legislature, as the case may be, that the Act or a provision thereof shall operate notwithstanding a provision included in section 2 or sections 7 to 15 of this Charter.

---

des droits et libertés, Cowansville: Editions Yvon Blais, 1989, pp. 255-292. On article 13 of the *European Convention*, see: *Boyle* et al. v. *United Kingdom*, 27 April 1988, Series A, No. 131; *Plattform "Ärzte für das Leben"* v. *Austria*, 21 June 1988, Series A, No. 139; *Powell and Rayner* v. *United Kingdom*, 21 February 1990, Series A, No. 172.

911 *König* v. *Federal Republic of Germany*, 10 March 1980, Series A, No. 36, 2 EHRR 170, 59 ILR 370, 17 *ILM* 1151; *Artico* v. *Italy*, 13 May 1980, Series A, No. 37, 3 EHRR 1; *Airey* v. *Ireland*, 2 February 1981, Series A, No. 41, 3 EHRR 592, 67 ILR 388; *Young, James and Webster* v. *United Kingdom* (App. Nos. 7601/76 and 7806/77), (1980) 9 DR 126, 3 EHRR 20; *Van Droogenbroeck* v. *Belgium*, 25 April 1983, Series A, No. 63; *Bagetta* v. *Italy*, 25 June 1987, Series A, No. 119, 10 EHRR 325; *Milasi* v. *Italy*, 25 June 1987, Series A, No. 119, 10 EHRR 333; *DeCubber* v. *Belgium (art. 50)*, 14 September 1987, Series A, No. 124; *Gillow* v. *United Kingdom (art 50)*, 14 September 1987, Series A, No. 124; *H.* v. *Belgium*, 30 November 1987, Series A, No. 127, 10 EHRR 339; *Feldbrugge* v. *The Netherlands (art. 50)*, 17 July 1987, Series A, No. 124; *O.* v. *United Kingdom (art. 50)*, 9 June 1988, Series A, No. 136; *H.* v. *United Kingdom, (art. 50)*, 9 June 1988, Series A, No. 136; *W.* v. *United Kingdom, (art. 50)*, 9 June 1988, Series A, No. 136; *B.* v. *United Kingdom, (art. 50)*, 9 June 1988, Series A, No. 136; *R.* v. *United Kingdom, (art. 50)*, 9 June 1988, Series A, No. 136; *Weeks* v. *United Kingdom (art. 50)*, 5 October 1988, Series A, No. 145; *Bozano* v. *France*, 2 December 1987, Series A, No. 124; *Olsson* v. *Sweden*, 24 March 1988, Series A, No. 130, 11 EHRR 259; *Bock* v. *Federal Republic of Germany*, 29 March 1989, Series A, No. 150; *Neves e Silva* v. *Portugal*, 27 April 1989, Series A, No. 153.

912 Not to be confused with the "limitation" clause found in section 1 of the *Charter*, as did the Alberta Court of Appeal in *Black* v. *Law Society of Alberta*, [1986] 3 WWR 591, 27 DLR (4th) 527, Alta LR (2d) 1, 68 AR 259, 20 Admin LR 140, 20 CRR 177 (CA), affirmed, [1989] 1 SCR 591, 58 DLR (4th) 317, 37 Admin LR 161, 38 CRR 193, [1989] 4 WWR 1, 66 Alta LR (2d) 97, 96 AR 352, 93 NR 266, at 545-547 (DLR). Limitation clauses and derogations clauses may often accomplish the same objective, and courts would almost certainly consider an "override" of certain rights in time of national emergency to be a "reasonably justified limitation": Rusen Ergec, *Les droits de l'homme à l'épreuve des circonstances exceptionnelles; Etude sur l'article 15 de la Convention européenne des droits de l'homme*, Brussels: Editions Bruylant, 1987, at 27, 222.

According to the Quebec Court of Appeal, this clause permits Parliament or a provincial legislature to reacquire the sovereignty that it lost with the proclamation of the *Charter*, providing of course that the declaration of derogation follows the requisite formalities.[913] The provision, according to Gérald-A. Beaudoin, "n'est pas une matière d'importation."[914]

Although it is true to state that Canada's derogation clause was inspired by political compromises of the federal system and the complexities of repatriation of the constitution,[915] and as well perhaps by a reluctance to break completely with the English tradition of Parliamentary sovereignty, it is not correct to suggest that there is no counterpart in the international instruments.[916] The *International Covenant on Civil and Political Rights*, the *European Convention* and the *American Convention* all provide for derogation in times of public emergency (the formulation varies somewhat in the three instruments).[917] Like the *Canadian Charter*, they also contemplate a mechanism of political control, whereby the derogation must be publicly denounced. In Canada, it is the legislature that must make the required declaration, which is valid only for five years, at which time it must be renewed. In the international documents, notification of the derogation must be made to other States parties as well as to the Secretary-General of the United Nations, the Council of Europe or the Organization of American States, as the case may be. Both the *Canadian Charter* and the

---

913 *Alliance des professeurs de Montréal* v. *PG Québec*, [1985] CA 376, 21 DLR (4th) 354, 18 CRR 195, [1985] RDJ 439.

914 Gérald-A. Beaudoin, "Les clauses dérogatoire et limitatives des instruments canadiens des droits de la personne", in Daniel Turp & Gérald-A. Beaudoin, *Perspectives canadiennes et européennes des droits de la personne*, Cowansville: Editions Yvon Blais, 1986, pp. 139-157, at 147. See also André Binette, "Le pouvoir dérogatoire de l'article 33 de la *Charte canadienne des droits et libertés* et la structure de la Constitution du Canada", (2003) *Revue du Barreau* (No. sp.) 107.

915 Roger Tassé, "Application de la Charte canadienne des droits et libertés", in Gérald-A. Beaudoin & Ed Ratushny, eds., *The Canadian Charter of Rights and Freedoms*, 2nd ed., Toronto: Carswell, 1989, pp. 75-142, at 117; James G. Matkin, "The Negotiation of the Charter of Rights: The Provincial Perspective", in Paul Weiler & Robin Elliott, eds., *Litigating the Values of a Nation: The Canadian Charter of Rights and Freedoms*, Toronto: Carswell, 1986, pp. 27-35.

916 See: Marie Paré, "La légitimité de la clause dérogatoire de la Charte canadienne des droits et libertés en regard du droit international", (1995) 29 *Revue juridique Thémis* 627.

917 *International Covenant on Civil and Political Rights, supra* note 905, art. 4(1); *European Convention on Human Rights, supra* note 907, art. 15(1); *American Convention on Human Rights, supra* note 905, art. 27(1). Also: *European Social Charter*, (1965) 529 UNTS 89, ETS 25, art. 30; "Document of the Copenhagen Meeting of the Conference on the Human Dimension of the CSCE", 1989, paras. 16, 25; "Document of the Moscow Meeting of the Conference on the Human Dimension of the CSCE", 1991, para. 28.

international instruments enumerate a number of rights which are non-derogable under any circumstances, although the Inter-American Court of Human Rights has identified at least one other right, that of *habeas corpus*, which is non-derogable and yet which is not enumerated as such.[918]

The *Canadian Charter* breaks with the international models in two respects. First, the enumeration of rights subject to derogation under the *Canadian Charter* differs substantially from the international models. Under the *Charter*, no derogation under section 33 is permitted with respect to democratic rights (section 3-5), mobility rights (section 6), equality of men and women (section 28) and the language and education rights set out in sections 16 to 23. The fundamental freedoms of section 2, and the legal rights of sections 7 to 15, are thus vulnerable to Parliamentary attack. The non-derogable rights in the international documents vary somewhat from one to another. The *International Covenant on Civil and Political Rights*, the *European Convention* and the *American Convention* all consider the right to life, the prohibition of torture and slavery, and the non-retroactivity of penal legislation to be immune from derogation, even in times of war and crisis. Individually, the *International Covenant on Civil and Political Rights* and the *American Convention* also provide for a number of other non-derogable rights, such as recognition of juridical personality, freedom of thought, conscience, and religion, the rights of children and of the family, imprisonment for debt, the right to a name and certain political rights.[919] It is unthinkable that a Canadian legislative assembly or Parliament would suspend such core rights as the prohibition of cruel and unusual punishment, but this is what section 33 appears to allow.

The Canadian government took the position, in its pleadings before the Human Rights Committee in the *Ballantiyne case*, that "while a legislative override in respect of abortion or military conscription would be permissible, s. 33 could never be invoked to permit acts clearly prohibited by international law, such as summary executions or disappearances".[920] It is reassuring that the Canadian government publicly proclaims this view, but it is not binding in law and certainly of no effect with respect to the provinces.

The other significant difference between the *Canadian Charter* and the international instruments is that in Canada no state of war or emergency is necessary for derogation. Indeed, no justification whatsoever is required. In

---

918 *Habeas corpus in Emergency Situations (Non Derogable Guarantee)*, Advisory Opinion OC-8/87, Series A No. 8, 9 *Human Rights Law Journal* 94, 27 *ILM* 1588, 11 EHRR 33. Similarly, "General Comment No. 29, States of Emergency (Art. 4)", UN Doc. CCPR/C/21/Rev.1/Add.11, paras. 14-15.

919 *International Covenant on Civil and Political Rights, supra* note 905, art. 4(2); *European Convention on Human Rights, supra* note 907, art. 15(2); *American Convention on Human Rights, supra* note 905, art. 27(2).

920 Quoted in: *Immeubles Claude Dupont Inc. v. Québec*, [1994] RJQ 1968 (SC), at 1974.

the European system, even where the required formalities are followed, an individual or State can still challenge the legality of the derogation before the court, in effect arguing that the judiciary should pass judgment on the fact situation and itself determine whether a state of war or emergency exists.[921] In Canada, the only judicial control on a section 33 derogation would be one of form.[922] Canada explained this to the Human Rights Committee in its fourth periodic report:

> To date, the Government of Canada has never sought to invoke the override power contained in section 33. The provision has been used by two provinces – Saskatchewan and Quebec. At this point, given the infrequency with which the provision has been invoked and the resultant absence of jurisprudence, the precise effects of section 33 remain uncertain. The only guidance thus far comes from a Supreme Court of Canada decision holding that a reference to the Charter provision(s) sought to be overridden is sufficient for an enactment to qualify under section 33, but that section 33 does not allow Parliament or a legislature to enact retroactive override provisions (Ford v. A.G. Québec). Beyond this, it remains uncertain what, if any, limitations beyond those set out in the provision itself (i.e. requirement of express declaration and the five-year limitation rule) the courts may see fit to impose upon the use of the notwithstanding clause.[923]

Following proclamation of the *Charter* on 17 April 1982, Quebec's National Assembly declared a section 33 derogation of all provincial legislation,[924] something that was not renewed upon its expiration in April 1987. In any case, the validity of the blanket derogation was successfully

---

921   In the European Commission's earliest interstate case, Greece challenged the behaviour of the United Kingdom colonial government in Cyprus: *Greece* v. *United Kingdom* (App. No. 176/56, 299/57), (1958-59) 2 European Convention on Human Rights Yearbook 182, 25 ILR 168. In its first case of an individual petition, the application of the *Offences of the State, [Amendment] Act 1940* in Ireland was contested: *Lawless* v. *United Kingdom*, 1 July 1961, Series A, No. 3, 1 EHRR 15. See also: *Ireland* v. *United Kingdom*, 18 January 1978, Series A, No. 25, 2 EHRR 25, 59 ILR 188; *Brogan* et al. v. *United Kingdom*, 29 November 1988, Series A, No. 145-B; *Fox, Campbell and Hartley* v. *United Kingdom*, 30 August 1990, Series A, No. 182; *Brannigan and McBride* v. *United Kingdom*, 28 May 1993, Series A, No. 258-B.

922   As in *Alliance des professeurs de Montréal* v. *PG Québec*, *supra* note 913.

923   UN Doc. CCPR/C/103/Add.5, para. 34.

924   *An Act respecting the Constitution Act, 1982*, SQ 1982, c. 21. Other specific statutes have invoked section 33 of the *Charter*: *An Act to amend the Act to promote the development of agricultural operations*, SQ 1986, c. 54, s. 16 derogates from section 15 in matters respecting age; *An Act to again amend the Education Act and the Act respecting the Conseil supérieur de l'éducation and to amend the Act respecting the Ministère de l'Education*, SQ 1986, c. 101, ss. 11, 12 and 13 derogates from section 2(a) and section 15; *An Act to amend various legislation respect the pension plans of the public and parapublic sectors*, SQ 1987, c. 47, s. 157 derogates from section 15; *SGEU Dispute Settlement Act*, S.S. 1984-85-86, c. 111 derogates from section 2(d).

attacked before the courts.[925] There has been occasional use of the notwith-standing clause by provincial legislatures on an *ad hoc* basis, of which the most well-known example was the Quebec National Assembly's measure in 1988 aimed at sheltering certain provisions of the *Charter of the French Language* from the *Canadian Charter* after they had been declared invalid by the Supreme Court of Canada. Quebec made a section 33 derogation from sections 2(b) and 15 of the *Charter* with respect to its language of sign legislation.[926] Three Quebec anglophone merchants immediately filed com-munications with the Human Rights Committee alleging a breach of their rights under the *Covenant*.

During presentation of Canada's reports to the Human Rights Com-mittee, in 1990, several members of the body expressed their concern about the use of section 33 and its potential incompatibility with the country's international obligations. The Human Rights Committee's views in the contentious cases were issued in 1993.[927] They were essentially the same as those reached by the Quebec Superior Court, the Quebec Court of Appeal and the Supreme Court of Canada, concerning the incompatibility of section 58 of the *Charter of the French Language* with the guarantee of freedom of expression. Unlike the Canadian courts, the Human Rights Committee was under no obligation to respect the use of the "notwithstanding" clause in the legislation by which the Quebec National Assembly neutralized the Supreme Court of Canada's judgment in *Ford*.

The Quebec government, which had "ratified" the *Covenant* in 1976,[928] responded appropriately by amending the *Charter of the French Language* so as to conform with the views of the Human Rights Committee.[929] Que-bec's decision to amend the *Charter of the French Language* following issuance of the Human Rights Committee's views in that case provides one of the best demonstrations of the effectiveness of the *Covenant* and its petition procedure. The National Assembly could live quite comfortably, given Quebec's political climate, with legislation that literally defied a unanimous judgment of the Supreme Court of Canada. It was, however,

---

925 *Alliance des professeurs de Montréal* v. *PG Québec, supra* note 913. Note that inter-national tribunals have been equally rigorous in their assessment of the validity of derogations: in *Habeas corpus in Emergency Situations (Non Derogable Guarantee), supra* note 918, the Inter-American Court stated: "rather than adopting a philosophy that favours the suspension of rights, the *Convention* establishes the contrary principle", at 98 (*HRLJ*).

926 *An Act to Amend the Charter of the French Language*, SQ 1988, c. 54, s. 10.

927 *Ballantyne and Davidson, and McIntyre* v. *Canada* (Nos. 359/1989 and 385/1989), UN Doc. CCPR/C/47/D/385/1989, UN Doc. A/48/40, Vol. II, p. 91, 14 *Human Rights Law Journal* 171, 11 *Netherlands Quarterly of Human Rights* 469.

928 REIQ (1984-89), no 1976 (5), p. 817.

929 A fact of which the Human Rights Committee took note in *Singer* v. *Canada*, (No. 455/1991), UN Doc. A/49/40, Vol. II, p. 155.

considerably more ill at ease with the conclusions of the majority of the Human Rights Committee, and took appropriate legislative action to comply with its views. Nevertheless, section 33 is for all practical purposes unattackable before Canadian courts, despite its incompatibility with the country's international obligations.[930]

Article 4 of the *International Covenant on Civil and Political Rights*, providing for derogation from specified rights in times of public emergency threatening the life of the nation and the existence of which is officially proclaimed, has not escaped the notice of Parliament. The preamble to the 1988 *Emergencies Act* declares that application of the *Charter* with respect to that specific law is to take into account the provisions of the *International Covenant on Civil and Political Rights*.[931] Parliament's intention is apparently to preserve the non-derogable rights in the *International Covenant* in time of public emergency. The scope of the *Emergencies Act* should therefore be construed by the courts in light of article 4 of the *Covenant*.[932] During presentation of Canada's third periodic report, there were questions from members of the Human Rights Committee about a reference in section 4(b) of the *Emergencies Act* suggesting it applied only to citizens and permanent residents. In the fourth periodic report, Canada replied: "This provision was inserted in the Emergencies Act for historical reasons and is meant to ensure that Canada will never again engage in practices such as those used against Canadians of Japanese origin during the Second World War. This provision does not mean that Canada could treat persons who are citizens or permanent residents in a discriminatory manner."[933]

---

930 For a rather ill-conceived attempt to challenge section 33 on this basis, see: *Immeubles Claude Dupont Inc.* v. *Québec (PG)*, *supra* note 920.

931 SC 1988, c. 29.

932 "The preamble of an enactment shall be read as a part thereof intended to assist in explaining its purport and object", *Interpretation Act*, RSC 1985, C. I-21, s. 12.

933 UN Doc. CCPR/C/103/Add.5, para. 37.

5

Conclusion

The relevance and importance of international sources was recognized by both Parliamentarians and legal scholars even prior to proclamation of the *Canadian Charter*. Clearly, international materials played a significant role in the drafting of the *Charter*, and also influenced other forms of Canadian human rights legislation, including the *Canadian Bill of Rights*, the Quebec *Charter of Human Rights and Freedoms* and the various provincial codes.

Following adoption of the *Canadian Charter* in 1982, international instruments, decisions and similar materials provided considerable assistance to lawyers and to the courts. It was discovered that the largely unfamiliar language of the new *Charter* had actually been considered in some details by bodies like the European Court of Human Rights. But as references to international authorities began to appear, there was also much debate about the legal basis for their consultation. International lawyers, mostly from the academic community, saw this as an opportunity to promote theories about domestic implementation of international law. In 1987, in the *Re Public Service Employee Relations Act*, Chief Justice Brian Dickson set out a methodology that in some ways reflected such an approach. He distinguished between legal instruments that bind Canada, such as the *International Covenants*, and those that do not. In the case of the former, he said that the *Charter* should be presumed to provide a protection that is at least equivalent to that included in Canada's international obligations. As for the latter, he said that international human rights sources were in general both relevant and persuasive elements to be considered in *Charter* interpretation.[1]

---

1 *Re Public Service Employee Relations Act (Alberta)*, [1987] 1 SCR 313, 51 Alta LR (2d) 97, [1987] 3 WWR 577, 28 CRR 305, 38 DLR (4th) 161, 74 NR 99, 78 AR 1, [1987] DLQ 225, 87 CLLC ¶14,021, at pp. 348-50 (SCR).

But since that time, although the Supreme Court has referred to international human rights law sources in scores of cases, the theoretical approach set out by the Chief Justice in 1987 has been largely ignored. Instead, the Canadian courts, with the Supreme Court at the helm, have used international legal sources as "relevant and persuasive" materials to assist in construing the *Charter*, but they have exchewed any special status or legal significance attached to treaties that are ratified, and that are therefore binding upon Canada. International law operates essentially as comparative law, rather than as some sort of superior or even merely competing normative system.

This may have been the source of dismay to some observers. But far from diminish the significance of international law, the approach currently followed by the Canadian courts almost certainly enhances it. Because they are not concerned with whether or not an instrument has been ratified or otherwise accepted by Canada, they feel comfortable consulting a broad range of sources. These include not only materials to which Canada is not bound at international law, but also materials to which Canada cannot be bound, such as the treaties of European regional system, and various "soft law" texts such as the documents of the Organization for Security and Cooperation in Europe and resolutions of the United Nations General Assembly.

In the 1998 *Secession Reference*, one of the *amici curiae* questioned whether the Supreme Court of Canada was authorized to consider a question of pure international law. The challenge was quickly disposed of. Indeed, the *Secession Reference* itself constitutes not only a landmark in Canadian constitutional jurisprudence, it is also consulted and cited elsewhere as a serious and in some ways profound judicial contemplation of what are extremely difficult issues in international law. The Court had been advised by some of the world's great international lawyers. The result showed that it can interpret and apply international law, making its own original contribution to the discipline.[2]

Along similar lines, the Supreme Court of Canada has also contributed to the development of international law concerning accountability for serious violations of human rights. In *Finta*, in 1994,[3] the Court presented the most detailed judicial consideration of the law concerning crimes against humanity since the judgment of the International Military Tribunal at Nu-

---

2 *Reference re Secession of Quebec*, [1998] 2 SCR 217, 161 DLR (4th) 385, 55 CRR (2d) 1.
3 *R. v. Finta*, (1992) 92 DLR (4th) 1 (Ont CA), affirmed, [1994] 1 SCR 701, 88 CCC (3d) 417, 112 DLR (4th) 513, 150 NR 370.

remberg,[4] and that of the Israeli courts in *Eichmann*.[5] For this reason, *Finta* became one of the key cases to be debated in prosecutions before the International Criminal Tribunal for the former Yugoslavia. The Supreme Court of Canada revisited the subject in 2005, in *Mugesera*, reflecting the rapidly evolving law in the field but also making a contribution of its own to the debate.[6] Clearly, the Court was anxious to make sure that its caselaw was in step with the contemporary international authorities.

Yet a third example presents itself in the cases concerning capital punishment. The second edition of this book, which was published in 1996, lamented the failure of the Supreme Court of Canada to show more leadership in the 1991 cases of *Kindler* and *Ng*.[7] It noted how the *Kindler* judgment had been criticized in other jurisdictions, including by the Judicial Committee of the Privy Council.[8] In 2001, the Supreme Court of Canada revisited the question and, in effect, overturned its earlier rulings.[9] This enhanced the Court's international prestige, and within weeks of the decision it was being cited by other constitutional courts.[10]

International human rights law is ripe with invitations to progressive judges, who may use its new and evolving norms to develop additional dimensions to Canadian jurisprudence. One area of particular interest is economic and social rights, which are apparently excluded from the *Charter*. In Justice Minister Trudeau's original proposal of January 1968, he explained that economic rights were included in the *Universal Declaration of Human Rights* and, of course, in the *International Covenant on Economic, Social and Cultural Rights*: He said:

> The guarantee of such economic rights is desirable and should be an ultimate objective for Canada. There are, however, good reasons for putting aside this issue at this stage and proceeding with the protection of political, legal, egalitarian and linguistic rights. It might take considerable time to reach agreement

---

4 *France* et al. v. *Goering* et al., (1946) 23 *Trial of the Major War Criminals before the International Military Tribunal*, 13 ILR 203.

5 *Attorney-General of the Government of Israel* v. *Eichmann*, (1961) 36 ILR 5.

6 *Mugesera* v. *Canada (Minister of Citizenship and Immigration)*, [2005] 2 SCR 100.

7 *Kindler* v. *Canada (Minister of Justice)*, [1989] 2 FC 492, 46 CCC (3d) 257, 91 NR 359, 42 CRR 262, 69 CR (3d) 38, 25 FTR 240n (CA), leave to appeal allowed, (1989) 102 NR 158n (S.C.C.), affirmed, [1991] 2 SCR 779, 67 CCC (3d) 1, 84 DLR (4th) 438, 6 CRR (2d) 193, 129 NR 81; *Reference re: Ng Extradition (Can.)*, [1991] 2 SCR 858, 67 CCC (3d) 61, 84 DLR (4th) 498.

8 *Pratt* et al. v. *Attorney General for Jamaica* et al., [1993] 4 All ER 769, [1993] 2 LRC 349, [1994] 2 AC 1, [1993] 3 WLR 995, 43 WIR 340, 14 *Human Rights Law Journal* 338, 33 ILM 364 (JCPC).

9 *United States* v. *Burns and Rafay*, [2001] 1 SCR 283, 195 DLR (4th) 1, [2001] 3 WWR 193, 151 CCC (3d) 97, 39 CR (5th) 205, 81 CRR (2d) 1, 85 BCLR (3d) 1.

10 *Mohamed* et al. v. *President of the Republic of South Africa* et al., CCT 17/01, 28 May 2001, para. 46.

on the rights to be guaranteed and on the feasibility of implementation. The United Nations recognized these problems when it prepared two separate Covenants on Human Rights – one on Civil and Political Rights and one on Economic, Social and Cultural Rights, thus giving nations an opportunity to accede to them one at a time.[11]

Walter Tarnopolsky, in his seminal study *The Canadian Bill of Rights*, devoted a mere four pages to a chapter entitled "Economic Civil Liberties and the Canadian Bill of Rights".[12] There was simply nothing to say on the subject. Yet Canada acceded to both *Covenants* at the same time and, moreover, international law has come to accept the fact that the distinction between the two categories, civil and political and economic, social and cultural, is an aberation of the Cold War. The 1993 Vienna Conference affirmed the "indivisibility" of human rights.[13] Justice Minister Trudeau's comments, valid as they may have been in 1968, no longer correspond to the state of the law, and interpretation of the *Charter* ought to begin to reflect this. There is, to be sure, plenty of room within section 7 of the *Charter*, as well as other provisions, for such innovation. But recently, when given the opportunity to promote progressive evolution of the law in this area, in the *Gosselin* case, the Supreme Court of Canada kept its powder dry.[14] One of the dissenters, Louise Arbour, left the Court shortly afterwards. She now promotes the indivisibility of economic, social and cultural rights from her prestigious position of United Nations High Commissioner for Human Rights. Predictions are always dangerous things. But let us take a bold leap, and suggest that just as *Kindler* was ultimately scrapped when the Supreme Court realized it was out of step with evolving international developments, so will *Gosselin* find itself set aside in the next decade or so, in favour of the approach advocated by Justice Arbour in the Supreme Court and Chief Justice Robert in the Quebec Court of Appeal.

Canada enjoys an excellent reputation internationally with respect to human rights law. It has ratified many of the important treaties, and participates with considerable diligence in the various mechanisms, including the production of periodic reports to treaty bodies. But it is not without its shortcomings, too. Canada's recent defiance of interim or provisional measures requests from human rights treaty bodies runs counter to evolving international law, including rulings of the International Court of Justice. It

---

11   Cited in Anne F. Bayefsky, *Canada's Constitution Act 1982 & Amendments, A Documentary History*, Toronto: McGraw-Hill Ryerson, 1989, at 60.

12   Walter S. Tarnopolsky, *The Canadian Bill of Rights*, 2nd ed., Toronto: McClelland and Stewart, 1975, pp. 218-221.

13   *Vienna Declaration and Programme of Action*, UN Doc. A/CONF.157/24, (1993) 14 *Human Rights Law Journal* 352, para. 5.

14   *Gosselin* v. *Quebec (Attorney General)*, [2002] 4 SCR 429, 221 DLR (4th) 257, 100 CRR (2d) 1, 44 CHRR D/363.

also sends a rather nasty message to states whose human rights record is less honourable that even a country like Canada treats international human rights organs with caution and even some disdain. Canada has also failed to participate genuinely in the regional human rights system of the Organization of American States. For objections that appear to have some validity but that can be overcome if Canada takes a more constructive approach, our country sits on the sidelines. Its refusal to sign or ratify the *American Convention on Human Rights* means that it also does not engage with the other normative instruments of the system.

In 2001, the Standing Senate Committee on Human Rights called for establishing of a Parliamentary Human Rights Committee, and said that "Canada needs to find a better framework to bring its international obligations into domestic law".[15] According to the Committee:

> While we, along with a number of the witnesses who appeared before us, applaud the increased effect that the courts seem to be giving to international human rights law through their decisions, we believe strongly that Canada cannot rely on the judiciary to solve its problem of inadequate implementation of its treaty obligations. Inadequate implementation of internaitonal human rights commitments is not fundamentally a legal or constitutional problem. Rather it is one of political will.
>
> The disjuncture between Canada's international human rights commitments and its domestic law cannot be allowed to go unaddressed. Nor is it either fair or proper to sit back and hope that the courts will rescue Canada from the inconsistencies of its approach to implementing international human rights. A new approach must be found. Otherwise, the continued failure of governments in Canada to systematically address the domestic legal implications of international human rights treaties it has voluntarily ratified could leave this country open to charges of hypocrisy and has the potential to diminish Canada's moral authority as a leading voice fo human rights in the international arena.[16]

It took this a step further four years later, urging that Parliament make a "declaration of intent to comply" with respect to international human rights treaty obligations.[17]

In 1948, Canada abstained in the vote in the Third Committee of the General Assembly on the *Universal Declaration of Human Rights*. A few

---

15   The Senate: *Promises to Keep: Implementing Canada's Human Rights Obligations*, Ottawa, December 2001, p. 34.

16   *Ibid.*, pp. 21-22.

17   Standing Senate Committee on Human Rights, *Who's in Charge Here? Effective Implementation of Canada's International Obligations with Respect to the Rights of Children*, Ottawa, November 2005, p. 78. The recommendation specifically concerned the *Convention on the Rights of the Child*, but logically it extends to the other major human rights treaties.

days later, Canadian diplomats changed their position after realizing the historic humiliation that might be involved. Official documents now show us that Canadian reticence came straight from the Cabinet, which was concerned not so much with trampling on provincial prerogatives as with substantive issues, such as freedom of religion and of association. A 2005 Press Release issued by the Department of Justice said: "Canada has been a consistently strong voice for the protection of human rights from its central role in the drafting of the Universal Declaration of Human Rights in 1947 and 1948 to its work at the UN today."[18] Though surely not a conscious effort to mislead, the statement reveals a satisfaction with Canada's record that is a bit too comfortable. Canada has, of course, largely corrected its *faux pas* of December 1948, but justifiable pride in many aspects of its contemporary record on human rights law should never lead to complacency. There is still much to be done, both on the judicial and the political level. Above all, it is not enough to stand still, because human rights law continues to evolve at a breathtaking pace.

---

18 "Canada Supports International Efforts Toward Abolition of the Death Penalty", Department of Justice Press Release No. 238, 25 November 2005.

Appendix

International Human Rights and Humanitarian Law Conventions to which Canada is a Party

(Chronologically, by date of entry into force for Canada)

1. *Convention for the Amelioration of the Condition of the Wounded and Sick in Armies in the Field*, [1942] CTS 6. Adopted by: Geneva Conference; Adoption: 22/8/1864; Date of accession by the United Kingdom on behalf of Canada: 18/2/1865; Entry into force for Canada: 18/2/1865.

2. *International Convention with respect to the Laws and Customs of War by Land* (Convention no 2), [1942] CTS 6. Adopted by: Hague Conference; Adoption: 29/7/1899; Ratification by the United Kingdom on behalf of Canada: 4/9/1900; Entry into force for Canada: 4/9/1900.

3. *Convention for Adapting to Maritime Warfare the Principles of the Geneva Convention of 1864 (Convention no 3)*, [1942] CTS 6. Adopted by: Hague Conference; Adoption: 29/7/1899; Ratification by the United Kingdom on behalf of Canada: 4/9/1900; Entry into force for Canada: 4/9/1900.

4.*Convention for the Revision of the Geneva Convention of 1864*, [1916] T.S. 1. Adoption: 6/7/06; Ratification by the United Kingdom on behalf of Canada: 16/4/07; Entry into force for Canada: 16/4/07.

5. *International Convention Concerning the Laws and Customs of War by Land*, [1910] B.T.S. 9. Adopted by: Hague Conference; Adoption: 18/10/

07; Ratification by the United Kingdom on behalf of Canada 27/11/09; Entry into force for Canada: 27/11/09.

6. *Treaty of Peace between the Allied and Associated Power and Germany* ("Treaty of Versailles"), [1919] T.S. 4. Adopted by: Paris Peace Conference; Adoption: 28/6/19; Entry into force: 28/6/19; Signature by Canada: 28/6/ 19; Ratification by the United Kingdom on behalf of Canada: 28/6/19; Entry into force for Canada: 28/6/19. Implementation: Treties of Peace Act, 1919 (Can. 2nd Sess.), c. 30.

7. *Slavery Convention (1926)*, (1926), 60 LNTS 253, [1928] CTS 5. Adopted by: Assembly of the League of Nations; Adoption: 25/9/26; Entry into force: 9/3/27; Signature by Canada: 25/9/26; Ratification by Canada 6/8/28; Entry into force for Canada: 6/8/28.

8. *Protocol for the Prohibition of the Use in War of Asphyxiating, Poisonous or Other Gases, and of Bacteriological Methods of Warfare*, (1925) 94 LNTS 65, [1939] CTS 3 Adopted by: Conference for the supervision of the International Trade in Arms and Ammunition; Adoption: 17/6/25; Entry into force: 8/2/28; Ratification by Canada: 6/5/30; Entry into force for Canada: 6/5/30.

9. *International Convention Relative to the Treatment of Prisoners of War* (1931-32), 118 LNTS 343, [1942] CTS 6. Adopted by: Geneva Conference; Adoption: 27/6/29; Entry into force: 19/6/31; Signature by Canada: 27/7/ 29; Ratification by Canada: 20/2/33; Entry into force for Canada: 20/8/33.

10. *International Convention for the Amelioration of the Condition of the Wounded and Sick in Armies in the Field* (1931-32), 118 LNTS 303, [1933] CTS 6, [1942] CTS 6. Adopted by: Geneva Conference; Adoption: 27/6/ 29; Entry into force: 19/6/31; Signature by Canada: 27/7/29; Ratification by Canada 20/2/33; Entry into force for Canada: 20/8/33.

11. *ILO Convention (No. 1) Limiting the Hours of Work in Industrial Undertakings to 8 Per Day and 48 Per Week* (1949), 38 UNTS 18. Adopted by: General Conference of the International Labour Organization; Adoption: 29/10/19; Entry into force: 13/6/21; Signature by Canada: 21/3/35; Ratification by Canada: 21/3/35; Entry into force for Canada: 21/3/35. Implementation: *Limitation of Hours of Work Act*, RS 1935, c. 63.

12. *ILO Convention (No. 14) Concerning the Application of the Weekly Rest in Industrial Undertakings* (1949), 38 UNTS 188. Adopted by: General Conference of the International Labour Organization; Adoption: 24/10/21;

Entry into force: 19/6/23; Signature by Canada: 21/3/35; Ratification by Canada: 21/3/35; Entry into force for Canada: 21/3/35. Implementation: *Weekly Rest in Industrial Undertakings Act*, RS 1935, c. 14.

13. *ILO Convention (No. 26) Concerning the Creation of Minimum Wage Fixing Machinery* (1949), 39 UNTS 3. Adopted by: General Conference of the International Labour Organization; Adoption: 30/5/28; Entry into force: 14/6/30; Signature by Canada: 25/4/35; Ratification by Canada: 25/4/35; Entry into force for Canada: 25/4/35. Implementation: *Minimum Wages Act* RS 1935, c. 44.

14. *Charter of the United Nations*, [1945] CTS 7, as amended by (1963), 557 UNTS 143, (1965), 638 UNTS 306, [1973] CTS 4. Adopted by: San Francisco Conference; Adoption: 26/6/45; Entry into force: 26/6/45; Ratification by Canada 9/11/45; Entry into force for Canada: 9/11/45.

15. *Instrument for the Amendment of the Constitution of the International Labour Organization*, (1946) 2 UNTS 17, [1946] CTS 28. Adopted by: General Conference of the International Labour Organization; Adoption: 5/11/45; Entry into force: 26/9/46; Ratification by Canada 22/7/46; Entry into force for Canada: 26/9/46.

16. *Instrument for the Amendment of the Constitution of the International Labour Organization, with Annexed Constitution*, (1946) 15 UNTS 15, [1946] CTS 48. Adopted by: General Conference of the International Labour Organization; Adoption: 9/10/46; Entry into force: 20/4/48; Ratification by Canada: 31/7/47; Entry into force for Canada: 20/4/48.

17. *UNESCO Constitution*, (1946) 4 UNTS 275, [1945] CTS 18. Adopted by: UNESCO; Adoption: 16/11/45; Entry into force: 4/11/46; Signature by Canada: 16/11/45; Entry into force for Canada: 4/11/46.

18. *Constitution of the International Refugee Organization*, (1946) 18 UNTS 3, [1946] CTS 47. Adopted by: United Nations General Assembly; Adoption: 15/12/46; Date d'entrée en vigueur: 20/8/48; Signature by Canada: 16/12/46; Ratification by Canada: 7/8/48; Entry into force for Canada: 20/8/48.

19. *ILO Convention (No. 88) Concerning the Organization of the Employment Service* (1950), 70 UNTS 85, [1951] CTS 20. Adopted by: General Conference of the International Labour Organization; Adoption: 9/7/48; Entry into force: 10/8/50; Ratification by Canada: 24/8/50; Entry into force for Canada: 24/8/51.

20. *Convention on the Prevention and Punishment of the Crime of Genocide*, (1951) 78 UNTS 277, [1949] CTS 27. Adopted by: United Nations General Assembly; Adoption: 9/12/48; Entry into force: 12/1/51; Signature by Canada: 28/11/49; Ratification by Canada: 3/9/52; Entry into force for Canada: 2/12/52. Implementation: *Act to Amend the Criminal Code*, S.C. 1969-70, c. 39; *Act to Amend the Criminal Code, the Immigration Act, 1976 and the Citizenship Act*, RS 1987, c. 37; *Crimes Against Humanity and War Crimes Act*, SC 2000, c. 24.

21. *Protocol Amending the Slavery Convention, Signed at Geneva on 25 September 1926*, (1955) 212 UNTS 17, [1953] CTS 26. Adopted by: United Nations General Assembly; Adoption: 23/10/53; Entry into force: 7/12/53; Binding signature by Canada: 17/12/53; Entry into force for Canada: 17/12/53.

22. *Instrument for the Amendment of the Constitution of the International Labour Organization*, (1954) 191 UNTS 143, [1954] CTS 5. Adopted by: General Conference of the International Labour Organization; Adoption: 25/6/53; Entry into force: 20/5/54; Ratification by Canada: 24/11/53; Entry into force for Canada: 20/5/54.

23. *Convention on the Political Rights of Women*, (1954) 193 UNTS 135, [1957] CTS 3[1]. Adopted by: United Nations General Assembly; Adoption: 20/12/52; Entry into force: 7/7/54; Date of accession by Canada: 30/1/57; Entry into force for Canada: 30/4/57.

24. *Convention on the Nationality of Married Women*, (1958) 309 UNTS 65, [1960] CTS 2. Adopted by: United Nations General Assembly; Adoption: 29/1/57; Entry into force: 11/8/58; Signature by Canada: 20/2/57; Ratification by Canada: 21/10/59; Entry into force for Canada: 19/1/60.

25. *ILO Convention (No. 105) Concerning the Abolition of Forced Labour*, (1958) 320 UNTS 291, [1960] CTS 21. Adopted by: General Conference of the International Labour Organization; Adoption: 25/6/57; Entry into force: 17/1/59; Ratification by Canada: 14/7/59; Entry into force for Canada: 14/7/60.

---

1 Canada made a reservation to the *Convention* upon accession: "Inasmuch as under the Canadian constitutional system legislative jurisdiction in respect of political rights is divided between the provinces and the Federal Government, the Government of Canada is obliged, in acceding to this Convention, to make a reservation in respect of rights within the legislative jurisdiction of the provinces." Canada also made an objection, at the time of its accession to the treaty, to reservations that had been made by several of the socialist countries.

26. *Supplementary Convention on the Abolition of Slavery, the Slave Trade, and Institutions and Practices Similar to Slavery,* (1957) 266 UNTS 3, [1963] CTS 7. Adopted by: United Nations Conference of Plenipotentiaries; Adoption: 7/9/56; Entry into force: 30/4/57; Signature by Canada: 17/9/56; Ratification by Canada: 10/1/63; Entry into force for Canada: 10/1/63.

27. *Geneva Convention for the Amelioration of the Condition of the Wounded and Sick in Armed Forces in the Field,* (1950) 75 UNTS 31, [1965] CTS 20. Adopted by: Diplomatic Conference convened by the Swiss Federal Council; Adoption: 12/8/49; Entry into force: 21/10/50; Signature by Canada: 8/12/49; Ratification by Canada: 14/5/65; Entry into force for Canada: 14/11/65. Implementation: *Geneva Conventions Act,* RSC., 1985, ch. G-3; *Crimes Against Humanity and War Crimes Act,* SC 2000, c. 24.

28. *Geneva Convention for the Amelioration of the Condition of the Wounded, Sick and Shipwrecked Members of the Armed Forces at Sea,* (1950) 75 UNTS 85, [1965] CTS 20. Adopted by: Diplomatic Conference convened by the Swiss Federal Council; Adoption: 12/8/49; Entry into force: 21/10/50; Signature by Canada: 8/12/49; Ratification by Canada: 14/5/65; Entry into force for Canada: 14/11/65. Implementation: *Geneva Conventions Act,* RSC., 1985, ch. G-3; *Crimes Against Humanity and War Crimes Act,* SC 2000, c. 24.

29. *Geneva Convention Relative to the Treatment of Prisoners of War,* (1950) 75 UNTS 135, [1965] CTS 20. Adopted by: Diplomatic Conference convened by the Swiss Federal Council; Adoption: 12/8/49; Entry into force: 21/10/50; Signature by Canada: 8/12/49; Ratification by Canada: 14/5/65; Entry into force for Canada: 14/11/65. Implementation: *Geneva Conventions Act,* RSC., 1985, ch. G-3; *Prisoner-of-War Status Determination Regulations,* DORS/91-134, G.C.II, 13/2/91, 843; *Crimes Against Humanity and War Crimes Act,* SC 2000, c. 24.

30. *Geneva Convention Relative to the Protection of Civilians,* (1950) 75 UNTS 287, [1965] CTS 20. Adopted by: Diplomatic Conference convened by the Swiss Federal Council; Adoption: 12/8/49; Entry into force: 21/10/50; Signature by Canada: 8/12/49; Ratification by Canada: 14/5/65; Entry into force for Canada: 14/11/65. Implementation: *Geneva Conventions Act,* RSC., 1985, ch. G-3; *Crimes Against Humanity and War Crimes Act,* SC 2000, c. 24.

31. *ILO Convention (No. 111) Concerning Discrimination in Respect of Employment and Occupation,* (1960) 361 UNTS 31. Adopted by: General Conference of the International Labour Organization; Adoption: 25/6/58;

Entry into force: 15/6/60; Ratification by Canada: 26/11/64; Entry into force for Canada: 26/11/65.

32. *ILO Convention (No. 122) Concerning Employment Policy*, (1966) 569 UNTS 65. Adopted by: General Conference of the International Labour Organization; Adoption: 9/7/64; Entry into force: 15/7/66; Ratification by Canada: 16/9/66; Entry into force for Canada: 16/9/67.

33. *Protocol Relating to the Status of Refugees*, (1967) 606 UNTS 267, [1969] CTS 6. Adopted by: United Nations General Assembly; Adoption: 31/1/67; Entry into force: 4/10/67; Date of accession by Canada: 4/6/69; Entry into force for Canada: 4/6/69. Implementation: *Immigration Act*, RSC., 1985, ch. I-2, ss. 2(1), 3(7).

34. *Agreement Relating to Refugee Seamen*, [1969] CTS 35. Adopted by: Hague Conference; Adoption: 23/11/57; Entry into force: 27/12/61; Date of accession by Canada: 30/5/69; Entry into force for Canada: 28/8/69.

35. *Convention Relating to the Status of Refugees*, (1954) 189 UNTS 137, [1969] CTS 29[2]. Adopted by: United Nations Conference of Plenipotentiaries; Adoption: 28/7/51; Entry into force: 22/4/54; Date of accession by Canada: 4/6/69; Entry into force for Canada: 2/9/69. Implementation: *Immigration Act*, RSC, 1985, ch. I-2, ss. 2(1), 3(7), replaced by *Immigration and Refugee Protection Act*, SC 2001, c. 27.

36. *International Convention on the Elimination of All Forms of Racial Discrimination*, (1969) 660 UNTS 195, [1970] CTS 28, REIQ (1984-89), no (1978) (8), p. 836. Adopted by: United Nations General Assembly; Adoption: 21/12/65; Entry into force: 4/1/69; Signature by Canada: 24/8/66; Ratification by Canada: 14/10/70; Ratification by Quebec: 10/5/78; Entry into force for Canada: 13/11/70; Entry into force for Québec: 13/11/70. Implementation: *Act to Amend the Criminal Code*, S.C. 1969-70, c. 39; *Canadian Multiculturalism Act*, RS 1988, c.31, preamble.

---

2 Upon accession, Canada formulated reservations to article 23 and 24: "Canada interprets the phrase 'lawfully staying' as referring only to refugees admitted for permanent residence; refugees admitted for temporary residence will be accorded the same treatment with respect to the matters dealt with in Articles 23 and 24 as is accorded visitors generally." On 23 October 1970, Canada made the following declaration: "The Government of Canada declares that for the purposes of its obligations under the Convention relating to the Status of Refugees done at Geneva on July 28, 1951, the words 'events occurring before 1 January 1951' in Article 1, Section B(1) of the said Convention shall be understood as meaning 'events occurring in Europe or elsewhere before 1 January 1951'."

37. *ILO Convention (No. 87) Concerning Freedom of Association and Protection of the Right to Organize*, (1950) 68 UNTS 17, [1973] CTS 14. Adopted by: General Conference of the International Labour Organization; Adoption: 9/7/48; Entry into force: 4/7/50; Ratification by Canada: 23/3/72; Entry into force for Canada: 23/3/73. Implementation: *Canadian Labour Code*, RSC., 1985, ch. L-2, Part V, Preamble.

38. *ILO Convention (No. 100) Concerning Equal Remuneration for Men and Women Workers for Work of Equal Value*, (1953) 165 UNTS 303, [1973] CTS 37. Adopted by: General Conference of the International Labour Organization; Adoption: 29/6/51; Entry into force: 23/5/53; Ratification by Canada: 16/11/72; Entry into force for Canada: 16/11/73.

39. *Instrument of Amendment of the Constitution of the International Labour Organization*, [1974] CTS 35. Adopted by: General Conference of the International Labour Organization; Adoption: 22/6/72; Entry into force: 1/11/74; Ratification by Canada: 9/11/72; Entry into force for Canada: 1/11/74.

40. *Protocol Relating to Refugee Seamen*, [1975] CTS 3. Adopted by: Hague Conference; Adoption: 12/6/73; Entry into force: 10/2/75; Date of accesion by Canada: 9/1/75; Entry into force for Canada: 10/2/75.

41. *International Covenant on Economic, Social and Cultural Rights*, (1976) 993 UNTS 3, [1976] CTS 46, REIQ (1984-89), no 1976 (3), p. 808. Adopted by: United Nations General Assembly; Adoption: 16/12/66; Entry into force: 3/1/76; Date of accession by Canada: 19/5/76; Entry into force for Canada: 19/8/76.

42. *International Covenant on Civil and Political Rights*, (1976) 999 UNTS 171, [1976] CTS 47, REIQ (1984-89), no 1976 (5), p. 817[3]. Adopted by: United Nations General Assembly; Adoption: 16/12/66; Entry into force: 23/3/76; Date of accession by Canada: 19/5/76; Entry into force for Canada:

---

3 Canada made an optional declaration under article 41 of the *International Covenant on Civil and Political Rights* on 29 October 1979: "The Government of Canada declares, under article 41 of the International Covenant on Civil and Political Rights, that it recognizes the competence of the Human Rights Committee referred to in article 28 of the said Covenant to receive and consider communications submitted by another State Party, provided that such State Party has not less than twelve months prior to the submission by it of a communication relating to Canada, made a declaration under article 41 recognized the competence of the Committee to receive and consider communications relating to itself."

19/8/76. Implementation: *Emergency Powers Act*, RS 1987, c. 29, Preamble; *Canadian Multiculturalism Act*, RS 1988, c.31, Preamble.

43. *Optional Protocol to the International Covenant on Civil and Political Rights*, (1976) 999 UNTS 171, [1976] CTS 47, REIQ (1984-89), no (1976) (4), p. 832. Adopted by: United Nations General Assembly; Adoption: 16/12/66; Entry into force: 23/3/76; Accession by Canada: 19/5/76; Entry into force for Canada: 19/8/76.

44. *Convention on the Reduction of Statelessness*, (1976) 989 UNTS 175, [1978] CTS 32. Adopted by: United Nations Conference on the Elimination or Reduction of Future Statelessness; Adoption: 30/8/61; Entry into force: 13/12/75; Accession by Canada: 17/7/78; Entry into force for Canada: 15/10/78.

45. *Convention on the Elimination of Discrimination Against Women*, (1981), 1249 UNTS 13, [1982] CTS 31, REIQ (1984-89), no (1981) (12), p. 850.[4] Adopted by: United Nations General Assembly; Adoption: 18/12/79; Entry into force: 3/9/81; Signature by Canada: 17/7/80; Ratification by Canada: 10/12/81; Entry into force for Canada: 10/1/82.

46. *Convention Against Torture and Other Cruel, Inhuman or Degrading Treatment or Punishment*, UN Doc. A/39/51, p. 197, REIQ (1984-89), no (1987) (16), p. 870[5]. Adopted by: United Nations General Assembly; Adop-

---

4   When it ratified the *Convention*, Canada made the following declaration: "The Government of Canada states that the competent legislative authorities within Canada have addressed the concept of equal pay referred to in article 11(1)(d) by legislation which requires the establishment of rates of remuneration without discrimination on the basis of sex. The competent legislative authorities within Canada will continue to implement the object and purpose of article 11(1)(d) and to that end have developed, and where appropriate will continue to develop, additional legislative and other measures." On 28 May 1992, the Government of Canada notified the Secretary-General of the United Nations of its decision to withdraw the declaration to article 11(1)(d) of the Convention, made upon ratification.

On 25 October 1994, Canada filed the following objection: "With regard to the reservations made by Maldives upon accession: 'In the view of the Government of Canada, this reservation is incompatible with the object and purpose of the Convention (article 28, paragraph 2). The Government of Canada therefore enters its formal objection to this reservation. This objection shall not preclude the entry into force of the Convention as between Canada and the Republic of Maldives.'"

5   In response to declarations formulated by the German Democratic Republic and Chile refusing to recognize the jurisdiction of the Committee Against Torture, Canada has filed objections. On 5 October 1988, Canada made the following declaration: "With regard to the declaration made by the German Democratic Republic: The Government of Canada considers that this declaration is incompatible with the object and purpose of the Convention Against Torture, and thus inadmissible under article 19(c) of the Vienna Convention

tion: 10/12/84; Entry into force: 26/6/87; Signature by Canada: 23/8/85; Ratification by Canada: 24/6/87; Entry into force for Canada: 24/7/87. Declaration recognizing the competence of the Committee Against Torture under arts, 21 and 22: 13/11/89. Implementation: *Criminal Code Amendment Act (torture)*, RS 1987, ch. 13.

47. *Charter of the Organization of American States, as amended*, (1951) 119 UNTS 4, [1990] CTS 23. Adopted by: Ninth Inter-American Conference, held at Bogota; Adoption: 30/4/48; Entry into force: 13/12/51; Signature by Canada: 13/11/89; Ratification by Canada: 8/1/90; Entry into force for Canada: 8/1/90.

48. *North American Agreement on Labour Cooperation*, [1994] CTS 2. Adoption: 15/9/93; Entry into Force: 1/1/94; Ratification by Canada: 14/9/93; Entry into force for Canada: 1/1/94.

49. *Protocol Additional I to the 1949 Geneva Conventions and Relating to The Protection of Victims of International Armed Conflicts*, (1979) 1125 UNTS 3, [1991] CTS 2[6]. Adopted by: Conférence diplomatique sur le droit

---

on the Law of Treaties. Through its functions and its activities, the Committee Against Torture plays an essential role in the execution of the obligations of States Parties to the Convention Against Torture. Any restriction whose effect is to hamper the activities of the Committee would thus be incompatible with the object and purpose of the Convention." On October 29, 1989, Canada made the following declaration: "With regard to reservations made by Child concerning article 2(3) and 3: The Government of Canada considers that this declaration is incompatible with the object and purpose of the Convention Against Torture, and thus inadmissible under article 19(c) of the Vienna Convention on the Law of Treaties." On November 13, 1989, Canada made declarations pursuant to articles 21 and 22 of the *Convention* recognizing the competence of the Committee Against Torture to receive and consider communications to the effect that a State Party claims that another State Party is not fulfilling its obligations under the *Convention* (art. 21), and to receive and consider communications from or on behalf of individuals subject to its jurisdiction who claim to be victims of a violation by a State Party of the provisions of the *Convention*.

6 Canada has formulated two reservations, ten statements of understanding, and one declaration:
   "Reservations
   "Article 11 – Protection of Persons
   "(Medical Procedures)
      "The Government of Canada does not intend to be bound by the prohibitions contained in Article 11 subparagraph 2(c) with respect to Canadian nationals or other persons ordinarily resident in Canada who may be interned, detained or otherwise deprived of liberty as a result of a situation referred to in Article 1, so long as the removal of tissue or organs for transplantation is in accordance with Canadian laws and applicable to the population generally and the operation is carried out in accordance with normal Canadian medical practices, standards and ethics.
   "Article 39 – Emblems of Nationality

humanitaire. Adoption: 8/6/77; Entry into force: 7/12/78; Signature by
Canada: 12/12/77; Ratification by Canada: 20/11/90; Entry into force for
Canada: 20/5/91. Implementation: *Act to Amend the Geneva Conventions
Act, the National Defence Act and the Trade-Marks Act*, RS 1990, c. 14;
Prisoner-of-War Status Determination Regulations, DORS/91-134, G.C.II,
13/2/91, 843; *Crimes Against Humanity and War Crimes Act*, SC 2000,
c. 24.

"(Enemy Uniforms)
"The Government of Canada does not intend to be bound by the prohibitions
contained in paragraph 2 of Article 39 to make use of military emblems, insignia or
uniforms of adverse parties in order to shield, favour, protect or impede military
operations.
"Statements of Understanding
"(Conventional Weapons)
"It is the understanding of the Government of Canada that the rules introduced
by Protocol I were intended to apply exclusively to conventional weapons. In particular, the rules so introduced do not have any effect on and do not regulate or
prohibit the use of nuclear weapons.
"Article 38 – Recognized Emblems
"Protective Emblems
"It is the understanding of the Government of Canada that, in relation to Article
38, in situations where the Medical Service of the armed force of a party to an
armed conflict is identified by another emblem than the emblem referred to in
Article 38 of the first Geneva Convention of August 12, 1949, that other
emblem, when notified, should be respected by the adverse party as a protective
emblem in the conflict, under analogous conditions to those imposed by the
Geneva Conventions of 1949 and the Additional Protocols of 1977 for the use
of emblems referred to in Article 38 of the first Geneva Convention and Protocol
I. In such situations, misuse of such an emblem should be considered as misuse
of emblems referred to in Article 38 of the first Geneva Convention and Protocol
I.
"Articles 41, 56, 57, 58, 78 and 86
"(Meaning of Feasible)
"It is the understanding of the Government of Canada that, in relation to Articles
41, 56, 57, 58, 78 and 86 the word "feasible" means that which is practicable
or practically possible, taking into account all circumstances ruling at the time,
including humanitarian and military considerations.
"Article 44 – Combatants and Prisoners of War
"(Combatant Status)
"It is the understanding of the Government of Canada that:
"a. the situation described in the second sentence of paragraph 3 of Article 44
can exist only in occupied territory or in armed conflicts covered by paragraph
4 of Article 1, and
"b. the word "deployment" in paragraph 3 of Article 44 includes any movement
towards a place from which an attack is to be launched.
"Part IV, Section I – General Protection Against Effects of Hostilities
"(Standard for Decision Making)
"It is the understanding of the Government of Canada that, in relation to Articles

50. *Protocol Additional II to the 1949 Geneva Conventions and Relating to The Protection of Victims of Non-International Armed Conflicts*, (1979) 1125 UNTS 3, [1991] CTS 2[7]. Adopted by: Conférence diplomatique sur le droit humanitaire. Adoption: 8/6/77; Entry into force: 7/12/78; Signature by Canada: 12/12/77; Ratification by Canada: 20/11/90; Entry into force for Canada: 20/5/91. Implementation: *Act to Amend the Geneva Conventions Act, the National Defence Act and the Trade-Marks Act*, RS 1990, c. 14; *Prisoner-of-War Status Determination Regulations*, DORS/91-134, G.C.II, 13/2/91, 843; *Crimes Against Humanity and War Crimes Act*, SC 2000, c. 24.

48, 51 to 60 inclusive, 62 and 67, military commanders and others responsible for planning, deciding upon or executing attacks have to reach decisions on the basis of their assessment of the information reasonably available to them at the relevant time and that such decisions cannot be judged on the basis of information which has subsequently come to light.

"Article 52 – General Protection of Civilian Objects
"(Military Objectives)
"It is the understanding of the Government of Canada in relation to Article 52 that:
"a. a specific area of land may be a military objective if, because of its location or other reasons specified in the Article as to what constitutes a military objective, its total or partial destruction, capture or neutralization in the circumstances governing at the time offers a definite military advantage, and
"b. the first sentence of paragraph 2 of the Article is not intended to, nor does it, deal with the question of incidental or collateral damage resulting from an attack directed against a military objective.
"Article 53 – Protection of Cultural Objects and of Places of Worship
"(Cultural Objects)
"It is the understanding of the Government of Canada in relation to Article 53 that:
"a. such protection as is afforded by the Article will be lost during such time as the protected property is used for military purposes, and
"b. the prohibitions contained in subparagraphs (a) and (b) of this Article can only be waived when military necessity imperatively requires such a waiver.
"Articles 51, subparagraph 5(b), 52 paragraph 2, and 57 clause 2(a)(iii)
"(Military Advantage)
"It is the understanding of the Government of Canada in relation to subparagraph 5(b) of Article 51, paragraph 2 of Article 52, and clause 2(a)(iii) of Article 57 that the military advantage anticipated from an attack is intended to refer to the advantage anticipated from the attack considered as a whole and not from isolated or particular parts of the attack.
"Article 62 – General Protection
"(Protection of Civil Defence Personnel)
"It is the understanding of the Government of Canada that nothing in Article 62 will prevent Canada from using assigned civil defence personnel or volunteer civil defence workers in Canada in accordance with nationally established priorities regardless of the military situation.

51. *Organization of American States Convention on the Nationality of Women*, [1991] CTS 28. Adopted by: Organization of American States. Adoption: 26/12/33; Entry into force: 29/8/34; Date of accession by Canada: 23/10/91; Entry into force for Canada: 23/10/91.

52. *Organization of American States Convention on the Granting of Civil Rights to Women*, [1991] CTS 30. Adopted by: Organization of American States. Adoption: 2/5/48; Entry into force: 17/3/49; Date of accession by Canada: 23/10/91; Entry into force for Canada: 23/10/91.

53. *Inter-American Convention on the Granding of Political Rights to Women*, [1991] CTS 29. Adopted by: Organization of American S tates. Adoption: 2/5/48; Entry into force: 17/3/49; Date of accession by Canada: 23/10/91; Entry into force for Canada: 23/10/91.

54. *Convention on the Rights of the Child*, [1992] CTS 3[8]. Adopted by: United Nations General Assembly. Adoption: 20/11/89; Entry into force:

"Article 96 – Treaty Relations upon Entry into Force of this Protocol, paragraph 3
"(Declaration by National Liberation Movement)
"It is the understanding of the Government of Canada that the making of a unilateral declaration does not, in itself, validate the credentials of the person or persons making such declaration and that States are entitled to satisfy themselves as to whether in fact the makers of such declaration constitute an authority referred to in Article 96. In this respect, the fact that such authority has or has not been recognized as such by an appropriate regional intergovernmental organization is relevant.
"Declaration
"Article 90 – International Fact Finding Commission
"The Government of Canada declares that it recognizes ipso facto and without special agreement, in relation to any other High Contracting Party accepting the same obligation, the competence of the Commission to enquire, as authorized by Article 90 of Protocol I, into allegations by such other Party that it has been the victim of violations amounting to a grave breach or other serious violation of the Geneva Convention of 1949 or of Protocol I."

7   Canada has formulated a statement of understanding:
"The Government of Canada understands that the undefined terms used in Additional Protocol II which are defined in Additional Protocol I shall, so far as relevant, be construed in the same sense as those definitions. The understandings expressed by the Government of Canada with respect to Additional Protocol I hall, as far as relevant, be applicable to the comparable terms and provisions contained in Additional Protocol II."

8   Canada formulated two reservations to the *Convention*:
"Reservations
"(i) Article 21
"With a view to ensuring full respect for the purposes and intent of article 20 (3) and article 30 of the Convention, the Government of Canada reserves the right not to apply the provisions of article 21 to the extent that they may be

2/9/90; Ratification by Canada: 9/12/91; Entry into force for Canada: 8/1/92.

55. *Convention on Prohibitions or Restrictions on the Use of Certain Conventional Weapons which may be deemed to be Excessively Injurious or to have Indiscriminate Effects*, (1983) 1342 UNTS 7. Adopted by: United Nations Conference on Prohibitions or Restrictions on the Use of Certain Conventional Weapons Which May be Deemed to be Excessively Injurious or to Have Indiscriminate Effects. Adoption: 10/10/80; Entry into force: 2/12/83; Ratification by Canada: 24/6/94.

56. *Protocol on Prohibitions or Restrictions on the Use of Incendiary Weapons*, (1983) 1342 UNTS 7. Adopted by: United Nations Conference on Prohibitions or Restrictions on the Use of Certain Conventional Weapons Which May be Deemed to be Excessively Injurious or to Have Indiscriminate Effects. Adoption: 10/10/80; Entry into force: 2/12/83; Ratification by Canada: 24/6/94.

57. *Protocol on Blinding Lasar Weapons*, (1983) 1342 UNTS 7. Adopted by: United Nations Conference on Prohibitions or Restrictions on the Use of Certain Conventional Weapons Which May be Deemed to be Excessively Injurious or to Have Indiscriminate Effects. Adoption: 10/10/80; Entry into force: 2/12/83; Ratification by Canada: 24/6/94.

58. *Protocol on Non-Detectable Fragments*, (1983) 1342 UNTS 7. Adopted by: United Nations Conference on Prohibitions or Restrictions on the Use of Certain Conventional Weapons Which May be Deemed to be Excessively Injurious or to Have Indiscriminate Effects. Adoption: 10/10/80; Entry into force: 2/12/83; Ratification by Canada: 24/6/94.

---

inconsistent with customary forms of care among aboriginal peoples in Canada.
"(ii) Article 37(c)
"The Government of Canada accepts the general principles of article 37(c) of the Convention, but reserves the right not to detain children separately from adults where this is not appropriate or feasible.
"Statement of understanding:
"Article 30:
"It is the understanding of the Government of Canada that, in matters relating to aboriginal peoples of Canada, the fulfillment of its responsibilities under article 4 of the Convention must take into account the provisions of article 30. In particular, in assessing what measures are appropriate to implement the rights recognized in the Convention for aboriginal children, due regard must be paid to not denying their right, in community with other members of their group, to enjoy their own culture, to profess and practice their own religion and to use their own language."

59. *Convention on the Prohibition of the Use, Stockpiling, Production and Transfer of Anti-Personnel Mines and on their Destruction,* [1999] CTS 4. Adoption: 18/9/97; Entry into force: 1/3/99; Signature by Canada: 3/12/97; Ratification by Canada: 3/12/97; Entry into force for Canada: 1/3/99. Implementation: *Anti-Personnel Mines Convention Implementation Act,* SC 1997, c. 33.

60. *Convention for the Protection of Cultural Property in the Event of Armed Conflict,* [1999] 4 CTS 52. Adoption: 14/5/54; Entry into force: 7/8/56; Accession by Canada: 11/12/98; Entry into force for Canada: 11/3/99.

61. *Optional Protocol to the Convention on the Rights of the Child on the Involvement of Children in Armed Conflict,* UN Doc. A/RES/54/263, [2002] CTS 5[9]. Adopted by: United Nations General Assembly; Adoption: 25/5/00; Entry into force: 12/2/02; Signature by Canada: 5/6/00; Ratification by Canada: 7/7/00; Entry into force for Canada: 12/2/02.

62. *Rome Statute of the International Criminal Court,* UN Doc. A/CONF.183/9, [2002] CTS 13. Adopted by: United Nations Diplomatic Conference of Plenipotentiaries on the Establishment of an International

---

9   Canada formulated the following Declaration: "Pursuant to article 3, paragraph 2, of the Optional Protocol to the Convention on the Rights of the Child on Involvement of Children in Armed Conflicts, Canada hereby declares:

    1. The Canadian Armed Forces permit voluntary recruitment at the minimum age of 16 years.

    2. The Canadian Armed Forces have adopted the following safeguards to ensure that recruitment of personnel under the age of 18 years is not forced or coerced:

    (a) all recruitment of personnel in the Canadian Forces is voluntary. Canada does not practice conscription or any form of forced or obligatory service. In this regard, recruitment campaigns of the Canadian Forces are informational in nature. If an individual wishes to enter the Canadian Forces, he or she fills in an application. If the Canadian Forces offer a particular position to the candidate, the latter is not obliged to accept the position;

    (b) recruitment of personnel under the age of 18 is done with the informed and written consent of the person's parents or legal guardians. Article 20, paragraph 3, of the National Defence Act states that "a person under the age of eighteen years shall not be enrolled without the consent of one of the parents or the guardian of that person",

    (c) personnel under the age of 18 are fully informed of the duties involved in military service. The Canadian Forces provide, among other things, a series of informational brochures and films on the duties involved in military service to those who wish to enter the Canadian Forces; and

    (d) personnel under the age of 18 must provide reliable proof of age prior to acceptance into national military service. An applicant must provide a legally recognized document, that is an original or a certified copy of their birth certificate or baptismal certificate, to prove his or her age."

Criminal Court; Adoption: 17/7/98; Entry into force: 1/7/02; Signature by Canada: 18/12/98; Ratification by Canada: 7/7/00; Entry into force for Canada: 1/7/02. Implementation: *Crimes Against Humanity and War Crimes Act*, SC 2000, c. 24; *International Criminal Court Privileges and Immunities Order*, SOR/2004-156; *Mutual Legal Assistance in Criminal Matters Act*, RS, 1985, c. 30 (4th Supp.).

63. *Optional Protocol to the Convention on the Elimination of Discrimination Against Women*, UN Doc. A/RES/54/4. Adopted by: United Nations General Assembly; Adoption: 6/10/99; Entry into force: 22/12/00; Accession by Canada: 18/10/02; Entry into force for Canada: 18/1/03.

64. *Amendment to Article 43(2) of the Convention on the Rights of the Child*, UN Doc. CRC/SP/1995/L.1/Rev.1. Adopted by: Conference of the States Parties; Adoption: 12/12/95; Approved by: United Nations General Assembly; Approval: 21/12/95; Entry into force: 18/11/02; Acceptance by Canada: 17/9/97; Entry into force for Canada: 18/11/02.

65. *Protocol to Prevent, Suppress and Punish Trafficking in Persons, Especially Women and Children, Supplementing the United Nations Convention Against Transnational Organized Crime*, UN Doc. A/55/383. Adopted by: United Nations General Assembly; Adoption: 15/11/00; Entry into force: 25/12/03; Signature by Canada: 14/12/00; Ratification by Canada: 13/5/02; Entry into force for Canada: 25/12/03.

66. *Protocol on Prohibitions or Restrictions on the Use of Mines, Booby-Traps and Other Devices*, [1998] CTS 41. Adopted by: United Nations Conference on Prohibitions or Restrictions on the Use of Certain Conventional Weapons Which May be Deemed to be Excessively Injurious or to Have Indiscriminate Effects; Adoption: 10/10/80; Entry into force: 2/12/83; Accession by Canada: 5/1/98; Entry into force for Canada: 3/12/98.

67. *Convention on the Prohibition of the Development, Production, Stockpiling and Use of Chemical Weapons and on their Destruction (with Annexes)*. Adoption: 31/1/93; Signature by Canada: 12/4/94; Ratification by Canada: 19/12/96; Entry into force for Canada: 29/4/97. Implementation: *Chemical Weapons Convention Implementation Act*, SC 1995, c. 25.

68. *Additional Protocol to the Convention on Prohibitions or Restrictions on the Use of Certain Conventional Weapons Which May be Deemed to be Excessively Injurious or to Have Indiscriminate Effects done at Geneva on October 10, 1980 (Protocol IV)*, [1998] CTS 31. Adoption: 13/10/95; Entry

into force: 30/6/98; Acceptance by Canada: 5/1/98; Entry into force for Canada: 30/6/98.

69. *Agreement Establishing the International Institute for Democracy and Electoral Assistance*, [1998] CTS 6. Adoption: 27/2/95; Accession by Canada: 23/1/98; Entry into force for Canada: 22/2/98.

70. *ILO Convention (No. 182) concerning the Prohibition and Immediate Action on the Elimination of the Worst Forms of Child Labour*, [2001] CTS 2. Adopted by: General Conference of the International Labour Organization; Adoption: 17/6/99; Entry into force: 19/11/00; Ratification by Canada: 6/6/00; Entry into force for Canada: 19/11/00.

71. *Second Optional Protocol to the International Covenant on Civil and Political Rights*, UN Doc. A/44/128. Adopted by: United Nations General Assembly; Adoption: 14/12/89; Entry into force: 11 July 1991; Accession by Canada: 15/11/05; Entry into force for Canada: 15/2/06.

72. *Optional Protocol to the Convention on the Rights of the Child on the Sale of Children, Child Prostitution and Child Pornography*, UN Doc. A/RES/54/263. Adopted by: United Nations General Assembly; Adoption: 25/05/00; Entry into force: 18/01/02; Signature by Canada: 10/11/01; Ratification by Canada: 14/09/05; Entry into force for Canada: 14/10/05.

73. *Amendment to article 20, paragraph 1 of the Convention on the Elimination of Discrimination Against Women*, UN Doc. CEDAW/SP/1995/2. Adopted by: Conference of the States Parties; Adoption: 22/5/95; Approved by: United Nations General Assembly; Approval: 22/12/95; Not yet in force; Acceptance by Canada: 3/11/97.

74. *Amendment to article 8 of the International Convention on the Elimination of All Forms of Racial Discrimination*, UN Doc. CERD/SP/45. Adopted by: Conference of the States Parties; Approved by: United Nations General Assembly; Approval: 16/12/95; Not yet in force; Acceptance by Canada: 8/2/95.

75. *Amendments to articles 17 (7) and 18 (5) of the Convention against Torture and Other Cruel, Inhuman or Degrading Treatment or Punishment*, UN Doc. CAT/SP/1992-L.1. Adopted by: Conference of the States Parties; Adoption: 8/9/92; Approved by: United Nations General Assembly; Approval: 16/12/92; Not yet in force; Acceptance by Canada: 8/2/95.

Bibliography

Abella, Rosalie S., "Limitations on the Right to Equality Before the Law", in Armand de Mestral et al., eds, *The Limitation of Human Rights in Comparative Constitutional Law*, Cowansville: Editions Yvon Blais, 1986, pp 223-236.

Adachi, Ken, *The Enemy that Never Was: A History of Japanese Canadians*, Toronto: McClelland & Stewart, 1991.

Aguilar-Urbina, Francisco José, "A Comparison Between the Covenant and the American Convention as Regards the Procedure", [1991] *Canadian Human Rights Yearbook* 127.

Akhavan, Payam, "Enforcement of the Genocide Convention: A Challenge to Civilization", (1995) 8 *Harvard Human Rights J.* 229.

Akhavan, Payam, "Lessons from Iraqi Kurdistan: Self-Determination and Humanitarian Intervention Against Genocide", (1993) 1 *Netherlands Quarterly of Human Rights* 41.

Alfredsson, Gudmunder & Asbjorn Eide, eds., *The Universal Declaration of Human Rights: A Commentary*, Oslo: Oxford University Press/Scandinavian University Press, 1992.

Alfredsson, Gudmundur & Asbjorn Eide, eds., *The Universal Declaration of Human Rights – A Common Standard of Achievement*, The Hague: Kluwer Academic, 1999.

Alston, Philip & Bruno Simma, "First Session of the U.N. Committee on Economic, Social and Cultural Rights", (1987) 81 *American Journal of International Law* 747.

Alston, Philip, "Neither Fish nor Fowl: The Quest to Define the Role of the UN High Commissioner for Human Rights", (1997) 8 *European Journal of International Law* 321.

Alston, Philip, ed., *The EU and Human Rights*, Oxford: Oxford University Press, 1999.

Anand, Sanjeev, "Beyond *Keegstra*: The Constitutionality of the Wilful Promotion of Hatred Revisited", (1997-1998) 9 *National Journal of Constitutional Law* 117.

Anaya, S. James, "Indigenous Rights Norms in Contemporary International Law", (1991) 8 *Arizona Journal of International and Comparative Law* 1.

Andrews, J., "Freedom of Speech and Politicians", (1986) 11 *European Law Reports* 491.

Arbess, Daniel J., "Limitations on Legislative Override Under the Canadian Charter of Rights and Freedoms: A Matter of Balancing Values", (1983) 21 *Osgoode Hall Law Journal* 113.

Arbour, Louise, *Commission of Inquiry into Certain Events at the Prison for Women at Kingston*, Canada, 1996.

Aust, Anthony, "The Theory and Practice of Informal International Instruments", (1986) 35 *International & Comparative Law Quarterly* 787.

Baehr, Peter, Cees Flinterman & Mignon Senders, eds., *Innovation and Inspiration: Fifty Years of the Universal Declaration of Human Rights*, Amsterdam: Royal Netherlands Academy of Arts and Sciences, 1999.

Balanda, Mikuin Leliel, "Le droit de vivre", in Daniel Prémont, ed., *Essais sur le concept de "droit de vivre" en mémoire de Yougindra Khushalani*, Brussels: Bruylant, 1988, pp. 31-41.

Bantekas, Ilias & Peter Hodgkinson, "Capital Punishment at the United Nations: Recent Developments", (2000) 11 *Criminal Law Forum* 23.

Banton, Michael, *International Action Against Racial Discrimination*, Oxford: Clarendon Press, 1996.

Barsh, Russell, "An Advocate's Guide to the Convention on Indigenous and Tribal Peoples", (1990) 15 *Oklahoma City University Law Review* 209.

Bassiouni, M. Cherif & Edward M. Wise, *Aut dedere aut judicare, the Duty to Extradite or Prosecute in International Law*, Dordrecht/Boston/London: Martinus Nijhoff, 1995.

Bassiouni, M. Cherif, *Crimes Against Humanity in International Law*, 2nd ed., The Hague: Kluwer Law International, 1999, p. 450.

Bastarache, Michel, "The Honourable G.V. La Forest's Use of Foreign Materials in the Supreme Court of Canada and His Influence on Foreign Courts", in Rebecca Johnson & John P. McEvoy, eds., *Gérard V. La Forest at the Supreme Court of Canada, 1985-1997*, Winnipeg: Canadian Legal History Project, 2000, pp. 433-447.

Bayefsky, Anne F., "The Human Rights Committee and the Case of Sandra Lovelace", [1982] *Canadian Yearbook of International Law* 244.

Bayefsky, Anne F., "The Principle of Equality or Non-Discrimination in International Law", (1990) 11 *Human Rights Law Journal* 1.

Bayefsky, Anne F., *Canada's Constitution Act 1982 & Amendments, A Documentary History*, Toronto: McGraw-Hill Ryerson, 1989.

Bayefsky, Anne F., ed., *Self-Determination in International Law – Quebec and Lessons Learned*, The Hague: Kluwer Law International, 2000.

Bayefsky, Anne F., ed., *The UN Human Rights Treaty System in the 21st Century*, The Hague/London/Boston: Kluwer Academic, 2000.

Bayefsky, Anne F., *International Human Rights Law, Use in Canadian Charter of Rights and Freedoms Litigation*, Toronto: Butterworths, 1992.

Beaudoin, Gérald-A., "L'équilibre délicat entre la sécurité publique et les droits individuels: le point de vue d'un législateur" ,[2003] *Revue du Barreau* (numéro spécial) 75.

Beaudoin, Gérald-A., "Les clauses dérogatoire et limitatives des instruments canadiens des droits de la personne", in Daniel Turp & Gérald-A. Beaudoin, eds., *Perspectives canadiennes et européennes des droits de la personne*, Cowansville: Editions Yvon Blais, 1986, pp. 139-157.

Beaudoin, Gérald-A., ed., *Vues canadiennes and européennes des droits de and libertés,* Cowansville: Éditions Yvon Blais, 1989.

Beaulac, Stéphane & Pierre-André Côté, "Driedger's 'Modern Principle' at the Supreme Court of Canada: Interpretation, Justification, Legitimization", (2006) 40 *Revue juridique Thémis*, 131.

Beaulac, Stéphane, "Arrêtons de dire que les tribunaux au Canada sont 'liés' par le droit international", (2004) 5 *Revue juridique Thémis* 359.

Beaulac, Stéphane, "Customary International Law in Domestic Courts: Imbroglio, Lord Denning, *Stare Decisis"*, in Christopher P.M. Waters, ed., *British and Canadian Perspectives on International Law*, Leiden & Boston: Martinus Nijhoff, pp. 379-392.

Beaulac, Stéphane, "Emer de Vattel and the Externalization of Sovereignty", (2003) 5 *Journal of the History of International Law* 237.

Beaulac, Stéphane, "International Law and Statutory Interpretation: Up with Context, Down with Presumption", in O. Fitzgerald, ed., *The Globalized Rule of Law: Relationships Between International and Domestic Law*, Toronto: Irwin Law, pp. 331-365.

Beaulac, Stéphane, "International Treaty Norms and Driedger's "Modern Principle" of Statutory Interpretation", in *Legitimacy and Accountability in International Law – Proceedings of the 33rd Annual Conference of the Canadian Council on International Law*, Ottawa: Canadian Council of International Law, 2005, pp. 141-163.

Beaulac, Stéphane, "L'interprétation de la Charte: reconsidération de l'approche téléologique et réévaluation du rôle du droit international", in Gérald.-A. Beaudoin & Erroll Mendes, eds., *Canadian Charter of Rights and Freedoms*, 4th ed., Markham, Ont.: LexisNexis Butterworths, 2005, pp. 27-69.

Beaulac, Stéphane, "Le Code civil commande-t-il une interprétation distincte?", (1999) 22 *Dalhousie Law Journal* 236.

Beaulac, Stéphane, "Le droit international comme élément contextuel en interprétation des lois", (2004) *Canadian International Lawyer* 1.

Beaulac, Stéphane, "Les bases constitutionnelles de la théorie de l'imprécision: partie d'un précaire dynamique globale de la Charte", (1995) 55 *Revue du Barreau* 257.

Beaulac, Stéphane, "National Application of International Law: The Statutory Interpretation Perspective", (2003) 41 *Canadian Yearbook of International Law* 225.

Beaulac, Stéphane, "Parliamentary Debates in Statutory Interpretation: A Question of Admissibility of of Weight?", (1998) 43 *McGill Law Journal* 287.

Beaulac, Stéphane, "Recent Developments on the Role of International Law in Canadian Statutory Interpretation", (2004) 25 *Statute Law Review* 19.

Beaulac, Stéphane, "The Canadian Federal Constitutional Framework and the Implementation of the Kyoto Protocol", (2005) 5 *Revue juridique polynésienne (hors série)* 125.

Beaulac, Stéphane, "The Social Power of Bodin's 'Sovereignty' and International Law", (2003) 4 *Melbourne Journal of International Law* 1.

Beaulac, Stéphane, "The *Suresh* Case and Unimplemented Treaty Norms", (2002) 15 *Revue québecoise de droit international* 221.

Beaulac, Stéphane, "The Westphalian Legal Orthodoxy – Myth or Reality?", (2000) 2 *Journal of the History of International Law* 148.

Beaulac, Stéphane, *The Power of Language in the Making of International Law – The Word Sovereignty in Bodin and Vattel and the Myth of Westphalia*, Leiden & Boston: Martinus Nijhoff Publishers, 2004.

Beckton, Clare, "Freedom of expression", in Walter S. Tarnopolsky & Gérald-A. Beaudoin, eds., *The Canadian Charter of Rights and Freedoms: Commentary*, Toronto: Carswell, 1982, pp. 75-125.

Bello, Emmanuel G., "The African Charter on Human and People's Rights. A Legal Analysis", (1985) 194 *Receuil de cours de l'Academie de droit international* 91.

Bendel, Michael, "The International Protection of Trade Union Rights: A Canadian Case Study", (1981) 13 *Ottawa Law Review* 169.

Bender, Paul, "The Canadian Charter of Rights and Freedoms and the United States Bill of Rights: a Comparison", (1982) 28 *McGill Law Journal* 811.

Benedet, Janice, "Children in Pornography after *Sharpe*", (2002) 43 *Cahiers de Droit* 327.

Benedet, Janice, "Little Sisters Book and Art Emporium v. Minister of Justice: Sex Equality and the Attack on R. v. Butler", (2001) 39 *Osgoode Hall Law Journal* 187.

Bennion, Francis A.R., *Statutory Interpretation A Code*, 4th ed., London: Butterworths, 2002.

Berenstein, Alexandre & David Harris, *The European Social Charter*, Charlottesville: University of Virginia Press, 1985.

Berenstein, Alexandre, "Les droits économiques and sociaux garantis par la Charte sociale européenne", in Daniel Turp & Gérald-A. Beaudoin, eds., *Perspectives canadiennes et européennes des droits de la personne*, Cowansville, Éditions Yvon Blais, 1986, p. 405.

Beres, Louis Rene, "Iraqi Crimes and International Law: The Imperative to Punish", (1993) 21 *Denver Journal of International Law & Policy* 335.

Beres, Louis Rene, "Prosecuting Iraqi Crimes: Fulfilling the Expectations of International Law After the Gulf War", (1992) 10 *Dickinson Journal of International Law* 425.

Berger, Vincent, *Jurisprudence de la Cour européenne des droits de l'homme*, Paris: Sirey, 1994.

Berlin, Marc & Luc Metivier, "Le droit international humanitaire comme source interprétative de la Charte canadienne des droits and libertés: l'incidence de la Convention européenne des droits de l'Homme", (1987) 64 *Revue de droit international et de droit constitutionnel* 36.

Berman, Paul Schiff, "The Globalization of Jurisdiction", (2002) 151 *University of Pennsylvania Law Review* 311.

Betten, L., "The European Social Charter", (1988) 6 *Netherlands Quarterly of Human Rights* 82.

Betten, L., "The Protocol to the European Social Charter: More Rights, A Better Impact?", (1988) 6 *Netherlands Quarterly of Human Rights* 9.

Bilder, Richard B., "The Status of International Human Rights Law: An Overview", (1978) *International Law & Practice* 1.

Binette, André, "Le pouvoir dérogatoire de l'article 33 de la *Charte canadienne des droits et libertés* et la structure de la Constitution du Canada", (2003) *Revue du Barreau* (No. sp.) 107.

Blache, Pierre, "Les libertés de circulation et d'établissement", in Gérald-A. Beaudoin & Errol P. Mendes, eds., *Canadian Charter of Rights and Freedoms*, 3rd ed., Toronto: Carswell, 1996, pp. 387-413.

Black, William & Lynn Smith, "The Equality Rights", in Gérald-A. Beaudoin & Errol P. Mendes, eds., *Canadian Charter of Rights and Freedoms*, 4th ed., Markham, Ont., LexisNexis Butterworths, 2005, pp. 925-1024.

Bloed, Arie, "The CSCE and the Protection of National Minorities", (1993) 1:3 *CSCE ODHIR Bulletin* 1.

Bloed, Arie, "The CSCE and the Protection of National Minorities", in Alan Phillips & Allan Rosas, eds., *The U.N. Minority Rights Declaration*, Abo: Abo Akademi University Institute for Human Rights, 1993, pp. 95-101.

Boerefijn, Ineke, *The Reporting Procedure under the Covenant on Civil and Political Rights: Practice and Procedure of the Human Rights Committee*, Antwerp/Groningen/Oxford: Hart, 1999.

Bonin, Jean-François, "La protection contre la torture et les traitements cruels, inhumains et dégradants: l'affirmation d'une norme et l'évolution d'une définition en droit international", (1986) 3 *Revue québecoise de droit international* 169.

Bonner, D., "Ireland v. United Kingdom", (1978) 27 *International & Comparative Law Quarterly* 897.

Bonner, D., "The Beginning of the End for Corporal Punishment", (1979) 42 *Modern Law Review* 580.

Borgwardt, Elizabeth, *A New Deal for the World, America's Vision for Human Rights*, Cambridge and London: Harvard University Press, 2005, pp. 14-45.

Bossuyt, Marc J., "La Convention des Nations Unies sur les droits de l'enfant", (1990) 2 *Revue universelle des droits de l'homme* 141.

Bossuyt, Marc J., *Guide to the "travaux préparatoires" of the International Covenant on Civil and Political Rights*, Dordrecht: Martinus Nijhoff, 1987.

Bossuyt, Marc J., *L'interdiction de la discrimination dans le droit international des droits de l'homme*, Brussels: Emile Bruylant, 1976.

Bothe, Michael, "La protection des droits fondementaux au Canada", *Jahrbuch des öffentlichen Rechts der Gegenwart*, 1986, pp. 292-294.

Boulesbaa, Ahcene, "An Analysis of the 1984 Draft Convention Against Torture and Other Cruel, Inhuman or Degrading Treatment or Punishment", (1986) 4 *Dickinson Journal of International Law* 185.

Boulesbaa, Ahcene, *The UN Convention on Torture and the Prospects for Enforcement*, The Hague: Martinus Nijhoff, 1999

Boyle, Christine, *Sexual Assault*, Toronto, Carswell, 1984.

Brandon, Elizabeth, "Does International Law Mean Anything in Canadian Courts", (2002) 11 *Journal of Environmental Law & Practice* 399.

Brant, Irving, *The Bill of Rights, Its Origin and Meaning*, Indianapolis: Bobbs-Merrill, 1965.

Brierly, James L., *The Law of Nations: An Introduction to the International Law of Peace*, 6th ed., Oxford: Clarendon Press, 1963 .

Broadfoot, Barry, *Years of Sorrow Years of Shame: The Story of Japanese Canadians in World War II*, Toronto: Doubleday, 1977.

Brode, Patrick, *Casual Slaughters and Accidental Judgments, Canadian War Crimes Prosecutions, 1944-1948*, Toronto: University of Toronto Press, 1997.

Brölmann, Catherine M. & Marjoleine Y.A. Zieck, "Some Remarks on the Draft Declaration on the Rights of Indigenous Peoples", (1995) 8 *Leiden Journal of International Law* 103.

Brown, L. Neville & Francis G. Jacobs, *The Court of Justice of the European Communities*, London: Sweet & Maxwell, 1977.

Brown, L. Neville, "Thalidomide, the 'Sunday Times' and the Reform of the English Law of Contempt of Court", in Daniel Turp & G.A. Beaudoin, eds., *Perspectives canadiennes et européennes des droits de la personne*, Cowansville: Editions Yvon Blais, 1986, pp. 527-541.

Brownlie, Ian, *Principles of Public International Law*, 6th ed., Oxford: Clarendon Press, 2003, p. 490.

Brunée, Jutta & Stephen J. Toope, "A Hesitant Embrace: The Application of International Law by Canadian Courts", (2002) 40 *Canadian Yearbook of International Law* 3.

Bruun, Lori Lyman, "Beyond the 1948 Convention – Emerging Principles of Genocide in Customary International Law", (1993) 17 *Maryland J. Int"l L. & Trade* 193.

Bryden, Philip, "*Blencoe* v. *British Columbia Human Rights Commission*", (1999) 33 *University of British Columbia Law Review* 153.

Buergenthal, Thomas, "The Advisory Practice of the Inter-American Court of Human Rights", (1985) 79 *American Journal of International Law* 11.

Buergenthal, Thomas, "The Inter-American Court of Human Rights", (1982) 76 *American Journal of International Law* 23.

Buergenthal, Thomas, "The Inter-American System for the Protection of Human Rights", in Theodor Meron, ed., *Human Rights and International Law Legal and Political Issues*, Oxford, Oxford University Press, 1985, pp. 439-460.

Buergenthal, Thomas, Robert Norris & Dinah Shelton, *Protecting Human Rights in the Americas: Selected Problems*, 4th ed., Kehl: N.P. Engel, 1996.

Burgers, J.H. & Hans Danelius, *The United Nations Convention Against Torture: A Handbook of the Convention Against Torture and Other Cruel, Inhuman or Degrading Treatment or Punishment*, Dordrecht: Martinus Nijhoff, 1988.

Burgorgue-Larsen, Laurence, Anne Levade & Fabrice Picod, *Traité établissant une Constitution pour l'Europe, Commentaire article par article*, Vol. II, Brussels: Bruylant, 2005.

Burkett, Brian W. "Canada and the ILO: Freedom of Association since 1982", (2003) 10 *Canadian Labour and Employment Law Journal* 231.

Burkett, Brian W., John D.R Craig & S. Jodi Gallagher, "Canada and the ILO: Freedom of Association since 1982", (2003) 10 *Canadian Labour & Employment Law Journal* 231.

Cameron, Jamie, "The 'Second Labour Trilogy': A Comment on *R.* v. *Advance Cutting*, *Dunmore* v. *Ontario*, and *RWDSU* v. *Pepsi-Cola*", (2002) 16 *Supreme Court Law Review* (2d) 67.

Cameron, Jamie, "The First Amendment and Section 1 of the Charter", (1990) 1 *Media & Communication Law Review* 59.

Cameron, Jamie, "The Motor Vehicle Reference and the Relevance of American Doctrine in Charter Adjudication," in Robert J. Sharpe, ed., *Charter Litigation*, Toronto & Vancouver: Butterworths, 1987, 69.

Cançado Trindade, A.A., "La protection des droits économiques, sociaux et culturels: évolutions et tendances particulièrement à l'échelle régionale", (1990) 94 *Revue générale de droit international public* 913.

Capotorti, F., *Study on the Rights of Persons Belonging to Ethnic, Religious and Linguistic Minorities*, UN Doc. E/CN.4/Sub.2/384/Add.1-7, U.N. Sales No. E.78.XIV.I.

Caron, Marie, "Les travaux du Comité pour l'élimination de la discrimination à l'égard des femmes", (1985) 2 *Revue québecoise de droit international* 295.

Carter, Mark, "Reconsidering the Charter and Electoral Boundaries", (1999) 22 *Dalhousie Law Journal* 53.

Cassel, Douglass W., Jr., "Somoza's Revenge: A New Judge for the Inter-American Court of Human Rights", (1992) 13 *Human Rights Law Journal* 137.

Cassese, Antonio, Paola Gaeta & John R.W.D. Jones, *The Rome Statute of the International Criminal Court, A Commentary*, Oxford: Oxford University Press, 2002.

Cassese, Antonio, *Self Determination of Peoples: A Legal Reappraisal*, Cambridge: Cambridge University Press, 1995.

Cassin, René, "La Déclaration universelle et la mise en œuvre des droits de l'homme", (1951) 79 *Receuil de cours de l'Academie de droit international* 237.

Castellino, Joshua, *International Law of Self-Determination: The Interplay of the Politics of Territorial Possession with Formulations of Post-Colonial "National" Identity*, London: Kluwer Law International, 2000.

Cavaluzzo, Paul J.J., "Freedom of Association and the Right to Bargain Collectively", in Paul Weiler, Robin Elliott, eds., *Litigating the Values of a Nation: The Canadian Charter of Rights and Freedoms*, Toronto: Carswell, 1986, pp. 195-220.

Cerna, Christina M., "La Cour interaméricaine des droits de l'Homme: les affaires récentes", (1987) 33 *Annuaire français de droit international* 351

Cerna, Christina M., "La Cour interaméricaine des droits de l'homme, ses premières affaires", (1983) 29 *Annuaire français de droit international* 300.

Chanet, Christina M., "Le Comité contre la torture", (1991) 37 *Annuaire français de droit international* 553.

Chevrette, François, "Arrestation, détention et incrimination rétroactive", in G.-A Beaudoin, E. Ratushny, eds., *Charte canadienne des droits et libertés*, 2nd ed., Montreal: Wilson & Lafleur, 1989, pp 443-502.

Chevrette, François, Hugo Cyr & François Tanguay-Renaud, "La protection lors de l'arrestation, la détention et la protection contre l'incrimination rétroactive", in Gérald-A. Beaudoin & Errol P. Mendes, eds., *Canadian Charter of Rights and Freedoms*, 4th ed., Markham, Ont., LexisNexis Butterworths, 2005, pp. 595-789.

Chinkin, Christine, "The Challenge of Soft Law: Development and Change in International Law", (1989) 38 *International & Comparative Law Quarterly* 850.

Choudhry, Sujit & Robert Howse, "Constitutional Theory and the Quebec Secession Reference", (2000) 13 *Canadian Journal of Law & Jurisprudence* 143.

Christakis, Théodore, *Le droit à l'autodétermination en dehors des situations de décolonisation*, Paris: La documentation française, 1999.

Christian, Timothy, "The Limitation of Liberty: A Consideration of Section 1 of the Charter of Rights and Freedoms", [1982] *Charter Edition University of British Columbia Law Review* 105.

Clapham, Andrew & Susan Marks, *International Human Rights Lexicon*, Oxford: Oxford University Press, 2005.

Clapham, Andrew, "Creating the High Commissioner for Human Rights: The Outside Story", (1994) 5 *European Journal of International Law* 556.

Clapham, Andrew, "The High Commissioner of Human Rights", in P. Alston, ed., *The United Nations and Human Rights*, Oxford: Clarendon Press, 2004.

Clapham, Andrew, *Human Rights Obligations of Non-State Actors*, Oxford: Oxford University Press, 2006.

Clark, Roger S., *The United Nations Crime Prevention and Criminal Justice Program, Formulation of Standards and Efforts at Their Implementation*, Philadelphia: Pennsylvania University Press, 1994.

Claydon, John E., "International Human Rights Law and the Interpretation of the Canadian Charter of Rights and Freedoms", (1982) 4 *Supreme Court Law Review* 287.

Claydon, John E., "The Application of International Human Rights Law by the Canadian Courts", (1981) 30 *Buffalo Law Review* 727.

Cliche, Guillaume, "L'utilisation de la Convention européenne des droits de l'Homme pour l'interprétation de la Charte canadienne", (1993) 7 *Revue juridique des étudiants de l'Université Laval* 93.

Cohen, Maxwell & Anne F. Bayefsky, "The Canadian Charter of Rights and Freedoms and International Law", (1983) 61 *Canadian Bar Review* 265.

Cohen, Maxwell, "Bill C-60 and International Law – The United Nations Charter – Declaration of Human Rights", (1959) 37 *Canadian Bar Review* 228.

Cohen, Maxwell, "Towards a Paradigm of Theory and Practice: The Canadian Charter of Rights and Freedoms – International Law Influences and Interactions", [1986] *Canadian Human Rights Yearbook* 47.

Cohen-Jonathan, Gérald & Jean-Paul Jacqué, "Obligations Assumed by the Helsinki Signatories", in Thomas Buergenthal, ed., *Human Rights, International Law and the Helsinki Accord*, Montclair, N.J.: Allenheld, Osman, 1975, pp. 43-70.

Cohen-Jonathan, Gérald, "Les "écoutes téléphoniques"", in *Protecting Human Rights: The European Dimension*, Cologne: Carl Heymanns, 1988, pp. 97-1095.

Cohen-Jonathan, Gérald, *La Convention européenne des droits de l'homme*, Paris: Economica, 1989.

Cohen-Jonathan, Gérard, "La Cour européenne et les écoutes téléphoniques. Les arrêts Kruslin et Huvig du 24 avril 1990", (1990) 2 *Revue universelle des droits de l'homme* 185.

Cook, Rebecca, "Reservations to the Convention on the Elimination of Discrimination Against Women", (1990) 30 *Virginia Journal of International Law* 643.

Corten, Olivier & Pierre Klein, "L'Assistance humanitaire face à la souveraineté des états", [1992] *Revue trimestrielle des droits de l'homme* 343.

Cossman, Brenda, "Disciplining the Unruly Sexual Outlaws, *Little Sisters* and the Legacy of *Butler*", (2003) 36 *University of British Columbia Law Review* 77.

Côté, Pierre-André, *Interprétation des lois*, 3rd ed., Montreal: Thémis, 1999.

Côté, Pierre-André, *Interpretation of Legislation in Canada*, 2nd ed., Cowansville: Éditions Yvon Blais, 1991, at pp. 290-291.

Cotler, Irwin, "Freedom of Conscience and Religion (Section 2(a))", in Gérald.-A. Beaudoin & Ed Ratushny, eds., *The Canadian Charter of Rights and Freedoms*, 2nd ed., Toronto: Carswell, 1989, pp. 165-193.

Cotler, Irwin, "Hate Speech, Equality, and Harm under the Charter: Towards a Jurisprudence of Respect for a 'Free and Democratic Society,'" in Gérald-A. Beaudoin & Errol P. Mendes, eds., *Canadian Charter of Rights and Freedoms*, 4th ed., Markham, Ont., LexisNexis Butterworths, 2005, pp. 1399-1490.

Cotler, Irwin, "R. v. Finta", (1996) 90 *American Journal of International Law* 460.

Coulter, Robert T., "The Draft U.N. Declaration on the Rights of Indigenous Peoples: What is it? What does it mean?", (1995) 13 *Netherlands Quarterly of Human Rights* 123.

Cremona, J.J., "The Thick Hide of Politicians and Article 10 of the European Convention on Human Rights", in *Présence du droit public et des droits de l'homme. Mélanges offerts à Jacques Vélu*, Vol. III, Brussels: Bruylant, 1992, pp. 1799-1811.

Crépeau, François, *Droit d'asile, de l'hospitalité aux contrôles migratoires*, Brussels: Éditions Bruylant, 1995.

Currie, John, "NATO's Humanitarian Intervention in Kosovo: Making or Breaking International Law?", (1998) 36 *Canadian Yearbook of International Law* 303.

D'Entrèves, Allessandro Passerin, *Natural Law*, 2nd ed., London: Hutchison, 1970.

Dadrian, Vahakn N., *The History of the Armenian Genocide: Ethnic Conflict rom the Balkans to Anatolia to the Caucasus*, 6th ed., New York & Oxford: Berghahn Books, 2003, p. 278.

Danelius, Hans, "The International Protection Against Torture and Inhuman or Degrading Treatment or Punishment", (1991) 2:2 *Collected Courses of the Academy of European Law* 151.

Danspeckgruber, W. & Arthur Watts, eds., *Self-Determination and Self-Administration: A Sourcebook*, Boulder, Colorado: Lynne Rienner Publishers, 1997.

David, Éric, *Principes de droit des conflits armés*, 2nd ed., Brussels: Bruylant, 1999, p. 694, para. 4.184c.

de Azcarate, Pablo, *League of Nations and National Minorities*, Washington: Carnegie Endowment for International Peace, 1945.

de Mestral, Armand & Jan Winter, "Mobility Rights in the European Union and Canada", (2001) 46 *McGill Law Journal* 979.

de Zayas, Alfred, "The Examination of Individual Complaints by the United Nations Human Rights Committee under the Optional Protocol to the International Covenant on Civil and Political Rights", in Gudmundur Alfredsson, Jonas Grimhelden, Bertrand Ramcharan & Alfred de Zayas, *International Human Rights Monitoring Mechanisms: Essays in Honour of Jakob Th. Möller*, The Hague/Boston/London: Kluwer Academic, 2001.

Decaux, Emmanuel, "Le Haut Commissaire de la CSCE pour les minorités nationales", in Linos-Alexandre Sicilianos, ed., *New Forms of Discrimination*, Paris: Pedone, 1995, pp. 269-280.

Decaux, Emmanuel, "Vers un nouveau droit des minorités nationales", *Gazette du palais*, 16-17 December 1994, p. 2.

Decaux, Emmanuel, ed., *Les Nations Unies et les droits de l'homme*, Paris : Pedone, 2006.

Decaux, Emmanuel, Pierre-Henri Imbert & Louis E. Pettiti, eds., *La Convention européenne des droits de l'Homme: commentaire article par article*, Paris: Economica, 1995.

Decaux, Emmanuel, Pierre-Henri Imbert & Louis E. Pettiti, eds., *La Convention européenne des droits de l'Homme: commentaire article par article*, Paris: Economica, 1999.

Des Rosiers, Nathalie, "From Québec Veto to Québec Secession: The Evolution of the Supreme Court of Canada on Québec-Canada Disputes", (2000) 13 *Canadian Journal of Law & Jurisprudence* 171.

Desch, Thomas, "The Concept and Dimensions of the Right to Life – As Defined in International Standards and in International and Comparative Jurisprudence", (1985-86) 36 *Osterreichische Zeitschrift für Offentliches Recht und Volkerrecht* 77.

Deschênes, Jules, "Proposal Concerning a Definition of the Term 'Minority'", UN Doc. E/CN.4/Sub.2/1985/31, para. 181.

Deschênes, Jules, *Commission of Inquiry on War Criminals Report*, Ottawa: Minister of Supply and Services, 1986.

Detric, Sharon, *et al.*, *The United Nations Convention on the Rights of the Child: a Guide to the "Travaux préparatoires"*, Dordrecht, Martinus Nijhoff, 1992.

Dominick, Mary Frances, *Human Rights and the Helsinki Accord*, Nashville: William S. Hein, 1981.

Dormenval, Agnès, *Procédures onusiennes de mise en oeuvre des droits de l'homme: limites ou défauts*, Geneva: Presses universitaires de France, 1991.

Doswald-Beck, Louise & Robert Kolb, *Judicial Process and Human Rights*, Kehl/Strasbourg/Arlington: N.P. Engel, 2004.

Doswald-Beck, Louise, "What does the Prohibition of 'Torture or Inhuman or Degrading Treatment or Punishment' Mean? The Interpretation of the European Commission and Court of Human Rights", (1978) 25 *Netherlands International Law Review* 24.

Driedger, Elmer A., *Construction of Statutes*, 2nd ed., Toronto: Butterworths, 1983.

Drzemczewski, A., & F. Wooldridge, "The Closed Shop Case in Strasbourg", (1982) 31 *International & Comparative Law Quarterly* 396.

Du Plessis, Lourens M., "The Bill of Rights in the Working Draft of the New Constitution: An Evaluation of Aspects of a Constitutional Text *Sui Generis*", (1995) 6 *Stellenbosch Law Review* 3.

Duffy, Peter J., "Article 3 of the European Convention on Human Rights", (1983) 32 *International & Comparative Law Quarterly* 316.

Eid, Elisabeth & Hoori Hamboyan, "Implementation by Canada of its International Human Rights Treaty Obligations: Making Sense out of the Nonsensical", in *Legitimacy and Accountability in International Law – Proceedings of the 33rd Annual Conference of the Canadian Council on International Law*, Ottawa: Canadian Council of International Law, 2005, 175-191.

Elberg, Brad A. & Mark C. Power, "Freedom of Conscience and Religion", in Gérald-A. Beaudoin & Errol P. Mendes, eds., *Canadian Charter of Rights and Freedoms*, 4th ed., Markham, Ont., LexisNexis Butterworths, 2005, pp. 217-256.

Eliadis, F. Pearl, "The Right to Work: Policy Alternatives for Spouses with Pending Permanent Residence Status", (1992) 11 Imm. L.R. (2d) 269.

Elliott, Robin, "Interpreting the Charter – Use of the Earlier Versions as an Aid", (1982) 16 *Charter Edition University of British Columbia Law Review* 11.

Ergec, Rusen, *Les droits de l'homme à l'épreuve des circonstances exceptionnelles; Etude sur l'article 15 de la Convention européenne des droits de l'homme*, Brussels: Editions Bruylant, 1987.

Ermacora, Felix, "Rights of Minorities and Self-determination in the Framework of the CSCE", in A. Bloed & Pieter Van Dijk, *The Human Dimension of the Helsinki Process*, Dordrecht: Nijhoff, 1991, p. 205.

Eser, Albin, "'Defences' in War Crime Trials", in Yoram Dinstein, Mala Tabory, eds., *War Crimes in International Law*, The Hague/Boston/London: Kluwer Law International, 1996, pp. 251-273.

Evans, Malcolm & Rod Morgan, *Preventing Torture: A Study of the European Convention for the Prevention of Torture and Inhuman or Degrading Treatment or Punishment*, Oxford: Clarendon Press, 1998.

Fawcett, J.E.S., *The Application of the European Convention on Human Rights*, 2nd ed., Oxford: Clarendon Press, 1987.

Feinberg, Nathan, "La juridiction et la jurisprudence de la Cour permanente de Justice internationale en matière de mandats et de minorités", [1937] I *Receuil de cours de l'Academie de droit international* 592.

Feingold, Cora, "The Little Red Schoolbook and the European Court of Human Rights", (1978) 11 *Revue des droits de l'homme* 21.

Fisher, Dana D., "Reporting Under the Covenant on Civil and Political Rights: the First Five Years of the H.R.C.", (1982) 76 *American Journal of International Law* 142.

Flauss, Jean-François, "Le droit à un recours effectif: l'art. 13 de la Convention européenne des droits de l'Homme dans la jurisprudence de la Commission et de la Cour", in Gérald-A. Beaudoin, *Vues canadiennes et européennes des droits et libertés*, Cowansville: Editions Yvon Blais, 1989, pp. 255-292.

Forsythe, David, *The Humanitarians*, Cambridge: Cambridge University Press, 2005.

Foster, Caroline E., "Articulating Self-Determination in the Draft Declaration on the Rights of Indigenous Peoples", (2001) 12 *European Journal of International Law* 141.

Fox, Gregory H., "Self-Determination in the Post-Cold War Era: A New Internal Focus", (1995) 16 *Michigan Journal of International Law* 733.

Franck, Thomas M., "Postmodern Tribalism and the Right to Secession", in Catherine M. Brölmann, Rene Lefeber & Marjoleine Y.A. Zieck, *Peoples and Minorities in International Law*, Dordrecht, Martinus Nijhoff Publishers, 1993, pp. 3-27.

Franck, Thomas M.. "The Emerging Right to Democratic Governance", (1992) 86 *American Journal of International Law* 46.

Freeman, Michael & Philip Veerman, *The Ideologies of Children's Rights*, Dordrecht, Martinus Nijhoff, 1992.

Fritz, Ronald E., "Challenging Electoral Boundaries under the Charter: Judicial Deference and Burden of Proof", (1999) 5 *Revue d'études constitutionnelles* 1.

Frowein, Jochen Abr., "The Interrelationship between the Helsinki Final Act, the International Covenants on Human Rights, and the European Convention on Human Rights", in Thomas Buergenthal, ed., *Human Rights, International Law and the Helsinki Accord*, Montclair, N.J.: Allenheld, Osman, 1975, pp. 71-82.

Fyfe, M.H., "Some Legal Aspects of the Report of the Royal Commission on Espionage", (1946) 24 *Canadian Bar Review* 777.

Gayim, Eyassu, *The UN Draft Declaration on Indigenous Peoples, Assessment of the Draft Prepared by the Working Group on Indigenous Populations*, Rovaniemi, Finland: University of Lapland, 1994.

Ghandi, S., "Spare the Rod: Corporal Punishment in Schools and the European Convention of Human Rights", (1984) 33 *International & Comparative Law Quarterly* 488.

Gherari, Habib, "Le Comité des droits économiques, sociaux et culturels", (1992) 96 *Revue générale de droit international public* 75.

Gibson, Dale, "Enforcement of the Canadian Charter of Rights and Freedoms", in Gérald-A. Beaudoin & Errol P. Mendes, eds., *Canadian Charter of Rights and Freedoms*, 4th ed., Markham, Ont., LexisNexis Butterworths, 2005, pp. 1321-1398.

Gibson, Dale, "Interpretation of the Canadian Charter of Rights and Freedoms: General Considerations," in Walter S. Tarnopolsky, Gérald-A. Beaudoin, eds., *The Canadian Charter of Rights and Freedoms: Commentary*, Toronto: Carswell, 1982, pp. 25-40.

Girard, Philip, "The Protection of the Rights of Homosexuals under the International Law of Human Rights: European Perspectives", [1986] *Canadian Human Rights Yearbook* 3.

Gittleman, Richard, "The African Charter on Human and Peoples' Rights: a Legal Analysis", (1982) 22 *Virginia Journal of International Law* 667.

Glendon, Mary Ann, *A World Made New, Eleanor Roosevelt and the Universal Declaration of Human Rights*, New York: Random House, 2001.

Glueck, Sheldon, *War Criminals. Their Prosecution and Punishment*, New York: Knopf, 1944.

Goldberg, George, *The Peace to End Peace, The Paris Peace Conference of 1919*, New York: Harcourt, Brace & World: 1969, p. 151.

Gomez del Prado, J.L., "United Nations Conventions on Human Rights: The Practice of the Human Rights Committee and the Committee on the Elimination of Racial Discrimination in Dealing with Reporting Obligations of States Parties", (1985) 7 *Human Rights Quarterly* 492.

Goodwin-Gill, Guy, *The Refugee in International Law*, Oxford: Oxford University Press, 1983.

Gordon, Melissa, "Justice on Trial: The Efficacy of the International Tribunal for Rwanda", (1995) 1 *ILSA Journal of International & Comparative Law* 217.

Grahl-Madsen, Atle, *The Status of Refugees in International Law*, Leyden: Sijthoff, 1966.

Grammond, Sébastien, "La justice secrète: information confidentielle et procès civil", (1996) 56 *Cahiers de Droit* 437.

Gray, Christine, "European Convention on Human Rights. Fredom of Expression and the Thalidomide Case", (1979) 38 *Commonwealth Law Journal* 242.

Grey, Julius H., *Immigration Law in Canada*, Toronto: Butterworths, 1984.

Gros-Espiell, Hector, "L'O.É.A.", in Karel Vasak, ed., *Les dimensions internationales des droits de l'Homme*, Paris, Unesco, 1978, p. 600.

Gros-Espiell, Hector, "Le système interaméricain comme régime régional de protection internationale des droits de l'Homme", (1975) 145 *Receuil de cours de l'Academie de droit international* 1.

Hannikainen, Lauri, *Peremptory Norms (Jus Cogens) in International Law: Historical Development, Criteria, Present Status*, Helsinki: Lakimiedliiten Kustannus, 1988.

Hannum, Hurst, "The Right of Self-Determination in the Twenty-First Century", (1998) 55 *Washington & Lee Law Review* 773.

Hannum, Hurst, *Autonomy, Sovereignty and Self-Determination: The Accommodation of Conflicting Rights*, Philadelphia: University of Pennsylvania Press, 1990.

Haquani, Z., "La Convention des Nations Unies contre la torture", (1986) *Revue générale de droit international public* 127.

Harrington, Joanna, "Punting Terrorists, Assassins and Other Undesirables: Canada, the Human Rights Committee and Requests for Interim Measures of Protection", (2003) 48 *McGill Law Journal* 55.

Harris, David J., "Decisions on the European Convention on Human Rights during 1976-1977", (1976-77) 48 *British Yearbook of International Law* 381.

Harris, David J., M. O'Boyle & Colin Warbrick, *Law of the European Convention on Human Rights*, London: Butterworths, 1995.

Hathaway, James C., "Canada and the Inter-American Rights System: What Contribution to Expect?", October, 1991.

Hathaway, James C., *The Law of Refugee Status*, Toronto: Butterworths, 1991.

Hathaway, James C., *The Rights of Refugees Under International Law*, Cambridge: Cambridge University Press, 2005.

Hayward, Ann M., "International Law and the Interpretation of the Canadian Charter of Rights and Freedoms: Uses and Justifications", (1985) 23 *University of Western Ontario Law Review* 9.

Helgesen, Jan, "Protection of Minorities in the Conference on Security and Co-operation in Europe (CSCE) Process", in A. Rosas & J. Helgesen, eds., *The Strength of Diversity: Human Rights and Pluralist Democracy*, Dordrecht: Nijhoff, 1992, pp. 159-186.

Henkin, Louis, ed., *The International Bill of Rights: The Covenant on Civil and Political Rights*, New York: Columbia University Press, 1981.

Hiebert, Janet L., "The Evolution of the Limitation Clause", (1990) 28 *Osgoode Hall Law Journal* 103.

Hilling, Carol, "La participation canadienne au système interaméricain de protection des droits and libertés : les obligations immédiates and les perspectives d'avenir", in *Canada and the Americas: Proceedings of the 1991 Annual Meeting of the Canadian Council of International Law*, Ottawa: C.C.D.I., 1992, p. 223.

Hobbins, Alan John & Ann H. Steward, "Bringing Individual Human Rights Issues to the United Nations: John Humphrey and th Quest for Compensation", (2003) 41 *Canadian Yearbook of International Law* 187-223,

Hobbins, Alan John, "Humphrey and the High Commissioners: The Genesis of the Office of the High Commissioner for Human Rights", (2001) 3 *Journal of the History of International Law* 37.

Hobbins, Alan John, ed., *On the Edge of Greatness, The Diaries of John Humphrey, First Director of the United Nations Division of Human Rights, Volume I, 1948-1949*, Montreal: McGill University Libraries, 1994.

Hochschild, Adam, *King Leopold's Ghost*, Boston & New York: Houghton Mifflin, 1998, p. 112.

Hogg, Peter W. & Allison A. Bushell, "The *Charter* Dialogue Between Courts and Legislatures", (1997) 35 *Osgoode Hall Law Journal* 75.

Hogg, Peter W., "Canadian Law in the Constitutional Court of South Africa", (1998) 13 *South African Publiekreg/Public Law* 1.

Hogg, Peter W., "Section one of the Canadian Charter of Rights and Freedoms", in Armand De Mestral et al., eds., *The Limitation of Human*

Rights in Comparative Constitutional Law, Cowansville: Editions Yvon Blais, 1986, pp. 3-40.

Hogg, Peter W., "The Charter of Rights and American Theories of Interpretation", (1987) *Osgoode Hall Law Journal* 87.

Hogg, Peter W., *Constitutional Law of Canada*, 2nd ed., Toronto: Carswell, 1985.

Hovannisian, Richard G., ed., *The Armenian Genocide, History, Politics, Ethics*, New York: St. Martin's Press, 1991.

Hovius, Berend & Robert Martin, "The Canadian Charter of Rights and Freedoms in the Supreme Court of Canada", (1983) 61 *Canadian Bar Review* 354.

Hovius, Berend, "The Limitation Clauses of the European Convention on Human Rights and Freedoms", (1986) 6 *Yearbook of European Law* 1.

Hovius, Berend, "The Limitation Clauses of the European Convention of Human Rights: A Guide for the Application of Section 1 of the Charter?", (1985) 17 *Ottawa Law Review* 213.

How, W.G., "Case for a Canadian Bill of Rights", (1948) 26 *Canadian Bar Review* 497.

Huaraka, Tunguru, "The African Charter on Human and Peoples' Rights: A Significant Contribution to the Development of International Human Rights Law", in Daniel Prémont, ed., *Essais sur le concept de "droit de vivre" en mémoire de Yougindra Khushalani*, Brussels: Bruylant, 1988, pp. 193-211.

Hudson, Michael, "La Convention no. 169 de l'O.I.T. – observation sur son importance et son actualité au Canada", (1989-90) 6 *Revue québecoise de droit international* 98.

Humphrey, John P., "La nature juridique de la Déclaration universelle des droits de l'Homme", (1981) 12 *Revue générale de droit* 397.

Humphrey, John P., "The Canadian Charter of Rights and Freedoms and International Law", (1985-86) 50 *Saskatchewan Law Review* 13.

Humphrey, John P., "The International Bill of Rights: Scope and Implementation", (1976) 17 *William & Mary Law Review* 527.

Humphrey, John P., "The Universal Declaration of Human Rights: Its History, Impact and Judicial Character," in Bertrand G. Ramcharan, ed., *Human Rights: Thirty Years After the Universal Declaration*, The Hague: Martinus Nijhoff, 1984.

Humphrey, John P., *Human Rights and the United Nations: A Great Adventure*, Dobbs Ferry, N.Y.: Transnational, 1984.

Jackson, Robert H., *Report of Robert H. Jackson, United States Representative to the International Conference on Military Trials*, Washington: U.S. Government Printing Office, 1949.

Jacobs, Francis G., "The European Convention on Human Rights", in *The Canadian Charter of Rights and Freedoms, Initial Experience, Emerging Issues, Future Challenges*, Cowansville: Editions Yvon Blais, 1983.

Jacobs, Francis G., "The Limitation Clauses of the European Convention on Human Rights", in Armand De Mestral et al., eds., *The Limitation of Human Rights in Comparative Constitutional Law*, Cowansville: Editions Yvon Blais, 1986, pp. 21-40.

Jacobs, Francis G., *The European Convention on Human Rights*, Oxford: Clarendon Press, 1975.

Jacobs, Francis G.. "The Impact of the European Convention on Human Rights on Judicial Decisions in the United Kingdom", in Daniel Turp & Gérald-A. Beaudoin, eds., *Perspectives canadiennes et européennes des droits de la personne*, Cowansville: Editions Yvon Blais, 1986, pp. 81-90.

Janis, Mark W., Richard S. Kay & Anthony W. Bradley, *European Human Rights Law*, Oxford: Oxford University Press, 2000.

Jaspers, A.Ph.C.M., L. Betten, eds., *25 Years, European Social Charter*, Deventer: Kluwer, 1988.

Jayawickrama, Nihal, *The Judicial Application of Human Rights Law – National, Regional and International Jurisprudence*, Cambridge, Cambridge University Press, 2002.

Jenks, Wilfred C., *Human Rights and International Labour Standards*, New York: Praeger, 1960.

Jhabvala, Farrock, "The Practice of the Covenant's Human Rights Committee, 1976-82: Review of State Party Reports", (1984) 6 *Human Rights Quarterly* 81.

Johnson, Glen, "La rédaction de la Déclaration universelle (1946-1948)", in *La Déclaration universelle des droits de l'homme*, Paris: UNESCO/ L'Harmattan, 1991.

Jones, R.H., "Jurisdiction and Extradition under the Genocide Convention", (1975) 16 *Harvard International Law Journal* 696.

Joseph, Sarah, "New Procedures Concerning the Human Rights Committee's Examination of State Reports", (1995) 13 *Netherlands Quarterly of Human Rights* 5.

Joseph, Sarah, Jenny Schultz & Melissa Castan, *The International Covenant on Civil and Political Rights – Cases, Materials, and Commentary*, 2nd ed., Oxford: Oxford University Press, 2005.

Joyal, Renée, "La notion d'intérêt supérieur de l'enfant : sa place dans la Convention des Nations Unies sur les droits de l'enfant", (1991) 62 *Revue international de droit public* 785.

Kaplan, William, *State and Salvation, The Jehovah's Witnesses and Their Fight for Civil Rights*, Toronto: University of Toronto Press, 1989.

Kearney, Michael, "The Prohibition of Propaganda for War in the International Covenant on Civil and Political Rights", (2005) 23 *Netherlands Quarterly of Human Rights* 551

Kelly, Michael J., "Political Downsizing: The Re-Emergence of Self-Determination, and the Movement toward Smaller, Ethnically Homogenous States", (1999) 47 *Drake Law Review* 209.

Kelsen, Hans, "Will the Judgment in the Nuremberg Trial Constitute a Precedent in International Law?", (1947) 1 *International Law Quarterly* 153.

Keresztezi, N., "Mexican Labour Laws and Practices Come to Canada: A Comment on the First Case Brought to Canada Under the North American Agreement on Labour Cooperation", (2000) 8 *Canadian Labour and Employment Law Journal* 411.

Khan, S. Aga, "Legal Problems Relating to Refugees and Displaced Persons", (1976) 149 *Receuil de cours de l'Academie de droit international* 287.

Khushalani, Yougindra, "Right to Live", in Daniel Prémont, ed., *Essais sur le concept de "droit de vivre" en mémoire de Yougindra Khushalani*, Brussels: Bruylant, 1988, 283.

Kindred, Hugh, "Canadians as Citizens of the International Community: Asserting Unimplemented Treaty Rights in the Courts", in Stephen G. Coughlan & Dawn Russell, eds., *Citizenship and Citizen Participation in the Administration of Justice*, Montreal: Thémis, 2002, pp. 263-287.

Kirsch, Philippe & John T. Holmes, "The Birth of the International Criminal Court: The 1998 Rome Conference", (1998) 36 *Canadian Yearbook of International Law* 3-39.

Kiss, Alexandre, "Commentary on Limitations Provisions", (1985) 7 *Human Rights Quarterly* 15.

Kiss, Alexandre, "Le problème de l'interception des communictions téléphoniques devant la Cour européene des droits de l'homme: l'affaire Malone", [1986] *Canadian Human Rights Yearbook* 77.

Knight, Amy, *How the Cold War Began, The Gouzenko Affair and the Hunt for Soviet Spies*, Toronto: McClelland & Stewart, 2005.

Knop, Karen, "Here and There: International Law in Domestic Courts", (2000) 32 *New York University Journal of International Law & Policy* 501.

Kochavi, Arieh J., *Prelude to Nuremberg, Allied War Crimes Policy and the Question of Punishment*, Chapel Hill and London: University of North Carolina Press, 1998.

Koh, Harold Hongju, "Transnational Legal Process", (1996) 75 *Nebraska Law Review* 181.

Kolb, Robert, "Aspects historique de la relation entre le droit international humanitaire et les droits de l'homme", (1999) 37 *Canadian Yearbook of International Law* 57.

Korey, William, *NGOs and the Universal Declaration of Human Rights*, New York: St. Martin's Press, 1998.

Koskenniemi, Martti, "National Self-determination Today: Problems of Legal Theory and Practice", (1994) 43 *International & Comparative Law Quarterly* 241.

L'Heureux-Dubé, Claire, "The Importance of Dialogue: Globalization and the International Impact of the Rehnquist Court", (1998) 34 *Tulsa Law Journal* 15.

La Forest, Anne W., "Domestic Application of International Law in *Charter* Cases: Are We There Yet?", (2004) 37 *University of British Columbia Law Review* 157.

La Forest, Gérard V., "May the Provinces Legislate in Violation of International Law?", (1961) 39 *Canadian Bar Review* 78.

La Forest, Gérard V., "The Canadian Charter of Rights and Freedoms: An Overview", (1983) 61 *Canadian Bar Review* 19.

La Forest, Gérard V., "The Use of International and Foreign Material in the Supreme Court of Canada", *Proceedings, XVIIth Annual Conference, Canadian Council on International Law*, 1988, pp. 230-241.

Lambert, Hélène, *Seeking Asylum: Comparative Law and Practice in Selected European Countries*, Dordrecht: Kluwer, 1995.

Landry, Yannick & Virginie Désilets, "Les garanties juridiques", in Gérald-A. Beaudoin & Errol P. Mendes, eds., *Canadian Charter of Rights and Freedoms*, 4th ed., Markham, Ont., LexisNexis Butterworths, 2005, pp. 875-921.

Larsen, Joan L., "Importing Constitutional Norms from a 'Wider Civilization': Lawrence and the Rehnquist Court's Use of Foreign and International Law in Domestic Constitutional Interpretation", (2004) 65 *Ohio State Law Journal* 1283.

Laski, Harold, "Civil Liberties in Great Britain and Canada during War", (1942) 55 *Harvard Law Review* 1006.

Lasok, K.P.E., *The European Court of Justice; Practice and Procedure*, London: Butterworths, 1984.

Lattanzi, Flavia & William A. Schabas, eds., *Essays on the Rome Statute of the ICC*, Rome: Editrice il Sirente, 2000.

Lauren, Paul Gorden, *the Evolution of International Human Rights, Visions Seen*, 2nd ed., Philadelphia: University of Pennsylvania Press, 2003.

Lauterpacht, Hersh, *An International Bill of the Rights of Man*, New York: Columbia University Press, 1945.

Law Reform Commission of Canada, *Medical Treatment and Criminal Law, Working Paper No. 26*, Ottawa: Supply and Service Canada, 1980.

Le Bel, Michel, "L'interprétation de la Charte canadienne des droits et libertés au regard du droit international des droits de la personne – Critique de la démarche suivie par la Cour suprême du Canada", (1988) 48 *Revue du barreau* 743.

LeBel, Louis & Gloria Chao, "The Rise of International Law in Canadian Constitutional Litigation: Fugue or Fusion? Recent Developments and Challenges in Internalizing International Law", (2002) 16 *Supreme Court Law Review (2nd)* 23.

Lee, Roy, ed., *The International Criminal Court, Elements of Crimes and Rules of Procedure and Evidence*, Ardsley, New York: Transnational Publishers, 2001.

Lee, Roy, ed., *The International Criminal Court, The Making of the Rome Statute, Issues, Negotiations, Results*, The Hague: Kluwer Law International, 1999.

Leir, Michael, ed., "Amendments to the Universal Declaration of Human Rights", (1999) 37 *Canadian Yearbook of International Law* 331.

Leir, Michael, ed., "Protocol to Prevent, Suppress, and Punish Trafficking in Persons, Especially Women and Children", (2000) 38 *Canadian Yearbook of International Law* 332.

Leir, Michael, ed., "Ratification of the American Convention on Human Rights", (1999) 37 *Canadian Yearbook of International Law* 327.

Lemkin, Raphael, "Genocide as a Crime in International Law", (1947) 41 *American Journal of International Law* 145.

Lerner, Natan, "The 1989 ILO Convention on Indigenous Populations: New Standards", in Yoram Dinstein, Mala Tabory, eds., *The Protection of Minorities in Human Rights*, Dordrecht: Nijhoff, 1992, pp. 213-231.

Lerner, Natan, "The 1989 ILO Convention on Indigenous Populations: New Standards", (1990) 20 *Israel Yearbook on Human Rights* 223.

Lerner, Natan, "The 1992 UN Declaration on Minorities", (1993) 23 *Israel Yearbook of Human Rights* 111.

Lerner, Natan, "Toward a Draft Declaration Against Religious Intolerance and Discrimination", (1981) 11 *Israel Yearbook of Human Rights* 82.

Lerner, Natan, *The U.N. Convention on the Elimination of all Forms of Racial Discrimination*, Alphen den Rijn: Sitjhoff and Noordhoof, 1989.

Lessard, Hester, "Farce or Tragedy?: Judicial Backlash and Justice McClung", (1999) 10 *Constitutional Forum* 65.

Link, Arthur S., ed., *The Papers of Woodrow Wilson*, Vol. 56, Princeton: Princeton University Press, 1987, p. 534.

Lippman, Matthew, "The 1948 Convention on the Prevention and Punishment of the Crime of Genocide: Forty-Five Years Later", (1994) 8 *Temple International and Comparative Law Journal* 1.

Lipstein, K., *The Law of the European Economic Community*, London: Butterworths, 1974.

Livingstone, Stephen & David J. Harris, *The Inter-American System of Human Rights*, Oxford: Oxford University Press, 1998; Scott Davidson, *The Inter-American Human Rights* System, Aldershot: Dartmouth, 1997.

Lopatka, Adam, "Convention relative aux droits de l'enfant", (1991) 62 *Revue international de droit public* 765.

Lubell, Noam, "Challenges in Applying Human Rights Law to Armed Conflict", (2005) 87 *International Review of the Red Cross* 737.

Lyon, Jennie Hatfield, John E. Claydon, "International and Comparative Sources for Interpreting the Charter: A selective annotated bibliographic guide", Canadian Bar Association-Ontario, Continuing Legal Education, 10 June 1986.

MacDonald, Ronald St. J., "Politicians and the Press", in *Protecting Human Rights: The European Dimension*, Cologne: Carl Heymanns, 1988, pp. 361-372.

MacDonald, Ronald St. J., "The Relationship Between International Law and Domestic Law in Canada", in Ronald St. J. MacDonald, Gerald L. Morris & Douglas J. Johnston, eds., *Canadian Perspectives on International Law and Organization*, Toronto: University of Toronto Press, 1974, pp. 88-136.

MacDonald, Ronald St. J., F. Matscher & Hubert Petzold, eds. *The European System for the Protection of Human Rights*, Dordrecht, Martinus Nijhoff, 1994.

MacIntyre, J.M., "The Use of American Cases in Canadian Courts", (1966) 2 *University of British Columbia Law Review* 478.

Mackay, Robert Alexander, *Canadian Foreign Policy, 1945-1954*, Toronto: McClelland & Stewart, 1971, pp. 163-165.

Mainwairing, John, *The International Labour Organization, A Canadian View*, Ottawa: Supply and Services Canada, 1986.

Major, Marie-France, "Reporting to the Human Rights Committee: The Canadian Experience", (2000) 38 *Canadian Yearbook of International Law* 261.

Malinverni, Giorgio, "Le projet de Convention pour la protection des minorités élaboré par la Commission européenne pour la démocratie par le droit", (1991) 3 *Revue universelle des droits de l'homme* 157.

Mann, Francis, "Contempt of Court in the House of Lords and the European Court of Human Rights", (1979) 95 *Law Quarterly Review* 348.

Manning, Morris, *Rights, Freedoms and the Courts: A Practical Analysis of the* Constitution Act, 1982, Toronto: Emond-Montgomery, 1983.

Margolian, Howard, *Conduct Unbecoming: The Story of the Murder of Canadian Prisoners of War in Normandy*, Toronto: University of Toronto Press, 1998.

Margolian, Howard, *Unauthorized Entry: The Truth about Nazi War Criminals in Canada, 1946-1956*, Toronto: University of Toronto Press, 2000.

Marie, Jean-Bernard, *La Commission des droits de l'homme de l'O.N.U.*, Paris: Pedone, 1975.

Marsh, Norman S., "What Rights are Fundamental – the United Kingdom's Dilemma," in Armand De Mestral et al., eds., *The Limitation of Human Rights in Comparative Constitutional Law*, Cowansville: Editions Yvon Blais, 1986, pp. 515-524.

Martin, Dianne L., "Extradition, the Charter, and Due Process: Is Procedural Fairness Enough?", (2002) 16 *Supreme Court Law Review (2d)* 161.

Martin, Robert, "*R.* v. Sharpe", (2001) 39 *Alberta Law Review* 585.

Matkin, James G., "The Negotiation of the Charter of Rights: The Provincial Perspective", in Paul Weiler, Robin Elliott, eds., *Litigating the Values of a Nation: The Canadian Charter of Rights and Freedoms*, Toronto: Carswell, 1986, pp. 27-35.

Maxwell, Peter B., *On the Interpretation of Statutes*, London: Sweet & Maxwell, 1896.

McCorquodale, Robert, ed., *Self-Determination in International Law*, Aldershot, United Kingdom: Ashgate/Dartmouth, 2000.

McDonald, David, *Legal Rights in the Canadian Charter of Rights and Freedoms: A Manual of Issues and Sources*, Toronto: Carswell, 1982.

McGoldrick, Dominic, "The United Nations Convention on the Rights of the Child", (1991) 5 *International Journal of the Law of the Family* 132.

McGoldrick, Dominic, *The Human Rights Committee, Its Role in the Development of the International Covenant on Civil and Political Rights*, 2nd ed., Oxford: Clarendon Press, 2000.

McGoldrick, Dominic, *The Human Rights Committee*, Oxford: Clarendon Press, 1991.

McWhinney, Edward, *The United Nations and a New World Order for a New Millenium: Self-Determination, State Succession and Humanitarian Intervention*, Boston: Kluwer Law International, 2000.

Medina, Cecilia, "Inter-American System", (1994) 12 *Netherlands Quarterly of Human Rights* 327.

Melson, Robert, *Revolution and Genocide: on the Origin of the Armenian Genocide and of the Holocaust*, Chicago: University of Chicago Press, 1992.

Mendes, Errol P., "Interpreting the Canadian Charter of Rights and Freedoms: Applying International and European Jurisprudence on the Law and Practice of Fundamental Rights", (1982) 20 *Alberta Law Review* 383.

Mendes, Errol P., "The Crucible of the Charter: Judicial Principles v. Judicial Deference in the Context of Section 1", in Gerald-A. Beaudoin & Errol P. Mendes, eds., *Canadian Charter of Rights and Freedoms*, 4th ed., Markham, Ont., LexisNexis Butterworths, 2005, pp. 163-214.

Meron, Theodor, "The Geneva Conventions as Customary Law", (1987) 81 *American Journal of International Law* 348.

Meron, Theodor, "The Meaning and Reach of the International Convention on the Elimination of All Forms of Racial Discrimination", (1985) 79 *American Journal of International Law* 283.

Mertens, P., "L'application de la Convention and de la Recommandation de l'UNESCO concernant la lutte contre la discrimination dans le domaine de l'enseignement, Un bilan provisoire", (1968) 1 *Revue des droits de l'homme* 91.

Möller, Jakob Th., "Recent Jurisprudence of the Human Rights Committee", [1991-92] *Canadian Human Rights Yearbook* 79.

Monahan, Patrick J., "The Public Policy Role of the Supreme Court of Canada in the *Secession Reference*", (1999) 11 *National Journal of Constitutional Law* 65.

Morel, André, "La Charte québécoise: un document unique dans l'histoire législative canadienne", (1987) 21 *Revue juridique Thémis* 1.

Morel, André, "La clause limitative de l'article 1 de la Charte canadienne des droits et libertés; une assurance contre le gouvernement des juges", (1983) 61 *Canadian Bar Review* 81.

Morel, André, "La recherche d'un équilibre entre les pouvoirs législatif et judiciaire – essai de psychologie judiciaire," in Armand De Mestral et al., eds., *The Limitation of Human Rights in Comparative Constitutional Law*, Cowansville: Editions Yvon Blais, 1986, pp 115-135.

Morsink, Johannes, "Cultural Genocide, the Universal Declaration, and Minority Rights", (1999) 21 *Human Rights Quarterly* 1009.

Morsink, Johannes, "World War Two and the Universal Declaration", (1993) 15 *Human Rights Quarterly* 357.

Morsink, Johannes, *The Universal Declaration of Human Rights: Origins, Drafting, and Intent*, Philadelphia: University of Pennsylvania Press, 1999.

Mullan, David J., "Quebec Unilateral Secession Reference: 'A Ruling that Will Stand the Test of Time'", (1998) 9 *Public Law Review* 231.

Murray, Rachel, *Human Rights in Africa: From the OAU to the African Union*, Cambridge: Cambridge University Press, 2004.

Musgrave, Thomas D., *Self Determination and National Minorities*, Oxford: Clarendon Press, 1997.

Myhall, Patricia J., "Canada's Unjustified Ratification of the Race Convention", (1972) 30 *University of Toronto Faculty of Law Review* 31.

Norman, Ken, "Freedom of Association (Section (d))", in Gérald-A. Beaudoin & Errol P. Mendes, eds., *Canadian Charter of Rights and Freedoms*, 4th ed., Markham, Ont., LexisNexis Butterworths, 2005, pp. 325-359.

Norman, Ken, "Freedom of Peaceful Assembly and Freedom of Association (Section 2(c) and (d))", in Gérald-A. Beaudoin, Ed Ratushny, eds., *The Canadian Charter of Rights and Freedoms*, Toronto: Carswell, pp. 227-264.

Norman, Ken, "Taking Human Rights Lightly: The Canadian Appraoch", (2001) 12 *National Journal of Constitutional Law* 291.

Norris, Robert, "The Individual Petition Procedure of the Inter-American System for the Protection of Human Rights", in Hurst Hannum, ed., *Guide to International Human Rights Law Practice*, Philadelphia, University of Pennsylvania Press, 1984, pp. 104-125.

Nowak, Manfred, "The African Charter on Human and Peoples' Rights", (1986) 7 *Human Rights Law Journal* 399.

Nowak, Manfred, *Covenant on Civil and Political Rights, CCPR Commentary*, 2nd ed., Kehl, Strasbourg, Arlington: N.P. Engel, 2005.

Nowak, Manfred, *Introduction to the International Human Rights Regime*, Leiden/Boston: Martinus Nijhoff, 2003.

O'Connell, Mary Ellen, "New International Legal Process", (1999) 93 *American Journal of International Law* 334.

O'Flaherty, Michael, *Human Rights and the United Nations: Practice Before the Treaty Bodies*, The Hague: Kluwer Academic, 2002.

O'Flaherty, Michael, The Concluding Observations of the United Nations Treaty Bodies", (2006) 6 *Human Rights Law Review* 27.

O'Halloran, W.O., "Inherent Rights", (1947-48) *Obiter Dicta*.

Ojo, Olosula & Amadu Sesay, "The OAU and Human Rights: Prospects for the 1980s and Beyond", (1986) 8 *Human Rights Quarterly* 89.

Omozurike, O.U., "The African Charter of Human Rights", (1983) 77 *American Journal of International Law* 511.

Opsahl, T., "The Human Rights Committee", in Philys Alston, ed., *The United Nations and Human Rights*, Oxford: Clarendon Press, 1992, pp. 369-443.

Ovey, Clare & Robin C.A. White, *Jacobs & White, The European Convention on Human Rights*, Oxford: Clarendon Press, 2002.

Pais, Marta Santos, "La Convention sur les droits de l'enfant", in Institut canadien d'études juridiques supérieures, *Droits de la personne: l'émergence des droits nouveaux, aspects canadiens et européens, Actes des Journées strasbourgeoises de 1992*, Cowansville: Éditions Yvon Blais, 1992, pp. 665-680.

Paré, Marie, "La légitimité de la clause dérogatoire de la Charte canadienne des droits et libertés en regard du droit international", (1995) 29 *Revue juridique Thémis* 627.

Parker, G., "The 'New' Sexual Offences", (1983) 31 CR (3d) 317.

Partsch, K.J., "The Contribution of Universal International Instruments on Human Rights," in Armand De Mestral et al., eds., *The Limitation of Human Rights in Comparative Constitutional Law*, Cowansville: Editions Yvon Blais, 1986, pp. 63-74.

Pasqualucci, Jo M., "Interim Measures in International Human Rights: Evolution and Harmonization", (2005) 38 *Vanderbilt Journal of Transnational Law* 1.

Pateyron, Eric, *La contribution française à la rédaction de la Déclaration universelle des droits de l'homme, René Cassin et la Commission consultative des droits de l'homme*, Paris : La documentation française. 1998.

Patrick Thornberry, "Confronting Racial Discrimination: A CERD Perspective", (2005) 5 *Human Rights Law Review* 239.

Pearson, Lester B., "Federalism for the Future: A Statement of Policy by the Government of Canada", in Anne F. Bayefsky, *Canada's Constitution Act 1982 & Amendments, A Documentary History*, Vol. I, Toronto: McGraw Hill Ryerson, 1989, pp. 61-74.

Peck, Sidney R., "An Analytical Framework for the Application of the Canadian Charter of Rights and Freedoms", (1987) 25 *Osgoode Hall Law Journal* 1.

Pellet, Alain, & Patrick Daillier, *Droit international public*, 6th ed., Paris: LGDJ, 1999.

Pelloux, R., "L'arrêt de la Cour européenne des droits de l'homme dans l'affaire linguistique belge (fond)", [1968] *Annuaire français de droit international* 201.

Pelloux, R., "Trois affaires syndicales devant la Cour européenne des droits de l'homme", [1976] *Annuaire français de droit international* 121.

Penton, M. James, *Jehovah's Witnesses in Canada, Champions of Freedom of Speech and Worship*, Toronto: Macmillan, 1976.

Petrenko, A., "The Human Rights Provisions of the United Nations Charter", (1978) 9 *Manitoba Law Journal* 53.

Pettiti, L.-E., "Écoutes téléphoniques et droits de l'homme", in *Fortschritt im Bewusstsein der Grund- und Menschenrechte. Festschrift für Felix Ermacora*, Kehl: Engel, 1988, pp. 455-474.

Phillips, Alan & Allan Rosas, *The U.N. Minority Rights Declaration*, Abo: Abo Akademi University Institute for Human Rights, 1993.

Phillips, B., "The Case for Corporal Punishment in the United Kingdom. Beaten Into Submission in Europe?", (1994) 43 *International & Comparative Law Quarterly* 153.

Pigeon, Louis-Philippe, *Rédaction et interprétation des lois*, Québec: Editeur officiel, 1986.

Politi, Mauro & Giuseppe Nesi, eds., *The Rome Statute of the International Criminal Court, A Challenge to Impunity*, Aldershot: Ashgate, 2001.

Pollock, Frederick, *Essays in Jurisprudence and Ethics*, London: Macmillan, 1882.

Pothier, Diane, "Twenty Years of Labour Law and the Charter", (2002) 40 *Osgoode Hall Law Journal* 369.

Power, Mark & Pierre Foucher, "Language Rights and Education", in Gérald-A. Beaudoin & Errol P. Mendes, eds., *Canadian Charter of Rights and Freedoms*, 4th ed., Markham, Ont., LexisNexis Butterworths, 2005, pp. 1093-1167.

Prémont, Daniel, ed., *Essais sur le concept de "droit de vivre" en mémoire de Yougindra Khushalani*, Brussels: Bruylant, 1988.

Price Cohen, Cynthia, "The U.N. Convention on the Rights of the Child: Developing an Information Model to Computerize the Monitoring of Treaty Compliance", (1992) 14 *Human Rights Law Journal* 216.

Provost, René, "Le juge mondialisé : légitimité judiciaire et droit international au Canada", in Marie-Claude Belleau & François Lacasse, eds., *Claire L'Heureux-Dubé à la Cour suprême du Canada, 1987-2002*, Montreal: Wilson & Lafleur, 2004, pp. 569-603.

Quane, Helen, "The United Nations and the Evolving Right to Self-Determination", (1998) 47 *International & Comparative Law Quarterly* 537.

Ramcharan, Bertrand G., "The Concept and Dimensions of the Right to Life", in B.G. Ramcharan, ed., *The Right to Life in International Law*, Dordrecht/Boston/Lancaster: Martinus Nijhoff Publishers, 1985, pp. 1-32.

Ramcharan, Bertrand G., "The Right to Life", (1983) 30 *Netherlands International Law Review* 297.

Ramcharan, Bertrand G., *The United Nations High Commissioner for Human Rights: The Challenges of International Protection*, The Hague: Kluwer Academic, 2002.

Randall, Maya Hertig, "Commercial Speech under the European Convention on Human Rights: Subordinate or Equal", (2006) 6 *Human Rights Law Review* 53.

Reid, Escott, *On Duty, A Canadian at the Making of the United Nations, 1945-1946*, Toronto: McClelland and Stewart, 1983, pp. 18-23.

Reid, Escott, *Radical Mandarin: The Memoirs of Escott Reid*, Toronto/ Buffalo/London: University of Toronto Press, 1989.

Rials, Stéphane, *La déclaration des droits de l'Homme et du citoyen*, Paris: Hachette, 1988.

Rigaldies, Francis & José Woehrling, "Le juge interne canadien et le droit international", (1980) 21 *Cahiers de Droit* 293.

Rigaux, F., "L'incrimination du prosélytisme face à la liberté d'expression", [1994] *Revue trimestrielle des droits de l'homme* 144.

Roach, Kent & David Schneiderman, "Freedom of Expression in Canada", in Gérald-A. Beaudoin & Errol P. Mendes, eds., *Canadian Charter of Rights and Freedoms*, 4th ed., Markham, Ont., LexisNexis Butterworths, 2005, pp. 257-323.

Roach, Kent, "Constitutional and Common Law Dialogues Between the Supreme Court and Canadian Legislatures", (2001) 81 *Canadian Bar Review* 481.

Roach, Kent, "Dialogic Judicial Review and its Critics", (2004) 23 *Supreme Court Law Review* (2d) 49.

Roach, Kent, *Constitutional Remedies in Canada* (looseleaf) Toronto: Canada Law Book, 1994.

Robert, Jacques, "La Commission européenne pour la démocratie par le droit, dite Commission de Venise", in Alexandre-Linos Sicilianos & Emmanuel Decaux, *La CSCE: Dimension humaine et règlement des différends*, Paris: Montchrestien, 1993, p. 255.

Robertson, A.H., *Human Rights in the World*, Manchester: Manchester University Press, 1972.

Robinson, Jacob, *And the Crooked Shall be Made Straight*, New York: MacMillan, 1965, pp. 72-73.

Robinson, Mary, *A Voice for Human Rights*, Philadelphia: University of Pennsylvania Press, 2006.

Robinson, Nehemiah, *The Genocide Convention: A Commentary*, New York: Institute of Jewish Affairs, 1960.

Rodley, Nigel, *The Treatment of Prisoners under International Law*, Oxford: Clareindon Press, 1999.

Rodriguez-Orellana, Manuel, "Human Rights Talk . . . and Self-Determination, Too!", (1998) 73 *Notre Dame Law Review* 1391.

Roth, S.J., "Comments on the Geneva CSCE Meeting of Experts on National Minorities", (1991) 12 *Human Rights Law Journal* 330.

Roy, Simon, "Le rôle de l'accusé dans la poursuite criminelle", in Gérald-A. Beaudoin & Errol P. Mendes, eds., *Canadian Charter of Rights and Freedoms*, 4th ed., Markham, Ont., LexisNexis Butterworths, 2005, pp. 791-874.

Safferling, Christoph J.M., "Public Prosecutor v. Djajic", (1998) 92 *American Journal of International Law* 528.

Sanders, Douglas, "A Text and New Process", [1994] 1 *C.N.L.R.* 48.

Santos Pais, Marta, "La Convention sur les droits de l'enfant", in Institut canadien d'études juridiques supérieures, *Droits de la personne: l'émergence des droits nouveaux, aspects canadiens et européens, Actes des Journées strasbourgeoises de 1992*, Cowansville, Éditions Yvon Blais, 1992, p. 665.

Sarkin, Jeremy, "The Drafting of South Africa's Final Constitution from a Human-Rights Perspective", (1999) 47 *American Journal of Comparative Law* 67.

Sauriol, Chantal, "Droit de vote des détenus: le Parlement est-il encore souverain?", in *Développements récents en droit administratif et constitutionnel (2003)*, Cowansville: Éditions Yvon Blais, 2003, pp. 119-141.

Schabas, William A. & Daniel Turp, "La *Charte canadienne des droits et libertés* et le droit international: les enseignements de la Cour suprême dans les affaires *Keegstra, Andrews* et *Taylor*", (1989-90) 6 *Revue québécoise de droit international* 12.

Schabas, William A., "Aspects of the Canadian Model: Self-determination, non-discrimination and international human rights protection", (2001) 1 *Wales Law Journal* 144.

Schabas, William A., "Canada and the Adoption of the *Universal Declaration of Human Rights*", (1998) 43 *McGill Law Journal* 403.

Schabas, William A., "Canada", in Ben Brandon & Max Du Plessis, eds., *The Prosecution of International Crimes, A Guide to Prosecuting ICC Crimes in Commonwealth States*, London: Commonwealth Secretariat, 2005, pp. 153-172.

Schabas, William A., "Canadian Implementing Legislation for the Rome Statute", (2000) 3 *Yearbook of International Humanitarian Law* 337.

Schabas, William A., "Canadian Implementing Legislation for the Rome Statute: Jurisdiction and Defences", in M. Neuner, ed., *National Legislation Incorporating International Crimes*, Berlin: Berliner Wissenschafts-Verlag/Wolf Legal Publishers, 2003, pp. 35-43.

Schabas, William A., "Canadian Ratification of the American Convention on Human Rights", (1998) 16 *Netherlands Quarterly of Human Rights* 315.

Schabas, William A., "Case Comment: *United States* v. *Burns*", (2001) 95 *American Journal of International Law* 666.

Schabas, William A., "Extradition et la peine de mort: le Canada renvoie deux fugitifs au couloir de la mort", (1992) 4 *Revue universelle des droits de l'homme* 65.

Schabas, William A., "Freedom from Want: How Can We Make Indivisibility More than a Mere Slogan", (2000) 11 *National Journal of Constitutional Law* 187-209.

Schabas, William A., "From *Kindler* to *Burns*: International Law is Nourishing the Constitutional Living Tree", in Gérard Cohen-Jonathan & William Schabas, eds., *La peine capitale et le droit international des droits de l'homme*, Paris: L.G.D.J. Diffuseur, 2003, pp. 143-156.

Schabas, William A., "International Human Rights / Les droits de la personne au plan international", in Donat Pharand, Don McRae & Yves

Le Bouthillier, eds., *Compendium*, Ottawa: Canadian Council on International Law, 1998, pp. 177-182.

Schabas, William A., "International Human Rights Law and the Canadian Courts", in Thomas A. Cromwell, Danielle Pinard & Hélène Dumont, eds., *Human Rights in the 21st Century: Prospects, Institutions and Processes*, Montréal: Les Éditions Thémis, 1997, at pp. 21-48.

Schabas, William A., "Kindler and Ng: Our Supreme Magistrates Take a Frightening Step into the Court of Public Opinion", (1991) 51 *Revue du Barreau* 673-682.

Schabas, William A., "*Kindler* v. *Canada*", (1993) 87 *American Journal of International Law* 128.

Schabas, William A., "L'influence de la Convention européenne des droits de l'homme sur la jurisprudence des Cours suprêmes du Commonwealth (A.F.S., Australie, Canada, Nouvelle-Zélande)", in Jean François Flauss, ed., *L'influence de la Convention européenne des droits de l'homme sur les États tiers*, Brussels: Nemesis/Bruylant, 2002, pp. 29-53.

Schabas, William A., "L'affaire Mugesera", (1996) 7 *Revue universelle des droits de l'homme* 193.

Schabas, William A., "Le renaissance du bref d'*habeas corpus* sous la *Charte canadienne des droits et libertés*", (1990) 50 *Revue du Barreau* 409.

Schabas, William A., "Le rôle du droit européen dans la jurisprudence des tribunaux canadiens", (1991-92) 7 *Revue québecoise de droit international* 235.

Schabas, William A., "Les droits des minorités: Une déclaration inachevée", in *Déclaration universelle des droits de l'homme 1948-98, Avenir d'un idéal commun*, Paris: La Documentation française, 1999, pp. 223-242.

Schabas, William A., "Les recours individuals en droit international des droits de la personne : problèmes et perspectives", in Canadian Council on International Law, *Selected Papers in International Law*, The Hague: Kluwer Law International, 1999, pp. 489-501.

Schabas, William A., "Les recours internationaux en matière des droits de la personne", in *Actes du Congrès du Barreau de Québec, 1982*, Cowansville, Éditions Yvon Blais, 1992, pp. 855-880.

Schabas, William A., "Mugesera v. Minister of Citizenship and Immigration", (1999) 93 *American Journal of International Law* 529-533.

Schabas, William A., "New Perspectives on International Human Rights Law for Administrative Tribunals", in Stephen G. Coughlan & Dawn Russell, eds., *Citizenship and Citizen Participation in the Administration of Justice*, Montreal: Editions Thémis, 2002, pp. 331-346.

Schabas, William A., "Passagers clandestins, travailleurs migrants et droits de la personne: le traité du 19e siècle triomphe sur les valeurs du 20e siècle", (1997) 2 *Canadian International Lawyer* 210.

Schabas, William A., "Reservations to International Human Rights Treaties", (1995) 32 *Canadian Yearbook of International Law* 39.

Schabas, William A., "Substantive and Procedural Issues in the Ratification by Canada of the *American Convention on Human Rights*", (1991) 12 *Human Rights Law Journal* 405.

Schabas, William A., "The Omission of the Right to Property in the International Covenants", in (1991) 4 *Hague Yearbook of International Law* 135.

Schabas, William A., "Twenty-Five Years of Public International Law at the Supreme Court of Canada", (2000) 79 *Canadian Bar Review* 174.

Schabas, William A., *Genocide in International Law*, Cambridge: Cambridge University Press, 2000.

Schabas, William A., *Introduction to the International Criminal Court*, 2nd ed., Cambridge: Cambridge University Press, 2004.

Schabas, William A., *The Abolition of the Death Penalty in International Law*, 3rd ed., Cambridge: Cambridge University Press, 2003.

Schabas, William A., *The UN International Criminal Tribunals: The former Yugoslavia, Rwanda and Sierra Leone*, Cambridge: Cambridge University Press, 2006.

Schachter, Oscar, "The Twilight Existence of Nonbinding International Agreements", (1977) 71 *American Journal of International Law* 296.

Schneiderman, David, ed., *The Quebec Decision: Perspectives on the Supreme Court Ruling on Secession*, Toronto: Lorimer, 1999.

Schwelb, Egon, "The International Court of Justice and the Human Rights Clauses of the Charter", (1972) 66 *American Journal of International Law* 336.

Schwelb, Egon, "The U.N. Convention on the Elimination of All Forms of Racial Discrimination", (1966) 15 *International & Comparative Law Quarterly* 996.

Shaw, Malcolm N., *International Law*, 4th ed., Cambridge: Cambridge University Press, 1997.

Shelton, Dinah, "Abortion and Right to Life in the Inter-American System: The Case of Baby Boy", (1981) 2 *Human Rights Law Journal* 309.

Shelton, Dinah, ed., *International Crimes, Peace, and Human Rights: The Role of the International Criminal Court*, Ardsley, New York: Transnational Publishers, 2000.

Sicilianos, Linos-Alexandre, "L'actualité et les potentialités de la Convention sur l'élimination de la discrimination raciale", (2005) 16 *Revue trimestrielle des droits de l'homme* 861.

Sieghart, Paul, *The International Law of Human Rights*, Oxford: Clarendon Press, 1983.

Simpson, A.W. Brian, *Human Rights and the End of Empire, Britain and the Genesis of the European Convention*, Oxford: Oxford University Press, 2001.

Slaughter, Anne-Marie, "A Typology of Transjudicial Communication", (1994) 29 *University of Richmond Law Review* 99.

Slaughter, Anne-Marie, "Judicial Globalization", (2000) 40 *Virginia Journal of International Law* 1103.

Smith, Rhona K.M. & Christien van den Anker, *The Essentials of Human Rights*, London: Hodder Arnold, 2005.

Sodini, Raphaël, *Le Comité des droits économiques, sociaux et culturels*, Paris : Montchrestien, 2000.

Sohn, Louis B., "How American International Lawyers Prepared for the San Francisco Bill of Rights", (1995) 89 *American Journal of International Law* 540.

Spencer, Robert A., *Canada in World Affairs, 1946-1949*, Toronto: Oxford University Press, 1959, pp. 162-163. The phrase "mild sensation" was used in the Canadian Press wire story: *The Globe and Mail*, 8 December 1948, p. 1.

Stanfield, P., "Right to Free Assistance of an Interpreter in Judicial Proceedings Concerning a "Regulatory Offence"/Öztürk Case", (1984) 4 *Human Rights Law Journal* 293.

Stewart, Bryce M., *Canadian Labor Laws and the Treaty*, New York: Columbia University Press, 1926.

Stone, Harlan, "The Common Law in the United States", (1936) 50 *Harvard Law Review* 4.

Sudre, Frédéric *et al.*, "Chronique de la jurisprudence de la Cour européenne des droits de l'homme. Première partie: janvier-mai 1993", (1993) 4 *Revue universelle des droits de l'homme* 217.

Sudre, Frédéric, *Droit international et européen des droits de l'homme*, 2nd. ed., Paris: Presses universitaires de France, 1994.

Sudre, Frédéric, *La Convention européenne des droits de l'homme*, Paris: Presses universitaires de France ("Que sais-je?"), 1990.

Sullivan, Ruth, "Some Implications of Plain Language Drafting", (2001) 22 *Statute Law Review* 145.

Sullivan, Ruth, "Statutory Interpretation in the Supreme Court of Canada", (1998-1999) 30 *Ottawa Law Review* 175.

Sullivan, Ruth, *Driedger on the Construction of Statutes*, 3rd ed., Toronto & Vancouver: Butterworths, 1994.

Sullivan, Ruth, *Sullivan and Driedger on the Construction of Statutes*, 4th ed., Markham, Ont. & Vancouver: Butterworths, 2002.

Sunahara, Ann Gomer, *The Politics of Racism: The Uprooting of Japanese Canadians During the Second World War*, Toronto: Lorimer, 1981.

Swepston, Lee, "A New Step in the International Law on Indigenous and Tribal Peoples: The ILO Convention 169 of 1989", (1990) 15 *Oklahoma City University Law Review* 677.

Swords, Colleen, ed., "Canadian Ratification Practice", (2002) 40 *Canadian Yearbook of International Law* 491.

Tabory, Mala, "Minority Rights in the CSCE Context", (1990) 20 *Israel Yearbook of Human Rights* 197.

Tabory, Mala, "Minority Rights in the CSCE Context", in Yoram Dinstein, Mala Tabory, eds., *The Protection of Minorities in Human Rights*, Dordrecht: Nijhoff, 1992, pp. 187-212.

Tarnopolsky, Walter S., "Human Rights, International Law and the International Bill of Rights", (1986) 50 *Saskatchewan Law Review* 21.

Tarnopolsky, Walter S., *The Canadian Bill of Rights*, 2nd ed., Toronto: McClelland and Stewart, 1975.

Tassé, Roger, "Application de la Charte canadienne des droits et libertés", in Gérald-A. Beaudoin & Ed Ratushny, eds., *The Canadian Charter of Rights and Freedoms*, 2nd ed., Toronto: Carswell, 1989, pp. 75-142.

Ténékidès, Georges, "L'action des Nations Unies contre la discrimination raciale", (1989) 180 *Receuil de cours de l'Academie de droit international* 269.

Thornberry, Patrick, "Poverty, Litigation and Fundamental Rights – A European perspective", (1980) 29 *International & Comparative Law Quarterly* 250.

Thornberry, Patrick, *Indigenous Peoples and Human Rights*, Manchester: Manchester University Press, 2002.

Thornberry, Patrick, *International Law and the Rights of Minorities*, Oxford: Clarendon Press, 1991.

Tinker, Catherine, "Human Rights for Women: the U.N. Convention on the Elimination of Discrimination Against Women", (1981) 3 *Human Rights Quarterly* 32.

Tittemore, Brian, "Canada and the OAS – The First Five Years", *Human Rights Brief*, Vol. 2, No. 1, p. 3.

Toman, Jiri, "The Treatment of Prisoners: Development of Legal Instruments and Quasi-Legal Standards", in Gudmundur Alfredsson, Peter Macalister-Smith, *The Living Law of Nations*, Kehl: Engel, 1996, pp. 421-439.

Tomuschat, Christian, ed., *Modern Law of Self-Determination*, Dordrecht: Martinus Nijhoff, 1993.

Toope, Stephen J., "Case Comment on the Reference Re Secession of Quebec", (1999) 93 *American Journal of International Law* 519.

Toope, Stephen J., "Inside and Out: The Stories of International Law and Domestic Law", (2001) 50 *University of New Brunswick Law Journal* 11.

Toope, Stephen J., "The Uses of Metaphor: International Law and the Supreme Court of Canada", (2001) 80 *Canadian Bar Review* 534.

Trechsel, Stefan, *Human Rights in Criminal Proceedings*, Oxford: Oxford University Press, 2005.

Tremblay, Guy, "La Charte canadienne des droits et libertés et quelques leçons tirées de la Convention européenne des droits de l'homme", (1982) 23 *Cahiers de Droit* 795.

Tremblay, Luc B., "Legitimacy of Judicial Review: The Limits of Dialogue Between Courts and Legislatures", (2005) 3 *International Journal of Constitutional Law* 617.

Triffterer, Otto, ed., *Commentary on the Rome Statute of the International Criminal Court, Observers' Notes, Article by Article*, Baden-Baden: Nomos, 1999.

Trudeau, Pierre Elliott, *A Canadian Charter of Human Rights*, Ottawa: Queen's Printer, 1968.

Turp, Daniel & Gérald-A. Beaudoin, eds. *Perspectives canadiennes and européennes des droits de la personne*, Cowansville: Éditions Yvon Blais, 1986.

Turp, Daniel, "L'examen des rapports périodiques du Canada en application du Pacte international relatif aux droits économiques, sociaux et culturels", (1991) 28 *Canadian Yearbook of International Law* 330.

Turp, Daniel, "La préparation des rapports périodiques du Canada en application des traités relatifs aux droits et libertés", (1986) 23 *Canadian Yearbook of International Law* 161.

Turp, Daniel, "Le contrôle du respect du Pacte international relatif aux droits économiques, sociaux et culturels", in *Le droit au service de la justice, de la paix et du développement: Mélanges Michel Virally*, Paris: Pedone, 1991, p. 465.

Turp, Daniel, "Le recours au droit international aux fins de l'interprétation de la Charte canadienne des droits et libertés: un bilan jurisprudentiel', (1984) 18 *Revue juridique Thémis* 353.

Turp, Daniel, *Le droit de choisir: Essais sur le droit du Québec à disposer de lui-même*, Montreal: Éditions Thémis, 2001.

Van Bueren, Geraldine, *The International Law on the Rights of the Child*, Dordrecht, Boston & London: Martinus Nijhoff Publishers, 1995.

Van Ert, Gibran, "What is Treaty Implementation?", in *Legitimacy and Accountability in International Law – Proceedings of the 33rd Annual Conference of the Canadian Council on International Law*, Ottawa: Canadian Council of International Law, 2005, pp. 165-174.

Van Ert, Gibran, "Using Treaties in Canadian Courts", (2000) 38 *Canadian Yearbook of International Law* 3-88.

Van Ert, Gibran, *Using International Law in Canadian Courts*, The Hague: Kluwer Law International, 2002.

van Zyl Smit, Dirk, "Life Imprisonment as an Ultimate Penalty in International Law: A Human Rights Perspective", (1999) 9 *Criminal Law Forum* 5.

Vanek, C., "Is International Law a Part of the Law of Canada?", (1949-50) 8 *University of Toronto Law Journal* 251.

Veerman, Philip E., *The Rights of the Child and the Changing Image of Childhood*, Dordrecht, Martinus Nijhoff, 1992.

Velu, Jacques & Rusen Ergec, *La Convention européenne des droits de l'Homme*, Brussels: Bruylant, 1990.

Verdoodt, Albert, "Influence des structures ethniques et linguistiques des pays membres des Nations Unites sur la rédaction de la Déclaration universelle des droits de l'homme", in *Liber Amicorum Discipulorumque René Cassin*, Paris: Pedone, 1969, pp. 403-416.

Verdoodt, Albert, *Naissance et signification de la Déclaration universelle des droits de l'homme*, Louvain, Paris: Nauwelaerts, 1963.

Verge, Pierre, *Le droit de grève*, Cowansville: Editions Yvon Blais, 1985.

Verhellen, Eugen, ed., *Monitoring Children's Rights*, Dordrecht: Martinus Nijhoff, 1996.

Verhoeven, Joe, "Le crime de génocide, originalité et ambiguïté", [1991] *Revue belge de droit international* 5.

von Hebel, Herman, Johan G. Lammers & Jolien Schukking, eds., *Reflections on the International Criminal Court: Essays in Honour of Adriaan Bos*, The Hague: T.M.C. Asser, 1999.

Wai, Robert, "Justice Gérard La Forest and the Internationalist Turn in Canadian Jurisprudence", in R. Johnson *et al.*, eds., *Gérard V. La Forest at the Supreme Court of Canada, 1985-1997*, Winnipeg: Faculty of Law: University of Manitoba, 2000.

Walters, Mark D., "Nationalism and the Pathology of Legal Systems: Considering the *Quebec Secession Reference* and the Lessons for the United Kingdom", (1999) 62 *Modern Law Review* 371.

Waters, Melissa A., "Mediating Norms and Identity: The Role of Transnational Judicial Dialogue in Creating and Enforcing International Law", (2005) 93 *Georgetown Law Journal* 487.

Watt, David, *The New Offences Against the Person: The Provisions of Bill C-127*, Toronto: Butterworths, 1984.

Waugh, David A., "The ILO and Human Rights", (1982) 5 *Comparative Labour Law* 186.

Weis, P., *The Refugee Convention, 1951: The travaux préparatoires Analyzed with Commentary*, Cambridge: Cambridge University Press, 1995.

Weiser, Irit, "Effect in Domestic Law of International Human Rights Treaties Ratified without Implementing Legislation," in *The Impact of International Law on the Practice of Law in Canada – Proceedings of the 27th Annual Conference of the Canadian Council on International Law*, The Hague: Kluwer Law International, 1999, p. 132.

Weiser, Irit, "Undressing the Window: Treating International Human Rights Law Meaningfully in the Canadian Commonwealth System", (2004) 37 *University of British Columbia Law Review* 113.

Weissbrodt, David, *The Right to a Fair Trial, Articles 8, 10 and 11 of the Universal Declaration of Human Rights*, The Hague/Boston/London: Martinus Nijhoff, 2001.

Whelan, Anthony, "Wilsonian Self Determination and the Versailles Settlement", (1994) 43 *International & Comparative Law Quarterly* 99.

Whitaker, Reg & Gary Marcuse, *Cold War Canada: The Making of a National Insecurity State, 1945-1957*, Toronto/Buffalo/London: University of Toronto Press, 1994.

Wiebringhaus, H., "La Charte sociale européenne: vingt ans après la conclusion du Traité", (1982) 86 *Annuaire français de droit international* 934.

Willis, James F., *Prologue to Nuremberg: The Politics and Diplomacy of Punishing War Criminals of the First World War*, Westport, Connecticut: Greenwood Press, 1982.

Wilson, Jerome, "Ethnic Groups and the Right to Self-Determination", (1996) *Connecticut Journal of International Law* 433.

Wiseman, David, "The Charter and Poverty: Beyond Injusticiability", (2001) *University of Toronto Law Journal* 425.

Woehrling, José, "L'accord du Lac Meech et l'application de la Charte canadienne des droits et libertés", in Gérald-A. Beaudoin, ed., *Vues canadiennes and européennes des droits de and libertés,* Cowansville: Éditions Yvon Blais, 1989, pp. 377-418.

Woehrling, José, "Le rôle du droit comparé dans la jurisprudence des droits de la personne – rapport canadien", in Armand De Mestral et al., eds., *The Limitation of Human Rights in Comparative Constitutional Law*, Cowansville: Editions Yvon Blais, 1986, pp. 449-514.

Young, Alan, "Fundamental Justice and Political Power: A Personal Reflection on Twenty Years in the Trenches", (2002) 16 *Supreme Court Law Review (2d)* 121.

Yourow, Howard Charles, *The Margin of Appreciation Doctrine in the Dynamics of European Human Rights Jurisprudence*, The Hague: Martinus Nijhoff, 1996.

Zander, Michael, *The Law-Making Process*, 4th ed., London: Butterworths, 1994.

Zellick, Graham, "Corporal punishment in the Isle of Man", (1978) 27 *International & Comparative Law Quarterly* 665.

Zellick, Graham, "The European Convention on Human Rights: Its Significance for Charter Litigation", in R.J. Sharpe, ed., *Charter Litigation*, Toronto: Butterworths, 1987, pp. 102-103.

INDEX

European regional systems — *continued*
  European Social Charter, 217-218
    legislative changes as result of its influence, 217
    nineteen rights and principles, 217
    no individual petition procedure, 217
    protocol adding four rights, 217-218
    states parties submitting biennial reports, 217
      "recommendations" to states parties, 217
  specialized instruments, 218
    Torture Convention, 218
  Venice Convention, 219
    expertise in constitutional law and policy, 219
    opinion on illegal detention centres and self-determination, 219
    "think tank" in areas of elections and minority rights, 219
European Union, 210-211, 220-221
  Amsterdam Treaty, 220
  Charter of Fundamental Rights of the European Union, 220-221
  economic integration, 220
  European Court of Justice, and Court of First Instance, 221
  foreign policy initiatives, 220
  international human rights, significant role in, 220
  normative provisions adopted within European Union, 221
    norms cited as guidelines in Canadian courts, 221
introduction, 210-211
  Council of Europe, 210
    demanding standards of democratic development and human rights, 211
    European Convention on Human Rights, 210
    European Court of Human Rights, 210
  European Union, 210-211
    issues of human rights becoming significant, 210-211
    strict human rights standards, 211
  Organization for Security and Cooperation in Europe (OSCE), 210, 211
    fifty-five "participating states", 211
Organization for Security and Cooperation in Europe (OSCE), 210, 211, 222-225
  Helsinki Final Act, 222, 223-224
    "commitment" and ongoing dialogue, 222
    right to self-determination within framework of existing sovereign states, 223
    Supreme Court of Canada citing it in *Succession Reference*, 223-224
      principle of territorial integrity of states, 223-224
  High Commissioner on National Minorities, 224-225
    rights of national, ethnic, linguistic and religious minorities, 224-225
  "human dimension", 222, 223
    Copenhagen Conference, 222
    ODIHR involved in human rights work, 223
  instruments containing detailed provisions covering rights, 222-223
    self-determination and rights of minorities, 222-223

Moscow mechanism, 222

Francophonie, 227
Fundamental freedoms, 291-327 *See also* **Charter of Rights and Freedoms caselaw and international human rights law**

Genesis of human rights protection
Canadian developments, 6-8
   anti-discrimination legislation in Ontario, 7
   Continuation of Transitional Powers Act suspending *habeus corpus*, 8
   human rights code in Saskatchewan, 7
   Quebec *Padlock Law* prohibiting activities of communists and Jehovah's Witnesses, 8
   ratification of several ILO conventions by Canadian Parliament, 6-7
      statutes under provincial legislation and declared *ultra vires*, 7
   War Measures Act prohibiting political activity and interning "enemy aliens", 7
      Japanese Canadians forced to live in internment camps, 7
         discriminatory measures not repealed until 1949, 7-8
English and American history, 2-3
   constitutional entrenchment of fundamental rights and freedoms, 2
   English *Bill of Rights*, 2
   European Court of Human Rights, British participation in, 3
   international human rights law, 3
      branch of public international law, 3
   Magna Carta (1215), 2, 3
      Parliamentary supremacy, struggle for, 2
      reinforced by *European Convention on Human Rights*, 3
   Petition of Right, 2
   public international law vs, private international law, 3
   U.S. *Bill of Rights*, 2
   Westminster Parliament moving toward modest form of entrenchment, 2-3
introduction, 1-2
   Charter of Rights and Freedoms, 1
      legislation in violation of rights and freedoms declared inoperative, 1
      Parliament's override pursuant to "notwithstanding clause", 1
      petition to courts for appropriate remedy, 1
   international law and protection of human rights and fundamental freedoms, 1-2
sources of international human rights law, 3-7
   General Act of the Berlin Conference on Central Africa, 4
      slave trade forbidden, 4
   Hague Conventions of 1899 and 1907, 5
      "international humanitarian law", 5
      law of armed conflict, 5
   international agreements on labour and working conditions, 4-5
   International Labour Organization (ILO), 6-7

Genesis of human rights protection — *continued*

ratification of several ILO conventions by Canadian Parliament, 6-7

statutes under provincial legislation and declared *ultra vires*, 7

rights of labour and working conditions, 6

guarantee of eight-hour working day, 6

natural law, 3

Peace of Westphalia of 1648, 3-4

guarantees for religious minorities, 4

Second World War marking turning point in international and Canadian law, 8-10

Atlantic Charter containing humans rights proclamation, 8-9

Charter of the United Nations, 9-10

human rights proposals from Canadian diplomat, 10

several references to human rights, 9-10

post-war system built upon "four essential human freedoms", 9

Universal Declaration of Human Rights, 9, 10-12

centerpiece of international law of human rights and fundamental freedoms, 10-11

Commission adopting text of *Declaration*, 11-12

draft declaration of human rights prepared by Humphrey, 11

General Assembly adopting text of *Declaration*, 12

treaties protecting minority rights, 6

Treaty of Paris (1763), 4

freedom of Catholic religion in Canada, 4

Treaty of Utrecht (1713), 4

protection of francophone Roman Catholics within British North America,

Treaty of Versailles, 5-6

Covenant of the League of Nations incorporated, 5

criminal responsibility of perpetrators of human rights abuses, 6

"fair and humane conditions of labour", 5-6

International Labour Organization (ILO), 6-7

rights of indigenous populations, 6

Human Rights Committee *See* **United Nations and human rights law**

International Covenant on Civil and Political Rights See **United Nations and human rights law**, treaty-based protection of human rights, and *Universal Declaration of Human Rights*

International Covenant on Economic, Social and Cultural Rights See **United Nations and human rights law**, treaty-based protection of human rights, and *Universal Declaration of Human Rights*

International Conventions where Canada being party, 441-456

Sources of international human rights law — *continued*
    slave trade forbidden, 4
    Hague Conventions of 1899 and 1907, 5
      "international humanitarian law", 5
      law of armed conflict, 5
    international agreements on labour and working conditions, 4-5
    International Labour Organization (ILO), 6-7
      ratification of several ILO conventions by Canadian Parliament, 6-7
        statutes under provincial legislation and declared *ultra vires*, 7
      rights of labour and working conditions, 6
        guarantee of eight-hour working day, 6
    natural law, 3
    Peace of Westphalia of 1648, 3-4
      guarantees for religious minorities, 4
    Second World War marking turning point in international and Canadian law, 8-10
      Atlantic Charter containing humans rights proclamation, 8-9
      Charter of the United Nations, 9-10
        human rights proposals from Canadian diplomat, 10
        several references to human rights, 9-10
      post-war system built upon "four essential human freedoms", 9
      Universal Declaration of Human Rights, 9, 10-12
        centerpiece of international law of human rights and fundamental freedoms, 10-11
        Commission adopting text of *Declaration*, 11-12
        draft declaration of human rights prepared by Humphrey, 11
        General Assembly adopting text of *Declaration*, 12
    treaties protecting minority rights, 6
    Treaty of Paris (1763), 4
      freedom of Catholic religion in Canada, 4
    Treaty of Utrecht (1713), 4
      protection of francophone Roman Catholics within British North America,
    Treaty of Versailles, 5-6
      Covenant of the League of Nations incorporated, 5
      criminal responsibility of perpetrators of human rights abuses, 6
      "fair and humane conditions of labour", 5-6
      International Labour Organization (ILO), 6-7
      rights of indigenous populations, 6
international criminal law, 114, 115
international human rights law and domestic protections of human rights, 113-114
    Charter of the United Nations, 114
    Universal Declaration of Human Rights, 114
international humanitarian law, 114-115
"international law" defined, 113